Presented

TO

Dad

BY

Kert, Tami & Konner

ON

Father's Day '97

Mr. Thomas Young
59833 Lee Ave.
Elkhart, IN 46517

Dad

Kat, Tami + Kerri

Father's Day '97

MEN'S
DEVOTIONAL
NEW TESTAMENT
WITH PSALMS & PROVERBS

NEW INTERNATIONAL VERSION

Zondervan Publishing House
Grand Rapids, Michigan 49530, U.S.A.

NIV Men's Devotional New Testament with Psalms and Proverbs
Copyright © 1993, 1994 by Zondervan Publishing House
All rights reserved

Devotional material copyright information can be found on page 549.

The Holy Bible, New International Version®
Copyright © 1973, 1978, 1984 by International Bible Society

The "NIV" and "New International Version" trademarks are registered in the
United States Patent and Trademark Office by International Bible Society. Use of
either trademark requires the permission of International Bible Society.

The NIV text may be quoted in any form (written, visual, electronic or audio), up to and inclusive of
five hundred (500) verses without express written permission of the publisher, providing the verses
quoted do not amount to a complete book of the Bible nor do the verses quoted account for 25
percent or more of the total text of the work in which they are quoted.

Notice of copyright must appear on the title or copyright page of the work as follows:

> Scripture taken from the HOLY BIBLE, NEW INTERNATIONAL VERSION®. Copyright ©
> 1973, 1978, 1984 by International Bible Society. Used by permission of Zondervan Publishing
> House. All rights reserved.
>
> The "NIV" and "New International Version" trademarks are registered in the United States
> Patent and Trademark Office by International Bible Society. Use of either trademark requires
> the permission of International Bible Society.

When quotations from the NIV text are used in non-saleable media, such as church bulletins, orders
of service, posters, transparencies or similar media, a complete copyright notice is not required, but
the initials (NIV) must appear at the end of each quotation.

Any commentary or other Biblical reference work produced for commercial sale that uses the New
International Version must obtain written permission for use of the NIV text.

Permission requests for commercial use within the U.S. and Canada that exceed the above guidelines
must be directed to, and approved in writing by, Zondervan Publishing House.

Permission requests for commercial use within the U.K., EEC, and EFTA countries that exceed the
above guidelines must be directed to, and approved in writing by, Hodder Headline Plc., Mill Road,
Dunton Green, Sevenoaks, Kent, TN13 2YA, England.

Permission requests for non-commercial use that exceed the above guidelines must be directed to,
and approved in writing by, International Bible Society, 1820 Jet Stream Drive, Colorado Springs, CO
80921.

Library of Congress Catalog Card Number 92-63054

Published by Zondervan Publishing House
Grand Rapids, Michigan 49530, U.S.A.
Printed in Belgium
All rights reserved

Edited by: Dirk R. Buursma, Martha Manikas-Foster
Illustrations by: Linda Rzoska
Cover photo: © M. Angelo/West Light

94 95 96 97 98 99   8 7 6 5 4 3 2 1

You will be pleased to know that a portion of the purchase price of your new NIV Bible has been
provided to the International Bible Society to help spread the gospel of Jesus Christ around the world!

CONTENTS

Introduction vi
Preface to The New International Version viii

THE NEW TESTAMENT
Matthew 1
Mark 45
Luke 73
John 119
Acts 156
Romans 196
1 Corinthians 218
2 Corinthians 240
Galatians 254
Ephesians 262
Philippians 272
Colossians 280
1 Thessalonians 288
2 Thessalonians 294
1 Timothy 299
2 Timothy 307
Titus 313
Philemon 317
Hebrews 320
James 338
1 Peter 347
2 Peter 356
1 John 363
2 John 370
3 John 372
Jude 375
Revelation 378

Psalms 401
Proverbs 507

Weights & Measures 548
Acknowledgments Index 549
Reading Plan 554
Author Biographies 558
Subject Index 563

INTRODUCTION
NIV MEN'S DEVOTIONAL

Becoming a real man in a fast-paced, demanding world is hard work. It's not easy to build relationships with family and friends, to stand up under job pressures, and still be true to who you are as a man made in God's image. What's a real man supposed to be? What your father was? What your peers want? What your wife and children need? Where can a man find answers to tough questions about being a man? Relax, your search is over! The NIV Men's Devotional New Testament is designed just for you—one of today's men tired of trying to measure up to society's standards of manhood and eager to discover the Biblical model of masculinity and maturity.

Written for, by and about today's man, the devotions in this New Testament will reach you right where you are. But it won't leave you there! With God's Word and the thoughtful reflections of many godly men, the NIV Men's Devotional New Testament will transport you step by step on a journey to Christian maturity.

Several features make the NIV Men's Devotional New Testament an exceptional devotional guide:

The Bible
The NIV Men's Devotional New Testament features the text of the New International Version. The NIV's accuracy and readability make it today's most popular modern translation.

The Devotions
All of the daily and weekend devotions are written by men—men who have struggled with what it means to be a man of integrity and vision; men who want to be good men, good workers, good husbands, good fathers; men who want to share what they've learned with other men. Each devotion is located within the text, in close proximity to the Scripture passage on which it is based.

The Introductions
The introduction to each Bible book succinctly highlights that book's practical themes. Each introduction gives you interesting facts and helpful background information, as well as a practical application to encourage you as you read that particular book and the devotions within it.

Ease of Use
The NIV Men's Devotional New Testament is designed to help you see how relevant the Bible is to your particular life situation as a man. The easy-to-use Bible reading/devotional meditation plan will get you into the Word and help you to leave a mark on your friends, your colleagues, your wife and your children.

The devotions in the NIV Men's Devotional New Testament take a distinctive pattern following the days of the week: Monday, Tuesday, Wednesday, Thursday, Friday. In recognition of your need for something different on the weekend, we've developed "Weekending"—combining brief, provocative devotional thoughts with short Scripture readings for both Saturday and Sunday.

No matter what day of the week you begin your reading, you simply turn to a devotion for that day. To proceed on to the next reading, look to the bottom of the devotion; you will be directed to the page number on which the next day's devotion can be found. For example, if you start on a Monday, you could turn to the first devotion in the book of Matthew, page 2. Glance at the bottom of Monday's devotion, and you will see the page number where Tuesday's devotion will be found—and so on as you keep reading on through Friday.

Friday's devotion will direct you to a "Weekending," which will provide you with a reflective insight for your weekend and a Scripture reading for both Saturday and Sunday. The bottom of the "Weekending" will send you to the next Monday's devotion. And you are well on your way—through a year of developing a vital relationship with the Lord as you spend time in his Word.

Reading Plan

On page 554 you will find a plan to help you read through the New Testament and the books of Psalms and Proverbs in one year. If you choose to follow this plan, you'll discover great riches as you read chapter by chapter and book by book.

Author Biographies

You will very likely recognize the names of many of the men who contributed to the NIV Men's Devotional New Testament. The author index, found on page 558, provides information about each man, as well as a list of the pages where his devotions appear.

Subject Index

You feel like a failure as a father; your spiritual discipline is waning; you're weary of the rat race; you're confused about how your sexuality relates to who you are as a man. Whatever your circumstances, the subject index will direct you to just the right words to encourage and motivate you. Look up a wide variety of subjects in this index on page 563, and turn to the listed page number for a devotion that fits your need.

So come on along. You're invited to open the pages of the NIV Men's Devotional New Testament and proceed along the road to authentic masculinity and maturity in Christ. The riches of God's Word await you every step of the way, and the meditations of the men who have shared a bit of themselves will give the encouragement you need to keep moving ahead. As you go, we pray you'll become all that God intends you to be as a man of God in today's world.

PREFACE

THE NEW INTERNATIONAL VERSION is a completely new translation of the Holy Bible made by over a hundred scholars working directly from the best available Hebrew, Aramaic and Greek texts. It had its beginning in 1965 when, after several years of exploratory study by committees from the Christian Reformed Church and the National Association of Evangelicals, a group of scholars met at Palos Heights, Illinois, and concurred in the need for a new translation of the Bible in contemporary English. This group, though not made up of official church representatives, was transdenominational. Its conclusion was endorsed by a large number of leaders from many denominations who met in Chicago in 1966.
Responsibility for the new version was delegated by the Palos Heights group to a self-governing body of fifteen, the Committee on Bible Translation, composed for the most part of biblical scholars from colleges, universities and seminaries. In 1967 the New York Bible Society (now the International Bible Society) generously undertook the financial sponsorship of the project—a sponsorship that made it possible to enlist the help of many distinguished scholars. The fact that participants from the United States, Great Britain, Canada, Australia and New Zealand worked together gave the project its international scope. That they were from many denominations—including Anglican, Assemblies of God, Baptist, Brethren, Christian Reformed, Church of Christ, Evangelical Free, Lutheran, Mennonite, Methodist, Nazarene, Presbyterian, Wesleyan and other churches—helped to safeguard the translation from sectarian bias.

How it was made helps to give the New International Version its distinctiveness. The translation of each book was assigned to a team of scholars. Next, one of the Intermediate Editorial Committees revised the initial translation, with constant reference to the Hebrew, Aramaic or Greek. Their work then went to one of the General Editorial Committees, which checked it in detail and made another thorough revision. This revision in turn was carefully reviewed by the Committee on Bible Translation, which made further changes and then released the final version for publication. In this way the entire Bible underwent three revisions, during each of which the translation was examined for its faithfulness to the original languages and for its English style.
All this involved many thousands of hours of research and discussion regarding the meaning of the texts and the precise way of putting them into English. It may well be that no other translation has been made by a more thorough process of review and revision from committee to committee than this one.

From the beginning of the project, the Committee on Bible Translation held to certain goals for the New International Version: that it would be an accurate translation and one that would have clarity and literary quality and so prove suitable for public and private reading, teaching, preaching, memorizing and liturgical use. The Committee also sought to preserve some measure of continuity with the long tradition of translating the Scriptures into English.
In working toward these goals, the translators were united in their commitment to the authority and infallibility of the Bible as God's Word in written form. They believe that it contains the divine answer to the deepest needs of humanity, that it sheds unique light on our path in a dark world, and that it sets forth the way to our eternal well-being.
The first concern of the translators has been the accuracy of the translation and its fidelity to the thought of the biblical writers. They have weighed the significance of the lexical and grammatical details of the Hebrew, Aramaic and Greek texts. At the same time, they have striven for more than a word-for-word translation. Because thought patterns and syntax differ from language to language, faithful communication of the meaning of the writers of the Bible demands frequent modifications in sentence structure and constant regard for the contextual meanings of words.
A sensitive feeling for style does not always accompany scholarship. Accordingly the Committee on Bible Translation submitted the developing version to a number of stylistic consultants. Two of them read every book of both Old and New Testaments twice—once before and once after the last major revision—and made invaluable suggestions. Samples of the translation were tested for clarity and ease of reading by various kinds of people—young and old, highly educated and less well educated, ministers and laymen.
Concern for clear and natural English—that the New International Version should be idiomatic but not idiosyncratic, contemporary but not dated—motivated the translators and consultants. At the same time, they tried to reflect the differing styles of the biblical writers. In view of

PREFACE

the international use of English, the translators sought to avoid obvious Americanisms on the one hand and obvious Anglicisms on the other. A British edition reflects the comparatively few differences of significant idiom and of spelling.

As for the traditional pronouns "thou," "thee" and "thine" in reference to the Deity, the translators judged that to use these archaisms (along with the old verb forms such as "doest," "wouldest" and "hadst") would violate accuracy in translation. Neither Hebrew, Aramaic nor Greek uses special pronouns for the persons of the Godhead. A present-day translation is not enhanced by forms that in the time of the King James Version were used in everyday speech, whether referring to God or man.

For the Old Testament the standard Hebrew text, the Masoretic Text as published in the latest editions of Biblia Hebraica, was used throughout. The Dead Sea Scrolls contain material bearing on an earlier stage of the Hebrew text. They were consulted, as were the Samaritan Pentateuch and the ancient scribal traditions relating to textual changes. Sometimes a variant Hebrew reading in the margin of the Masoretic Text was followed instead of the text itself. Such instances, being variants within the Masoretic tradition, are not specified by footnotes. In rare cases, words in the consonantal text were divided differently from the way they appear in the Masoretic Text. Footnotes indicate this. The translators also consulted the more important early versions—the Septuagint; Aquila, Symmachus and Theodotion; the Vulgate; the Syriac Peshitta; the Targums; and for the Psalms the Juxta Hebraica of Jerome. Readings from these versions were occasionally followed where the Masoretic Text seemed doubtful and where accepted principles of textual criticism showed that one or more of these textual witnesses appeared to provide the correct reading. Such instances are footnoted. Sometimes vowel letters and vowel signs did not, in the judgment of the translators, represent the correct vowels for the original consonantal text. Accordingly some words were read with a different set of vowels. These instances are usually not indicated by footnotes.

The Greek text used in translating the New Testament was an eclectic one. No other piece of ancient literature has such an abundance of manuscript witnesses as does the New Testament. Where existing manuscripts differ, the translators made their choice of readings according to accepted principles of New Testament textual criticism. Footnotes call attention to places where there was uncertainty about what the original text was. The best current printed texts of the Greek New Testament were used.

There is a sense in which the work of translation is never wholly finished. This applies to all great literature and uniquely so to the Bible. In 1973 the New Testament in the New International Version was published. Since then, suggestions for corrections and revisions have been received from various sources. The Committee on Bible Translation carefully considered the suggestions and adopted a number of them. These were incorporated in the first printing of the entire Bible in 1978. Additional revisions were made by the Committee on Bible Translation in 1983 and appear in printings after that date.

As in other ancient documents, the precise meaning of the biblical texts is sometimes uncertain. This is more often the case with the Hebrew and Aramaic texts than with the Greek text. Although archaeological and linguistic discoveries in this century aid in understanding difficult passages, some uncertainties remain. The more significant of these have been called to the reader's attention in the footnotes.

In regard to the divine name YHWH, commonly referred to as the Tetragrammaton, the translators adopted the device used in most English versions of rendering that name as "LORD" in capital letters to distinguish it from Adonai, another Hebrew word rendered "Lord," for which small letters are used. Wherever the two names stand together in the Old Testament as a compound name of God, they are rendered "Sovereign LORD."

Because for most readers today the phrases "the LORD of hosts" and "God of hosts" have little meaning, this version renders them "the LORD Almighty" and "God Almighty." These renderings convey the sense of the Hebrew, namely, "he who is sovereign over all the 'hosts' (powers) in heaven and on earth, especially over the 'hosts' (armies) of Israel." For readers unacquainted with Hebrew this does not make clear the distinction between Sabaoth ("hosts" or "Almighty") and Shaddai (which can also be translated "Almighty"), but the latter occurs infrequently and is always footnoted. When Adonai and YHWH Sabaoth occur together, they are rendered "the Lord, the LORD Almighty."

As for other proper nouns, the familiar spellings of the King James Version are generally retained. Names traditionally spelled with "ch," except where it is final, are usually spelled in this translation with "k" or "c," since the biblical languages do not have the sound that "ch" frequently indicates in English—for example, in chant. For well-known names such as Zechariah, however, the traditional spelling has been retained. Variation in the spelling of names in the original languages has usually not been indicated. Where a person or place has two or more different names in the Hebrew, Aramaic or Greek texts, the more familiar one has generally been used, with footnotes where needed.

To achieve clarity the translators sometimes supplied words not in the original texts but required by the context. If there was uncertainty about such material, it is enclosed in brackets. Also for the sake of clarity or style, nouns, including some proper nouns, are sometimes substituted for pronouns, and vice versa. And though the Hebrew writers often shifted back and forth between first, second and third personal pronouns without change of antecedent, this translation often makes them uniform, in accordance with English style and without the use of footnotes.

Poetical passages are printed as poetry, that is, with indentation of lines with separate stanzas. These are generally designed to reflect the structure of Hebrew poetry. This poetry is normally characterized by parallelism in balanced lines. Most of the poetry in the Bible is in the Old Testament, and scholars differ regarding the scansion of Hebrew lines. The translators determined the stanza divisions for the most part by analysis of the subject matter. The stanzas therefore serve as poetic paragraphs.

As an aid to the reader, italicized sectional headings are inserted in most of the books. They are not to be regarded as part of the NIV text, are not for oral reading, and are not intended to dictate the interpretation of the sections they head.

The footnotes in this version are of several kinds, most of which need no explanation. Those giving alternative translations begin with "Or" and generally introduce the alternative with the last word preceding it in the text, except when it is a single-word alternative; in poetry quoted in a footnote a slant mark indicates a line division. Footnotes introduced by "Or" do not have uniform significance. In some cases two possible translations were considered to have about equal validity. In other cases, though the translators were convinced that the translation in the text was correct, they judged that another interpretation was possible and of sufficient importance to be represented in a footnote.

In the New Testament, footnotes that refer to uncertainty regarding the original text are introduced by "Some manuscripts" or similar expressions. In the Old Testament, evidence for the reading chosen is given first and evidence for the alternative is added after a semicolon (for example: Septuagint; Hebrew father). In such notes the term "Hebrew" refers to the Masoretic Text.

It should be noted that minerals, flora and fauna, architectural details, articles of clothing and jewelry, musical instruments and other articles cannot always be identified with precision. Also measures of capacity in the biblical period are particularly uncertain (see the table of weights and measures following the text).

Like all translations of the Bible, made as they are by imperfect man, this one undoubtedly falls short of its goals. Yet we are grateful to God for the extent to which he has enabled us to realize these goals and for the strength he has given us and our colleagues to complete our task. We offer this version of the Bible to him in whose name and for whose glory it has been made. We pray that it will lead many into a better understanding of the Holy Scriptures and a fuller knowledge of Jesus Christ the incarnate Word, of whom the Scriptures so faithfully testify.

The Committee on Bible Translation

June 1978
(Revised August 1983)

Names of the translators and editors may be secured
from the International Bible Society,
translation sponsors of the New International Version,
P.O. Box 62970, Colorado Springs, Colorado
80962-2970 U.S.A.

NEW TESTAMENT

NEW TESTAMENT

MATTHEW writes this Gospel to emphasize how Jesus fulfills God's promises from the Old Testament. He includes numerous sayings of Jesus about living as one of his disciples and as a member of the church, concluding with the command of Jesus to make disciples of all nations. As you read this book, ask yourself whether you are living as a disciple of Jesus, as well as how you can tell others the story of Jesus.

MATTHEW

The Genealogy of Jesus

1 A record of the genealogy of Jesus Christ the son of David, the son of Abraham:

²Abraham was the father of Isaac,
Isaac the father of Jacob,
Jacob the father of Judah and his brothers,
³Judah the father of Perez and Zerah, whose mother was Tamar,
Perez the father of Hezron,
Hezron the father of Ram,
⁴Ram the father of Amminadab,
Amminadab the father of Nahshon,
Nahshon the father of Salmon,
⁵Salmon the father of Boaz, whose mother was Rahab,
Boaz the father of Obed, whose mother was Ruth,
Obed the father of Jesse,
⁶and Jesse the father of King David.

David was the father of Solomon, whose mother had been Uriah's wife,
⁷Solomon the father of Rehoboam,
Rehoboam the father of Abijah,
Abijah the father of Asa,
⁸Asa the father of Jehoshaphat,
Jehoshaphat the father of Jehoram,
Jehoram the father of Uzziah,
⁹Uzziah the father of Jotham,
Jotham the father of Ahaz,
Ahaz the father of Hezekiah,

MONDAY

VERSE FOR THE DAY:
Matthew 1:1

AUTHOR:
Walter Trobisch

PASSAGE FOR THE DAY:
Matthew 1:1-17

The Sheltered Man

IN CONTRAST to the frustrated man who would like to run away from his responsibilities stands the redeemed man who feels safe and secure. He can be a shelter to others because he himself is sheltered. He is not afraid even if at times he should lose or suffer defeat. He simply gets up again and keeps on keeping on. He is a man who has accepted himself not only with his strengths but also with his weaknesses. His secret: he knows he has been accepted by the heavenly Father. He has a roof over his head. He knows where his home is. He has a place where he can put his feet under the table. He can say with the psalmist, "You prepare a table before me in the presence of my enemies" (Psalm 23:5). He can say, "You have been my refuge, a strong tower against the foe. I long to dwell in your tent forever and take refuge in the shelter of your wings" (Psalm 61:3–4).

This is the longing of all mankind—to have security, to know where one's place is. God created man and then he created a place for him, the Garden of Eden. When man lost God, he lost at the same time his place. Since then, the longing for a place where he belongs, where he feels at home, is in the heart of every human being. Those who have not found a place, the uprooted, the eternal Gypsies will find a place nowhere, not even in marriage. On the other hand, those who have found a place, married or unmarried, will be able to become a place where others feel at home, thus filling one of the deepest needs of our time. In light of this, Jesus' promise "to prepare a place" for us is filled with new meaning (John 14:2). Those who have found him have found their place . . .

The redeemed man . . . is a whole man. He is whole first of all because he *belongs* to a family, the family of God. God, his Father, makes him one of his sons.

He is a whole man because he feels *worthy*. Christ died to give him birth and therefore he can take as his own the worthiness of Christ.

He is a whole man because he feels *competent*. This competence comes from the Holy Spirit. "God did not give us a spirit of timidity, but a spirit of power, of love and of self-discipline" (2 Timothy 1:7).

Additional Scripture Readings:
Psalm 1; Romans 8:1–4

Go to page 4 for your next devotional reading.

¹⁰Hezekiah the father of Manasseh,
Manasseh the father of Amon,
Amon the father of Josiah,
¹¹and Josiah the father of Jeconiah[a] and his brothers at the time of the exile to Babylon.

¹²After the exile to Babylon:
Jeconiah was the father of Shealtiel,
Shealtiel the father of Zerubbabel,
¹³Zerubbabel the father of Abiud,
Abiud the father of Eliakim,
Eliakim the father of Azor,
¹⁴Azor the father of Zadok,
Zadok the father of Akim,
Akim the father of Eliud,
¹⁵Eliud the father of Eleazar,
Eleazar the father of Matthan,
Matthan the father of Jacob,
¹⁶and Jacob the father of Joseph, the husband of Mary, of whom was born Jesus, who is called Christ.

¹⁷Thus there were fourteen generations in all from Abraham to David, fourteen from David to the exile to Babylon, and fourteen from the exile to the Christ.[b]

The Birth of Jesus Christ

¹⁸This is how the birth of Jesus Christ came about: His mother Mary was pledged to be married to Joseph, but before they came together, she was found to be with child through the Holy Spirit. ¹⁹Because Joseph her husband was a righteous man and did not want to expose her to public disgrace, he had in mind to divorce her quietly.

²⁰But after he had considered this, an angel of the Lord appeared to him in a dream and said, "Joseph son of David, do not be afraid to take Mary home as your wife, because what is conceived in her is from the Holy Spirit. ²¹She will give birth to a son, and you are to give him the name Jesus,[c] because he will save his people from their sins."

²²All this took place to fulfill what the Lord had said through the prophet: ²³"The virgin will be with child and will give birth to a son, and they will call him Immanuel"[d]—which means, "God with us."

²⁴When Joseph woke up, he did what the angel of the Lord had commanded him and took Mary home as his wife. ²⁵But he had no union with her until she gave birth to a son. And he gave him the name Jesus.

The Visit of the Magi

2 After Jesus was born in Bethlehem in Judea, during the time of King Herod, Magi[e] from the east came to Jerusalem ²and asked, "Where is the one who has been born king of the Jews? We saw his star in the east[f] and have come to worship him."

³When King Herod heard this he was disturbed, and all Jerusalem with him. ⁴When he had called together all the people's chief priests and teachers of the law, he asked them where the Christ[g] was to be born. ⁵"In Bethlehem in Judea," they replied, "for this is what the prophet has written:

⁶" 'But you, Bethlehem, in the land of Judah,
are by no means least among the rulers of Judah;
for out of you will come a ruler
who will be the shepherd of my people Israel.'[h]"

⁷Then Herod called the Magi secretly and found out from them the exact time the star had appeared. ⁸He sent them to Bethlehem and said, "Go and make a careful search for the child. As soon as you find him, report to me, so that I too may go and worship him."

⁹After they had heard the king, they went on their way, and the star they had seen in the east[i] went ahead of them until it stopped over the place where the child was. ¹⁰When they saw the star, they were overjoyed. ¹¹On coming to the house, they saw the child with his mother Mary, and they bowed down and worshiped him. Then they opened their treasures and presented him with gifts of gold and of incense and of myrrh. ¹²And having been warned in a dream not to go back to Herod, they returned to their country by another route.

The Escape to Egypt

¹³When they had gone, an angel of the Lord appeared to Joseph in a dream. "Get up," he said, "take the child and his mother and escape to Egypt. Stay there until I

---

[a]11 That is, Jehoiachin; also in verse 12   [b]17 Or *Messiah.* "The Christ" (Greek) and "the Messiah" (Hebrew) both mean "the Anointed One."   [c]21 *Jesus* is the Greek form of *Joshua,* which means *the L*ORD *saves.*   [d]23 Isaiah 7:14   [e]1 Traditionally *Wise Men*   [f]2 Or *star when it rose*   [g]4 Or *Messiah*   [h]6 Micah 5:2   [i]9 Or *seen when it rose*

tell you, for Herod is going to search for the child to kill him."

¹⁴So he got up, took the child and his mother during the night and left for Egypt, ¹⁵where he stayed until the death of Herod. And so was fulfilled what the Lord had said through the prophet: "Out of Egypt I called my son."ᵃ

¹⁶When Herod realized that he had been outwitted by the Magi, he was furious, and he gave orders to kill all the boys in Bethlehem and its vicinity who were two years old and under, in accordance with the time he had learned from the Magi. ¹⁷Then what was said through the prophet Jeremiah was fulfilled:

¹⁸"A voice is heard in Ramah,

a15 Hosea 11:1

TUESDAY

VERSE FOR THE DAY:
Matthew 1:20

AUTHOR:
Michael Card

PASSAGE FOR THE DAY:
Matthew 1:18–25

How Could It Be?

JOSEPH was the first person to really struggle with the Incarnation. Mary's momentary "How will this be?" [see Luke 1:34] seemed to come and go, like a cool breeze. But Joseph saw no angels. He only dreamed dreams. He had no quickening in his belly to tell him that life had indeed been conceived without his flesh. We know almost nothing about Joseph, apart from his gentleness and willingness to say "No" to himself for Mary's sake and for God's.

Imagine the dilemma of that simple man, finding himself cast in the role of father to the Son of God. Though that beautiful infant was not part of his body, the baby must have quickly taken over Joseph's heart, as most adopted children have a way of doing. As he held that squirming bundle in his arms, Joseph must have asked the question every new father asks himself and God, "How could it be?" . . .

It is an impossible task, being a parent. Not just difficult . . . impossible. To take a life from its first breath on through to maturity—to feed, clothe, educate, and all the rest. How could it be? . . .

How did Joseph do? We regretfully have no scenes of him with Jesus in the carpenter shop. But since Jesus was also known as a carpenter, he must have learned his trade somewhere, and why not from Joseph? We know for certain that Jesus made it to manhood with a wonderfully strong and simple vision of what *father* meant. He must have learned it at least in part from Joseph. Before he shrieked, "Abba!" with a man's tormented voice in the garden of Gethsemane, he must have tenderly called out that same name in an innocent child's voice to that man in the shadows, Joseph.

Additional Scripture Readings:
Mark 14:32–36; Romans 8:12–17

Go to page 7 for your next devotional reading.

weeping and great mourning,
Rachel weeping for her children
   and refusing to be comforted,
because they are no more."[a]

The Return to Nazareth

19After Herod died, an angel of the Lord appeared in a dream to Joseph in Egypt **20**and said, "Get up, take the child and his mother and go to the land of Israel, for those who were trying to take the child's life are dead."

21So he got up, took the child and his mother and went to the land of Israel. **22**But when he heard that Archelaus was reigning in Judea in place of his father Herod, he was afraid to go there. Having been warned in a dream, he withdrew to the district of Galilee, **23**and he went and lived in a town called Nazareth. So was fulfilled what was said through the prophets: "He will be called a Nazarene."

John the Baptist Prepares the Way

3 In those days John the Baptist came, preaching in the Desert of Judea **2**and saying, "Repent, for the kingdom of heaven is near." **3**This is he who was spoken of through the prophet Isaiah:

"A voice of one calling in the desert,
'Prepare the way for the Lord,
   make straight paths for him.'"[b]

4John's clothes were made of camel's hair, and he had a leather belt around his waist. His food was locusts and wild honey. **5**People went out to him from Jerusalem and all Judea and the whole region of the Jordan. **6**Confessing their sins, they were baptized by him in the Jordan River.

7But when he saw many of the Pharisees and Sadducees coming to where he was baptizing, he said to them: "You brood of vipers! Who warned you to flee from the coming wrath? **8**Produce fruit in keeping with repentance. **9**And do not think you can say to yourselves, 'We have Abraham as our father.' I tell you that out of these stones God can raise up children for Abraham. **10**The ax is already at the root of the trees, and every tree that does not produce good fruit will be cut down and thrown into the fire.

11"I baptize you with[c] water for repentance. But after me will come one who is more powerful than I, whose sandals I am not fit to carry. He will baptize you with the Holy Spirit and with fire. **12**His winnowing fork is in his hand, and he will clear his threshing floor, gathering his wheat into the barn and burning up the chaff with unquenchable fire."

The Baptism of Jesus

13Then Jesus came from Galilee to the Jordan to be baptized by John. **14**But John tried to deter him, saying, "I need to be baptized by you, and do you come to me?"

15Jesus replied, "Let it be so now; it is proper for us to do this to fulfill all righteousness." Then John consented.

16As soon as Jesus was baptized, he went up out of the water. At that moment heaven was opened, and he saw the Spirit of God descending like a dove and lighting on him. **17**And a voice from heaven said, "This is my Son, whom I love; with him I am well pleased."

The Temptation of Jesus

4 Then Jesus was led by the Spirit into the desert to be tempted by the devil. **2**After fasting forty days and forty nights, he was hungry. **3**The tempter came to him and said, "If you are the Son of God, tell these stones to become bread."

4Jesus answered, "It is written: 'Man does not live on bread alone, but on every word that comes from the mouth of God.'[d]"

5Then the devil took him to the holy city and had him stand on the highest point of the temple. **6**"If you are the Son of God," he said, "throw yourself down. For it is written:

" 'He will command his angels
      concerning you,
   and they will lift you up in their
      hands,
so that you will not strike your foot
   against a stone.'[e]"

7Jesus answered him, "It is also written: 'Do not put the Lord your God to the test.'[f]"

8Again, the devil took him to a very high mountain and showed him all the kingdoms of the world and their splendor. **9**"All this I will give you," he said, "if you will bow down and worship me."

10Jesus said to him, "Away from me, Satan! For it is written: 'Worship the Lord your God, and serve him only.'[g]"

---

[a]18 Jer. 31:15 [b]3 Isaiah 40:3 [c]11 Or *in* [d]4 Deut. 8:3 [e]6 Psalm 91:11,12 [f]7 Deut. 6:16
[g]10 Deut. 6:13

¹¹Then the devil left him, and angels came and attended him.

Jesus Begins to Preach

¹²When Jesus heard that John had been put in prison, he returned to Galilee. ¹³Leaving Nazareth, he went and lived in Capernaum, which was by the lake in the area of Zebulun and Naphtali — ¹⁴to fulfill what was said through the prophet Isaiah:

¹⁵"Land of Zebulun and land of
    Naphtali,
the way to the sea, along the
    Jordan,
Galilee of the Gentiles —
¹⁶the people living in darkness
    have seen a great light;
on those living in the land of the
    shadow of death
    a light has dawned."[a]

¹⁷From that time on Jesus began to preach, "Repent, for the kingdom of heaven is near."

The Calling of the First Disciples

¹⁸As Jesus was walking beside the Sea of Galilee, he saw two brothers, Simon called Peter and his brother Andrew. They were casting a net into the lake, for they were fishermen. ¹⁹"Come, follow me," Jesus said, "and I will make you fishers of men." ²⁰At once they left their nets and followed him.

²¹Going on from there, he saw two other brothers, James son of Zebedee and his brother John. They were in a boat with their father Zebedee, preparing their nets. Jesus called them, ²²and immediately they left the boat and their father and followed him.

Jesus Heals the Sick

²³Jesus went throughout Galilee, teaching in their synagogues, preaching the good news of the kingdom, and healing every disease and sickness among the people. ²⁴News about him spread all over Syria, and people brought to him all who were ill with various diseases, those suffering severe pain, the demon-possessed, those having seizures, and the paralyzed, and he healed them. ²⁵Large crowds from Galilee, the Decapolis,[b] Jerusalem, Judea and the region across the Jordan followed him.

The Beatitudes

5 Now when he saw the crowds, he went up on a mountainside and sat down. His disciples came to him, ²and he began to teach them, saying:

³"Blessed are the poor in spirit,
    for theirs is the kingdom of heaven.
⁴Blessed are those who mourn,
    for they will be comforted.
⁵Blessed are the meek,
    for they will inherit the earth.
⁶Blessed are those who hunger and
    thirst for righteousness,
    for they will be filled.
⁷Blessed are the merciful,
    for they will be shown mercy.
⁸Blessed are the pure in heart,
    for they will see God.
⁹Blessed are the peacemakers,
    for they will be called sons of God.
¹⁰Blessed are those who are persecuted
    because of righteousness,
    for theirs is the kingdom of heaven.

¹¹"Blessed are you when people insult you, persecute you and falsely say all kinds of evil against you because of me. ¹²Rejoice and be glad, because great is your reward in heaven, for in the same way they persecuted the prophets who were before you.

Salt and Light

¹³"You are the salt of the earth. But if the salt loses its saltiness, how can it be made salty again? It is no longer good for anything, except to be thrown out and trampled by men.

¹⁴"You are the light of the world. A city on a hill cannot be hidden. ¹⁵Neither do people light a lamp and put it under a bowl. Instead they put it on its stand, and it gives light to everyone in the house. ¹⁶In the same way, let your light shine before men, that they may see your good deeds and praise your Father in heaven.

The Fulfillment of the Law

¹⁷"Do not think that I have come to abolish the Law or the Prophets; I have not come to abolish them but to fulfill them. ¹⁸I tell you the truth, until heaven and earth disappear, not the smallest letter, not the least stroke of a pen, will by any means disappear from the Law until everything is accomplished. ¹⁹Anyone who breaks one of the least of these com-

---

[a] 16 Isaiah 9:1,2   [b] 25 That is, the Ten Cities

mandments and teaches others to do the same will be called least in the kingdom of heaven, but whoever practices and teaches these commands will be called great in the kingdom of heaven. **20**For I tell you that unless your righteousness surpasses that of the Pharisees and the teachers of the law, you will certainly not enter the kingdom of heaven.

Murder

21"You have heard that it was said to the people long ago, 'Do not murder,[a] and anyone who murders will be subject to judgment.' **22**But I tell you that anyone who is angry with his brother[b] will be subject to judgment. Again, anyone who says to his brother, 'Raca,[c]' is answerable to the Sanhedrin. But anyone who says, 'You fool!' will be in danger of the fire of hell.

23"Therefore, if you are offering your gift at the altar and there remember that your brother has something against you, **24**leave your gift there in front of the altar. First go and be reconciled to your brother; then come and offer your gift.

25"Settle matters quickly with your adversary who is taking you to court. Do it while you are still with him on the way, or

[a]21 Exodus 20:13   [b]22 Some manuscripts *brother without cause*   [c]22 An Aramaic term of contempt

WEDNESDAY

VERSE FOR THE DAY:
Matthew 5:14

AUTHOR:
Thomas Merton

PASSAGE FOR THE DAY:
Matthew 5:14–16

Give Us the Light

ALL of us who have been baptized in Christ and have "put on Christ" as a new identity are bound to be holy as he is holy. We are bound to live worthy lives, and our actions should bear witness to our union with him. He should manifest his presence in us and through us . . .

We are supposed to be the light of the world. We are supposed to be a light to ourselves and to others. That may well be what accounts for the fact that the world is in darkness! What then is meant by the light of Christ in our lives? What is "holiness"? What is divine sonship? Are we really seriously supposed to be saints? Can a man even desire such a thing without making a complete fool of himself in the eyes of everyone else? Is it not presumptuous? Is such a thing even possible at all? To tell the truth, many laypeople and even a good many religious do not believe, in practice, that sanctity is possible for them. Is this just plain common sense? Is it perhaps humility? Or is it defection, defeatism and despair?

If we are called by God to holiness of life and if holiness is beyond our natural power to achieve (which it certainly is) then it follows that God himself must give us the light, the strength and the courage to fulfill the task he requires of us. He will certainly give us the grace we need. If we do not become saints it is because we do not avail ourselves of his gift.

Additional Scripture Readings:
John 1:1–14; 2 Corinthians 4:1–6

Go to page 9 for your next devotional reading.

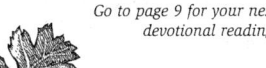

he may hand you over to the judge, and the judge may hand you over to the officer, and you may be thrown into prison. ²⁶I tell you the truth, you will not get out until you have paid the last penny.ᵃ

Adultery

²⁷"You have heard that it was said, 'Do not commit adultery.'ᵇ ²⁸But I tell you that anyone who looks at a woman lustfully has already committed adultery with her in his heart. ²⁹If your right eye causes you to sin, gouge it out and throw it away. It is better for you to lose one part of your body than for your whole body to be thrown into hell. ³⁰And if your right hand causes you to sin, cut it off and throw it away. It is better for you to lose one part of your body than for your whole body to go into hell.

Divorce

³¹"It has been said, 'Anyone who divorces his wife must give her a certificate of divorce.'ᶜ ³²But I tell you that anyone who divorces his wife, except for marital unfaithfulness, causes her to become an adulteress, and anyone who marries the divorced woman commits adultery.

Oaths

³³"Again, you have heard that it was said to the people long ago, 'Do not break your oath, but keep the oaths you have made to the Lord.' ³⁴But I tell you, Do not swear at all: either by heaven, for it is God's throne; ³⁵or by the earth, for it is his footstool; or by Jerusalem, for it is the city of the Great King. ³⁶And do not swear by your head, for you cannot make even one hair white or black. ³⁷Simply let your 'Yes' be 'Yes,' and your 'No,' 'No'; anything beyond this comes from the evil one.

An Eye for an Eye

³⁸"You have heard that it was said, 'Eye for eye, and tooth for tooth.'ᵈ ³⁹But I tell you, Do not resist an evil person. If someone strikes you on the right cheek, turn to him the other also. ⁴⁰And if someone wants to sue you and take your tunic, let him have your cloak as well. ⁴¹If someone forces you to go one mile, go with him two miles. ⁴²Give to the one who asks you, and do not turn away from the one who wants to borrow from you.

Love for Enemies

⁴³"You have heard that it was said, 'Love your neighborᵉ and hate your enemy.' ⁴⁴But I tell you: Love your enemiesᶠ and pray for those who persecute you, ⁴⁵that you may be sons of your Father in heaven. He causes his sun to rise on the evil and the good, and sends rain on the righteous and the unrighteous. ⁴⁶If you love those who love you, what reward will you get? Are not even the tax collectors doing that? ⁴⁷And if you greet only your brothers, what are you doing more than others? Do not even pagans do that? ⁴⁸Be perfect, therefore, as your heavenly Father is perfect.

Giving to the Needy

6 "Be careful not to do your 'acts of righteousness' before men, to be seen by them. If you do, you will have no reward from your Father in heaven.

²"So when you give to the needy, do not announce it with trumpets, as the hypocrites do in the synagogues and on the streets, to be honored by men. I tell you the truth, they have received their reward in full. ³But when you give to the needy, do not let your left hand know what your right hand is doing, ⁴so that your giving may be in secret. Then your Father, who sees what is done in secret, will reward you.

Prayer

⁵"And when you pray, do not be like the hypocrites, for they love to pray standing in the synagogues and on the street corners to be seen by men. I tell you the truth, they have received their reward in full. ⁶But when you pray, go into your room, close the door and pray to your Father, who is unseen. Then your Father, who sees what is done in secret, will reward you. ⁷And when you pray, do not keep on babbling like pagans, for they think they will be heard because of their many words. ⁸Do not be like them, for your Father knows what you need before you ask him.

⁹"This, then, is how you should pray:

" 'Our Father in heaven,
hallowed be your name,
¹⁰your kingdom come,
your will be done

ᵃ26 Greek *kodrantes*   ᵇ27 Exodus 20:14   ᶜ31 Deut. 24:1   ᵈ38 Exodus 21:24; Lev. 24:20; Deut. 19:21   ᵉ43 Lev. 19:18   ᶠ44 Some late manuscripts *enemies, bless those who curse you, do good to those who hate you*

on earth as it is in heaven. ¹¹Give us today our daily bread. ¹²Forgive us our debts, as we also have forgiven our debtors. ¹³And lead us not into temptation, but deliver us from the evil one.*ᵃ*'

¹⁴For if you forgive men when they sin against you, your heavenly Father will also forgive you. ¹⁵But if you do not forgive men their sins, your Father will not forgive your sins.

Fasting

¹⁶"When you fast, do not look somber as the hypocrites do, for they disfigure their faces to show men they are fasting.

ᵃ13 Or from evil; some late manuscripts *one, / for yours is the kingdom and the power and the glory forever. Amen.*

THURSDAY

VERSE FOR THE DAY:
Matthew 6:10

AUTHOR:
Jack Perry

PASSAGE FOR THE DAY:
Matthew 6:5–15

A Most Tragic Search

IN HIS own life, Jesus asked what was the will of God. He received a most searing answer. We can easily say that he was the Son of God, and came into the world to save sinners, and thus had to die on the cross. Yes, but he was the Son of Man as well, and he prayed that the cup might pass from him, and he asked why God had forsaken him, and his suffering as he undertook to do the will of God was suffering such as we mortals know. So we cannot take refuge from hard choices in the divinity of Jesus. Nor can we hide behind some division of the world into the part Jesus was talking about and the part he was not. At Calvary, all came together.

Therefore when Jesus told us to say, "Your kingdom come, your will be done" (Matthew 6:10), he was telling us to embark upon a most tragic search for the will of God in our lives. Try as I might, I cannot find any place to hide in those crystal, bleeding sentences. Human words find it hard to express the depth of Jesus' divine words. But he was saying, in the most literal way, that God's will should be sought and it should be obeyed.

To obey God's will for my life—what a shattering thought! If I took Jesus at his word, would I not be helping the poor, or giving all I had to the needy, or learning to care for the sick, or proclaiming the acceptable day of the Lord on the public streets, or binding the wounds of the war-torn—would I not be about my Father's business, rather than going on about my daily routine? If I took Jesus seriously, and truly asked God to let me do his will in my life, would I be where I am right now?

Additional Scripture Readings:
Ephesians 5:15–20;
Colossians 1:9–14

Go to page 11 for your next devotional reading.

I tell you the truth, they have received their reward in full. ¹⁷But when you fast, put oil on your head and wash your face, ¹⁸so that it will not be obvious to men that you are fasting, but only to your Father, who is unseen; and your Father, who sees what is done in secret, will reward you.

Treasures in Heaven

¹⁹"Do not store up for yourselves treasures on earth, where moth and rust destroy, and where thieves break in and steal. ²⁰But store up for yourselves treasures in heaven, where moth and rust do not destroy, and where thieves do not break in and steal. ²¹For where your treasure is, there your heart will be also.

²²"The eye is the lamp of the body. If your eyes are good, your whole body will be full of light. ²³But if your eyes are bad, your whole body will be full of darkness. If then the light within you is darkness, how great is that darkness!

²⁴"No one can serve two masters. Either he will hate the one and love the other, or he will be devoted to the one and despise the other. You cannot serve both God and Money.

Do Not Worry

²⁵"Therefore I tell you, do not worry about your life, what you will eat or drink; or about your body, what you will wear. Is not life more important than food, and the body more important than clothes? ²⁶Look at the birds of the air; they do not sow or reap or store away in barns, and yet your heavenly Father feeds them. Are you not much more valuable than they? ²⁷Who of you by worrying can add a single hour to his life*ᵃ*?

²⁸"And why do you worry about clothes? See how the lilies of the field grow. They do not labor or spin. ²⁹Yet I tell you that not even Solomon in all his splendor was dressed like one of these. ³⁰If that is how God clothes the grass of the field, which is here today and tomorrow is thrown into the fire, will he not much more clothe you, O you of little faith? ³¹So do not worry, saying, 'What shall we eat?' or 'What shall we drink?' or 'What shall we wear?' ³²For the pagans run after all these things, and your heavenly Father knows that you need them. ³³But seek first his kingdom and his righteousness, and all these things will be given to you as well. ³⁴Therefore do not worry about tomorrow, for tomorrow will worry about itself. Each day has enough trouble of its own.

Judging Others

7 "Do not judge, or you too will be judged. ²For in the same way you judge others, you will be judged, and with the measure you use, it will be measured to you.

³"Why do you look at the speck of sawdust in your brother's eye and pay no attention to the plank in your own eye? ⁴How can you say to your brother, 'Let me take the speck out of your eye,' when all the time there is a plank in your own eye? ⁵You hypocrite, first take the plank out of your own eye, and then you will see clearly to remove the speck from your brother's eye.

⁶"Do not give dogs what is sacred; do not throw your pearls to pigs. If you do, they may trample them under their feet, and then turn and tear you to pieces.

Ask, Seek, Knock

⁷"Ask and it will be given to you; seek and you will find; knock and the door will be opened to you. ⁸For everyone who asks receives; he who seeks finds; and to him who knocks, the door will be opened.

⁹"Which of you, if his son asks for bread, will give him a stone? ¹⁰Or if he asks for a fish, will give him a snake? ¹¹If you, then, though you are evil, know how to give good gifts to your children, how much more will your Father in heaven give good gifts to those who ask him! ¹²So in everything, do to others what you would have them do to you, for this sums up the Law and the Prophets.

The Narrow and Wide Gates

¹³"Enter through the narrow gate. For wide is the gate and broad is the road that leads to destruction, and many enter through it. ¹⁴But small is the gate and narrow the road that leads to life, and only a few find it.

A Tree and Its Fruit

¹⁵"Watch out for false prophets. They come to you in sheep's clothing, but inwardly they are ferocious wolves. ¹⁶By their fruit you will recognize them. Do people pick grapes from thornbushes, or figs from thistles? ¹⁷Likewise every good tree bears good fruit, but a bad tree bears

---

a27 Or single cubit to his height

FRIDAY

VERSE FOR THE DAY:
Matthew 7:24

AUTHOR:
Tom Landry

PASSAGE FOR THE DAY:
Matthew 7:24–27

Spiritual Crossroads

I HAD always considered myself a Christian, yet so much of what I now discovered in the Bible went against the grain of the life philosophy I had lived by . . .

All my life I had made my football career the number-one priority and let it dictate the direction of my life. Now here was the Bible saying I needed to make God and his will first and follow his direction for my life.

Gradually I realized the crossroads I faced in my life was really a spiritual crossroads. I had to decide whether or not I believed what the Bible said. All my other questions hung on that one.

The more of the Bible I read and studied, the more it all made sense. The more pieces of life fit together. The more I wanted to believe. And yet that analytical part of my nature kept asking questions, trying to dispel all doubt.

One day I came across a short passage of a poem by Robert Browning that said: "You call for faith, I give you doubt, to prove that faith exists. The greater the doubt, the stronger the faith, I say, if faith overcomes doubt."

When I read that, something clicked in me and I began to understand faith in a new light.

I can't point to a specific moment or a specific time when I had a sudden "born-again" experience. For me, coming to my own personal faith in God took place over a period of months in 1959. But I finally reached a point where faith outweighed the doubts, and I was willing to commit my entire life to God.

I can't say that decision made an immediately visible difference in my life. I can't even say it instantly transformed me into a much better person; I had a lot yet to learn—and I still do—about how God wants me to live my life. But what my new Christian experience did do for me was to place football behind the priorities of my faith and my family and give me a sense of confidence and peace about the future—whatever it would be.

Additional Scripture Readings:
Romans 12:1–2;
1 Thessalonians 4:1–7

Go to page 13 for your next devotional reading.

bad fruit. **18**A good tree cannot bear bad fruit, and a bad tree cannot bear good fruit. **19**Every tree that does not bear good fruit is cut down and thrown into the fire. **20**Thus, by their fruit you will recognize them.

21"Not everyone who says to me, 'Lord, Lord,' will enter the kingdom of heaven, but only he who does the will of my Father who is in heaven. **22**Many will say to me on that day, 'Lord, Lord, did we not prophesy in your name, and in your name drive out demons and perform many miracles?' **23**Then I will tell them plainly, 'I never knew you. Away from me, you evildoers!'

The Wise and Foolish Builders

24"Therefore everyone who hears these words of mine and puts them into practice is like a wise man who built his house on the rock. **25**The rain came down, the streams rose, and the winds blew and beat against that house; yet it did not fall, because it had its foundation on the rock. **26**But everyone who hears these words of mine and does not put them into practice is like a foolish man who built his house on sand. **27**The rain came down, the streams rose, and the winds blew and beat against that house, and it fell with a great crash."

28When Jesus had finished saying these things, the crowds were amazed at his teaching, **29**because he taught as one who had authority, and not as their teachers of the law.

The Man With Leprosy

8 When he came down from the mountainside, large crowds followed him. **2**A man with leprosy[a] came and knelt before him and said, "Lord, if you are willing, you can make me clean."
3Jesus reached out his hand and touched the man. "I am willing," he said. "Be clean!" Immediately he was cured[b] of his leprosy. **4**Then Jesus said to him, "See that you don't tell anyone. But go, show yourself to the priest and offer the gift Moses commanded, as a testimony to them."

The Faith of the Centurion

5When Jesus had entered Capernaum, a centurion came to him, asking for help. **6**"Lord," he said, "my servant lies at home paralyzed and in terrible suffering."
7Jesus said to him, "I will go and heal him."
8The centurion replied, "Lord, I do not deserve to have you come under my roof. But just say the word, and my servant will be healed. **9**For I myself am a man under authority, with soldiers under me. I tell this one, 'Go,' and he goes; and that one, 'Come,' and he comes. I say to my servant, 'Do this,' and he does it."

10When Jesus heard this, he was astonished and said to those following him, "I tell you the truth, I have not found anyone in Israel with such great faith. **11**I say to you that many will come from the east and the west, and will take their places at the feast with Abraham, Isaac and Jacob in the kingdom of heaven. **12**But the subjects of the kingdom will be thrown outside, into the darkness, where there will be weeping and gnashing of teeth."

13Then Jesus said to the centurion, "Go! It will be done just as you believed it would." And his servant was healed at that very hour.

Jesus Heals Many

14When Jesus came into Peter's house, he saw Peter's mother-in-law lying in bed with a fever. **15**He touched her hand and the fever left her, and she got up and began to wait on him.

16When evening came, many who were demon-possessed were brought to him, and he drove out the spirits with a word and healed all the sick. **17**This was to fulfill what was spoken through the prophet Isaiah:

"He took up our infirmities
and carried our diseases."[c]

The Cost of Following Jesus

18When Jesus saw the crowd around him, he gave orders to cross to the other side of the lake. **19**Then a teacher of the law came to him and said, "Teacher, I will follow you wherever you go."
20Jesus replied, "Foxes have holes and birds of the air have nests, but the Son of Man has no place to lay his head."
21Another disciple said to him, "Lord, first let me go and bury my father."
22But Jesus told him, "Follow me, and let the dead bury their own dead."

---

[a] 2 The Greek word was used for various diseases affecting the skin—not necessarily leprosy.   [b] 3 Greek *made clean*   [c] 17 Isaiah 53:4

WEEKENDING

RENEW

As long as Jesus is one of many options, he is no option. As long as you can carry your burdens alone, you don't need a burden bearer. As long as your situation brings you no grief, you will receive no comfort. And as long as you can take him or leave him, you might as well leave him, because he won't be taken half-heartedly.

But when you mourn, when you get to the point of sorrow for your sins, when you admit that you have no other option but to cast all your cares on him, and when there is truly no other name that you can call, then cast all your cares on him, for he is waiting in the midst of the storm.

– *Max Lucado*

REVIVE
Saturday: Matthew 14:22–33
Sunday: 1 Peter 5:5–7

Go to page 14 for your next devotional reading.

MATTHEW 8

Jesus Calms the Storm

²³Then he got into the boat and his disciples followed him. ²⁴Without warning, a furious storm came up on the lake, so that the waves swept over the boat. But Jesus was sleeping. ²⁵The disciples went and woke him, saying, "Lord, save us! We're going to drown!"

²⁶He replied, "You of little faith, why are you so afraid?" Then he got up and rebuked the winds and the waves, and it was completely calm.

²⁷The men were amazed and asked, "What kind of man is this? Even the winds and the waves obey him!"

The Healing of Two Demon-possessed Men

²⁸When he arrived at the other side in the region of the Gadarenes,ᵃ two demon-possessed men coming from the tombs met him. They were so violent that no one could pass that way. ²⁹"What do you want with us, Son of God?" they shouted. "Have you come here to torture us before the appointed time?"

³⁰Some distance from them a large herd of pigs was feeding. ³¹The demons begged Jesus, "If you drive us out, send us into the herd of pigs."

³²He said to them, "Go!" So they came

ᵃ28 Some manuscripts Gergesenes; others Gerasenes

MONDAY

VERSE FOR THE DAY:
Matthew 8:0

AUTHOR:
Charles Colson

PASSAGE FOR THE DAY:
Matthew 8:18–22

Identifying with Jesus

TIME after time I find that men and women in the prisons of America want nothing to do with the church or with Christianity. They cannot relate to our lavish buildings and stained-glass windows because they see the church as a manifestation of the culture that has rejected them and holds them prisoner. But I see those same people come alive when I talk about Jesus the prisoner, the outcast who was followed by a dirty dozen, the One who was laid in a borrowed manger, rode on a borrowed donkey, was arrested, hung on a cross between two thieves, and then buried in a borrowed tomb. They can understand and identify with the Jesus of the Scriptures, not with a Christ who appears to have just stepped out of a Brooks Brothers catalog.

The longer I'm a Christian, the more I realize that the vague deity of American civil religion is a heretical rejection of the Christ of Holy Scripture. So don't confuse your loyalties —never assume the will of the majority and the will of God are synonymous. They may be different—and frequently are.

The Christian is committed to work for justice and righteousness, to bring the gospel of Christ to bear in all areas of life to make a difference in society. But we do it by the integrity of our witness, not by resorting to quick, simplistic clichés.

Additional Scripture Readings:
Luke 4:16–20; Philippians 2:1–11

Go to page 18 for your next devotional reading.

out and went into the pigs, and the whole herd rushed down the steep bank into the lake and died in the water. ³³Those tending the pigs ran off, went into the town and reported all this, including what had happened to the demon-possessed men. ³⁴Then the whole town went out to meet Jesus. And when they saw him, they pleaded with him to leave their region.

Jesus Heals a Paralytic

9 Jesus stepped into a boat, crossed over and came to his own town. ²Some men brought to him a paralytic, lying on a mat. When Jesus saw their faith, he said to the paralytic, "Take heart, son; your sins are forgiven."

³At this, some of the teachers of the law said to themselves, "This fellow is blaspheming!"

⁴Knowing their thoughts, Jesus said, "Why do you entertain evil thoughts in your hearts? ⁵Which is easier: to say, 'Your sins are forgiven,' or to say, 'Get up and walk'? ⁶But so that you may know that the Son of Man has authority on earth to forgive sins...." Then he said to the paralytic, "Get up, take your mat and go home." ⁷And the man got up and went home. ⁸When the crowd saw this, they were filled with awe; and they praised God, who had given such authority to men.

The Calling of Matthew

⁹As Jesus went on from there, he saw a man named Matthew sitting at the tax collector's booth. "Follow me," he told him, and Matthew got up and followed him.

¹⁰While Jesus was having dinner at Matthew's house, many tax collectors and "sinners" came and ate with him and his disciples. ¹¹When the Pharisees saw this, they asked his disciples, "Why does your teacher eat with tax collectors and 'sinners'?"

¹²On hearing this, Jesus said, "It is not the healthy who need a doctor, but the sick. ¹³But go and learn what this means: 'I desire mercy, not sacrifice.'*a* For I have not come to call the righteous, but sinners."

Jesus Questioned About Fasting

¹⁴Then John's disciples came and asked him, "How is it that we and the Pharisees fast, but your disciples do not fast?"

¹⁵Jesus answered, "How can the guests of the bridegroom mourn while he is with them? The time will come when the bridegroom will be taken from them; then they will fast.

¹⁶"No one sews a patch of unshrunk cloth on an old garment, for the patch will pull away from the garment, making the tear worse. ¹⁷Neither do men pour new wine into old wineskins. If they do, the skins will burst, the wine will run out and the wineskins will be ruined. No, they pour new wine into new wineskins, and both are preserved."

A Dead Girl and a Sick Woman

¹⁸While he was saying this, a ruler came and knelt before him and said, "My daughter has just died. But come and put your hand on her, and she will live." ¹⁹Jesus got up and went with him, and so did his disciples.

²⁰Just then a woman who had been subject to bleeding for twelve years came up behind him and touched the edge of his cloak. ²¹She said to herself, "If I only touch his cloak, I will be healed."

²²Jesus turned and saw her. "Take heart, daughter," he said, "your faith has healed you." And the woman was healed from that moment.

²³When Jesus entered the ruler's house and saw the flute players and the noisy crowd, ²⁴he said, "Go away. The girl is not dead but asleep." But they laughed at him. ²⁵After the crowd had been put outside, he went in and took the girl by the hand, and she got up. ²⁶News of this spread through all that region.

Jesus Heals the Blind and Mute

²⁷As Jesus went on from there, two blind men followed him, calling out, "Have mercy on us, Son of David!"

²⁸When he had gone indoors, the blind men came to him, and he asked them, "Do you believe that I am able to do this?"

"Yes, Lord," they replied.

²⁹Then he touched their eyes and said, "According to your faith will it be done to you"; ³⁰and their sight was restored. Jesus warned them sternly, "See that no one knows about this." ³¹But they went out and spread the news about him all over that region.

³²While they were going out, a man who was demon-possessed and could not talk was brought to Jesus. ³³And when the demon was driven out, the man who had

a13 Hosea 6:6

been mute spoke. The crowd was amazed and said, "Nothing like this has ever been seen in Israel."

34But the Pharisees said, "It is by the prince of demons that he drives out demons."

The Workers Are Few

35Jesus went through all the towns and villages, teaching in their synagogues, preaching the good news of the kingdom and healing every disease and sickness. **36**When he saw the crowds, he had compassion on them, because they were harassed and helpless, like sheep without a shepherd. **37**Then he said to his disciples, "The harvest is plentiful but the workers are few. **38**Ask the Lord of the harvest, therefore, to send out workers into his harvest field."

Jesus Sends Out the Twelve

10 He called his twelve disciples to him and gave them authority to drive out evil*a* spirits and to heal every disease and sickness.

2These are the names of the twelve apostles: first, Simon (who is called Peter) and his brother Andrew; James son of Zebedee, and his brother John; **3**Philip and Bartholomew; Thomas and Matthew the tax collector; James son of Alphaeus, and Thaddaeus; **4**Simon the Zealot and Judas Iscariot, who betrayed him.

5These twelve Jesus sent out with the following instructions: "Do not go among the Gentiles or enter any town of the Samaritans. **6**Go rather to the lost sheep of Israel. **7**As you go, preach this message: 'The kingdom of heaven is near.' **8**Heal the sick, raise the dead, cleanse those who have leprosy,*b* drive out demons. Freely you have received, freely give. **9**Do not take along any gold or silver or copper in your belts; **10**take no bag for the journey, or extra tunic, or sandals or a staff; for the worker is worth his keep.

11"Whatever town or village you enter, search for some worthy person there and stay at his house until you leave. **12**As you enter the home, give it your greeting. **13**If the home is deserving, let your peace rest on it; if it is not, let your peace return to you. **14**If anyone will not welcome you or listen to your words, shake the dust off your feet when you leave that home or town. **15**I tell you the truth, it will be more bearable for Sodom and Gomorrah on the day of judgment than for that town. **16**I am sending you out like sheep among wolves. Therefore be as shrewd as snakes and as innocent as doves.

17"Be on your guard against men; they will hand you over to the local councils and flog you in their synagogues. **18**On my account you will be brought before governors and kings as witnesses to them and to the Gentiles. **19**But when they arrest you, do not worry about what to say or how to say it. At that time you will be given what to say, **20**for it will not be you speaking, but the Spirit of your Father speaking through you.

21"Brother will betray brother to death, and a father his child; children will rebel against their parents and have them put to death. **22**All men will hate you because of me, but he who stands firm to the end will be saved. **23**When you are persecuted in one place, flee to another. I tell you the truth, you will not finish going through the cities of Israel before the Son of Man comes.

24"A student is not above his teacher, nor a servant above his master. **25**It is enough for the student to be like his teacher, and the servant like his master. If the head of the house has been called Beelzebub,*c* how much more the members of his household!

26"So do not be afraid of them. There is nothing concealed that will not be disclosed, or hidden that will not be made known. **27**What I tell you in the dark, speak in the daylight; what is whispered in your ear, proclaim from the roofs. **28**Do not be afraid of those who kill the body but cannot kill the soul. Rather, be afraid of the One who can destroy both soul and body in hell. **29**Are not two sparrows sold for a penny*d*? Yet not one of them will fall to the ground apart from the will of your Father. **30**And even the very hairs of your head are all numbered. **31**So don't be afraid; you are worth more than many sparrows.

32"Whoever acknowledges me before men, I will also acknowledge him before my Father in heaven. **33**But whoever disowns me before men, I will disown him before my Father in heaven.

34"Do not suppose that I have come to bring peace to the earth. I did not come to

---

a1 Greek *unclean*   *b8* The Greek word was used for various diseases affecting the skin—not necessarily leprosy.   *c25* Greek *Beezeboul* or *Beelzeboul*   *d29* Greek *an assarion*

bring peace, but a sword. **35**For I have come to turn

" 'a man against his father,
a daughter against her mother,
a daughter-in-law against her mother-in-law —
36 a man's enemies will be the members of his own household.'*a*

37"Anyone who loves his father or mother more than me is not worthy of me; anyone who loves his son or daughter more than me is not worthy of me; **38**and anyone who does not take his cross and follow me is not worthy of me. **39**Whoever finds his life will lose it, and whoever loses his life for my sake will find it.

40"He who receives you receives me, and he who receives me receives the one who sent me. **41**Anyone who receives a prophet because he is a prophet will receive a prophet's reward, and anyone who receives a righteous man because he is a righteous man will receive a righteous man's reward. **42**And if anyone gives even a cup of cold water to one of these little ones because he is my disciple, I tell you the truth, he will certainly not lose his reward."

Jesus and John the Baptist

11 After Jesus had finished instructing his twelve disciples, he went on from there to teach and preach in the towns of Galilee.*b*

2When John heard in prison what Christ was doing, he sent his disciples **3**to ask him, "Are you the one who was to come, or should we expect someone else?"

4Jesus replied, "Go back and report to John what you hear and see: **5**The blind receive sight, the lame walk, those who have leprosy*c* are cured, the deaf hear, the dead are raised, and the good news is preached to the poor. **6**Blessed is the man who does not fall away on account of me."

7As John's disciples were leaving, Jesus began to speak to the crowd about John: "What did you go out into the desert to see? A reed swayed by the wind? **8**If not, what did you go out to see? A man dressed in fine clothes? No, those who wear fine clothes are in kings' palaces. **9**Then what did you go out to see? A prophet? Yes, I tell you, and more than a prophet. **10**This is the one about whom it is written:

" 'I will send my messenger ahead of you,
who will prepare your way before you.'*d*

11I tell you the truth: Among those born of women there has not risen anyone greater than John the Baptist; yet he who is least in the kingdom of heaven is greater than he. **12**From the days of John the Baptist until now, the kingdom of heaven has been forcefully advancing, and forceful men lay hold of it. **13**For all the Prophets and the Law prophesied until John. **14**And if you are willing to accept it, he is the Elijah who was to come. **15**He who has ears, let him hear.

16"To what can I compare this generation? They are like children sitting in the marketplaces and calling out to others:

17" 'We played the flute for you,
and you did not dance;
we sang a dirge,
and you did not mourn.'

18For John came neither eating nor drinking, and they say, 'He has a demon.' **19**The Son of Man came eating and drinking, and they say, 'Here is a glutton and a drunkard, a friend of tax collectors and "sinners." ' But wisdom is proved right by her actions."

Woe on Unrepentant Cities

20Then Jesus began to denounce the cities in which most of his miracles had been performed, because they did not repent. **21**"Woe to you, Korazin! Woe to you, Bethsaida! If the miracles that were performed in you had been performed in Tyre and Sidon, they would have repented long ago in sackcloth and ashes. **22**But I tell you, it will be more bearable for Tyre and Sidon on the day of judgment than for you. **23**And you, Capernaum, will you be lifted up to the skies? No, you will go down to the depths.*e* If the miracles that were performed in you had been performed in Sodom, it would have remained to this day. **24**But I tell you that it will be more bearable for Sodom on the day of judgment than for you."

---

a 36 Micah 7:6   *b 1* Greek *in their towns*   *c 5* The Greek word was used for various diseases affecting the skin—not necessarily leprosy.   *d 10* Mal. 3:1   *e 23* Greek *Hades*

MATTHEW 11–12

Rest for the Weary

25At that time Jesus said, "I praise you, Father, Lord of heaven and earth, because you have hidden these things from the wise and learned, and revealed them to little children. **26**Yes, Father, for this was your good pleasure.

27"All things have been committed to me by my Father. No one knows the Son except the Father, and no one knows the Father except the Son and those to whom the Son chooses to reveal him.

28"Come to me, all you who are weary and burdened, and I will give you rest. **29**Take my yoke upon you and learn from me, for I am gentle and humble in heart, and you will find rest for your souls. **30**For my yoke is easy and my burden is light."

Lord of the Sabbath

12 At that time Jesus went through the grainfields on the Sabbath. His disciples were hungry and began to pick some heads of grain and eat them. **2**When the Pharisees saw this, they said to him, "Look! Your disciples are doing what is unlawful on the Sabbath."

3He answered, "Haven't you read what David did when he and his companions were hungry? **4**He entered the house of God, and he and his companions ate the consecrated bread—which was not lawful for them to do, but only for the priests. **5**Or haven't you read in the Law that on the Sabbath the priests in the temple desecrate the day and yet are innocent? **6**I tell you that one*a* greater than the temple is

*a*6 Or *something*; also in verses 41 and 42

TUESDAY

VERSE FOR THE DAY:
Matthew 11:30

AUTHOR:
Dietrich Bonhoeffer

PASSAGE FOR THE DAY:
Matthew 11:28–30

Christ's Kindly Yoke

WHEN the Bible speaks of following Jesus, it is proclaiming a discipleship that will liberate mankind from all man-made dogmas, from every burden and oppression, from every anxiety and torture that afflicts the conscience. If they follow Jesus, men escape from the hard yoke of their own laws, and submit to the kindly yoke of Jesus Christ. But does this mean that we ignore the seriousness of his commands? Far from it. We can only achieve perfect liberty and enjoy fellowship with Jesus when his command, his call to absolute discipleship, is appreciated in its entirety. Only the man who follows the command of Jesus single-mindedly, and unresistingly lets his yoke rest upon him, finds his burden easy, and under its gentle pressure receives the power to persevere in the right way. The command of Jesus is hard, unutterably hard, for those who try to resist it. But for those who willingly submit, the yoke is easy and the burden is light. "His commands are not burdensome" (1 John 5:3). The commandment of Jesus is not a sort of spiritual shock treatment. Jesus asks nothing of us without giving us the strength to perform it. His commandment never seeks to destroy life, but to foster, strengthen and heal it.

Additional Scripture Readings:
Galatians 3:1–14; 1 John 5:1–5

Go to page 23 for your next devotional reading.

here. ⁷If you had known what these words mean, 'I desire mercy, not sacrifice,'*a* you would not have condemned the innocent. ⁸For the Son of Man is Lord of the Sabbath."

⁹Going on from that place, he went into their synagogue, ¹⁰and a man with a shriveled hand was there. Looking for a reason to accuse Jesus, they asked him, "Is it lawful to heal on the Sabbath?"

¹¹He said to them, "If any of you has a sheep and it falls into a pit on the Sabbath, will you not take hold of it and lift it out? ¹²How much more valuable is a man than a sheep! Therefore it is lawful to do good on the Sabbath."

¹³Then he said to the man, "Stretch out your hand." So he stretched it out and it was completely restored, just as sound as the other. ¹⁴But the Pharisees went out and plotted how they might kill Jesus.

God's Chosen Servant

¹⁵Aware of this, Jesus withdrew from that place. Many followed him, and he healed all their sick, ¹⁶warning them not to tell who he was. ¹⁷This was to fulfill what was spoken through the prophet Isaiah:

¹⁸"Here is my servant whom I have chosen,
the one I love, in whom I delight;
I will put my Spirit on him,
and he will proclaim justice to the nations.
¹⁹He will not quarrel or cry out;
no one will hear his voice in the streets.
²⁰A bruised reed he will not break,
and a smoldering wick he will not snuff out,
till he leads justice to victory.
21   In his name the nations will put their hope."*b*

Jesus and Beelzebub

²²Then they brought him a demon-possessed man who was blind and mute, and Jesus healed him, so that he could both talk and see. ²³All the people were astonished and said, "Could this be the Son of David?"

²⁴But when the Pharisees heard this, they said, "It is only by Beelzebub,*c* the prince of demons, that this fellow drives out demons."

²⁵Jesus knew their thoughts and said to them, "Every kingdom divided against itself will be ruined, and every city or household divided against itself will not stand. ²⁶If Satan drives out Satan, he is divided against himself. How then can his kingdom stand? ²⁷And if I drive out demons by Beelzebub, by whom do your people drive them out? So then, they will be your judges. ²⁸But if I drive out demons by the Spirit of God, then the kingdom of God has come upon you.

²⁹"Or again, how can anyone enter a strong man's house and carry off his possessions unless he first ties up the strong man? Then he can rob his house.

³⁰"He who is not with me is against me, and he who does not gather with me scatters. ³¹And so I tell you, every sin and blasphemy will be forgiven men, but the blasphemy against the Spirit will not be forgiven. ³²Anyone who speaks a word against the Son of Man will be forgiven, but anyone who speaks against the Holy Spirit will not be forgiven, either in this age or in the age to come.

³³"Make a tree good and its fruit will be good, or make a tree bad and its fruit will be bad, for a tree is recognized by its fruit. ³⁴You brood of vipers, how can you who are evil say anything good? For out of the overflow of the heart the mouth speaks. ³⁵The good man brings good things out of the good stored up in him, and the evil man brings evil things out of the evil stored up in him. ³⁶But I tell you that men will have to give account on the day of judgment for every careless word they have spoken. ³⁷For by your words you will be acquitted, and by your words you will be condemned."

The Sign of Jonah

³⁸Then some of the Pharisees and teachers of the law said to him, "Teacher, we want to see a miraculous sign from you."

³⁹He answered, "A wicked and adulterous generation asks for a miraculous sign! But none will be given it except the sign of the prophet Jonah. ⁴⁰For as Jonah was three days and three nights in the belly of a huge fish, so the Son of Man will be three days and three nights in the heart of the earth. ⁴¹The men of Nineveh will stand up at the judgment with this generation and condemn it; for they repented at

---

a 7 Hosea 6:6   *b 21* Isaiah 42:1-4   *c 24* Greek *Beezeboul* or *Beelzeboul*; also in verse 27

the preaching of Jonah, and now one[a] greater than Jonah is here. **42**The Queen of the South will rise at the judgment with this generation and condemn it; for she came from the ends of the earth to listen to Solomon's wisdom, and now one greater than Solomon is here.

43"When an evil[b] spirit comes out of a man, it goes through arid places seeking rest and does not find it. **44**Then it says, 'I will return to the house I left.' When it arrives, it finds the house unoccupied, swept clean and put in order. **45**Then it goes and takes with it seven other spirits more wicked than itself, and they go in and live there. And the final condition of that man is worse than the first. That is how it will be with this wicked generation."

Jesus' Mother and Brothers

46While Jesus was still talking to the crowd, his mother and brothers stood outside, wanting to speak to him. **47**Someone told him, "Your mother and brothers are standing outside, wanting to speak to you."[c]

48He replied to him, "Who is my mother, and who are my brothers?" **49**Pointing to his disciples, he said, "Here are my mother and my brothers. **50**For whoever does the will of my Father in heaven is my brother and sister and mother."

The Parable of the Sower

13 That same day Jesus went out of the house and sat by the lake. **2**Such large crowds gathered around him that he got into a boat and sat in it, while all the people stood on the shore. **3**Then he told them many things in parables, saying: "A farmer went out to sow his seed. **4**As he was scattering the seed, some fell along the path, and the birds came and ate it up. **5**Some fell on rocky places, where it did not have much soil. It sprang up quickly, because the soil was shallow. **6**But when the sun came up, the plants were scorched, and they withered because they had no root. **7**Other seed fell among thorns, which grew up and choked the plants. **8**Still other seed fell on good soil, where it produced a crop—a hundred, sixty or thirty times what was sown. **9**He who has ears, let him hear."

10The disciples came to him and asked, "Why do you speak to the people in parables?"

11He replied, "The knowledge of the secrets of the kingdom of heaven has been given to you, but not to them. **12**Whoever has will be given more, and he will have an abundance. Whoever does not have, even what he has will be taken from him. **13**This is why I speak to them in parables:

"Though seeing, they do not see;
though hearing, they do not hear or understand.

14In them is fulfilled the prophecy of Isaiah:

" 'You will be ever hearing but never understanding;
you will be ever seeing but never perceiving.
15For this people's heart has become calloused;
they hardly hear with their ears,
and they have closed their eyes.
Otherwise they might see with their eyes,
hear with their ears,
understand with their hearts
and turn, and I would heal them.'[d]

16But blessed are your eyes because they see, and your ears because they hear. **17**For I tell you the truth, many prophets and righteous men longed to see what you see but did not see it, and to hear what you hear but did not hear it.

18"Listen then to what the parable of the sower means: **19**When anyone hears the message about the kingdom and does not understand it, the evil one comes and snatches away what was sown in his heart. This is the seed sown along the path. **20**The one who received the seed that fell on rocky places is the man who hears the word and at once receives it with joy. **21**But since he has no root, he lasts only a short time. When trouble or persecution comes because of the word, he quickly falls away. **22**The one who received the seed that fell among the thorns is the man who hears the word, but the worries of this life and the deceitfulness of wealth choke it, making it unfruitful. **23**But the one who received the seed that fell on good soil is the man who hears the word and understands it. He produces a crop, yielding a hundred, sixty or thirty times what was sown."

---

[a]41 Or *something*; also in verse 42   [b]43 Greek *unclean*   [c]47 Some manuscripts do not have verse 47.   [d]15 Isaiah 6:9,10

MATTHEW 13

The Parable of the Weeds

24Jesus told them another parable: "The kingdom of heaven is like a man who sowed good seed in his field. **25**But while everyone was sleeping, his enemy came and sowed weeds among the wheat, and went away. **26**When the wheat sprouted and formed heads, then the weeds also appeared.

27"The owner's servants came to him and said, 'Sir, didn't you sow good seed in your field? Where then did the weeds come from?'

28" 'An enemy did this,' he replied.

"The servants asked him, 'Do you want us to go and pull them up?'

29" 'No,' he answered, 'because while you are pulling the weeds, you may root up the wheat with them. **30**Let both grow together until the harvest. At that time I will tell the harvesters: First collect the weeds and tie them in bundles to be burned; then gather the wheat and bring it into my barn.' "

The Parables of the Mustard Seed and the Yeast

31He told them another parable: "The kingdom of heaven is like a mustard seed, which a man took and planted in his field. **32**Though it is the smallest of all your seeds, yet when it grows, it is the largest of garden plants and becomes a tree, so that the birds of the air come and perch in its branches."

33He told them still another parable: "The kingdom of heaven is like yeast that a woman took and mixed into a large amount^a of flour until it worked all through the dough."

34Jesus spoke all these things to the crowd in parables; he did not say anything to them without using a parable. **35**So was fulfilled what was spoken through the prophet:

"I will open my mouth in parables,
 I will utter things hidden since the creation of the world."^b

The Parable of the Weeds Explained

36Then he left the crowd and went into the house. His disciples came to him and said, "Explain to us the parable of the weeds in the field."

37He answered, "The one who sowed the good seed is the Son of Man. **38**The field is the world, and the good seed stands for the sons of the kingdom. The weeds are the sons of the evil one, **39**and the enemy who sows them is the devil. The harvest is the end of the age, and the harvesters are angels.

40"As the weeds are pulled up and burned in the fire, so it will be at the end of the age. **41**The Son of Man will send out his angels, and they will weed out of his kingdom everything that causes sin and all who do evil. **42**They will throw them into the fiery furnace, where there will be weeping and gnashing of teeth. **43**Then the righteous will shine like the sun in the kingdom of their Father. He who has ears, let him hear.

The Parables of the Hidden Treasure and the Pearl

44"The kingdom of heaven is like treasure hidden in a field. When a man found it, he hid it again, and then in his joy went and sold all he had and bought that field.

45"Again, the kingdom of heaven is like a merchant looking for fine pearls. **46**When he found one of great value, he went away and sold everything he had and bought it.

The Parable of the Net

47"Once again, the kingdom of heaven is like a net that was let down into the lake and caught all kinds of fish. **48**When it was full, the fishermen pulled it up on the shore. Then they sat down and collected the good fish in baskets, but threw the bad away. **49**This is how it will be at the end of the age. The angels will come and separate the wicked from the righteous **50**and throw them into the fiery furnace, where there will be weeping and gnashing of teeth.

51"Have you understood all these things?" Jesus asked.

"Yes," they replied.

52He said to them, "Therefore every teacher of the law who has been instructed about the kingdom of heaven is like the owner of a house who brings out of his storeroom new treasures as well as old."

A Prophet Without Honor

53When Jesus had finished these parables, he moved on from there. **54**Coming to his hometown, he began teaching the people in their synagogue, and they were amazed. "Where did this man get this wisdom and these miraculous powers?" they

---

^a33 Greek *three satas* (probably about 1/2 bushel or 22 liters)   ^b35 Psalm 78:2

asked. ⁵⁵"Isn't this the carpenter's son? Isn't his mother's name Mary, and aren't his brothers James, Joseph, Simon and Judas? ⁵⁶Aren't all his sisters with us? Where then did this man get all these things?" ⁵⁷And they took offense at him.

But Jesus said to them, "Only in his hometown and in his own house is a prophet without honor."

⁵⁸And he did not do many miracles there because of their lack of faith.

John the Baptist Beheaded

14 At that time Herod the tetrarch heard the reports about Jesus, ²and he said to his attendants, "This is John the Baptist; he has risen from the dead! That is why miraculous powers are at work in him."

³Now Herod had arrested John and bound him and put him in prison because of Herodias, his brother Philip's wife, ⁴for John had been saying to him: "It is not lawful for you to have her." ⁵Herod wanted to kill John, but he was afraid of the people, because they considered him a prophet.

⁶On Herod's birthday the daughter of Herodias danced for them and pleased Herod so much ⁷that he promised with an oath to give her whatever she asked. ⁸Prompted by her mother, she said, "Give me here on a platter the head of John the Baptist." ⁹The king was distressed, but because of his oaths and his dinner guests, he ordered that her request be granted ¹⁰and had John beheaded in the prison. ¹¹His head was brought in on a platter and given to the girl, who carried it to her mother. ¹²John's disciples came and took his body and buried it. Then they went and told Jesus.

Jesus Feeds the Five Thousand

¹³When Jesus heard what had happened, he withdrew by boat privately to a solitary place. Hearing of this, the crowds followed him on foot from the towns. ¹⁴When Jesus landed and saw a large crowd, he had compassion on them and healed their sick.

¹⁵As evening approached, the disciples came to him and said, "This is a remote place, and it's already getting late. Send the crowds away, so they can go to the villages and buy themselves some food."

¹⁶Jesus replied, "They do not need to go away. You give them something to eat."

¹⁷"We have here only five loaves of bread and two fish," they answered.

¹⁸"Bring them here to me," he said. ¹⁹And he directed the people to sit down on the grass. Taking the five loaves and the two fish and looking up to heaven, he gave thanks and broke the loaves. Then he gave them to the disciples, and the disciples gave them to the people. ²⁰They all ate and were satisfied, and the disciples picked up twelve basketfuls of broken pieces that were left over. ²¹The number of those who ate was about five thousand men, besides women and children.

Jesus Walks on the Water

²²Immediately Jesus made the disciples get into the boat and go on ahead of him to the other side, while he dismissed the crowd. ²³After he had dismissed them, he went up on a mountainside by himself to pray. When evening came, he was there alone, ²⁴but the boat was already a considerable distance^a from land, buffeted by the waves because the wind was against it.

²⁵During the fourth watch of the night Jesus went out to them, walking on the lake. ²⁶When the disciples saw him walking on the lake, they were terrified. "It's a ghost," they said, and cried out in fear.

²⁷But Jesus immediately said to them: "Take courage! It is I. Don't be afraid."

²⁸"Lord, if it's you," Peter replied, "tell me to come to you on the water."

²⁹"Come," he said.

Then Peter got down out of the boat, walked on the water and came toward Jesus. ³⁰But when he saw the wind, he was afraid and, beginning to sink, cried out, "Lord, save me!"

³¹Immediately Jesus reached out his hand and caught him. "You of little faith," he said, "why did you doubt?"

³²And when they climbed into the boat, the wind died down. ³³Then those who were in the boat worshiped him, saying, "Truly you are the Son of God."

³⁴When they had crossed over, they landed at Gennesaret. ³⁵And when the men of that place recognized Jesus, they sent word to all the surrounding country. People brought all their sick to him ³⁶and begged him to let the sick just touch the edge of his cloak, and all who touched him were healed.

---

a24 Greek *many stadia*

WEDNESDAY

VERSE FOR THE DAY:
Matthew 14:14

AUTHOR:
Thomas Hale

PASSAGE FOR THE DAY:
Matthew 14:13–21

Giving All We Have

FROM *his home in Nepal, missionary surgeon Thomas Hale looks to the future.*

The watchword for us all, no matter where God leads us, will be "love." Love is the one quality the world can discern that sets Christians apart and makes Christianity distinct from every other religion. If we fail to act on this truth, we will lose our right to be heard and will enter the post-Christian era for good.

What is our own personal role to be as we face the travail of the coming years? The problems of overpopulation and hunger, already upon us, are too great even for governments to handle, let alone individual Christians. It is one thing to minister to a handful of hungry Nepalis at our door by giving them food, money, seeds or a job, but when individuals become multitudes, what will we do? . . .

It seems that God is telling us simply to share with them whatever we have, and when it runs low, to try to get more, and when there is no more, to leave the issue to him. He is telling us to enter into their suffering without concern for the outcome. He is reminding us that, whatever we have done for the least of our brothers, we have done for him [see Matthew 25:40]. We cannot, as some do, restrict the interpretation of "brothers" to mean fellow-Christians alone. We wince when we hear Christians refer to much of the agony of mankind as the judgment of God; it may be, but it is not for us to say or even to think.

There are moments when we long for Christ to come again and feed the multitudes, not five thousand only, but fifty thousand, even fifty million. He could do it. Those first disciples had only two fish and a few loaves, but they gave him all they had. Is this not his word to us today—to give him all our loaves and fish, to give him everything we have? Then, who can say what he would be able to accomplish in our time through us?

Additional Scripture Readings:
Matthew 25:31–40;
2 Corinthians 9:6–15

Go to page 27 for your next devotional reading.

Clean and Unclean

15 Then some Pharisees and teachers of the law came to Jesus from Jerusalem and asked, **2**"Why do your disciples break the tradition of the elders? They don't wash their hands before they eat!"

3Jesus replied, "And why do you break the command of God for the sake of your tradition? **4**For God said, 'Honor your father and mother'*a* and 'Anyone who curses his father or mother must be put to death.'*b* **5**But you say that if a man says to his father or mother, 'Whatever help you might otherwise have received from me is a gift devoted to God,' **6**he is not to 'honor his father*c*' with it. Thus you nullify the word of God for the sake of your tradition. **7**You hypocrites! Isaiah was right when he prophesied about you:

8" 'These people honor me with their lips,
but their hearts are far from me.
9They worship me in vain;
their teachings are but rules taught by men.'*d*"

10Jesus called the crowd to him and said, "Listen and understand. **11**What goes into a man's mouth does not make him 'unclean,' but what comes out of his mouth, that is what makes him 'unclean.' "

12Then the disciples came to him and asked, "Do you know that the Pharisees were offended when they heard this?"

13He replied, "Every plant that my heavenly Father has not planted will be pulled up by the roots. **14**Leave them; they are blind guides.*e* If a blind man leads a blind man, both will fall into a pit."

15Peter said, "Explain the parable to us."

16"Are you still so dull?" Jesus asked them. **17**"Don't you see that whatever enters the mouth goes into the stomach and then out of the body? **18**But the things that come out of the mouth come from the heart, and these make a man 'unclean.' **19**For out of the heart come evil thoughts, murder, adultery, sexual immorality, theft, false testimony, slander. **20**These are what make a man 'unclean'; but eating with unwashed hands does not make him 'unclean.' "

The Faith of the Canaanite Woman

21Leaving that place, Jesus withdrew to the region of Tyre and Sidon. **22**A Canaanite woman from that vicinity came to him, crying out, "Lord, Son of David, have mercy on me! My daughter is suffering terribly from demon-possession."

23Jesus did not answer a word. So his disciples came to him and urged him, "Send her away, for she keeps crying out after us."

24He answered, "I was sent only to the lost sheep of Israel."

25The woman came and knelt before him. "Lord, help me!" she said.

26He replied, "It is not right to take the children's bread and toss it to their dogs."

27"Yes, Lord," she said, "but even the dogs eat the crumbs that fall from their masters' table."

28Then Jesus answered, "Woman, you have great faith! Your request is granted." And her daughter was healed from that very hour.

Jesus Feeds the Four Thousand

29Jesus left there and went along the Sea of Galilee. Then he went up on a mountainside and sat down. **30**Great crowds came to him, bringing the lame, the blind, the crippled, the mute and many others, and laid them at his feet; and he healed them. **31**The people were amazed when they saw the mute speaking, the crippled made well, the lame walking and the blind seeing. And they praised the God of Israel.

32Jesus called his disciples to him and said, "I have compassion for these people; they have already been with me three days and have nothing to eat. I do not want to send them away hungry, or they may collapse on the way."

33His disciples answered, "Where could we get enough bread in this remote place to feed such a crowd?"

34"How many loaves do you have?" Jesus asked.

"Seven," they replied, "and a few small fish."

35He told the crowd to sit down on the ground. **36**Then he took the seven loaves and the fish, and when he had given thanks, he broke them and gave them to the disciples, and they in turn to the people. **37**They all ate and were satisfied. Af-

---

*a*4 Exodus 20:12; Deut. 5:16   *b*4 Exodus 21:17; Lev. 20:9   *c*6 Some manuscripts *father or his mother*
*d*9 Isaiah 29:13   *e*14 Some manuscripts *guides of the blind*

terward the disciples picked up seven basketfuls of broken pieces that were left over. ⁳⁸The number of those who ate was four thousand, besides women and children. ³⁹After Jesus had sent the crowd away, he got into the boat and went to the vicinity of Magadan.

The Demand for a Sign

16 The Pharisees and Sadducees came to Jesus and tested him by asking him to show them a sign from heaven.

²He replied,ᵃ "When evening comes, you say, 'It will be fair weather, for the sky is red,' ³and in the morning, 'Today it will be stormy, for the sky is red and overcast.' You know how to interpret the appearance of the sky, but you cannot interpret the signs of the times. ⁴A wicked and adulterous generation looks for a miraculous sign, but none will be given it except the sign of Jonah." Jesus then left them and went away.

The Yeast of the Pharisees and Sadducees

⁵When they went across the lake, the disciples forgot to take bread. ⁶"Be careful," Jesus said to them. "Be on your guard against the yeast of the Pharisees and Sadducees."

⁷They discussed this among themselves and said, "It is because we didn't bring any bread."

⁸Aware of their discussion, Jesus asked, "You of little faith, why are you talking among yourselves about having no bread? ⁹Do you still not understand? Don't you remember the five loaves for the five thousand, and how many basketfuls you gathered? ¹⁰Or the seven loaves for the four thousand, and how many basketfuls you gathered? ¹¹How is it you don't understand that I was not talking to you about bread? But be on your guard against the yeast of the Pharisees and Sadducees." ¹²Then they understood that he was not telling them to guard against the yeast used in bread, but against the teaching of the Pharisees and Sadducees.

Peter's Confession of Christ

¹³When Jesus came to the region of Caesarea Philippi, he asked his disciples, "Who do people say the Son of Man is?"

¹⁴They replied, "Some say John the Baptist; others say Elijah; and still others, Jeremiah or one of the prophets."

¹⁵"But what about you?" he asked. "Who do you say I am?"

¹⁶Simon Peter answered, "You are the Christ,ᵇ the Son of the living God."

¹⁷Jesus replied, "Blessed are you, Simon son of Jonah, for this was not revealed to you by man, but by my Father in heaven. ¹⁸And I tell you that you are Peter,ᶜ and on this rock I will build my church, and the gates of Hadesᵈ will not overcome it.ᵉ ¹⁹I will give you the keys of the kingdom of heaven; whatever you bind on earth will beᶠ bound in heaven, and whatever you loose on earth will beᶠ loosed in heaven." ²⁰Then he warned his disciples not to tell anyone that he was the Christ.

Jesus Predicts His Death

²¹From that time on Jesus began to explain to his disciples that he must go to Jerusalem and suffer many things at the hands of the elders, chief priests and teachers of the law, and that he must be killed and on the third day be raised to life.

²²Peter took him aside and began to rebuke him. "Never, Lord!" he said. "This shall never happen to you!"

²³Jesus turned and said to Peter, "Get behind me, Satan! You are a stumbling block to me; you do not have in mind the things of God, but the things of men."

²⁴Then Jesus said to his disciples, "If anyone would come after me, he must deny himself and take up his cross and follow me. ²⁵For whoever wants to save his lifeᵍ will lose it, but whoever loses his life for me will find it. ²⁶What good will it be for a man if he gains the whole world, yet forfeits his soul? Or what can a man give in exchange for his soul? ²⁷For the Son of Man is going to come in his Father's glory with his angels, and then he will reward each person according to what he has done. ²⁸I tell you the truth, some who are standing here will not taste death before they see the Son of Man coming in his kingdom."

The Transfiguration

17 After six days Jesus took with him Peter, James and John the brother of James, and led them up a high moun-

---

ᵃ2 Some early manuscripts do not have the rest of verse 2 and all of verse 3.　ᵇ16 Or *Messiah*; also in verse 20　ᶜ18 *Peter* means *rock*.　ᵈ18 Or *hell*　ᵉ18 Or *not prove stronger than it*　ᶠ19 Or *have been*　ᵍ25 The Greek word means either *life* or *soul*; also in verse 26.

tain by themselves. ²There he was transfigured before them. His face shone like the sun, and his clothes became as white as the light. ³Just then there appeared before them Moses and Elijah, talking with Jesus.

⁴Peter said to Jesus, "Lord, it is good for us to be here. If you wish, I will put up three shelters—one for you, one for Moses and one for Elijah."

⁵While he was still speaking, a bright cloud enveloped them, and a voice from the cloud said, "This is my Son, whom I love; with him I am well pleased. Listen to him!"

⁶When the disciples heard this, they fell facedown to the ground, terrified. ⁷But Jesus came and touched them. "Get up," he said. "Don't be afraid." ⁸When they looked up, they saw no one except Jesus.

⁹As they were coming down the mountain, Jesus instructed them, "Don't tell anyone what you have seen, until the Son of Man has been raised from the dead."

¹⁰The disciples asked him, "Why then do the teachers of the law say that Elijah must come first?"

¹¹Jesus replied, "To be sure, Elijah comes and will restore all things. ¹²But I tell you, Elijah has already come, and they did not recognize him, but have done to him everything they wished. In the same way the Son of Man is going to suffer at their hands." ¹³Then the disciples understood that he was talking to them about John the Baptist.

The Healing of a Boy With a Demon

¹⁴When they came to the crowd, a man approached Jesus and knelt before him. ¹⁵"Lord, have mercy on my son," he said. "He has seizures and is suffering greatly. He often falls into the fire or into the water. ¹⁶I brought him to your disciples, but they could not heal him."

¹⁷"O unbelieving and perverse generation," Jesus replied, "how long shall I stay with you? How long shall I put up with you? Bring the boy here to me." ¹⁸Jesus rebuked the demon, and it came out of the boy, and he was healed from that moment.

¹⁹Then the disciples came to Jesus in private and asked, "Why couldn't we drive it out?"

²⁰He replied, "Because you have so little faith. I tell you the truth, if you have faith as small as a mustard seed, you can say to this mountain, 'Move from here to there' and it will move. Nothing will be impossible for you.ᵃ"

²²When they came together in Galilee, he said to them, "The Son of Man is going to be betrayed into the hands of men. ²³They will kill him, and on the third day he will be raised to life." And the disciples were filled with grief.

The Temple Tax

²⁴After Jesus and his disciples arrived in Capernaum, the collectors of the two-drachma tax came to Peter and asked, "Doesn't your teacher pay the temple taxᵇ?"

²⁵"Yes, he does," he replied.

When Peter came into the house, Jesus was the first to speak. "What do you think, Simon?" he asked. "From whom do the kings of the earth collect duty and taxes—from their own sons or from others?"

²⁶"From others," Peter answered.

"Then the sons are exempt," Jesus said to him. ²⁷"But so that we may not offend them, go to the lake and throw out your line. Take the first fish you catch; open its mouth and you will find a four-drachma coin. Take it and give it to them for my tax and yours."

The Greatest in the Kingdom of Heaven

18 At that time the disciples came to Jesus and asked, "Who is the greatest in the kingdom of heaven?"

²He called a little child and had him stand among them. ³And he said: "I tell you the truth, unless you change and become like little children, you will never enter the kingdom of heaven. ⁴Therefore, whoever humbles himself like this child is the greatest in the kingdom of heaven.

⁵"And whoever welcomes a little child like this in my name welcomes me. ⁶But if anyone causes one of these little ones who believe in me to sin, it would be better for him to have a large millstone hung around his neck and to be drowned in the depths of the sea.

⁷"Woe to the world because of the things that cause people to sin! Such things must come, but woe to the man through whom they come! ⁸If your hand or your foot causes you to sin, cut it off

---

ᵃ20 Some manuscripts *you.* ²¹*But this kind does not go out except by prayer and fasting.*   ᵇ24 Greek *the two drachmas*

and throw it away. It is better for you to enter life maimed or crippled than to have two hands or two feet and be thrown into eternal fire. **9**And if your eye causes you to sin, gouge it out and throw it away. It is better for you to enter life with one eye than to have two eyes and be thrown into the fire of hell.

The Parable of the Lost Sheep

10"See that you do not look down on one of these little ones. For I tell you that their angels in heaven always see the face of my Father in heaven.*a*

12"What do you think? If a man owns a hundred sheep, and one of them wanders away, will he not leave the ninety-nine on the hills and go to look for the one that wandered off? **13**And if he finds it, I tell you the truth, he is happier about that one sheep than about the ninety-nine that did not wander off. **14**In the same way your Father in heaven is not willing that any of these little ones should be lost.

a10 Some manuscripts *heaven. 11The Son of Man came to save what was lost.*

THURSDAY

VERSE FOR THE DAY:
Matthew 17:20

AUTHOR:
Philip W. Williams

PASSAGE FOR THE DAY:
Matthew 17:14–23

"Father" on Our Lips

"IF ONLY I had more faith, I'd be able to handle myself in this situation." How much faith is enough in our mourning? Some of us feel that it is always more than what we have. Jesus said that the amount of faith isn't important: "I tell you the truth, if you have faith as small as a mustard seed, you can say to this mountain, 'Move from here to there' and it will move. Nothing will be impossible for you" [Matthew 17:20].

A grain of mustard seed! Do you recall how small a mustard seed is? Necklaces used to be worn with a mustard seed in the bulb, which magnified it so that it could be seen with normal eyesight. Now if we have faith, though it be that small, nothing will be impossible.

I interpret faith in this instance as basic trust. We don't need a huge quantity of it in order to get on with our bereavement. In fact, if we worry about having a lot of faith, we may miss the mustard seed we do have.

The giver of this grain of faith is God, whose Son, though despondent and despairing in his crisis, maintained his faith. He went through his Gethsemane of grief with the word "Father" still on his lips.

We too can go through the valleys and mountains of our bereavement journey with "Father" on our lips. Our hearts may wonder, doubt and cry out in pain, but these feelings will not obliterate our faith. Even when we think we have lost that mustard seed, we do well to remember that our Father is faithful, for he has loved us first.

Additional Scripture Readings:
Mark 14:32–40; Ephesians 3:14–21

Go to page 29 for your next devotional reading.

A Brother Who Sins Against You

¹⁵"If your brother sins against you,^a go and show him his fault, just between the two of you. If he listens to you, you have won your brother over. ¹⁶But if he will not listen, take one or two others along, so that 'every matter may be established by the testimony of two or three witnesses.'^b ¹⁷If he refuses to listen to them, tell it to the church; and if he refuses to listen even to the church, treat him as you would a pagan or a tax collector.

¹⁸"I tell you the truth, whatever you bind on earth will be^c bound in heaven, and whatever you loose on earth will be^c loosed in heaven.

¹⁹"Again, I tell you that if two of you on earth agree about anything you ask for, it will be done for you by my Father in heaven. ²⁰For where two or three come together in my name, there am I with them."

The Parable of the Unmerciful Servant

²¹Then Peter came to Jesus and asked, "Lord, how many times shall I forgive my brother when he sins against me? Up to seven times?"

²²Jesus answered, "I tell you, not seven times, but seventy-seven times.^d

²³"Therefore, the kingdom of heaven is like a king who wanted to settle accounts with his servants. ²⁴As he began the settlement, a man who owed him ten thousand talents^e was brought to him. ²⁵Since he was not able to pay, the master ordered that he and his wife and his children and all that he had be sold to repay the debt.

²⁶"The servant fell on his knees before him. 'Be patient with me,' he begged, 'and I will pay back everything.' ²⁷The servant's master took pity on him, canceled the debt and let him go.

²⁸"But when that servant went out, he found one of his fellow servants who owed him a hundred denarii.^f He grabbed him and began to choke him. 'Pay back what you owe me!' he demanded.

²⁹"His fellow servant fell to his knees and begged him, 'Be patient with me, and I will pay you back.'

³⁰"But he refused. Instead, he went off and had the man thrown into prison until he could pay the debt. ³¹When the other servants saw what had happened, they were greatly distressed and went and told their master everything that had happened.

³²"Then the master called the servant in. 'You wicked servant,' he said, 'I canceled all that debt of yours because you begged me to. ³³Shouldn't you have had mercy on your fellow servant just as I had on you?' ³⁴In anger his master turned him over to the jailers to be tortured, until he should pay back all he owed.

³⁵"This is how my heavenly Father will treat each of you unless you forgive your brother from your heart."

Divorce

19 When Jesus had finished saying these things, he left Galilee and went into the region of Judea to the other side of the Jordan. ²Large crowds followed him, and he healed them there.

³Some Pharisees came to him to test him. They asked, "Is it lawful for a man to divorce his wife for any and every reason?"

⁴"Haven't you read," he replied, "that at the beginning the Creator 'made them male and female,'^g ⁵and said, 'For this reason a man will leave his father and mother and be united to his wife, and the two will become one flesh'^h? ⁶So they are no longer two, but one. Therefore what God has joined together, let man not separate."

⁷"Why then," they asked, "did Moses command that a man give his wife a certificate of divorce and send her away?"

⁸Jesus replied, "Moses permitted you to divorce your wives because your hearts were hard. But it was not this way from the beginning. ⁹I tell you that anyone who divorces his wife, except for marital unfaithfulness, and marries another woman commits adultery."

¹⁰The disciples said to him, "If this is the situation between a husband and wife, it is better not to marry."

¹¹Jesus replied, "Not everyone can accept this word, but only those to whom it has been given. ¹²For some are eunuchs because they were born that way; others were made that way by men; and others have renounced marriageⁱ because of the kingdom of heaven. The one who can accept this should accept it."

---

^a15 Some manuscripts do not have *against you.*   ^b16 Deut. 19:15   ^c18 Or *have been*   ^d22 Or *seventy times seven*   ^e24 That is, millions of dollars   ^f28 That is, a few dollars   ^g4 Gen. 1:27   ^h5 Gen. 2:24   ⁱ12 Or *have made themselves eunuchs*

The Little Children and Jesus

¹³Then little children were brought to Jesus for him to place his hands on them and pray for them. But the disciples rebuked those who brought them. ¹⁴Jesus said, "Let the little children come to me, and do not hinder them, for the kingdom of heaven belongs to such as these." ¹⁵When he had placed his hands on them, he went on from there.

FRIDAY

VERSE FOR THE DAY:
Matthew 19:26

AUTHOR:
Bill Hybels

PASSAGE FOR THE DAY:
Matthew 19:16–30

Cultivating Vision

THE disciples once thought that they had heard Jesus say that respectable, well-to-do, upstanding community leaders could not be saved. If that were true, then their chances of being saved were not very good either. The disciples, who had not yet become visionaries, immediately gave up hope. They saw no solution; salvation was obviously out of reach. Jesus looked at them and said, "Fellas, you're right. With human beings, some problems have no solutions. But with God all things are possible" (Matthew 19:26).

Does your problem seem bigger than life, bigger than God himself? It isn't. God is infinitely bigger than any problem you ever had or will have, and every time you call a problem unsolvable, you mock God. "With God all things are possible." Visionary people face the same problems everyone else faces; but rather than get paralyzed by their problems, visionaries immediately commit themselves to finding a solution. Almost as a reflex reaction to the problem they say, "The situation is bad, all right, but no problem is bigger than God. And right now, before I get bogged down, I need to start down the path of solving it." More often than not, visionaries find a way, with God's help, to deal with their problems and overcome them rather than surrender their lives to them.

Vision is a vitally important quality to cultivate, because life is really just a series of problems, challenges, trials and disappointments. If you allow yourself to be overwhelmed by difficulties, your future is not bright. You will get stuck first on one problem and then on another... If, on the other hand, you cultivate vision—if, whenever you are faced with a problem, you immediately explore ways to deal with it—you will not only avert all sorts of discouragement, but you will also discover just how much creativity and wisdom God wants to give his children who look to him for help.

Additional Scripture Readings:
Ephesians 3:14–21;
Philippians 4:10–13

Go to page 31 for your next devotional reading.

The Rich Young Man

16Now a man came up to Jesus and asked, "Teacher, what good thing must I do to get eternal life?"

17"Why do you ask me about what is good?" Jesus replied. "There is only One who is good. If you want to enter life, obey the commandments."

18"Which ones?" the man inquired.

Jesus replied, " 'Do not murder, do not commit adultery, do not steal, do not give false testimony, **19**honor your father and mother,'*a* and 'love your neighbor as yourself.'*b*"

20"All these I have kept," the young man said. "What do I still lack?"

21Jesus answered, "If you want to be perfect, go, sell your possessions and give to the poor, and you will have treasure in heaven. Then come, follow me."

22When the young man heard this, he went away sad, because he had great wealth.

23Then Jesus said to his disciples, "I tell you the truth, it is hard for a rich man to enter the kingdom of heaven. **24**Again I tell you, it is easier for a camel to go through the eye of a needle than for a rich man to enter the kingdom of God."

25When the disciples heard this, they were greatly astonished and asked, "Who then can be saved?"

26Jesus looked at them and said, "With man this is impossible, but with God all things are possible."

27Peter answered him, "We have left everything to follow you! What then will there be for us?"

28Jesus said to them, "I tell you the truth, at the renewal of all things, when the Son of Man sits on his glorious throne, you who have followed me will also sit on twelve thrones, judging the twelve tribes of Israel. **29**And everyone who has left houses or brothers or sisters or father or mother*c* or children or fields for my sake will receive a hundred times as much and will inherit eternal life. **30**But many who are first will be last, and many who are last will be first.

The Parable of the Workers in the Vineyard

20 "For the kingdom of heaven is like a landowner who went out early in the morning to hire men to work in his vineyard. **2**He agreed to pay them a denarius for the day and sent them into his vineyard.

3"About the third hour he went out and saw others standing in the marketplace doing nothing. **4**He told them, 'You also go and work in my vineyard, and I will pay you whatever is right.' **5**So they went.

"He went out again about the sixth hour and the ninth hour and did the same thing. **6**About the eleventh hour he went out and found still others standing around. He asked them, 'Why have you been standing here all day long doing nothing?'

7" 'Because no one has hired us,' they answered.

"He said to them, 'You also go and work in my vineyard.'

8"When evening came, the owner of the vineyard said to his foreman, 'Call the workers and pay them their wages, beginning with the last ones hired and going on to the first.'

9"The workers who were hired about the eleventh hour came and each received a denarius. **10**So when those came who were hired first, they expected to receive more. But each one of them also received a denarius. **11**When they received it, they began to grumble against the landowner. **12**'These men who were hired last worked only one hour,' they said, 'and you have made them equal to us who have borne the burden of the work and the heat of the day.'

13"But he answered one of them, 'Friend, I am not being unfair to you. Didn't you agree to work for a denarius? **14**Take your pay and go. I want to give the man who was hired last the same as I gave you. **15**Don't I have the right to do what I want with my own money? Or are you envious because I am generous?'

16"So the last will be first, and the first will be last."

Jesus Again Predicts His Death

17Now as Jesus was going up to Jerusalem, he took the twelve disciples aside and said to them, **18**"We are going up to Jerusalem, and the Son of Man will be betrayed to the chief priests and the teachers of the law. They will condemn him to death **19**and will turn him over to the Gentiles to be mocked and flogged and crucified. On the third day he will be raised to life!"

---

*a*19 Exodus 20:12-16; Deut. 5:16-20   *b*19 Lev. 19:18   *c*29 Some manuscripts *mother or wife*

WEEKENDING

REALIZE

Forgiving is love's revolution against love's unfairness. When we forgive, we ignore the normal laws that strap us to the natural law of getting even and, by the alchemy of love, we release ourselves from our own painful pasts.

We fly over a dues-paying morality in order to create a new future out of the past's unfairness. We free ourselves from the wrong that is locked into our private histories; we unshackle our spirits from malice; and, maybe, if we are lucky, we also restore a relationship that would otherwise be lost forever.
– *Lewis B. Smedes*

REVIVE
Saturday: Matthew 18:21–35
Sunday: Ephesians 4:29—5:2

Go to page 33 for your next devotional reading.

A Mother's Request

20Then the mother of Zebedee's sons came to Jesus with her sons and, kneeling down, asked a favor of him.

21"What is it you want?" he asked.

She said, "Grant that one of these two sons of mine may sit at your right and the other at your left in your kingdom."

22"You don't know what you are asking," Jesus said to them. "Can you drink the cup I am going to drink?"

"We can," they answered.

23Jesus said to them, "You will indeed drink from my cup, but to sit at my right or left is not for me to grant. These places belong to those for whom they have been prepared by my Father."

24When the ten heard about this, they were indignant with the two brothers. **25**Jesus called them together and said, "You know that the rulers of the Gentiles lord it over them, and their high officials exercise authority over them. **26**Not so with you. Instead, whoever wants to become great among you must be your servant, **27**and whoever wants to be first must be your slave— **28**just as the Son of Man did not come to be served, but to serve, and to give his life as a ransom for many."

Two Blind Men Receive Sight

29As Jesus and his disciples were leaving Jericho, a large crowd followed him. **30**Two blind men were sitting by the roadside, and when they heard that Jesus was going by, they shouted, "Lord, Son of David, have mercy on us!"

31The crowd rebuked them and told them to be quiet, but they shouted all the louder, "Lord, Son of David, have mercy on us!"

32Jesus stopped and called them. "What do you want me to do for you?" he asked.

33"Lord," they answered, "we want our sight."

34Jesus had compassion on them and touched their eyes. Immediately they received their sight and followed him.

The Triumphal Entry

21 As they approached Jerusalem and came to Bethphage on the Mount of Olives, Jesus sent two disciples, **2**saying to them, "Go to the village ahead of you, and at once you will find a donkey tied there, with her colt by her. Untie them and bring them to me. **3**If anyone says anything to you, tell him that the Lord needs them, and he will send them right away."

4This took place to fulfill what was spoken through the prophet:

5"Say to the Daughter of Zion,
  'See, your king comes to you,
gentle and riding on a donkey,
  on a colt, the foal of a donkey.' "[a]

6The disciples went and did as Jesus had instructed them. **7**They brought the donkey and the colt, placed their cloaks on them, and Jesus sat on them. **8**A very large crowd spread their cloaks on the road, while others cut branches from the trees and spread them on the road. **9**The crowds that went ahead of him and those that followed shouted,

"Hosanna[b] to the Son of David!"

"Blessed is he who comes in the name of the Lord!"[c]

"Hosanna[b] in the highest!"

10When Jesus entered Jerusalem, the whole city was stirred and asked, "Who is this?"

11The crowds answered, "This is Jesus, the prophet from Nazareth in Galilee."

Jesus at the Temple

12Jesus entered the temple area and drove out all who were buying and selling there. He overturned the tables of the money changers and the benches of those selling doves. **13**"It is written," he said to them, " 'My house will be called a house of prayer,'[d] but you are making it a 'den of robbers.'[e]"

14The blind and the lame came to him at the temple, and he healed them. **15**But when the chief priests and the teachers of the law saw the wonderful things he did and the children shouting in the temple area, "Hosanna to the Son of David," they were indignant.

16"Do you hear what these children are saying?" they asked him.

"Yes," replied Jesus, "have you never read,

" 'From the lips of children and
    infants
you have ordained praise'[f]?"

17And he left them and went out of the city to Bethany, where he spent the night.

---

[a]5 Zech. 9:9   [b]9 A Hebrew expression meaning "Save!" which became an exclamation of praise; also in verse 15   [c]9 Psalm 118:26   [d]13 Isaiah 56:7   [e]13 Jer. 7:11   [f]16 Psalm 8:2

The Fig Tree Withers

[18]Early in the morning, as he was on his way back to the city, he was hungry. [19]Seeing a fig tree by the road, he went up to it but found nothing on it except leaves. Then he said to it, "May you never bear fruit again!" Immediately the tree withered.

[20]When the disciples saw this, they were amazed. "How did the fig tree wither so quickly?" they asked.

[21]Jesus replied, "I tell you the truth, if you have faith and do not doubt, not only can you do what was done to the fig tree, but also you can say to this mountain, 'Go, throw yourself into the sea,' and it will be done. [22]If you believe, you will receive whatever you ask for in prayer."

MONDAY

VERSE FOR THE DAY:
Matthew 20:26

AUTHOR:
Mike Singletary

PASSAGE FOR THE DAY:
Matthew 20:20–28

Love and the Real Man

TOO many people say love is impossible to understand or define. Love is action. A real man will love a woman the way the Bible says to. The most militant feminist would not condemn a love like that.

I would never say that I am the definition of what a real man is, but I'm not ashamed to say I'm working toward it. I want to be the best man I can be, and before it's over I'm trying to come close. A real man will treat his wife right. He will be a servant rather than a master. He will do the right thing because it's the right thing. He will give a hundred percent no matter what he's called upon to do.

And how will a man know when he's a real man? When he seeks to serve. When he can sit down with his wife and honestly look to fulfill her needs before his own. He should ask, "What can I do for you?"

Society says a man should find a gorgeous wife who will take care of his needs, make him happy and serve him. She becomes part of his orbit, makes him proud, and he gives her everything he thinks she wants. But she's miserable. She's in second place. He can't put her first because that goes against everything he feels and has been taught. Just like everything else God made perfect, the world has flipped this around. There's a counterfeit of the real thing being sold on the market, and it's called lust.

It's exciting. It looks good. It's even satisfying for a while. But it's not true love. It's backwards. It fulfills *our* desires first, even at the expense of the person we're supposed to love. There is a big difference, and we men need to learn and know it. Lust takes, for our benefit. Love gives, for the benefit of the one we love.

Additional Scripture Readings:
Mark 9:33–37; 1 Corinthians 13:1–7

Go to page 37 for your next devotional reading.

The Authority of Jesus Questioned

²³Jesus entered the temple courts, and, while he was teaching, the chief priests and the elders of the people came to him. "By what authority are you doing these things?" they asked. "And who gave you this authority?"

²⁴Jesus replied, "I will also ask you one question. If you answer me, I will tell you by what authority I am doing these things. ²⁵John's baptism—where did it come from? Was it from heaven, or from men?"

They discussed it among themselves and said, "If we say, 'From heaven,' he will ask, 'Then why didn't you believe him?' ²⁶But if we say, 'From men'—we are afraid of the people, for they all hold that John was a prophet."

²⁷So they answered Jesus, "We don't know."

Then he said, "Neither will I tell you by what authority I am doing these things.

The Parable of the Two Sons

²⁸"What do you think? There was a man who had two sons. He went to the first and said, 'Son, go and work today in the vineyard.'

²⁹" 'I will not,' he answered, but later he changed his mind and went.

³⁰"Then the father went to the other son and said the same thing. He answered, 'I will, sir,' but he did not go.

³¹"Which of the two did what his father wanted?"

"The first," they answered.

Jesus said to them, "I tell you the truth, the tax collectors and the prostitutes are entering the kingdom of God ahead of you. ³²For John came to you to show you the way of righteousness, and you did not believe him, but the tax collectors and the prostitutes did. And even after you saw this, you did not repent and believe him.

The Parable of the Tenants

³³"Listen to another parable: There was a landowner who planted a vineyard. He put a wall around it, dug a winepress in it and built a watchtower. Then he rented the vineyard to some farmers and went away on a journey. ³⁴When the harvest time approached, he sent his servants to the tenants to collect his fruit.

³⁵"The tenants seized his servants; they beat one, killed another, and stoned a third. ³⁶Then he sent other servants to them, more than the first time, and the tenants treated them the same way. ³⁷Last of all, he sent his son to them. 'They will respect my son,' he said.

³⁸"But when the tenants saw the son, they said to each other, 'This is the heir. Come, let's kill him and take his inheritance.' ³⁹So they took him and threw him out of the vineyard and killed him.

⁴⁰"Therefore, when the owner of the vineyard comes, what will he do to those tenants?"

⁴¹"He will bring those wretches to a wretched end," they replied, "and he will rent the vineyard to other tenants, who will give him his share of the crop at harvest time."

⁴²Jesus said to them, "Have you never read in the Scriptures:

" 'The stone the builders rejected
has become the capstone*ᵃ*;
the Lord has done this,
and it is marvelous in our eyes'*ᵇ*?

⁴³"Therefore I tell you that the kingdom of God will be taken away from you and given to a people who will produce its fruit. ⁴⁴He who falls on this stone will be broken to pieces, but he on whom it falls will be crushed."*ᶜ*

⁴⁵When the chief priests and the Pharisees heard Jesus' parables, they knew he was talking about them. ⁴⁶They looked for a way to arrest him, but they were afraid of the crowd because the people held that he was a prophet.

The Parable of the Wedding Banquet

22 Jesus spoke to them again in parables, saying: ²"The kingdom of heaven is like a king who prepared a wedding banquet for his son. ³He sent his servants to those who had been invited to the banquet to tell them to come, but they refused to come.

⁴"Then he sent some more servants and said, 'Tell those who have been invited that I have prepared my dinner: My oxen and fattened cattle have been butchered, and everything is ready. Come to the wedding banquet.'

⁵"But they paid no attention and went off—one to his field, another to his business. ⁶The rest seized his servants, mistreated them and killed them. ⁷The king was enraged. He sent his army and destroyed those murderers and burned their city.

---

*ᵃ*42 Or *cornerstone*   *ᵇ*42 Psalm 118:22,23   *ᶜ*44 Some manuscripts do not have verse 44.

⁸"Then he said to his servants, 'The wedding banquet is ready, but those I invited did not deserve to come. ⁹Go to the street corners and invite to the banquet anyone you find.' ¹⁰So the servants went out into the streets and gathered all the people they could find, both good and bad, and the wedding hall was filled with guests.

¹¹"But when the king came in to see the guests, he noticed a man there who was not wearing wedding clothes. ¹²'Friend,' he asked, 'how did you get in here without wedding clothes?' The man was speechless.

¹³"Then the king told the attendants, 'Tie him hand and foot, and throw him outside, into the darkness, where there will be weeping and gnashing of teeth.'

¹⁴"For many are invited, but few are chosen."

Paying Taxes to Caesar

¹⁵Then the Pharisees went out and laid plans to trap him in his words. ¹⁶They sent their disciples to him along with the Herodians. "Teacher," they said, "we know you are a man of integrity and that you teach the way of God in accordance with the truth. You aren't swayed by men, because you pay no attention to who they are. ¹⁷Tell us then, what is your opinion? Is it right to pay taxes to Caesar or not?"

¹⁸But Jesus, knowing their evil intent, said, "You hypocrites, why are you trying to trap me? ¹⁹Show me the coin used for paying the tax." They brought him a denarius, ²⁰and he asked them, "Whose portrait is this? And whose inscription?"

²¹"Caesar's," they replied.

Then he said to them, "Give to Caesar what is Caesar's, and to God what is God's."

²²When they heard this, they were amazed. So they left him and went away.

Marriage at the Resurrection

²³That same day the Sadducees, who say there is no resurrection, came to him with a question. ²⁴"Teacher," they said, "Moses told us that if a man dies without having children, his brother must marry the widow and have children for him. ²⁵Now there were seven brothers among us. The first one married and died, and since he had no children, he left his wife to his brother. ²⁶The same thing happened to the second and third brother, right on down to the seventh. ²⁷Finally, the woman died. ²⁸Now then, at the resurrection, whose wife will she be of the seven, since all of them were married to her?"

²⁹Jesus replied, "You are in error because you do not know the Scriptures or the power of God. ³⁰At the resurrection people will neither marry nor be given in marriage; they will be like the angels in heaven. ³¹But about the resurrection of the dead—have you not read what God said to you, ³²'I am the God of Abraham, the God of Isaac, and the God of Jacob'ᵃ? He is not the God of the dead but of the living."

³³When the crowds heard this, they were astonished at his teaching.

The Greatest Commandment

³⁴Hearing that Jesus had silenced the Sadducees, the Pharisees got together. ³⁵One of them, an expert in the law, tested him with this question: ³⁶"Teacher, which is the greatest commandment in the Law?"

³⁷Jesus replied: "'Love the Lord your God with all your heart and with all your soul and with all your mind.'ᵇ ³⁸This is the first and greatest commandment. ³⁹And the second is like it: 'Love your neighbor as yourself.'ᶜ ⁴⁰All the Law and the Prophets hang on these two commandments."

Whose Son Is the Christ?

⁴¹While the Pharisees were gathered together, Jesus asked them, ⁴²"What do you think about the Christᵈ? Whose son is he?"

"The son of David," they replied.

⁴³He said to them, "How is it then that David, speaking by the Spirit, calls him 'Lord'? For he says,

⁴⁴"'The Lord said to my Lord:
  "Sit at my right hand
until I put your enemies
  under your feet."'ᵉ

⁴⁵If then David calls him 'Lord,' how can he be his son?" ⁴⁶No one could say a word in reply, and from that day on no one dared to ask him any more questions.

Seven Woes

23 Then Jesus said to the crowds and to his disciples: ²"The teachers of the law and the Pharisees sit in Moses'

ᵃ32 Exodus 3:6   ᵇ37 Deut. 6:5   ᶜ39 Lev. 19:18   ᵈ42 Or *Messiah*   ᵉ44 Psalm 110:1

seat. ³So you must obey them and do everything they tell you. But do not do what they do, for they do not practice what they preach. ⁴They tie up heavy loads and put them on men's shoulders, but they themselves are not willing to lift a finger to move them.

⁵"Everything they do is done for men to see: They make their phylacteries*a* wide and the tassels on their garments long; ⁶they love the place of honor at banquets and the most important seats in the synagogues; ⁷they love to be greeted in the marketplaces and to have men call them 'Rabbi.'

⁸"But you are not to be called 'Rabbi,' for you have only one Master and you are all brothers. ⁹And do not call anyone on earth 'father,' for you have one Father, and he is in heaven. ¹⁰Nor are you to be called 'teacher,' for you have one Teacher, the Christ.*b* ¹¹The greatest among you will be your servant. ¹²For whoever exalts himself will be humbled, and whoever humbles himself will be exalted.

¹³"Woe to you, teachers of the law and Pharisees, you hypocrites! You shut the kingdom of heaven in men's faces. You yourselves do not enter, nor will you let those enter who are trying to.*c*

¹⁵"Woe to you, teachers of the law and Pharisees, you hypocrites! You travel over land and sea to win a single convert, and when he becomes one, you make him twice as much a son of hell as you are.

¹⁶"Woe to you, blind guides! You say, 'If anyone swears by the temple, it means nothing; but if anyone swears by the gold of the temple, he is bound by his oath.' ¹⁷You blind fools! Which is greater: the gold, or the temple that makes the gold sacred? ¹⁸You also say, 'If anyone swears by the altar, it means nothing; but if anyone swears by the gift on it, he is bound by his oath.' ¹⁹You blind men! Which is greater: the gift, or the altar that makes the gift sacred? ²⁰Therefore, he who swears by the altar swears by it and by everything on it. ²¹And he who swears by the temple swears by it and by the one who dwells in it. ²²And he who swears by heaven swears by God's throne and by the one who sits on it.

²³"Woe to you, teachers of the law and Pharisees, you hypocrites! You give a tenth of your spices — mint, dill and cummin. But you have neglected the more important matters of the law — justice, mercy and faithfulness. You should have practiced the latter, without neglecting the former. ²⁴You blind guides! You strain out a gnat but swallow a camel.

²⁵"Woe to you, teachers of the law and Pharisees, you hypocrites! You clean the outside of the cup and dish, but inside they are full of greed and self-indulgence. ²⁶Blind Pharisee! First clean the inside of the cup and dish, and then the outside also will be clean.

²⁷"Woe to you, teachers of the law and Pharisees, you hypocrites! You are like whitewashed tombs, which look beautiful on the outside but on the inside are full of dead men's bones and everything unclean. ²⁸In the same way, on the outside you appear to people as righteous but on the inside you are full of hypocrisy and wickedness.

²⁹"Woe to you, teachers of the law and Pharisees, you hypocrites! You build tombs for the prophets and decorate the graves of the righteous. ³⁰And you say, 'If we had lived in the days of our forefathers, we would not have taken part with them in shedding the blood of the prophets.' ³¹So you testify against yourselves that you are the descendants of those who murdered the prophets. ³²Fill up, then, the measure of the sin of your forefathers!

³³"You snakes! You brood of vipers! How will you escape being condemned to hell? ³⁴Therefore I am sending you prophets and wise men and teachers. Some of them you will kill and crucify; others you will flog in your synagogues and pursue from town to town. ³⁵And so upon you will come all the righteous blood that has been shed on earth, from the blood of righteous Abel to the blood of Zechariah son of Berekiah, whom you murdered between the temple and the altar. ³⁶I tell you the truth, all this will come upon this generation.

³⁷"O Jerusalem, Jerusalem, you who kill the prophets and stone those sent to you, how often I have longed to gather your children together, as a hen gathers her chicks under her wings, but you were

---

a 5 That is, boxes containing Scripture verses, worn on forehead and arm   *b* 10 Or *Messiah*
c 13 Some manuscripts *to.* ¹⁴*Woe to you, teachers of the law and Pharisees, you hypocrites! You devour widows' houses and for a show make lengthy prayers. Therefore you will be punished more severely.*

not willing. **38**Look, your house is left to you desolate. **39**For I tell you, you will not see me again until you say, 'Blessed is he who comes in the name of the Lord.'*a*"

a39 Psalm 118:26

Signs of the End of the Age

24 Jesus left the temple and was walking away when his disciples came up to him to call his attention to its buildings. **2**"Do you see all these things?" he

TUESDAY

VERSE FOR THE DAY:
Matthew 23:28

AUTHOR:
John Fischer

PASSAGE FOR THE DAY:
Matthew 23:25–28

R-rated Hearts

THE way I feel about being around unbelievers will tell me a whole lot about my concept of God and how I stand before him. Jesus put it this way: "Do not judge, or you too will be judged. For in the same way you judge others, you will be judged, and with the measure you use, it will be measured to you" (Matthew 7:1–2).

In other words, you get what you give out. You want a loving God? Then be loving. You want a merciful God? Then be merciful. Want God to forgive you? Then forgive your fellowman. Want God to condemn you? Then be an accusatory person. Want to put yourself above the rest of the world? Then get ready for a God who is going to strain out every judgmental thought you've ever had and measure all the thoughts and intents of your hidden heart by the same standard.

That's enough to send me to my knees, because I know my heart. You and I as Christians need to realize that however acceptable our lives may be for the general audience, we still possess an R-rated heart, and we're as good as dead if we want God to meet us on any other ground than his grace and forgiveness.

The joy of this truth is that once I can believe that forgiveness for myself, then I can believe it for anybody. I have new eyes to see beyond my neighbor's sin and love him or her with the love of Christ.

When we search the Gospels, we never find a place where Jesus was offended by a sinful person. But there are repeated accounts of his being offended by the self-righteousness of so-called holy people who set themselves apart from the rest of humanity in their own eyes. For these people, he didn't even have the time of day, except to warn them of the judgment to come, a judgment brought about by their refusal to see themselves as needy as the next guy.

Additional Scripture Readings:
Luke 6:37–42; Luke 18:9–14

Go to page 48 for your next devotional reading.

asked. "I tell you the truth, not one stone here will be left on another; every one will be thrown down."

³As Jesus was sitting on the Mount of Olives, the disciples came to him privately. "Tell us," they said, "when will this happen, and what will be the sign of your coming and of the end of the age?"

⁴Jesus answered: "Watch out that no one deceives you. ⁵For many will come in my name, claiming, 'I am the Christ,*ᵃ*' and will deceive many. ⁶You will hear of wars and rumors of wars, but see to it that you are not alarmed. Such things must happen, but the end is still to come. ⁷Nation will rise against nation, and kingdom against kingdom. There will be famines and earthquakes in various places. ⁸All these are the beginning of birth pains.

⁹"Then you will be handed over to be persecuted and put to death, and you will be hated by all nations because of me. ¹⁰At that time many will turn away from the faith and will betray and hate each other, ¹¹and many false prophets will appear and deceive many people. ¹²Because of the increase of wickedness, the love of most will grow cold, ¹³but he who stands firm to the end will be saved. ¹⁴And this gospel of the kingdom will be preached in the whole world as a testimony to all nations, and then the end will come.

¹⁵"So when you see standing in the holy place 'the abomination that causes desolation,'*ᵇ* spoken of through the prophet Daniel—let the reader understand—¹⁶then let those who are in Judea flee to the mountains. ¹⁷Let no one on the roof of his house go down to take anything out of the house. ¹⁸Let no one in the field go back to get his cloak. ¹⁹How dreadful it will be in those days for pregnant women and nursing mothers! ²⁰Pray that your flight will not take place in winter or on the Sabbath. ²¹For then there will be great distress, unequaled from the beginning of the world until now—and never to be equaled again. ²²If those days had not been cut short, no one would survive, but for the sake of the elect those days will be shortened. ²³At that time if anyone says to you, 'Look, here is the Christ!' or, 'There he is!' do not believe it. ²⁴For false Christs and false prophets will appear and perform great signs and miracles to deceive even the elect—if that were possible. ²⁵See, I have told you ahead of time.

²⁶"So if anyone tells you, 'There he is, out in the desert,' do not go out; or, 'Here he is, in the inner rooms,' do not believe it. ²⁷For as lightning that comes from the east is visible even in the west, so will be the coming of the Son of Man. ²⁸Wherever there is a carcass, there the vultures will gather.

²⁹"Immediately after the distress of those days

" 'the sun will be darkened,
    and the moon will not give its light;
the stars will fall from the sky,
    and the heavenly bodies will be shaken.'*ᶜ*

³⁰"At that time the sign of the Son of Man will appear in the sky, and all the nations of the earth will mourn. They will see the Son of Man coming on the clouds of the sky, with power and great glory. ³¹And he will send his angels with a loud trumpet call, and they will gather his elect from the four winds, from one end of the heavens to the other.

³²"Now learn this lesson from the fig tree: As soon as its twigs get tender and its leaves come out, you know that summer is near. ³³Even so, when you see all these things, you know that it*ᵈ* is near, right at the door. ³⁴I tell you the truth, this generation*ᵉ* will certainly not pass away until all these things have happened. ³⁵Heaven and earth will pass away, but my words will never pass away.

The Day and Hour Unknown

³⁶"No one knows about that day or hour, not even the angels in heaven, nor the Son,*ᶠ* but only the Father. ³⁷As it was in the days of Noah, so it will be at the coming of the Son of Man. ³⁸For in the days before the flood, people were eating and drinking, marrying and giving in marriage, up to the day Noah entered the ark; ³⁹and they knew nothing about what would happen until the flood came and took them all away. That is how it will be at the coming of the Son of Man. ⁴⁰Two men will be in the field; one will be taken and the other left. ⁴¹Two women will be grinding with a hand mill; one will be taken and the other left.

⁴²"Therefore keep watch, because you do not know on what day your Lord will come. ⁴³But understand this: If the owner of the house had known at what time of

---

ᵃ5 Or *Messiah*; also in verse 23   *ᵇ15* Daniel 9:27; 11:31; 12:11   *ᶜ29* Isaiah 13:10; 34:4   *ᵈ33* Or *he*
ᵉ34 Or *race*   *ᶠ36* Some manuscripts do not have *nor the Son.*

night the thief was coming, he would have kept watch and would not have let his house be broken into. **44**So you also must be ready, because the Son of Man will come at an hour when you do not expect him.

45"Who then is the faithful and wise servant, whom the master has put in charge of the servants in his household to give them their food at the proper time? **46**It will be good for that servant whose master finds him doing so when he returns. **47**I tell you the truth, he will put him in charge of all his possessions. **48**But suppose that servant is wicked and says to himself, 'My master is staying away a long time,' **49**and he then begins to beat his fellow servants and to eat and drink with drunkards. **50**The master of that servant will come on a day when he does not expect him and at an hour he is not aware of. **51**He will cut him to pieces and assign him a place with the hypocrites, where there will be weeping and gnashing of teeth.

The Parable of the Ten Virgins

25 "At that time the kingdom of heaven will be like ten virgins who took their lamps and went out to meet the bridegroom. **2**Five of them were foolish and five were wise. **3**The foolish ones took their lamps but did not take any oil with them. **4**The wise, however, took oil in jars along with their lamps. **5**The bridegroom was a long time in coming, and they all became drowsy and fell asleep.

6"At midnight the cry rang out: 'Here's the bridegroom! Come out to meet him!'

7"Then all the virgins woke up and trimmed their lamps. **8**The foolish ones said to the wise, 'Give us some of your oil; our lamps are going out.'

9" 'No,' they replied, 'there may not be enough for both us and you. Instead, go to those who sell oil and buy some for yourselves.'

10"But while they were on their way to buy the oil, the bridegroom arrived. The virgins who were ready went in with him to the wedding banquet. And the door was shut.

11"Later the others also came. 'Sir! Sir!' they said. 'Open the door for us!'

12"But he replied, 'I tell you the truth, I don't know you.'

13"Therefore keep watch, because you do not know the day or the hour.

The Parable of the Talents

14"Again, it will be like a man going on a journey, who called his servants and entrusted his property to them. **15**To one he gave five talents[a] of money, to another two talents, and to another one talent, each according to his ability. Then he went on his journey. **16**The man who had received the five talents went at once and put his money to work and gained five more. **17**So also, the one with the two talents gained two more. **18**But the man who had received the one talent went off, dug a hole in the ground and hid his master's money.

19"After a long time the master of those servants returned and settled accounts with them. **20**The man who had received the five talents brought the other five. 'Master,' he said, 'you entrusted me with five talents. See, I have gained five more.'

21"His master replied, 'Well done, good and faithful servant! You have been faithful with a few things; I will put you in charge of many things. Come and share your master's happiness!'

22"The man with the two talents also came. 'Master,' he said, 'you entrusted me with two talents; see, I have gained two more.'

23"His master replied, 'Well done, good and faithful servant! You have been faithful with a few things; I will put you in charge of many things. Come and share your master's happiness!'

24"Then the man who had received the one talent came. 'Master,' he said, 'I knew that you are a hard man, harvesting where you have not sown and gathering where you have not scattered seed. **25**So I was afraid and went out and hid your talent in the ground. See, here is what belongs to you.'

26"His master replied, 'You wicked, lazy servant! So you knew that I harvest where I have not sown and gather where I have not scattered seed? **27**Well then, you should have put my money on deposit with the bankers, so that when I returned I would have received it back with interest.

28" 'Take the talent from him and give it to the one who has the ten talents. **29**For everyone who has will be given more, and he will have an abundance. Whoever does not have, even what he has will be taken from him. **30**And throw that worthless ser-

---

[a] 15 A talent was worth more than a thousand dollars.

vant outside, into the darkness, where there will be weeping and gnashing of teeth.'

The Sheep and the Goats

³¹"When the Son of Man comes in his glory, and all the angels with him, he will sit on his throne in heavenly glory. ³²All the nations will be gathered before him, and he will separate the people one from another as a shepherd separates the sheep from the goats. ³³He will put the sheep on his right and the goats on his left.

³⁴"Then the King will say to those on his right, 'Come, you who are blessed by my Father; take your inheritance, the kingdom prepared for you since the creation of the world. ³⁵For I was hungry and you gave me something to eat, I was thirsty and you gave me something to drink, I was a stranger and you invited me in, ³⁶I needed clothes and you clothed me, I was sick and you looked after me, I was in prison and you came to visit me.'

³⁷"Then the righteous will answer him, 'Lord, when did we see you hungry and feed you, or thirsty and give you something to drink? ³⁸When did we see you a stranger and invite you in, or needing clothes and clothe you? ³⁹When did we see you sick or in prison and go to visit you?'

⁴⁰"The King will reply, 'I tell you the truth, whatever you did for one of the least of these brothers of mine, you did for me.'

⁴¹"Then he will say to those on his left, 'Depart from me, you who are cursed, into the eternal fire prepared for the devil and his angels. ⁴²For I was hungry and you gave me nothing to eat, I was thirsty and you gave me nothing to drink, ⁴³I was a stranger and you did not invite me in, I needed clothes and you did not clothe me, I was sick and in prison and you did not look after me.'

⁴⁴"They also will answer, 'Lord, when did we see you hungry or thirsty or a stranger or needing clothes or sick or in prison, and did not help you?'

⁴⁵"He will reply, 'I tell you the truth, whatever you did not do for one of the least of these, you did not do for me.'

⁴⁶"Then they will go away to eternal punishment, but the righteous to eternal life."

The Plot Against Jesus

26 When Jesus had finished saying all these things, he said to his disciples, ²"As you know, the Passover is two days away—and the Son of Man will be handed over to be crucified."

³Then the chief priests and the elders of the people assembled in the palace of the high priest, whose name was Caiaphas, ⁴and they plotted to arrest Jesus in some sly way and kill him. ⁵"But not during the Feast," they said, "or there may be a riot among the people."

Jesus Anointed at Bethany

⁶While Jesus was in Bethany in the home of a man known as Simon the Leper, ⁷a woman came to him with an alabaster jar of very expensive perfume, which she poured on his head as he was reclining at the table.

⁸When the disciples saw this, they were indignant. "Why this waste?" they asked. ⁹"This perfume could have been sold at a high price and the money given to the poor."

¹⁰Aware of this, Jesus said to them, "Why are you bothering this woman? She has done a beautiful thing to me. ¹¹The poor you will always have with you, but you will not always have me. ¹²When she poured this perfume on my body, she did it to prepare me for burial. ¹³I tell you the truth, wherever this gospel is preached throughout the world, what she has done will also be told, in memory of her."

Judas Agrees to Betray Jesus

¹⁴Then one of the Twelve—the one called Judas Iscariot—went to the chief priests ¹⁵and asked, "What are you willing to give me if I hand him over to you?" So they counted out for him thirty silver coins. ¹⁶From then on Judas watched for an opportunity to hand him over.

The Lord's Supper

¹⁷On the first day of the Feast of Unleavened Bread, the disciples came to Jesus and asked, "Where do you want us to make preparations for you to eat the Passover?"

¹⁸He replied, "Go into the city to a certain man and tell him, 'The Teacher says: My appointed time is near. I am going to celebrate the Passover with my disciples at your house.' " ¹⁹So the disciples did as Jesus had directed them and prepared the Passover.

²⁰When evening came, Jesus was reclining at the table with the Twelve. ²¹And while they were eating, he said, "I tell you the truth, one of you will betray me."

MATTHEW 26

²²They were very sad and began to say to him one after the other, "Surely not I, Lord?"

²³Jesus replied, "The one who has dipped his hand into the bowl with me will betray me. ²⁴The Son of Man will go just as it is written about him. But woe to that man who betrays the Son of Man! It would be better for him if he had not been born."

²⁵Then Judas, the one who would betray him, said, "Surely not I, Rabbi?"

Jesus answered, "Yes, it is you."ᵃ

²⁶While they were eating, Jesus took bread, gave thanks and broke it, and gave it to his disciples, saying, "Take and eat; this is my body."

²⁷Then he took the cup, gave thanks and offered it to them, saying, "Drink from it, all of you. ²⁸This is my blood of theᵇ covenant, which is poured out for many for the forgiveness of sins. ²⁹I tell you, I will not drink of this fruit of the vine from now on until that day when I drink it anew with you in my Father's kingdom."

³⁰When they had sung a hymn, they went out to the Mount of Olives.

Jesus Predicts Peter's Denial

³¹Then Jesus told them, "This very night you will all fall away on account of me, for it is written:

" 'I will strike the shepherd,
and the sheep of the flock will be scattered.'ᶜ

³²But after I have risen, I will go ahead of you into Galilee."

³³Peter replied, "Even if all fall away on account of you, I never will."

³⁴"I tell you the truth," Jesus answered, "this very night, before the rooster crows, you will disown me three times."

³⁵But Peter declared, "Even if I have to die with you, I will never disown you." And all the other disciples said the same.

Gethsemane

³⁶Then Jesus went with his disciples to a place called Gethsemane, and he said to them, "Sit here while I go over there and pray." ³⁷He took Peter and the two sons of Zebedee along with him, and he began to be sorrowful and troubled. ³⁸Then he said to them, "My soul is overwhelmed with sorrow to the point of death. Stay here and keep watch with me."

³⁹Going a little farther, he fell with his face to the ground and prayed, "My Father, if it is possible, may this cup be taken from me. Yet not as I will, but as you will."

⁴⁰Then he returned to his disciples and found them sleeping. "Could you men not keep watch with me for one hour?" he asked Peter. ⁴¹"Watch and pray so that you will not fall into temptation. The spirit is willing, but the body is weak."

⁴²He went away a second time and prayed, "My Father, if it is not possible for this cup to be taken away unless I drink it, may your will be done."

⁴³When he came back, he again found them sleeping, because their eyes were heavy. ⁴⁴So he left them and went away once more and prayed the third time, saying the same thing.

⁴⁵Then he returned to the disciples and said to them, "Are you still sleeping and resting? Look, the hour is near, and the Son of Man is betrayed into the hands of sinners. ⁴⁶Rise, let us go! Here comes my betrayer!"

Jesus Arrested

⁴⁷While he was still speaking, Judas, one of the Twelve, arrived. With him was a large crowd armed with swords and clubs, sent from the chief priests and the elders of the people. ⁴⁸Now the betrayer had arranged a signal with them: "The one I kiss is the man; arrest him." ⁴⁹Going at once to Jesus, Judas said, "Greetings, Rabbi!" and kissed him.

⁵⁰Jesus replied, "Friend, do what you came for."ᵈ

Then the men stepped forward, seized Jesus and arrested him. ⁵¹With that, one of Jesus' companions reached for his sword, drew it out and struck the servant of the high priest, cutting off his ear.

⁵²"Put your sword back in its place," Jesus said to him, "for all who draw the sword will die by the sword. ⁵³Do you think I cannot call on my Father, and he will at once put at my disposal more than twelve legions of angels? ⁵⁴But how then would the Scriptures be fulfilled that say it must happen in this way?"

⁵⁵At that time Jesus said to the crowd, "Am I leading a rebellion, that you have come out with swords and clubs to capture me? Every day I sat in the temple

---

ᵃ25 Or *"You yourself have said it"*   ᵇ28 Some manuscripts *the new*   ᶜ31 Zech. 13:7   ᵈ50 Or *"Friend, why have you come?"*

courts teaching, and you did not arrest me. **56**But this has all taken place that the writings of the prophets might be fulfilled." Then all the disciples deserted him and fled.

Before the Sanhedrin

57Those who had arrested Jesus took him to Caiaphas, the high priest, where the teachers of the law and the elders had assembled. **58**But Peter followed him at a distance, right up to the courtyard of the high priest. He entered and sat down with the guards to see the outcome.

59The chief priests and the whole Sanhedrin were looking for false evidence against Jesus so that they could put him to death. **60**But they did not find any, though many false witnesses came forward.

Finally two came forward **61**and declared, "This fellow said, 'I am able to destroy the temple of God and rebuild it in three days.'"

62Then the high priest stood up and said to Jesus, "Are you not going to answer? What is this testimony that these men are bringing against you?" **63**But Jesus remained silent.

The high priest said to him, "I charge you under oath by the living God: Tell us if you are the Christ,*a* the Son of God."

64"Yes, it is as you say," Jesus replied. "But I say to all of you: In the future you will see the Son of Man sitting at the right hand of the Mighty One and coming on the clouds of heaven."

65Then the high priest tore his clothes and said, "He has spoken blasphemy! Why do we need any more witnesses? Look, now you have heard the blasphemy. **66**What do you think?"

"He is worthy of death," they answered. **67**Then they spit in his face and struck him with their fists. Others slapped him **68**and said, "Prophesy to us, Christ. Who hit you?"

Peter Disowns Jesus

69Now Peter was sitting out in the courtyard, and a servant girl came to him. "You also were with Jesus of Galilee," she said.

70But he denied it before them all. "I don't know what you're talking about," he said.

71Then he went out to the gateway, where another girl saw him and said to the people there, "This fellow was with Jesus of Nazareth."

72He denied it again, with an oath: "I don't know the man!"

73After a little while, those standing there went up to Peter and said, "Surely you are one of them, for your accent gives you away."

74Then he began to call down curses on himself and he swore to them, "I don't know the man!"

Immediately a rooster crowed. **75**Then Peter remembered the word Jesus had spoken: "Before the rooster crows, you will disown me three times." And he went outside and wept bitterly.

Judas Hangs Himself

27 Early in the morning, all the chief priests and the elders of the people came to the decision to put Jesus to death. **2**They bound him, led him away and handed him over to Pilate, the governor.

3When Judas, who had betrayed him, saw that Jesus was condemned, he was seized with remorse and returned the thirty silver coins to the chief priests and the elders. **4**"I have sinned," he said, "for I have betrayed innocent blood."

"What is that to us?" they replied. "That's your responsibility."

5So Judas threw the money into the temple and left. Then he went away and hanged himself.

6The chief priests picked up the coins and said, "It is against the law to put this into the treasury, since it is blood money." **7**So they decided to use the money to buy the potter's field as a burial place for foreigners. **8**That is why it has been called the Field of Blood to this day. **9**Then what was spoken by Jeremiah the prophet was fulfilled: "They took the thirty silver coins, the price set on him by the people of Israel, **10**and they used them to buy the potter's field, as the Lord commanded me."*b*

Jesus Before Pilate

11Meanwhile Jesus stood before the governor, and the governor asked him, "Are you the king of the Jews?"

"Yes, it is as you say," Jesus replied.

12When he was accused by the chief priests and the elders, he gave no answer. **13**Then Pilate asked him, "Don't you hear the testimony they are bringing against you?" **14**But Jesus made no reply, not even to a single charge—to the great amazement of the governor.

15Now it was the governor's custom at

*a*63 Or *Messiah;* also in verse 68   *b*10 See Zech. 11:12,13; Jer. 19:1-13; 32:6-9.

the Feast to release a prisoner chosen by the crowd. **16**At that time they had a notorious prisoner, called Barabbas. **17**So when the crowd had gathered, Pilate asked them, "Which one do you want me to release to you: Barabbas, or Jesus who is called Christ?" **18**For he knew it was out of envy that they had handed Jesus over to him.

19While Pilate was sitting on the judge's seat, his wife sent him this message: "Don't have anything to do with that innocent man, for I have suffered a great deal today in a dream because of him."

20But the chief priests and the elders persuaded the crowd to ask for Barabbas and to have Jesus executed.

21"Which of the two do you want me to release to you?" asked the governor.

"Barabbas," they answered.

22"What shall I do, then, with Jesus who is called Christ?" Pilate asked.

They all answered, "Crucify him!"

23"Why? What crime has he committed?" asked Pilate.

But they shouted all the louder, "Crucify him!"

24When Pilate saw that he was getting nowhere, but that instead an uproar was starting, he took water and washed his hands in front of the crowd. "I am innocent of this man's blood," he said. "It is your responsibility!"

25All the people answered, "Let his blood be on us and on our children!"

26Then he released Barabbas to them. But he had Jesus flogged, and handed him over to be crucified.

The Soldiers Mock Jesus

27Then the governor's soldiers took Jesus into the Praetorium and gathered the whole company of soldiers around him. **28**They stripped him and put a scarlet robe on him, **29**and then twisted together a crown of thorns and set it on his head. They put a staff in his right hand and knelt in front of him and mocked him. "Hail, king of the Jews!" they said. **30**They spit on him, and took the staff and struck him on the head again and again. **31**After they had mocked him, they took off the robe and put his own clothes on him. Then they led him away to crucify him.

The Crucifixion

32As they were going out, they met a man from Cyrene, named Simon, and they forced him to carry the cross. **33**They came to a place called Golgotha (which means The Place of the Skull). **34**There they offered Jesus wine to drink, mixed with gall; but after tasting it, he refused to drink it. **35**When they had crucified him, they divided up his clothes by casting lots.[a] **36**And sitting down, they kept watch over him there. **37**Above his head they placed the written charge against him: THIS IS JESUS, THE KING OF THE JEWS. **38**Two robbers were crucified with him, one on his right and one on his left. **39**Those who passed by hurled insults at him, shaking their heads **40**and saying, "You who are going to destroy the temple and build it in three days, save yourself! Come down from the cross, if you are the Son of God!"

41In the same way the chief priests, the teachers of the law and the elders mocked him. **42**"He saved others," they said, "but he can't save himself! He's the King of Israel! Let him come down now from the cross, and we will believe in him. **43**He trusts in God. Let God rescue him now if he wants him, for he said, 'I am the Son of God.' " **44**In the same way the robbers who were crucified with him also heaped insults on him.

The Death of Jesus

45From the sixth hour until the ninth hour darkness came over all the land. **46**About the ninth hour Jesus cried out in a loud voice, *"Eloi, Eloi,[b] lama sabachthani?"* — which means, "My God, my God, why have you forsaken me?"[c]

47When some of those standing there heard this, they said, "He's calling Elijah."

48Immediately one of them ran and got a sponge. He filled it with wine vinegar, put it on a stick, and offered it to Jesus to drink. **49**The rest said, "Now leave him alone. Let's see if Elijah comes to save him."

50And when Jesus had cried out again in a loud voice, he gave up his spirit.

51At that moment the curtain of the temple was torn in two from top to bottom. The earth shook and the rocks split. **52**The tombs broke open and the bodies of many holy people who had died were

---

[a]35 A few late manuscripts *lots that the word spoken by the prophet might be fulfilled: "They divided my garments among themselves and cast lots for my clothing"* (Psalm 22:18)   [b]46 Some manuscripts *Eli, Eli*   [c]46 Psalm 22:1

raised to life. ⁵³They came out of the tombs, and after Jesus' resurrection they went into the holy city and appeared to many people.

⁵⁴When the centurion and those with him who were guarding Jesus saw the earthquake and all that had happened, they were terrified, and exclaimed, "Surely he was the Son*ᵃ* of God!"

⁵⁵Many women were there, watching from a distance. They had followed Jesus from Galilee to care for his needs. ⁵⁶Among them were Mary Magdalene, Mary the mother of James and Joses, and the mother of Zebedee's sons.

The Burial of Jesus

⁵⁷As evening approached, there came a rich man from Arimathea, named Joseph, who had himself become a disciple of Jesus. ⁵⁸Going to Pilate, he asked for Jesus' body, and Pilate ordered that it be given to him. ⁵⁹Joseph took the body, wrapped it in a clean linen cloth, ⁶⁰and placed it in his own new tomb that he had cut out of the rock. He rolled a big stone in front of the entrance to the tomb and went away. ⁶¹Mary Magdalene and the other Mary were sitting there opposite the tomb.

The Guard at the Tomb

⁶²The next day, the one after Preparation Day, the chief priests and the Pharisees went to Pilate. ⁶³"Sir," they said, "we remember that while he was still alive that deceiver said, 'After three days I will rise again.' ⁶⁴So give the order for the tomb to be made secure until the third day. Otherwise, his disciples may come and steal the body and tell the people that he has been raised from the dead. This last deception will be worse than the first."

⁶⁵"Take a guard," Pilate answered. "Go, make the tomb as secure as you know how." ⁶⁶So they went and made the tomb secure by putting a seal on the stone and posting the guard.

The Resurrection

28 After the Sabbath, at dawn on the first day of the week, Mary Magdalene and the other Mary went to look at the tomb.

²There was a violent earthquake, for an angel of the Lord came down from heaven and, going to the tomb, rolled back the stone and sat on it. ³His appearance was like lightning, and his clothes were white as snow. ⁴The guards were so afraid of him that they shook and became like dead men.

⁵The angel said to the women, "Do not be afraid, for I know that you are looking for Jesus, who was crucified. ⁶He is not here; he has risen, just as he said. Come and see the place where he lay. ⁷Then go quickly and tell his disciples: 'He has risen from the dead and is going ahead of you into Galilee. There you will see him.' Now I have told you."

⁸So the women hurried away from the tomb, afraid yet filled with joy, and ran to tell his disciples. ⁹Suddenly Jesus met them. "Greetings," he said. They came to him, clasped his feet and worshiped him. ¹⁰Then Jesus said to them, "Do not be afraid. Go and tell my brothers to go to Galilee; there they will see me."

The Guards' Report

¹¹While the women were on their way, some of the guards went into the city and reported to the chief priests everything that had happened. ¹²When the chief priests had met with the elders and devised a plan, they gave the soldiers a large sum of money, ¹³telling them, "You are to say, 'His disciples came during the night and stole him away while we were asleep.' ¹⁴If this report gets to the governor, we will satisfy him and keep you out of trouble." ¹⁵So the soldiers took the money and did as they were instructed. And this story has been widely circulated among the Jews to this very day.

The Great Commission

¹⁶Then the eleven disciples went to Galilee, to the mountain where Jesus had told them to go. ¹⁷When they saw him, they worshiped him; but some doubted. ¹⁸Then Jesus came to them and said, "All authority in heaven and on earth has been given to me. ¹⁹Therefore go and make disciples of all nations, baptizing them in*ᵇ* the name of the Father and of the Son and of the Holy Spirit, ²⁰and teaching them to obey everything I have commanded you. And surely I am with you always, to the very end of the age."

ᵃ 54 Or *a son*   *ᵇ 19* Or *into*; see Acts 8:16; 19:5; Romans 6:3; 1 Cor. 1:13; 10:2 and Gal. 3:27.

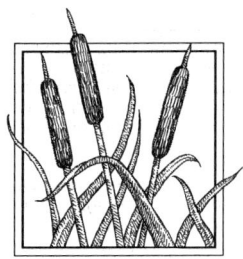

*M*ARK writes this Gospel to tell the basic story about Jesus. He recounts miracles, parables and other sayings of Jesus. Almost half of his book deals with the final week of Jesus' life, ending with his death on the cross and his resurrection from the dead. As you read this book, notice how full of life and emotion Jesus is and how caring he is. Note too why he came into the world—to give his life for you (Mark 10:45). God wants you to accept his Son Jesus as your own personal Savior and Lord.

MARK

John the Baptist Prepares the Way

1 The beginning of the gospel about Jesus Christ, the Son of God.[a]

2It is written in Isaiah the prophet:

"I will send my messenger ahead of you,
 who will prepare your way"[b]—
3"a voice of one calling in the desert,
'Prepare the way for the Lord,
 make straight paths for him.' "[c]

4And so John came, baptizing in the desert region and preaching a baptism of repentance for the forgiveness of sins. **5**The whole Judean countryside and all the people of Jerusalem went out to him. Confessing their sins, they were baptized by him in the Jordan River. **6**John wore clothing made of camel's hair, with a leather belt around his waist, and he ate locusts and wild honey. **7**And this was his message: "After me will come one more powerful than I, the thongs of whose sandals I am not worthy to stoop down and untie. **8**I baptize you with[d] water,

---

[a]1 Some manuscripts do not have *the Son of God.*   [b]2 Mal. 3:1   [c]3 Isaiah 40:3   [d]8 Or *in*

but he will baptize you with the Holy Spirit."

The Baptism and Temptation of Jesus

⁹At that time Jesus came from Nazareth in Galilee and was baptized by John in the Jordan. ¹⁰As Jesus was coming up out of the water, he saw heaven being torn open and the Spirit descending on him like a dove. ¹¹And a voice came from heaven: "You are my Son, whom I love; with you I am well pleased."

¹²At once the Spirit sent him out into the desert, ¹³and he was in the desert forty days, being tempted by Satan. He was with the wild animals, and angels attended him.

The Calling of the First Disciples

¹⁴After John was put in prison, Jesus went into Galilee, proclaiming the good news of God. ¹⁵"The time has come," he said. "The kingdom of God is near. Repent and believe the good news!"

¹⁶As Jesus walked beside the Sea of Galilee, he saw Simon and his brother Andrew casting a net into the lake, for they were fishermen. ¹⁷"Come, follow me," Jesus said, "and I will make you fishers of men." ¹⁸At once they left their nets and followed him.

¹⁹When he had gone a little farther, he saw James son of Zebedee and his brother John in a boat, preparing their nets. ²⁰Without delay he called them, and they left their father Zebedee in the boat with the hired men and followed him.

Jesus Drives Out an Evil Spirit

²¹They went to Capernaum, and when the Sabbath came, Jesus went into the synagogue and began to teach. ²²The people were amazed at his teaching, because he taught them as one who had authority, not as the teachers of the law. ²³Just then a man in their synagogue who was possessed by an evil[a] spirit cried out, ²⁴"What do you want with us, Jesus of Nazareth? Have you come to destroy us? I know who you are—the Holy One of God!"

²⁵"Be quiet!" said Jesus sternly. "Come out of him!" ²⁶The evil spirit shook the man violently and came out of him with a shriek.

²⁷The people were all so amazed that they asked each other, "What is this? A new teaching—and with authority! He even gives orders to evil spirits and they obey him." ²⁸News about him spread quickly over the whole region of Galilee.

Jesus Heals Many

²⁹As soon as they left the synagogue, they went with James and John to the home of Simon and Andrew. ³⁰Simon's mother-in-law was in bed with a fever, and they told Jesus about her. ³¹So he went to her, took her hand and helped her up. The fever left her and she began to wait on them.

³²That evening after sunset the people brought to Jesus all the sick and demon-possessed. ³³The whole town gathered at the door, ³⁴and Jesus healed many who had various diseases. He also drove out many demons, but he would not let the demons speak because they knew who he was.

Jesus Prays in a Solitary Place

³⁵Very early in the morning, while it was still dark, Jesus got up, left the house and went off to a solitary place, where he prayed. ³⁶Simon and his companions went to look for him, ³⁷and when they found him, they exclaimed: "Everyone is looking for you!"

³⁸Jesus replied, "Let us go somewhere else—to the nearby villages—so I can preach there also. That is why I have come." ³⁹So he traveled throughout Galilee, preaching in their synagogues and driving out demons.

A Man With Leprosy

⁴⁰A man with leprosy[b] came to him and begged him on his knees, "If you are willing, you can make me clean."

⁴¹Filled with compassion, Jesus reached out his hand and touched the man. "I am willing," he said. "Be clean!" ⁴²Immediately the leprosy left him and he was cured.

⁴³Jesus sent him away at once with a strong warning: ⁴⁴"See that you don't tell this to anyone. But go, show yourself to the priest and offer the sacrifices that Moses commanded for your cleansing, as a testimony to them." ⁴⁵Instead he went out and began to talk freely, spreading the news. As a result, Jesus could no longer enter a town openly but stayed outside in

---

[a] 23 Greek *unclean*; also in verses 26 and 27 affecting the skin—not necessarily leprosy. [b] 40 The Greek word was used for various diseases

lonely places. Yet the people still came to him from everywhere.

Jesus Heals a Paralytic

2 A few days later, when Jesus again entered Capernaum, the people heard that he had come home. ²So many gathered that there was no room left, not even outside the door, and he preached the word to them. ³Some men came, bringing to him a paralytic, carried by four of them. ⁴Since they could not get him to Jesus because of the crowd, they made an opening in the roof above Jesus and, after digging through it, lowered the mat the paralyzed man was lying on. ⁵When Jesus saw their faith, he said to the paralytic, "Son, your sins are forgiven."

⁶Now some teachers of the law were sitting there, thinking to themselves, ⁷"Why does this fellow talk like that? He's blaspheming! Who can forgive sins but God alone?"

⁸Immediately Jesus knew in his spirit that this was what they were thinking in their hearts, and he said to them, "Why are you thinking these things? ⁹Which is easier: to say to the paralytic, 'Your sins are forgiven,' or to say, 'Get up, take your mat and walk'? ¹⁰But that you may know that the Son of Man has authority on earth to forgive sins . . . ." He said to the paralytic, ¹¹"I tell you, get up, take your mat and go home." ¹²He got up, took his mat and walked out in full view of them all. This amazed everyone and they praised God, saying, "We have never seen anything like this!"

The Calling of Levi

¹³Once again Jesus went out beside the lake. A large crowd came to him, and he began to teach them. ¹⁴As he walked along, he saw Levi son of Alphaeus sitting at the tax collector's booth. "Follow me," Jesus told him, and Levi got up and followed him.

¹⁵While Jesus was having dinner at Levi's house, many tax collectors and "sinners" were eating with him and his disciples, for there were many who followed him. ¹⁶When the teachers of the law who were Pharisees saw him eating with the "sinners" and tax collectors, they asked his disciples: "Why does he eat with tax collectors and 'sinners'?"

¹⁷On hearing this, Jesus said to them, "It is not the healthy who need a doctor, but the sick. I have not come to call the righteous, but sinners."

Jesus Questioned About Fasting

¹⁸Now John's disciples and the Pharisees were fasting. Some people came and asked Jesus, "How is it that John's disciples and the disciples of the Pharisees are fasting, but yours are not?"

¹⁹Jesus answered, "How can the guests of the bridegroom fast while he is with them? They cannot, so long as they have him with them. ²⁰But the time will come when the bridegroom will be taken from them, and on that day they will fast.

²¹"No one sews a patch of unshrunk cloth on an old garment. If he does, the new piece will pull away from the old, making the tear worse. ²²And no one pours new wine into old wineskins. If he does, the wine will burst the skins, and both the wine and the wineskins will be ruined. No, he pours new wine into new wineskins."

Lord of the Sabbath

²³One Sabbath Jesus was going through the grainfields, and as his disciples walked along, they began to pick some heads of grain. ²⁴The Pharisees said to him, "Look, why are they doing what is unlawful on the Sabbath?"

²⁵He answered, "Have you never read what David did when he and his companions were hungry and in need? ²⁶In the days of Abiathar the high priest, he entered the house of God and ate the consecrated bread, which is lawful only for priests to eat. And he also gave some to his companions."

²⁷Then he said to them, "The Sabbath was made for man, not man for the Sabbath. ²⁸So the Son of Man is Lord even of the Sabbath."

3 Another time he went into the synagogue, and a man with a shriveled hand was there. ²Some of them were looking for a reason to accuse Jesus, so they watched him closely to see if he would heal him on the Sabbath. ³Jesus said to the man with the shriveled hand, "Stand up in front of everyone."

⁴Then Jesus asked them, "Which is lawful on the Sabbath: to do good or to do evil, to save life or to kill?" But they remained silent.

⁵He looked around at them in anger and, deeply distressed at their stubborn hearts, said to the man, "Stretch out your hand." He stretched it out, and his hand was completely restored. ⁶Then the Phari-

sees went out and plot with the Herodians how they might kill Jesus.

Crowds Follow Jesus

⁷Jesus withdrew with his disciples to the lake, and a large crowd from Galilee followed. ⁸When they heard all he was doing, many people came to him from Judea, Jerusalem, Idumea, and the regions across the Jordan and around Tyre and Sidon. ⁹Because of the crowd he told his disciples to have a small boat ready for him, to keep the people from crowding him. ¹⁰For he had healed many, so that those

---

WEDNESDAY

VERSE FOR THE DAY:　　AUTHOR:　　PASSAGE FOR THE DAY:
Mark 2:14　　Dietrich Bonhoeffer　　Mark 2:13–17

No Other Road

THE call goes forth, and is at once followed by the response of obedience. The response of the disciples is an act of obedience, not a confession of faith in Jesus. How could the call immediately evoke obedience? The story is a stumbling block for the natural reason, and it is no wonder that frantic attempts have been made to separate the two events. By hook or by crook a bridge must be found between them. Something must have happened in between, some psychological or historical event. Thus we get the stupid question: Surely the tax collector must have known Jesus before, and that previous acquaintance explains his readiness to hear the Master's call. Unfortunately our text is ruthlessly silent on this point, and in fact it regards the immediate sequence of call and response as a matter of crucial importance. It displays not the slightest interest in the psychological reasons for a man's religious decisions. And why? For the simple reason that the cause behind the immediate following of call by response is Jesus Christ himself. It is Jesus who calls, and because it is Jesus, Levi follows at once.

This encounter is a testimony to the absolute, direct and unaccountable authority of Jesus. There is no need of any preliminaries, and no other consequence but obedience to the call. Because Jesus is the Christ, he has the authority to call and to demand obedience to his word. Jesus summons men to follow him, not as a teacher or a pattern of the good life, but as the Christ, the Son of God. In this short text Jesus Christ and his claim are proclaimed to men. Not a word of praise is given to the disciple for his decision for Christ. We are not expected to contemplate the disciple, but only him who calls, and his absolute authority. According to our text, there is no road to faith or discipleship, no other road—only obedience to the call of Jesus.

Additional Scripture Readings:
Luke 9:18–27; John 12:23–26

Go to page 50 for your next devotional reading.

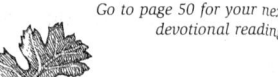

with diseases were pushing forward to touch him. ¹¹Whenever the evil[a] spirits saw him, they fell down before him and cried out, "You are the Son of God." ¹²But he gave them strict orders not to tell who he was.

The Appointing of the Twelve Apostles

¹³Jesus went up on a mountainside and called to him those he wanted, and they came to him. ¹⁴He appointed twelve—designating them apostles[b]—that they might be with him and that he might send them out to preach ¹⁵and to have authority to drive out demons. ¹⁶These are the twelve he appointed: Simon (to whom he gave the name Peter); ¹⁷James son of Zebedee and his brother John (to them he gave the name Boanerges, which means Sons of Thunder); ¹⁸Andrew, Philip, Bartholomew, Matthew, Thomas, James son of Alphaeus, Thaddaeus, Simon the Zealot ¹⁹and Judas Iscariot, who betrayed him.

Jesus and Beelzebub

²⁰Then Jesus entered a house, and again a crowd gathered, so that he and his disciples were not even able to eat. ²¹When his family heard about this, they went to take charge of him, for they said, "He is out of his mind."

²²And the teachers of the law who came down from Jerusalem said, "He is possessed by Beelzebub[c]! By the prince of demons he is driving out demons."

²³So Jesus called them and spoke to them in parables: "How can Satan drive out Satan? ²⁴If a kingdom is divided against itself, that kingdom cannot stand. ²⁵If a house is divided against itself, that house cannot stand. ²⁶And if Satan opposes himself and is divided, he cannot stand; his end has come. ²⁷In fact, no one can enter a strong man's house and carry off his possessions unless he first ties up the strong man. Then he can rob his house. ²⁸I tell you the truth, all the sins and blasphemies of men will be forgiven them. ²⁹But whoever blasphemes against the Holy Spirit will never be forgiven; he is guilty of an eternal sin."

³⁰He said this because they were saying, "He has an evil spirit."

Jesus' Mother and Brothers

³¹Then Jesus' mother and brothers arrived. Standing outside, they sent someone in to call him. ³²A crowd was sitting around him, and they told him, "Your mother and brothers are outside looking for you."

³³"Who are my mother and my brothers?" he asked.

³⁴Then he looked at those seated in a circle around him and said, "Here are my mother and my brothers! ³⁵Whoever does God's will is my brother and sister and mother."

The Parable of the Sower

4 Again Jesus began to teach by the lake. The crowd that gathered around him was so large that he got into a boat and sat in it out on the lake, while all the people were along the shore at the water's edge. ²He taught them many things by parables, and in his teaching said: ³"Listen! A farmer went out to sow his seed. ⁴As he was scattering the seed, some fell along the path, and the birds came and ate it up. ⁵Some fell on rocky places, where it did not have much soil. It sprang up quickly, because the soil was shallow. ⁶But when the sun came up, the plants were scorched, and they withered because they had no root. ⁷Other seed fell among thorns, which grew up and choked the plants, so that they did not bear grain. ⁸Still other seed fell on good soil. It came up, grew and produced a crop, multiplying thirty, sixty, or even a hundred times."

⁹Then Jesus said, "He who has ears to hear, let him hear."

¹⁰When he was alone, the Twelve and the others around him asked him about the parables. ¹¹He told them, "The secret of the kingdom of God has been given to you. But to those on the outside everything is said in parables ¹²so that,

" 'they may be ever seeing but never perceiving,
and ever hearing but never understanding;
otherwise they might turn and be forgiven!' [d]"

¹³Then Jesus said to them, "Don't you understand this parable? How then will you understand any parable? ¹⁴The farmer sows the word. ¹⁵Some people are like seed along the path, where the word is sown. As soon as they hear it, Satan comes and takes away the word that was

---

[a]11 Greek *unclean*; also in verse 30   [b]14 Some manuscripts do not have *designating them apostles*.
[c]22 Greek *Beezeboul* or *Beelzeboul*   [d]12 Isaiah 6:9,10

sown in them. ⁱ⁶Others, like seed sown on rocky places, hear the word and at once receive it with joy. ¹⁷But since they have no root, they last only a short time. When trouble or persecution comes because of the word, they quickly fall away. ¹⁸Still others, like seed sown among thorns, hear the word; ¹⁹but the worries of this life, the deceitfulness of wealth and the desires for other things come in and choke the word, making it unfruitful. ²⁰Others, like seed sown on good soil, hear the word, accept it, and produce a crop—thirty, sixty or even a hundred times what was sown."

A Lamp on a Stand

²¹He said to them, "Do you bring in a lamp to put it under a bowl or a bed? Instead, don't you put it on its stand? ²²For whatever is hidden is meant to be disclosed, and whatever is concealed is meant to be brought out into the open. ²³If anyone has ears to hear, let him hear."

²⁴"Consider carefully what you hear," he continued. "With the measure you use,

---

THURSDAY

VERSE FOR THE DAY:
Mark 3:14

AUTHOR:
Stephen Arterburn and
David Stoop

PASSAGE FOR THE DAY:
Mark 3:13–19

Being Christ's Men

A MAN'S identity (as well as a woman's) is based on who he is apart from what he does. Identity is a matter of character, not accomplishment, a matter of being and relating, not doing. This is apparent in the call of Jesus Christ to his disciples, as recorded in the Bible in Mark 3:14–15: "He appointed twelve —designating them apostles—that they might be with him and that he might send them out to preach and to have authority to drive out demons."

Notice that Jesus definitely called the apostles to *do something*: to preach the gospel and drive out demons. But his first call was for them to *be someone*—his men. He wanted a mutually loving, nurturing, caring relationship with these men.

Christ's acceptance and approval of his disciples was always based on the being part of discipleship, not the doing part. The disciples enjoyed some successes in their mission. But they also experienced some failures, particularly during Christ's arrest, trial and crucifixion when "all the disciples deserted him and fled" (Matthew 26:56). Had the disciples based their identity on their performance, they would have reason to consider themselves failures.

But after his resurrection, Jesus didn't reprimand them for what they did or didn't do. Instead he met privately with them several times before his ascension to assure them that they were still his men. Then he gave them the Great Commission (Matthew 28:16–20), and the disciples successfully carried it out because they had a firm grasp on their identity in Christ.

Additional Scripture Readings:
John 20:19–23; Acts 17:24–28

Go to page 53 for your next devotional reading.

it will be measured to you—and even more. ²⁵Whoever has will be given more; whoever does not have, even what he has will be taken from him."

The Parable of the Growing Seed

²⁶He also said, "This is what the kingdom of God is like. A man scatters seed on the ground. ²⁷Night and day, whether he sleeps or gets up, the seed sprouts and grows, though he does not know how. ²⁸All by itself the soil produces grain— first the stalk, then the head, then the full kernel in the head. ²⁹As soon as the grain is ripe, he puts the sickle to it, because the harvest has come."

The Parable of the Mustard Seed

³⁰Again he said, "What shall we say the kingdom of God is like, or what parable shall we use to describe it? ³¹It is like a mustard seed, which is the smallest seed you plant in the ground. ³²Yet when planted, it grows and becomes the largest of all garden plants, with such big branches that the birds of the air can perch in its shade."

³³With many similar parables Jesus spoke the word to them, as much as they could understand. ³⁴He did not say anything to them without using a parable. But when he was alone with his own disciples, he explained everything.

Jesus Calms the Storm

³⁵That day when evening came, he said to his disciples, "Let us go over to the other side." ³⁶Leaving the crowd behind, they took him along, just as he was, in the boat. There were also other boats with him. ³⁷A furious squall came up, and the waves broke over the boat, so that it was nearly swamped. ³⁸Jesus was in the stern, sleeping on a cushion. The disciples woke him and said to him, "Teacher, don't you care if we drown?"

³⁹He got up, rebuked the wind and said to the waves, "Quiet! Be still!" Then the wind died down and it was completely calm.

⁴⁰He said to his disciples, "Why are you so afraid? Do you still have no faith?"

⁴¹They were terrified and asked each other, "Who is this? Even the wind and the waves obey him!"

The Healing of a Demon-possessed Man

5 They went across the lake to the region of the Gerasenes.ᵃ ²When Jesus got out of the boat, a man with an evilᵇ spirit came from the tombs to meet him. ³This man lived in the tombs, and no one could bind him any more, not even with a chain. ⁴For he had often been chained hand and foot, but he tore the chains apart and broke the irons on his feet. No one was strong enough to subdue him. ⁵Night and day among the tombs and in the hills he would cry out and cut himself with stones.

⁶When he saw Jesus from a distance, he ran and fell on his knees in front of him. ⁷He shouted at the top of his voice, "What do you want with me, Jesus, Son of the Most High God? Swear to God that you won't torture me!" ⁸For Jesus had said to him, "Come out of this man, you evil spirit!"

⁹Then Jesus asked him, "What is your name?"

"My name is Legion," he replied, "for we are many." ¹⁰And he begged Jesus again and again not to send them out of the area.

¹¹A large herd of pigs was feeding on the nearby hillside. ¹²The demons begged Jesus, "Send us among the pigs; allow us to go into them." ¹³He gave them permission, and the evil spirits came out and went into the pigs. The herd, about two thousand in number, rushed down the steep bank into the lake and were drowned.

¹⁴Those tending the pigs ran off and reported this in the town and countryside, and the people went out to see what had happened. ¹⁵When they came to Jesus, they saw the man who had been possessed by the legion of demons, sitting there, dressed and in his right mind; and they were afraid. ¹⁶Those who had seen it told the people what had happened to the demon-possessed man—and told about the pigs as well. ¹⁷Then the people began to plead with Jesus to leave their region.

¹⁸As Jesus was getting into the boat, the man who had been demon-possessed begged to go with him. ¹⁹Jesus did not let him, but said, "Go home to your family and tell them how much the Lord has done for you, and how he has had mercy

---

ᵃ1 Some manuscripts *Gadarenes*; other manuscripts *Gergesenes*   ᵇ2 Greek *unclean*; also in verses 8 and 13

on you." ²⁰So the man went away and began to tell in the Decapolis[a] how much Jesus had done for him. And all the people were amazed.

A Dead Girl and a Sick Woman

²¹When Jesus had again crossed over by boat to the other side of the lake, a large crowd gathered around him while he was by the lake. ²²Then one of the synagogue rulers, named Jairus, came there. Seeing Jesus, he fell at his feet ²³and pleaded earnestly with him, "My little daughter is dying. Please come and put your hands on her so that she will be healed and live." ²⁴So Jesus went with him.

A large crowd followed and pressed around him. ²⁵And a woman was there who had been subject to bleeding for twelve years. ²⁶She had suffered a great deal under the care of many doctors and had spent all she had, yet instead of getting better she grew worse. ²⁷When she heard about Jesus, she came up behind him in the crowd and touched his cloak, ²⁸because she thought, "If I just touch his clothes, I will be healed." ²⁹Immediately her bleeding stopped and she felt in her body that she was freed from her suffering.

³⁰At once Jesus realized that power had gone out from him. He turned around in the crowd and asked, "Who touched my clothes?"

³¹"You see the people crowding against you," his disciples answered, "and yet you can ask, 'Who touched me?' "

³²But Jesus kept looking around to see who had done it. ³³Then the woman, knowing what had happened to her, came and fell at his feet and, trembling with fear, told him the whole truth. ³⁴He said to her, "Daughter, your faith has healed you. Go in peace and be freed from your suffering."

³⁵While Jesus was still speaking, some men came from the house of Jairus, the synagogue ruler. "Your daughter is dead," they said. "Why bother the teacher any more?"

³⁶Ignoring what they said, Jesus told the synagogue ruler, "Don't be afraid; just believe."

³⁷He did not let anyone follow him except Peter, James and John the brother of James. ³⁸When they came to the home of the synagogue ruler, Jesus saw a commotion, with people crying and wailing loudly. ³⁹He went in and said to them, "Why all this commotion and wailing? The child is not dead but asleep." ⁴⁰But they laughed at him.

After he put them all out, he took the child's father and mother and the disciples who were with him, and went in where the child was. ⁴¹He took her by the hand and said to her, *"Talitha koum!"* (which means, "Little girl, I say to you, get up!"). ⁴²Immediately the girl stood up and walked around (she was twelve years old). At this they were completely astonished. ⁴³He gave strict orders not to let anyone know about this, and told them to give her something to eat.

A Prophet Without Honor

6 Jesus left there and went to his hometown, accompanied by his disciples. ²When the Sabbath came, he began to teach in the synagogue, and many who heard him were amazed.

"Where did this man get these things?" they asked. "What's this wisdom that has been given him, that he even does miracles! ³Isn't this the carpenter? Isn't this Mary's son and the brother of James, Joseph,[b] Judas and Simon? Aren't his sisters here with us?" And they took offense at him.

⁴Jesus said to them, "Only in his hometown, among his relatives and in his own house is a prophet without honor." ⁵He could not do any miracles there, except lay his hands on a few sick people and heal them. ⁶And he was amazed at their lack of faith.

Jesus Sends Out the Twelve

Then Jesus went around teaching from village to village. ⁷Calling the Twelve to him, he sent them out two by two and gave them authority over evil[c] spirits.

⁸These were his instructions: "Take nothing for the journey except a staff—no bread, no bag, no money in your belts. ⁹Wear sandals but not an extra tunic. ¹⁰Whenever you enter a house, stay there until you leave that town. ¹¹And if any place will not welcome you or listen to you, shake the dust off your feet when you leave, as a testimony against them."

¹²They went out and preached that people should repent. ¹³They drove out many demons and anointed many sick people with oil and healed them.

---

[a]20 That is, the Ten Cities   [b]3 Greek *Joses*, a variant of *Joseph*   [c]7 Greek *unclean*

FRIDAY

VERSE FOR THE DAY:
Mark 5:23

AUTHOR:
John E. Crawford

PASSAGE FOR THE DAY:
Mark 5:21–24,35–43

Fathers . . . and Daughters

EVERY thoughtful father knows that girls, as well as boys, can go terribly far wrong without the right guidance at home. The best counseling services in the finest school facilities have rarely been able to make up for a lack of guidance from a good father and mother who love their children and who tackle the job as a team.

Your daughter wants you to be the chief executive of the household on some matters, with her mother the chief on other matters. She wants you both to be intelligent executives so the household runs as smoothly as it can.

She wants to see in her mother a wise, mature woman who loves you, respects you and can talk to you about all important issues in the family. She needs to find a woman's kind of wisdom and courage in her mother . . .

At the same time, that daughter of yours wants to see in you an intelligent man's viewpoint about life, plus the ability to head up the family in fatherly ways. Then she can really love you as her father as well as a fine man . . .

You are the most important man in her young life. She ought to be able to build her life according to what she sees in yours:

- *your kindness* towards others who have not been able to get along in life due to no real fault of their own;
- *your forgiveness* that flows freely and does not allow you to hold tight to grudges or revenge;
- *your wisdom to withhold judgment* until all the facts have come into view;
- *your quiet courage* that wells up out of deep faith in God;
- *your uncommon sense* that probably is a mixture of these traits.

Nobody can show her these facets of a good father nearly as well as you can, if you put your brainpower to it. Her mother can show her the comparable facets of a fine woman, and she can copy them in her own young life. But your example of what a good man is like will be priceless to her. . . even if you sing off tune beside her in the Sunday morning worship.

Additional Scripture Readings:
1 Corinthians 16:13–14;
Colossians 3:12–14

Go to page 57 for your next devotional reading.

John the Baptist Beheaded

14King Herod heard about this, for Jesus' name had become well known. Some were saying,*a* "John the Baptist has been raised from the dead, and that is why miraculous powers are at work in him."

15Others said, "He is Elijah."

And still others claimed, "He is a prophet, like one of the prophets of long ago."

16But when Herod heard this, he said, "John, the man I beheaded, has been raised from the dead!"

17For Herod himself had given orders to have John arrested, and he had him bound and put in prison. He did this because of Herodias, his brother Philip's wife, whom he had married. **18**For John had been saying to Herod, "It is not lawful for you to have your brother's wife." **19**So Herodias nursed a grudge against John and wanted to kill him. But she was not able to, **20**because Herod feared John and protected him, knowing him to be a righteous and holy man. When Herod heard John, he was greatly puzzled*b*; yet he liked to listen to him.

21Finally the opportune time came. On his birthday Herod gave a banquet for his high officials and military commanders and the leading men of Galilee. **22**When the daughter of Herodias came in and danced, she pleased Herod and his dinner guests.

The king said to the girl, "Ask me for anything you want, and I'll give it to you." **23**And he promised her with an oath, "Whatever you ask I will give you, up to half my kingdom."

24She went out and said to her mother, "What shall I ask for?"

"The head of John the Baptist," she answered.

25At once the girl hurried in to the king with the request: "I want you to give me right now the head of John the Baptist on a platter."

26The king was greatly distressed, but because of his oaths and his dinner guests, he did not want to refuse her. **27**So he immediately sent an executioner with orders to bring John's head. The man went, beheaded John in the prison, **28**and brought back his head on a platter. He presented it to the girl, and she gave it to her mother. **29**On hearing of this, John's disciples came and took his body and laid it in a tomb.

Jesus Feeds the Five Thousand

30The apostles gathered around Jesus and reported to him all they had done and taught. **31**Then, because so many people were coming and going that they did not even have a chance to eat, he said to them, "Come with me by yourselves to a quiet place and get some rest."

32So they went away by themselves in a boat to a solitary place. **33**But many who saw them leaving recognized them and ran on foot from all the towns and got there ahead of them. **34**When Jesus landed and saw a large crowd, he had compassion on them, because they were like sheep without a shepherd. So he began teaching them many things.

35By this time it was late in the day, so his disciples came to him. "This is a remote place," they said, "and it's already very late. **36**Send the people away so they can go to the surrounding countryside and villages and buy themselves something to eat."

37But he answered, "You give them something to eat."

They said to him, "That would take eight months of a man's wages*c*! Are we to go and spend that much on bread and give it to them to eat?"

38"How many loaves do you have?" he asked. "Go and see."

When they found out, they said, "Five—and two fish."

39Then Jesus directed them to have all the people sit down in groups on the green grass. **40**So they sat down in groups of hundreds and fifties. **41**Taking the five loaves and the two fish and looking up to heaven, he gave thanks and broke the loaves. Then he gave them to his disciples to set before the people. He also divided the two fish among them all. **42**They all ate and were satisfied, **43**and the disciples picked up twelve basketfuls of broken pieces of bread and fish. **44**The number of the men who had eaten was five thousand.

Jesus Walks on the Water

45Immediately Jesus made his disciples get into the boat and go on ahead of him to Bethsaida, while he dismissed the

---

a 14 Some early manuscripts *He was saying* *b* 20 Some early manuscripts *he did many things*
c 37 Greek *take two hundred denarii*

crowd. **46**After leaving them, he went up on a mountainside to pray.

47When evening came, the boat was in the middle of the lake, and he was alone on land. **48**He saw the disciples straining at the oars, because the wind was against them. About the fourth watch of the night he went out to them, walking on the lake. He was about to pass by them, **49**but when they saw him walking on the lake, they thought he was a ghost. They cried out, **50**because they all saw him and were terrified.

Immediately he spoke to them and said, "Take courage! It is I. Don't be afraid." **51**Then he climbed into the boat with them, and the wind died down. They were completely amazed, **52**for they had not understood about the loaves; their hearts were hardened.

53When they had crossed over, they landed at Gennesaret and anchored there. **54**As soon as they got out of the boat, people recognized Jesus. **55**They ran throughout that whole region and carried the sick on mats to wherever they heard he was. **56**And wherever he went — into villages, towns or countryside — they placed the sick in the marketplaces. They begged him to let them touch even the edge of his cloak, and all who touched him were healed.

Clean and Unclean

7 The Pharisees and some of the teachers of the law who had come from Jerusalem gathered around Jesus and **2**saw some of his disciples eating food with hands that were "unclean," that is, unwashed. **3**(The Pharisees and all the Jews do not eat unless they give their hands a ceremonial washing, holding to the tradition of the elders. **4**When they come from the marketplace they do not eat unless they wash. And they observe many other traditions, such as the washing of cups, pitchers and kettles.*a*)

5So the Pharisees and teachers of the law asked Jesus, "Why don't your disciples live according to the tradition of the elders instead of eating their food with 'unclean' hands?"

6He replied, "Isaiah was right when he prophesied about you hypocrites; as it is written:

" 'These people honor me with their lips,
but their hearts are far from me.
7They worship me in vain;
their teachings are but rules taught by men.'*b*

8You have let go of the commands of God and are holding on to the traditions of men."

9And he said to them: "You have a fine way of setting aside the commands of God in order to observe*c* your own traditions! **10**For Moses said, 'Honor your father and your mother,'*d* and, 'Anyone who curses his father or mother must be put to death.'*e* **11**But you say that if a man says to his father or mother: 'Whatever help you might otherwise have received from me is Corban' (that is, a gift devoted to God), **12**then you no longer let him do anything for his father or mother. **13**Thus you nullify the word of God by your tradition that you have handed down. And you do many things like that."

14Again Jesus called the crowd to him and said, "Listen to me, everyone, and understand this. **15**Nothing outside a man can make him 'unclean' by going into him. Rather, it is what comes out of a man that makes him 'unclean.'*f*

17After he had left the crowd and entered the house, his disciples asked him about this parable. **18**"Are you so dull?" he asked. "Don't you see that nothing that enters a man from the outside can make him 'unclean'? **19**For it doesn't go into his heart but into his stomach, and then out of his body." (In saying this, Jesus declared all foods "clean.")

20He went on: "What comes out of a man is what makes him 'unclean.' **21**For from within, out of men's hearts, come evil thoughts, sexual immorality, theft, murder, adultery, **22**greed, malice, deceit, lewdness, envy, slander, arrogance and folly. **23**All these evils come from inside and make a man 'unclean.' "

The Faith of a Syrophoenician Woman

24Jesus left that place and went to the vicinity of Tyre.*g* He entered a house and did not want anyone to know it; yet he could not keep his presence secret. **25**In

---

a 4 Some early manuscripts *pitchers, kettles and dining couches*   *b 6,7* Isaiah 29:13   *c 9* Some manuscripts *set up*   *d 10* Exodus 20:12; Deut. 5:16   *e 10* Exodus 21:17; Lev. 20:9   *f 15* Some early manuscripts *'unclean.' 16If anyone has ears to hear, let him hear.*   *g 24* Many early manuscripts *Tyre and Sidon*

fact, as soon as she heard about him, a woman whose little daughter was possessed by an evil[a] spirit came and fell at his feet. 26The woman was a Greek, born in Syrian Phoenicia. She begged Jesus to drive the demon out of her daughter.

27"First let the children eat all they want," he told her, "for it is not right to take the children's bread and toss it to their dogs."

28"Yes, Lord," she replied, "but even the dogs under the table eat the children's crumbs."

29Then he told her, "For such a reply, you may go; the demon has left your daughter."

30She went home and found her child lying on the bed, and the demon gone.

The Healing of a Deaf and Mute Man

31Then Jesus left the vicinity of Tyre and went through Sidon, down to the Sea of Galilee and into the region of the Decapolis.[b] 32There some people brought to him a man who was deaf and could hardly talk, and they begged him to place his hand on the man.

33After he took him aside, away from the crowd, Jesus put his fingers into the man's ears. Then he spit and touched the man's tongue. 34He looked up to heaven and with a deep sigh said to him, *"Ephphatha!"* (which means, "Be opened!"). 35At this, the man's ears were opened, his tongue was loosened and he began to speak plainly.

36Jesus commanded them not to tell anyone. But the more he did so, the more they kept talking about it. 37People were overwhelmed with amazement. "He has done everything well," they said. "He even makes the deaf hear and the mute speak."

Jesus Feeds the Four Thousand

8 During those days another large crowd gathered. Since they had nothing to eat, Jesus called his disciples to him and said, 2"I have compassion for these people; they have already been with me three days and have nothing to eat. 3If I send them home hungry, they will collapse on the way, because some of them have come a long distance."

4His disciples answered, "But where in this remote place can anyone get enough bread to feed them?"

5"How many loaves do you have?" Jesus asked.

"Seven," they replied.

6He told the crowd to sit down on the ground. When he had taken the seven loaves and given thanks, he broke them and gave them to his disciples to set before the people, and they did so. 7They had a few small fish as well; he gave thanks for them also and told the disciples to distribute them. 8The people ate and were satisfied. Afterward the disciples picked up seven basketfuls of broken pieces that were left over. 9About four thousand men were present. And having sent them away, 10he got into the boat with his disciples and went to the region of Dalmanutha.

11The Pharisees came and began to question Jesus. To test him, they asked him for a sign from heaven. 12He sighed deeply and said, "Why does this generation ask for a miraculous sign? I tell you the truth, no sign will be given to it." 13Then he left them, got back into the boat and crossed to the other side.

The Yeast of the Pharisees and Herod

14The disciples had forgotten to bring bread, except for one loaf they had with them in the boat. 15"Be careful," Jesus warned them. "Watch out for the yeast of the Pharisees and that of Herod."

16They discussed this with one another and said, "It is because we have no bread."

17Aware of their discussion, Jesus asked them: "Why are you talking about having no bread? Do you still not see or understand? Are your hearts hardened? 18Do you have eyes but fail to see, and ears but fail to hear? And don't you remember? 19When I broke the five loaves for the five thousand, how many basketfuls of pieces did you pick up?"

"Twelve," they replied.

20"And when I broke the seven loaves for the four thousand, how many basketfuls of pieces did you pick up?"

They answered, "Seven."

21He said to them, "Do you still not understand?"

The Healing of a Blind Man at Bethsaida

22They came to Bethsaida, and some people brought a blind man and begged Jesus to touch him. 23He took the blind man by the hand and led him outside the

---

[a]25 Greek *unclean*   [b]31 That is, the Ten Cities

WEEKENDING

RECOGNIZE

What was it that drew men to Jesus? Yes, he spoke with authority and he did miraculous and wonderful deeds, but I think the one thing that men could not ignore was the compassion and love that came from his heart and on to his face and into his words and deeds.

If we abide in him as he abides in us, we begin to see things differently. We begin to look at things with his eyes.

– *Bob Benson*

REVIVE
Saturday: Mark 1:40–45
Sunday: Colossians 3:12–17

Go to page 59 for your next devotional reading.

village. When he had spit on the man's eyes and put his hands on him, Jesus asked, "Do you see anything?"

²⁴He looked up and said, "I see people; they look like trees walking around."

²⁵Once more Jesus put his hands on the man's eyes. Then his eyes were opened, his sight was restored, and he saw everything clearly. ²⁶Jesus sent him home, saying, "Don't go into the village.*ᵃ*"

Peter's Confession of Christ

²⁷Jesus and his disciples went on to the villages around Caesarea Philippi. On the way he asked them, "Who do people say I am?"

²⁸They replied, "Some say John the Baptist; others say Elijah; and still others, one of the prophets."

²⁹"But what about you?" he asked. "Who do you say I am?"

Peter answered, "You are the Christ.*ᵇ*"

³⁰Jesus warned them not to tell anyone about him.

Jesus Predicts His Death

³¹He then began to teach them that the Son of Man must suffer many things and be rejected by the elders, chief priests and teachers of the law, and that he must be killed and after three days rise again. ³²He spoke plainly about this, and Peter took him aside and began to rebuke him.

³³But when Jesus turned and looked at his disciples, he rebuked Peter. "Get behind me, Satan!" he said. "You do not have in mind the things of God, but the things of men."

³⁴Then he called the crowd to him along with his disciples and said: "If anyone would come after me, he must deny himself and take up his cross and follow me. ³⁵For whoever wants to save his life*ᶜ* will lose it, but whoever loses his life for me and for the gospel will save it. ³⁶What good is it for a man to gain the whole world, yet forfeit his soul? ³⁷Or what can a man give in exchange for his soul? ³⁸If anyone is ashamed of me and my words in this adulterous and sinful generation, the Son of Man will be ashamed of him when he comes in his Father's glory with the holy angels."

9 And he said to them, "I tell you the truth, some who are standing here will not taste death before they see the kingdom of God come with power."

The Transfiguration

²After six days Jesus took Peter, James and John with him and led them up a high mountain, where they were all alone. There he was transfigured before them. ³His clothes became dazzling white, whiter than anyone in the world could bleach them. ⁴And there appeared before them Elijah and Moses, who were talking with Jesus.

⁵Peter said to Jesus, "Rabbi, it is good for us to be here. Let us put up three shelters—one for you, one for Moses and one for Elijah." ⁶(He did not know what to say, they were so frightened.)

⁷Then a cloud appeared and enveloped them, and a voice came from the cloud: "This is my Son, whom I love. Listen to him!"

⁸Suddenly, when they looked around, they no longer saw anyone with them except Jesus.

⁹As they were coming down the mountain, Jesus gave them orders not to tell anyone what they had seen until the Son of Man had risen from the dead. ¹⁰They kept the matter to themselves, discussing what "rising from the dead" meant.

¹¹And they asked him, "Why do the teachers of the law say that Elijah must come first?"

¹²Jesus replied, "To be sure, Elijah does come first, and restores all things. Why then is it written that the Son of Man must suffer much and be rejected? ¹³But I tell you, Elijah has come, and they have done to him everything they wished, just as it is written about him."

The Healing of a Boy With an Evil Spirit

¹⁴When they came to the other disciples, they saw a large crowd around them and the teachers of the law arguing with them. ¹⁵As soon as all the people saw Jesus, they were overwhelmed with wonder and ran to greet him.

¹⁶"What are you arguing with them about?" he asked.

¹⁷A man in the crowd answered, "Teacher, I brought you my son, who is possessed by a spirit that has robbed him of speech. ¹⁸Whenever it seizes him, it

---

ᵃ26 Some manuscripts *Don't go and tell anyone in the village* and "the Messiah" (Hebrew) both mean "the Anointed One."   *ᵇ29* Or *Messiah.* "The Christ" (Greek)   *ᶜ35* The Greek word means either *life* or *soul;* also in verse 36.

throws him to the ground. He foams at the mouth, gnashes his teeth and becomes rigid. I asked your disciples to drive out the spirit, but they could not."

19"O unbelieving generation," Jesus replied, "how long shall I stay with you? How long shall I put up with you? Bring the boy to me."

20So they brought him. When the spirit saw Jesus, it immediately threw the boy into a convulsion. He fell to the ground and rolled around, foaming at the mouth.

21Jesus asked the boy's father, "How long has he been like this?"

"From childhood," he answered. **22**"It has often thrown him into fire or water to kill him. But if you can do anything, take pity on us and help us."

23" 'If you can'?" said Jesus. "Everything is possible for him who believes."

24Immediately the boy's father exclaimed, "I do believe; help me overcome my unbelief!"

25When Jesus saw that a crowd was running to the scene, he rebuked the evil[a] spirit. "You deaf and mute spirit," he said, "I command you, come out of him and never enter him again."

26The spirit shrieked, convulsed him violently and came out. The boy looked so much like a corpse that many said, "He's dead." **27**But Jesus took him by the hand

[a]25 Greek *unclean*

MONDAY

VERSE FOR THE DAY:
Mark 9:2

AUTHOR:
Jim Conway

PASSAGE FOR THE DAY:
Mark 9:2–13

Equal Sharing

YOU don't need to be a friend to everyone. Remember the model of Jesus. He preached to, ministered to, and healed thousands of people, but he only had twelve disciples. Of those twelve, only three were invited with him when he was transfigured on the mountain.

Don't torture yourself by thinking you have to relate equally to everyone. In fact, don't waste your precious friendship time on relationships that won't be productive.

It's one thing to reach out to a needy person, but it's another to have a friendship. In the first situation you're doing social work or a spiritual ministry of caring. When you are truly a friend, you and your friend will be giving equally to each other. Both of you will be nourished by the relationship.

In your life you should always have some people whom you nourish and who return little or nothing to you. You should also have people who nourish you, but you may return nothing to them. A third kind of relationship is equal sharing. This is friendship.

All three categories are important, but don't refer to the first two as friendships. The first one is your ministry to someone else, the second type is someone's ministry to you. Only the third—equal sharing—is true friendship.

Additional Scripture Readings:
Proverbs 18:24; John 15:9-17

Go to page 61 for your next devotional reading.

and lifted him to his feet, and he stood up.

²⁸After Jesus had gone indoors, his disciples asked him privately, "Why couldn't we drive it out?"

²⁹He replied, "This kind can come out only by prayer.ᵃ"

³⁰They left that place and passed through Galilee. Jesus did not want anyone to know where they were, ³¹because he was teaching his disciples. He said to them, "The Son of Man is going to be betrayed into the hands of men. They will kill him, and after three days he will rise." ³²But they did not understand what he meant and were afraid to ask him about it.

Who Is the Greatest?

³³They came to Capernaum. When he was in the house, he asked them, "What were you arguing about on the road?" ³⁴But they kept quiet because on the way they had argued about who was the greatest.

³⁵Sitting down, Jesus called the Twelve and said, "If anyone wants to be first, he must be the very last, and the servant of all."

³⁶He took a little child and had him stand among them. Taking him in his arms, he said to them, ³⁷"Whoever welcomes one of these little children in my name welcomes me; and whoever welcomes me does not welcome me but the one who sent me."

Whoever Is Not Against Us Is for Us

³⁸"Teacher," said John, "we saw a man driving out demons in your name and we told him to stop, because he was not one of us."

³⁹"Do not stop him," Jesus said. "No one who does a miracle in my name can in the next moment say anything bad about me, ⁴⁰for whoever is not against us is for us. ⁴¹I tell you the truth, anyone who gives you a cup of water in my name because you belong to Christ will certainly not lose his reward.

Causing to Sin

⁴²"And if anyone causes one of these little ones who believe in me to sin, it would be better for him to be thrown into the sea with a large millstone tied around his neck. ⁴³If your hand causes you to sin, cut it off. It is better for you to enter life maimed than with two hands to go into hell, where the fire never goes out.ᵇ ⁴⁵And if your foot causes you to sin, cut it off. It is better for you to enter life crippled than to have two feet and be thrown into hell.ᶜ ⁴⁷And if your eye causes you to sin, pluck it out. It is better for you to enter the kingdom of God with one eye than to have two eyes and be thrown into hell, ⁴⁸where

" 'their worm does not die,
    and the fire is not quenched.'ᵈ

⁴⁹Everyone will be salted with fire.

⁵⁰"Salt is good, but if it loses its saltiness, how can you make it salty again? Have salt in yourselves, and be at peace with each other."

Divorce

10 Jesus then left that place and went into the region of Judea and across the Jordan. Again crowds of people came to him, and as was his custom, he taught them.

²Some Pharisees came and tested him by asking, "Is it lawful for a man to divorce his wife?"

³"What did Moses command you?" he replied.

⁴They said, "Moses permitted a man to write a certificate of divorce and send her away."

⁵"It was because your hearts were hard that Moses wrote you this law," Jesus replied. ⁶"But at the beginning of creation God 'made them male and female.'ᵉ ⁷'For this reason a man will leave his father and mother and be united to his wife,ᶠ ⁸and the two will become one flesh.'ᵍ So they are no longer two, but one. ⁹Therefore what God has joined together, let man not separate."

¹⁰When they were in the house again, the disciples asked Jesus about this. ¹¹He answered, "Anyone who divorces his wife and marries another woman commits adultery against her. ¹²And if she divorces her husband and marries another man, she commits adultery."

The Little Children and Jesus

¹³People were bringing little children to Jesus to have him touch them, but the dis-

---

ᵃ29 Some manuscripts *prayer and fasting*   ᵇ43 Some manuscripts *out,* ⁴⁴*where* / " '*their worm does not die,* / *and the fire is not quenched.*'   ᶜ45 Some manuscripts *hell,* ⁴⁶*where* / " '*their worm does not die,* / *and the fire is not quenched.*'   ᵈ48 Isaiah 66:24   ᵉ6 Gen. 1:27   ᶠ7 Some early manuscripts do not have *and be united to his wife.*   ᵍ8 Gen. 2:24

ciples rebuked them. **14**When Jesus saw this, he was indignant. He said to them, "Let the little children come to me, and do not hinder them, for the kingdom of God belongs to such as these. **15**I tell you the truth, anyone who will not receive the kingdom of God like a little child will never enter it." **16**And he took the children in his arms, put his hands on them and blessed them.

The Rich Young Man

17As Jesus started on his way, a man ran up to him and fell on his knees before him. "Good teacher," he asked, "what must I do to inherit eternal life?"

18"Why do you call me good?" Jesus answered. "No one is good—except God alone. **19**You know the commandments: 'Do not murder, do not commit adultery, do not steal, do not give false testimony, do not defraud, honor your father and mother.'*a*"

20"Teacher," he declared, "all these I have kept since I was a boy."

21Jesus looked at him and loved him. "One thing you lack," he said. "Go, sell everything you have and give to the poor, and you will have treasure in heaven. Then come, follow me."

a 19 Exodus 20:12-16; Deut. 5:16-20

TUESDAY

VERSE FOR THE DAY:
Mark 10:9

AUTHOR:
Donald M. Joy

PASSAGE FOR THE DAY:
Mark 10:1–12

Jesus' View of Sex

IF YOU want to see the highest respect for human sexuality and marriage, read it in the words and actions of Jesus. He says, "What God joins together sexually, be careful not to rip apart." Jesus announces the warning in the face of easy divorce in his teaching recorded in Matthew 19 [and in Mark 10]. He restates the Genesis 2 picture of one man and one woman forming one flesh unity, and suggests that the only alternative to the kind of beautiful sexual intimacy is holy celibacy: being single for the glory of God and the service of God's purposes in the world. It is clear that to be single and sexually unattached is an expression of high human responsibility and high respect for humans everywhere.

Jesus teaches responsible "looking" in the famous "lust" teaching in Matthew 5. We are to sanctify our sexual imagination and to be careful not to fantasize sexual intimacy with inappropriate people. This high target, which keeps all of us focused on our own lifelong intimacy covenant, means looking ahead toward marriage when we are young and looking back to reconstruct a lifelong fidelity for the rest of our lives. This sex-positive focusing of sexual imagination and energy is an invitation to clear and exclusive thinking as the highest respect we can show for everyone. No one has a higher, more positive view of sex than Jesus.

Additional Scripture Readings:
Matthew 5:27–30; Matthew 19:1–12

Go to page 63 for your next devotional reading.

²²At this the man's face fell. He went away sad, because he had great wealth.

²³Jesus looked around and said to his disciples, "How hard it is for the rich to enter the kingdom of God!"

²⁴The disciples were amazed at his words. But Jesus said again, "Children, how hard it is[a] to enter the kingdom of God! ²⁵It is easier for a camel to go through the eye of a needle than for a rich man to enter the kingdom of God."

²⁶The disciples were even more amazed, and said to each other, "Who then can be saved?"

²⁷Jesus looked at them and said, "With man this is impossible, but not with God; all things are possible with God."

²⁸Peter said to him, "We have left everything to follow you!"

²⁹"I tell you the truth," Jesus replied, "no one who has left home or brothers or sisters or mother or father or children or fields for me and the gospel ³⁰will fail to receive a hundred times as much in this present age (homes, brothers, sisters, mothers, children and fields — and with them, persecutions) and in the age to come, eternal life. ³¹But many who are first will be last, and the last first."

Jesus Again Predicts His Death

³²They were on their way up to Jerusalem, with Jesus leading the way, and the disciples were astonished, while those who followed were afraid. Again he took the Twelve aside and told them what was going to happen to him. ³³"We are going up to Jerusalem," he said, "and the Son of Man will be betrayed to the chief priests and teachers of the law. They will condemn him to death and will hand him over to the Gentiles, ³⁴who will mock him and spit on him, flog him and kill him. Three days later he will rise."

The Request of James and John

³⁵Then James and John, the sons of Zebedee, came to him. "Teacher," they said, "we want you to do for us whatever we ask."

³⁶"What do you want me to do for you?" he asked.

³⁷They replied, "Let one of us sit at your right and the other at your left in your glory."

³⁸"You don't know what you are asking," Jesus said. "Can you drink the cup I drink or be baptized with the baptism I am baptized with?"

³⁹"We can," they answered.

Jesus said to them, "You will drink the cup I drink and be baptized with the baptism I am baptized with, ⁴⁰but to sit at my right or left is not for me to grant. These places belong to those for whom they have been prepared."

⁴¹When the ten heard about this, they became indignant with James and John. ⁴²Jesus called them together and said, "You know that those who are regarded as rulers of the Gentiles lord it over them, and their high officials exercise authority over them. ⁴³Not so with you. Instead, whoever wants to become great among you must be your servant, ⁴⁴and whoever wants to be first must be slave of all. ⁴⁵For even the Son of Man did not come to be served, but to serve, and to give his life as a ransom for many."

Blind Bartimaeus Receives His Sight

⁴⁶Then they came to Jericho. As Jesus and his disciples, together with a large crowd, were leaving the city, a blind man, Bartimaeus (that is, the Son of Timaeus), was sitting by the roadside begging. ⁴⁷When he heard that it was Jesus of Nazareth, he began to shout, "Jesus, Son of David, have mercy on me!"

⁴⁸Many rebuked him and told him to be quiet, but he shouted all the more, "Son of David, have mercy on me!"

⁴⁹Jesus stopped and said, "Call him."

So they called to the blind man, "Cheer up! On your feet! He's calling you." ⁵⁰Throwing his cloak aside, he jumped to his feet and came to Jesus.

⁵¹"What do you want me to do for you?" Jesus asked him.

The blind man said, "Rabbi, I want to see."

⁵²"Go," said Jesus, "your faith has healed you." Immediately he received his sight and followed Jesus along the road.

The Triumphal Entry

11 As they approached Jerusalem and came to Bethphage and Bethany at the Mount of Olives, Jesus sent two of his disciples, ²saying to them, "Go to the village ahead of you, and just as you enter it, you will find a colt tied there, which no one has ever ridden. Untie it and bring it here. ³If anyone asks you, 'Why are you

---

[a]24 Some manuscripts *is for those who trust in riches*

doing this?' tell him, 'The Lord needs it and will send it back here shortly.'"

⁴They went and found a colt outside in the street, tied at a doorway. As they untied it, ⁵some people standing there asked, "What are you doing, untying that colt?" ⁶They answered as Jesus had told them to, and the people let them go. ⁷When they brought the colt to Jesus and threw their cloaks over it, he sat on it. ⁸Many people spread their cloaks on the road, while others spread branches they had cut in the fields. ⁹Those who went ahead and those who followed shouted,

"Hosanna!ᵃ"

"Blessed is he who comes in the name of the Lord!"ᵇ

¹⁰"Blessed is the coming kingdom of our father David!"

"Hosanna in the highest!"

ᵃ9 A Hebrew expression meaning "Save!" which became an exclamation of praise; also in verse 10
ᵇ9 Psalm 118:25,26

WEDNESDAY

VERSE FOR THE DAY:
Mark 10:43

AUTHOR:
Ron Blue

PASSAGE FOR THE DAY:
Mark 10:35–45

A Different Attitude

BOTH the Christian and the non-Christian are concerned with success, but in each case success is always relative to goals. The difference is in perspective. One view sees only the here and now, the other sees the unseen. What one's perspective is (or to put it another way, what one believes) will determine attitudes and actions. That is why the Christian, in managing his or her money, is different.

Individually, God has called us to be: salt and light (see Matthew 5:13–16), servants (see Mark 10:45) and stewards (see Matthew 25:14–30).

The idea of being salt and light says that God wants me to be *not* better than, *but* different from. The Christian, therefore, may or may not have more than his neighbor, but that does not distinguish him. What does distinguish the Christian from the world is the absence of any anxiety, which might have come as a result of the loss of something he has managed or even God's denial of something he wants. Why? Because the Christian's treasure is not on earth. The world and its temporal toys do not possess him. He is prayerful, but not the least bit anxious about the tremendous uncertainty facing our national and world economy.

Obviously that attitude is not "normal" but rather "different," and it comes from having an entirely different perspective. The Christian's perspective is eternal, the attitude is one of holding possessions lightly, and the lifestyle is free from worry and anxiety. Truly that is different!

Additional Scripture Readings:
Matthew 6:19–27; 1 Timothy 6:3–10

Go to page 66 for your next devotional reading.

¹¹Jesus entered Jerusalem and went to the temple. He looked around at everything, but since it was already late, he went out to Bethany with the Twelve.

Jesus Clears the Temple

¹²The next day as they were leaving Bethany, Jesus was hungry. ¹³Seeing in the distance a fig tree in leaf, he went to find out if it had any fruit. When he reached it, he found nothing but leaves, because it was not the season for figs. ¹⁴Then he said to the tree, "May no one ever eat fruit from you again." And his disciples heard him say it.

¹⁵On reaching Jerusalem, Jesus entered the temple area and began driving out those who were buying and selling there. He overturned the tables of the money changers and the benches of those selling doves, ¹⁶and would not allow anyone to carry merchandise through the temple courts. ¹⁷And as he taught them, he said, "Is it not written:

" 'My house will be called
a house of prayer for all nations'*a*?

But you have made it 'a den of robbers.'*b*"

¹⁸The chief priests and the teachers of the law heard this and began looking for a way to kill him, for they feared him, because the whole crowd was amazed at his teaching.

¹⁹When evening came, they*c* went out of the city.

The Withered Fig Tree

²⁰In the morning, as they went along, they saw the fig tree withered from the roots. ²¹Peter remembered and said to Jesus, "Rabbi, look! The fig tree you cursed has withered!"

²²"Have*d* faith in God," Jesus answered. ²³"I tell you the truth, if anyone says to this mountain, 'Go, throw yourself into the sea,' and does not doubt in his heart but believes that what he says will happen, it will be done for him. ²⁴Therefore I tell you, whatever you ask for in prayer, believe that you have received it, and it will be yours. ²⁵And when you stand praying, if you hold anything against anyone, forgive him, so that your Father in heaven may forgive you your sins.*e*"

The Authority of Jesus Questioned

²⁷They arrived again in Jerusalem, and while Jesus was walking in the temple courts, the chief priests, the teachers of the law and the elders came to him. ²⁸"By what authority are you doing these things?" they asked. "And who gave you authority to do this?"

²⁹Jesus replied, "I will ask you one question. Answer me, and I will tell you by what authority I am doing these things. ³⁰John's baptism—was it from heaven, or from men? Tell me!"

³¹They discussed it among themselves and said, "If we say, 'From heaven,' he will ask, 'Then why didn't you believe him?' ³²But if we say, 'From men' . . . ." (They feared the people, for everyone held that John really was a prophet.)

³³So they answered Jesus, "We don't know."

Jesus said, "Neither will I tell you by what authority I am doing these things."

The Parable of the Tenants

12 He then began to speak to them in parables: "A man planted a vineyard. He put a wall around it, dug a pit for the winepress and built a watchtower. Then he rented the vineyard to some farmers and went away on a journey. ²At harvest time he sent a servant to the tenants to collect from them some of the fruit of the vineyard. ³But they seized him, beat him and sent him away empty-handed. ⁴Then he sent another servant to them; they struck this man on the head and treated him shamefully. ⁵He sent still another, and that one they killed. He sent many others; some of them they beat, others they killed.

⁶"He had one left to send, a son, whom he loved. He sent him last of all, saying, 'They will respect my son.'

⁷"But the tenants said to one another, 'This is the heir. Come, let's kill him, and the inheritance will be ours.' ⁸So they took him and killed him, and threw him out of the vineyard.

⁹"What then will the owner of the vineyard do? He will come and kill those tenants and give the vineyard to others. ¹⁰Haven't you read this scripture:

" 'The stone the builders rejected
has become the capstone*f*;

---

a 17 Isaiah 56:7   *b* 17 Jer. 7:11   *c* 19 Some early manuscripts *he*   *d* 22 Some early manuscripts *If you have*   *e* 25 Some manuscripts *sins.* ²⁶*But if you do not forgive, neither will your Father who is in heaven forgive your sins.*   *f* 10 Or *cornerstone*

¹¹the Lord has done this,
and it is marvelous in our eyes'ᵃ?"

¹²Then they looked for a way to arrest him because they knew he had spoken the parable against them. But they were afraid of the crowd; so they left him and went away.

Paying Taxes to Caesar

¹³Later they sent some of the Pharisees and Herodians to Jesus to catch him in his words. ¹⁴They came to him and said, "Teacher, we know you are a man of integrity. You aren't swayed by men, because you pay no attention to who they are; but you teach the way of God in accordance with the truth. Is it right to pay taxes to Caesar or not? ¹⁵Should we pay or shouldn't we?"

But Jesus knew their hypocrisy. "Why are you trying to trap me?" he asked. "Bring me a denarius and let me look at it." ¹⁶They brought the coin, and he asked them, "Whose portrait is this? And whose inscription?"

"Caesar's," they replied.

¹⁷Then Jesus said to them, "Give to Caesar what is Caesar's and to God what is God's."

And they were amazed at him.

Marriage at the Resurrection

¹⁸Then the Sadducees, who say there is no resurrection, came to him with a question. ¹⁹"Teacher," they said, "Moses wrote for us that if a man's brother dies and leaves a wife but no children, the man must marry the widow and have children for his brother. ²⁰Now there were seven brothers. The first one married and died without leaving any children. ²¹The second one married the widow, but he also died, leaving no child. It was the same with the third. ²²In fact, none of the seven left any children. Last of all, the woman died too. ²³At the resurrectionᵇ whose wife will she be, since the seven were married to her?"

²⁴Jesus replied, "Are you not in error because you do not know the Scriptures or the power of God? ²⁵When the dead rise, they will neither marry nor be given in marriage; they will be like the angels in heaven. ²⁶Now about the dead rising—have you not read in the book of Moses, in the account of the bush, how God said to him, 'I am the God of Abraham, the God of Isaac, and the God of Jacob'ᶜ? ²⁷He is not the God of the dead, but of the living. You are badly mistaken!"

The Greatest Commandment

²⁸One of the teachers of the law came and heard them debating. Noticing that Jesus had given them a good answer, he asked, "Of all the commandments, which is the most important?"

²⁹"The most important one," answered Jesus, "is this: 'Hear, O Israel, the Lord our God, the Lord is one.ᵈ ³⁰Love the Lord your God with all your heart and with all your soul and with all your mind and with all your strength.'ᵉ ³¹The second is this: 'Love your neighbor as yourself.'ᶠ There is no commandment greater than these."

³²"Well said, teacher," the man replied. "You are right in saying that God is one and there is no other but him. ³³To love him with all your heart, with all your understanding and with all your strength, and to love your neighbor as yourself is more important than all burnt offerings and sacrifices."

³⁴When Jesus saw that he had answered wisely, he said to him, "You are not far from the kingdom of God." And from then on no one dared ask him any more questions.

Whose Son Is the Christ?

³⁵While Jesus was teaching in the temple courts, he asked, "How is it that the teachers of the law say that the Christᵍ is the son of David? ³⁶David himself, speaking by the Holy Spirit, declared:

" 'The Lord said to my Lord:
    "Sit at my right hand
until I put your enemies
    under your feet." 'ʰ

³⁷David himself calls him 'Lord.' How then can he be his son?"

The large crowd listened to him with delight.

³⁸As he taught, Jesus said, "Watch out for the teachers of the law. They like to walk around in flowing robes and be greeted in the marketplaces, ³⁹and have the most important seats in the synagogues and the places of honor at banquets. ⁴⁰They devour widows' houses and

---

ᵃ11 Psalm 118:22,23   ᵇ23 Some manuscripts *resurrection, when men rise from the dead,*
ᶜ26 Exodus 3:6   ᵈ29 Or *the Lord our God is one Lord*   ᵉ30 Deut. 6:4,5   ᶠ31 Lev. 19:18
ᵍ35 Or *Messiah*   ʰ36 Psalm 110:1

for a show make lengthy prayers. Such men will be punished most severely."

The Widow's Offering

⁴¹Jesus sat down opposite the place where the offerings were put and watched the crowd putting their money into the temple treasury. Many rich people threw in large amounts. ⁴²But a poor widow came and put in two very small copper

---

THURSDAY

VERSE FOR THE DAY:
Mark 12:33

AUTHOR:
Thomas Hale

PASSAGE FOR THE DAY:
Mark 12:28–34

No Greater Commandment

GOD'S immediate purpose is to communicate his love to people everywhere, and we believe that is why he sent us to Nepal. But though communicating love through medicine may discharge our responsibility as medical workers, it does little for the sick person coming for treatment if all he has to look forward to after recovery is a life of continuing unhappiness and hopelessness. The only way we know to help our Nepali friends in a lasting way is to put them in touch with the God who is the source of love and who sent his Son Jesus into the world to demonstrate it.

We know from personal experience that God's love changes lives; the faith we share with our Nepali friends is not a hand-me-down or merely theoretical faith. His love changed our lives and sent us to Nepal; his love has kept us here. Many are attracted to Nepal by the spectacular mountains, the anticipation of adventure, the dramatic needs—and undoubtedly we were too—but such attractions will never keep people here. Only the love of Christ can do that. There are too many frustrations, too many insurmountable hurdles, for one to be able to carry on for long on one's own. Humanitarian motives are not enough. The humanitarian needs to be able to measure his accomplishments and see the fruit of his labor. But when there is little to show for his efforts, as is so often the case with work in developing countries, the humanitarian becomes discouraged and his idealism starts to fade. With us, however, the primary motive is to serve Christ. Thus, if our service to men is frustrated, rebuffed or wiped away, we need not be disheartened. We are merely instruments to render *his* service. We share *his* love, not our own, and his love never runs dry.

What does Christ's love mean to us? To a Nepali? It means life, abundant life, that begins now and will never end. Jesus came that we "may have life, and have it to the full" [John 10:10]. And after 2,000 years, his offer still stands.

Additional Scripture Readings:
John 10:7–10; 1 John 4:7–12

Go to page 75 for your next devotional reading.

coins,[a] worth only a fraction of a penny.[b] ⁴³Calling his disciples to him, Jesus said, "I tell you the truth, this poor widow has put more into the treasury than all the others. ⁴⁴They all gave out of their wealth; but she, out of her poverty, put in everything—all she had to live on."

Signs of the End of the Age

13 As he was leaving the temple, one of his disciples said to him, "Look, Teacher! What massive stones! What magnificent buildings!"

²"Do you see all these great buildings?" replied Jesus. "Not one stone here will be left on another; every one will be thrown down."

³As Jesus was sitting on the Mount of Olives opposite the temple, Peter, James, John and Andrew asked him privately, ⁴"Tell us, when will these things happen? And what will be the sign that they are all about to be fulfilled?"

⁵Jesus said to them: "Watch out that no one deceives you. ⁶Many will come in my name, claiming, 'I am he,' and will deceive many. ⁷When you hear of wars and rumors of wars, do not be alarmed. Such things must happen, but the end is still to come. ⁸Nation will rise against nation, and kingdom against kingdom. There will be earthquakes in various places, and famines. These are the beginning of birth pains.

⁹"You must be on your guard. You will be handed over to the local councils and flogged in the synagogues. On account of me you will stand before governors and kings as witnesses to them. ¹⁰And the gospel must first be preached to all nations. ¹¹Whenever you are arrested and brought to trial, do not worry beforehand about what to say. Just say whatever is given you at the time, for it is not you speaking, but the Holy Spirit.

¹²"Brother will betray brother to death, and a father his child. Children will rebel against their parents and have them put to death. ¹³All men will hate you because of me, but he who stands firm to the end will be saved.

¹⁴"When you see 'the abomination that causes desolation'[c] standing where it[d] does not belong—let the reader understand—then let those who are in Judea flee to the mountains. ¹⁵Let no one on the roof of his house go down or enter the house to take anything out. ¹⁶Let no one in the field go back to get his cloak. ¹⁷How dreadful it will be in those days for pregnant women and nursing mothers! ¹⁸Pray that this will not take place in winter, ¹⁹because those will be days of distress unequaled from the beginning, when God created the world, until now—and never to be equaled again. ²⁰If the Lord had not cut short those days, no one would survive. But for the sake of the elect, whom he has chosen, he has shortened them. ²¹At that time if anyone says to you, 'Look, here is the Christ[e]!' or, 'Look, there he is!' do not believe it. ²²For false Christs and false prophets will appear and perform signs and miracles to deceive the elect—if that were possible. ²³So be on your guard; I have told you everything ahead of time.

²⁴"But in those days, following that distress,

" 'the sun will be darkened,
  and the moon will not give its light;
²⁵the stars will fall from the sky,
  and the heavenly bodies will be shaken.'[f]

²⁶"At that time men will see the Son of Man coming in clouds with great power and glory. ²⁷And he will send his angels and gather his elect from the four winds, from the ends of the earth to the ends of the heavens.

²⁸"Now learn this lesson from the fig tree: As soon as its twigs get tender and its leaves come out, you know that summer is near. ²⁹Even so, when you see these things happening, you know that it is near, right at the door. ³⁰I tell you the truth, this generation[g] will certainly not pass away until all these things have happened. ³¹Heaven and earth will pass away, but my words will never pass away.

The Day and Hour Unknown

³²"No one knows about that day or hour, not even the angels in heaven, nor the Son, but only the Father. ³³Be on guard! Be alert[h]! You do not know when that time will come. ³⁴It's like a man going away: He leaves his house and puts his servants in charge, each with his assigned

---

[a]42 Greek *two lepta*   [b]42 Greek *kodrantes*   [c]14 Daniel 9:27; 11:31; 12:11   [d]14 Or *he*; also in verse 29   [e]21 Or *Messiah*   [f]25 Isaiah 13:10; 34:4   [g]30 Or *race*   [h]33 Some manuscripts *alert and pray*

task, and tells the one at the door to keep watch.

[35]"Therefore keep watch because you do not know when the owner of the house will come back—whether in the evening, or at midnight, or when the rooster crows, or at dawn. [36]If he comes suddenly, do not let him find you sleeping. [37]What I say to you, I say to everyone: 'Watch!'"

Jesus Anointed at Bethany

14 Now the Passover and the Feast of Unleavened Bread were only two days away, and the chief priests and the teachers of the law were looking for some sly way to arrest Jesus and kill him. [2]"But not during the Feast," they said, "or the people may riot."

[3]While he was in Bethany, reclining at the table in the home of a man known as Simon the Leper, a woman came with an alabaster jar of very expensive perfume, made of pure nard. She broke the jar and poured the perfume on his head.

[4]Some of those present were saying indignantly to one another, "Why this waste of perfume? [5]It could have been sold for more than a year's wages[a] and the money given to the poor." And they rebuked her harshly.

[6]"Leave her alone," said Jesus. "Why are you bothering her? She has done a beautiful thing to me. [7]The poor you will always have with you, and you can help them any time you want. But you will not always have me. [8]She did what she could. She poured perfume on my body beforehand to prepare for my burial. [9]I tell you the truth, wherever the gospel is preached throughout the world, what she has done will also be told, in memory of her."

[10]Then Judas Iscariot, one of the Twelve, went to the chief priests to betray Jesus to them. [11]They were delighted to hear this and promised to give him money. So he watched for an opportunity to hand him over.

The Lord's Supper

[12]On the first day of the Feast of Unleavened Bread, when it was customary to sacrifice the Passover lamb, Jesus' disciples asked him, "Where do you want us to go and make preparations for you to eat the Passover?"

[13]So he sent two of his disciples, telling them, "Go into the city, and a man carrying a jar of water will meet you. Follow him. [14]Say to the owner of the house he enters, 'The Teacher asks: Where is my guest room, where I may eat the Passover with my disciples?' [15]He will show you a large upper room, furnished and ready. Make preparations for us there."

[16]The disciples left, went into the city and found things just as Jesus had told them. So they prepared the Passover.

[17]When evening came, Jesus arrived with the Twelve. [18]While they were reclining at the table eating, he said, "I tell you the truth, one of you will betray me—one who is eating with me."

[19]They were saddened, and one by one they said to him, "Surely not I?"

[20]"It is one of the Twelve," he replied, "one who dips bread into the bowl with me. [21]The Son of Man will go just as it is written about him. But woe to that man who betrays the Son of Man! It would be better for him if he had not been born."

[22]While they were eating, Jesus took bread, gave thanks and broke it, and gave it to his disciples, saying, "Take it; this is my body."

[23]Then he took the cup, gave thanks and offered it to them, and they all drank from it.

[24]"This is my blood of the[b] covenant, which is poured out for many," he said to them. [25]"I tell you the truth, I will not drink again of the fruit of the vine until that day when I drink it anew in the kingdom of God."

[26]When they had sung a hymn, they went out to the Mount of Olives.

Jesus Predicts Peter's Denial

[27]"You will all fall away," Jesus told them, "for it is written:

" 'I will strike the shepherd,
 and the sheep will be scattered.'[c]

[28]But after I have risen, I will go ahead of you into Galilee."

[29]Peter declared, "Even if all fall away, I will not."

[30]"I tell you the truth," Jesus answered, "today—yes, tonight—before the rooster crows twice[d] you yourself will disown me three times."

[31]But Peter insisted emphatically, "Even if I have to die with you, I will never disown you." And all the others said the same.

---

[a]5 Greek *than three hundred denarii*   [b]24 Some manuscripts *the new*   [c]27 Zech. 13:7   [d]30 Some early manuscripts do not have *twice.*

Gethsemane

32They went to a place called Gethsemane, and Jesus said to his disciples, "Sit here while I pray." **33**He took Peter, James and John along with him, and he began to be deeply distressed and troubled. **34**"My soul is overwhelmed with sorrow to the point of death," he said to them. "Stay here and keep watch."

35Going a little farther, he fell to the ground and prayed that if possible the hour might pass from him. **36**"*Abba,*[a] Father," he said, "everything is possible for you. Take this cup from me. Yet not what I will, but what you will."

37Then he returned to his disciples and found them sleeping. "Simon," he said to Peter, "are you asleep? Could you not keep watch for one hour? **38**Watch and pray so that you will not fall into temptation. The spirit is willing, but the body is weak."

39Once more he went away and prayed the same thing. **40**When he came back, he again found them sleeping, because their eyes were heavy. They did not know what to say to him.

41Returning the third time, he said to them, "Are you still sleeping and resting? Enough! The hour has come. Look, the Son of Man is betrayed into the hands of sinners. **42**Rise! Let us go! Here comes my betrayer!"

Jesus Arrested

43Just as he was speaking, Judas, one of the Twelve, appeared. With him was a crowd armed with swords and clubs, sent from the chief priests, the teachers of the law, and the elders.

44Now the betrayer had arranged a signal with them: "The one I kiss is the man; arrest him and lead him away under guard." **45**Going at once to Jesus, Judas said, "Rabbi!" and kissed him. **46**The men seized Jesus and arrested him. **47**Then one of those standing near drew his sword and struck the servant of the high priest, cutting off his ear.

48"Am I leading a rebellion," said Jesus, "that you have come out with swords and clubs to capture me? **49**Every day I was with you, teaching in the temple courts, and you did not arrest me. But the Scriptures must be fulfilled." **50**Then everyone deserted him and fled.

51A young man, wearing nothing but a linen garment, was following Jesus. When they seized him, **52**he fled naked, leaving his garment behind.

Before the Sanhedrin

53They took Jesus to the high priest, and all the chief priests, elders and teachers of the law came together. **54**Peter followed him at a distance, right into the courtyard of the high priest. There he sat with the guards and warmed himself at the fire.

55The chief priests and the whole Sanhedrin were looking for evidence against Jesus so that they could put him to death, but they did not find any. **56**Many testified falsely against him, but their statements did not agree.

57Then some stood up and gave this false testimony against him: **58**"We heard him say, 'I will destroy this man-made temple and in three days will build another, not made by man.' " **59**Yet even then their testimony did not agree.

60Then the high priest stood up before them and asked Jesus, "Are you not going to answer? What is this testimony that these men are bringing against you?" **61**But Jesus remained silent and gave no answer.

Again the high priest asked him, "Are you the Christ,[b] the Son of the Blessed One?"

62"I am," said Jesus. "And you will see the Son of Man sitting at the right hand of the Mighty One and coming on the clouds of heaven."

63The high priest tore his clothes. "Why do we need any more witnesses?" he asked. **64**"You have heard the blasphemy. What do you think?"

They all condemned him as worthy of death. **65**Then some began to spit at him; they blindfolded him, struck him with their fists, and said, "Prophesy!" And the guards took him and beat him.

Peter Disowns Jesus

66While Peter was below in the courtyard, one of the servant girls of the high priest came by. **67**When she saw Peter warming himself, she looked closely at him.

"You also were with that Nazarene, Jesus," she said.

68But he denied it. "I don't know or un-

---

a 36 Aramaic for *Father*   *b 61* Or *Messiah*

derstand what you're talking about," he said, and went out into the entryway.[a]

⁶⁹When the servant girl saw him there, she said again to those standing around, "This fellow is one of them." ⁷⁰Again he denied it.

After a little while, those standing near said to Peter, "Surely you are one of them, for you are a Galilean."

⁷¹He began to call down curses on himself, and he swore to them, "I don't know this man you're talking about."

⁷²Immediately the rooster crowed the second time.[b] Then Peter remembered the word Jesus had spoken to him: "Before the rooster crows twice[c] you will disown me three times." And he broke down and wept.

Jesus Before Pilate

15 Very early in the morning, the chief priests, with the elders, the teachers of the law and the whole Sanhedrin, reached a decision. They bound Jesus, led him away and handed him over to Pilate.

²"Are you the king of the Jews?" asked Pilate.

"Yes, it is as you say," Jesus replied.

³The chief priests accused him of many things. ⁴So again Pilate asked him, "Aren't you going to answer? See how many things they are accusing you of."

⁵But Jesus still made no reply, and Pilate was amazed.

⁶Now it was the custom at the Feast to release a prisoner whom the people requested. ⁷A man called Barabbas was in prison with the insurrectionists who had committed murder in the uprising. ⁸The crowd came up and asked Pilate to do for them what he usually did.

⁹"Do you want me to release to you the king of the Jews?" asked Pilate, ¹⁰knowing it was out of envy that the chief priests had handed Jesus over to him. ¹¹But the chief priests stirred up the crowd to have Pilate release Barabbas instead.

¹²"What shall I do, then, with the one you call the king of the Jews?" Pilate asked them.

¹³"Crucify him!" they shouted.

¹⁴"Why? What crime has he committed?" asked Pilate.

But they shouted all the louder, "Crucify him!"

¹⁵Wanting to satisfy the crowd, Pilate released Barabbas to them. He had Jesus flogged, and handed him over to be crucified.

The Soldiers Mock Jesus

¹⁶The soldiers led Jesus away into the palace (that is, the Praetorium) and called together the whole company of soldiers. ¹⁷They put a purple robe on him, then twisted together a crown of thorns and set it on him. ¹⁸And they began to call out to him, "Hail, king of the Jews!" ¹⁹Again and again they struck him on the head with a staff and spit on him. Falling on their knees, they paid homage to him. ²⁰And when they had mocked him, they took off the purple robe and put his own clothes on him. Then they led him out to crucify him.

The Crucifixion

²¹A certain man from Cyrene, Simon, the father of Alexander and Rufus, was passing by on his way in from the country, and they forced him to carry the cross. ²²They brought Jesus to the place called Golgotha (which means The Place of the Skull). ²³Then they offered him wine mixed with myrrh, but he did not take it. ²⁴And they crucified him. Dividing up his clothes, they cast lots to see what each would get.

²⁵It was the third hour when they crucified him. ²⁶The written notice of the charge against him read: THE KING OF THE JEWS. ²⁷They crucified two robbers with him, one on his right and one on his left.[d] ²⁹Those who passed by hurled insults at him, shaking their heads and saying, "So! You who are going to destroy the temple and build it in three days, ³⁰come down from the cross and save yourself!"

³¹In the same way the chief priests and the teachers of the law mocked him among themselves. "He saved others," they said, "but he can't save himself! ³²Let this Christ,[e] this King of Israel, come down now from the cross, that we may see and believe." Those crucified with him also heaped insults on him.

The Death of Jesus

³³At the sixth hour darkness came over the whole land until the ninth hour. ³⁴And

---

[a]68 Some early manuscripts *entryway and the rooster crowed*   [b]72 Some early manuscripts do not have *the second time.*   [c]72 Some early manuscripts do not have *twice.*   [d]27 Some manuscripts *left,* ²⁸*and the scripture was fulfilled which says, "He was counted with the lawless ones"* (Isaiah 53:12)   [e]32 Or *Messiah*

at the ninth hour Jesus cried out in a loud voice, *"Eloi, Eloi, lama sabachthani?"*—which means, "My God, my God, why have you forsaken me?"*a*

³⁵When some of those standing near heard this, they said, "Listen, he's calling Elijah."

³⁶One man ran, filled a sponge with wine vinegar, put it on a stick, and offered it to Jesus to drink. "Now leave him alone. Let's see if Elijah comes to take him down," he said.

³⁷With a loud cry, Jesus breathed his last.

³⁸The curtain of the temple was torn in two from top to bottom. ³⁹And when the centurion, who stood there in front of Jesus, heard his cry and*b* saw how he died, he said, "Surely this man was the Son*c* of God!"

⁴⁰Some women were watching from a distance. Among them were Mary Magdalene, Mary the mother of James the younger and of Joses, and Salome. ⁴¹In Galilee these women had followed him and cared for his needs. Many other women who had come up with him to Jerusalem were also there.

The Burial of Jesus

⁴²It was Preparation Day (that is, the day before the Sabbath). So as evening approached, ⁴³Joseph of Arimathea, a prominent member of the Council, who was himself waiting for the kingdom of God, went boldly to Pilate and asked for Jesus' body. ⁴⁴Pilate was surprised to hear that he was already dead. Summoning the centurion, he asked him if Jesus had already died. ⁴⁵When he learned from the centurion that it was so, he gave the body to Joseph. ⁴⁶So Joseph bought some linen cloth, took down the body, wrapped it in the linen, and placed it in a tomb cut out of rock. Then he rolled a stone against the entrance of the tomb. ⁴⁷Mary Magdalene and Mary the mother of Joses saw where he was laid.

The Resurrection

16 When the Sabbath was over, Mary Magdalene, Mary the mother of James, and Salome bought spices so that they might go to anoint Jesus' body. ²Very early on the first day of the week, just after sunrise, they were on their way to the tomb ³and they asked each other, "Who will roll the stone away from the entrance of the tomb?"

⁴But when they looked up, they saw that the stone, which was very large, had been rolled away. ⁵As they entered the tomb, they saw a young man dressed in a white robe sitting on the right side, and they were alarmed.

⁶"Don't be alarmed," he said. "You are looking for Jesus the Nazarene, who was crucified. He has risen! He is not here. See the place where they laid him. ⁷But go, tell his disciples and Peter, 'He is going ahead of you into Galilee. There you will see him, just as he told you.'"

⁸Trembling and bewildered, the women went out and fled from the tomb. They said nothing to anyone, because they were afraid.

[The most reliable early manuscripts and other ancient witnesses do not have Mark 16:9–20.]

⁹When Jesus rose early on the first day of the week, he appeared first to Mary Magdalene, out of whom he had driven seven demons. ¹⁰She went and told those who had been with him and who were mourning and weeping. ¹¹When they heard that Jesus was alive and that she had seen him, they did not believe it.

¹²Afterward Jesus appeared in a different form to two of them while they were walking in the country. ¹³These returned and reported it to the rest; but they did not believe them either.

¹⁴Later Jesus appeared to the Eleven as they were eating; he rebuked them for their lack of faith and their stubborn refusal to believe those who had seen him after he had risen.

¹⁵He said to them, "Go into all the world and preach the good news to all creation. ¹⁶Whoever believes and is baptized will be saved, but whoever does not believe will be condemned. ¹⁷And these signs will accompany those who believe: In my name they will drive out demons; they will speak in new tongues; ¹⁸they will pick up snakes with their hands; and when

---

a 34 Psalm 22:1   *b* 39 Some manuscripts do not have *heard his cry and*   *c* 39 Or *a son*

they drink deadly poison, it will not hurt them at all; they will place their hands on sick people, and they will get well."

[19]After the Lord Jesus had spoken to them, he was taken up into heaven and he sat at the right hand of God. [20]Then the disciples went out and preached everywhere, and the Lord worked with them and confirmed his word by the signs that accompanied it.

LUKE writes this Gospel to present Jesus as a Savior for the whole human race. The stories emphasize how kind and loving Jesus is to those despised by society (such as tax collectors, Samaritans, the poor, and women). He stresses the importance of prayer in Jesus' life. As you read this book, be sure that you have repented of your sins and have claimed Jesus as your own personal Savior. Ask yourself whether you show the same sort of compassion to others that Jesus showed.

LUKE

Introduction

1 Many have undertaken to draw up an account of the things that have been fulfilled[a] among us, **2** just as they were handed down to us by those who from the first were eyewitnesses and servants of the word. **3** Therefore, since I myself have carefully investigated everything from the beginning, it seemed good also to me to write an orderly account for you, most excellent Theophilus, **4** so that you may know the certainty of the things you have been taught.

The Birth of John the Baptist Foretold

5 In the time of Herod king of Judea there was a priest named Zechariah, who belonged to the priestly division of Abijah; his wife Elizabeth was also a descendant of Aaron. **6** Both of them were upright in the sight of God, observing all the Lord's commandments and regulations blamelessly. **7** But they had no children, because Elizabeth was barren; and they were both well along in years.

8 Once when Zechariah's division was

---

a 1 Or been surely believed

on duty and he was serving as priest before God, ⁹he was chosen by lot, according to the custom of the priesthood, to go into the temple of the Lord and burn incense. ¹⁰And when the time for the burning of incense came, all the assembled worshipers were praying outside.

¹¹Then an angel of the Lord appeared to him, standing at the right side of the altar of incense. ¹²When Zechariah saw him, he was startled and was gripped with fear. ¹³But the angel said to him: "Do not be afraid, Zechariah; your prayer has been heard. Your wife Elizabeth will bear you a son, and you are to give him the name John. ¹⁴He will be a joy and delight to you, and many will rejoice because of his birth, ¹⁵for he will be great in the sight of the Lord. He is never to take wine or other fermented drink, and he will be filled with the Holy Spirit even from birth.ᵃ ¹⁶Many of the people of Israel will he bring back to the Lord their God. ¹⁷And he will go on before the Lord, in the spirit and power of Elijah, to turn the hearts of the fathers to their children and the disobedient to the wisdom of the righteous—to make ready a people prepared for the Lord."

¹⁸Zechariah asked the angel, "How can I be sure of this? I am an old man and my wife is well along in years."

¹⁹The angel answered, "I am Gabriel. I stand in the presence of God, and I have been sent to speak to you and to tell you this good news. ²⁰And now you will be silent and not able to speak until the day this happens, because you did not believe my words, which will come true at their proper time."

²¹Meanwhile, the people were waiting for Zechariah and wondering why he stayed so long in the temple. ²²When he came out, he could not speak to them. They realized he had seen a vision in the temple, for he kept making signs to them but remained unable to speak.

²³When his time of service was completed, he returned home. ²⁴After this his wife Elizabeth became pregnant and for five months remained in seclusion. ²⁵"The Lord has done this for me," she said. "In these days he has shown his favor and taken away my disgrace among the people."

The Birth of Jesus Foretold

²⁶In the sixth month, God sent the angel Gabriel to Nazareth, a town in Galilee, ²⁷to a virgin pledged to be married to a man named Joseph, a descendant of David. The virgin's name was Mary. ²⁸The angel went to her and said, "Greetings, you who are highly favored! The Lord is with you."

²⁹Mary was greatly troubled at his words and wondered what kind of greeting this might be. ³⁰But the angel said to her, "Do not be afraid, Mary, you have found favor with God. ³¹You will be with child and give birth to a son, and you are to give him the name Jesus. ³²He will be great and will be called the Son of the Most High. The Lord God will give him the throne of his father David, ³³and he will reign over the house of Jacob forever; his kingdom will never end."

³⁴"How will this be," Mary asked the angel, "since I am a virgin?"

³⁵The angel answered, "The Holy Spirit will come upon you, and the power of the Most High will overshadow you. So the holy one to be born will be calledᵇ the Son of God. ³⁶Even Elizabeth your relative is going to have a child in her old age, and she who was said to be barren is in her sixth month. ³⁷For nothing is impossible with God."

³⁸"I am the Lord's servant," Mary answered. "May it be to me as you have said." Then the angel left her.

Mary Visits Elizabeth

³⁹At that time Mary got ready and hurried to a town in the hill country of Judea, ⁴⁰where she entered Zechariah's home and greeted Elizabeth. ⁴¹When Elizabeth heard Mary's greeting, the baby leaped in her womb, and Elizabeth was filled with the Holy Spirit. ⁴²In a loud voice she exclaimed: "Blessed are you among women, and blessed is the child you will bear! ⁴³But why am I so favored, that the mother of my Lord should come to me? ⁴⁴As soon as the sound of your greeting reached my ears, the baby in my womb leaped for joy. ⁴⁵Blessed is she who has believed that what the Lord has said to her will be accomplished!"

Mary's Song

⁴⁶And Mary said:

"My soul glorifies the Lord
⁴⁷ and my spirit rejoices in God my Savior,
⁴⁸for he has been mindful
of the humble state of his servant.

ᵃ15 Or *from his mother's womb*   ᵇ35 Or *So the child to be born will be called holy,*

From now on all generations will call
me blessed,
⁴⁹ for the Mighty One has done great
things for me —
holy is his name.
⁵⁰His mercy extends to those who fear
him,
from generation to generation.
⁵¹He has performed mighty deeds with
his arm;
he has scattered those who are
proud in their inmost thoughts.
⁵²He has brought down rulers from
their thrones
but has lifted up the humble.
⁵³He has filled the hungry with good
things
but has sent the rich away
empty.
⁵⁴He has helped his servant Israel,
remembering to be merciful
⁵⁵to Abraham and his descendants
forever,
even as he said to our fathers."

FRIDAY

VERSE FOR THE DAY:
Luke 1:17

AUTHOR:
John E. Crawford

PASSAGE FOR THE DAY:
Luke 1:8–17

Do It Now!

THERE is a fine art to being available to a youngster who might want to talk to you about what has been troubling her. Of course, she has to know that you love and value her. Otherwise she could not afford to tell you how she really feels about anything important. We rarely confide in anyone we think may not truly care about us. Neither do most of us open up to people who pry. Communication flows most freely when children and parents feel safe and secure with one another.

Teenagers as well as younger children often need to be able to spill out deeper anxieties and fears. Without safety valves, emotional tensions can rise to such levels that something has to go. Our children are no different from the rest of us in this need. The right words and conversation not only can ventilate the mind and heart and diminish neurotic fear and anguish of spirit, but also can mend and heal.

Pleasant and relaxing excursions with her father can let a girl see what intelligent, mature men really are like. Every girl needs a father she can talk to, argue with, race at a picnic, play ball with in the cool of evening, hug and kiss. These things are worth doing even if you have to make room in your time schedule. She is growing up just as swiftly as you are adding years to yourself. Waiting until next year or the year after that will find her older and that much less inclined to talk or swim or go to the concert with you. Out of these experiences come the kind of deep mutual ties and understanding that have kept thousands of girls right-minded and trustworthy about sex, even in a world where morals and ethics sometimes seem extinct.

Additional Scripture Readings:
Proverbs 15:1–5; Colossians 4:2–6

Go to page 77 for your next devotional reading.

⁵⁶Mary stayed with Elizabeth for about three months and then returned home.

The Birth of John the Baptist

⁵⁷When it was time for Elizabeth to have her baby, she gave birth to a son. ⁵⁸Her neighbors and relatives heard that the Lord had shown her great mercy, and they shared her joy.

⁵⁹On the eighth day they came to circumcise the child, and they were going to name him after his father Zechariah, ⁶⁰but his mother spoke up and said, "No! He is to be called John."

⁶¹They said to her, "There is no one among your relatives who has that name."

⁶²Then they made signs to his father, to find out what he would like to name the child. ⁶³He asked for a writing tablet, and to everyone's astonishment he wrote, "His name is John." ⁶⁴Immediately his mouth was opened and his tongue was loosed, and he began to speak, praising God. ⁶⁵The neighbors were all filled with awe, and throughout the hill country of Judea people were talking about all these things. ⁶⁶Everyone who heard this wondered about it, asking, "What then is this child going to be?" For the Lord's hand was with him.

Zechariah's Song

⁶⁷His father Zechariah was filled with the Holy Spirit and prophesied:

⁶⁸"Praise be to the Lord, the God of Israel,
 because he has come and has redeemed his people.
⁶⁹He has raised up a horn[a] of salvation for us
 in the house of his servant David
⁷⁰(as he said through his holy prophets of long ago),
⁷¹salvation from our enemies
 and from the hand of all who hate us —
⁷²to show mercy to our fathers
 and to remember his holy covenant,
⁷³ the oath he swore to our father Abraham:
⁷⁴to rescue us from the hand of our enemies,
 and to enable us to serve him without fear
⁷⁵ in holiness and righteousness before him all our days.

⁷⁶And you, my child, will be called a prophet of the Most High;
 for you will go on before the Lord to prepare the way for him,
⁷⁷to give his people the knowledge of salvation
 through the forgiveness of their sins,
⁷⁸because of the tender mercy of our God,
 by which the rising sun will come to us from heaven
⁷⁹to shine on those living in darkness and in the shadow of death,
 to guide our feet into the path of peace."

⁸⁰And the child grew and became strong in spirit; and he lived in the desert until he appeared publicly to Israel.

The Birth of Jesus

2 In those days Caesar Augustus issued a decree that a census should be taken of the entire Roman world. ²(This was the first census that took place while Quirinius was governor of Syria.) ³And everyone went to his own town to register.

⁴So Joseph also went up from the town of Nazareth in Galilee to Judea, to Bethlehem the town of David, because he belonged to the house and line of David. ⁵He went there to register with Mary, who was pledged to be married to him and was expecting a child. ⁶While they were there, the time came for the baby to be born, ⁷and she gave birth to her firstborn, a son. She wrapped him in cloths and placed him in a manger, because there was no room for them in the inn.

The Shepherds and the Angels

⁸And there were shepherds living out in the fields nearby, keeping watch over their flocks at night. ⁹An angel of the Lord appeared to them, and the glory of the Lord shone around them, and they were terrified. ¹⁰But the angel said to them, "Do not be afraid. I bring you good news of great joy that will be for all the people. ¹¹Today in the town of David a Savior has been born to you; he is Christ[b] the Lord. ¹²This will be a sign to you: You will find a baby wrapped in cloths and lying in a manger."

¹³Suddenly a great company of the

---

a 69 *Horn* here symbolizes strength.   *b* 11 Or *Messiah.* "The Christ" (Greek) and "the Messiah" (Hebrew) both mean "the Anointed One"; also in verse 26.

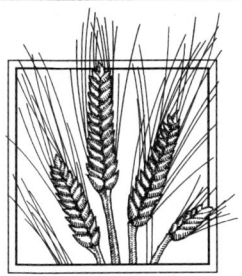

WEEKENDING

RECALL

When Jesus promised his return, he did not intend to scare us out of our wits . . . He placed himself firmly ahead of us, as end, just as he had established himself at the beginning . . . If we cannot join our beginning to our end, we will live scattered and incoherent lives. The expectation of Jesus' coming provides a goal that shapes and unifies life in accordance with its origins in Christ, in patterns that are consonant with its completion in Christ. This urgency is liberating, for it compels us to stay awake, deeply and earnestly aware of who we are and what we are doing, keeping us free from trivia that . . . can make prisoners of us as effectively as any ball and chain.
– *Eugene H. Peterson*

REVIVE
Saturday: Mark 13:32–37
Sunday: Revelation 1:17–18

Go to page 79 for your next devotional reading.

heavenly host appeared with the angel, praising God and saying,

¹⁴"Glory to God in the highest,
and on earth peace to men on whom his favor rests."

¹⁵When the angels had left them and gone into heaven, the shepherds said to one another, "Let's go to Bethlehem and see this thing that has happened, which the Lord has told us about."

¹⁶So they hurried off and found Mary and Joseph, and the baby, who was lying in the manger. ¹⁷When they had seen him, they spread the word concerning what had been told them about this child, ¹⁸and all who heard it were amazed at what the shepherds said to them. ¹⁹But Mary treasured up all these things and pondered them in her heart. ²⁰The shepherds returned, glorifying and praising God for all the things they had heard and seen, which were just as they had been told.

Jesus Presented in the Temple

²¹On the eighth day, when it was time to circumcise him, he was named Jesus, the name the angel had given him before he had been conceived.

²²When the time of their purification according to the Law of Moses had been completed, Joseph and Mary took him to Jerusalem to present him to the Lord ²³(as it is written in the Law of the Lord, "Every firstborn male is to be consecrated to the Lord"^a), ²⁴and to offer a sacrifice in keeping with what is said in the Law of the Lord: "a pair of doves or two young pigeons."^b

²⁵Now there was a man in Jerusalem called Simeon, who was righteous and devout. He was waiting for the consolation of Israel, and the Holy Spirit was upon him. ²⁶It had been revealed to him by the Holy Spirit that he would not die before he had seen the Lord's Christ. ²⁷Moved by the Spirit, he went into the temple courts. When the parents brought in the child Jesus to do for him what the custom of the Law required, ²⁸Simeon took him in his arms and praised God, saying:

²⁹"Sovereign Lord, as you have promised,
you now dismiss^c your servant in peace.
³⁰For my eyes have seen your salvation,
³¹which you have prepared in the sight of all people,
³²a light for revelation to the Gentiles
and for glory to your people Israel."

³³The child's father and mother marveled at what was said about him. ³⁴Then Simeon blessed them and said to Mary, his mother: "This child is destined to cause the falling and rising of many in Israel, and to be a sign that will be spoken against, ³⁵so that the thoughts of many hearts will be revealed. And a sword will pierce your own soul too."

³⁶There was also a prophetess, Anna, the daughter of Phanuel, of the tribe of Asher. She was very old; she had lived with her husband seven years after her marriage, ³⁷and then was a widow until she was eighty-four.^d She never left the temple but worshiped night and day, fasting and praying. ³⁸Coming up to them at that very moment, she gave thanks to God and spoke about the child to all who were looking forward to the redemption of Jerusalem.

³⁹When Joseph and Mary had done everything required by the Law of the Lord, they returned to Galilee to their own town of Nazareth. ⁴⁰And the child grew and became strong; he was filled with wisdom, and the grace of God was upon him.

The Boy Jesus at the Temple

⁴¹Every year his parents went to Jerusalem for the Feast of the Passover. ⁴²When he was twelve years old, they went up to the Feast, according to the custom. ⁴³After the Feast was over, while his parents were returning home, the boy Jesus stayed behind in Jerusalem, but they were unaware of it. ⁴⁴Thinking he was in their company, they traveled on for a day. Then they began looking for him among their relatives and friends. ⁴⁵When they did not find him, they went back to Jerusalem to look for him. ⁴⁶After three days they found him in the temple courts, sitting among the teachers, listening to them and asking them questions. ⁴⁷Everyone who heard him was amazed at his understanding and his answers. ⁴⁸When his parents saw him, they were astonished. His mother said to him, "Son, why have you treated us like this? Your father and I have been anxiously searching for you."

---

^a23 Exodus 13:2,12   ^b24 Lev. 12:8   ^c29 Or *promised, / now dismiss*   ^d37 Or *widow for eighty-four years*

LUKE 2-3

⁴⁹"Why were you searching for me?" he asked. "Didn't you know I had to be in my Father's house?" ⁵⁰But they did not understand what he was saying to them.

⁵¹Then he went down to Nazareth with them and was obedient to them. But his mother treasured all these things in her heart. ⁵²And Jesus grew in wisdom and stature, and in favor with God and men.

John the Baptist Prepares the Way

3 In the fifteenth year of the reign of Tiberius Caesar—when Pontius Pilate was governor of Judea, Herod tetrarch of Galilee, his brother Philip tetrarch of Iturea and Traconitis, and Lysanias tetrarch of Abilene— ²during the high priesthood of Annas and Caiaphas, the word of God came to John son of Zechariah in the desert. ³He went into all the country

---

MONDAY

VERSE FOR THE DAY:
Luke 2:8

AUTHOR:
Max Lucado

PASSAGE FOR THE DAY:
Luke 2:8–15

You Have to Stoop

THE announcement went first to the shepherds. They didn't ask God if he was sure he knew what he was doing. Had the angel gone to the theologians, they would have first consulted their commentaries. Had he gone to the elite, they would have looked around to see if anyone was watching. Had he gone to the successful, they would have first looked at their calendars.

So he went to the shepherds. Men who didn't have a reputation to protect or an ax to grind or a ladder to climb. Men who didn't know enough to tell God that angels don't sing to sheep and that messiahs aren't found wrapped in rags and sleeping in a feed trough.

A small cathedral outside Bethlehem marks the supposed birthplace of Jesus. Behind a high altar in the church is a cave, a little cavern lit by silver lamps.

You can enter the main edifice and admire the ancient church. You can also enter the quiet cave where a star embedded in the floor recognizes the birth of the King. There is one stipulation, however. You have to stoop. The door is so low you can't go in standing up.

The same is true of the Christ. You can see the world standing tall, but to witness the Savior, you have to get on your knees.

So . . .
while the theologians were sleeping
and the elite were dreaming
and the successful were snoring,
the meek were kneeling.

They were kneeling before the One only the meek will see. They were kneeling in front of Jesus.

Additional Scripture Readings:
Matthew 5:1–10; Ephesians 4:1–6

Go to page 84 for your next devotional reading.

around the Jordan, preaching a baptism of repentance for the forgiveness of sins. ⁴As is written in the book of the words of Isaiah the prophet:

"A voice of one calling in the desert,
'Prepare the way for the Lord,
   make straight paths for him.
⁵Every valley shall be filled in,
   every mountain and hill made low.
The crooked roads shall become straight,
   the rough ways smooth.
⁶And all mankind will see God's salvation.' "ᵃ

⁷John said to the crowds coming out to be baptized by him, "You brood of vipers! Who warned you to flee from the coming wrath? ⁸Produce fruit in keeping with repentance. And do not begin to say to yourselves, 'We have Abraham as our father.' For I tell you that out of these stones God can raise up children for Abraham. ⁹The ax is already at the root of the trees, and every tree that does not produce good fruit will be cut down and thrown into the fire."

¹⁰"What should we do then?" the crowd asked.

¹¹John answered, "The man with two tunics should share with him who has none, and the one who has food should do the same."

¹²Tax collectors also came to be baptized. "Teacher," they asked, "what should we do?"

¹³"Don't collect any more than you are required to," he told them.

¹⁴Then some soldiers asked him, "And what should we do?"

He replied, "Don't extort money and don't accuse people falsely — be content with your pay."

¹⁵The people were waiting expectantly and were all wondering in their hearts if John might possibly be the Christ.ᵇ ¹⁶John answered them all, "I baptize you withᶜ water. But one more powerful than I will come, the thongs of whose sandals I am not worthy to untie. He will baptize you with the Holy Spirit and with fire. ¹⁷His winnowing fork is in his hand to clear his threshing floor and to gather the wheat into his barn, but he will burn up the chaff with unquenchable fire." ¹⁸And with many other words John exhorted the people and preached the good news to them.

¹⁹But when John rebuked Herod the tetrarch because of Herodias, his brother's wife, and all the other evil things he had done, ²⁰Herod added this to them all: He locked John up in prison.

The Baptism and Genealogy of Jesus

²¹When all the people were being baptized, Jesus was baptized too. And as he was praying, heaven was opened ²²and the Holy Spirit descended on him in bodily form like a dove. And a voice came from heaven: "You are my Son, whom I love; with you I am well pleased."

²³Now Jesus himself was about thirty years old when he began his ministry. He was the son, so it was thought, of Joseph,

the son of Heli, ²⁴the son of Matthat,
   the son of Levi, the son of Melki,
   the son of Jannai, the son of Joseph,
²⁵the son of Mattathias, the son of Amos,
   the son of Nahum, the son of Esli,
   the son of Naggai, ²⁶the son of Maath,
   the son of Mattathias, the son of Semein,
   the son of Josech, the son of Joda,
²⁷the son of Joanan, the son of Rhesa,
   the son of Zerubbabel, the son of Shealtiel,
   the son of Neri, ²⁸the son of Melki,
   the son of Addi, the son of Cosam,
   the son of Elmadam, the son of Er,
²⁹the son of Joshua, the son of Eliezer,
   the son of Jorim, the son of Matthat,
   the son of Levi, ³⁰the son of Simeon,
   the son of Judah, the son of Joseph,
   the son of Jonam, the son of Eliakim,
³¹the son of Melea, the son of Menna,
   the son of Mattatha, the son of Nathan,
   the son of David, ³²the son of Jesse,
   the son of Obed, the son of Boaz,
   the son of Salmon,ᵈ the son of Nahshon,
³³the son of Amminadab, the son of Ram,ᵉ
   the son of Hezron, the son of Perez,
   the son of Judah, ³⁴the son of Jacob,
   the son of Isaac, the son of Abraham,
   the son of Terah, the son of Nahor,
³⁵the son of Serug, the son of Reu,
   the son of Peleg, the son of Eber,

ᵃ6 Isaiah 40:3-5   ᵇ15 Or Messiah   ᶜ16 Or in   ᵈ32 Some early manuscripts Sala   ᵉ33 Some manuscripts Amminadab, the son of Admin, the son of Arni; other manuscripts vary widely.

the son of Shelah, ³⁶the son of Cainan,
the son of Arphaxad, the son of Shem,
the son of Noah, the son of Lamech,
³⁷the son of Methuselah, the son of Enoch,
the son of Jared, the son of Mahalalel,
the son of Kenan, ³⁸the son of Enosh,
the son of Seth, the son of Adam,
the son of God.

The Temptation of Jesus

4 Jesus, full of the Holy Spirit, returned from the Jordan and was led by the Spirit in the desert, ²where for forty days he was tempted by the devil. He ate nothing during those days, and at the end of them he was hungry.

³The devil said to him, "If you are the Son of God, tell this stone to become bread."

⁴Jesus answered, "It is written: 'Man does not live on bread alone.'ᵃ"

⁵The devil led him up to a high place and showed him in an instant all the kingdoms of the world. ⁶And he said to him, "I will give you all their authority and splendor, for it has been given to me, and I can give it to anyone I want to. ⁷So if you worship me, it will all be yours."

⁸Jesus answered, "It is written: 'Worship the Lord your God and serve him only.'ᵇ"

⁹The devil led him to Jerusalem and had him stand on the highest point of the temple. "If you are the Son of God," he said, "throw yourself down from here. ¹⁰For it is written:

" 'He will command his angels
   concerning you
 to guard you carefully;
¹¹they will lift you up in their hands,
 so that you will not strike your foot
   against a stone.'ᶜ"

¹²Jesus answered, "It says: 'Do not put the Lord your God to the test.'ᵈ"

¹³When the devil had finished all this tempting, he left him until an opportune time.

Jesus Rejected at Nazareth

¹⁴Jesus returned to Galilee in the power of the Spirit, and news about him spread through the whole countryside. ¹⁵He taught in their synagogues, and everyone praised him.

¹⁶He went to Nazareth, where he had been brought up, and on the Sabbath day he went into the synagogue, as was his custom. And he stood up to read. ¹⁷The scroll of the prophet Isaiah was handed to him. Unrolling it, he found the place where it is written:

¹⁸"The Spirit of the Lord is on me,
  because he has anointed me
  to preach good news to the poor.
 He has sent me to proclaim freedom
    for the prisoners
  and recovery of sight for the blind,
 to release the oppressed,
¹⁹ to proclaim the year of the Lord's
    favor."ᵉ

²⁰Then he rolled up the scroll, gave it back to the attendant and sat down. The eyes of everyone in the synagogue were fastened on him, ²¹and he began by saying to them, "Today this scripture is fulfilled in your hearing."

²²All spoke well of him and were amazed at the gracious words that came from his lips. "Isn't this Joseph's son?" they asked.

²³Jesus said to them, "Surely you will quote this proverb to me: 'Physician, heal yourself! Do here in your hometown what we have heard that you did in Capernaum.' "

²⁴"I tell you the truth," he continued, "no prophet is accepted in his hometown. ²⁵I assure you that there were many widows in Israel in Elijah's time, when the sky was shut for three and a half years and there was a severe famine throughout the land. ²⁶Yet Elijah was not sent to any of them, but to a widow in Zarephath in the region of Sidon. ²⁷And there were many in Israel with leprosyᶠ in the time of Elisha the prophet, yet not one of them was cleansed — only Naaman the Syrian."

²⁸All the people in the synagogue were furious when they heard this. ²⁹They got up, drove him out of the town, and took him to the brow of the hill on which the town was built, in order to throw him down the cliff. ³⁰But he walked right through the crowd and went on his way.

Jesus Drives Out an Evil Spirit

³¹Then he went down to Capernaum, a town in Galilee, and on the Sabbath began

---

ᵃ4 Deut. 8:3   ᵇ8 Deut. 6:13   ᶜ11 Psalm 91:11,12   ᵈ12 Deut. 6:16   ᵉ19 Isaiah 61:1,2
ᶠ27 The Greek word was used for various diseases affecting the skin—not necessarily leprosy.

to teach the people. **32**They were amazed at his teaching, because his message had authority.

33In the synagogue there was a man possessed by a demon, an evil*a* spirit. He cried out at the top of his voice, **34**"Ha! What do you want with us, Jesus of Nazareth? Have you come to destroy us? I know who you are—the Holy One of God!"

35"Be quiet!" Jesus said sternly. "Come out of him!" Then the demon threw the man down before them all and came out without injuring him.

36All the people were amazed and said to each other, "What is this teaching? With authority and power he gives orders to evil spirits and they come out!" **37**And the news about him spread throughout the surrounding area.

Jesus Heals Many

38Jesus left the synagogue and went to the home of Simon. Now Simon's mother-in-law was suffering from a high fever, and they asked Jesus to help her. **39**So he bent over her and rebuked the fever, and it left her. She got up at once and began to wait on them.

40When the sun was setting, the people brought to Jesus all who had various kinds of sickness, and laying his hands on each one, he healed them. **41**Moreover, demons came out of many people, shouting, "You are the Son of God!" But he rebuked them and would not allow them to speak, because they knew he was the Christ.*b*

42At daybreak Jesus went out to a solitary place. The people were looking for him and when they came to where he was, they tried to keep him from leaving them. **43**But he said, "I must preach the good news of the kingdom of God to the other towns also, because that is why I was sent." **44**And he kept on preaching in the synagogues of Judea.*c*

The Calling of the First Disciples

5 One day as Jesus was standing by the Lake of Gennesaret,*d* with the people crowding around him and listening to the word of God, **2**he saw at the water's edge two boats, left there by the fishermen, who were washing their nets. **3**He got into one of the boats, the one belonging to Simon, and asked him to put out a little from shore. Then he sat down and taught the people from the boat.

4When he had finished speaking, he said to Simon, "Put out into deep water, and let down*e* the nets for a catch."

5Simon answered, "Master, we've worked hard all night and haven't caught anything. But because you say so, I will let down the nets."

6When they had done so, they caught such a large number of fish that their nets began to break. **7**So they signaled their partners in the other boat to come and help them, and they came and filled both boats so full that they began to sink.

8When Simon Peter saw this, he fell at Jesus' knees and said, "Go away from me, Lord; I am a sinful man!" **9**For he and all his companions were astonished at the catch of fish they had taken, **10**and so were James and John, the sons of Zebedee, Simon's partners.

Then Jesus said to Simon, "Don't be afraid; from now on you will catch men." **11**So they pulled their boats up on shore, left everything and followed him.

The Man With Leprosy

12While Jesus was in one of the towns, a man came along who was covered with leprosy.*f* When he saw Jesus, he fell with his face to the ground and begged him, "Lord, if you are willing, you can make me clean."

13Jesus reached out his hand and touched the man. "I am willing," he said. "Be clean!" And immediately the leprosy left him.

14Then Jesus ordered him, "Don't tell anyone, but go, show yourself to the priest and offer the sacrifices that Moses commanded for your cleansing, as a testimony to them."

15Yet the news about him spread all the more, so that crowds of people came to hear him and to be healed of their sicknesses. **16**But Jesus often withdrew to lonely places and prayed.

Jesus Heals a Paralytic

17One day as he was teaching, Pharisees and teachers of the law, who had come from every village of Galilee and from Judea and Jerusalem, were sitting there. And the power of the Lord was present for him to heal the sick. **18**Some men came

---

*a*33 Greek *unclean;* also in verse 36   *b*41 Or *Messiah*   *c*44 Or *the land of the Jews;* some manuscripts *Galilee*   *d*1 That is, Sea of Galilee   *e*4 The Greek verb is plural.   *f*12 The Greek word was used for various diseases affecting the skin—not necessarily leprosy.

carrying a paralytic on a mat and tried to take him into the house to lay him before Jesus. ¹⁹When they could not find a way to do this because of the crowd, they went up on the roof and lowered him on his mat through the tiles into the middle of the crowd, right in front of Jesus.

²⁰When Jesus saw their faith, he said, "Friend, your sins are forgiven."

²¹The Pharisees and the teachers of the law began thinking to themselves, "Who is this fellow who speaks blasphemy? Who can forgive sins but God alone?"

²²Jesus knew what they were thinking and asked, "Why are you thinking these things in your hearts? ²³Which is easier: to say, 'Your sins are forgiven,' or to say, 'Get up and walk'? ²⁴But that you may know that the Son of Man has authority on earth to forgive sins...." He said to the paralyzed man, "I tell you, get up, take your mat and go home." ²⁵Immediately he stood up in front of them, took what he had been lying on and went home praising God. ²⁶Everyone was amazed and gave praise to God. They were filled with awe and said, "We have seen remarkable things today."

The Calling of Levi

²⁷After this, Jesus went out and saw a tax collector by the name of Levi sitting at his tax booth. "Follow me," Jesus said to him, ²⁸and Levi got up, left everything and followed him.

²⁹Then Levi held a great banquet for Jesus at his house, and a large crowd of tax collectors and others were eating with them. ³⁰But the Pharisees and the teachers of the law who belonged to their sect complained to his disciples, "Why do you eat and drink with tax collectors and 'sinners'?"

³¹Jesus answered them, "It is not the healthy who need a doctor, but the sick. ³²I have not come to call the righteous, but sinners to repentance."

Jesus Questioned About Fasting

³³They said to him, "John's disciples often fast and pray, and so do the disciples of the Pharisees, but yours go on eating and drinking."

³⁴Jesus answered, "Can you make the guests of the bridegroom fast while he is with them? ³⁵But the time will come when the bridegroom will be taken from them; in those days they will fast."

³⁶He told them this parable: "No one tears a patch from a new garment and sews it on an old one. If he does, he will have torn the new garment, and the patch from the new will not match the old. ³⁷And no one pours new wine into old wineskins. If he does, the new wine will burst the skins, the wine will run out and the wineskins will be ruined. ³⁸No, new wine must be poured into new wineskins. ³⁹And no one after drinking old wine wants the new, for he says, 'The old is better.' "

Lord of the Sabbath

6 One Sabbath Jesus was going through the grainfields, and his disciples began to pick some heads of grain, rub them in their hands and eat the kernels. ²Some of the Pharisees asked, "Why are you doing what is unlawful on the Sabbath?"

³Jesus answered them, "Have you never read what David did when he and his companions were hungry? ⁴He entered the house of God, and taking the consecrated bread, he ate what is lawful only for priests to eat. And he also gave some to his companions." ⁵Then Jesus said to them, "The Son of Man is Lord of the Sabbath."

⁶On another Sabbath he went into the synagogue and was teaching, and a man was there whose right hand was shriveled. ⁷The Pharisees and the teachers of the law were looking for a reason to accuse Jesus, so they watched him closely to see if he would heal on the Sabbath. ⁸But Jesus knew what they were thinking and said to the man with the shriveled hand, "Get up and stand in front of everyone." So he got up and stood there.

⁹Then Jesus said to them, "I ask you, which is lawful on the Sabbath: to do good or to do evil, to save life or to destroy it?"

¹⁰He looked around at them all, and then said to the man, "Stretch out your hand." He did so, and his hand was completely restored. ¹¹But they were furious and began to discuss with one another what they might do to Jesus.

The Twelve Apostles

¹²One of those days Jesus went out to a mountainside to pray, and spent the night praying to God. ¹³When morning came, he called his disciples to him and chose twelve of them, whom he also designated apostles: ¹⁴Simon (whom he named Peter), his brother Andrew, James, John, Philip, Bartholomew, ¹⁵Matthew, Thomas, James son of Alphaeus, Simon who was

called the Zealot, **16**Judas son of James, and Judas Iscariot, who became a traitor.

Blessings and Woes

17He went down with them and stood on a level place. A large crowd of his disciples was there and a great number of people from all over Judea, from Jerusalem, and from the coast of Tyre and Sidon, **18**who had come to hear him and to be healed of their diseases. Those troubled by evil*a* spirits were cured, **19**and the people all tried to touch him, because power was coming from him and healing them all.

20Looking at his disciples, he said:

"Blessed are you who are poor,
 for yours is the kingdom of God.
21Blessed are you who hunger now,

a18 Greek *unclean*

TUESDAY

| VERSE FOR THE DAY: | AUTHOR: | PASSAGE FOR THE DAY: |
| Luke 5:27 | John Fischer | Luke 5:27–32 |

No Messianic Magic Show

TO EACH of his disciples, Jesus simply said, "Follow me." That was an invitation, not a requirement. An invitation respects the freedom of the invitee to accept or decline. Indeed, the "no" answer is perhaps the greatest expression of human dignity possible. That men and women can go to heaven is an expression of God's love; that they can go to hell is an expression of the value he places on their freedom.

God desires—not requires—a relationship with us. It is not a one-sided affair; we are co-participants with him, both in our relationship with him and in our work in the world.

A woman with a hemorrhage struggled through the press of the crowd in order to touch his garment; four men opened a hole in the ceiling of a crowded house and let down their paralyzed friend in front of Jesus; a centurion soldier asked that Jesus only speak a word so his servant would be healed; a blind man went and washed the clay and the darkness from his eyes; a little boy offered his meager lunch to feed a multitude. Even the miracles of Jesus involved human participation. This was not just a Messianic Magic Show; this was God interacting in human experience—giving and taking, relating with us as Son of Man.

God does not pull all the strings. He counts us as too important for that. To find without seeking, to hear without listening, to say yes without the possibility of saying no is to negate the value of my seeking, my hearing and my participating. I am not a puppet.

Nor does he put all the pieces together. He leaves holes; he raises questions. He wants me to ask.

Additional Scripture Readings:
Matthew 22:1–14; Mark 10:17–31

Go to page 86 for your next devotional reading.

for you will be satisfied.
Blessed are you who weep now,
for you will laugh.
22Blessed are you when men hate you,
when they exclude you and insult you
and reject your name as evil,
because of the Son of Man.

23"Rejoice in that day and leap for joy, because great is your reward in heaven. For that is how their fathers treated the prophets.

24"But woe to you who are rich,
for you have already received your comfort.
25Woe to you who are well fed now,
for you will go hungry.
Woe to you who laugh now,
for you will mourn and weep.
26Woe to you when all men speak well of you,
for that is how their fathers treated the false prophets.

Love for Enemies

27"But I tell you who hear me: Love your enemies, do good to those who hate you, **28**bless those who curse you, pray for those who mistreat you. **29**If someone strikes you on one cheek, turn to him the other also. If someone takes your cloak, do not stop him from taking your tunic. **30**Give to everyone who asks you, and if anyone takes what belongs to you, do not demand it back. **31**Do to others as you would have them do to you.

32"If you love those who love you, what credit is that to you? Even 'sinners' love those who love them. **33**And if you do good to those who are good to you, what credit is that to you? Even 'sinners' do that. **34**And if you lend to those from whom you expect repayment, what credit is that to you? Even 'sinners' lend to 'sinners,' expecting to be repaid in full. **35**But love your enemies, do good to them, and lend to them without expecting to get anything back. Then your reward will be great, and you will be sons of the Most High, because he is kind to the ungrateful and wicked. **36**Be merciful, just as your Father is merciful.

Judging Others

37"Do not judge, and you will not be judged. Do not condemn, and you will not be condemned. Forgive, and you will be forgiven. **38**Give, and it will be given to you. A good measure, pressed down, shaken together and running over, will be poured into your lap. For with the measure you use, it will be measured to you."

39He also told them this parable: "Can a blind man lead a blind man? Will they not both fall into a pit? **40**A student is not above his teacher, but everyone who is fully trained will be like his teacher.

41"Why do you look at the speck of sawdust in your brother's eye and pay no attention to the plank in your own eye? **42**How can you say to your brother, 'Brother, let me take the speck out of your eye,' when you yourself fail to see the plank in your own eye? You hypocrite, first take the plank out of your eye, and then you will see clearly to remove the speck from your brother's eye.

A Tree and Its Fruit

43"No good tree bears bad fruit, nor does a bad tree bear good fruit. **44**Each tree is recognized by its own fruit. People do not pick figs from thornbushes, or grapes from briers. **45**The good man brings good things out of the good stored up in his heart, and the evil man brings evil things out of the evil stored up in his heart. For out of the overflow of his heart his mouth speaks.

The Wise and Foolish Builders

46"Why do you call me, 'Lord, Lord,' and do not do what I say? **47**I will show you what he is like who comes to me and hears my words and puts them into practice. **48**He is like a man building a house, who dug down deep and laid the foundation on rock. When a flood came, the torrent struck that house but could not shake it, because it was well built. **49**But the one who hears my words and does not put them into practice is like a man who built a house on the ground without a foundation. The moment the torrent struck that house, it collapsed and its destruction was complete."

The Faith of the Centurion

7 When Jesus had finished saying all this in the hearing of the people, he entered Capernaum. **2**There a centurion's servant, whom his master valued highly, was sick and about to die. **3**The centurion heard of Jesus and sent some elders of the Jews to him, asking him to come and heal his servant. **4**When they came to Jesus, they pleaded earnestly with him, "This man deserves to have you do this, **5**because he loves our nation and has built our synagogue." ⁶So Jesus went with them.

He was not far from the house when the centurion sent friends to say to him: "Lord, don't trouble yourself, for I do not deserve to have you come under my roof. ⁷That is why I did not even consider myself worthy to come to you. But say the word, and my servant will be healed. ⁸For I myself am a man under authority, with soldiers under me. I tell this one, 'Go,' and he goes; and that one, 'Come,' and he comes. I say to my servant, 'Do this,' and he does it."

⁹When Jesus heard this, he was amazed at him, and turning to the crowd following him, he said, "I tell you, I have not found such great faith even in Israel." ¹⁰Then the men who had been sent returned to the house and found the servant well.

Jesus Raises a Widow's Son

¹¹Soon afterward, Jesus went to a town called Nain, and his disciples and a large crowd went along with him. ¹²As he approached the town gate, a dead person was being carried out — the only son of his mother, and she was a widow. And a large crowd from the town was with her. ¹³When the Lord saw her, his heart went out to her and he said, "Don't cry."

¹⁴Then he went up and touched the cof-

WEDNESDAY

VERSE FOR THE DAY:
Luke 6:38

AUTHOR:
Tim LaHaye

PASSAGE FOR THE DAY:
Luke 6:37–42

True Riches

NEVER settle for second-rate or selfish goals. Earl Nightingale, who probably has helped to motivate more people than any other living person, advises that people desiring success should never try to get rich. Above all, set goals for yourself that involve helping other people; the riches will follow. He has certainly captured the Biblical principle, "Give, and it will be given to you" (Luke 6:38). The richest people I know are those who have given themselves unselfishly to other people. Such motivation will affect the way you sell, cook, teach or ply your particular trade. True riches, of course, are totally unrelated to money or material reward. In fact, if a person has earned money without helping people, his money will not buy him happiness.

A perceptive real-estate friend who sold rather expensive homes observed that a big house never brought happiness. But if the people bought a big home with money they earned helping other people, they tended to enjoy that home. He expressed his homespun philosophy in these words, "Instead of being a status symbol, a home should be an expression of how much help a person has been to his fellowman." Of one thing I am sure: happy people have strong goals—and somehow these include helping other people. They can also be assured that they will never run out of people to help.

Additional Scripture Readings:
2 Corinthians 9:6–15;
Galatians 6:7–10

Go to page 88 for your next devotional reading.

fin, and those carrying it stood still. He said, "Young man, I say to you, get up!" ¹⁵The dead man sat up and began to talk, and Jesus gave him back to his mother.

¹⁶They were all filled with awe and praised God. "A great prophet has appeared among us," they said. "God has come to help his people." ¹⁷This news about Jesus spread throughout Judea[a] and the surrounding country.

Jesus and John the Baptist

¹⁸John's disciples told him about all these things. Calling two of them, ¹⁹he sent them to the Lord to ask, "Are you the one who was to come, or should we expect someone else?"

²⁰When the men came to Jesus, they said, "John the Baptist sent us to you to ask, 'Are you the one who was to come, or should we expect someone else?'"

²¹At that very time Jesus cured many who had diseases, sicknesses and evil spirits, and gave sight to many who were blind. ²²So he replied to the messengers, "Go back and report to John what you have seen and heard: The blind receive sight, the lame walk, those who have leprosy[b] are cured, the deaf hear, the dead are raised, and the good news is preached to the poor. ²³Blessed is the man who does not fall away on account of me."

²⁴After John's messengers left, Jesus began to speak to the crowd about John: "What did you go out into the desert to see? A reed swayed by the wind? ²⁵If not, what did you go out to see? A man dressed in fine clothes? No, those who wear expensive clothes and indulge in luxury are in palaces. ²⁶But what did you go out to see? A prophet? Yes, I tell you, and more than a prophet. ²⁷This is the one about whom it is written:

" 'I will send my messenger ahead of you,
    who will prepare your way before you.'[c]

²⁸I tell you, among those born of women there is no one greater than John; yet the one who is least in the kingdom of God is greater than he."

²⁹(All the people, even the tax collectors, when they heard Jesus' words, acknowledged that God's way was right, because they had been baptized by John. ³⁰But the Pharisees and experts in the law rejected God's purpose for themselves, because they had not been baptized by John.)

³¹"To what, then, can I compare the people of this generation? What are they like? ³²They are like children sitting in the marketplace and calling out to each other:

" 'We played the flute for you,
    and you did not dance;
we sang a dirge,
    and you did not cry.'

³³For John the Baptist came neither eating bread nor drinking wine, and you say, 'He has a demon.' ³⁴The Son of Man came eating and drinking, and you say, 'Here is a glutton and a drunkard, a friend of tax collectors and "sinners." ' ³⁵But wisdom is proved right by all her children."

Jesus Anointed by a Sinful Woman

³⁶Now one of the Pharisees invited Jesus to have dinner with him, so he went to the Pharisee's house and reclined at the table. ³⁷When a woman who had lived a sinful life in that town learned that Jesus was eating at the Pharisee's house, she brought an alabaster jar of perfume, ³⁸and as she stood behind him at his feet weeping, she began to wet his feet with her tears. Then she wiped them with her hair, kissed them and poured perfume on them.

³⁹When the Pharisee who had invited him saw this, he said to himself, "If this man were a prophet, he would know who is touching him and what kind of woman she is—that she is a sinner."

⁴⁰Jesus answered him, "Simon, I have something to tell you."

"Tell me, teacher," he said.

⁴¹"Two men owed money to a certain moneylender. One owed him five hundred denarii,[d] and the other fifty. ⁴²Neither of them had the money to pay him back, so he canceled the debts of both. Now which of them will love him more?"

⁴³Simon replied, "I suppose the one who had the bigger debt canceled."

"You have judged correctly," Jesus said. ⁴⁴Then he turned toward the woman and said to Simon, "Do you see this woman? I came into your house. You did not give me any water for my feet, but she wet my feet with her tears and wiped them with her hair. ⁴⁵You did not give me a kiss,

---

[a]17 Or *the land of the Jews*   [b]22 The Greek word was used for various diseases affecting the skin—not necessarily leprosy.   [c]27 Mal. 3:1   [d]41 A denarius was a coin worth about a day's wages.

but this woman, from the time I entered, has not stopped kissing my feet. ⁴⁶You did not put oil on my head, but she has poured perfume on my feet. ⁴⁷Therefore, I tell you, her many sins have been forgiven—for she loved much. But he who has been forgiven little loves little."

⁴⁸Then Jesus said to her, "Your sins are forgiven."

⁴⁹The other guests began to say among themselves, "Who is this who even forgives sins?"

THURSDAY

VERSE FOR THE DAY:
Luke 7:28

AUTHOR:
D. Stuart Briscoe

PASSAGE FOR THE DAY:
Luke 7:24–28

Be Men of Vision

[ONE] characteristic which qualified John as a real man was his vision. In describing him, Jesus had asked, "What did you go out into the desert to see? A reed swayed by the wind? . . . A man dressed in fine clothes? No . . . But what did you go out to see? A prophet? Yes, I tell you, and more than a prophet" [Luke 7:24–26].

What is a prophet? In Jesus' day a prophet was also called a seer—a person who sees. A seer looks past the immediate to the ultimate. He has been given the perspective of God himself and is able to see the meaning behind events. Unfortunately, because we are committed to the cult of immediacy, in the fast pace of our modern day we often do not realize the consequences of what we do. All we are interested in is an immediate solution to a present problem. So we need to develop the ability to see the consequences of our actions—to see past the immediate to the ultimate . . .

A seer has a vision for possibilities. He or she looks through the situation and envisions how it can glorify God, looking past people's exterior to discover what is really making them tick. The seer is a real man, the kind of gifted person we need in our families, homes, work places, and society. We moderns seem to be more concerned about quick fixes and immediacy than we are about the long-term consequences. That is why cosmetic firms are doing so well. As long as we look good we are likely to feel good about ourselves. If we look good and feel good about ourselves, nothing else matters.

Unfortunately, we've bought into a lie. What really matters is not so much whether I look or feel good, but whether I *am* good. The true seer can see *past* the cosmetic (looking good); he can see *through* the feeling good; and he can concentrate on the issues that determine whether we *are good or evil*. This was the vision of John the Baptist, and it has to be the vision of anyone who claims to be a real man.

Additional Scripture Readings:
Psalm 139:23–24; Ephesians 3:14–21

Go to page 90 for your next devotional reading.

⁵⁰Jesus said to the woman, "Your faith has saved you; go in peace."

The Parable of the Sower

8 After this, Jesus traveled about from one town and village to another, proclaiming the good news of the kingdom of God. The Twelve were with him, ²and also some women who had been cured of evil spirits and diseases: Mary (called Magdalene) from whom seven demons had come out; ³Joanna the wife of Cuza, the manager of Herod's household; Susanna; and many others. These women were helping to support them out of their own means.

⁴While a large crowd was gathering and people were coming to Jesus from town after town, he told this parable: ⁵"A farmer went out to sow his seed. As he was scattering the seed, some fell along the path; it was trampled on, and the birds of the air ate it up. ⁶Some fell on rock, and when it came up, the plants withered because they had no moisture. ⁷Other seed fell among thorns, which grew up with it and choked the plants. ⁸Still other seed fell on good soil. It came up and yielded a crop, a hundred times more than was sown."

When he said this, he called out, "He who has ears to hear, let him hear."

⁹His disciples asked him what this parable meant. ¹⁰He said, "The knowledge of the secrets of the kingdom of God has been given to you, but to others I speak in parables, so that,

" 'though seeing, they may not see;
though hearing, they may not
understand.'ᵃ

¹¹"This is the meaning of the parable: The seed is the word of God. ¹²Those along the path are the ones who hear, and then the devil comes and takes away the word from their hearts, so that they may not believe and be saved. ¹³Those on the rock are the ones who receive the word with joy when they hear it, but they have no root. They believe for a while, but in the time of testing they fall away. ¹⁴The seed that fell among thorns stands for those who hear, but as they go on their way they are choked by life's worries, riches and pleasures, and they do not mature. ¹⁵But the seed on good soil stands for those with a noble and good heart, who hear the word, retain it, and by persevering produce a crop.

A Lamp on a Stand

¹⁶"No one lights a lamp and hides it in a jar or puts it under a bed. Instead, he puts it on a stand, so that those who come in can see the light. ¹⁷For there is nothing hidden that will not be disclosed, and nothing concealed that will not be known or brought out into the open. ¹⁸Therefore consider carefully how you listen. Whoever has will be given more; whoever does not have, even what he thinks he has will be taken from him."

Jesus' Mother and Brothers

¹⁹Now Jesus' mother and brothers came to see him, but they were not able to get near him because of the crowd. ²⁰Someone told him, "Your mother and brothers are standing outside, wanting to see you."

²¹He replied, "My mother and brothers are those who hear God's word and put it into practice."

Jesus Calms the Storm

²²One day Jesus said to his disciples, "Let's go over to the other side of the lake." So they got into a boat and set out. ²³As they sailed, he fell asleep. A squall came down on the lake, so that the boat was being swamped, and they were in great danger.

²⁴The disciples went and woke him, saying, "Master, Master, we're going to drown!"

He got up and rebuked the wind and the raging waters; the storm subsided, and all was calm. ²⁵"Where is your faith?" he asked his disciples.

In fear and amazement they asked one another, "Who is this? He commands even the winds and the water, and they obey him."

The Healing of a Demon-possessed Man

²⁶They sailed to the region of the Gerasenes,ᵇ which is across the lake from Galilee. ²⁷When Jesus stepped ashore, he was met by a demon-possessed man from the town. For a long time this man had not worn clothes or lived in a house, but had lived in the tombs. ²⁸When he saw Jesus, he cried out and fell at his feet, shouting at the top of his voice, "What do you want with me, Jesus, Son of the Most High God? I beg you, don't torture me!" ²⁹For Jesus

---

ᵃ10 Isaiah 6:9   ᵇ26 Some manuscripts *Gadarenes*; other manuscripts *Gergesenes*; also in verse 37

had commanded the evil[a] spirit to come out of the man. Many times it had seized him, and though he was chained hand and foot and kept under guard, he had broken his chains and had been driven by the demon into solitary places.

³⁰Jesus asked him, "What is your name?"

"Legion," he replied, because many demons had gone into him. ³¹And they begged him repeatedly not to order them to go into the Abyss.

³²A large herd of pigs was feeding there on the hillside. The demons begged Jesus to let them go into them, and he gave them permission. ³³When the demons came out of the man, they went into the pigs, and the herd rushed down the steep bank into the lake and was drowned.

³⁴When those tending the pigs saw what had happened, they ran off and reported this in the town and countryside, ³⁵and the people went out to see what had happened. When they came to Jesus, they found the man from whom the demons had gone out, sitting at Jesus' feet, dressed and in his right mind; and they were afraid. ³⁶Those who had seen it told the people how the demon-possessed man had been cured. ³⁷Then all the peo-

[a]29 Greek *unclean*

FRIDAY

VERSE FOR THE DAY:
Luke 7:47

AUTHOR:
Philip W. Williams

PASSAGE FOR THE DAY:
Luke 7:36–50

Real Guilt, Real Grace

THERE is always some guilt when any of us loses a loved one. This isn't unusual. None of us can live close to another person and love deeply without hurting that person. We do and say things we later regret. We know they hurt our loved one.

Intimacy, closeness, is built by loving and hurting and reconciling. We can't really learn to love unless we are willing to run the risks of hurting and failing. Losing someone we love reminds us of those hurts and failings, of words we regret saying, incidents we'd like to forget, actions we'd like to take back. We feel guilty.

God has provided some beautiful resources to help us in our guilt. Church worship contains public or private confession and absolution. The Scriptures proclaim an accepting Lord who continually forgives people. This same Lord and Savior died for us in an ultimate act of forgiveness, and he rose to give us new life. He has given us the Lord's Supper to strengthen us and to reconcile us with God.

Guilt is real. The Bible shows us our guilt, but it also reveals a gracious God who forgives us. A college professor once said something that speaks to many life crises, certainly to the guilt of "if only." He said, "The greatest prayer anyone can pray is, 'Create in me a pure heart, O God, and renew a steadfast spirit within me'" [Psalm 51:10].

Additional Scripture Readings:
Psalm 51:1–12; Ephesians 1:3–10

Go to page 94 for your next devotional reading.

ple of the region of the Gerasenes asked Jesus to leave them, because they were overcome with fear. So he got into the boat and left.

38The man from whom the demons had gone out begged to go with him, but Jesus sent him away, saying, **39**"Return home and tell how much God has done for you." So the man went away and told all over town how much Jesus had done for him.

A Dead Girl and a Sick Woman

40Now when Jesus returned, a crowd welcomed him, for they were all expecting him. **41**Then a man named Jairus, a ruler of the synagogue, came and fell at Jesus' feet, pleading with him to come to his house **42**because his only daughter, a girl of about twelve, was dying.

As Jesus was on his way, the crowds almost crushed him. **43**And a woman was there who had been subject to bleeding for twelve years,*a* but no one could heal her. **44**She came up behind him and touched the edge of his cloak, and immediately her bleeding stopped.

45"Who touched me?" Jesus asked.

When they all denied it, Peter said, "Master, the people are crowding and pressing against you."

46But Jesus said, "Someone touched me; I know that power has gone out from me."

47Then the woman, seeing that she could not go unnoticed, came trembling and fell at his feet. In the presence of all the people, she told why she had touched him and how she had been instantly healed. **48**Then he said to her, "Daughter, your faith has healed you. Go in peace."

49While Jesus was still speaking, someone came from the house of Jairus, the synagogue ruler. "Your daughter is dead," he said. "Don't bother the teacher any more."

50Hearing this, Jesus said to Jairus, "Don't be afraid; just believe, and she will be healed."

51When he arrived at the house of Jairus, he did not let anyone go in with him except Peter, John and James, and the child's father and mother. **52**Meanwhile, all the people were wailing and mourning for her. "Stop wailing," Jesus said. "She is not dead but asleep."

53They laughed at him, knowing that she was dead. **54**But he took her by the hand and said, "My child, get up!" **55**Her spirit returned, and at once she stood up. Then Jesus told them to give her something to eat. **56**Her parents were astonished, but he ordered them not to tell anyone what had happened.

Jesus Sends Out the Twelve

9 When Jesus had called the Twelve together, he gave them power and authority to drive out all demons and to cure diseases, **2**and he sent them out to preach the kingdom of God and to heal the sick. **3**He told them: "Take nothing for the journey—no staff, no bag, no bread, no money, no extra tunic. **4**Whatever house you enter, stay there until you leave that town. **5**If people do not welcome you, shake the dust off your feet when you leave their town, as a testimony against them." **6**So they set out and went from village to village, preaching the gospel and healing people everywhere.

7Now Herod the tetrarch heard about all that was going on. And he was perplexed, because some were saying that John had been raised from the dead, **8**others that Elijah had appeared, and still others that one of the prophets of long ago had come back to life. **9**But Herod said, "I beheaded John. Who, then, is this I hear such things about?" And he tried to see him.

Jesus Feeds the Five Thousand

10When the apostles returned, they reported to Jesus what they had done. Then he took them with him and they withdrew by themselves to a town called Bethsaida, **11**but the crowds learned about it and followed him. He welcomed them and spoke to them about the kingdom of God, and healed those who needed healing.

12Late in the afternoon the Twelve came to him and said, "Send the crowd away so they can go to the surrounding villages and countryside and find food and lodging, because we are in a remote place here."

13He replied, "You give them something to eat."

They answered, "We have only five loaves of bread and two fish—unless we go and buy food for all this crowd." **14**(About five thousand men were there.)

But he said to his disciples, "Have them sit down in groups of about fifty each." **15**The disciples did so, and everybody sat down. **16**Taking the five loaves and the

---

a43 Many manuscripts *years, and she had spent all she had on doctors*

two fish and looking up to heaven, he gave thanks and broke them. Then he gave them to the disciples to set before the people. ¹⁷They all ate and were satisfied, and the disciples picked up twelve basketfuls of broken pieces that were left over.

Peter's Confession of Christ

¹⁸Once when Jesus was praying in private and his disciples were with him, he asked them, "Who do the crowds say I am?"

¹⁹They replied, "Some say John the Baptist; others say Elijah; and still others, that one of the prophets of long ago has come back to life."

²⁰"But what about you?" he asked. "Who do you say I am?"

Peter answered, "The Christ[a] of God."

²¹Jesus strictly warned them not to tell this to anyone. ²²And he said, "The Son of Man must suffer many things and be rejected by the elders, chief priests and teachers of the law, and he must be killed and on the third day be raised to life."

²³Then he said to them all: "If anyone would come after me, he must deny himself and take up his cross daily and follow me. ²⁴For whoever wants to save his life will lose it, but whoever loses his life for me will save it. ²⁵What good is it for a man to gain the whole world, and yet lose or forfeit his very self? ²⁶If anyone is ashamed of me and my words, the Son of Man will be ashamed of him when he comes in his glory and in the glory of the Father and of the holy angels. ²⁷I tell you the truth, some who are standing here will not taste death before they see the kingdom of God."

The Transfiguration

²⁸About eight days after Jesus said this, he took Peter, John and James with him and went up onto a mountain to pray. ²⁹As he was praying, the appearance of his face changed, and his clothes became as bright as a flash of lightning. ³⁰Two men, Moses and Elijah, ³¹appeared in glorious splendor, talking with Jesus. They spoke about his departure, which he was about to bring to fulfillment at Jerusalem. ³²Peter and his companions were very sleepy, but when they became fully awake, they saw his glory and the two men standing with him. ³³As the men were leaving Jesus, Peter said to him, "Master, it is good for us to be here. Let us put up three shelters—one for you, one for Moses and one for Elijah." (He did not know what he was saying.)

³⁴While he was speaking, a cloud appeared and enveloped them, and they were afraid as they entered the cloud. ³⁵A voice came from the cloud, saying, "This is my Son, whom I have chosen; listen to him." ³⁶When the voice had spoken, they found that Jesus was alone. The disciples kept this to themselves, and told no one at that time what they had seen.

The Healing of a Boy With an Evil Spirit

³⁷The next day, when they came down from the mountain, a large crowd met him. ³⁸A man in the crowd called out, "Teacher, I beg you to look at my son, for he is my only child. ³⁹A spirit seizes him and he suddenly screams; it throws him into convulsions so that he foams at the mouth. It scarcely ever leaves him and is destroying him. ⁴⁰I begged your disciples to drive it out, but they could not."

⁴¹"O unbelieving and perverse generation," Jesus replied, "how long shall I stay with you and put up with you? Bring your son here."

⁴²Even while the boy was coming, the demon threw him to the ground in a convulsion. But Jesus rebuked the evil[b] spirit, healed the boy and gave him back to his father. ⁴³And they were all amazed at the greatness of God.

While everyone was marveling at all that Jesus did, he said to his disciples, ⁴⁴"Listen carefully to what I am about to tell you: The Son of Man is going to be betrayed into the hands of men." ⁴⁵But they did not understand what this meant. It was hidden from them, so that they did not grasp it, and they were afraid to ask him about it.

Who Will Be the Greatest?

⁴⁶An argument started among the disciples as to which of them would be the greatest. ⁴⁷Jesus, knowing their thoughts, took a little child and had him stand beside him. ⁴⁸Then he said to them, "Whoever welcomes this little child in my name welcomes me; and whoever welcomes me welcomes the one who sent me. For he who is least among you all—he is the greatest."

⁴⁹"Master," said John, "we saw a man driving out demons in your name and we

---

a20 Or *Messiah*   *b42* Greek *unclean*

tried to stop him, because he is not one of us."

⁵⁰"Do not stop him," Jesus said, "for whoever is not against you is for you."

Samaritan Opposition

⁵¹As the time approached for him to be taken up to heaven, Jesus resolutely set out for Jerusalem. ⁵²And he sent messengers on ahead, who went into a Samaritan village to get things ready for him; ⁵³but the people there did not welcome him, because he was heading for Jerusalem. ⁵⁴When the disciples James and John saw this, they asked, "Lord, do you want us to call fire down from heaven to destroy them*a*?" ⁵⁵But Jesus turned and rebuked them, ⁵⁶and*b* they went to another village.

The Cost of Following Jesus

⁵⁷As they were walking along the road, a man said to him, "I will follow you wherever you go."

⁵⁸Jesus replied, "Foxes have holes and birds of the air have nests, but the Son of Man has no place to lay his head."

⁵⁹He said to another man, "Follow me." But the man replied, "Lord, first let me go and bury my father."

⁶⁰Jesus said to him, "Let the dead bury their own dead, but you go and proclaim the kingdom of God."

⁶¹Still another said, "I will follow you, Lord; but first let me go back and say good-by to my family."

⁶²Jesus replied, "No one who puts his hand to the plow and looks back is fit for service in the kingdom of God."

Jesus Sends Out the Seventy-two

10 After this the Lord appointed seventy-two*c* others and sent them two by two ahead of him to every town and place where he was about to go. ²He told them, "The harvest is plentiful, but the workers are few. Ask the Lord of the harvest, therefore, to send out workers into his harvest field. ³Go! I am sending you out like lambs among wolves. ⁴Do not take a purse or bag or sandals; and do not greet anyone on the road.

⁵"When you enter a house, first say, 'Peace to this house.' ⁶If a man of peace is there, your peace will rest on him; if not, it will return to you. ⁷Stay in that house, eating and drinking whatever they give you, for the worker deserves his wages. Do not move around from house to house.

⁸"When you enter a town and are welcomed, eat what is set before you. ⁹Heal the sick who are there and tell them, 'The kingdom of God is near you.' ¹⁰But when you enter a town and are not welcomed, go into its streets and say, ¹¹'Even the dust of your town that sticks to our feet we wipe off against you. Yet be sure of this: The kingdom of God is near.' ¹²I tell you, it will be more bearable on that day for Sodom than for that town.

¹³"Woe to you, Korazin! Woe to you, Bethsaida! For if the miracles that were performed in you had been performed in Tyre and Sidon, they would have repented long ago, sitting in sackcloth and ashes. ¹⁴But it will be more bearable for Tyre and Sidon at the judgment than for you. ¹⁵And you, Capernaum, will you be lifted up to the skies? No, you will go down to the depths.*d*

¹⁶"He who listens to you listens to me; he who rejects you rejects me; but he who rejects me rejects him who sent me."

¹⁷The seventy-two returned with joy and said, "Lord, even the demons submit to us in your name."

¹⁸He replied, "I saw Satan fall like lightning from heaven. ¹⁹I have given you authority to trample on snakes and scorpions and to overcome all the power of the enemy; nothing will harm you. ²⁰However, do not rejoice that the spirits submit to you, but rejoice that your names are written in heaven."

²¹At that time Jesus, full of joy through the Holy Spirit, said, "I praise you, Father, Lord of heaven and earth, because you have hidden these things from the wise and learned, and revealed them to little children. Yes, Father, for this was your good pleasure.

²²"All things have been committed to me by my Father. No one knows who the Son is except the Father, and no one knows who the Father is except the Son and those to whom the Son chooses to reveal him."

²³Then he turned to his disciples and said privately, "Blessed are the eyes that see what you see. ²⁴For I tell you that many prophets and kings wanted to see

---

a 54 Some manuscripts *them, even as Elijah did*   *b* 55,56 Some manuscripts *them. And he said, "You do not know what kind of spirit you are of, for the Son of Man did not come to destroy men's lives, but to save them."* ⁵⁶*And*   *c* 1 Some manuscripts *seventy*; also in verse 17   *d* 15 Greek *Hades*

WEEKENDING

RENEW

Help me to understand that only a few things really *are* necessary in life. And when you get right down to it, only one: to sit at your feet . . . listening . . . looking into your eyes . . . and loving you.

Thank you for the privilege of sitting at those nail-scarred feet. Grant me the grace never to regard that privilege casually, nor to neglect it, but to come there humbly, and to come there often . . . because you are worthy to be adored, O beautiful Savior . . . because you are worthy to be adored.

– *Ken Gire*

REVIVE
Saturday: Psalm 27
Sunday: Luke 10:38–42

Go to page 98 for your next devotional reading.

what you see but did not see it, and to hear what you hear but did not hear it."

The Parable of the Good Samaritan

25On one occasion an expert in the law stood up to test Jesus. "Teacher," he asked, "what must I do to inherit eternal life?"

26"What is written in the Law?" he replied. "How do you read it?"

27He answered: " 'Love the Lord your God with all your heart and with all your soul and with all your strength and with all your mind'*a*; and, 'Love your neighbor as yourself.'*b* "

28"You have answered correctly," Jesus replied. "Do this and you will live."

29But he wanted to justify himself, so he asked Jesus, "And who is my neighbor?"

30In reply Jesus said: "A man was going down from Jerusalem to Jericho, when he fell into the hands of robbers. They stripped him of his clothes, beat him and went away, leaving him half dead. **31**A priest happened to be going down the same road, and when he saw the man, he passed by on the other side. **32**So too, a Levite, when he came to the place and saw him, passed by on the other side. **33**But a Samaritan, as he traveled, came where the man was; and when he saw him, he took pity on him. **34**He went to him and bandaged his wounds, pouring on oil and wine. Then he put the man on his own donkey, took him to an inn and took care of him. **35**The next day he took out two silver coins*c* and gave them to the innkeeper. 'Look after him,' he said, 'and when I return, I will reimburse you for any extra expense you may have.'

36"Which of these three do you think was a neighbor to the man who fell into the hands of robbers?"

37The expert in the law replied, "The one who had mercy on him."

Jesus told him, "Go and do likewise."

At the Home of Martha and Mary

38As Jesus and his disciples were on their way, he came to a village where a woman named Martha opened her home to him. **39**She had a sister called Mary, who sat at the Lord's feet listening to what he said. **40**But Martha was distracted by all the preparations that had to be made. She came to him and asked, "Lord, don't you care that my sister has left me to do the work by myself? Tell her to help me!"

41"Martha, Martha," the Lord answered, "you are worried and upset about many things, **42**but only one thing is needed.*d* Mary has chosen what is better, and it will not be taken away from her."

Jesus' Teaching on Prayer

11 One day Jesus was praying in a certain place. When he finished, one of his disciples said to him, "Lord, teach us to pray, just as John taught his disciples."

2He said to them, "When you pray, say:

" 'Father,*e*
hallowed be your name,
your kingdom come.*f*
3Give us each day our daily bread.
4Forgive us our sins,
 for we also forgive everyone who
  sins against us.*g*
And lead us not into temptation.*h* ' "

5Then he said to them, "Suppose one of you has a friend, and he goes to him at midnight and says, 'Friend, lend me three loaves of bread, **6**because a friend of mine on a journey has come to me, and I have nothing to set before him.'

7"Then the one inside answers, 'Don't bother me. The door is already locked, and my children are with me in bed. I can't get up and give you anything.' **8**I tell you, though he will not get up and give him the bread because he is his friend, yet because of the man's boldness*i* he will get up and give him as much as he needs.

9"So I say to you: Ask and it will be given to you; seek and you will find; knock and the door will be opened to you. **10**For everyone who asks receives; he who seeks finds; and to him who knocks, the door will be opened.

11"Which of you fathers, if your son asks for*j* a fish, will give him a snake instead? **12**Or if he asks for an egg, will give him a scorpion? **13**If you then, though you are evil, know how to give good gifts to your children, how much more will your Father in heaven give the Holy Spirit to those who ask him!"

---

*a*27 Deut. 6:5   *b*27 Lev. 19:18   *c*35 Greek *two denarii*   *d*42 Some manuscripts *but few things are needed—or only one*   *e*2 Some manuscripts *Our Father in heaven*   *f*2 Some manuscripts *come. May your will be done on earth as it is in heaven.*   *g*4 Greek *everyone who is indebted to us*   *h*4 Some manuscripts *temptation but deliver us from the evil one*   *i*8 Or *persistence*   *j*11 Some manuscripts *for bread, will give him a stone; or if he asks for*

Jesus and Beelzebub

14Jesus was driving out a demon that was mute. When the demon left, the man who had been mute spoke, and the crowd was amazed. **15**But some of them said, "By Beelzebub,[a] the prince of demons, he is driving out demons." **16**Others tested him by asking for a sign from heaven.

17Jesus knew their thoughts and said to them: "Any kingdom divided against itself will be ruined, and a house divided against itself will fall. **18**If Satan is divided against himself, how can his kingdom stand? I say this because you claim that I drive out demons by Beelzebub. **19**Now if I drive out demons by Beelzebub, by whom do your followers drive them out? So then, they will be your judges. **20**But if I drive out demons by the finger of God, then the kingdom of God has come to you.

21"When a strong man, fully armed, guards his own house, his possessions are safe. **22**But when someone stronger attacks and overpowers him, he takes away the armor in which the man trusted and divides up the spoils.

23"He who is not with me is against me, and he who does not gather with me, scatters.

24"When an evil[b] spirit comes out of a man, it goes through arid places seeking rest and does not find it. Then it says, 'I will return to the house I left.' **25**When it arrives, it finds the house swept clean and put in order. **26**Then it goes and takes seven other spirits more wicked than itself, and they go in and live there. And the final condition of that man is worse than the first."

27As Jesus was saying these things, a woman in the crowd called out, "Blessed is the mother who gave you birth and nursed you."

28He replied, "Blessed rather are those who hear the word of God and obey it."

The Sign of Jonah

29As the crowds increased, Jesus said, "This is a wicked generation. It asks for a miraculous sign, but none will be given it except the sign of Jonah. **30**For as Jonah was a sign to the Ninevites, so also will the Son of Man be to this generation. **31**The Queen of the South will rise at the judgment with the men of this generation and condemn them; for she came from the ends of the earth to listen to Solomon's wisdom, and now one[c] greater than Solomon is here. **32**The men of Nineveh will stand up at the judgment with this generation and condemn it; for they repented at the preaching of Jonah, and now one greater than Jonah is here.

The Lamp of the Body

33"No one lights a lamp and puts it in a place where it will be hidden, or under a bowl. Instead he puts it on its stand, so that those who come in may see the light. **34**Your eye is the lamp of your body. When your eyes are good, your whole body also is full of light. But when they are bad, your body also is full of darkness. **35**See to it, then, that the light within you is not darkness. **36**Therefore, if your whole body is full of light, and no part of it dark, it will be completely lighted, as when the light of a lamp shines on you."

Six Woes

37When Jesus had finished speaking, a Pharisee invited him to eat with him; so he went in and reclined at the table. **38**But the Pharisee, noticing that Jesus did not first wash before the meal, was surprised.

39Then the Lord said to him, "Now then, you Pharisees clean the outside of the cup and dish, but inside you are full of greed and wickedness. **40**You foolish people! Did not the one who made the outside make the inside also? **41**But give what is inside the dish,[d] to the poor, and everything will be clean for you.

42"Woe to you Pharisees, because you give God a tenth of your mint, rue and all other kinds of garden herbs, but you neglect justice and the love of God. You should have practiced the latter without leaving the former undone.

43"Woe to you Pharisees, because you love the most important seats in the synagogues and greetings in the marketplaces.

44"Woe to you, because you are like unmarked graves, which men walk over without knowing it."

45One of the experts in the law answered him, "Teacher, when you say these things, you insult us also."

46Jesus replied, "And you experts in the law, woe to you, because you load people down with burdens they can hardly carry, and you yourselves will not lift one finger to help them.

---

[a] 15 Greek *Beezeboul* or *Beelzeboul*; also in verses 18 and 19   [b] 24 Greek *unclean*   [c] 31 Or *something*; also in verse 32   [d] 41 Or *what you have*

⁴⁷"Woe to you, because you build tombs for the prophets, and it was your forefathers who killed them. ⁴⁸So you testify that you approve of what your forefathers did; they killed the prophets, and you build their tombs. ⁴⁹Because of this, God in his wisdom said, 'I will send them prophets and apostles, some of whom they will kill and others they will persecute.' ⁵⁰Therefore this generation will be held responsible for the blood of all the prophets that has been shed since the beginning of the world, ⁵¹from the blood of Abel to the blood of Zechariah, who was killed between the altar and the sanctuary. Yes, I tell you, this generation will be held responsible for it all.

⁵²"Woe to you experts in the law, because you have taken away the key to knowledge. You yourselves have not entered, and you have hindered those who were entering."

⁵³When Jesus left there, the Pharisees and the teachers of the law began to oppose him fiercely and to besiege him with questions, ⁵⁴waiting to catch him in something he might say.

Warnings and Encouragements

12 Meanwhile, when a crowd of many thousands had gathered, so that they were trampling on one another, Jesus began to speak first to his disciples, saying: "Be on your guard against the yeast of the Pharisees, which is hypocrisy. ²There is nothing concealed that will not be disclosed, or hidden that will not be made known. ³What you have said in the dark will be heard in the daylight, and what you have whispered in the ear in the inner rooms will be proclaimed from the roofs.

⁴"I tell you, my friends, do not be afraid of those who kill the body and after that can do no more. ⁵But I will show you whom you should fear: Fear him who, after the killing of the body, has power to throw you into hell. Yes, I tell you, fear him. ⁶Are not five sparrows sold for two pennies*ᵃ*? Yet not one of them is forgotten by God. ⁷Indeed, the very hairs of your head are all numbered. Don't be afraid; you are worth more than many sparrows.

⁸"I tell you, whoever acknowledges me before men, the Son of Man will also acknowledge him before the angels of God. ⁹But he who disowns me before men will be disowned before the angels of God. ¹⁰And everyone who speaks a word against the Son of Man will be forgiven, but anyone who blasphemes against the Holy Spirit will not be forgiven.

¹¹"When you are brought before synagogues, rulers and authorities, do not worry about how you will defend yourselves or what you will say, ¹²for the Holy Spirit will teach you at that time what you should say."

The Parable of the Rich Fool

¹³Someone in the crowd said to him, "Teacher, tell my brother to divide the inheritance with me."

¹⁴Jesus replied, "Man, who appointed me a judge or an arbiter between you?" ¹⁵Then he said to them, "Watch out! Be on your guard against all kinds of greed; a man's life does not consist in the abundance of his possessions."

¹⁶And he told them this parable: "The ground of a certain rich man produced a good crop. ¹⁷He thought to himself, 'What shall I do? I have no place to store my crops.'

¹⁸"Then he said, 'This is what I'll do. I will tear down my barns and build bigger ones, and there I will store all my grain and my goods. ¹⁹And I'll say to myself, "You have plenty of good things laid up for many years. Take life easy; eat, drink and be merry." '

²⁰"But God said to him, 'You fool! This very night your life will be demanded from you. Then who will get what you have prepared for yourself?'

²¹"This is how it will be with anyone who stores up things for himself but is not rich toward God."

Do Not Worry

²²Then Jesus said to his disciples: "Therefore I tell you, do not worry about your life, what you will eat; or about your body, what you will wear. ²³Life is more than food, and the body more than clothes. ²⁴Consider the ravens: They do not sow or reap, they have no storeroom or barn; yet God feeds them. And how much more valuable you are than birds! ²⁵Who of you by worrying can add a single hour to his life*ᵇ*? ²⁶Since you cannot do this very little thing, why do you worry about the rest?

²⁷"Consider how the lilies grow. They do not labor or spin. Yet I tell you, not even Solomon in all his splendor was

---

ᵃ6 Greek *two assaria*   *ᵇ25* Or *single cubit to his height* dressed like one of these. **28**If that is how God clothes the grass of the field, which is here today, and tomorrow is thrown into the fire, how much more will he clothe you, O you of little faith! **29**And do not set your heart on what you will eat or drink; do not worry about it. **30**For the pagan world runs after all such things, and your Father knows that you need them. **31**But seek his kingdom, and these things will be given to you as well.

32"Do not be afraid, little flock, for your Father has been pleased to give you the kingdom. **33**Sell your possessions and give to the poor. Provide purses for yourselves that will not wear out, a treasure in heaven that will not be exhausted, where no thief comes near and no moth destroys. **34**For where your treasure is, there your heart will be also.

Watchfulness

35"Be dressed ready for service and keep your lamps burning, **36**like men wait-

---

MONDAY

VERSE FOR THE DAY:
Luke 12:15

AUTHOR:
Ron Blue

PASSAGE FOR THE DAY:
Luke 12:13–21

Needs, or Greeds?

PROVERBS 22:7 says, "The rich rule over the poor, and the borrower is servant to the lender." Anyone who has borrowed or been in bondage to debt knows the truth of this verse. The reality is that whenever you have borrowed from anyone, you are a servant to that person. This verse does not prohibit debt, of course, but it certainly cautions against the use of debt. We could say that anyone who uses debt for any purpose, at the very least, is not using Biblical wisdom and, in fact, may be a "fool." Again, a great caution, but not a prohibition, against debt.

1 Timothy 5:8 says, "If anyone does not provide for his relatives, and especially for his immediate family, he has denied the faith and is worse than an unbeliever." The underlying Biblical principle relative to debt in this verse is that by taking on debt you may run the risk of not providing for your own. Because debt mortgages the future and because the negative compound of debt works against you, you may very well end up in the future not providing for your own. Therefore, this verse says that you have denied the faith and are worse than an unbeliever. Obviously, the danger is great and needs to be avoided.

Luke 12:15 says, "Watch out! Be on your guard against all kinds of greed; a man's life does not consist in the abundance of his possessions." The caution in this verse is clear: "Beware, and be on your guard against *every form of greed*." Debt makes it very easy to fund greeds; yet in doing so, we may violate the Biblical principle set forth in this verse. The question to ask is, "Am I funding my *needs* or my *greeds?*"

Additional Scripture Readings:
Matthew 6:28–34; James 4:1–6

Go to page 104 for your next devotional reading.

ing for their master to return from a wedding banquet, so that when he comes and knocks they can immediately open the door for him. ³⁷It will be good for those servants whose master finds them watching when he comes. I tell you the truth, he will dress himself to serve, will have them recline at the table and will come and wait on them. ³⁸It will be good for those servants whose master finds them ready, even if he comes in the second or third watch of the night. ³⁹But understand this: If the owner of the house had known at what hour the thief was coming, he would not have let his house be broken into. ⁴⁰You also must be ready, because the Son of Man will come at an hour when you do not expect him."

⁴¹Peter asked, "Lord, are you telling this parable to us, or to everyone?"

⁴²The Lord answered, "Who then is the faithful and wise manager, whom the master puts in charge of his servants to give them their food allowance at the proper time? ⁴³It will be good for that servant whom the master finds doing so when he returns. ⁴⁴I tell you the truth, he will put him in charge of all his possessions. ⁴⁵But suppose the servant says to himself, 'My master is taking a long time in coming,' and he then begins to beat the menservants and maidservants and to eat and drink and get drunk. ⁴⁶The master of that servant will come on a day when he does not expect him and at an hour he is not aware of. He will cut him to pieces and assign him a place with the unbelievers.

⁴⁷"That servant who knows his master's will and does not get ready or does not do what his master wants will be beaten with many blows. ⁴⁸But the one who does not know and does things deserving punishment will be beaten with few blows. From everyone who has been given much, much will be demanded; and from the one who has been entrusted with much, much more will be asked.

Not Peace but Division

⁴⁹"I have come to bring fire on the earth, and how I wish it were already kindled! ⁵⁰But I have a baptism to undergo, and how distressed I am until it is completed! ⁵¹Do you think I came to bring peace on earth? No, I tell you, but division. ⁵²From now on there will be five in one family divided against each other, three against two and two against three. ⁵³They will be divided, father against son and son against father, mother against daughter and daughter against mother, mother-in-law against daughter-in-law and daughter-in-law against mother-in-law."

Interpreting the Times

⁵⁴He said to the crowd: "When you see a cloud rising in the west, immediately you say, 'It's going to rain,' and it does. ⁵⁵And when the south wind blows, you say, 'It's going to be hot,' and it is. ⁵⁶Hypocrites! You know how to interpret the appearance of the earth and the sky. How is it that you don't know how to interpret this present time?

⁵⁷"Why don't you judge for yourselves what is right? ⁵⁸As you are going with your adversary to the magistrate, try hard to be reconciled to him on the way, or he may drag you off to the judge, and the judge turn you over to the officer, and the officer throw you into prison. ⁵⁹I tell you, you will not get out until you have paid the last penny.ᵃ"

Repent or Perish

13 Now there were some present at that time who told Jesus about the Galileans whose blood Pilate had mixed with their sacrifices. ²Jesus answered, "Do you think that these Galileans were worse sinners than all the other Galileans because they suffered this way? ³I tell you, no! But unless you repent, you too will all perish. ⁴Or those eighteen who died when the tower in Siloam fell on them—do you think they were more guilty than all the others living in Jerusalem? ⁵I tell you, no! But unless you repent, you too will all perish."

⁶Then he told this parable: "A man had a fig tree, planted in his vineyard, and he went to look for fruit on it, but did not find any. ⁷So he said to the man who took care of the vineyard, 'For three years now I've been coming to look for fruit on this fig tree and haven't found any. Cut it down! Why should it use up the soil?'

⁸" 'Sir,' the man replied, 'leave it alone for one more year, and I'll dig around it and fertilize it. ⁹If it bears fruit next year, fine! If not, then cut it down.' "

A Crippled Woman Healed on the Sabbath

¹⁰On a Sabbath Jesus was teaching in

ᵃ59 Greek *lepton*

one of the synagogues, ¹¹and a woman was there who had been crippled by a spirit for eighteen years. She was bent over and could not straighten up at all. ¹²When Jesus saw her, he called her forward and said to her, "Woman, you are set free from your infirmity." ¹³Then he put his hands on her, and immediately she straightened up and praised God.

¹⁴Indignant because Jesus had healed on the Sabbath, the synagogue ruler said to the people, "There are six days for work. So come and be healed on those days, not on the Sabbath."

¹⁵The Lord answered him, "You hypocrites! Doesn't each of you on the Sabbath untie his ox or donkey from the stall and lead it out to give it water? ¹⁶Then should not this woman, a daughter of Abraham, whom Satan has kept bound for eighteen long years, be set free on the Sabbath day from what bound her?"

¹⁷When he said this, all his opponents were humiliated, but the people were delighted with all the wonderful things he was doing.

The Parables of the Mustard Seed and the Yeast

¹⁸Then Jesus asked, "What is the kingdom of God like? What shall I compare it to? ¹⁹It is like a mustard seed, which a man took and planted in his garden. It grew and became a tree, and the birds of the air perched in its branches."

²⁰Again he asked, "What shall I compare the kingdom of God to? ²¹It is like yeast that a woman took and mixed into a large amount[a] of flour until it worked all through the dough."

The Narrow Door

²²Then Jesus went through the towns and villages, teaching as he made his way to Jerusalem. ²³Someone asked him, "Lord, are only a few people going to be saved?"

He said to them, ²⁴"Make every effort to enter through the narrow door, because many, I tell you, will try to enter and will not be able to. ²⁵Once the owner of the house gets up and closes the door, you will stand outside knocking and pleading, 'Sir, open the door for us.'

"But he will answer, 'I don't know you or where you come from.'

²⁶"Then you will say, 'We ate and drank with you, and you taught in our streets.'

²⁷"But he will reply, 'I don't know you or where you come from. Away from me, all you evildoers!'

²⁸"There will be weeping there, and gnashing of teeth, when you see Abraham, Isaac and Jacob and all the prophets in the kingdom of God, but you yourselves thrown out. ²⁹People will come from east and west and north and south, and will take their places at the feast in the kingdom of God. ³⁰Indeed there are those who are last who will be first, and first who will be last."

Jesus' Sorrow for Jerusalem

³¹At that time some Pharisees came to Jesus and said to him, "Leave this place and go somewhere else. Herod wants to kill you."

³²He replied, "Go tell that fox, 'I will drive out demons and heal people today and tomorrow, and on the third day I will reach my goal.' ³³In any case, I must keep going today and tomorrow and the next day—for surely no prophet can die outside Jerusalem!

³⁴"O Jerusalem, Jerusalem, you who kill the prophets and stone those sent to you, how often I have longed to gather your children together, as a hen gathers her chicks under her wings, but you were not willing! ³⁵Look, your house is left to you desolate. I tell you, you will not see me again until you say, 'Blessed is he who comes in the name of the Lord.'[b]"

Jesus at a Pharisee's House

14 One Sabbath, when Jesus went to eat in the house of a prominent Pharisee, he was being carefully watched. ²There in front of him was a man suffering from dropsy. ³Jesus asked the Pharisees and experts in the law, "Is it lawful to heal on the Sabbath or not?" ⁴But they remained silent. So taking hold of the man, he healed him and sent him away.

⁵Then he asked them, "If one of you has a son[c] or an ox that falls into a well on the Sabbath day, will you not immediately pull him out?" ⁶And they had nothing to say.

⁷When he noticed how the guests picked the places of honor at the table, he told them this parable: ⁸"When someone invites you to a wedding feast, do not take the place of honor, for a person more dis-

---

[a]21 Greek *three satas* (probably about 1/2 bushel or 22 liters)   [b]35 Psalm 118:26   [c]5 Some manuscripts *donkey*

tinguished than you may have been invited. **9**If so, the host who invited both of you will come and say to you, 'Give this man your seat.' Then, humiliated, you will have to take the least important place. **10**But when you are invited, take the lowest place, so that when your host comes, he will say to you, 'Friend, move up to a better place.' Then you will be honored in the presence of all your fellow guests. **11**For everyone who exalts himself will be humbled, and he who humbles himself will be exalted."

12Then Jesus said to his host, "When you give a luncheon or dinner, do not invite your friends, your brothers or relatives, or your rich neighbors; if you do, they may invite you back and so you will be repaid. **13**But when you give a banquet, invite the poor, the crippled, the lame, the blind, **14**and you will be blessed. Although they cannot repay you, you will be repaid at the resurrection of the righteous."

The Parable of the Great Banquet

15When one of those at the table with him heard this, he said to Jesus, "Blessed is the man who will eat at the feast in the kingdom of God."

16Jesus replied: "A certain man was preparing a great banquet and invited many guests. **17**At the time of the banquet he sent his servant to tell those who had been invited, 'Come, for everything is now ready.'

18"But they all alike began to make excuses. The first said, 'I have just bought a field, and I must go and see it. Please excuse me.'

19"Another said, 'I have just bought five yoke of oxen, and I'm on my way to try them out. Please excuse me.'

20"Still another said, 'I just got married, so I can't come.'

21"The servant came back and reported this to his master. Then the owner of the house became angry and ordered his servant, 'Go out quickly into the streets and alleys of the town and bring in the poor, the crippled, the blind and the lame.'

22" 'Sir,' the servant said, 'what you ordered has been done, but there is still room.'

23"Then the master told his servant, 'Go out to the roads and country lanes and make them come in, so that my house will be full. **24**I tell you, not one of those men who were invited will get a taste of my banquet.' "

The Cost of Being a Disciple

25Large crowds were traveling with Jesus, and turning to them he said: **26**"If anyone comes to me and does not hate his father and mother, his wife and children, his brothers and sisters—yes, even his own life—he cannot be my disciple. **27**And anyone who does not carry his cross and follow me cannot be my disciple.

28"Suppose one of you wants to build a tower. Will he not first sit down and estimate the cost to see if he has enough money to complete it? **29**For if he lays the foundation and is not able to finish it, everyone who sees it will ridicule him, **30**saying, 'This fellow began to build and was not able to finish.'

31"Or suppose a king is about to go to war against another king. Will he not first sit down and consider whether he is able with ten thousand men to oppose the one coming against him with twenty thousand? **32**If he is not able, he will send a delegation while the other is still a long way off and will ask for terms of peace. **33**In the same way, any of you who does not give up everything he has cannot be my disciple.

34"Salt is good, but if it loses its saltiness, how can it be made salty again? **35**It is fit neither for the soil nor for the manure pile; it is thrown out.

"He who has ears to hear, let him hear."

The Parable of the Lost Sheep

15 Now the tax collectors and "sinners" were all gathering around to hear him. **2**But the Pharisees and the teachers of the law muttered, "This man welcomes sinners and eats with them."

3Then Jesus told them this parable: **4**"Suppose one of you has a hundred sheep and loses one of them. Does he not leave the ninety-nine in the open country and go after the lost sheep until he finds it? **5**And when he finds it, he joyfully puts it on his shoulders **6**and goes home. Then he calls his friends and neighbors together and says, 'Rejoice with me; I have found my lost sheep.' **7**I tell you that in the same way there will be more rejoicing in heaven over one sinner who repents than over ninety-nine righteous persons who do not need to repent.

The Parable of the Lost Coin

8"Or suppose a woman has ten silver

coins[a] and loses one. Does she not light a lamp, sweep the house and search carefully until she finds it? ⁹And when she finds it, she calls her friends and neighbors together and says, 'Rejoice with me; I have found my lost coin.' ¹⁰In the same way, I tell you, there is rejoicing in the presence of the angels of God over one sinner who repents."

The Parable of the Lost Son

¹¹Jesus continued: "There was a man who had two sons. ¹²The younger one said to his father, 'Father, give me my share of the estate.' So he divided his property between them.

¹³"Not long after that, the younger son got together all he had, set off for a distant country and there squandered his wealth in wild living. ¹⁴After he had spent everything, there was a severe famine in that whole country, and he began to be in need. ¹⁵So he went and hired himself out to a citizen of that country, who sent him to his fields to feed pigs. ¹⁶He longed to fill his stomach with the pods that the pigs were eating, but no one gave him anything.

¹⁷"When he came to his senses, he said, 'How many of my father's hired men have food to spare, and here I am starving to death! ¹⁸I will set out and go back to my father and say to him: Father, I have sinned against heaven and against you. ¹⁹I am no longer worthy to be called your son; make me like one of your hired men.' ²⁰So he got up and went to his father.

"But while he was still a long way off, his father saw him and was filled with compassion for him; he ran to his son, threw his arms around him and kissed him.

²¹"The son said to him, 'Father, I have sinned against heaven and against you. I am no longer worthy to be called your son.[b]'

²²"But the father said to his servants, 'Quick! Bring the best robe and put it on him. Put a ring on his finger and sandals on his feet. ²³Bring the fattened calf and kill it. Let's have a feast and celebrate. ²⁴For this son of mine was dead and is alive again; he was lost and is found.' So they began to celebrate.

²⁵"Meanwhile, the older son was in the field. When he came near the house, he heard music and dancing. ²⁶So he called one of the servants and asked him what was going on. ²⁷'Your brother has come,' he replied, 'and your father has killed the fattened calf because he has him back safe and sound.'

²⁸"The older brother became angry and refused to go in. So his father went out and pleaded with him. ²⁹But he answered his father, 'Look! All these years I've been slaving for you and never disobeyed your orders. Yet you never gave me even a young goat so I could celebrate with my friends. ³⁰But when this son of yours who has squandered your property with prostitutes comes home, you kill the fattened calf for him!'

³¹" 'My son,' the father said, 'you are always with me, and everything I have is yours. ³²But we had to celebrate and be glad, because this brother of yours was dead and is alive again; he was lost and is found.' "

The Parable of the Shrewd Manager

16 Jesus told his disciples: "There was a rich man whose manager was accused of wasting his possessions. ²So he called him in and asked him, 'What is this I hear about you? Give an account of your management, because you cannot be manager any longer.'

³"The manager said to himself, 'What shall I do now? My master is taking away my job. I'm not strong enough to dig, and I'm ashamed to beg— ⁴I know what I'll do so that, when I lose my job here, people will welcome me into their houses.'

⁵"So he called in each one of his master's debtors. He asked the first, 'How much do you owe my master?'

⁶" 'Eight hundred gallons[c] of olive oil,' he replied.

"The manager told him, 'Take your bill, sit down quickly, and make it four hundred.'

⁷"Then he asked the second, 'And how much do you owe?'

" 'A thousand bushels[d] of wheat,' he replied.

"He told him, 'Take your bill and make it eight hundred.'

⁸"The master commended the dishonest manager because he had acted shrewdly. For the people of this world are more shrewd in dealing with their own

---

[a] 8 Greek *ten drachmas*, each worth about a day's wages   [b] 21 Some early manuscripts *son. Make me like one of your hired men.*   [c] 6 Greek *one hundred batous* (probably about 3 kiloliters)   [d] 7 Greek *one hundred korous* (probably about 35 kiloliters)

kind than are the people of the light. ⁹I tell you, use worldly wealth to gain friends for yourselves, so that when it is gone, you will be welcomed into eternal dwellings.

¹⁰"Whoever can be trusted with very little can also be trusted with much, and whoever is dishonest with very little will also be dishonest with much. ¹¹So if you have not been trustworthy in handling worldly wealth, who will trust you with true riches? ¹²And if you have not been trustworthy with someone else's property, who will give you property of your own?

¹³"No servant can serve two masters. Either he will hate the one and love the other, or he will be devoted to the one and despise the other. You cannot serve both God and Money."

¹⁴The Pharisees, who loved money, heard all this and were sneering at Jesus. ¹⁵He said to them, "You are the ones who justify yourselves in the eyes of men, but God knows your hearts. What is highly valued among men is detestable in God's sight.

Additional Teachings

¹⁶"The Law and the Prophets were proclaimed until John. Since that time, the good news of the kingdom of God is being preached, and everyone is forcing his way into it. ¹⁷It is easier for heaven and earth to disappear than for the least stroke of a pen to drop out of the Law.

¹⁸"Anyone who divorces his wife and marries another woman commits adultery, and the man who marries a divorced woman commits adultery.

The Rich Man and Lazarus

¹⁹"There was a rich man who was dressed in purple and fine linen and lived in luxury every day. ²⁰At his gate was laid a beggar named Lazarus, covered with sores ²¹and longing to eat what fell from the rich man's table. Even the dogs came and licked his sores.

²²"The time came when the beggar died and the angels carried him to Abraham's side. The rich man also died and was buried. ²³In hell,ᵃ where he was in torment, he looked up and saw Abraham far away, with Lazarus by his side. ²⁴So he called to him, 'Father Abraham, have pity on me and send Lazarus to dip the tip of his finger in water and cool my tongue, because I am in agony in this fire.'

²⁵"But Abraham replied, 'Son, remember that in your lifetime you received your good things, while Lazarus received bad things, but now he is comforted here and you are in agony. ²⁶And besides all this, between us and you a great chasm has been fixed, so that those who want to go from here to you cannot, nor can anyone cross over from there to us.'

²⁷"He answered, 'Then I beg you, father, send Lazarus to my father's house, ²⁸for I have five brothers. Let him warn them, so that they will not also come to this place of torment.'

²⁹"Abraham replied, 'They have Moses and the Prophets; let them listen to them.'

³⁰" 'No, father Abraham,' he said, 'but if someone from the dead goes to them, they will repent.'

³¹"He said to him, 'If they do not listen to Moses and the Prophets, they will not be convinced even if someone rises from the dead.' "

Sin, Faith, Duty

17 Jesus said to his disciples: "Things that cause people to sin are bound to come, but woe to that person through whom they come. ²It would be better for him to be thrown into the sea with a millstone tied around his neck than for him to cause one of these little ones to sin. ³So watch yourselves.

"If your brother sins, rebuke him, and if he repents, forgive him. ⁴If he sins against you seven times in a day, and seven times comes back to you and says, 'I repent,' forgive him."

⁵The apostles said to the Lord, "Increase our faith!"

⁶He replied, "If you have faith as small as a mustard seed, you can say to this mulberry tree, 'Be uprooted and planted in the sea,' and it will obey you.

⁷"Suppose one of you had a servant plowing or looking after the sheep. Would he say to the servant when he comes in from the field, 'Come along now and sit down to eat'? ⁸Would he not rather say, 'Prepare my supper, get yourself ready and wait on me while I eat and drink; after that you may eat and drink'? ⁹Would he thank the servant because he did what he was told to do? ¹⁰So you also, when you have done everything you were told to do, should say, 'We are unworthy servants; we have only done our duty.' "

ᵃ*23* Greek *Hades*

TUESDAY

VERSE FOR THE DAY:
Luke 16:9

AUTHOR:
Bill Hybels

PASSAGE FOR THE DAY:
Luke 16:1–13

A Most Unusual Reaction

IN LUKE 16:1–9 Jesus tells a parable so unusual that many teachers would rather turn the page and go on than try to understand it. It is the parable of a crooked accountant (traditionally, an "unjust steward") who used creative bookkeeping techniques. His boss eventually caught on and decided to give him his termination notice. But while the accountant still had a few days left to work, he said to himself, "I have a problem. I'm going to lose my steady paycheck. I'm too old to dig ditches and too proud to panhandle. I'm going to have to solve this somehow."

So the accountant did an unethical but ingenious thing: he called some of the people who owed his boss money. "How much do you owe us?" he asked.

One man answered, "A hundred measures of wheat."

"I'll tell you what," the accountant said. "Change your copy of the invoice, and I'll change mine. Put down that you owe us only fifty measures."

"Well, thanks," said the man. "That's a very nice thing for you to do. If you ever need a favor, call me up."

"Don't worry," said the accountant, "I will." Then he called another debtor, and another, and repeated his generous offer.

What was the crooked accountant doing? Plainly, the man was using the company's capital to build up a reserve of personal favors so that when he lost his job he would be able to find another one. His boss quickly saw what he was doing, too, and he had a most unusual reaction—he praised his accountant's ingenuity and shrewdness!

Now neither Jesus nor the boss ever praised deceitfulness, dishonesty or creative bookkeeping. But both of them recognized the accountant's vision. When faced with a serious problem, he did not hide, blame somebody, run to the bottle or jump off a cliff. Instead, he faced his problem and came up with a shrewd way to solve it. Jesus commended him because, as soon as he saw his problem, he became solution oriented.

Additional Scripture Readings:
Matthew 10:5–16;
Philippians 4:10–13

Go to page 107 for your next devotional reading.

Ten Healed of Leprosy

11Now on his way to Jerusalem, Jesus traveled along the border between Samaria and Galilee. **12**As he was going into a village, ten men who had leprosy*a* met him. They stood at a distance **13**and called out in a loud voice, "Jesus, Master, have pity on us!"

14When he saw them, he said, "Go, show yourselves to the priests." And as they went, they were cleansed.

15One of them, when he saw he was healed, came back, praising God in a loud voice. **16**He threw himself at Jesus' feet and thanked him — and he was a Samaritan.

17Jesus asked, "Were not all ten cleansed? Where are the other nine? **18**Was no one found to return and give praise to God except this foreigner?" **19**Then he said to him, "Rise and go; your faith has made you well."

The Coming of the Kingdom of God

20Once, having been asked by the Pharisees when the kingdom of God would come, Jesus replied, "The kingdom of God does not come with your careful observation, **21**nor will people say, 'Here it is,' or 'There it is,' because the kingdom of God is within*b* you."

22Then he said to his disciples, "The time is coming when you will long to see one of the days of the Son of Man, but you will not see it. **23**Men will tell you, 'There he is!' or 'Here he is!' Do not go running off after them. **24**For the Son of Man in his day*c* will be like the lightning, which flashes and lights up the sky from one end to the other. **25**But first he must suffer many things and be rejected by this generation.

26"Just as it was in the days of Noah, so also will it be in the days of the Son of Man. **27**People were eating, drinking, marrying and being given in marriage up to the day Noah entered the ark. Then the flood came and destroyed them all.

28"It was the same in the days of Lot. People were eating and drinking, buying and selling, planting and building. **29**But the day Lot left Sodom, fire and sulfur rained down from heaven and destroyed them all.

30"It will be just like this on the day the Son of Man is revealed. **31**On that day no one who is on the roof of his house, with his goods inside, should go down to get them. Likewise, no one in the field should go back for anything. **32**Remember Lot's wife! **33**Whoever tries to keep his life will lose it, and whoever loses his life will preserve it. **34**I tell you, on that night two people will be in one bed; one will be taken and the other left. **35**Two women will be grinding grain together; one will be taken and the other left.*d*"

37"Where, Lord?" they asked.

He replied, "Where there is a dead body, there the vultures will gather."

The Parable of the Persistent Widow

18 Then Jesus told his disciples a parable to show them that they should always pray and not give up. **2**He said: "In a certain town there was a judge who neither feared God nor cared about men. **3**And there was a widow in that town who kept coming to him with the plea, 'Grant me justice against my adversary.'

4"For some time he refused. But finally he said to himself, 'Even though I don't fear God or care about men, **5**yet because this widow keeps bothering me, I will see that she gets justice, so that she won't eventually wear me out with her coming!'"

6And the Lord said, "Listen to what the unjust judge says. **7**And will not God bring about justice for his chosen ones, who cry out to him day and night? Will he keep putting them off? **8**I tell you, he will see that they get justice, and quickly. However, when the Son of Man comes, will he find faith on the earth?"

The Parable of the Pharisee and the Tax Collector

9To some who were confident of their own righteousness and looked down on everybody else, Jesus told this parable: **10**"Two men went up to the temple to pray, one a Pharisee and the other a tax collector. **11**The Pharisee stood up and prayed about*e* himself: 'God, I thank you that I am not like other men — robbers, evildoers, adulterers — or even like this tax collector. **12**I fast twice a week and give a tenth of all I get.'

13"But the tax collector stood at a distance. He would not even look up to heav-

---

*a*12 The Greek word was used for various diseases affecting the skin — not necessarily leprosy.   *b*21 Or among   *c*24 Some manuscripts do not have *in his day.*   *d*35 Some manuscripts *left. 36Two men will be in the field; one will be taken and the other left.*   *e*11 Or to

en, but beat his breast and said, 'God, have mercy on me, a sinner.'

¹⁴"I tell you that this man, rather than the other, went home justified before God. For everyone who exalts himself will be humbled, and he who humbles himself will be exalted."

The Little Children and Jesus

¹⁵People were also bringing babies to Jesus to have him touch them. When the disciples saw this, they rebuked them. ¹⁶But Jesus called the children to him and said, "Let the little children come to me, and do not hinder them, for the kingdom of God belongs to such as these. ¹⁷I tell you the truth, anyone who will not receive the kingdom of God like a little child will never enter it."

The Rich Ruler

¹⁸A certain ruler asked him, "Good teacher, what must I do to inherit eternal life?"

¹⁹"Why do you call me good?" Jesus answered. "No one is good—except God alone. ²⁰You know the commandments: 'Do not commit adultery, do not murder, do not steal, do not give false testimony, honor your father and mother.'[a]"

²¹"All these I have kept since I was a boy," he said.

²²When Jesus heard this, he said to him, "You still lack one thing. Sell everything you have and give to the poor, and you will have treasure in heaven. Then come, follow me."

²³When he heard this, he became very sad, because he was a man of great wealth. ²⁴Jesus looked at him and said, "How hard it is for the rich to enter the kingdom of God! ²⁵Indeed, it is easier for a camel to go through the eye of a needle than for a rich man to enter the kingdom of God."

²⁶Those who heard this asked, "Who then can be saved?"

²⁷Jesus replied, "What is impossible with men is possible with God."

²⁸Peter said to him, "We have left all we had to follow you!"

²⁹"I tell you the truth," Jesus said to them, "no one who has left home or wife or brothers or parents or children for the sake of the kingdom of God ³⁰will fail to receive many times as much in this age and, in the age to come, eternal life."

Jesus Again Predicts His Death

³¹Jesus took the Twelve aside and told them, "We are going up to Jerusalem, and everything that is written by the prophets about the Son of Man will be fulfilled. ³²He will be handed over to the Gentiles. They will mock him, insult him, spit on him, flog him and kill him. ³³On the third day he will rise again."

³⁴The disciples did not understand any of this. Its meaning was hidden from them, and they did not know what he was talking about.

A Blind Beggar Receives His Sight

³⁵As Jesus approached Jericho, a blind man was sitting by the roadside begging. ³⁶When he heard the crowd going by, he asked what was happening. ³⁷They told him, "Jesus of Nazareth is passing by."

³⁸He called out, "Jesus, Son of David, have mercy on me!"

³⁹Those who led the way rebuked him and told him to be quiet, but he shouted all the more, "Son of David, have mercy on me!"

⁴⁰Jesus stopped and ordered the man to be brought to him. When he came near, Jesus asked him, ⁴¹"What do you want me to do for you?"

"Lord, I want to see," he replied.

⁴²Jesus said to him, "Receive your sight; your faith has healed you." ⁴³Immediately he received his sight and followed Jesus, praising God. When all the people saw it, they also praised God.

Zacchaeus the Tax Collector

19 Jesus entered Jericho and was passing through. ²A man was there by the name of Zacchaeus; he was a chief tax collector and was wealthy. ³He wanted to see who Jesus was, but being a short man he could not, because of the crowd. ⁴So he ran ahead and climbed a sycamore-fig tree to see him, since Jesus was coming that way.

⁵When Jesus reached the spot, he looked up and said to him, "Zacchaeus, come down immediately. I must stay at your house today." ⁶So he came down at once and welcomed him gladly.

⁷All the people saw this and began to mutter, "He has gone to be the guest of a 'sinner.' "

⁸But Zacchaeus stood up and said to the Lord, "Look, Lord! Here and now I give

---

a 20 Exodus 20:12-16; Deut. 5:16-20

half of my possessions to the poor, and if I have cheated anybody out of anything, I will pay back four times the amount."

⁹Jesus said to him, "Today salvation has come to this house, because this man, too, is a son of Abraham. ¹⁰For the Son of Man came to seek and to save what was lost."

The Parable of the Ten Minas

¹¹While they were listening to this, he went on to tell them a parable, because he was near Jerusalem and the people thought that the kingdom of God was going to appear at once. ¹²He said: "A man of noble birth went to a distant country to

---

WEDNESDAY

VERSE FOR THE DAY:
Luke 18:22

AUTHOR:
Thomas Hale

PASSAGE FOR THE DAY:
Luke 18:18–30

Dim Lights, Glittering Goods

IT IS hard for friends back home to appreciate just how rich even the poorest missionaries are compared with those around them. Our light is dimmed by the glitter of our goods. We are asked every day for a shirt, money, a tin can, a pair of old shoes, food. If we give to them who ask, we have "rice Christians" and a bigger crowd at our door the next day. If we say no, we feel uneasy because we know full well there are seven shirts in the closet we don't really need. The solution for some has been to sell all and live at the level of their neighbors. The rest of us have managed to strike a compromise between that ideal and what we euphemistically call practicality. I am not implying that we are all called to possess nothing, but I am suggesting that if we did, it would help clarify many of Jesus' sayings pertaining not only to poverty but also to discipleship. We can transform everything Jesus said into symbols and metaphors or we can qualify it into thin air; however, in the end the words remain, "Give to the one who asks you, and do not turn away from the one who wants to borrow from you" (Matthew 5:42); "sell everything you have and give to the poor . . . Then come, follow me" (Mark 10:21).

Surely there is a clue here as to how we might remove the barrier between our wealth and their poverty, a barrier that obscures our Christian testimony. Yet in our experience, problems more basic than wealth affect our Christian testimony. Before worrying ourselves over how many shirts to give and how many to keep, we should make sure we are in a place where we can hear what God is saying to us and that we would be willing to "sell everything" if he told us to. If we have really died to self and aren't just kidding ourselves, and if the compassion of Christ is discernible in our lives, then the number of shirts we give and keep is no longer so important, and the barriers created by our wealth largely disappear.

Additional Scripture Readings:
Matthew 5:38–42; Romans 6:1–14

Go to page 109 for your next devotional reading.

have himself appointed king and then to return. ¹³So he called ten of his servants and gave them ten minas.[a] 'Put this money to work,' he said, 'until I come back.'

¹⁴"But his subjects hated him and sent a delegation after him to say, 'We don't want this man to be our king.'

¹⁵"He was made king, however, and returned home. Then he sent for the servants to whom he had given the money, in order to find out what they had gained with it.

¹⁶"The first one came and said, 'Sir, your mina has earned ten more.'

¹⁷" 'Well done, my good servant!' his master replied. 'Because you have been trustworthy in a very small matter, take charge of ten cities.'

¹⁸"The second came and said, 'Sir, your mina has earned five more.'

¹⁹"His master answered, 'You take charge of five cities.'

²⁰"Then another servant came and said, 'Sir, here is your mina; I have kept it laid away in a piece of cloth. ²¹I was afraid of you, because you are a hard man. You take out what you did not put in and reap what you did not sow.'

²²"His master replied, 'I will judge you by your own words, you wicked servant! You knew, did you, that I am a hard man, taking out what I did not put in, and reaping what I did not sow? ²³Why then didn't you put my money on deposit, so that when I came back, I could have collected it with interest?'

²⁴"Then he said to those standing by, 'Take his mina away from him and give it to the one who has ten minas.'

²⁵" 'Sir,' they said, 'he already has ten!'

²⁶"He replied, 'I tell you that to everyone who has, more will be given, but as for the one who has nothing, even what he has will be taken away. ²⁷But those enemies of mine who did not want me to be king over them — bring them here and kill them in front of me.' "

The Triumphal Entry

²⁸After Jesus had said this, he went on ahead, going up to Jerusalem. ²⁹As he approached Bethphage and Bethany at the hill called the Mount of Olives, he sent two of his disciples, saying to them, ³⁰"Go to the village ahead of you, and as you enter it, you will find a colt tied there, which no one has ever ridden. Untie it and bring it here. ³¹If anyone asks you, 'Why are you untying it?' tell him, 'The Lord needs it.' "

³²Those who were sent ahead went and found it just as he had told them. ³³As they were untying the colt, its owners asked them, "Why are you untying the colt?"

³⁴They replied, "The Lord needs it."

³⁵They brought it to Jesus, threw their cloaks on the colt and put Jesus on it. ³⁶As he went along, people spread their cloaks on the road.

³⁷When he came near the place where the road goes down the Mount of Olives, the whole crowd of disciples began joyfully to praise God in loud voices for all the miracles they had seen:

³⁸"Blessed is the king who comes in the name of the Lord!"[b]

"Peace in heaven and glory in the highest!"

³⁹Some of the Pharisees in the crowd said to Jesus, "Teacher, rebuke your disciples!"

⁴⁰"I tell you," he replied, "if they keep quiet, the stones will cry out."

⁴¹As he approached Jerusalem and saw the city, he wept over it ⁴²and said, "If you, even you, had only known on this day what would bring you peace — but now it is hidden from your eyes. ⁴³The days will come upon you when your enemies will build an embankment against you and encircle you and hem you in on every side. ⁴⁴They will dash you to the ground, you and the children within your walls. They will not leave one stone on another, because you did not recognize the time of God's coming to you."

Jesus at the Temple

⁴⁵Then he entered the temple area and began driving out those who were selling. ⁴⁶"It is written," he said to them, " 'My house will be a house of prayer'[c]; but you have made it 'a den of robbers.'[d]"

⁴⁷Every day he was teaching at the temple. But the chief priests, the teachers of the law and the leaders among the people were trying to kill him. ⁴⁸Yet they could not find any way to do it, because all the people hung on his words.

The Authority of Jesus Questioned

20 One day as he was teaching the people in the temple courts and preaching the gospel, the chief priests

---

[a]13 A mina was about three months' wages. [b]38 Psalm 118:26 [c]46 Isaiah 56:7 [d]46 Jer. 7:11

and the teachers of the law, together with the elders, came up to him. **2**"Tell us by what authority you are doing these things," they said. "Who gave you this authority?"

3He replied, "I will also ask you a question. Tell me, **4**John's baptism—was it from heaven, or from men?"

5They discussed it among themselves and said, "If we say, 'From heaven,' he will ask, 'Why didn't you believe him?' **6**But if we say, 'From men,' all the people will stone us, because they are persuaded that John was a prophet."

7So they answered, "We don't know where it was from."

8Jesus said, "Neither will I tell you by what authority I am doing these things."

The Parable of the Tenants

9He went on to tell the people this parable: "A man planted a vineyard, rented it to some farmers and went away for a long time. **10**At harvest time he sent a servant to the tenants so they would give him some of the fruit of the vineyard. But the tenants beat him and sent him away empty-handed. **11**He sent another servant, but that one

---

THURSDAY

| VERSE FOR THE DAY: | AUTHOR: | PASSAGE FOR THE DAY: |
| Luke 19:8 | Jim Conway | Luke 19:1–10 |

Overwhelming Acceptance

ZACCHAEUS was fascinated with Jesus. Perhaps he was awed by his power with the people, or maybe he saw in Jesus an opportunity for personal wholeness.

As Jesus moved through the town, he saw Zacchaeus up in a tree. But Jesus saw more than that. He saw [as Duncan Buchanan puts it] "a human being, unloved, unloving, bruised and hurt by the circumstances of life, unsuited to his wealth, . . . unacceptable to those around him, unacceptable to himself."

Jesus then did the unexpected, the dramatic. He invited himself to Zacchaeus's house for a meal. Jesus' acceptance of this shriveled little man so overwhelmed Zacchaeus that he repented on the spot and promised a changed lifestyle. "Here and now I give half of my possessions to the poor, and if I have cheated anybody out of anything, I will pay back four times the amount."

Jesus responded with a statement of affirmation and forgiveness that reinstated Zacchaeus not only with God, but with his community: "Today salvation has come to this house." What a great transformation! This man, so rejected by others and himself, found a new acceptance of himself and with God and others.

As you read accounts of Jesus working with a great variety of people, courageously talk to Jesus as you would with any human being. Tell him your needs and ask him to bring about in you the same feelings of love and acceptance that you see taking place in the people of the New Testament.

Additional Scripture Readings:
Luke 8:26–39; John 7:53—8:11

Go to page 115 for your next devotional reading.

also they beat and treated shamefully and sent away empty-handed. ¹²He sent still a third, and they wounded him and threw him out.

¹³"Then the owner of the vineyard said, 'What shall I do? I will send my son, whom I love; perhaps they will respect him.'

¹⁴"But when the tenants saw him, they talked the matter over. 'This is the heir,' they said. 'Let's kill him, and the inheritance will be ours.' ¹⁵So they threw him out of the vineyard and killed him.

"What then will the owner of the vineyard do to them? ¹⁶He will come and kill those tenants and give the vineyard to others."

When the people heard this, they said, "May this never be!"

¹⁷Jesus looked directly at them and asked, "Then what is the meaning of that which is written:

" 'The stone the builders rejected
has become the capstone[a][b]?

¹⁸Everyone who falls on that stone will be broken to pieces, but he on whom it falls will be crushed."

¹⁹The teachers of the law and the chief priests looked for a way to arrest him immediately, because they knew he had spoken this parable against them. But they were afraid of the people.

Paying Taxes to Caesar

²⁰Keeping a close watch on him, they sent spies, who pretended to be honest. They hoped to catch Jesus in something he said so that they might hand him over to the power and authority of the governor. ²¹So the spies questioned him: "Teacher, we know that you speak and teach what is right, and that you do not show partiality but teach the way of God in accordance with the truth. ²²Is it right for us to pay taxes to Caesar or not?"

²³He saw through their duplicity and said to them, ²⁴"Show me a denarius. Whose portrait and inscription are on it?"

²⁵"Caesar's," they replied.

He said to them, "Then give to Caesar what is Caesar's, and to God what is God's."

²⁶They were unable to trap him in what he had said there in public. And astonished by his answer, they became silent.

The Resurrection and Marriage

²⁷Some of the Sadducees, who say there is no resurrection, came to Jesus with a question. ²⁸"Teacher," they said, "Moses wrote for us that if a man's brother dies and leaves a wife but no children, the man must marry the widow and have children for his brother. ²⁹Now there were seven brothers. The first one married a woman and died childless. ³⁰The second ³¹and then the third married her, and in the same way the seven died, leaving no children. ³²Finally, the woman died too. ³³Now then, at the resurrection whose wife will she be, since the seven were married to her?"

³⁴Jesus replied, "The people of this age marry and are given in marriage. ³⁵But those who are considered worthy of taking part in that age and in the resurrection from the dead will neither marry nor be given in marriage, ³⁶and they can no longer die; for they are like the angels. They are God's children, since they are children of the resurrection. ³⁷But in the account of the bush, even Moses showed that the dead rise, for he calls the Lord 'the God of Abraham, and the God of Isaac, and the God of Jacob.'[c] ³⁸He is not the God of the dead, but of the living, for to him all are alive."

³⁹Some of the teachers of the law responded, "Well said, teacher!" ⁴⁰And no one dared to ask him any more questions.

Whose Son Is the Christ?

⁴¹Then Jesus said to them, "How is it that they say the Christ[d] is the Son of David? ⁴²David himself declares in the Book of Psalms:

" 'The Lord said to my Lord:
"Sit at my right hand
⁴³until I make your enemies
a footstool for your feet." '[e]

⁴⁴David calls him 'Lord.' How then can he be his son?"

⁴⁵While all the people were listening, Jesus said to his disciples, ⁴⁶"Beware of the teachers of the law. They like to walk around in flowing robes and love to be greeted in the marketplaces and have the most important seats in the synagogues and the places of honor at banquets. ⁴⁷They devour widows' houses and for a show make lengthy prayers. Such men will be punished most severely."

---

[a]17 Or cornerstone   [b]17 Psalm 118:22   [c]37 Exodus 3:6   [d]41 Or Messiah   [e]43 Psalm 110:1

The Widow's Offering

21 As he looked up, Jesus saw the rich putting their gifts into the temple treasury. ²He also saw a poor widow put in two very small copper coins.[a] ³"I tell you the truth," he said, "this poor widow has put in more than all the others. ⁴All these people gave their gifts out of their wealth; but she out of her poverty put in all she had to live on."

Signs of the End of the Age

⁵Some of his disciples were remarking about how the temple was adorned with beautiful stones and with gifts dedicated to God. But Jesus said, ⁶"As for what you see here, the time will come when not one stone will be left on another; every one of them will be thrown down."

⁷"Teacher," they asked, "when will these things happen? And what will be the sign that they are about to take place?"

⁸He replied: "Watch out that you are not deceived. For many will come in my name, claiming, 'I am he,' and, 'The time is near.' Do not follow them. ⁹When you hear of wars and revolutions, do not be frightened. These things must happen first, but the end will not come right away."

¹⁰Then he said to them: "Nation will rise against nation, and kingdom against kingdom. ¹¹There will be great earthquakes, famines and pestilences in various places, and fearful events and great signs from heaven.

¹²"But before all this, they will lay hands on you and persecute you. They will deliver you to synagogues and prisons, and you will be brought before kings and governors, and all on account of my name. ¹³This will result in your being witnesses to them. ¹⁴But make up your mind not to worry beforehand how you will defend yourselves. ¹⁵For I will give you words and wisdom that none of your adversaries will be able to resist or contradict. ¹⁶You will be betrayed even by parents, brothers, relatives and friends, and they will put some of you to death. ¹⁷All men will hate you because of me. ¹⁸But not a hair of your head will perish. ¹⁹By standing firm you will gain life.

²⁰"When you see Jerusalem being surrounded by armies, you will know that its desolation is near. ²¹Then let those who are in Judea flee to the mountains, let those in the city get out, and let those in the country not enter the city. ²²For this is the time of punishment in fulfillment of all that has been written. ²³How dreadful it will be in those days for pregnant women and nursing mothers! There will be great distress in the land and wrath against this people. ²⁴They will fall by the sword and will be taken as prisoners to all the nations. Jerusalem will be trampled on by the Gentiles until the times of the Gentiles are fulfilled.

²⁵"There will be signs in the sun, moon and stars. On the earth, nations will be in anguish and perplexity at the roaring and tossing of the sea. ²⁶Men will faint from terror, apprehensive of what is coming on the world, for the heavenly bodies will be shaken. ²⁷At that time they will see the Son of Man coming in a cloud with power and great glory. ²⁸When these things begin to take place, stand up and lift up your heads, because your redemption is drawing near."

²⁹He told them this parable: "Look at the fig tree and all the trees. ³⁰When they sprout leaves, you can see for yourselves and know that summer is near. ³¹Even so, when you see these things happening, you know that the kingdom of God is near.

³²"I tell you the truth, this generation[b] will certainly not pass away until all these things have happened. ³³Heaven and earth will pass away, but my words will never pass away.

³⁴"Be careful, or your hearts will be weighed down with dissipation, drunkenness and the anxieties of life, and that day will close on you unexpectedly like a trap. ³⁵For it will come upon all those who live on the face of the whole earth. ³⁶Be always on the watch, and pray that you may be able to escape all that is about to happen, and that you may be able to stand before the Son of Man."

³⁷Each day Jesus was teaching at the temple, and each evening he went out to spend the night on the hill called the Mount of Olives, ³⁸and all the people came early in the morning to hear him at the temple.

Judas Agrees to Betray Jesus

22 Now the Feast of Unleavened Bread, called the Passover, was approaching, ²and the chief priests and the teachers of the law were looking for some

---

a 2 Greek *two lepta*   *b 32* Or *race*

way to get rid of Jesus, for they were afraid of the people. ³Then Satan entered Judas, called Iscariot, one of the Twelve. ⁴And Judas went to the chief priests and the officers of the temple guard and discussed with them how he might betray Jesus. ⁵They were delighted and agreed to give him money. ⁶He consented, and watched for an opportunity to hand Jesus over to them when no crowd was present.

The Last Supper

⁷Then came the day of Unleavened Bread on which the Passover lamb had to be sacrificed. ⁸Jesus sent Peter and John, saying, "Go and make preparations for us to eat the Passover."

⁹"Where do you want us to prepare for it?" they asked.

¹⁰He replied, "As you enter the city, a man carrying a jar of water will meet you. Follow him to the house that he enters, ¹¹and say to the owner of the house, 'The Teacher asks: Where is the guest room, where I may eat the Passover with my disciples?' ¹²He will show you a large upper room, all furnished. Make preparations there."

¹³They left and found things just as Jesus had told them. So they prepared the Passover.

¹⁴When the hour came, Jesus and his apostles reclined at the table. ¹⁵And he said to them, "I have eagerly desired to eat this Passover with you before I suffer. ¹⁶For I tell you, I will not eat it again until it finds fulfillment in the kingdom of God."

¹⁷After taking the cup, he gave thanks and said, "Take this and divide it among you. ¹⁸For I tell you I will not drink again of the fruit of the vine until the kingdom of God comes."

¹⁹And he took bread, gave thanks and broke it, and gave it to them, saying, "This is my body given for you; do this in remembrance of me."

²⁰In the same way, after the supper he took the cup, saying, "This cup is the new covenant in my blood, which is poured out for you. ²¹But the hand of him who is going to betray me is with mine on the table. ²²The Son of Man will go as it has been decreed, but woe to that man who betrays him." ²³They began to question among themselves which of them it might be who would do this.

²⁴Also a dispute arose among them as to which of them was considered to be greatest. ²⁵Jesus said to them, "The kings of the Gentiles lord it over them; and those who exercise authority over them call themselves Benefactors. ²⁶But you are not to be like that. Instead, the greatest among you should be like the youngest, and the one who rules like the one who serves. ²⁷For who is greater, the one who is at the table or the one who serves? Is it not the one who is at the table? But I am among you as one who serves. ²⁸You are those who have stood by me in my trials. ²⁹And I confer on you a kingdom, just as my Father conferred one on me, ³⁰so that you may eat and drink at my table in my kingdom and sit on thrones, judging the twelve tribes of Israel.

³¹"Simon, Simon, Satan has asked to sift you*ᵃ* as wheat. ³²But I have prayed for you, Simon, that your faith may not fail. And when you have turned back, strengthen your brothers."

³³But he replied, "Lord, I am ready to go with you to prison and to death."

³⁴Jesus answered, "I tell you, Peter, before the rooster crows today, you will deny three times that you know me."

³⁵Then Jesus asked them, "When I sent you without purse, bag or sandals, did you lack anything?"

"Nothing," they answered.

³⁶He said to them, "But now if you have a purse, take it, and also a bag; and if you don't have a sword, sell your cloak and buy one. ³⁷It is written: 'And he was numbered with the transgressors'*ᵇ*; and I tell you that this must be fulfilled in me. Yes, what is written about me is reaching its fulfillment."

³⁸The disciples said, "See, Lord, here are two swords."

"That is enough," he replied.

Jesus Prays on the Mount of Olives

³⁹Jesus went out as usual to the Mount of Olives, and his disciples followed him. ⁴⁰On reaching the place, he said to them, "Pray that you will not fall into temptation." ⁴¹He withdrew about a stone's throw beyond them, knelt down and prayed, ⁴²"Father, if you are willing, take this cup from me; yet not my will, but yours be done." ⁴³An angel from heaven appeared to him and strengthened him. ⁴⁴And being in anguish, he prayed more

---

ᵃ31 The Greek is plural.   *ᵇ37* Isaiah 53:12

earnestly, and his sweat was like drops of blood falling to the ground.[a]

⁴⁵When he rose from prayer and went back to the disciples, he found them asleep, exhausted from sorrow. ⁴⁶"Why are you sleeping?" he asked them. "Get up and pray so that you will not fall into temptation."

Jesus Arrested

⁴⁷While he was still speaking a crowd came up, and the man who was called Judas, one of the Twelve, was leading them. He approached Jesus to kiss him, ⁴⁸but Jesus asked him, "Judas, are you betraying the Son of Man with a kiss?"

⁴⁹When Jesus' followers saw what was going to happen, they said, "Lord, should we strike with our swords?" ⁵⁰And one of them struck the servant of the high priest, cutting off his right ear.

⁵¹But Jesus answered, "No more of this!" And he touched the man's ear and healed him.

⁵²Then Jesus said to the chief priests, the officers of the temple guard, and the elders, who had come for him, "Am I leading a rebellion, that you have come with swords and clubs? ⁵³Every day I was with you in the temple courts, and you did not lay a hand on me. But this is your hour — when darkness reigns."

Peter Disowns Jesus

⁵⁴Then seizing him, they led him away and took him into the house of the high priest. Peter followed at a distance. ⁵⁵But when they had kindled a fire in the middle of the courtyard and had sat down together, Peter sat down with them. ⁵⁶A servant girl saw him seated there in the firelight. She looked closely at him and said, "This man was with him."

⁵⁷But he denied it. "Woman, I don't know him," he said.

⁵⁸A little later someone else saw him and said, "You also are one of them."

"Man, I am not!" Peter replied.

⁵⁹About an hour later another asserted, "Certainly this fellow was with him, for he is a Galilean."

⁶⁰Peter replied, "Man, I don't know what you're talking about!" Just as he was speaking, the rooster crowed. ⁶¹The Lord turned and looked straight at Peter. Then Peter remembered the word the Lord had spoken to him: "Before the rooster crows today, you will disown me three times." ⁶²And he went outside and wept bitterly.

The Guards Mock Jesus

⁶³The men who were guarding Jesus began mocking and beating him. ⁶⁴They blindfolded him and demanded, "Prophesy! Who hit you?" ⁶⁵And they said many other insulting things to him.

Jesus Before Pilate and Herod

⁶⁶At daybreak the council of the elders of the people, both the chief priests and teachers of the law, met together, and Jesus was led before them. ⁶⁷"If you are the Christ,[b]" they said, "tell us."

Jesus answered, "If I tell you, you will not believe me, ⁶⁸and if I asked you, you would not answer. ⁶⁹But from now on, the Son of Man will be seated at the right hand of the mighty God."

⁷⁰They all asked, "Are you then the Son of God?"

He replied, "You are right in saying I am."

⁷¹Then they said, "Why do we need any more testimony? We have heard it from his own lips."

23 Then the whole assembly rose and led him off to Pilate. ²And they began to accuse him, saying, "We have found this man subverting our nation. He opposes payment of taxes to Caesar and claims to be Christ,[c] a king."

³So Pilate asked Jesus, "Are you the king of the Jews?"

"Yes, it is as you say," Jesus replied.

⁴Then Pilate announced to the chief priests and the crowd, "I find no basis for a charge against this man."

⁵But they insisted, "He stirs up the people all over Judea[d] by his teaching. He started in Galilee and has come all the way here."

⁶On hearing this, Pilate asked if the man was a Galilean. ⁷When he learned that Jesus was under Herod's jurisdiction, he sent him to Herod, who was also in Jerusalem at that time.

⁸When Herod saw Jesus, he was greatly pleased, because for a long time he had been wanting to see him. From what he had heard about him, he hoped to see him perform some miracle. ⁹He plied him with many questions, but Jesus gave him no answer. ¹⁰The chief priests and the teachers of the law were standing there, vehe-

---

[a]44 Some early manuscripts do not have verses 43 and 44.   [b]67 Or *Messiah*   [c]2 Or *Messiah*; also in verses 35 and 39   [d]5 Or *over the land of the Jews*

mently accusing him. ¹¹Then Herod and his soldiers ridiculed and mocked him. Dressing him in an elegant robe, they sent him back to Pilate. ¹²That day Herod and Pilate became friends—before this they had been enemies.

¹³Pilate called together the chief priests, the rulers and the people, ¹⁴and said to them, "You brought me this man as one who was inciting the people to rebellion. I have examined him in your presence and have found no basis for your charges against him. ¹⁵Neither has Herod, for he sent him back to us; as you can see, he has done nothing to deserve death. ¹⁶Therefore, I will punish him and then release him.ᵃ"

¹⁸With one voice they cried out, "Away with this man! Release Barabbas to us!" ¹⁹(Barabbas had been thrown into prison for an insurrection in the city, and for murder.)

²⁰Wanting to release Jesus, Pilate appealed to them again. ²¹But they kept shouting, "Crucify him! Crucify him!"

²²For the third time he spoke to them: "Why? What crime has this man committed? I have found in him no grounds for the death penalty. Therefore I will have him punished and then release him."

²³But with loud shouts they insistently demanded that he be crucified, and their shouts prevailed. ²⁴So Pilate decided to grant their demand. ²⁵He released the man who had been thrown into prison for insurrection and murder, the one they asked for, and surrendered Jesus to their will.

The Crucifixion

²⁶As they led him away, they seized Simon from Cyrene, who was on his way in from the country, and put the cross on him and made him carry it behind Jesus. ²⁷A large number of people followed him, including women who mourned and wailed for him. ²⁸Jesus turned and said to them, "Daughters of Jerusalem, do not weep for me; weep for yourselves and for your children. ²⁹For the time will come when you will say, 'Blessed are the barren women, the wombs that never bore and the breasts that never nursed!' ³⁰Then

" 'they will say to the mountains, "Fall on us!"

and to the hills, "Cover us!" 'ᵇ

³¹For if men do these things when the tree is green, what will happen when it is dry?"

³²Two other men, both criminals, were also led out with him to be executed. ³³When they came to the place called the Skull, there they crucified him, along with the criminals—one on his right, the other on his left. ³⁴Jesus said, "Father, forgive them, for they do not know what they are doing."ᶜ And they divided up his clothes by casting lots.

³⁵The people stood watching, and the rulers even sneered at him. They said, "He saved others; let him save himself if he is the Christ of God, the Chosen One."

³⁶The soldiers also came up and mocked him. They offered him wine vinegar ³⁷and said, "If you are the king of the Jews, save yourself."

³⁸There was a written notice above him, which read: THIS IS THE KING OF THE JEWS.

³⁹One of the criminals who hung there hurled insults at him: "Aren't you the Christ? Save yourself and us!"

⁴⁰But the other criminal rebuked him. "Don't you fear God," he said, "since you are under the same sentence? ⁴¹We are punished justly, for we are getting what our deeds deserve. But this man has done nothing wrong."

⁴²Then he said, "Jesus, remember me when you come into your kingdom.ᵈ"

⁴³Jesus answered him, "I tell you the truth, today you will be with me in paradise."

Jesus' Death

⁴⁴It was now about the sixth hour, and darkness came over the whole land until the ninth hour, ⁴⁵for the sun stopped shining. And the curtain of the temple was torn in two. ⁴⁶Jesus called out with a loud voice, "Father, into your hands I commit my spirit." When he had said this, he breathed his last.

⁴⁷The centurion, seeing what had happened, praised God and said, "Surely this was a righteous man." ⁴⁸When all the people who had gathered to witness this sight saw what took place, they beat their breasts and went away. ⁴⁹But all those who knew him, including the women who had followed him from Galilee, stood at a distance, watching these things.

ᵃ16 Some manuscripts him." ¹⁷Now he was obliged to release one man to them at the Feast.   ᵇ30 Hosea 10:8   ᶜ34 Some early manuscripts do not have this sentence.   ᵈ42 Some manuscripts come with your kingly power

Jesus' Burial

50Now there was a man named Joseph, a member of the Council, a good and upright man, **51**who had not consented to their decision and action. He came from the Judean town of Arimathea and he was waiting for the kingdom of God. **52**Going to Pilate, he asked for Jesus' body. **53**Then he took it down, wrapped it in linen cloth and placed it in a tomb cut in the rock, one in which no one had yet been laid. **54**It was Preparation Day, and the Sabbath was about to begin.

55The women who had come with Jesus from Galilee followed Joseph and saw the tomb and how his body was laid in it. **56**Then they went home and prepared spices and perfumes. But they rested on the Sabbath in obedience to the commandment.

The Resurrection

24 On the first day of the week, very early in the morning, the women took the spices they had prepared and went to the tomb. **2**They found the stone rolled away from the tomb, **3**but when they entered, they did not find the body of the Lord Jesus. **4**While they were wondering about this, suddenly two men in clothes that gleamed like lightning stood beside them. **5**In their fright the women bowed down with their faces to the ground, but the men said to them, "Why do you look for the living among the dead? **6**He is not here; he has risen! Remember how he told you, while he was

---

| FRIDAY |

VERSE FOR THE DAY: *AUTHOR:* *PASSAGE FOR THE DAY:*
Luke 23:34   Larry Crabb   Luke 23:32–43

The Mind of Christ

IT'S more than interesting to notice how unblemished humanity responds to aloneness and mistreatment. As our Lord hung on the cross, he didn't require others to treat him fairly. Even though he was alone and wrongly treated beyond imagination and even though he mightily wished his pain could be avoided, his commitment to the Father's purpose and to rescuing us from judgment never became secondary to his desire for immediate relief. It would never have occurred to him to use suffering to excuse self-interest.

When *we* hurt, however, we *do* use suffering to excuse our self-interest. Self-centeredness seems understandable. A command to think of another's happiness seems cruel and absurd. When our Lord hurt, other-centeredness came naturally: "Father, forgive them, for they do not know what they are doing" [Luke 23:34]. In us, loneliness and abuse justify whatever effort we make to recover our sense of dignity and worth, to preserve our meager quality of life. In Christ, however, loneliness and abuse provided a backdrop for highlighting the difference between a character that justifies self-interest and one that delights to love: "Today you will be with me in paradise" [Luke 23:43].

Additional Scripture Readings:
Romans 12:9–16;
Philippians 2:1–11

Go to page 117 for your next devotional reading.

still with you in Galilee: ⁷'The Son of Man must be delivered into the hands of sinful men, be crucified and on the third day be raised again.' " ⁸Then they remembered his words.

⁹When they came back from the tomb, they told all these things to the Eleven and to all the others. ¹⁰It was Mary Magdalene, Joanna, Mary the mother of James, and the others with them who told this to the apostles. ¹¹But they did not believe the women, because their words seemed to them like nonsense. ¹²Peter, however, got up and ran to the tomb. Bending over, he saw the strips of linen lying by themselves, and he went away, wondering to himself what had happened.

On the Road to Emmaus

¹³Now that same day two of them were going to a village called Emmaus, about seven miles[a] from Jerusalem. ¹⁴They were talking with each other about everything that had happened. ¹⁵As they talked and discussed these things with each other, Jesus himself came up and walked along with them; ¹⁶but they were kept from recognizing him.

¹⁷He asked them, "What are you discussing together as you walk along?"

They stood still, their faces downcast. ¹⁸One of them, named Cleopas, asked him, "Are you only a visitor to Jerusalem and do not know the things that have happened there in these days?"

¹⁹"What things?" he asked.

"About Jesus of Nazareth," they replied. "He was a prophet, powerful in word and deed before God and all the people. ²⁰The chief priests and our rulers handed him over to be sentenced to death, and they crucified him; ²¹but we had hoped that he was the one who was going to redeem Israel. And what is more, it is the third day since all this took place. ²²In addition, some of our women amazed us. They went to the tomb early this morning ²³but didn't find his body. They came and told us that they had seen a vision of angels, who said he was alive. ²⁴Then some of our companions went to the tomb and found it just as the women had said, but him they did not see."

²⁵He said to them, "How foolish you are, and how slow of heart to believe all that the prophets have spoken! ²⁶Did not the Christ[b] have to suffer these things and then enter his glory?" ²⁷And beginning with Moses and all the Prophets, he explained to them what was said in all the Scriptures concerning himself.

²⁸As they approached the village to which they were going, Jesus acted as if he were going farther. ²⁹But they urged him strongly, "Stay with us, for it is nearly evening; the day is almost over." So he went in to stay with them.

³⁰When he was at the table with them, he took bread, gave thanks, broke it and began to give it to them. ³¹Then their eyes were opened and they recognized him, and he disappeared from their sight. ³²They asked each other, "Were not our hearts burning within us while he talked with us on the road and opened the Scriptures to us?"

³³They got up and returned at once to Jerusalem. There they found the Eleven and those with them, assembled together ³⁴and saying, "It is true! The Lord has risen and has appeared to Simon." ³⁵Then the two told what had happened on the way, and how Jesus was recognized by them when he broke the bread.

Jesus Appears to the Disciples

³⁶While they were still talking about this, Jesus himself stood among them and said to them, "Peace be with you."

³⁷They were startled and frightened, thinking they saw a ghost. ³⁸He said to them, "Why are you troubled, and why do doubts rise in your minds? ³⁹Look at my hands and my feet. It is I myself! Touch me and see; a ghost does not have flesh and bones, as you see I have."

⁴⁰When he had said this, he showed them his hands and feet. ⁴¹And while they still did not believe it because of joy and amazement, he asked them, "Do you have anything here to eat?" ⁴²They gave him a piece of broiled fish, ⁴³and he took it and ate it in their presence.

⁴⁴He said to them, "This is what I told you while I was still with you: Everything must be fulfilled that is written about me in the Law of Moses, the Prophets and the Psalms."

⁴⁵Then he opened their minds so they could understand the Scriptures. ⁴⁶He told them, "This is what is written: The Christ will suffer and rise from the dead on the third day, ⁴⁷and repentance and forgiveness of sins will be preached in his name to all nations, beginning at Jerusalem. ⁴⁸You are witnesses of these things. ⁴⁹I am

---

[a] 13 Greek *sixty stadia* (about 11 kilometers)   [b] 26 Or *Messiah*; also in verse 46

WEEKENDING

REJOICE

You have a present Savior with whom to meet and wrestle a present death. Surely, in such company you need not ignore this enemy as the fearful world does. And the more you recognize death around you, the sweeter will seem the love of the Lord. You will know him better; you will realize the pragmatic and immediate power of his salvation—for wherever death is, there can also be the manifestation of his glorious victory. And you, child—you may stride with freedom, even *through* the difficulties, grief and the hard road, mourning and bereavement.
– *Walter Wangerin, Jr.*

REVIVE
Saturday: Psalm 42:5–11
Sunday: 1 Corinthians 15:55–57

Go to page 121 for your next devotional reading.

going to send you what my Father has promised; but stay in the city until you have been clothed with power from on high."

The Ascension

⁵⁰When he had led them out to the vicinity of Bethany, he lifted up his hands and blessed them. ⁵¹While he was blessing them, he left them and was taken up into heaven. ⁵²Then they worshiped him and returned to Jerusalem with great joy. ⁵³And they stayed continually at the temple, praising God.

*J*OHN *writes this Gospel to present Jesus, the powerful Son of God, who comes in human flesh, gives his life on the cross, and then returns to the Father—all with a view that we may believe in him and receive eternal life. His coming shows us how much the Father and the Son love us, and his parting command is that we should show the same sacrificial love to one another. As you read this book, be sure that you believe that Jesus is the Christ, the Son of God, and promise him that you will love others as he loves you.*

JOHN

The Word Became Flesh

1 In the beginning was the Word, and the Word was with God, and the Word was God. **2**He was with God in the beginning.

3Through him all things were made; without him nothing was made that has been made. **4**In him was life, and that life was the light of men. **5**The light shines in the darkness, but the darkness has not understood*a* it.

6There came a man who was sent from God; his name was John. **7**He came as a witness to testify concerning that light, so that through him all men might believe. **8**He himself was not the light; he came only as a witness to the light. **9**The true light that gives light to every man was coming into the world.*b*

---

*a*5 Or *darkness, and the darkness has not overcome every man who comes into the world*

*b*9 Or *This was the true light that gives light to*

[10]He was in the world, and though the world was made through him, the world did not recognize him. [11]He came to that which was his own, but his own did not receive him. [12]Yet to all who received him, to those who believed in his name, he gave the right to become children of God— [13]children born not of natural descent,[a] nor of human decision or a husband's will, but born of God.

[14]The Word became flesh and made his dwelling among us. We have seen his glory, the glory of the One and Only,[b] who came from the Father, full of grace and truth.

[15]John testifies concerning him. He cries out, saying, "This was he of whom I said, 'He who comes after me has surpassed me because he was before me.'" [16]From the fullness of his grace we have all received one blessing after another. [17]For the law was given through Moses; grace and truth came through Jesus Christ. [18]No one has ever seen God, but God the One and Only,[b,c] who is at the Father's side, has made him known.

John the Baptist Denies Being the Christ

[19]Now this was John's testimony when the Jews of Jerusalem sent priests and Levites to ask him who he was. [20]He did not fail to confess, but confessed freely, "I am not the Christ.[d]"

[21]They asked him, "Then who are you? Are you Elijah?"

He said, "I am not."

"Are you the Prophet?"

He answered, "No."

[22]Finally they said, "Who are you? Give us an answer to take back to those who sent us. What do you say about yourself?"

[23]John replied in the words of Isaiah the prophet, "I am the voice of one calling in the desert, 'Make straight the way for the Lord.'"[e]

[24]Now some Pharisees who had been sent [25]questioned him, "Why then do you baptize if you are not the Christ, nor Elijah, nor the Prophet?"

[26]"I baptize with[f] water," John replied, "but among you stands one you do not know. [27]He is the one who comes after me, the thongs of whose sandals I am not worthy to untie."

[28]This all happened at Bethany on the other side of the Jordan, where John was baptizing.

Jesus the Lamb of God

[29]The next day John saw Jesus coming toward him and said, "Look, the Lamb of God, who takes away the sin of the world! [30]This is the one I meant when I said, 'A man who comes after me has surpassed me because he was before me.' [31]I myself did not know him, but the reason I came baptizing with water was that he might be revealed to Israel."

[32]Then John gave this testimony: "I saw the Spirit come down from heaven as a dove and remain on him. [33]I would not have known him, except that the one who sent me to baptize with water told me, 'The man on whom you see the Spirit come down and remain is he who will baptize with the Holy Spirit.' [34]I have seen and I testify that this is the Son of God."

Jesus' First Disciples

[35]The next day John was there again with two of his disciples. [36]When he saw Jesus passing by, he said, "Look, the Lamb of God!"

[37]When the two disciples heard him say this, they followed Jesus. [38]Turning around, Jesus saw them following and asked, "What do you want?"

They said, "Rabbi" (which means Teacher), "where are you staying?"

[39]"Come," he replied, "and you will see."

So they went and saw where he was staying, and spent that day with him. It was about the tenth hour.

[40]Andrew, Simon Peter's brother, was one of the two who heard what John had said and who had followed Jesus. [41]The first thing Andrew did was to find his brother Simon and tell him, "We have found the Messiah" (that is, the Christ). [42]And he brought him to Jesus.

Jesus looked at him and said, "You are Simon son of John. You will be called Cephas" (which, when translated, is Peter[g]).

Jesus Calls Philip and Nathanael

[43]The next day Jesus decided to leave for Galilee. Finding Philip, he said to him, "Follow me."

---

[a]13 Greek *of bloods*   [b]14,18 Or *the Only Begotten begotten) Son*   [c]18 Some manuscripts *but the only* (or *only begotten) Son*   [d]20 Or *Messiah.* "The Christ" (Greek) and "the Messiah" (Hebrew) both mean "the Anointed One"; also in verse 25.   [e]23 Isaiah 40:3   [f]26 Or *in*; also in verses 31 and 33   [g]42 Both *Cephas* (Aramaic) and *Peter* (Greek) mean *rock*.

⁴⁴Philip, like Andrew and Peter, was from the town of Bethsaida. ⁴⁵Philip found Nathanael and told him, "We have found the one Moses wrote about in the Law, and about whom the prophets also wrote—Jesus of Nazareth, the son of Joseph."

⁴⁶"Nazareth! Can anything good come from there?" Nathanael asked.

"Come and see," said Philip.

⁴⁷When Jesus saw Nathanael approaching, he said of him, "Here is a true Israelite, in whom there is nothing false."

⁴⁸"How do you know me?" Nathanael asked.

Jesus answered, "I saw you while you were still under the fig tree before Philip called you."

⁴⁹Then Nathanael declared, "Rabbi, you are the Son of God; you are the King of Israel."

⁵⁰Jesus said, "You believe[a] because I told you I saw you under the fig tree. You shall see greater things than that." ⁵¹He then added, "I tell you[b] the truth, you[b] shall see heaven open, and the angels of God ascending and descending on the Son of Man."

Jesus Changes Water to Wine

2 On the third day a wedding took place at Cana in Galilee. Jesus' mother was there, ²and Jesus and his disciples had

a50 Or *Do you believe . . . ?*   *b51* The Greek is plural.

MONDAY

VERSE FOR THE DAY:
John 2:16

AUTHOR:
Stephen Arterburn and David Stoop

PASSAGE FOR THE DAY:
John 2:13–17

Suppressed Anger

A LOT of people, especially Christians, have a problem with Jesus being angry. They may call his outburst in the temple "righteous indignation," but they won't admit that he was angry because "everybody knows that anger is a sin."

This mentality has caused many men to push their anger out of bounds in another direction—denying it, suppressing it, or pretending it isn't there, because to them it's wrong to be angry . . . Suppressed anger is just as harmful to an angry man as explosive hostility and aggression is to those around an angry man.

Jesus didn't suppress his anger any more than he exploded with rage that day in the temple. His anger was up front, out in the open. He responded to the situation quickly, positively and appropriately, then went on with his business.

If a man buries his anger inside, he's only storing up pressure for a later implosion (hurting himself) and/or explosion (hurting others). If he doesn't bring his anger to the surface and deal with it, someday, somewhere, somehow it will express itself in an out-of-bounds manner, and somebody will get hurt.

Additional Scripture Readings:
Ephesians 4:25–32; James 1:19–21

Go to page 123 for your next devotional reading.

also been invited to the wedding. ³When the wine was gone, Jesus' mother said to him, "They have no more wine."

⁴"Dear woman, why do you involve me?" Jesus replied. "My time has not yet come."

⁵His mother said to the servants, "Do whatever he tells you."

⁶Nearby stood six stone water jars, the kind used by the Jews for ceremonial washing, each holding from twenty to thirty gallons.ᵃ

⁷Jesus said to the servants, "Fill the jars with water"; so they filled them to the brim.

⁸Then he told them, "Now draw some out and take it to the master of the banquet."

They did so, ⁹and the master of the banquet tasted the water that had been turned into wine. He did not realize where it had come from, though the servants who had drawn the water knew. Then he called the bridegroom aside ¹⁰and said, "Everyone brings out the choice wine first and then the cheaper wine after the guests have had too much to drink; but you have saved the best till now."

¹¹This, the first of his miraculous signs, Jesus performed at Cana in Galilee. He thus revealed his glory, and his disciples put their faith in him.

Jesus Clears the Temple

¹²After this he went down to Capernaum with his mother and brothers and his disciples. There they stayed for a few days.

¹³When it was almost time for the Jewish Passover, Jesus went up to Jerusalem. ¹⁴In the temple courts he found men selling cattle, sheep and doves, and others sitting at tables exchanging money. ¹⁵So he made a whip out of cords, and drove all from the temple area, both sheep and cattle; he scattered the coins of the money changers and overturned their tables. ¹⁶To those who sold doves he said, "Get these out of here! How dare you turn my Father's house into a market!"

¹⁷His disciples remembered that it is written: "Zeal for your house will consume me."ᵇ

¹⁸Then the Jews demanded of him, "What miraculous sign can you show us to prove your authority to do all this?"

¹⁹Jesus answered them, "Destroy this temple, and I will raise it again in three days."

²⁰The Jews replied, "It has taken forty-six years to build this temple, and you are going to raise it in three days?" ²¹But the temple he had spoken of was his body. ²²After he was raised from the dead, his disciples recalled what he had said. Then they believed the Scripture and the words that Jesus had spoken.

²³Now while he was in Jerusalem at the Passover Feast, many people saw the miraculous signs he was doing and believed in his name.ᶜ ²⁴But Jesus would not entrust himself to them, for he knew all men. ²⁵He did not need man's testimony about man, for he knew what was in a man.

Jesus Teaches Nicodemus

3 Now there was a man of the Pharisees named Nicodemus, a member of the Jewish ruling council. ²He came to Jesus at night and said, "Rabbi, we know you are a teacher who has come from God. For no one could perform the miraculous signs you are doing if God were not with him."

³In reply Jesus declared, "I tell you the truth, no one can see the kingdom of God unless he is born again.ᵈ"

⁴"How can a man be born when he is old?" Nicodemus asked. "Surely he cannot enter a second time into his mother's womb to be born!"

⁵Jesus answered, "I tell you the truth, no one can enter the kingdom of God unless he is born of water and the Spirit. ⁶Flesh gives birth to flesh, but the Spiritᵉ gives birth to spirit. ⁷You should not be surprised at my saying, 'Youᶠ must be born again.' ⁸The wind blows wherever it pleases. You hear its sound, but you cannot tell where it comes from or where it is going. So it is with everyone born of the Spirit."

⁹"How can this be?" Nicodemus asked.

¹⁰"You are Israel's teacher," said Jesus, "and you do not understand these things? ¹¹I tell you the truth, we speak of what we know, and we testify to what we have seen, but still you people do not accept our testimony. ¹²I have spoken to you of earthly things and you do not believe; how then will you believe if I speak of heavenly things? ¹³No one has ever gone into heaven except the one who came

---

ᵃ6 Greek *two to three metretes* (probably about 75 to 115 liters)   ᵇ17 Psalm 69:9   ᶜ23 Or *and believed in him*   ᵈ3 Or *born from above*; also in verse 7   ᵉ6 Or *but spirit*   ᶠ7 The Greek is plural.

from heaven—the Son of Man.[a] **14**Just as Moses lifted up the snake in the desert, so the Son of Man must be lifted up, **15**that everyone who believes in him may have eternal life.[b]

16"For God so loved the world that he gave his one and only Son,[c] that whoever believes in him shall not perish but have eternal life. **17**For God did not send his Son into the world to condemn the world, but to save the world through him. **18**Whoever believes in him is not condemned, but whoever does not believe stands condemned already because he has not believed in the name of God's one and only Son.[d] **19**This is the verdict: Light has come into the world, but men loved darkness instead of light because their deeds were evil. **20**Everyone who does evil hates the light, and will not come into the light for fear that his deeds will be exposed. **21**But whoever lives by the truth comes

---

[a]13 Some manuscripts *Man, who is in heaven*   [b]15 Or *believes may have eternal life in him*   [c]16 Or *his only begotten Son*   [d]18 Or *God's only begotten Son*

TUESDAY

VERSE FOR THE DAY:
John 3:3

AUTHOR:
Jim Conway

PASSAGE FOR THE DAY:
John 3:3–6

The New Has Come

YOU have been marked, not only by your genetic background but also by the environment in which you were raised. The people who affirmed you gave you a positive view of other human beings. The people who put you down or belittled you have caused you to feel uncertain about yourself and others . . .

Genesis 1 tells us that God created living things to bring forth according to their own kind. Not only are we likely to look like our parents, but it is also inferred that we will respond to life as our parents did. But take heart. The Bible also says, "So God created man in his own image" (Genesis 1:27). You were not only created in your parents' image, but also in God's.

Yes, you have your past, but you also have God. Remember the classic verse: "Therefore, if anyone is in Christ, he is a new creation; the old has gone, the new has come!" (2 Corinthians 5:17).

You are not trapped with your old experiences and genes. You do have the capacity for change! You can be different! But I won't kid you. You must take charge of your life! You must stop saying, "I'll never be different," and begin saying, "I can be different because of God's love working in me."

If you've invited Christ into your life, you have been reborn and the Holy Spirit is working to help you become all that God wants you to be.

Additional Scripture Readings:
2 Corinthians 5:16–21;
Ephesians 4:20–24

Go to page 125 for your next devotional reading.

John the Baptist's Testimony About Jesus

into the light, so that it may be seen plainly that what he has done has been done through God."[a]

22After this, Jesus and his disciples went out into the Judean countryside, where he spent some time with them, and baptized. **23**Now John also was baptizing at Aenon near Salim, because there was plenty of water, and people were constantly coming to be baptized. **24**(This was before John was put in prison.) **25**An argument developed between some of John's disciples and a certain Jew[b] over the matter of ceremonial washing. **26**They came to John and said to him, "Rabbi, that man who was with you on the other side of the Jordan—the one you testified about—well, he is baptizing, and everyone is going to him."

27To this John replied, "A man can receive only what is given him from heaven. **28**You yourselves can testify that I said, 'I am not the Christ[c] but am sent ahead of him.' **29**The bride belongs to the bridegroom. The friend who attends the bridegroom waits and listens for him, and is full of joy when he hears the bridegroom's voice. That joy is mine, and it is now complete. **30**He must become greater; I must become less.

31"The one who comes from above is above all; the one who is from the earth belongs to the earth, and speaks as one from the earth. The one who comes from heaven is above all. **32**He testifies to what he has seen and heard, but no one accepts his testimony. **33**The man who has accepted it has certified that God is truthful. **34**For the one whom God has sent speaks the words of God, for God[d] gives the Spirit without limit. **35**The Father loves the Son and has placed everything in his hands. **36**Whoever believes in the Son has eternal life, but whoever rejects the Son will not see life, for God's wrath remains on him."[e]

Jesus Talks With a Samaritan Woman

4 The Pharisees heard that Jesus was gaining and baptizing more disciples than John, **2**although in fact it was not Jesus who baptized, but his disciples. **3**When the Lord learned of this, he left Judea and went back once more to Galilee. **4**Now he had to go through Samaria. **5**So he came to a town in Samaria called Sychar, near the plot of ground Jacob had given to his son Joseph. **6**Jacob's well was there, and Jesus, tired as he was from the journey, sat down by the well. It was about the sixth hour.

7When a Samaritan woman came to draw water, Jesus said to her, "Will you give me a drink?" **8**(His disciples had gone into the town to buy food.)

9The Samaritan woman said to him, "You are a Jew and I am a Samaritan woman. How can you ask me for a drink?" (For Jews do not associate with Samaritans.[f])

10Jesus answered her, "If you knew the gift of God and who it is that asks you for a drink, you would have asked him and he would have given you living water."

11"Sir," the woman said, "you have nothing to draw with and the well is deep. Where can you get this living water? **12**Are you greater than our father Jacob, who gave us the well and drank from it himself, as did also his sons and his flocks and herds?"

13Jesus answered, "Everyone who drinks this water will be thirsty again, **14**but whoever drinks the water I give him will never thirst. Indeed, the water I give him will become in him a spring of water welling up to eternal life."

15The woman said to him, "Sir, give me this water so that I won't get thirsty and have to keep coming here to draw water."

16He told her, "Go, call your husband and come back."

17"I have no husband," she replied.

Jesus said to her, "You are right when you say you have no husband. **18**The fact is, you have had five husbands, and the man you now have is not your husband. What you have just said is quite true."

19"Sir," the woman said, "I can see that you are a prophet. **20**Our fathers worshiped on this mountain, but you Jews claim that the place where we must worship is in Jerusalem."

21Jesus declared, "Believe me, woman, a time is coming when you will worship the Father neither on this mountain nor in Jerusalem. **22**You Samaritans worship what you do not know; we worship what we do know, for salvation is from the Jews. **23**Yet a time is coming and has now

---

a21 Some interpreters end the quotation after verse 15. *b25* Some manuscripts *and certain Jews* *c28* Or *Messiah* *d34* Greek *he* *e36* Some interpreters end the quotation after verse 30. *f9* Or *do not use dishes Samaritans have used*

come when the true worshipers will worship the Father in spirit and truth, for they are the kind of worshipers the Father seeks. ²⁴God is spirit, and his worshipers must worship in spirit and in truth."

²⁵The woman said, "I know that Messiah" (called Christ) "is coming. When he comes, he will explain everything to us."

²⁶Then Jesus declared, "I who speak to you am he."

The Disciples Rejoin Jesus

²⁷Just then his disciples returned and were surprised to find him talking with a woman. But no one asked, "What do you want?" or "Why are you talking with her?"

²⁸Then, leaving her water jar, the woman went back to the town and said to the people, ²⁹"Come, see a man who told me everything I ever did. Could this be the

---

WEDNESDAY

VERSE FOR THE DAY:
John 3:30

AUTHOR:
D. Stuart Briscoe

PASSAGE FOR THE DAY:
John 3:22–36

The Vulnerable Man

SOCIETY'S definition of a real man is erroneous and its requirements of him are so burdensome that he really finds it difficult to *be* a man. He knows inwardly that he isn't able to cope with these heavy demands. For that reason it's time to reevaluate the question, "What is a real man?"

The answer comes loud and clear from Jesus. "Hey! If you want to see a real man, take a look at John the Baptist. Because, of all the men born of women, there's never been a greater one than John" [see Luke 7:28]. John had six characteristics which qualified him as a real man: sincerity, simplicity, conviction, courage, vision and vulnerability . . .

Modern "macho" man in American society is not supposed to be vulnerable. According to research, the five most difficult statements for the modern man to make are (1) I don't know; (2) I was wrong; (3) I need help; (4) I'm afraid; and (5) I'm sorry. In other words, according to the world's definition, real men do not admit any vulnerability. And if they do, their masculinity is in question. But John was not afraid to admit his vulnerability . . .

John the Baptist's vulnerability is shown in two ways—his honesty and his humility. His humility is unbelievable. One of his best-known statements was in reference to Jesus: "He must become greater; I must become less" (John 3:30) . . .

There's nothing phony about John's humility—it's real. He has come to grips with who he really is in relation to Jesus. A humble man is not afraid to admit it. Such a man admits openly, "I must go on decreasing. He must go on increasing."

Additional Scripture Readings:
1 Corinthians 1:26–31;
Colossians 3:12–14

Go to page 127 for your next devotional reading.

Christ*a*?" ³⁰They came out of the town and made their way toward him.

³¹Meanwhile his disciples urged him, "Rabbi, eat something."

³²But he said to them, "I have food to eat that you know nothing about."

³³Then his disciples said to each other, "Could someone have brought him food?"

³⁴"My food," said Jesus, "is to do the will of him who sent me and to finish his work. ³⁵Do you not say, 'Four months more and then the harvest'? I tell you, open your eyes and look at the fields! They are ripe for harvest. ³⁶Even now the reaper draws his wages, even now he harvests the crop for eternal life, so that the sower and the reaper may be glad together. ³⁷Thus the saying 'One sows and another reaps' is true. ³⁸I sent you to reap what you have not worked for. Others have done the hard work, and you have reaped the benefits of their labor."

Many Samaritans Believe

³⁹Many of the Samaritans from that town believed in him because of the woman's testimony, "He told me everything I ever did." ⁴⁰So when the Samaritans came to him, they urged him to stay with them, and he stayed two days. ⁴¹And because of his words many more became believers.

⁴²They said to the woman, "We no longer believe just because of what you said; now we have heard for ourselves, and we know that this man really is the Savior of the world."

Jesus Heals the Official's Son

⁴³After the two days he left for Galilee. ⁴⁴(Now Jesus himself had pointed out that a prophet has no honor in his own country.) ⁴⁵When he arrived in Galilee, the Galileans welcomed him. They had seen all that he had done in Jerusalem at the Passover Feast, for they also had been there.

⁴⁶Once more he visited Cana in Galilee, where he had turned the water into wine. And there was a certain royal official whose son lay sick at Capernaum. ⁴⁷When this man heard that Jesus had arrived in Galilee from Judea, he went to him and begged him to come and heal his son, who was close to death.

⁴⁸"Unless you people see miraculous signs and wonders," Jesus told him, "you will never believe."

⁴⁹The royal official said, "Sir, come down before my child dies."

⁵⁰Jesus replied, "You may go. Your son will live."

The man took Jesus at his word and departed. ⁵¹While he was still on the way, his servants met him with the news that his boy was living. ⁵²When he inquired as to the time when his son got better, they said to him, "The fever left him yesterday at the seventh hour."

⁵³Then the father realized that this was the exact time at which Jesus had said to him, "Your son will live." So he and all his household believed.

⁵⁴This was the second miraculous sign that Jesus performed, having come from Judea to Galilee.

The Healing at the Pool

5 Some time later, Jesus went up to Jerusalem for a feast of the Jews. ²Now there is in Jerusalem near the Sheep Gate a pool, which in Aramaic is called Bethesda*b* and which is surrounded by five covered colonnades. ³Here a great number of disabled people used to lie—the blind, the lame, the paralyzed.*c* ⁵One who was there had been an invalid for thirty-eight years. ⁶When Jesus saw him lying there and learned that he had been in this condition for a long time, he asked him, "Do you want to get well?"

⁷"Sir," the invalid replied, "I have no one to help me into the pool when the water is stirred. While I am trying to get in, someone else goes down ahead of me."

⁸Then Jesus said to him, "Get up! Pick up your mat and walk." ⁹At once the man was cured; he picked up his mat and walked.

The day on which this took place was a Sabbath, ¹⁰and so the Jews said to the man who had been healed, "It is the Sabbath; the law forbids you to carry your mat."

¹¹But he replied, "The man who made me well said to me, 'Pick up your mat and walk.'"

¹²So they asked him, "Who is this fellow who told you to pick it up and walk?"

---

*a*29 Or *Messiah*   *b*2 Some manuscripts *Bethzatha*; other manuscripts *Bethsaida*   *c*3 Some less important manuscripts *paralyzed—and they waited for the moving of the waters.* ⁴*From time to time an angel of the Lord would come down and stir up the waters. The first one into the pool after each such disturbance would be cured of whatever disease he had.*

¹³The man who was healed had no idea who it was, for Jesus had slipped away into the crowd that was there.

¹⁴Later Jesus found him at the temple and said to him, "See, you are well again. Stop sinning or something worse may happen to you." ¹⁵The man went away and told the Jews that it was Jesus who had made him well.

Life Through the Son

¹⁶So, because Jesus was doing these things on the Sabbath, the Jews persecuted him. ¹⁷Jesus said to them, "My Father is always at his work to this very day, and I, too, am working." ¹⁸For this reason the Jews tried all the harder to kill him; not only was he breaking the Sabbath, but he was even calling God his own Father, making himself equal with God.

¹⁹Jesus gave them this answer: "I tell you the truth, the Son can do nothing by himself; he can do only what he sees his Father doing, because whatever the Father does the Son also does. ²⁰For the Father loves the Son and shows him all he does. Yes, to your amazement he will show him even greater things than these. ²¹For just as the Father raises the dead and gives them life, even so the Son gives life to whom he is pleased to give it. ²²Moreover, the Father judges no one, but has entrusted all judgment to the Son, ²³that all may honor the Son just as they honor the Father. He who does not honor the Son does not honor the Father, who sent him.

²⁴"I tell you the truth, whoever hears my word and believes him who sent me has eternal life and will not be condemned; he has crossed over from death to life. ²⁵I tell you the truth, a time is coming and has now come when the dead will hear the voice of the Son of God and those

---

THURSDAY

VERSE FOR THE DAY:
John 4:42

AUTHOR:
Michael Card

PASSAGE FOR THE DAY:
John 4:39–42

Savior of the World

IF CHRISTMAS means anything to you, then it must mean everything. It is a beginning and an end. It is a time of darkness and inexpressible light. It is a time of blessed relief at finally seeing all God's promises come true in one person . . . As our family [each year visits a real barn and] gathers around our faint, flickering candle to read the Christmas story, the loneliness of the stable reminds us of the loneliness of another place on a hill outside Jerusalem. The rough trough seems almost as cruel a place as the cross. The infant cries we hear coming from the stable seem no less desperate than his final cry, and no less forsaken.

Celebrate? you say. Yes, most heartily, amidst the dung of the stable, which is, of course, the refuse of the world. Celebrate at the foot of that ghastly cross because it is the hope of the world. Gather around a cattle trough and celebrate a baby born in poverty and rejected, because he is the Savior of the world!

Additional Scripture Readings:
Matthew 27:45–50; Luke 2:1–14

Go to page 131 for your next devotional reading.

who hear will live. ²⁶For as the Father has life in himself, so he has granted the Son to have life in himself. ²⁷And he has given him authority to judge because he is the Son of Man.

²⁸"Do not be amazed at this, for a time is coming when all who are in their graves will hear his voice ²⁹and come out—those who have done good will rise to live, and those who have done evil will rise to be condemned. ³⁰By myself I can do nothing; I judge only as I hear, and my judgment is just, for I seek not to please myself but him who sent me.

Testimonies About Jesus

³¹"If I testify about myself, my testimony is not valid. ³²There is another who testifies in my favor, and I know that his testimony about me is valid.

³³"You have sent to John and he has testified to the truth. ³⁴Not that I accept human testimony; but I mention it that you may be saved. ³⁵John was a lamp that burned and gave light, and you chose for a time to enjoy his light.

³⁶"I have testimony weightier than that of John. For the very work that the Father has given me to finish, and which I am doing, testifies that the Father has sent me. ³⁷And the Father who sent me has himself testified concerning me. You have never heard his voice nor seen his form, ³⁸nor does his word dwell in you, for you do not believe the one he sent. ³⁹You diligently study*ᵃ* the Scriptures because you think that by them you possess eternal life. These are the Scriptures that testify about me, ⁴⁰yet you refuse to come to me to have life.

⁴¹"I do not accept praise from men, ⁴²but I know you. I know that you do not have the love of God in your hearts. ⁴³I have come in my Father's name, and you do not accept me; but if someone else comes in his own name, you will accept him. ⁴⁴How can you believe if you accept praise from one another, yet make no effort to obtain the praise that comes from the only God*ᵇ*?

⁴⁵"But do not think I will accuse you before the Father. Your accuser is Moses, on whom your hopes are set. ⁴⁶If you believed Moses, you would believe me, for he wrote about me. ⁴⁷But since you do not believe what he wrote, how are you going to believe what I say?"

Jesus Feeds the Five Thousand

6 Some time after this, Jesus crossed to the far shore of the Sea of Galilee (that is, the Sea of Tiberias), ²and a great crowd of people followed him because they saw the miraculous signs he had performed on the sick. ³Then Jesus went up on a mountainside and sat down with his disciples. ⁴The Jewish Passover Feast was near.

⁵When Jesus looked up and saw a great crowd coming toward him, he said to Philip, "Where shall we buy bread for these people to eat?" ⁶He asked this only to test him, for he already had in mind what he was going to do.

⁷Philip answered him, "Eight months' wages*ᶜ* would not buy enough bread for each one to have a bite!"

⁸Another of his disciples, Andrew, Simon Peter's brother, spoke up, ⁹"Here is a boy with five small barley loaves and two small fish, but how far will they go among so many?"

¹⁰Jesus said, "Have the people sit down." There was plenty of grass in that place, and the men sat down, about five thousand of them. ¹¹Jesus then took the loaves, gave thanks, and distributed to those who were seated as much as they wanted. He did the same with the fish.

¹²When they had all had enough to eat, he said to his disciples, "Gather the pieces that are left over. Let nothing be wasted." ¹³So they gathered them and filled twelve baskets with the pieces of the five barley loaves left over by those who had eaten.

¹⁴After the people saw the miraculous sign that Jesus did, they began to say, "Surely this is the Prophet who is to come into the world." ¹⁵Jesus, knowing that they intended to come and make him king by force, withdrew again to a mountain by himself.

Jesus Walks on the Water

¹⁶When evening came, his disciples went down to the lake, ¹⁷where they got into a boat and set off across the lake for Capernaum. By now it was dark, and Jesus had not yet joined them. ¹⁸A strong wind was blowing and the waters grew rough. ¹⁹When they had rowed three or three and a half miles,*ᵈ* they saw Jesus approaching the boat, walking on the water; and they were terrified. ²⁰But he said to them, "It is I; don't be afraid." ²¹Then

---

*ᵃ*39 Or *Study diligently* (the imperative) *ᵇ*44 Some early manuscripts *the Only One* *ᶜ*7 Greek *two hundred denarii* *ᵈ*19 Greek *rowed twenty-five or thirty stadia* (about 5 or 6 kilometers)

they were willing to take him into the boat, and immediately the boat reached the shore where they were heading.

²²The next day the crowd that had stayed on the opposite shore of the lake realized that only one boat had been there, and that Jesus had not entered it with his disciples, but that they had gone away alone. ²³Then some boats from Tiberias landed near the place where the people had eaten the bread after the Lord had given thanks. ²⁴Once the crowd realized that neither Jesus nor his disciples were there, they got into the boats and went to Capernaum in search of Jesus.

Jesus the Bread of Life

²⁵When they found him on the other side of the lake, they asked him, "Rabbi, when did you get here?"

²⁶Jesus answered, "I tell you the truth, you are looking for me, not because you saw miraculous signs but because you ate the loaves and had your fill. ²⁷Do not work for food that spoils, but for food that endures to eternal life, which the Son of Man will give you. On him God the Father has placed his seal of approval."

²⁸Then they asked him, "What must we do to do the works God requires?"

²⁹Jesus answered, "The work of God is this: to believe in the one he has sent."

³⁰So they asked him, "What miraculous sign then will you give that we may see it and believe you? What will you do? ³¹Our forefathers ate the manna in the desert; as it is written: 'He gave them bread from heaven to eat.'ᵃ"

³²Jesus said to them, "I tell you the truth, it is not Moses who has given you the bread from heaven, but it is my Father who gives you the true bread from heaven. ³³For the bread of God is he who comes down from heaven and gives life to the world."

³⁴"Sir," they said, "from now on give us this bread."

³⁵Then Jesus declared, "I am the bread of life. He who comes to me will never go hungry, and he who believes in me will never be thirsty. ³⁶But as I told you, you have seen me and still you do not believe. ³⁷All that the Father gives me will come to me, and whoever comes to me I will never drive away. ³⁸For I have come down from heaven not to do my will but to do the will of him who sent me. ³⁹And this is the will of him who sent me, that I shall lose none of all that he has given me, but raise them up at the last day. ⁴⁰For my Father's will is that everyone who looks to the Son and believes in him shall have eternal life, and I will raise him up at the last day."

⁴¹At this the Jews began to grumble about him because he said, "I am the bread that came down from heaven." ⁴²They said, "Is this not Jesus, the son of Joseph, whose father and mother we know? How can he now say, 'I came down from heaven'?"

⁴³"Stop grumbling among yourselves," Jesus answered. ⁴⁴"No one can come to me unless the Father who sent me draws him, and I will raise him up at the last day. ⁴⁵It is written in the Prophets: 'They will all be taught by God.'ᵇ Everyone who listens to the Father and learns from him comes to me. ⁴⁶No one has seen the Father except the one who is from God; only he has seen the Father. ⁴⁷I tell you the truth, he who believes has everlasting life. ⁴⁸I am the bread of life. ⁴⁹Your forefathers ate the manna in the desert, yet they died. ⁵⁰But here is the bread that comes down from heaven, which a man may eat and not die. ⁵¹I am the living bread that came down from heaven. If anyone eats of this bread, he will live forever. This bread is my flesh, which I will give for the life of the world."

⁵²Then the Jews began to argue sharply among themselves, "How can this man give us his flesh to eat?"

⁵³Jesus said to them, "I tell you the truth, unless you eat the flesh of the Son of Man and drink his blood, you have no life in you. ⁵⁴Whoever eats my flesh and drinks my blood has eternal life, and I will raise him up at the last day. ⁵⁵For my flesh is real food and my blood is real drink. ⁵⁶Whoever eats my flesh and drinks my blood remains in me, and I in him. ⁵⁷Just as the living Father sent me and I live because of the Father, so the one who feeds on me will live because of me. ⁵⁸This is the bread that came down from heaven. Your forefathers ate manna and died, but he who feeds on this bread will live forever." ⁵⁹He said this while teaching in the synagogue in Capernaum.

Many Disciples Desert Jesus

⁶⁰On hearing it, many of his disciples said, "This is a hard teaching. Who can accept it?"

⁶¹Aware that his disciples were grum-

ᵃ*31* Exodus 16:4; Neh. 9:15; Psalm 78:24,25   ᵇ*45* Isaiah 54:13

bling about this, Jesus said to them, "Does this offend you? ⁶²What if you see the Son of Man ascend to where he was before! ⁶³The Spirit gives life; the flesh counts for nothing. The words I have spoken to you are spirit[a] and they are life. ⁶⁴Yet there are some of you who do not believe." For Jesus had known from the beginning which of them did not believe and who would betray him. ⁶⁵He went on to say, "This is why I told you that no one can come to me unless the Father has enabled him."

⁶⁶From this time many of his disciples turned back and no longer followed him.

⁶⁷"You do not want to leave too, do you?" Jesus asked the Twelve.

⁶⁸Simon Peter answered him, "Lord, to whom shall we go? You have the words of eternal life. ⁶⁹We believe and know that you are the Holy One of God."

⁷⁰Then Jesus replied, "Have I not chosen you, the Twelve? Yet one of you is a devil!" ⁷¹(He meant Judas, the son of Simon Iscariot, who, though one of the Twelve, was later to betray him.)

Jesus Goes to the Feast of Tabernacles

7 After this, Jesus went around in Galilee, purposely staying away from Judea because the Jews there were waiting to take his life. ²But when the Jewish Feast of Tabernacles was near, ³Jesus' brothers said to him, "You ought to leave here and go to Judea, so that your disciples may see the miracles you do. ⁴No one who wants to become a public figure acts in secret. Since you are doing these things, show yourself to the world." ⁵For even his own brothers did not believe in him.

⁶Therefore Jesus told them, "The right time for me has not yet come; for you any time is right. ⁷The world cannot hate you, but it hates me because I testify that what it does is evil. ⁸You go to the Feast. I am not yet[b] going up to this Feast, because for me the right time has not yet come." ⁹Having said this, he stayed in Galilee.

¹⁰However, after his brothers had left for the Feast, he went also, not publicly, but in secret. ¹¹Now at the Feast the Jews were watching for him and asking, "Where is that man?"

¹²Among the crowds there was widespread whispering about him. Some said, "He is a good man."

Others replied, "No, he deceives the people." ¹³But no one would say anything publicly about him for fear of the Jews.

Jesus Teaches at the Feast

¹⁴Not until halfway through the Feast did Jesus go up to the temple courts and begin to teach. ¹⁵The Jews were amazed and asked, "How did this man get such learning without having studied?"

¹⁶Jesus answered, "My teaching is not my own. It comes from him who sent me. ¹⁷If anyone chooses to do God's will, he will find out whether my teaching comes from God or whether I speak on my own. ¹⁸He who speaks on his own does so to gain honor for himself, but he who works for the honor of the one who sent him is a man of truth; there is nothing false about him. ¹⁹Has not Moses given you the law? Yet not one of you keeps the law. Why are you trying to kill me?"

²⁰"You are demon-possessed," the crowd answered. "Who is trying to kill you?"

²¹Jesus said to them, "I did one miracle, and you are all astonished. ²²Yet, because Moses gave you circumcision (though actually it did not come from Moses, but from the patriarchs), you circumcise a child on the Sabbath. ²³Now if a child can be circumcised on the Sabbath so that the law of Moses may not be broken, why are you angry with me for healing the whole man on the Sabbath? ²⁴Stop judging by mere appearances, and make a right judgment."

Is Jesus the Christ?

²⁵At that point some of the people of Jerusalem began to ask, "Isn't this the man they are trying to kill? ²⁶Here he is, speaking publicly, and they are not saying a word to him. Have the authorities really concluded that he is the Christ[c]? ²⁷But we know where this man is from; when the Christ comes, no one will know where he is from."

²⁸Then Jesus, still teaching in the temple courts, cried out, "Yes, you know me, and you know where I am from. I am not here on my own, but he who sent me is true. You do not know him, ²⁹but I know him because I am from him and he sent me."

³⁰At this they tried to seize him, but no one laid a hand on him, because his time

---

[a]63 Or *Spirit* [b]8 Some early manuscripts do not have *yet.* [c]26 Or *Messiah;* also in verses 27, 31, 41 and 42

had not yet come. **31**Still, many in the crowd put their faith in him. They said, "When the Christ comes, will he do more miraculous signs than this man?"

32The Pharisees heard the crowd whispering such things about him. Then the chief priests and the Pharisees sent temple guards to arrest him.

33Jesus said, "I am with you for only a short time, and then I go to the one who sent me. **34**You will look for me, but you will not find me; and where I am, you cannot come."

35The Jews said to one another, "Where does this man intend to go that we cannot find him? Will he go where our people live scattered among the Greeks, and teach the Greeks? **36**What did he mean when he said, 'You will look for me, but you will not find me,' and 'Where I am, you cannot come'?"

37On the last and greatest day of the Feast, Jesus stood and said in a loud voice, "If anyone is thirsty, let him come to me and drink. **38**Whoever believes in me, as*a* the Scripture has said, streams of living

---

a 37,38 Or / If anyone is thirsty, let him come to me. / And let him drink, 38who believes in me. / As

---

FRIDAY

VERSE FOR THE DAY:
John 7:37

AUTHOR:
Max Lucado

PASSAGE FOR THE DAY:
John 7:37–44

Thirsty for Righteousness

"IF ANYONE is thirsty," Jesus once said, "let him come to me and drink" (John 7:37).

Admission of thirst doesn't come easy for us. False fountains pacify our cravings with sugary swallows of pleasure. But there comes a time when pleasure doesn't satisfy. There comes a dark hour in every life when the world caves in and we are left trapped in the rubble of reality, parched and dying.

Some would rather die than admit it. Others admit it and escape death.

"God, I need help."

So the thirsty come. A ragged lot we are, bound together by broken dreams and collapsed promises. Fortunes that were never made. Families that were never built. Promises that were never kept . . .

And we are very thirsty.

Not thirsty for fame, possessions, passion or romance. We've drunk from those pools. They are salt water in the desert. They don't quench—they kill.

"Blessed are those who hunger and thirst for righteousness . . ."

Righteousness. That's it. That's what we are thirsty for. We're thirsty for a clean conscience. We crave a clean slate. We yearn for a fresh start. We pray for a hand which will enter the dark cavern of our world and do for us the one thing we can't do for ourselves—make us right again.

Additional Scripture Readings:
Matthew 5:1–10; 1 Timothy 6:6–11

Go to page 133 for your next devotional reading.

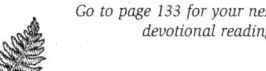

water will flow from within him." ³⁹By this he meant the Spirit, whom those who believed in him were later to receive. Up to that time the Spirit had not been given, since Jesus had not yet been glorified.

⁴⁰On hearing his words, some of the people said, "Surely this man is the Prophet."

⁴¹Others said, "He is the Christ."

Still others asked, "How can the Christ come from Galilee? ⁴²Does not the Scripture say that the Christ will come from David's family*ᵃ* and from Bethlehem, the town where David lived?" ⁴³Thus the people were divided because of Jesus. ⁴⁴Some wanted to seize him, but no one laid a hand on him.

Unbelief of the Jewish Leaders

⁴⁵Finally the temple guards went back to the chief priests and Pharisees, who asked them, "Why didn't you bring him in?"

⁴⁶"No one ever spoke the way this man does," the guards declared.

⁴⁷"You mean he has deceived you also?" the Pharisees retorted. ⁴⁸"Has any of the rulers or of the Pharisees believed in him? ⁴⁹No! But this mob that knows nothing of the law—there is a curse on them."

⁵⁰Nicodemus, who had gone to Jesus earlier and who was one of their own number, asked, ⁵¹"Does our law condemn anyone without first hearing him to find out what he is doing?"

⁵²They replied, "Are you from Galilee, too? Look into it, and you will find that a prophet*ᵇ* does not come out of Galilee."

[The earliest and most reliable manuscripts and other ancient witnesses do not have John 7:53–8:11.]

⁵³Then each went to his own home.

8 But Jesus went to the Mount of Olives. ²At dawn he appeared again in the temple courts, where all the people gathered around him, and he sat down to teach them. ³The teachers of the law and the Pharisees brought in a woman caught in adultery. They made her stand before the group ⁴and said to Jesus, "Teacher, this woman was caught in the act of adultery. ⁵In the Law Moses commanded us to stone such women. Now what do you say?" ⁶They were using this question as a trap, in order to have a basis for accusing him.

But Jesus bent down and started to write on the ground with his finger. ⁷When they kept on questioning him, he straightened up and said to them, "If any one of you is without sin, let him be the first to throw a stone at her." ⁸Again he stooped down and wrote on the ground.

⁹At this, those who heard began to go away one at a time, the older ones first, until only Jesus was left, with the woman still standing there. ¹⁰Jesus straightened up and asked her, "Woman, where are they? Has no one condemned you?"

¹¹"No one, sir," she said.

"Then neither do I condemn you," Jesus declared. "Go now and leave your life of sin."

The Validity of Jesus' Testimony

¹²When Jesus spoke again to the people, he said, "I am the light of the world. Whoever follows me will never walk in darkness, but will have the light of life."

¹³The Pharisees challenged him, "Here you are, appearing as your own witness; your testimony is not valid."

¹⁴Jesus answered, "Even if I testify on my own behalf, my testimony is valid, for I know where I came from and where I am going. But you have no idea where I come from or where I am going. ¹⁵You judge by human standards; I pass judgment on no one. ¹⁶But if I do judge, my decisions are right, because I am not alone. I stand with the Father, who sent me. ¹⁷In your own Law it is written that the testimony of two men is valid. ¹⁸I am one who testifies for myself; my other witness is the Father, who sent me."

¹⁹Then they asked him, "Where is your father?"

"You do not know me or my Father," Jesus replied. "If you knew me, you would know my Father also." ²⁰He spoke these words while teaching in the temple area near the place where the offerings were put. Yet no one seized him, because his time had not yet come.

²¹Once more Jesus said to them, "I am going away, and you will look for me, and you will die in your sin. Where I go, you cannot come."

---

*ᵃ*42 Greek *seed*   *ᵇ*52 Two early manuscripts *the Prophet*

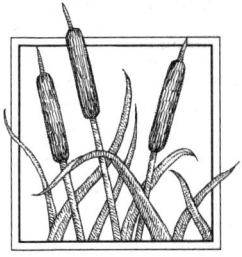

WEEKENDING

REMIND

Father, we need reminders. I need reminders. And so we are thankful for the reminders you give us daily in the form of our children. Reminders, first, of your generosity, for children are a gift from you. But reminders, as well, of our finitude, or our place in this world that you have created. Reminders that we are stewards of your creation, not its gods. Reminders that we tend the seeds that you have sown, but we do not determine the plant's growth. Reminders that our final duty is to honor you through our acts of service to one another, not to serve and honor ourselves. *May God grant us the wisdom to be parents whose treasure lies in heaven and not in the applause of others.*

– S.D. Gaede

REVIVE
Saturday: Psalm 145:1–7
Sunday: John 3:27–36

Go to page 135 for your next devotional reading.

²²This made the Jews ask, "Will he kill himself? Is that why he says, 'Where I go, you cannot come'?"

²³But he continued, "You are from below; I am from above. You are of this world; I am not of this world. ²⁴I told you that you would die in your sins; if you do not believe that I am ₁the one I claim to be₁,ᵃ you will indeed die in your sins."

²⁵"Who are you?" they asked.

"Just what I have been claiming all along," Jesus replied. ²⁶"I have much to say in judgment of you. But he who sent me is reliable, and what I have heard from him I tell the world."

²⁷They did not understand that he was telling them about his Father. ²⁸So Jesus said, "When you have lifted up the Son of Man, then you will know that I am ₁the one I claim to be₁ and that I do nothing on my own but speak just what the Father has taught me. ²⁹The one who sent me is with me; he has not left me alone, for I always do what pleases him." ³⁰Even as he spoke, many put their faith in him.

The Children of Abraham

³¹To the Jews who had believed him, Jesus said, "If you hold to my teaching, you are really my disciples. ³²Then you will know the truth, and the truth will set you free."

³³They answered him, "We are Abraham's descendantsᵇ and have never been slaves of anyone. How can you say that we shall be set free?"

³⁴Jesus replied, "I tell you the truth, everyone who sins is a slave to sin. ³⁵Now a slave has no permanent place in the family, but a son belongs to it forever. ³⁶So if the Son sets you free, you will be free indeed. ³⁷I know you are Abraham's descendants. Yet you are ready to kill me, because you have no room for my word. ³⁸I am telling you what I have seen in the Father's presence, and you do what you have heard from your father.ᶜ"

³⁹"Abraham is our father," they answered.

"If you were Abraham's children," said Jesus, "then you wouldᵈ do the things Abraham did. ⁴⁰As it is, you are determined to kill me, a man who has told you the truth that I heard from God. Abraham did not do such things. ⁴¹You are doing the things your own father does."

"We are not illegitimate children," they protested. "The only Father we have is God himself."

The Children of the Devil

⁴²Jesus said to them, "If God were your Father, you would love me, for I came from God and now am here. I have not come on my own; but he sent me. ⁴³Why is my language not clear to you? Because you are unable to hear what I say. ⁴⁴You belong to your father, the devil, and you want to carry out your father's desire. He was a murderer from the beginning, not holding to the truth, for there is no truth in him. When he lies, he speaks his native language, for he is a liar and the father of lies. ⁴⁵Yet because I tell the truth, you do not believe me! ⁴⁶Can any of you prove me guilty of sin? If I am telling the truth, why don't you believe me? ⁴⁷He who belongs to God hears what God says. The reason you do not hear is that you do not belong to God."

The Claims of Jesus About Himself

⁴⁸The Jews answered him, "Aren't we right in saying that you are a Samaritan and demon-possessed?"

⁴⁹"I am not possessed by a demon," said Jesus, "but I honor my Father and you dishonor me. ⁵⁰I am not seeking glory for myself; but there is one who seeks it, and he is the judge. ⁵¹I tell you the truth, if anyone keeps my word, he will never see death."

⁵²At this the Jews exclaimed, "Now we know that you are demon-possessed! Abraham died and so did the prophets, yet you say that if anyone keeps your word, he will never taste death. ⁵³Are you greater than our father Abraham? He died, and so did the prophets. Who do you think you are?"

⁵⁴Jesus replied, "If I glorify myself, my glory means nothing. My Father, whom you claim as your God, is the one who glorifies me. ⁵⁵Though you do not know him, I know him. If I said I did not, I would be a liar like you, but I do know him and keep his word. ⁵⁶Your father Abraham rejoiced at the thought of seeing my day; he saw it and was glad."

⁵⁷"You are not yet fifty years old," the Jews said to him, "and you have seen Abraham!"

ᵃ24 Or *I am he*; also in verse 28   ᵇ33 Greek *seed*; also in verse 37   ᶜ38 Or *presence. Therefore do what you have heard from the Father.*   ᵈ39 Some early manuscripts *"If you are Abraham's children," said Jesus, "then*

⁵⁸"I tell you the truth," Jesus answered, "before Abraham was born, I am!" ⁵⁹At this, they picked up stones to stone him, but Jesus hid himself, slipping away from the temple grounds.

Jesus Heals a Man Born Blind

9 As he went along, he saw a man blind from birth. ²His disciples asked him, "Rabbi, who sinned, this man or his parents, that he was born blind?"

³"Neither this man nor his parents sinned," said Jesus, "but this happened so that the work of God might be displayed in his life. ⁴As long as it is day, we must do the work of him who sent me. Night is coming, when no one can work. ⁵While I am in the world, I am the light of the world."

MONDAY

VERSE FOR THE DAY:
John 8:36

AUTHOR:
Mark Ritchie

PASSAGE FOR THE DAY:
John 8:32–41

Set Free!

MARK Ritchie reflects on God and the death of friends as he visits his hometown cemetery.

I had the overwhelming sense that I knew a God who had his act together, who knew the end from the beginning, who was indeed in the process of putting all the little pieces of this puzzle of human drama together to form a big picture. And the picture was starting to make sense.

Following God had turned out to be nothing but a bargain for me. And the bargain was totally in nonfinancial terms. Of course, I could hardly complain about the financial end of things either. I could still recall the tough times: the old potato I had found and eaten in my college days; the old car with no alternator or reverse; a very pregnant Nancy pushing the car back out of an intersection. They were tough times to be sure, but I wasn't going to say that God hadn't done right by me. I know where I came from, who I am, and where I'm going.

Amazing, I thought to myself . . . The creator of all this majesty of the universe—I know him, he's my friend. I've felt his comfort in my distress. I saw his care that day in Afghanistan when a poor man reached into his pocket to offer me money. I remember well the incredibly comforting feelings he gave me when I had those awful financial setbacks.

And most of all, I had complete freedom from guilt. The carpenter-preacher had said that he could by his death on a cross make people free of their guilt. He had been so credible in other things, I tried him on this one and found he delivered. The same forgiveness he extended to his executioners, he now handed me. My lifelong quest for truth and meaning has truly been met. I have been literally saved by his life.

Additional Scripture Readings:
Romans 8:1–4; 1 Peter 1:3–9

Go to page 137 for your next devotional reading.

⁶Having said this, he spit on the ground, made some mud with the saliva, and put it on the man's eyes. ⁷"Go," he told him, "wash in the Pool of Siloam" (this word means Sent). So the man went and washed, and came home seeing.

⁸His neighbors and those who had formerly seen him begging asked, "Isn't this the same man who used to sit and beg?" ⁹Some claimed that he was.

Others said, "No, he only looks like him."

But he himself insisted, "I am the man."

¹⁰"How then were your eyes opened?" they demanded.

¹¹He replied, "The man they call Jesus made some mud and put it on my eyes. He told me to go to Siloam and wash. So I went and washed, and then I could see."

¹²"Where is this man?" they asked him. "I don't know," he said.

The Pharisees Investigate the Healing

¹³They brought to the Pharisees the man who had been blind. ¹⁴Now the day on which Jesus had made the mud and opened the man's eyes was a Sabbath. ¹⁵Therefore the Pharisees also asked him how he had received his sight. "He put mud on my eyes," the man replied, "and I washed, and now I see."

¹⁶Some of the Pharisees said, "This man is not from God, for he does not keep the Sabbath."

But others asked, "How can a sinner do such miraculous signs?" So they were divided.

¹⁷Finally they turned again to the blind man, "What have you to say about him? It was your eyes he opened."

The man replied, "He is a prophet."

¹⁸The Jews still did not believe that he had been blind and had received his sight until they sent for the man's parents. ¹⁹"Is this your son?" they asked. "Is this the one you say was born blind? How is it that now he can see?"

²⁰"We know he is our son," the parents answered, "and we know he was born blind. ²¹But how he can see now, or who opened his eyes, we don't know. Ask him. He is of age; he will speak for himself." ²²His parents said this because they were afraid of the Jews, for already the Jews had decided that anyone who acknowledged that Jesus was the Christ[a] would be put out of the synagogue. ²³That was why his parents said, "He is of age; ask him."

²⁴A second time they summoned the man who had been blind. "Give glory to God,[b]" they said. "We know this man is a sinner."

²⁵He replied, "Whether he is a sinner or not, I don't know. One thing I do know. I was blind but now I see!"

²⁶Then they asked him, "What did he do to you? How did he open your eyes?"

²⁷He answered, "I have told you already and you did not listen. Why do you want to hear it again? Do you want to become his disciples, too?"

²⁸Then they hurled insults at him and said, "You are this fellow's disciple! We are disciples of Moses! ²⁹We know that God spoke to Moses, but as for this fellow, we don't even know where he comes from."

³⁰The man answered, "Now that is remarkable! You don't know where he comes from, yet he opened my eyes. ³¹We know that God does not listen to sinners. He listens to the godly man who does his will. ³²Nobody has ever heard of opening the eyes of a man born blind. ³³If this man were not from God, he could do nothing."

³⁴To this they replied, "You were steeped in sin at birth; how dare you lecture us!" And they threw him out.

Spiritual Blindness

³⁵Jesus heard that they had thrown him out, and when he found him, he said, "Do you believe in the Son of Man?"

³⁶"Who is he, sir?" the man asked. "Tell me so that I may believe in him."

³⁷Jesus said, "You have now seen him; in fact, he is the one speaking with you."

³⁸Then the man said, "Lord, I believe," and he worshiped him.

³⁹Jesus said, "For judgment I have come into this world, so that the blind will see and those who see will become blind."

⁴⁰Some Pharisees who were with him heard him say this and asked, "What? Are we blind too?"

⁴¹Jesus said, "If you were blind, you would not be guilty of sin; but now that you claim you can see, your guilt remains.

The Shepherd and His Flock

10 "I tell you the truth, the man who does not enter the sheep pen by the gate, but climbs in by some other way, is a thief and a robber. ²The man who enters

---

a 22 Or *Messiah*   *b 24* A solemn charge to tell the truth (see Joshua 7:19)

by the gate is the shepherd of his sheep. ³The watchman opens the gate for him, and the sheep listen to his voice. He calls his own sheep by name and leads them out. ⁴When he has brought out all his own, he goes on ahead of them, and his sheep follow him because they know his voice. ⁵But they will never follow a stranger; in fact, they will run away from him because they do not recognize a stranger's voice." ⁶Jesus used this figure of speech, but they did not understand what he was telling them.

⁷Therefore Jesus said again, "I tell you the truth, I am the gate for the sheep. ⁸All who ever came before me were thieves and robbers, but the sheep did not listen to them. ⁹I am the gate; whoever enters through me will be saved.ᵃ He will come in and go out, and find pasture. ¹⁰The thief

ᵃ9 Or *kept safe*

TUESDAY

VERSE FOR THE DAY:
John 10:10

AUTHOR:
Tim LaHaye

PASSAGE FOR THE DAY:
John 10:1–10

God's Special Remedy

MOST miserable or depressed people are not conscious of the fact that their misery emanates from the God-vacuum within them. This spiritual deficiency or God-void makes them vulnerable to a variety of mental, emotional and physical maladies or disorders. Whether they are antagonistic to God or just neglect his presence in their lives seems to make no difference. They experience an empty hunger within them for God, but they lack the spiritual resources to help them cope with the problems caused by their ego-dominated decisions. This God-void is universally as old as man. The Bible calls it "death." In the Garden of Eden when Adam and Eve rebelled and disobeyed God, they died spiritually. That spiritual death has been transmitted from generation to generation, conferring a serious void within the life of every human being. Although man can gain momentary happiness on the mental, emotional or physical planes of life, he will never attain lasting happiness as long as the God-void in his spiritual nature is unfulfilled. He will never know abiding joy or have power to control those weaker parts of his nature.

Jesus Christ is God's special remedy to fill the God-void in every human being. That he lived over 1,900 years ago is a matter of historical fact. Why he lived, however, is too often a source of confusion, even though the only authentic record of his life gives us the answer. Jesus Christ himself said, "I have come that they may have life, and have it to the full" (John 10:10). The abundant life he offers not only fills the God-void in a person's spirit, but also provides him with power to eliminate depression and other emotional problems.

Additional Scripture Readings:
Psalm 42:1–8; Philippians 3:7–11

Go to page 140 for your next devotional reading.

comes only to steal and kill and destroy; I have come that they may have life, and have it to the full.

¹¹"I am the good shepherd. The good shepherd lays down his life for the sheep. ¹²The hired hand is not the shepherd who owns the sheep. So when he sees the wolf coming, he abandons the sheep and runs away. Then the wolf attacks the flock and scatters it. ¹³The man runs away because he is a hired hand and cares nothing for the sheep.

¹⁴"I am the good shepherd; I know my sheep and my sheep know me— ¹⁵just as the Father knows me and I know the Father—and I lay down my life for the sheep. ¹⁶I have other sheep that are not of this sheep pen. I must bring them also. They too will listen to my voice, and there shall be one flock and one shepherd. ¹⁷The reason my Father loves me is that I lay down my life—only to take it up again. ¹⁸No one takes it from me, but I lay it down of my own accord. I have authority to lay it down and authority to take it up again. This command I received from my Father."

¹⁹At these words the Jews were again divided. ²⁰Many of them said, "He is demon-possessed and raving mad. Why listen to him?"

²¹But others said, "These are not the sayings of a man possessed by a demon. Can a demon open the eyes of the blind?"

The Unbelief of the Jews

²²Then came the Feast of Dedication*ᵃ* at Jerusalem. It was winter, ²³and Jesus was in the temple area walking in Solomon's Colonnade. ²⁴The Jews gathered around him, saying, "How long will you keep us in suspense? If you are the Christ,*ᵇ* tell us plainly."

²⁵Jesus answered, "I did tell you, but you do not believe. The miracles I do in my Father's name speak for me, ²⁶but you do not believe because you are not my sheep. ²⁷My sheep listen to my voice; I know them, and they follow me. ²⁸I give them eternal life, and they shall never perish; no one can snatch them out of my hand. ²⁹My Father, who has given them to me, is greater than all*ᶜ*; no one can snatch them out of my Father's hand. ³⁰I and the Father are one."

³¹Again the Jews picked up stones to stone him, ³²but Jesus said to them, "I have shown you many great miracles from the Father. For which of these do you stone me?"

³³"We are not stoning you for any of these," replied the Jews, "but for blasphemy, because you, a mere man, claim to be God."

³⁴Jesus answered them, "Is it not written in your Law, 'I have said you are gods'*ᵈ*? ³⁵If he called them 'gods,' to whom the word of God came—and the Scripture cannot be broken— ³⁶what about the one whom the Father set apart as his very own and sent into the world? Why then do you accuse me of blasphemy because I said, 'I am God's Son'? ³⁷Do not believe me unless I do what my Father does. ³⁸But if I do it, even though you do not believe me, believe the miracles, that you may know and understand that the Father is in me, and I in the Father." ³⁹Again they tried to seize him, but he escaped their grasp.

⁴⁰Then Jesus went back across the Jordan to the place where John had been baptizing in the early days. Here he stayed ⁴¹and many people came to him. They said, "Though John never performed a miraculous sign, all that John said about this man was true." ⁴²And in that place many believed in Jesus.

The Death of Lazarus

11 Now a man named Lazarus was sick. He was from Bethany, the village of Mary and her sister Martha. ²This Mary, whose brother Lazarus now lay sick, was the same one who poured perfume on the Lord and wiped his feet with her hair. ³So the sisters sent word to Jesus, "Lord, the one you love is sick."

⁴When he heard this, Jesus said, "This sickness will not end in death. No, it is for God's glory so that God's Son may be glorified through it." ⁵Jesus loved Martha and her sister and Lazarus. ⁶Yet when he heard that Lazarus was sick, he stayed where he was two more days.

⁷Then he said to his disciples, "Let us go back to Judea."

⁸"But Rabbi," they said, "a short while ago the Jews tried to stone you, and yet you are going back there?"

⁹Jesus answered, "Are there not twelve hours of daylight? A man who walks by day will not stumble, for he sees by this world's light. ¹⁰It is when he walks by

---

ᵃ22 That is, Hanukkah   *ᵇ24* Or *Messiah*   *ᶜ29* Many early manuscripts *What my Father has given me is greater than all*   *ᵈ34* Psalm 82:6

night that he stumbles, for he has no light."

¹¹After he had said this, he went on to tell them, "Our friend Lazarus has fallen asleep; but I am going there to wake him up."

¹²His disciples replied, "Lord, if he sleeps, he will get better." ¹³Jesus had been speaking of his death, but his disciples thought he meant natural sleep.

¹⁴So then he told them plainly, "Lazarus is dead, ¹⁵and for your sake I am glad I was not there, so that you may believe. But let us go to him."

¹⁶Then Thomas (called Didymus) said to the rest of the disciples, "Let us also go, that we may die with him."

Jesus Comforts the Sisters

¹⁷On his arrival, Jesus found that Lazarus had already been in the tomb for four days. ¹⁸Bethany was less than two miles*a* from Jerusalem, ¹⁹and many Jews had come to Martha and Mary to comfort them in the loss of their brother. ²⁰When Martha heard that Jesus was coming, she went out to meet him, but Mary stayed at home.

²¹"Lord," Martha said to Jesus, "if you had been here, my brother would not have died. ²²But I know that even now God will give you whatever you ask."

²³Jesus said to her, "Your brother will rise again."

²⁴Martha answered, "I know he will rise again in the resurrection at the last day."

²⁵Jesus said to her, "I am the resurrection and the life. He who believes in me will live, even though he dies; ²⁶and whoever lives and believes in me will never die. Do you believe this?"

²⁷"Yes, Lord," she told him, "I believe that you are the Christ,*b* the Son of God, who was to come into the world."

²⁸And after she had said this, she went back and called her sister Mary aside. "The Teacher is here," she said, "and is asking for you." ²⁹When Mary heard this, she got up quickly and went to him. ³⁰Now Jesus had not yet entered the village, but was still at the place where Martha had met him. ³¹When the Jews who had been with Mary in the house, comforting her, noticed how quickly she got up and went out, they followed her, supposing she was going to the tomb to mourn there.

³²When Mary reached the place where Jesus was and saw him, she fell at his feet and said, "Lord, if you had been here, my brother would not have died."

³³When Jesus saw her weeping, and the Jews who had come along with her also weeping, he was deeply moved in spirit and troubled. ³⁴"Where have you laid him?" he asked.

"Come and see, Lord," they replied.

³⁵Jesus wept.

³⁶Then the Jews said, "See how he loved him!"

³⁷But some of them said, "Could not he who opened the eyes of the blind man have kept this man from dying?"

Jesus Raises Lazarus From the Dead

³⁸Jesus, once more deeply moved, came to the tomb. It was a cave with a stone laid across the entrance. ³⁹"Take away the stone," he said.

"But, Lord," said Martha, the sister of the dead man, "by this time there is a bad odor, for he has been there four days."

⁴⁰Then Jesus said, "Did I not tell you that if you believed, you would see the glory of God?"

⁴¹So they took away the stone. Then Jesus looked up and said, "Father, I thank you that you have heard me. ⁴²I knew that you always hear me, but I said this for the benefit of the people standing here, that they may believe that you sent me."

⁴³When he had said this, Jesus called in a loud voice, "Lazarus, come out!" ⁴⁴The dead man came out, his hands and feet wrapped with strips of linen, and a cloth around his face.

Jesus said to them, "Take off the grave clothes and let him go."

The Plot to Kill Jesus

⁴⁵Therefore many of the Jews who had come to visit Mary, and had seen what Jesus did, put their faith in him. ⁴⁶But some of them went to the Pharisees and told them what Jesus had done. ⁴⁷Then the chief priests and the Pharisees called a meeting of the Sanhedrin.

"What are we accomplishing?" they asked. "Here is this man performing many miraculous signs. ⁴⁸If we let him go on like this, everyone will believe in him, and then the Romans will come and take away both our place*c* and our nation."

⁴⁹Then one of them, named Caiaphas, who was high priest that year, spoke up, "You know nothing at all! ⁵⁰You do not re-

---

a18 Greek *fifteen stadia* (about 3 kilometers)   *b27* Or *Messiah*   *c48* Or *temple* alize that it is better for you that one man die for the people than that the whole nation perish."

⁵¹He did not say this on his own, but as high priest that year he prophesied that Jesus would die for the Jewish nation, ⁵²and not only for that nation but also for the scattered children of God, to bring them together and make them one. ⁵³So from that day on they plotted to take his life.

⁵⁴Therefore Jesus no longer moved about publicly among the Jews. Instead he withdrew to a region near the desert, to a village called Ephraim, where he stayed with his disciples.

⁵⁵When it was almost time for the Jewish Passover, many went up from the country to Jerusalem for their ceremonial cleansing before the Passover. ⁵⁶They kept looking for Jesus, and as they stood in the temple area they asked one another,

WEDNESDAY

VERSE FOR THE DAY:
John 11:35

AUTHOR:
Haddon W. Robinson

PASSAGE FOR THE DAY:
John 11:32–37

Big Boys Do Cry

MARY, a follower of Jesus, approached her Lord at the sudden death of her brother and with some bitterness and hostility said, "If you had been here, my brother would not have died." Jesus, deeply moved by her tears, asked, "Where have you laid him?" When Mary and her companions took him to the town cemetery, Christ stood before the tomb, and the text states simply and profoundly, "Jesus wept." Seeing his tears, friends of the family remarked, "See how he loved him!" In that incident, once and for all, Jesus refuted by his tears the notion that "big boys don't cry." He who remains history's perfect and complete man stood by a graveside and wept.

A passage from the pen of Paul has been seriously misunderstood. Paul wrote to his friends in Thessalonica, "We do not want you to be ignorant about those who fall asleep, or to grieve like the rest of men, who have no hope" (1 Thessalonians 4:13). Unfortunately, some Christians struggle under "bad grief" because they have left off the last phrase of the sentence and have missed Paul's point completely. Paul does not say we are not to grieve. Grief is an emotion like love, or fear, guilt or anger and probably a mixture of all of these. Religion does not make us immune from or to emotions, and it is as pointless to deny grief as it is to deny laughter. Christians, in company with all men, experience grief, but unlike others, Christians do not grieve as people without hope. The assurance of the resurrection and the trust in God's power to turn bad Fridays into Good Fridays keep grief from being overwhelming; but nonetheless, God gives no crowns to those who refuse to weep.

Additional Scripture Readings:
John 16:19–24;
1 Thessalonians 4:13–18

Go to page 143 for your next devotional reading.

"What do you think? Isn't he coming to the Feast at all?" ⁵⁷But the chief priests and Pharisees had given orders that if anyone found out where Jesus was, he should report it so that they might arrest him.

Jesus Anointed at Bethany

12 Six days before the Passover, Jesus arrived at Bethany, where Lazarus lived, whom Jesus had raised from the dead. ²Here a dinner was given in Jesus' honor. Martha served, while Lazarus was among those reclining at the table with him. ³Then Mary took about a pint[a] of pure nard, an expensive perfume; she poured it on Jesus' feet and wiped his feet with her hair. And the house was filled with the fragrance of the perfume.

⁴But one of his disciples, Judas Iscariot, who was later to betray him, objected, ⁵"Why wasn't this perfume sold and the money given to the poor? It was worth a year's wages.[b]" ⁶He did not say this because he cared about the poor but because he was a thief; as keeper of the money bag, he used to help himself to what was put into it.

⁷"Leave her alone," Jesus replied. "It was intended that she should save this perfume for the day of my burial. ⁸You will always have the poor among you, but you will not always have me."

⁹Meanwhile a large crowd of Jews found out that Jesus was there and came, not only because of him but also to see Lazarus, whom he had raised from the dead. ¹⁰So the chief priests made plans to kill Lazarus as well, ¹¹for on account of him many of the Jews were going over to Jesus and putting their faith in him.

The Triumphal Entry

¹²The next day the great crowd that had come for the Feast heard that Jesus was on his way to Jerusalem. ¹³They took palm branches and went out to meet him, shouting,

"Hosanna![c]"

"Blessed is he who comes in the name of the Lord!"[d]

"Blessed is the King of Israel!"

¹⁴Jesus found a young donkey and sat upon it, as it is written,

¹⁵"Do not be afraid, O Daughter of Zion;
see, your king is coming,
seated on a donkey's colt."[e]

¹⁶At first his disciples did not understand all this. Only after Jesus was glorified did they realize that these things had been written about him and that they had done these things to him.

¹⁷Now the crowd that was with him when he called Lazarus from the tomb and raised him from the dead continued to spread the word. ¹⁸Many people, because they had heard that he had given this miraculous sign, went out to meet him. ¹⁹So the Pharisees said to one another, "See, this is getting us nowhere. Look how the whole world has gone after him!"

Jesus Predicts His Death

²⁰Now there were some Greeks among those who went up to worship at the Feast. ²¹They came to Philip, who was from Bethsaida in Galilee, with a request. "Sir," they said, "we would like to see Jesus." ²²Philip went to tell Andrew; Andrew and Philip in turn told Jesus.

²³Jesus replied, "The hour has come for the Son of Man to be glorified. ²⁴I tell you the truth, unless a kernel of wheat falls to the ground and dies, it remains only a single seed. But if it dies, it produces many seeds. ²⁵The man who loves his life will lose it, while the man who hates his life in this world will keep it for eternal life. ²⁶Whoever serves me must follow me; and where I am, my servant also will be. My Father will honor the one who serves me.

²⁷"Now my heart is troubled, and what shall I say? 'Father, save me from this hour'? No, it was for this very reason I came to this hour. ²⁸Father, glorify your name!"

Then a voice came from heaven, "I have glorified it, and will glorify it again." ²⁹The crowd that was there and heard it said it had thundered; others said an angel had spoken to him.

³⁰Jesus said, "This voice was for your benefit, not mine. ³¹Now is the time for judgment on this world; now the prince of this world will be driven out. ³²But I, when I am lifted up from the earth, will draw all men to myself." ³³He said this to show the kind of death he was going to die.

---

[a] 3 Greek *a litra* (probably about 0.5 liter)   [b] 5 Greek *three hundred denarii*   [c] 13 A Hebrew expression meaning "Save!" which became an exclamation of praise   [d] 13 Psalm 118:25, 26   [e] 15 Zech. 9:9

³⁴The crowd spoke up, "We have heard from the Law that the Christ[a] will remain forever, so how can you say, 'The Son of Man must be lifted up'? Who is this 'Son of Man'?"

³⁵Then Jesus told them, "You are going to have the light just a little while longer. Walk while you have the light, before darkness overtakes you. The man who walks in the dark does not know where he is going. ³⁶Put your trust in the light while you have it, so that you may become sons of light." When he had finished speaking, Jesus left and hid himself from them.

The Jews Continue in Their Unbelief

³⁷Even after Jesus had done all these miraculous signs in their presence, they still would not believe in him. ³⁸This was to fulfill the word of Isaiah the prophet:

"Lord, who has believed our message
 and to whom has the arm of the
  Lord been revealed?"[b]

³⁹For this reason they could not believe, because, as Isaiah says elsewhere:

⁴⁰"He has blinded their eyes
 and deadened their hearts,
so they can neither see with their
  eyes,
 nor understand with their hearts,
 nor turn—and I would heal
  them."[c]

⁴¹Isaiah said this because he saw Jesus' glory and spoke about him.

⁴²Yet at the same time many even among the leaders believed in him. But because of the Pharisees they would not confess their faith for fear they would be put out of the synagogue; ⁴³for they loved praise from men more than praise from God.

⁴⁴Then Jesus cried out, "When a man believes in me, he does not believe in me only, but in the one who sent me. ⁴⁵When he looks at me, he sees the one who sent me. ⁴⁶I have come into the world as a light, so that no one who believes in me should stay in darkness.

⁴⁷"As for the person who hears my words but does not keep them, I do not judge him. For I did not come to judge the world, but to save it. ⁴⁸There is a judge for the one who rejects me and does not accept my words; that very word which I spoke will condemn him at the last day. ⁴⁹For I did not speak of my own accord, but the Father who sent me commanded me what to say and how to say it. ⁵⁰I know that his command leads to eternal life. So whatever I say is just what the Father has told me to say."

Jesus Washes His Disciples' Feet

13 It was just before the Passover Feast. Jesus knew that the time had come for him to leave this world and go to the Father. Having loved his own who were in the world, he now showed them the full extent of his love.[d]

²The evening meal was being served, and the devil had already prompted Judas Iscariot, son of Simon, to betray Jesus. ³Jesus knew that the Father had put all things under his power, and that he had come from God and was returning to God; ⁴so he got up from the meal, took off his outer clothing, and wrapped a towel around his waist. ⁵After that, he poured water into a basin and began to wash his disciples' feet, drying them with the towel that was wrapped around him.

⁶He came to Simon Peter, who said to him, "Lord, are you going to wash my feet?"

⁷Jesus replied, "You do not realize now what I am doing, but later you will understand."

⁸"No," said Peter, "you shall never wash my feet."

Jesus answered, "Unless I wash you, you have no part with me."

⁹"Then, Lord," Simon Peter replied, "not just my feet but my hands and my head as well!"

¹⁰Jesus answered, "A person who has had a bath needs only to wash his feet; his whole body is clean. And you are clean, though not every one of you." ¹¹For he knew who was going to betray him, and that was why he said not every one was clean.

¹²When he had finished washing their feet, he put on his clothes and returned to his place. "Do you understand what I have done for you?" he asked them. ¹³"You call me 'Teacher' and 'Lord,' and rightly so, for that is what I am. ¹⁴Now that I, your Lord and Teacher, have washed your feet, you also should wash one another's feet. ¹⁵I have set you an example that you should do as I have done for you. ¹⁶I tell you the truth, no servant is greater than his master, nor is a messenger greater than the one who sent him. ¹⁷Now that

---

[a]34 Or *Messiah*   [b]38 Isaiah 53:1   [c]40 Isaiah 6:10   [d]1 Or *he loved them to the last*

you know these things, you will be blessed if you do them.

Jesus Predicts His Betrayal

18"I am not referring to all of you; I know those I have chosen. But this is to fulfill the scripture: 'He who shares my bread has lifted up his heel against me.'[a]

19"I am telling you now before it happens, so that when it does happen you will believe that I am He. **20**I tell you the truth, whoever accepts anyone I send accepts me; and whoever accepts me accepts the one who sent me."

21After he had said this, Jesus was troubled in spirit and testified, "I tell you the truth, one of you is going to betray me."

22His disciples stared at one another, at a loss to know which of them he meant. **23**One of them, the disciple whom Jesus loved, was reclining next to him. **24**Simon Peter motioned to this disciple and said, "Ask him which one he means."

25Leaning back against Jesus, he asked him, "Lord, who is it?"

26Jesus answered, "It is the one to whom I will give this piece of bread when I have dipped it in the dish." Then, dipping the piece of bread, he gave it to Judas Iscariot, son of Simon. **27**As soon as Judas took the bread, Satan entered into him.

"What you are about to do, do quickly," Jesus told him, **28**but no one at the meal understood why Jesus said this to him. **29**Since Judas had charge of the money, some thought Jesus was telling him to buy

[a]18 Psalm 41:9

THURSDAY

VERSE FOR THE DAY:
John 13:14

AUTHOR:
Oswald Chambers

PASSAGE FOR THE DAY:
John 13:1–17

Half Mechanical, Half Mysterious

WE HAVE to recognize that we are one-half mechanical and one-half mysterious; to live in either domain and ignore the other is to be a fool or a fanatic. The great supernatural work of God's grace is in the incalculable part of our nature; we have to work out in the mechanical realm what God works in the mysterious realm. People accept creeds, but they will not accept the holy standards of Jesus Christ's teaching. To build on the fundamental work of God's grace and ignore the fact that we have to work it out in a mechanical life produces humbugs, those who make a divorce between the mysterious life and the practical life. In John 13 the mysterious and the mechanical are closely welded together.

You can't wash anybody's feet mysteriously; it is a purely mechanical matter-of-fact job; you can't do it by giving him devotional books or by praying for him; you can only wash anybody's feet by doing something mechanical. Our Lord did not tell the disciples how they were to do it: He simply says—"Do it." He is not questioning whether or not they can do it; he is saying that they must do what the mastery of his ruling shows them they should do.

Additional Scripture Readings:
Philippians 2:12–14; 1 John 3:11–24

Go to page 146 for your next devotional reading.

Jesus Predicts Peter's Denial

31When he was gone, Jesus said, "Now is the Son of Man glorified and God is glorified in him. **32**If God is glorified in him,*a* God will glorify the Son in himself, and will glorify him at once.

33"My children, I will be with you only a little longer. You will look for me, and just as I told the Jews, so I tell you now: Where I am going, you cannot come.

34"A new command I give you: Love one another. As I have loved you, so you must love one another. **35**By this all men will know that you are my disciples, if you love one another."

36Simon Peter asked him, "Lord, where are you going?"

Jesus replied, "Where I am going, you cannot follow now, but you will follow later."

37Peter asked, "Lord, why can't I follow you now? I will lay down my life for you."

38Then Jesus answered, "Will you really lay down your life for me? I tell you the truth, before the rooster crows, you will disown me three times!

Jesus Comforts His Disciples

14 "Do not let your hearts be troubled. Trust in God*b*; trust also in me. **2**In my Father's house are many rooms; if it were not so, I would have told you. I am going there to prepare a place for you. **3**And if I go and prepare a place for you, I will come back and take you to be with me that you also may be where I am. **4**You know the way to the place where I am going."

Jesus the Way to the Father

5Thomas said to him, "Lord, we don't know where you are going, so how can we know the way?"

6Jesus answered, "I am the way and the truth and the life. No one comes to the Father except through me. **7**If you really knew me, you would know*c* my Father as well. From now on, you do know him and have seen him."

8Philip said, "Lord, show us the Father and that will be enough for us."

9Jesus answered: "Don't you know me, Philip, even after I have been among you such a long time? Anyone who has seen me has seen the Father. How can you say, 'Show us the Father'? **10**Don't you believe that I am in the Father, and that the Father is in me? The words I say to you are not just my own. Rather, it is the Father, living in me, who is doing his work. **11**Believe me when I say that I am in the Father and the Father is in me; or at least believe on the evidence of the miracles themselves. **12**I tell you the truth, anyone who has faith in me will do what I have been doing. He will do even greater things than these, because I am going to the Father. **13**And I will do whatever you ask in my name, so that the Son may bring glory to the Father. **14**You may ask me for anything in my name, and I will do it.

Jesus Promises the Holy Spirit

15"If you love me, you will obey what I command. **16**And I will ask the Father, and he will give you another Counselor to be with you forever— **17**the Spirit of truth. The world cannot accept him, because it neither sees him nor knows him. But you know him, for he lives with you and will be*d* in you. **18**I will not leave you as orphans; I will come to you. **19**Before long, the world will not see me anymore, but you will see me. Because I live, you also will live. **20**On that day you will realize that I am in my Father, and you are in me, and I am in you. **21**Whoever has my commands and obeys them, he is the one who loves me. He who loves me will be loved by my Father, and I too will love him and show myself to him."

22Then Judas (not Judas Iscariot) said, "But, Lord, why do you intend to show yourself to us and not to the world?"

23Jesus replied, "If anyone loves me, he will obey my teaching. My Father will love him, and we will come to him and make our home with him. **24**He who does not love me will not obey my teaching. These words you hear are not my own; they belong to the Father who sent me.

25"All this I have spoken while still with you. **26**But the Counselor, the Holy Spirit, whom the Father will send in my name, will teach you all things and will remind you of everything I have said to you. **27**Peace I leave with you; my peace I give

---

*a*32 Many early manuscripts do not have *If God is glorified in him.*   *b*1 Or *You trust in God*
*c*7 Some early manuscripts *If you really have known me, you will know*   *d*17 Some early manuscripts *and is*

you. I do not give to you as the world gives. Do not let your hearts be troubled and do not be afraid.

²⁸"You heard me say, 'I am going away and I am coming back to you.' If you loved me, you would be glad that I am going to the Father, for the Father is greater than I. ²⁹I have told you now before it happens, so that when it does happen you will believe. ³⁰I will not speak with you much longer, for the prince of this world is coming. He has no hold on me, ³¹but the world must learn that I love the Father and that I do exactly what my Father has commanded me.

"Come now; let us leave.

The Vine and the Branches

15 "I am the true vine, and my Father is the gardener. ²He cuts off every branch in me that bears no fruit, while every branch that does bear fruit he prunes[a] so that it will be even more fruitful. ³You are already clean because of the word I have spoken to you. ⁴Remain in me, and I will remain in you. No branch can bear fruit by itself; it must remain in the vine. Neither can you bear fruit unless you remain in me.

⁵"I am the vine; you are the branches. If a man remains in me and I in him, he will bear much fruit; apart from me you can do nothing. ⁶If anyone does not remain in me, he is like a branch that is thrown away and withers; such branches are picked up, thrown into the fire and burned. ⁷If you remain in me and my words remain in you, ask whatever you wish, and it will be given you. ⁸This is to my Father's glory, that you bear much fruit, showing yourselves to be my disciples.

⁹"As the Father has loved me, so have I loved you. Now remain in my love. ¹⁰If you obey my commands, you will remain in my love, just as I have obeyed my Father's commands and remain in his love. ¹¹I have told you this so that my joy may be in you and that your joy may be complete. ¹²My command is this: Love each other as I have loved you. ¹³Greater love has no one than this, that he lay down his life for his friends. ¹⁴You are my friends if you do what I command. ¹⁵I no longer call you servants, because a servant does not know his master's business. Instead, I have called you friends, for everything that I learned from my Father I have made known to you. ¹⁶You did not choose me, but I chose you and appointed you to go and bear fruit—fruit that will last. Then the Father will give you whatever you ask in my name. ¹⁷This is my command: Love each other.

The World Hates the Disciples

¹⁸"If the world hates you, keep in mind that it hated me first. ¹⁹If you belonged to the world, it would love you as its own. As it is, you do not belong to the world, but I have chosen you out of the world. That is why the world hates you. ²⁰Remember the words I spoke to you: 'No servant is greater than his master.'[b] If they persecuted me, they will persecute you also. If they obeyed my teaching, they will obey yours also. ²¹They will treat you this way because of my name, for they do not know the One who sent me. ²²If I had not come and spoken to them, they would not be guilty of sin. Now, however, they have no excuse for their sin. ²³He who hates me hates my Father as well. ²⁴If I had not done among them what no one else did, they would not be guilty of sin. But now they have seen these miracles, and yet they have hated both me and my Father. ²⁵But this is to fulfill what is written in their Law: 'They hated me without reason.'[c]

²⁶"When the Counselor comes, whom I will send to you from the Father, the Spirit of truth who goes out from the Father, he will testify about me. ²⁷And you also must testify, for you have been with me from the beginning.

16 "All this I have told you so that you will not go astray. ²They will put you out of the synagogue; in fact, a time is coming when anyone who kills you will think he is offering a service to God. ³They will do such things because they have not known the Father or me. ⁴I have told you this, so that when the time comes you will remember that I warned you. I did not tell you this at first because I was with you.

The Work of the Holy Spirit

⁵"Now I am going to him who sent me, yet none of you asks me, 'Where are you going?' ⁶Because I have said these things, you are filled with grief. ⁷But I tell you the truth: It is for your good that I am going away. Unless I go away, the Counselor will not come to you; but if I go, I will send him to you. ⁸When he comes, he will con-

---

[a]2 The Greek for *prunes* also means *cleans*.   [b]20 John 13:16   [c]25 Psalms 35:19; 69:4

vict the world of guilt*a* in regard to sin and righteousness and judgment: **9**in regard to sin, because men do not believe in me; **10**in regard to righteousness, because I am going to the Father, where you can see me no longer; **11**and in regard to judgment, because the prince of this world now stands condemned.

12"I have much more to say to you, more than you can now bear. **13**But when he, the Spirit of truth, comes, he will guide you into all truth. He will not speak on his own; he will speak only what he hears, and he will tell you what is yet to come. **14**He will bring glory to me by taking from what is mine and making it known to you. **15**All that belongs to the Father is mine. That is why I said the Spirit will take from what is mine and make it known to you.

16"In a little while you will see me no more, and then after a little while you will see me."

The Disciples' Grief Will Turn to Joy

17Some of his disciples said to one another, "What does he mean by saying, 'In

*a*8 Or *will expose the guilt of the world*

FRIDAY

VERSE FOR THE DAY:
John 15:5

AUTHOR:
Patrick Morley

PASSAGE FOR THE DAY:
John 15:1–8

A Man's Most Innate Need

WHAT do you think is man's greatest need? Someone recently mentioned they would like their tombstone to read, "He made a difference." Whether we speak of achieving our full potential, or only of surviving to the next paycheck, men invariably talk about their need to be significant. A man's most innate need is his need to be significant—to find purpose and meaning . . .

The difference in men is in how we go about satisfying our need to be significant. Some men, eager for the spoils of this life, pursue significance by gratifying only their own ambitions. Others, trained by the Scriptures, find it in obeying God.

How we answer the questions, *"Who am I?"* and *"Why do I exist?"* determines how we pursue our significance. Our answers divide us succinctly into two groups: those who pursue significance in appropriate ways and those who pursue significance in inappropriate ways. Our desire to satisfy this need can take us close to or far away from the things of God.

Authentic, lasting significance is hid with Christ. Jesus said, "I am the vine; you are the branches. If a man remains in me and I in him, he will bear much fruit; *apart from me you can do nothing*" (John 15:5, italics added). That is to say, a man cannot find significance in any lasting way apart from Christ. So, if a man is in Christ, and submitted to God's plan and purpose, then he can satisfy his greatest need in a way that endures.

Additional Scripture Readings:
Luke 12:13-21;
Philippians 3:7–11

Go to page 147 for your next devotional reading.

WEEKENDING

RENEW

There is a striking difference between knowing about God and knowing God. We may know the right God-words yet not experience God. Only in Jesus, the Son of God, can we truly know God the Father . . .

What we think of God makes a tremendous difference in our lives. Where we get our ideas of God makes a tremendous difference too. We can gather up data and develop our own image of God, or we can allow God to reveal himself in a self-portrait — his Son, Jesus Christ . . .

Yes, Jesus, yes. If God is like you, my heart says yes! But it is hard to let go of old ideas, feelings and images. Give me the grace to bring them all to you. Let your Holy Spirit cleanse and replace the false God-images I have carried so long. Let him fill my heart and mind with the vision of yourself. Amen.

— Reuben R. Welch

REVIVE
Saturday: Psalm 145:1–7
Sunday: John 3:27–36

Go to page 149 for your next devotional reading.

a little while you will see me no more, and then after a little while you will see me,' and 'Because I am going to the Father'?" ¹⁸They kept asking, "What does he mean by 'a little while'? We don't understand what he is saying."

¹⁹Jesus saw that they wanted to ask him about this, so he said to them, "Are you asking one another what I meant when I said, 'In a little while you will see me no more, and then after a little while you will see me'? ²⁰I tell you the truth, you will weep and mourn while the world rejoices. You will grieve, but your grief will turn to joy. ²¹A woman giving birth to a child has pain because her time has come; but when her baby is born she forgets the anguish because of her joy that a child is born into the world. ²²So with you: Now is your time of grief, but I will see you again and you will rejoice, and no one will take away your joy. ²³In that day you will no longer ask me anything. I tell you the truth, my Father will give you whatever you ask in my name. ²⁴Until now you have not asked for anything in my name. Ask and you will receive, and your joy will be complete.

²⁵"Though I have been speaking figuratively, a time is coming when I will no longer use this kind of language but will tell you plainly about my Father. ²⁶In that day you will ask in my name. I am not saying that I will ask the Father on your behalf. ²⁷No, the Father himself loves you because you have loved me and have believed that I came from God. ²⁸I came from the Father and entered the world; now I am leaving the world and going back to the Father."

²⁹Then Jesus' disciples said, "Now you are speaking clearly and without figures of speech. ³⁰Now we can see that you know all things and that you do not even need to have anyone ask you questions. This makes us believe that you came from God."

³¹"You believe at last!"ᵃ Jesus answered. ³²"But a time is coming, and has come, when you will be scattered, each to his own home. You will leave me all alone. Yet I am not alone, for my Father is with me.

³³"I have told you these things, so that in me you may have peace. In this world you will have trouble. But take heart! I have overcome the world."

Jesus Prays for Himself

17 After Jesus said this, he looked toward heaven and prayed:

"Father, the time has come. Glorify your Son, that your Son may glorify you. ²For you granted him authority over all people that he might give eternal life to all those you have given him. ³Now this is eternal life: that they may know you, the only true God, and Jesus Christ, whom you have sent. ⁴I have brought you glory on earth by completing the work you gave me to do. ⁵And now, Father, glorify me in your presence with the glory I had with you before the world began.

Jesus Prays for His Disciples

⁶"I have revealed youᵇ to those whom you gave me out of the world. They were yours; you gave them to me and they have obeyed your word. ⁷Now they know that everything you have given me comes from you. ⁸For I gave them the words you gave me and they accepted them. They knew with certainty that I came from you, and they believed that you sent me. ⁹I pray for them. I am not praying for the world, but for those you have given me, for they are yours. ¹⁰All I have is yours, and all you have is mine. And glory has come to me through them. ¹¹I will remain in the world no longer, but they are still in the world, and I am coming to you. Holy Father, protect them by the power of your name—the name you gave me—so that they may be one as we are one. ¹²While I was with them, I protected them and kept them safe by that name you gave me. None has been lost except the one doomed to destruction so that Scripture would be fulfilled.

¹³"I am coming to you now, but I say these things while I am still in the world, so that they may have the full measure of my joy within them. ¹⁴I have given them your word and the world has hated them, for they are not of the world any more than I am of the world. ¹⁵My prayer is not that you take them out of the world but

---

ᵃ31 Or *"Do you now believe?"*   ᵇ6 Greek *your name*; also in verse 26

that you protect them from the evil one. ⁱ⁶They are not of the world, even as I am not of it. ⁱ⁷Sanctify[a] them by the truth; your word is truth. ⁱ⁸As you sent me into the world, I have sent them into the world. ⁱ⁹For them I sanctify myself, that they too may be truly sanctified.

[a]17 Greek *hagiazo* (*set apart for sacred use* or *make holy*); also in verse 19

MONDAY

VERSE FOR THE DAY:
John 17:11

AUTHOR:
Paul Brand

PASSAGE FOR THE DAY:
John 17:6–12

Unlikely Seekers

I THINK of the churches I have known: Is there another institution in town with such a mosaic assortment of unlikes? Young radicals, uniformed in jeans, share the pews with Republican bankers in three-piece suits. Bored teenagers tune out the sermon even as their eager grandparents turn up their hearing aids. Some members gather as methodically as a school of fish, then quickly break apart to return to their jobs and homes. Others want close communities and migrate together like social amoebae.

I could easily cluck my tongue at the absurdity of the whole enterprise, seemingly doomed to fail. Jesus prayed that we "may be one" as he and God the Father are one (John 17:11). How can any organism composed of such diversity attain even a semblance of unity?

As the doubts rumble inside me, a sober and quieting voice replies, "You have not chosen me, I have chosen you" [see John 15:16]. The chuckle at Christ's Body is caught in my throat like cotton. For if anything is to be believed about the collection of people who follow him, it is that we were called by him. The word church, *ekklēsia*, means "the called-out ones." Our crew of comedians from central casting is the group God wants.

During my life as a missionary surgeon in India and now as a member of the tiny chapel on the grounds of the Carville leprosy hospital, I have seen my share of unlikely seekers after God. And I must admit that most of my worship in the last thirty years has not taken place among people who have shared my taste in music, speech, or even thought. But over those years I have been profoundly—and humbly—impressed that I find God in the faces of my fellow worshipers by sharing with people who are shockingly different from each other and from me.

Additional Scripture Readings:
Romans 12:4–8;
1 Corinthians 12:12–27

Go to page 154 for your next devotional reading.

Jesus Prays for All Believers

20"My prayer is not for them alone. I pray also for those who will believe in me through their message, **21**that all of them may be one, Father, just as you are in me and I am in you. May they also be in us so that the world may believe that you have sent me. **22**I have given them the glory that you gave me, that they may be one as we are one: **23**I in them and you in me. May they be brought to complete unity to let the world know that you sent me and have loved them even as you have loved me.

24"Father, I want those you have given me to be with me where I am, and to see my glory, the glory you have given me because you loved me before the creation of the world.

25"Righteous Father, though the world does not know you, I know you, and they know that you have sent me. **26**I have made you known to them, and will continue to make you known in order that the love you have for me may be in them and that I myself may be in them."

Jesus Arrested

18 When he had finished praying, Jesus left with his disciples and crossed the Kidron Valley. On the other side there was an olive grove, and he and his disciples went into it.

2Now Judas, who betrayed him, knew the place, because Jesus had often met there with his disciples. **3**So Judas came to the grove, guiding a detachment of soldiers and some officials from the chief priests and Pharisees. They were carrying torches, lanterns and weapons.

4Jesus, knowing all that was going to happen to him, went out and asked them, "Who is it you want?"

5"Jesus of Nazareth," they replied.

"I am he," Jesus said. (And Judas the traitor was standing there with them.) **6**When Jesus said, "I am he," they drew back and fell to the ground.

7Again he asked them, "Who is it you want?"

And they said, "Jesus of Nazareth."

8"I told you that I am he," Jesus answered. "If you are looking for me, then let these men go." **9**This happened so that the words he had spoken would be fulfilled: "I have not lost one of those you gave me."[a]

10Then Simon Peter, who had a sword, drew it and struck the high priest's servant, cutting off his right ear. (The servant's name was Malchus.)

11Jesus commanded Peter, "Put your sword away! Shall I not drink the cup the Father has given me?"

Jesus Taken to Annas

12Then the detachment of soldiers with its commander and the Jewish officials arrested Jesus. They bound him **13**and brought him first to Annas, who was the father-in-law of Caiaphas, the high priest that year. **14**Caiaphas was the one who had advised the Jews that it would be good if one man died for the people.

Peter's First Denial

15Simon Peter and another disciple were following Jesus. Because this disciple was known to the high priest, he went with Jesus into the high priest's courtyard, **16**but Peter had to wait outside at the door. The other disciple, who was known to the high priest, came back, spoke to the girl on duty there and brought Peter in.

17"You are not one of his disciples, are you?" the girl at the door asked Peter.

He replied, "I am not."

18It was cold, and the servants and officials stood around a fire they had made to keep warm. Peter also was standing with them, warming himself.

The High Priest Questions Jesus

19Meanwhile, the high priest questioned Jesus about his disciples and his teaching.

20"I have spoken openly to the world," Jesus replied. "I always taught in synagogues or at the temple, where all the Jews come together. I said nothing in secret. **21**Why question me? Ask those who heard me. Surely they know what I said."

22When Jesus said this, one of the officials nearby struck him in the face. "Is this the way you answer the high priest?" he demanded.

23"If I said something wrong," Jesus replied, "testify as to what is wrong. But if I spoke the truth, why did you strike me?" **24**Then Annas sent him, still bound, to Caiaphas the high priest.[b]

---

[a] 9 John 6:39 [b] 24 Or *(Now Annas had sent him, still bound, to Caiaphas the high priest.)*

Peter's Second and Third Denials

²⁵As Simon Peter stood warming himself, he was asked, "You are not one of his disciples, are you?"

He denied it, saying, "I am not."

²⁶One of the high priest's servants, a relative of the man whose ear Peter had cut off, challenged him, "Didn't I see you with him in the olive grove?" ²⁷Again Peter denied it, and at that moment a rooster began to crow.

Jesus Before Pilate

²⁸Then the Jews led Jesus from Caiaphas to the palace of the Roman governor. By now it was early morning, and to avoid ceremonial uncleanness the Jews did not enter the palace; they wanted to be able to eat the Passover. ²⁹So Pilate came out to them and asked, "What charges are you bringing against this man?"

³⁰"If he were not a criminal," they replied, "we would not have handed him over to you."

³¹Pilate said, "Take him yourselves and judge him by your own law."

"But we have no right to execute anyone," the Jews objected. ³²This happened so that the words Jesus had spoken indicating the kind of death he was going to die would be fulfilled.

³³Pilate then went back inside the palace, summoned Jesus and asked him, "Are you the king of the Jews?"

³⁴"Is that your own idea," Jesus asked, "or did others talk to you about me?"

³⁵"Am I a Jew?" Pilate replied. "It was your people and your chief priests who handed you over to me. What is it you have done?"

³⁶Jesus said, "My kingdom is not of this world. If it were, my servants would fight to prevent my arrest by the Jews. But now my kingdom is from another place."

³⁷"You are a king, then!" said Pilate.

Jesus answered, "You are right in saying I am a king. In fact, for this reason I was born, and for this I came into the world, to testify to the truth. Everyone on the side of truth listens to me."

³⁸"What is truth?" Pilate asked. With this he went out again to the Jews and said, "I find no basis for a charge against him. ³⁹But it is your custom for me to release to you one prisoner at the time of the Passover. Do you want me to release 'the king of the Jews'?"

⁴⁰They shouted back, "No, not him! Give us Barabbas!" Now Barabbas had taken part in a rebellion.

Jesus Sentenced to be Crucified

19 Then Pilate took Jesus and had him flogged. ²The soldiers twisted together a crown of thorns and put it on his head. They clothed him in a purple robe ³and went up to him again and again, saying, "Hail, king of the Jews!" And they struck him in the face.

⁴Once more Pilate came out and said to the Jews, "Look, I am bringing him out to you to let you know that I find no basis for a charge against him." ⁵When Jesus came out wearing the crown of thorns and the purple robe, Pilate said to them, "Here is the man!"

⁶As soon as the chief priests and their officials saw him, they shouted, "Crucify! Crucify!"

But Pilate answered, "You take him and crucify him. As for me, I find no basis for a charge against him."

⁷The Jews insisted, "We have a law, and according to that law he must die, because he claimed to be the Son of God."

⁸When Pilate heard this, he was even more afraid, ⁹and he went back inside the palace. "Where do you come from?" he asked Jesus, but Jesus gave him no answer. ¹⁰"Do you refuse to speak to me?" Pilate said. "Don't you realize I have power either to free you or to crucify you?"

¹¹Jesus answered, "You would have no power over me if it were not given to you from above. Therefore the one who handed me over to you is guilty of a greater sin."

¹²From then on, Pilate tried to set Jesus free, but the Jews kept shouting, "If you let this man go, you are no friend of Caesar. Anyone who claims to be a king opposes Caesar."

¹³When Pilate heard this, he brought Jesus out and sat down on the judge's seat at a place known as the Stone Pavement (which in Aramaic is Gabbatha). ¹⁴It was the day of Preparation of Passover Week, about the sixth hour.

"Here is your king," Pilate said to the Jews.

¹⁵But they shouted, "Take him away! Take him away! Crucify him!"

"Shall I crucify your king?" Pilate asked.

"We have no king but Caesar," the chief priests answered.

¹⁶Finally Pilate handed him over to them to be crucified.

The Crucifixion

So the soldiers took charge of Jesus. **17**Carrying his own cross, he went out to the place of the Skull (which in Aramaic is called Golgotha). **18**Here they crucified him, and with him two others—one on each side and Jesus in the middle.

19Pilate had a notice prepared and fastened to the cross. It read: JESUS OF NAZARETH, THE KING OF THE JEWS. **20**Many of the Jews read this sign, for the place where Jesus was crucified was near the city, and the sign was written in Aramaic, Latin and Greek. **21**The chief priests of the Jews protested to Pilate, "Do not write 'The King of the Jews,' but that this man claimed to be king of the Jews."

22Pilate answered, "What I have written, I have written."

23When the soldiers crucified Jesus, they took his clothes, dividing them into four shares, one for each of them, with the undergarment remaining. This garment was seamless, woven in one piece from top to bottom.

24"Let's not tear it," they said to one another. "Let's decide by lot who will get it."

This happened that the scripture might be fulfilled which said,

"They divided my garments among them
and cast lots for my clothing."[a]

So this is what the soldiers did.

25Near the cross of Jesus stood his mother, his mother's sister, Mary the wife of Clopas, and Mary Magdalene. **26**When Jesus saw his mother there, and the disciple whom he loved standing nearby, he said to his mother, "Dear woman, here is your son," **27**and to the disciple, "Here is your mother." From that time on, this disciple took her into his home.

The Death of Jesus

28Later, knowing that all was now completed, and so that the Scripture would be fulfilled, Jesus said, "I am thirsty." **29**A jar of wine vinegar was there, so they soaked a sponge in it, put the sponge on a stalk of the hyssop plant, and lifted it to Jesus' lips. **30**When he had received the drink, Jesus said, "It is finished." With that, he bowed his head and gave up his spirit.

31Now it was the day of Preparation, and the next day was to be a special Sabbath. Because the Jews did not want the bodies left on the crosses during the Sabbath, they asked Pilate to have the legs broken and the bodies taken down. **32**The soldiers therefore came and broke the legs of the first man who had been crucified with Jesus, and then those of the other. **33**But when they came to Jesus and found that he was already dead, they did not break his legs. **34**Instead, one of the soldiers pierced Jesus' side with a spear, bringing a sudden flow of blood and water. **35**The man who saw it has given testimony, and his testimony is true. He knows that he tells the truth, and he testifies so that you also may believe. **36**These things happened so that the scripture would be fulfilled: "Not one of his bones will be broken,"[b] **37**and, as another scripture says, "They will look on the one they have pierced."[c]

The Burial of Jesus

38Later, Joseph of Arimathea asked Pilate for the body of Jesus. Now Joseph was a disciple of Jesus, but secretly because he feared the Jews. With Pilate's permission, he came and took the body away. **39**He was accompanied by Nicodemus, the man who earlier had visited Jesus at night. Nicodemus brought a mixture of myrrh and aloes, about seventy-five pounds.[d] **40**Taking Jesus' body, the two of them wrapped it, with the spices, in strips of linen. This was in accordance with Jewish burial customs. **41**At the place where Jesus was crucified, there was a garden, and in the garden a new tomb, in which no one had ever been laid. **42**Because it was the Jewish day of Preparation and since the tomb was nearby, they laid Jesus there.

The Empty Tomb

20 Early on the first day of the week, while it was still dark, Mary Magdalene went to the tomb and saw that the stone had been removed from the entrance. **2**So she came running to Simon Peter and the other disciple, the one Jesus loved, and said, "They have taken the Lord out of the tomb, and we don't know where they have put him!"

3So Peter and the other disciple started for the tomb. **4**Both were running, but the other disciple outran Peter and reached the tomb first. **5**He bent over and looked

---

*a*24 Psalm 22:18   *b*36 Exodus 12:46; Num. 9:12; Psalm 34:20   *c*37 Zech. 12:10   *d*39 Greek *a hundred litrai* (about 34 kilograms)

in at the strips of linen lying there but did not go in. ⁶Then Simon Peter, who was behind him, arrived and went into the tomb. He saw the strips of linen lying there, ⁷as well as the burial cloth that had been around Jesus' head. The cloth was folded up by itself, separate from the linen. ⁸Finally the other disciple, who had reached the tomb first, also went inside. He saw and believed. ⁹(They still did not understand from Scripture that Jesus had to rise from the dead.)

Jesus Appears to Mary Magdalene

¹⁰Then the disciples went back to their homes, ¹¹but Mary stood outside the tomb crying. As she wept, she bent over to look into the tomb ¹²and saw two angels in white, seated where Jesus' body had been, one at the head and the other at the foot.

¹³They asked her, "Woman, why are you crying?"

"They have taken my Lord away," she said, "and I don't know where they have put him." ¹⁴At this, she turned around and saw Jesus standing there, but she did not realize that it was Jesus.

¹⁵"Woman," he said, "why are you crying? Who is it you are looking for?"

Thinking he was the gardener, she said, "Sir, if you have carried him away, tell me where you have put him, and I will get him."

¹⁶Jesus said to her, "Mary."

She turned toward him and cried out in Aramaic, "Rabboni!" (which means Teacher).

¹⁷Jesus said, "Do not hold on to me, for I have not yet returned to the Father. Go instead to my brothers and tell them, 'I am returning to my Father and your Father, to my God and your God.' "

¹⁸Mary Magdalene went to the disciples with the news: "I have seen the Lord!" And she told them that he had said these things to her.

Jesus Appears to His Disciples

¹⁹On the evening of that first day of the week, when the disciples were together, with the doors locked for fear of the Jews, Jesus came and stood among them and said, "Peace be with you!" ²⁰After he said this, he showed them his hands and side. The disciples were overjoyed when they saw the Lord.

²¹Again Jesus said, "Peace be with you! As the Father has sent me, I am sending you." ²²And with that he breathed on them and said, "Receive the Holy Spirit. ²³If you forgive anyone his sins, they are forgiven; if you do not forgive them, they are not forgiven."

Jesus Appears to Thomas

²⁴Now Thomas (called Didymus), one of the Twelve, was not with the disciples when Jesus came. ²⁵So the other disciples told him, "We have seen the Lord!"

But he said to them, "Unless I see the nail marks in his hands and put my finger where the nails were, and put my hand into his side, I will not believe it."

²⁶A week later his disciples were in the house again, and Thomas was with them. Though the doors were locked, Jesus came and stood among them and said, "Peace be with you!" ²⁷Then he said to Thomas, "Put your finger here; see my hands. Reach out your hand and put it into my side. Stop doubting and believe."

²⁸Thomas said to him, "My Lord and my God!"

²⁹Then Jesus told him, "Because you have seen me, you have believed; blessed are those who have not seen and yet have believed."

³⁰Jesus did many other miraculous signs in the presence of his disciples, which are not recorded in this book. ³¹But these are written that you may*a* believe that Jesus is the Christ, the Son of God, and that by believing you may have life in his name.

Jesus and the Miraculous Catch of Fish

21 Afterward Jesus appeared again to his disciples, by the Sea of Tiberias.*b* It happened this way: ²Simon Peter, Thomas (called Didymus), Nathanael from Cana in Galilee, the sons of Zebedee, and two other disciples were together. ³"I'm going out to fish," Simon Peter told them, and they said, "We'll go with you." So they went out and got into the boat, but that night they caught nothing.

⁴Early in the morning, Jesus stood on the shore, but the disciples did not realize that it was Jesus.

⁵He called out to them, "Friends, haven't you any fish?"

"No," they answered.

⁶He said, "Throw your net on the right side of the boat and you will find some." When they did, they were unable to haul

---

a 31 Some manuscripts *may continue to*   *b 1* That is, Sea of Galilee the net in because of the large number of fish.

⁷Then the disciple whom Jesus loved said to Peter, "It is the Lord!" As soon as Simon Peter heard him say, "It is the Lord," he wrapped his outer garment around him (for he had taken it off) and jumped into the water. ⁸The other disciples followed in the boat, towing the net full of fish, for they were not far from shore, about a hundred yards.ᵃ ⁹When they landed, they saw a fire of burning coals there with fish on it, and some bread.

¹⁰Jesus said to them, "Bring some of the fish you have just caught."

¹¹Simon Peter climbed aboard and dragged the net ashore. It was full of large fish, 153, but even with so many the net was not torn. ¹²Jesus said to them, "Come

ᵃ8 Greek *about two hundred cubits* (about 90 meters)

TUESDAY

VERSE FOR THE DAY:
John 20:20

AUTHOR:
Michael Card

PASSAGE FOR THE DAY:
John 20:19–23

Known by the Scars

[AFTER the crucifixion,] Mary recognized his [Jesus'] familiar voice. The disciples at Emmaus recognized him in the breaking of the bread. The weary fishermen knew it was him because of a miraculous catch. We, too, can recognize the resurrected Jesus in all these ways, by his voice, at his Table, by the miracles he still performs.

When Jesus wanted to be recognized the first thing the Bible says he did was show them his scars. He didn't point to his face and say, "Look, it's me." He showed them his hands and feet and side and gently said, "Look, it's me." Jesus is known by his scars . . .

At the far end of history, John, weeping because no one could open the special scroll, was told by an elder standing beside him in the heavenly crowd, "Do not weep! See, the Lion of the tribe of Judah" [Revelation 5:5].

John looked up, expecting to see a lion. But what did he see? A Lamb. And he knew who that Lamb was precisely because it was wounded.

Jesus is known by his scars. When we stand in his presence he won't point to his face but to his scars and say, "Look, it's me!"

Modern-day heretics point to material wealth and say, "Look, it's Jesus!" But the true followers of all ages . . . will tell you, "This is Jesus, for I bear in my own body the marks of his death" [see Galatians 6:17]. As Jesus' resurrected body was recognized by its scars, so his body, the church, should be known by its scars and tears and the unspeakable joy it knows in spite of, and indeed because of, it all.

Additional Scripture Readings:
Galatians 6:11–18; Revelation 5:1–10

Go to page 157 for your next devotional reading.

and have breakfast." None of the disciples dared ask him, "Who are you?" They knew it was the Lord. [13]Jesus came, took the bread and gave it to them, and did the same with the fish. [14]This was now the third time Jesus appeared to his disciples after he was raised from the dead.

Jesus Reinstates Peter

[15]When they had finished eating, Jesus said to Simon Peter, "Simon son of John, do you truly love me more than these?"

"Yes, Lord," he said, "you know that I love you."

Jesus said, "Feed my lambs."

[16]Again Jesus said, "Simon son of John, do you truly love me?"

He answered, "Yes, Lord, you know that I love you."

Jesus said, "Take care of my sheep."

[17]The third time he said to him, "Simon son of John, do you love me?"

Peter was hurt because Jesus asked him the third time, "Do you love me?" He said, "Lord, you know all things; you know that I love you."

Jesus said, "Feed my sheep. [18]I tell you the truth, when you were younger you dressed yourself and went where you wanted; but when you are old you will stretch out your hands, and someone else will dress you and lead you where you do not want to go." [19]Jesus said this to indicate the kind of death by which Peter would glorify God. Then he said to him, "Follow me!"

[20]Peter turned and saw that the disciple whom Jesus loved was following them. (This was the one who had leaned back against Jesus at the supper and had said, "Lord, who is going to betray you?") [21]When Peter saw him, he asked, "Lord, what about him?"

[22]Jesus answered, "If I want him to remain alive until I return, what is that to you? You must follow me." [23]Because of this, the rumor spread among the brothers that this disciple would not die. But Jesus did not say that he would not die; he only said, "If I want him to remain alive until I return, what is that to you?"

[24]This is the disciple who testifies to these things and who wrote them down. We know that his testimony is true.

[25]Jesus did many other things as well. If every one of them were written down, I suppose that even the whole world would not have room for the books that would be written.

*L*UKE begins the second volume of his history of Christianity (Acts 1:1–3) by telling how Jesus pours out the Holy Spirit on the apostles. The Spirit in turn inspires them to spread the message of salvation from Jerusalem to Rome. In his story Luke stresses how unity and love prevail in the church and how God protects the missionaries from their enemies. As you read this book, think about how powerful the Holy Spirit still is in the church and in your own life and how God protects you against the forces of evil.

ACTS

Jesus Taken Up Into Heaven

1 In my former book, Theophilus, I wrote about all that Jesus began to do and to teach ²until the day he was taken up to heaven, after giving instructions through the Holy Spirit to the apostles he had chosen. ³After his suffering, he showed himself to these men and gave many convincing proofs that he was alive. He appeared to them over a period of forty days and spoke about the kingdom of God. ⁴On one occasion, while he was eating with them, he gave them this command: "Do not leave Jerusalem, but wait for the gift my Father promised, which you have heard me speak about. ⁵For John baptized with*a* water, but in a few days you will be baptized with the Holy Spirit."

⁶So when they met together, they asked him, "Lord, are you at this time going to restore the kingdom to Israel?"

⁷He said to them: "It is not for you to

a 5 Or *in*

know the times or dates the Father has set by his own authority. **8**But you will receive power when the Holy Spirit comes on you; and you will be my witnesses in Jerusalem, and in all Judea and Samaria, and to the ends of the earth."

9After he said this, he was taken up before their very eyes, and a cloud hid him from their sight.

10They were looking intently up into the sky as he was going, when suddenly two men dressed in white stood beside them. **11**"Men of Galilee," they said, "why do you stand here looking into the sky? This same Jesus, who has been taken from you into heaven, will come back in the same way you have seen him go into heaven."

Matthias Chosen to Replace Judas

12Then they returned to Jerusalem from the hill called the Mount of Olives, a Sab-

---

WEDNESDAY

VERSE FOR THE DAY:
Acts 1:8

AUTHOR:
Reggie White

PASSAGE FOR THE DAY:
Acts 1:1–8

Playground Platform

ON A regular basis Philadelphia Eagles' defensive lineman Reggie White visits Philadelphia's inner city to talk to the kids.

I remind them that I grew up in a neighborhood just like theirs. I know what it's like to feel frustrated, to search for peace and a sense of security. I tell them about my upbringing and the most important thing I learned as a kid. I tell them about God and about his love for me.

I tell them that I love them with the love of the Lord Jesus Christ who loved them so much that he gave his life for them. I share that nothing in life satisfies like he does, that they may think power or money or important friends may fill the need they have. I read a few passages of Scripture and then relay to them the plan of salvation. As their heads are bowed on that dirty, old, hot playground, several of the kids pray to receive Christ as their Lord and Savior.

The rest of the crowd is dismissed as I remind them that we will be back the next Friday and that they should tell their friends and bring them back with them. Then I take the kids who have prayed to receive Christ over to the side and explain to them further what has just happened to their lives as a result of asking Jesus to come into their hearts. The next week I talk with them again about the problems they have, about what being a Christian is all about. What a glorious time we have on those Fridays.

Why do I take time out of my hectic schedule to be with these kids in North Philadelphia? Because God has given me a platform, and if I don't use it, I commit sin. Therefore, I choose to obey my Lord. And I enjoy it.

Additional Scripture Readings:
Romans 1:11–17; 2 Timothy 1:3–14

Go to page 162 for your next devotional reading.

bath day's walk[a] from the city. ¹³When they arrived, they went upstairs to the room where they were staying. Those present were Peter, John, James and Andrew; Philip and Thomas, Bartholomew and Matthew; James son of Alphaeus and Simon the Zealot, and Judas son of James. ¹⁴They all joined together constantly in prayer, along with the women and Mary the mother of Jesus, and with his brothers.

¹⁵In those days Peter stood up among the believers[b] (a group numbering about a hundred and twenty) ¹⁶and said, "Brothers, the Scripture had to be fulfilled which the Holy Spirit spoke long ago through the mouth of David concerning Judas, who served as guide for those who arrested Jesus— ¹⁷he was one of our number and shared in this ministry."

¹⁸(With the reward he got for his wickedness, Judas bought a field; there he fell headlong, his body burst open and all his intestines spilled out. ¹⁹Everyone in Jerusalem heard about this, so they called that field in their language Akeldama, that is, Field of Blood.)

²⁰"For," said Peter, "it is written in the book of Psalms,

" 'May his place be deserted;
    let there be no one to dwell in it,'[c]

and,

" 'May another take his place of
    leadership.'[d]

²¹Therefore it is necessary to choose one of the men who have been with us the whole time the Lord Jesus went in and out among us, ²²beginning from John's baptism to the time when Jesus was taken up from us. For one of these must become a witness with us of his resurrection."

²³So they proposed two men: Joseph called Barsabbas (also known as Justus) and Matthias. ²⁴Then they prayed, "Lord, you know everyone's heart. Show us which of these two you have chosen ²⁵to take over this apostolic ministry, which Judas left to go where he belongs." ²⁶Then they cast lots, and the lot fell to Matthias; so he was added to the eleven apostles.

The Holy Spirit Comes at Pentecost

2 When the day of Pentecost came, they were all together in one place. ²Suddenly a sound like the blowing of a violent wind came from heaven and filled the whole house where they were sitting. ³They saw what seemed to be tongues of fire that separated and came to rest on each of them. ⁴All of them were filled with the Holy Spirit and began to speak in other tongues[e] as the Spirit enabled them.

⁵Now there were staying in Jerusalem God-fearing Jews from every nation under heaven. ⁶When they heard this sound, a crowd came together in bewilderment, because each one heard them speaking in his own language. ⁷Utterly amazed, they asked: "Are not all these men who are speaking Galileans? ⁸Then how is it that each of us hears them in his own native language? ⁹Parthians, Medes and Elamites; residents of Mesopotamia, Judea and Cappadocia, Pontus and Asia, ¹⁰Phrygia and Pamphylia, Egypt and the parts of Libya near Cyrene; visitors from Rome ¹¹(both Jews and converts to Judaism); Cretans and Arabs—we hear them declaring the wonders of God in our own tongues!" ¹²Amazed and perplexed, they asked one another, "What does this mean?"

¹³Some, however, made fun of them and said, "They have had too much wine.[f]"

Peter Addresses the Crowd

¹⁴Then Peter stood up with the Eleven, raised his voice and addressed the crowd: "Fellow Jews and all of you who live in Jerusalem, let me explain this to you; listen carefully to what I say. ¹⁵These men are not drunk, as you suppose. It's only nine in the morning! ¹⁶No, this is what was spoken by the prophet Joel:

¹⁷" 'In the last days, God says,
    I will pour out my Spirit on all
        people.
Your sons and daughters will
        prophesy,
    your young men will see visions,
    your old men will dream dreams.
¹⁸Even on my servants, both men and
        women,
    I will pour out my Spirit in those
        days,
    and they will prophesy.
¹⁹I will show wonders in the heaven
        above
    and signs on the earth below,

---

[a]12 That is, about 3/4 mile (about 1,100 meters)   [b]15 Greek *brothers*   [c]20 Psalm 69:25
[d]20 Psalm 109:8   [e]4 Or *languages*; also in verse 11   [f]13 Or *sweet wine*

blood and fire and billows of smoke.
²⁰The sun will be turned to darkness
and the moon to blood
before the coming of the great and glorious day of the Lord.
²¹And everyone who calls
on the name of the Lord will be saved.'ᵃ

²²"Men of Israel, listen to this: Jesus of Nazareth was a man accredited by God to you by miracles, wonders and signs, which God did among you through him, as you yourselves know. ²³This man was handed over to you by God's set purpose and foreknowledge; and you, with the help of wicked men,ᵇ put him to death by nailing him to the cross. ²⁴But God raised him from the dead, freeing him from the agony of death, because it was impossible for death to keep its hold on him. ²⁵David said about him:

" 'I saw the Lord always before me.
Because he is at my right hand,
I will not be shaken.
²⁶Therefore my heart is glad and my tongue rejoices;
my body also will live in hope,
²⁷because you will not abandon me to the grave,
nor will you let your Holy One see decay.
²⁸You have made known to me the paths of life;
you will fill me with joy in your presence.'ᶜ

²⁹"Brothers, I can tell you confidently that the patriarch David died and was buried, and his tomb is here to this day. ³⁰But he was a prophet and knew that God had promised him on oath that he would place one of his descendants on his throne. ³¹Seeing what was ahead, he spoke of the resurrection of the Christ,ᵈ that he was not abandoned to the grave, nor did his body see decay. ³²God has raised this Jesus to life, and we are all witnesses of the fact. ³³Exalted to the right hand of God, he has received from the Father the promised Holy Spirit and has poured out what you now see and hear. ³⁴For David did not ascend to heaven, and yet he said,

" 'The Lord said to my Lord:
"Sit at my right hand
³⁵until I make your enemies
a footstool for your feet." 'ᵉ

³⁶"Therefore let all Israel be assured of this: God has made this Jesus, whom you crucified, both Lord and Christ."

³⁷When the people heard this, they were cut to the heart and said to Peter and the other apostles, "Brothers, what shall we do?"

³⁸Peter replied, "Repent and be baptized, every one of you, in the name of Jesus Christ for the forgiveness of your sins. And you will receive the gift of the Holy Spirit. ³⁹The promise is for you and your children and for all who are far off— for all whom the Lord our God will call."

⁴⁰With many other words he warned them; and he pleaded with them, "Save yourselves from this corrupt generation." ⁴¹Those who accepted his message were baptized, and about three thousand were added to their number that day.

The Fellowship of the Believers

⁴²They devoted themselves to the apostles' teaching and to the fellowship, to the breaking of bread and to prayer. ⁴³Everyone was filled with awe, and many wonders and miraculous signs were done by the apostles. ⁴⁴All the believers were together and had everything in common. ⁴⁵Selling their possessions and goods, they gave to anyone as he had need. ⁴⁶Every day they continued to meet together in the temple courts. They broke bread in their homes and ate together with glad and sincere hearts, ⁴⁷praising God and enjoying the favor of all the people. And the Lord added to their number daily those who were being saved.

Peter Heals the Crippled Beggar

3 One day Peter and John were going up to the temple at the time of prayer—at three in the afternoon. ²Now a man crippled from birth was being carried to the temple gate called Beautiful, where he was put every day to beg from those going into the temple courts. ³When he saw Peter and John about to enter, he asked them for money. ⁴Peter looked straight at him, as did John. Then Peter said, "Look at us!" ⁵So the man gave them his attention, expecting to get something from them.

ᵃ21 Joel 2:28-32   ᵇ23 Or *of those not having the law* (that is, Gentiles)   ᶜ28 Psalm 16:8-11
ᵈ31 Or *Messiah.* "The Christ" (Greek) and "the Messiah" (Hebrew) both mean "the Anointed One"; also in verse 36.   ᵉ35 Psalm 110:1

⁶Then Peter said, "Silver or gold I do not have, but what I have I give you. In the name of Jesus Christ of Nazareth, walk." ⁷Taking him by the right hand, he helped him up, and instantly the man's feet and ankles became strong. ⁸He jumped to his feet and began to walk. Then he went with them into the temple courts, walking and jumping, and praising God. ⁹When all the people saw him walking and praising God, ¹⁰they recognized him as the same man who used to sit begging at the temple gate called Beautiful, and they were filled with wonder and amazement at what had happened to him.

Peter Speaks to the Onlookers

¹¹While the beggar held on to Peter and John, all the people were astonished and came running to them in the place called Solomon's Colonnade. ¹²When Peter saw this, he said to them: "Men of Israel, why does this surprise you? Why do you stare at us as if by our own power or godliness we had made this man walk? ¹³The God of Abraham, Isaac and Jacob, the God of our fathers, has glorified his servant Jesus. You handed him over to be killed, and you disowned him before Pilate, though he had decided to let him go. ¹⁴You disowned the Holy and Righteous One and asked that a murderer be released to you. ¹⁵You killed the author of life, but God raised him from the dead. We are witnesses of this. ¹⁶By faith in the name of Jesus, this man whom you see and know was made strong. It is Jesus' name and the faith that comes through him that has given this complete healing to him, as you can all see.

¹⁷"Now, brothers, I know that you acted in ignorance, as did your leaders. ¹⁸But this is how God fulfilled what he had foretold through all the prophets, saying that his Christ*ᵃ* would suffer. ¹⁹Repent, then, and turn to God, so that your sins may be wiped out, that times of refreshing may come from the Lord, ²⁰and that he may send the Christ, who has been appointed for you — even Jesus. ²¹He must remain in heaven until the time comes for God to restore everything, as he promised long ago through his holy prophets. ²²For Moses said, 'The Lord your God will raise up for you a prophet like me from among your own people; you must listen to everything he tells you. ²³Anyone who does not listen to him will be completely cut off from among his people.'*ᵇ*

²⁴"Indeed, all the prophets from Samuel on, as many as have spoken, have foretold these days. ²⁵And you are heirs of the prophets and of the covenant God made with your fathers. He said to Abraham, 'Through your offspring all peoples on earth will be blessed.'*ᶜ* ²⁶When God raised up his servant, he sent him first to you to bless you by turning each of you from your wicked ways."

Peter and John Before the Sanhedrin

4 The priests and the captain of the temple guard and the Sadducees came up to Peter and John while they were speaking to the people. ²They were greatly disturbed because the apostles were teaching the people and proclaiming in Jesus the resurrection of the dead. ³They seized Peter and John, and because it was evening, they put them in jail until the next day. ⁴But many who heard the message believed, and the number of men grew to about five thousand.

⁵The next day the rulers, elders and teachers of the law met in Jerusalem. ⁶Annas the high priest was there, and so were Caiaphas, John, Alexander and the other men of the high priest's family. ⁷They had Peter and John brought before them and began to question them: "By what power or what name did you do this?"

⁸Then Peter, filled with the Holy Spirit, said to them: "Rulers and elders of the people! ⁹If we are being called to account today for an act of kindness shown to a cripple and are asked how he was healed, ¹⁰then know this, you and all the people of Israel: It is by the name of Jesus Christ of Nazareth, whom you crucified but whom God raised from the dead, that this man stands before you healed. ¹¹He is

" 'the stone you builders rejected,
which has become the
capstone.*ᵈ*'*ᵉ*

¹²Salvation is found in no one else, for there is no other name under heaven given to men by which we must be saved."

¹³When they saw the courage of Peter and John and realized that they were unschooled, ordinary men, they were astonished and they took note that these men had been with Jesus. ¹⁴But since they could see the man who had been healed

---

ᵃ18 Or *Messiah*; also in verse 20   *ᵇ23* Deut. 18:15,18,19   *ᶜ25* Gen. 22:18; 26:4   *ᵈ11* Or *cornerstone*   *ᵉ11* Psalm 118:22

standing there with them, there was nothing they could say. ¹⁵So they ordered them to withdraw from the Sanhedrin and then conferred together. ¹⁶"What are we going to do with these men?" they asked. "Everybody living in Jerusalem knows they have done an outstanding miracle, and we cannot deny it. ¹⁷But to stop this thing from spreading any further among the people, we must warn these men to speak no longer to anyone in this name."

¹⁸Then they called them in again and commanded them not to speak or teach at all in the name of Jesus. ¹⁹But Peter and John replied, "Judge for yourselves whether it is right in God's sight to obey you rather than God. ²⁰For we cannot help speaking about what we have seen and heard."

²¹After further threats they let them go. They could not decide how to punish them, because all the people were praising God for what had happened. ²²For the man who was miraculously healed was over forty years old.

The Believers' Prayer

²³On their release, Peter and John went back to their own people and reported all that the chief priests and elders had said to them. ²⁴When they heard this, they raised their voices together in prayer to God. "Sovereign Lord," they said, "you made the heaven and the earth and the sea, and everything in them. ²⁵You spoke by the Holy Spirit through the mouth of your servant, our father David:

" 'Why do the nations rage
 and the peoples plot in vain?
²⁶The kings of the earth take their stand
 and the rulers gather together
against the Lord
 and against his Anointed One.*ᵃ* ' *ᵇ*

²⁷Indeed Herod and Pontius Pilate met together with the Gentiles and the people*ᶜ* of Israel in this city to conspire against your holy servant Jesus, whom you anointed. ²⁸They did what your power and will had decided beforehand should happen. ²⁹Now, Lord, consider their threats and enable your servants to speak your word with great boldness. ³⁰Stretch out your hand to heal and perform miraculous signs and wonders through the name of your holy servant Jesus."

³¹After they prayed, the place where they were meeting was shaken. And they were all filled with the Holy Spirit and spoke the word of God boldly.

The Believers Share Their Possessions

³²All the believers were one in heart and mind. No one claimed that any of his possessions was his own, but they shared everything they had. ³³With great power the apostles continued to testify to the resurrection of the Lord Jesus, and much grace was upon them all. ³⁴There were no needy persons among them. For from time to time those who owned lands or houses sold them, brought the money from the sales ³⁵and put it at the apostles' feet, and it was distributed to anyone as he had need.

³⁶Joseph, a Levite from Cyprus, whom the apostles called Barnabas (which means Son of Encouragement), ³⁷sold a field he owned and brought the money and put it at the apostles' feet.

Ananias and Sapphira

5 Now a man named Ananias, together with his wife Sapphira, also sold a piece of property. ²With his wife's full knowledge he kept back part of the money for himself, but brought the rest and put it at the apostles' feet.

³Then Peter said, "Ananias, how is it that Satan has so filled your heart that you have lied to the Holy Spirit and have kept for yourself some of the money you received for the land? ⁴Didn't it belong to you before it was sold? And after it was sold, wasn't the money at your disposal? What made you think of doing such a thing? You have not lied to men but to God."

⁵When Ananias heard this, he fell down and died. And great fear seized all who heard what had happened. ⁶Then the young men came forward, wrapped up his body, and carried him out and buried him.

⁷About three hours later his wife came in, not knowing what had happened. ⁸Peter asked her, "Tell me, is this the price you and Ananias got for the land?"

"Yes," she said, "that is the price."

⁹Peter said to her, "How could you agree to test the Spirit of the Lord? Look! The feet of the men who buried your husband are at the door, and they will carry you out also."

¹⁰At that moment she fell down at his feet and died. Then the young men came in and, finding her dead, carried her out

---

ᵃ26 That is, Christ or Messiah *ᵇ26* Psalm 2:1,2 *ᶜ27* The Greek is plural.

and buried her beside her husband. ¹¹Great fear seized the whole church and all who heard about these events.

The Apostles Heal Many

¹²The apostles performed many miraculous signs and wonders among the people. And all the believers used to meet together in Solomon's Colonnade. ¹³No one else dared join them, even though they were highly regarded by the people. ¹⁴Nevertheless, more and more men and women believed in the Lord and were added to their number. ¹⁵As a result, peo-

---

THURSDAY

VERSE FOR THE DAY:
Acts 4:13

AUTHOR:
Richard Halverson

PASSAGE FOR THE DAY:
Acts 4:8–20

God with a Face

"I WANT a God with a face on," said a little girl to her minister one day—thereby expressing a *childlike*, nevertheless *profound*, desire for reality in religion. She was not satisfied with some nebulous, ethereal abstraction for God.

She wanted something definite, tangible. She wanted a *someone* for a God . . . not a *something*.

Perhaps that is why men do not take God more seriously. They hold a *theory about God*: Their notion of God is foggy, hazy, remote—an idea that is beyond them with *no connection with the everyday*.

A man wants a God with a face on!

"Who is the God you worship?" I have asked men this question on many occasions. "Tell me about him. What is he like? Where does he dwell? Is he real to you?"

Again and again they stop after a few confused mutterings and admit God is quite unreal. When pinned down they have little to say. Why should a man bother about God if that is all he means to him?

But consider Jesus Christ!

Jesus Christ is God in focus! In him we see God clearly, distinctly, sharply, *down to earth*! . . .

If you want to know what God is like, look at his Son. If you want to hear God, listen to his Son! *A man will make no mistake following Christ*!

Let a man begin with Jesus wherever he must to be honest with himself; let him investigate Jesus all the way. Let him go along with Jesus as far as truth dictates—as far as honest inquiry leads.

He will begin to realize that *Jesus is God in focus* . . .

You can't go wrong trusting Christ, following Christ, worshiping Christ! He will lead you to a personal, dynamic experience of God.

Additional Scripture Readings:
Hebrews 1:1–4; 1 John 1:1–4

Go to page 168 for your next devotional reading.

ple brought the sick into the streets and laid them on beds and mats so that at least Peter's shadow might fall on some of them as he passed by. ¹⁶Crowds gathered also from the towns around Jerusalem, bringing their sick and those tormented by evil[a] spirits, and all of them were healed.

The Apostles Persecuted

¹⁷Then the high priest and all his associates, who were members of the party of the Sadducees, were filled with jealousy. ¹⁸They arrested the apostles and put them in the public jail. ¹⁹But during the night an angel of the Lord opened the doors of the jail and brought them out. ²⁰"Go, stand in the temple courts," he said, "and tell the people the full message of this new life."

²¹At daybreak they entered the temple courts, as they had been told, and began to teach the people.

When the high priest and his associates arrived, they called together the Sanhedrin — the full assembly of the elders of Israel — and sent to the jail for the apostles. ²²But on arriving at the jail, the officers did not find them there. So they went back and reported, ²³"We found the jail securely locked, with the guards standing at the doors; but when we opened them, we found no one inside." ²⁴On hearing this report, the captain of the temple guard and the chief priests were puzzled, wondering what would come of this.

²⁵Then someone came and said, "Look! The men you put in jail are standing in the temple courts teaching the people." ²⁶At that, the captain went with his officers and brought the apostles. They did not use force, because they feared that the people would stone them.

²⁷Having brought the apostles, they made them appear before the Sanhedrin to be questioned by the high priest. ²⁸"We gave you strict orders not to teach in this name," he said. "Yet you have filled Jerusalem with your teaching and are determined to make us guilty of this man's blood."

²⁹Peter and the other apostles replied: "We must obey God rather than men! ³⁰The God of our fathers raised Jesus from the dead — whom you had killed by hanging him on a tree. ³¹God exalted him to his own right hand as Prince and Savior that he might give repentance and forgiveness of sins to Israel. ³²We are witnesses of these things, and so is the Holy Spirit, whom God has given to those who obey him."

³³When they heard this, they were furious and wanted to put them to death. ³⁴But a Pharisee named Gamaliel, a teacher of the law, who was honored by all the people, stood up in the Sanhedrin and ordered that the men be put outside for a little while. ³⁵Then he addressed them: "Men of Israel, consider carefully what you intend to do to these men. ³⁶Some time ago Theudas appeared, claiming to be somebody, and about four hundred men rallied to him. He was killed, all his followers were dispersed, and it all came to nothing. ³⁷After him, Judas the Galilean appeared in the days of the census and led a band of people in revolt. He too was killed, and all his followers were scattered. ³⁸Therefore, in the present case I advise you: Leave these men alone! Let them go! For if their purpose or activity is of human origin, it will fail. ³⁹But if it is from God, you will not be able to stop these men; you will only find yourselves fighting against God."

⁴⁰His speech persuaded them. They called the apostles in and had them flogged. Then they ordered them not to speak in the name of Jesus, and let them go.

⁴¹The apostles left the Sanhedrin, rejoicing because they had been counted worthy of suffering disgrace for the Name. ⁴²Day after day, in the temple courts and from house to house, they never stopped teaching and proclaiming the good news that Jesus is the Christ.[b]

The Choosing of the Seven

6 In those days when the number of disciples was increasing, the Grecian Jews among them complained against the Hebraic Jews because their widows were being overlooked in the daily distribution of food. ²So the Twelve gathered all the disciples together and said, "It would not be right for us to neglect the ministry of the word of God in order to wait on tables. ³Brothers, choose seven men from among you who are known to be full of the Spirit and wisdom. We will turn this responsibility over to them ⁴and will give our attention to prayer and the ministry of the word."

⁵This proposal pleased the whole group. They chose Stephen, a man full of faith and of the Holy Spirit; also Philip,

---

[a] 16 Greek *unclean*   [b] 42 Or *Messiah*

Procorus, Nicanor, Timon, Parmenas, and Nicolas from Antioch, a convert to Judaism. ⁶They presented these men to the apostles, who prayed and laid their hands on them.

⁷So the word of God spread. The number of disciples in Jerusalem increased rapidly, and a large number of priests became obedient to the faith.

Stephen Seized

⁸Now Stephen, a man full of God's grace and power, did great wonders and miraculous signs among the people. ⁹Opposition arose, however, from members of the Synagogue of the Freedmen (as it was called) — Jews of Cyrene and Alexandria as well as the provinces of Cilicia and Asia. These men began to argue with Stephen, ¹⁰but they could not stand up against his wisdom or the Spirit by whom he spoke.

¹¹Then they secretly persuaded some men to say, "We have heard Stephen speak words of blasphemy against Moses and against God."

¹²So they stirred up the people and the elders and the teachers of the law. They seized Stephen and brought him before the Sanhedrin. ¹³They produced false witnesses, who testified, "This fellow never stops speaking against this holy place and against the law. ¹⁴For we have heard him say that this Jesus of Nazareth will destroy this place and change the customs Moses handed down to us."

¹⁵All who were sitting in the Sanhedrin looked intently at Stephen, and they saw that his face was like the face of an angel.

Stephen's Speech to the Sanhedrin

7 Then the high priest asked him, "Are these charges true?"

²To this he replied: "Brothers and fathers, listen to me! The God of glory appeared to our father Abraham while he was still in Mesopotamia, before he lived in Haran. ³'Leave your country and your people,' God said, 'and go to the land I will show you.'[a]

⁴"So he left the land of the Chaldeans and settled in Haran. After the death of his father, God sent him to this land where you are now living. ⁵He gave him no inheritance here, not even a foot of ground. But God promised him that he and his descendants after him would possess the land, even though at that time Abraham had no child. ⁶God spoke to him in this way: 'Your descendants will be strangers in a country not their own, and they will be enslaved and mistreated four hundred years. ⁷But I will punish the nation they serve as slaves,' God said, 'and afterward they will come out of that country and worship me in this place.'[b] ⁸Then he gave Abraham the covenant of circumcision. And Abraham became the father of Isaac and circumcised him eight days after his birth. Later Isaac became the father of Jacob, and Jacob became the father of the twelve patriarchs.

⁹"Because the patriarchs were jealous of Joseph, they sold him as a slave into Egypt. But God was with him ¹⁰and rescued him from all his troubles. He gave Joseph wisdom and enabled him to gain the goodwill of Pharaoh king of Egypt; so he made him ruler over Egypt and all his palace.

¹¹"Then a famine struck all Egypt and Canaan, bringing great suffering, and our fathers could not find food. ¹²When Jacob heard that there was grain in Egypt, he sent our fathers on their first visit. ¹³On their second visit, Joseph told his brothers who he was, and Pharaoh learned about Joseph's family. ¹⁴After this, Joseph sent for his father Jacob and his whole family, seventy-five in all. ¹⁵Then Jacob went down to Egypt, where he and our fathers died. ¹⁶Their bodies were brought back to Shechem and placed in the tomb that Abraham had bought from the sons of Hamor at Shechem for a certain sum of money.

¹⁷"As the time drew near for God to fulfill his promise to Abraham, the number of our people in Egypt greatly increased. ¹⁸Then another king, who knew nothing about Joseph, became ruler of Egypt. ¹⁹He dealt treacherously with our people and oppressed our forefathers by forcing them to throw out their newborn babies so that they would die.

²⁰"At that time Moses was born, and he was no ordinary child.[c] For three months he was cared for in his father's house. ²¹When he was placed outside, Pharaoh's daughter took him and brought him up as her own son. ²²Moses was educated in all the wisdom of the Egyptians and was powerful in speech and action.

²³"When Moses was forty years old, he decided to visit his fellow Israelites. ²⁴He saw one of them being mistreated by an

---

a 3 Gen. 12:1   *b* 7 Gen. 15:13,14   *c* 20 Or *was fair in the sight of God*

Egyptian, so he went to his defense and avenged him by killing the Egyptian. **25**Moses thought that his own people would realize that God was using him to rescue them, but they did not. **26**The next day Moses came upon two Israelites who were fighting. He tried to reconcile them by saying, 'Men, you are brothers; why do you want to hurt each other?'

27"But the man who was mistreating the other pushed Moses aside and said, 'Who made you ruler and judge over us? **28**Do you want to kill me as you killed the Egyptian yesterday?'[a] **29**When Moses heard this, he fled to Midian, where he settled as a foreigner and had two sons.

30"After forty years had passed, an angel appeared to Moses in the flames of a burning bush in the desert near Mount Sinai. **31**When he saw this, he was amazed at the sight. As he went over to look more closely, he heard the Lord's voice: **32**'I am the God of your fathers, the God of Abraham, Isaac and Jacob.'[b] Moses trembled with fear and did not dare to look.

33"Then the Lord said to him, 'Take off your sandals; the place where you are standing is holy ground. **34**I have indeed seen the oppression of my people in Egypt. I have heard their groaning and have come down to set them free. Now come, I will send you back to Egypt.'[c]

35"This is the same Moses whom they had rejected with the words, 'Who made you ruler and judge?' He was sent to be their ruler and deliverer by God himself, through the angel who appeared to him in the bush. **36**He led them out of Egypt and did wonders and miraculous signs in Egypt, at the Red Sea[d] and for forty years in the desert.

37"This is that Moses who told the Israelites, 'God will send you a prophet like me from your own people.'[e] **38**He was in the assembly in the desert, with the angel who spoke to him on Mount Sinai, and with our fathers; and he received living words to pass on to us.

39"But our fathers refused to obey him. Instead, they rejected him and in their hearts turned back to Egypt. **40**They told Aaron, 'Make us gods who will go before us. As for this fellow Moses who led us out of Egypt—we don't know what has happened to him!'[f] **41**That was the time they made an idol in the form of a calf. They brought sacrifices to it and held a celebration in honor of what their hands had made. **42**But God turned away and gave them over to the worship of the heavenly bodies. This agrees with what is written in the book of the prophets:

> " 'Did you bring me sacrifices and offerings
>   forty years in the desert, O house of Israel?
> **43**You have lifted up the shrine of Molech
>   and the star of your god Rephan,
>   the idols you made to worship.
> Therefore I will send you into exile'[g]
>   beyond Babylon.

44"Our forefathers had the tabernacle of the Testimony with them in the desert. It had been made as God directed Moses, according to the pattern he had seen. **45**Having received the tabernacle, our fathers under Joshua brought it with them when they took the land from the nations God drove out before them. It remained in the land until the time of David, **46**who enjoyed God's favor and asked that he might provide a dwelling place for the God of Jacob.[h] **47**But it was Solomon who built the house for him.

48"However, the Most High does not live in houses made by men. As the prophet says:

> **49**" 'Heaven is my throne,
>   and the earth is my footstool.
> What kind of house will you build for me?
>   says the Lord.
> Or where will my resting place be?
> **50**Has not my hand made all these things?'[i]

51"You stiff-necked people, with uncircumcised hearts and ears! You are just like your fathers: You always resist the Holy Spirit! **52**Was there ever a prophet your fathers did not persecute? They even killed those who predicted the coming of the Righteous One. And now you have betrayed and murdered him— **53**you who have received the law that was put into effect through angels but have not obeyed it."

The Stoning of Stephen

54When they heard this, they were furi-

---

[a]28 Exodus 2:14   [b]32 Exodus 3:6   [c]34 Exodus 3:5,7,8,10   [d]36 That is, Sea of Reeds   [e]37 Deut. 18:15   [f]40 Exodus 32:1   [g]43 Amos 5:25-27   [h]46 Some early manuscripts *the house of Jacob*   [i]50 Isaiah 66:1,2

ous and gnashed their teeth at him. ⁵⁵But Stephen, full of the Holy Spirit, looked up to heaven and saw the glory of God, and Jesus standing at the right hand of God. ⁵⁶"Look," he said, "I see heaven open and the Son of Man standing at the right hand of God."

⁵⁷At this they covered their ears and, yelling at the top of their voices, they all rushed at him, ⁵⁸dragged him out of the city and began to stone him. Meanwhile, the witnesses laid their clothes at the feet of a young man named Saul.

⁵⁹While they were stoning him, Stephen prayed, "Lord Jesus, receive my spirit." ⁶⁰Then he fell on his knees and cried out, "Lord, do not hold this sin against them." When he had said this, he fell asleep.

8 And Saul was there, giving approval to his death.

The Church Persecuted and Scattered

On that day a great persecution broke out against the church at Jerusalem, and all except the apostles were scattered throughout Judea and Samaria. ²Godly men buried Stephen and mourned deeply for him. ³But Saul began to destroy the church. Going from house to house, he dragged off men and women and put them in prison.

Philip in Samaria

⁴Those who had been scattered preached the word wherever they went. ⁵Philip went down to a city in Samaria and proclaimed the Christ*ᵃ* there. ⁶When the crowds heard Philip and saw the miraculous signs he did, they all paid close attention to what he said. ⁷With shrieks, evil*ᵇ* spirits came out of many, and many paralytics and cripples were healed. ⁸So there was great joy in that city.

Simon the Sorcerer

⁹Now for some time a man named Simon had practiced sorcery in the city and amazed all the people of Samaria. He boasted that he was someone great, ¹⁰and all the people, both high and low, gave him their attention and exclaimed, "This man is the divine power known as the Great Power." ¹¹They followed him because he had amazed them for a long time with his magic. ¹²But when they believed Philip as he preached the good news of the kingdom of God and the name of Jesus Christ, they were baptized, both men and women. ¹³Simon himself believed and was baptized. And he followed Philip everywhere, astonished by the great signs and miracles he saw.

¹⁴When the apostles in Jerusalem heard that Samaria had accepted the word of God, they sent Peter and John to them. ¹⁵When they arrived, they prayed for them that they might receive the Holy Spirit, ¹⁶because the Holy Spirit had not yet come upon any of them; they had simply been baptized into*ᶜ* the name of the Lord Jesus. ¹⁷Then Peter and John placed their hands on them, and they received the Holy Spirit.

¹⁸When Simon saw that the Spirit was given at the laying on of the apostles' hands, he offered them money ¹⁹and said, "Give me also this ability so that everyone on whom I lay my hands may receive the Holy Spirit."

²⁰Peter answered: "May your money perish with you, because you thought you could buy the gift of God with money! ²¹You have no part or share in this ministry, because your heart is not right before God. ²²Repent of this wickedness and pray to the Lord. Perhaps he will forgive you for having such a thought in your heart. ²³For I see that you are full of bitterness and captive to sin."

²⁴Then Simon answered, "Pray to the Lord for me so that nothing you have said may happen to me."

²⁵When they had testified and proclaimed the word of the Lord, Peter and John returned to Jerusalem, preaching the gospel in many Samaritan villages.

Philip and the Ethiopian

²⁶Now an angel of the Lord said to Philip, "Go south to the road—the desert road—that goes down from Jerusalem to Gaza." ²⁷So he started out, and on his way he met an Ethiopian*ᵈ* eunuch, an important official in charge of all the treasury of Candace, queen of the Ethiopians. This man had gone to Jerusalem to worship, ²⁸and on his way home was sitting in his chariot reading the book of Isaiah the prophet. ²⁹The Spirit told Philip, "Go to that chariot and stay near it."

³⁰Then Philip ran up to the chariot and heard the man reading Isaiah the prophet. "Do you understand what you are reading?" Philip asked.

³¹"How can I," he said, "unless some-

---

*ᵃ*5 Or *Messiah*   *ᵇ*7 Greek *unclean*   *ᶜ*16 Or *in*   *ᵈ*27 That is, from the upper Nile region

one explains it to me?" So he invited Philip to come up and sit with him.

32The eunuch was reading this passage of Scripture:

"He was led like a sheep to the
    slaughter,
and as a lamb before the shearer is
    silent,
so he did not open his mouth.
33In his humiliation he was deprived of
    justice.
Who can speak of his descendants?
For his life was taken from the
    earth."*a*

34The eunuch asked Philip, "Tell me, please, who is the prophet talking about, himself or someone else?" **35**Then Philip began with that very passage of Scripture and told him the good news about Jesus.

36As they traveled along the road, they came to some water and the eunuch said, "Look, here is water. Why shouldn't I be baptized?"*b* **38**And he gave orders to stop the chariot. Then both Philip and the eunuch went down into the water and Philip baptized him. **39**When they came up out of the water, the Spirit of the Lord suddenly took Philip away, and the eunuch did not see him again, but went on his way rejoicing. **40**Philip, however, appeared at Azotus and traveled about, preaching the gospel in all the towns until he reached Caesarea.

Saul's Conversion

9 Meanwhile, Saul was still breathing out murderous threats against the Lord's disciples. He went to the high priest **2**and asked him for letters to the synagogues in Damascus, so that if he found any there who belonged to the Way, whether men or women, he might take them as prisoners to Jerusalem. **3**As he neared Damascus on his journey, suddenly a light from heaven flashed around him. **4**He fell to the ground and heard a voice say to him, "Saul, Saul, why do you persecute me?"

5"Who are you, Lord?" Saul asked.

"I am Jesus, whom you are persecuting," he replied. **6**"Now get up and go into the city, and you will be told what you must do."

7The men traveling with Saul stood there speechless; they heard the sound but did not see anyone. **8**Saul got up from the ground, but when he opened his eyes he could see nothing. So they led him by the hand into Damascus. **9**For three days he was blind, and did not eat or drink anything.

10In Damascus there was a disciple named Ananias. The Lord called to him in a vision, "Ananias!"

"Yes, Lord," he answered.

11The Lord told him, "Go to the house of Judas on Straight Street and ask for a man from Tarsus named Saul, for he is praying. **12**In a vision he has seen a man named Ananias come and place his hands on him to restore his sight."

13"Lord," Ananias answered, "I have heard many reports about this man and all the harm he has done to your saints in Jerusalem. **14**And he has come here with authority from the chief priests to arrest all who call on your name."

15But the Lord said to Ananias, "Go! This man is my chosen instrument to carry my name before the Gentiles and their kings and before the people of Israel. **16**I will show him how much he must suffer for my name."

17Then Ananias went to the house and entered it. Placing his hands on Saul, he said, "Brother Saul, the Lord—Jesus, who appeared to you on the road as you were coming here—has sent me so that you may see again and be filled with the Holy Spirit." **18**Immediately, something like scales fell from Saul's eyes, and he could see again. He got up and was baptized, **19**and after taking some food, he regained his strength.

Saul in Damascus and Jerusalem

Saul spent several days with the disciples in Damascus. **20**At once he began to preach in the synagogues that Jesus is the Son of God. **21**All those who heard him were astonished and asked, "Isn't he the man who raised havoc in Jerusalem among those who call on this name? And hasn't he come here to take them as prisoners to the chief priests?" **22**Yet Saul grew more and more powerful and baffled the Jews living in Damascus by proving that Jesus is the Christ.*c*

23After many days had gone by, the Jews conspired to kill him, **24**but Saul learned of their plan. Day and night they kept close watch on the city gates in order to kill him. **25**But his followers took him

---

a33 Isaiah 53:7,8   *b36* Some late manuscripts *baptized?"* *37Philip said, "If you believe with all your heart, you may." The eunuch answered, "I believe that Jesus Christ is the Son of God."*   *c22* Or *Messiah*

FRIDAY

VERSE FOR THE DAY:
Acts 9:15

AUTHOR:
Bill McCartney

PASSAGE FOR THE DAY:
Acts 9:1–16

Overpowered by His Presence

I'VE spent a lot of time reading Bible stories about this remarkable man [Paul]. He began as the bitterest enemy the gospel had. He was a murderer, a bigot, he hated Christianity and everything about it and he almost single-handedly drove the church out of Jerusalem. And he was on his way to Damascus to do the same thing there—to find Christians and bind them and bring them back to a kangaroo court and put them to death. Then, at the doorway of Damascus, the Lord Jesus Christ appeared to him in person and struck him down and transformed his life. From then on, Paul was a completely changed man. All his old war buddies, his cronies, were amazed. They couldn't understand what had happened to him. But he stayed true all the rest of his days.

In 2 Corinthians, there's a list as long as a tall man's arm relating all the things Paul endured. He was beaten, stoned, shipwrecked three times, imprisoned, and there were many attempts on his life before he was finally killed, beheaded in Rome because of his love for the gospel. And just before the end of his life, he was able to write to Timothy: "I have fought the good fight, I have finished the race, I have kept the faith. Now there is in store for me the crown of righteousness, which the Lord, the righteous Judge, will award to me on that day —and not only to me, but also to all who have longed for his appearing" (2 Timothy 4:7–8).

Paul said in Colossians that Christ is our life and in Galatians that Christ lives in us and again in Colossians that Christ in us is the hope of glory. I want more than anything in the world for Jesus Christ to live out his life through me. Without him I am nothing; with him I have the promise of everlasting life. Is there any better deal you can cut? Does anything else give you that assurance? It boggles my mind that someone can see life breathed into a baby, watch the grass die and then come to life again, see leaves fall and watch the rebirth of a tree, or gaze on any of the majestic splendor that is this earth and not be overpowered by the presence of an Almighty God!

Additional Scripture Readings:
Philippians 3:7–11;
Colossians 1:24–29

Go to page 170 for your next devotional reading.

by night and lowered him in a basket through an opening in the wall.

26When he came to Jerusalem, he tried to join the disciples, but they were all afraid of him, not believing that he really was a disciple. 27But Barnabas took him and brought him to the apostles. He told them how Saul on his journey had seen the Lord and that the Lord had spoken to him, and how in Damascus he had preached fearlessly in the name of Jesus. 28So Saul stayed with them and moved about freely in Jerusalem, speaking boldly in the name of the Lord. 29He talked and debated with the Grecian Jews, but they tried to kill him. 30When the brothers learned of this, they took him down to Caesarea and sent him off to Tarsus.

31Then the church throughout Judea, Galilee and Samaria enjoyed a time of peace. It was strengthened; and encouraged by the Holy Spirit, it grew in numbers, living in the fear of the Lord.

Aeneas and Dorcas

32As Peter traveled about the country, he went to visit the saints in Lydda. 33There he found a man named Aeneas, a paralytic who had been bedridden for eight years. 34"Aeneas," Peter said to him, "Jesus Christ heals you. Get up and take care of your mat." Immediately Aeneas got up. 35All those who lived in Lydda and Sharon saw him and turned to the Lord.

36In Joppa there was a disciple named Tabitha (which, when translated, is Dorcas*a*), who was always doing good and helping the poor. 37About that time she became sick and died, and her body was washed and placed in an upstairs room. 38Lydda was near Joppa; so when the disciples heard that Peter was in Lydda, they sent two men to him and urged him, "Please come at once!"

39Peter went with them, and when he arrived he was taken upstairs to the room. All the widows stood around him, crying and showing him the robes and other clothing that Dorcas had made while she was still with them.

40Peter sent them all out of the room; then he got down on his knees and prayed. Turning toward the dead woman, he said, "Tabitha, get up." She opened her eyes, and seeing Peter she sat up. 41He took her by the hand and helped her to her feet. Then he called the believers and the widows and presented her to them alive. 42This became known all over Joppa, and many people believed in the Lord. 43Peter stayed in Joppa for some time with a tanner named Simon.

Cornelius Calls for Peter

10 At Caesarea there was a man named Cornelius, a centurion in what was known as the Italian Regiment. 2He and all his family were devout and God-fearing; he gave generously to those in need and prayed to God regularly. 3One day at about three in the afternoon he had a vision. He distinctly saw an angel of God, who came to him and said, "Cornelius!"

4Cornelius stared at him in fear. "What is it, Lord?" he asked.

The angel answered, "Your prayers and gifts to the poor have come up as a memorial offering before God. 5Now send men to Joppa to bring back a man named Simon who is called Peter. 6He is staying with Simon the tanner, whose house is by the sea."

7When the angel who spoke to him had gone, Cornelius called two of his servants and a devout soldier who was one of his attendants. 8He told them everything that had happened and sent them to Joppa.

Peter's Vision

9About noon the following day as they were on their journey and approaching the city, Peter went up on the roof to pray. 10He became hungry and wanted something to eat, and while the meal was being prepared, he fell into a trance. 11He saw heaven opened and something like a large sheet being let down to earth by its four corners. 12It contained all kinds of fourfooted animals, as well as reptiles of the earth and birds of the air. 13Then a voice told him, "Get up, Peter. Kill and eat."

14"Surely not, Lord!" Peter replied. "I have never eaten anything impure or unclean."

15The voice spoke to him a second time, "Do not call anything impure that God has made clean."

16This happened three times, and immediately the sheet was taken back to heaven.

17While Peter was wondering about the meaning of the vision, the men sent by Cornelius found out where Simon's house was and stopped at the gate. 18They called

---

a 36 Both *Tabitha* (Aramaic) and *Dorcas* (Greek) mean *gazelle*.

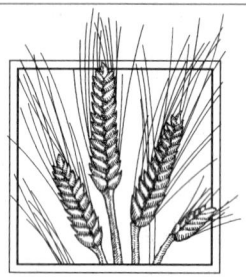

WEEKENDING

RESOLVE

I'm part of the fellowship of the unashamed. I have the Holy Spirit power. The die has been cast. I have stepped over the line. The decision has been made—I'm a disciple of his. I won't look back, let up, slow down, back away, or be still. My past is redeemed, my present makes sense, my future is secure. I'm finished and done with low living, sight walking, smooth knees, colorless dreams, tamed visions, worldly talking, cheap giving and dwarfed goals.

I no longer need preeminence, prosperity, position, promotions, plaudits or popularity. I don't have to be right, first, tops, recognized, praised, regarded or rewarded. I now live by faith, lean in his presence, walk by patience, am uplifted by prayer, and I labor with power.
– *A young pastor in Zimbabwe, Africa, later martyred for his faith in Christ*

REVIVE
Saturday: Luke 14:25–35
Sunday: Acts 7:54—8:1a

Go to page 172 for your next devotional reading.

out, asking if Simon who was known as Peter was staying there.

¹⁹While Peter was still thinking about the vision, the Spirit said to him, "Simon, three[a] men are looking for you. ²⁰So get up and go downstairs. Do not hesitate to go with them, for I have sent them."

²¹Peter went down and said to the men, "I'm the one you're looking for. Why have you come?"

²²The men replied, "We have come from Cornelius the centurion. He is a righteous and God-fearing man, who is respected by all the Jewish people. A holy angel told him to have you come to his house so that he could hear what you have to say." ²³Then Peter invited the men into the house to be his guests.

Peter at Cornelius' House

The next day Peter started out with them, and some of the brothers from Joppa went along. ²⁴The following day he arrived in Caesarea. Cornelius was expecting them and had called together his relatives and close friends. ²⁵As Peter entered the house, Cornelius met him and fell at his feet in reverence. ²⁶But Peter made him get up. "Stand up," he said, "I am only a man myself."

²⁷Talking with him, Peter went inside and found a large gathering of people. ²⁸He said to them: "You are well aware that it is against our law for a Jew to associate with a Gentile or visit him. But God has shown me that I should not call any man impure or unclean. ²⁹So when I was sent for, I came without raising any objection. May I ask why you sent for me?"

³⁰Cornelius answered: "Four days ago I was in my house praying at this hour, at three in the afternoon. Suddenly a man in shining clothes stood before me ³¹and said, 'Cornelius, God has heard your prayer and remembered your gifts to the poor. ³²Send to Joppa for Simon who is called Peter. He is a guest in the home of Simon the tanner, who lives by the sea.' ³³So I sent for you immediately, and it was good of you to come. Now we are all here in the presence of God to listen to everything the Lord has commanded you to tell us."

³⁴Then Peter began to speak: "I now realize how true it is that God does not show favoritism ³⁵but accepts men from every nation who fear him and do what is right. ³⁶You know the message God sent to the people of Israel, telling the good news of peace through Jesus Christ, who is Lord of all. ³⁷You know what has happened throughout Judea, beginning in Galilee after the baptism that John preached— ³⁸how God anointed Jesus of Nazareth with the Holy Spirit and power, and how he went around doing good and healing all who were under the power of the devil, because God was with him.

³⁹"We are witnesses of everything he did in the country of the Jews and in Jerusalem. They killed him by hanging him on a tree, ⁴⁰but God raised him from the dead on the third day and caused him to be seen. ⁴¹He was not seen by all the people, but by witnesses whom God had already chosen—by us who ate and drank with him after he rose from the dead. ⁴²He commanded us to preach to the people and to testify that he is the one whom God appointed as judge of the living and the dead. ⁴³All the prophets testify about him that everyone who believes in him receives forgiveness of sins through his name."

⁴⁴While Peter was still speaking these words, the Holy Spirit came on all who heard the message. ⁴⁵The circumcised believers who had come with Peter were astonished that the gift of the Holy Spirit had been poured out even on the Gentiles. ⁴⁶For they heard them speaking in tongues[b] and praising God.

Then Peter said, ⁴⁷"Can anyone keep these people from being baptized with water? They have received the Holy Spirit just as we have." ⁴⁸So he ordered that they be baptized in the name of Jesus Christ. Then they asked Peter to stay with them for a few days.

Peter Explains His Actions

11 The apostles and the brothers throughout Judea heard that the Gentiles also had received the word of God. ²So when Peter went up to Jerusalem, the circumcised believers criticized him ³and said, "You went into the house of uncircumcised men and ate with them."

⁴Peter began and explained everything to them precisely as it had happened: ⁵"I was in the city of Joppa praying, and in a trance I saw a vision. I saw something like a large sheet being let down from heaven by its four corners, and it came down to where I was. ⁶I looked into it and saw

---

[a]19 One early manuscript *two*; other manuscripts do not have the number.   [b]46 Or *other languages*

four-footed animals of the earth, wild beasts, reptiles, and birds of the air. ⁷Then I heard a voice telling me, 'Get up, Peter. Kill and eat.'

⁸"I replied, 'Surely not, Lord! Nothing impure or unclean has ever entered my mouth.'

⁹"The voice spoke from heaven a second time, 'Do not call anything impure that God has made clean.' ¹⁰This happened three times, and then it was all pulled up to heaven again.

¹¹"Right then three men who had been sent to me from Caesarea stopped at the house where I was staying. ¹²The Spirit told me to have no hesitation about going with them. These six brothers also went with me, and we entered the man's house. ¹³He told us how he had seen an angel appear in his house and say, 'Send to Joppa for Simon who is called Peter. ¹⁴He will bring you a message through which you and all your household will be saved.'

¹⁵"As I began to speak, the Holy Spirit came on them as he had come on us at the beginning. ¹⁶Then I remembered what the Lord had said: 'John baptized with*ᵃ* water, but you will be baptized with the Holy Spirit.' ¹⁷So if God gave them the same gift as he gave us, who believed in the Lord Jesus Christ, who was I to think that I could oppose God?"

¹⁸When they heard this, they had no further objections and praised God, say-

ᵃ16 Or in

MONDAY

VERSE FOR THE DAY:
Acts 10:43

AUTHOR:
Charles Stanley

PASSAGE FOR THE DAY:
Acts 10:34–43

Whoever Enters

GOD'S gift of forgiveness must be appropriated; that is, it must be accepted on an individual basis. Although it is a universal offer, it has no effect on the sin debt of a man or a woman who has not personally put trust in Christ. It is like a paycheck that is never picked up; it is like a gift certificate that is not redeemed; it is like a lifeline that is ignored by a drowning person.

Christ creatively communicated the concept of appropriation. Through the use of word pictures and parables, he drove home his point to "trust in God; trust also in me" (John 14:1). He told the woman at the well to ask for "living water" (John 4:10). He instructed the Jews to come to him to receive "life" (John 5:40). He told one group they would have to "eat the flesh of the Son of Man and drink his blood" (John 6:53). To the leaders of the Jews, he said, "If anyone keeps my word, he will never see death" (John 8:51). He presented himself to the Pharisees in this way: "I am the gate; whoever enters through me will be saved. He will come in and go out, and find pasture" (John 10:9). He used every conceivable illustration to show his audience that they needed to personally and individually appropriate God's gift of eternal life for themselves.

Additional Scripture Readings:
John 10:1–10; John 15:1–8

Go to page 176 for your next devotional reading.

ing, "So then, God has granted even the Gentiles repentance unto life."

The Church in Antioch

[19]Now those who had been scattered by the persecution in connection with Stephen traveled as far as Phoenicia, Cyprus and Antioch, telling the message only to Jews. [20]Some of them, however, men from Cyprus and Cyrene, went to Antioch and began to speak to Greeks also, telling them the good news about the Lord Jesus. [21]The Lord's hand was with them, and a great number of people believed and turned to the Lord.

[22]News of this reached the ears of the church at Jerusalem, and they sent Barnabas to Antioch. [23]When he arrived and saw the evidence of the grace of God, he was glad and encouraged them all to remain true to the Lord with all their hearts. [24]He was a good man, full of the Holy Spirit and faith, and a great number of people were brought to the Lord.

[25]Then Barnabas went to Tarsus to look for Saul, [26]and when he found him, he brought him to Antioch. So for a whole year Barnabas and Saul met with the church and taught great numbers of people. The disciples were called Christians first at Antioch.

[27]During this time some prophets came down from Jerusalem to Antioch. [28]One of them, named Agabus, stood up and through the Spirit predicted that a severe famine would spread over the entire Roman world. (This happened during the reign of Claudius.) [29]The disciples, each according to his ability, decided to provide help for the brothers living in Judea. [30]This they did, sending their gift to the elders by Barnabas and Saul.

Peter's Miraculous Escape From Prison

12 It was about this time that King Herod arrested some who belonged to the church, intending to persecute them. [2]He had James, the brother of John, put to death with the sword. [3]When he saw that this pleased the Jews, he proceeded to seize Peter also. This happened during the Feast of Unleavened Bread. [4]After arresting him, he put him in prison, handing him over to be guarded by four squads of four soldiers each. Herod intended to bring him out for public trial after the Passover.

[5]So Peter was kept in prison, but the church was earnestly praying to God for him.

[6]The night before Herod was to bring him to trial, Peter was sleeping between two soldiers, bound with two chains, and sentries stood guard at the entrance. [7]Suddenly an angel of the Lord appeared and a light shone in the cell. He struck Peter on the side and woke him up. "Quick, get up!" he said, and the chains fell off Peter's wrists.

[8]Then the angel said to him, "Put on your clothes and sandals." And Peter did so. "Wrap your cloak around you and follow me," the angel told him. [9]Peter followed him out of the prison, but he had no idea that what the angel was doing was really happening; he thought he was seeing a vision. [10]They passed the first and second guards and came to the iron gate leading to the city. It opened for them by itself, and they went through it. When they had walked the length of one street, suddenly the angel left him.

[11]Then Peter came to himself and said, "Now I know without a doubt that the Lord sent his angel and rescued me from Herod's clutches and from everything the Jewish people were anticipating."

[12]When this had dawned on him, he went to the house of Mary the mother of John, also called Mark, where many people had gathered and were praying. [13]Peter knocked at the outer entrance, and a servant girl named Rhoda came to answer the door. [14]When she recognized Peter's voice, she was so overjoyed she ran back without opening it and exclaimed, "Peter is at the door!"

[15]"You're out of your mind," they told her. When she kept insisting that it was so, they said, "It must be his angel."

[16]But Peter kept on knocking, and when they opened the door and saw him, they were astonished. [17]Peter motioned with his hand for them to be quiet and described how the Lord had brought him out of prison. "Tell James and the brothers about this," he said, and then he left for another place.

[18]In the morning, there was no small commotion among the soldiers as to what had become of Peter. [19]After Herod had a thorough search made for him and did not find him, he cross-examined the guards and ordered that they be executed.

Herod's Death

Then Herod went from Judea to Caesarea and stayed there a while. [20]He had been quarreling with the people of Tyre and Sidon; they now joined together and sought an audience with him. Having secured the support of Blastus, a trusted personal servant of the king, they asked for peace, because they depended on the king's country for their food supply.

21On the appointed day Herod, wearing his royal robes, sat on his throne and delivered a public address to the people. 22They shouted, "This is the voice of a god, not of a man." 23Immediately, because Herod did not give praise to God, an angel of the Lord struck him down, and he was eaten by worms and died.

24But the word of God continued to increase and spread.

25When Barnabas and Saul had finished their mission, they returned from[a] Jerusalem, taking with them John, also called Mark.

Barnabas and Saul Sent Off

13 In the church at Antioch there were prophets and teachers: Barnabas, Simeon called Niger, Lucius of Cyrene, Manaen (who had been brought up with Herod the tetrarch) and Saul. 2While they were worshiping the Lord and fasting, the Holy Spirit said, "Set apart for me Barnabas and Saul for the work to which I have called them." 3So after they had fasted and prayed, they placed their hands on them and sent them off.

On Cyprus

4The two of them, sent on their way by the Holy Spirit, went down to Seleucia and sailed from there to Cyprus. 5When they arrived at Salamis, they proclaimed the word of God in the Jewish synagogues. John was with them as their helper.

6They traveled through the whole island until they came to Paphos. There they met a Jewish sorcerer and false prophet named Bar-Jesus, 7who was an attendant of the proconsul, Sergius Paulus. The proconsul, an intelligent man, sent for Barnabas and Saul because he wanted to hear the word of God. 8But Elymas the sorcerer (for that is what his name means) opposed them and tried to turn the proconsul from the faith. 9Then Saul, who was also called Paul, filled with the Holy Spirit, looked straight at Elymas and said, 10"You are a child of the devil and an enemy of everything that is right! You are full of all kinds of deceit and trickery. Will you never stop perverting the right ways of the Lord? 11Now the hand of the Lord is against you. You are going to be blind, and for a time you will be unable to see the light of the sun."

Immediately mist and darkness came over him, and he groped about, seeking someone to lead him by the hand. 12When the proconsul saw what had happened, he believed, for he was amazed at the teaching about the Lord.

In Pisidian Antioch

13From Paphos, Paul and his companions sailed to Perga in Pamphylia, where John left them to return to Jerusalem. 14From Perga they went on to Pisidian Antioch. On the Sabbath they entered the synagogue and sat down. 15After the reading from the Law and the Prophets, the synagogue rulers sent word to them, saying, "Brothers, if you have a message of encouragement for the people, please speak."

16Standing up, Paul motioned with his hand and said: "Men of Israel and you Gentiles who worship God, listen to me! 17The God of the people of Israel chose our fathers; he made the people prosper during their stay in Egypt, with mighty power he led them out of that country, 18he endured their conduct[b] for about forty years in the desert, 19he overthrew seven nations in Canaan and gave their land to his people as their inheritance. 20All this took about 450 years.

"After this, God gave them judges until the time of Samuel the prophet. 21Then the people asked for a king, and he gave them Saul son of Kish, of the tribe of Benjamin, who ruled forty years. 22After removing Saul, he made David their king. He testified concerning him: 'I have found David son of Jesse a man after my own heart; he will do everything I want him to do.'

23"From this man's descendants God has brought to Israel the Savior Jesus, as he promised. 24Before the coming of Jesus, John preached repentance and baptism to all the people of Israel. 25As John was completing his work, he said: 'Who do you think I am? I am not that one. No, but he is coming after me, whose sandals I am not worthy to untie.'

26"Brothers, children of Abraham, and you God-fearing Gentiles, it is to us that this message of salvation has been sent.

---

[a]25 Some manuscripts *to*   [b]18 Some manuscripts *and cared for them*

²⁷The people of Jerusalem and their rulers did not recognize Jesus, yet in condemning him they fulfilled the words of the prophets that are read every Sabbath. ²⁸Though they found no proper ground for a death sentence, they asked Pilate to have him executed. ²⁹When they had carried out all that was written about him, they took him down from the tree and laid him in a tomb. ³⁰But God raised him from the dead, ³¹and for many days he was seen by those who had traveled with him from Galilee to Jerusalem. They are now his witnesses to our people.

³²"We tell you the good news: What God promised our fathers ³³he has fulfilled for us, their children, by raising up Jesus. As it is written in the second Psalm:

> " 'You are my Son;
> today I have become your
>   Father.'ᵃ'ᵇ

³⁴The fact that God raised him from the dead, never to decay, is stated in these words:

> " 'I will give you the holy and sure
>   blessings promised to David.'ᶜ

³⁵So it is stated elsewhere:

> " 'You will not let your Holy One see
>   decay.'ᵈ

³⁶"For when David had served God's purpose in his own generation, he fell asleep; he was buried with his fathers and his body decayed. ³⁷But the one whom God raised from the dead did not see decay.

³⁸"Therefore, my brothers, I want you to know that through Jesus the forgiveness of sins is proclaimed to you. ³⁹Through him everyone who believes is justified from everything you could not be justified from by the law of Moses. ⁴⁰Take care that what the prophets have said does not happen to you:

⁴¹" 'Look, you scoffers,
     wonder and perish,
for I am going to do something in
     your days
that you would never believe,
     even if someone told you.'ᵉ"

⁴²As Paul and Barnabas were leaving the synagogue, the people invited them to speak further about these things on the next Sabbath. ⁴³When the congregation was dismissed, many of the Jews and devout converts to Judaism followed Paul and Barnabas, who talked with them and urged them to continue in the grace of God.

⁴⁴On the next Sabbath almost the whole city gathered to hear the word of the Lord. ⁴⁵When the Jews saw the crowds, they were filled with jealousy and talked abusively against what Paul was saying.

⁴⁶Then Paul and Barnabas answered them boldly: "We had to speak the word of God to you first. Since you reject it and do not consider yourselves worthy of eternal life, we now turn to the Gentiles. ⁴⁷For this is what the Lord has commanded us:

> " 'I have made youᶠ a light for the
>   Gentiles,
> that youᶠ may bring salvation to
>   the ends of the earth.'ᵍ"

⁴⁸When the Gentiles heard this, they were glad and honored the word of the Lord; and all who were appointed for eternal life believed.

⁴⁹The word of the Lord spread through the whole region. ⁵⁰But the Jews incited the God-fearing women of high standing and the leading men of the city. They stirred up persecution against Paul and Barnabas, and expelled them from their region. ⁵¹So they shook the dust from their feet in protest against them and went to Iconium. ⁵²And the disciples were filled with joy and with the Holy Spirit.

In Iconium

14 At Iconium Paul and Barnabas went as usual into the Jewish synagogue. There they spoke so effectively that a great number of Jews and Gentiles believed. ²But the Jews who refused to believe stirred up the Gentiles and poisoned their minds against the brothers. ³So Paul and Barnabas spent considerable time there, speaking boldly for the Lord, who confirmed the message of his grace by enabling them to do miraculous signs and wonders. ⁴The people of the city were divided; some sided with the Jews, others with the apostles. ⁵There was a plot afoot among the Gentiles and Jews, together with their leaders, to mistreat them and stone them. ⁶But they found out about it and fled to the Lycaonian cities of Lystra and Derbe and to the surrounding coun-

---

ᵃ33 Or *have begotten you*   ᵇ33 Psalm 2:7   ᶜ34 Isaiah 55:3   ᵈ35 Psalm 16:10   ᵉ41 Hab. 1:5
ᶠ47 The Greek is singular.   ᵍ47 Isaiah 49:6

try, ⁷where they continued to preach the good news.

In Lystra and Derbe

⁸In Lystra there sat a man crippled in his feet, who was lame from birth and had never walked. ⁹He listened to Paul as he was speaking. Paul looked directly at him, saw that he had faith to be healed ¹⁰and called out, "Stand up on your feet!" At that, the man jumped up and began to walk.

¹¹When the crowd saw what Paul had done, they shouted in the Lycaonian language, "The gods have come down to us in human form!" ¹²Barnabas they called Zeus, and Paul they called Hermes because he was the chief speaker. ¹³The priest of Zeus, whose temple was just outside the city, brought bulls and wreaths to the city gates because he and the crowd wanted to offer sacrifices to them.

¹⁴But when the apostles Barnabas and Paul heard of this, they tore their clothes and rushed out into the crowd, shouting: ¹⁵"Men, why are you doing this? We too are only men, human like you. We are bringing you good news, telling you to turn from these worthless things to the living God, who made heaven and earth and sea and everything in them. ¹⁶In the past, he let all nations go their own way. ¹⁷Yet he has not left himself without testimony: He has shown kindness by giving

---

TUESDAY

VERSE FOR THE DAY:
Acts 13:39

AUTHOR:
Bill McCartney

PASSAGE FOR THE DAY:
Acts 13:38–41

A Personal Relationship

ON A retreat weekend with Christian university students, many of whom he coached, Bill McCartney was confronted with vibrant Christianity.

That day, for the first time in my life, I was confronted with questions about my faith. Did I have a personal relationship with Jesus Christ? Had I surrendered control of my life to Jesus? Had I made him Lord of my life?

In summary, I began to realize that I had been totally without a clue about what it's like to be a wholehearted, committed Christian—to have the true spirit of the Lord in my heart.

Right then and there, I made a decision. I decided to commit my life to Jesus Christ.

You see, I've always been a wholehearted guy, and I've always wanted a full measure of whatever was out there. I've never wanted just part of the package, part of the prize. I want it all! Over the previous ten years I'd been a daily communicant in the Catholic Church. You don't have that kind of resolve unless you want something really enthusiastically. I knew I wanted a deeper walk with the Lord. And that day, I realized what I had been missing—I hadn't been born again!

I wanted more. I wanted all of it. Right then and there, I prayed hard to receive the full measure of God's love. It was the most exciting moment of my life!

Additional Scripture Readings:
John 3:1–21; Romans 10:5–13

Go to page 181 for your next devotional reading.

you rain from heaven and crops in their seasons; he provides you with plenty of food and fills your hearts with joy." ¹⁸Even with these words, they had difficulty keeping the crowd from sacrificing to them.

¹⁹Then some Jews came from Antioch and Iconium and won the crowd over. They stoned Paul and dragged him outside the city, thinking he was dead. ²⁰But after the disciples had gathered around him, he got up and went back into the city. The next day he and Barnabas left for Derbe.

The Return to Antioch in Syria

²¹They preached the good news in that city and won a large number of disciples. Then they returned to Lystra, Iconium and Antioch, ²²strengthening the disciples and encouraging them to remain true to the faith. "We must go through many hardships to enter the kingdom of God," they said. ²³Paul and Barnabas appointed elders[a] for them in each church and, with prayer and fasting, committed them to the Lord, in whom they had put their trust. ²⁴After going through Pisidia, they came into Pamphylia, ²⁵and when they had preached the word in Perga, they went down to Attalia.

²⁶From Attalia they sailed back to Antioch, where they had been committed to the grace of God for the work they had now completed. ²⁷On arriving there, they gathered the church together and reported all that God had done through them and how he had opened the door of faith to the Gentiles. ²⁸And they stayed there a long time with the disciples.

The Council at Jerusalem

15 Some men came down from Judea to Antioch and were teaching the brothers: "Unless you are circumcised, according to the custom taught by Moses, you cannot be saved." ²This brought Paul and Barnabas into sharp dispute and debate with them. So Paul and Barnabas were appointed, along with some other believers, to go up to Jerusalem to see the apostles and elders about this question. ³The church sent them on their way, and as they traveled through Phoenicia and Samaria, they told how the Gentiles had been converted. This news made all the brothers very glad. ⁴When they came to Jerusalem, they were welcomed by the church and the apostles and elders, to whom they reported everything God had done through them.

⁵Then some of the believers who belonged to the party of the Pharisees stood up and said, "The Gentiles must be circumcised and required to obey the law of Moses."

⁶The apostles and elders met to consider this question. ⁷After much discussion, Peter got up and addressed them: "Brothers, you know that some time ago God made a choice among you that the Gentiles might hear from my lips the message of the gospel and believe. ⁸God, who knows the heart, showed that he accepted them by giving the Holy Spirit to them, just as he did to us. ⁹He made no distinction between us and them, for he purified their hearts by faith. ¹⁰Now then, why do you try to test God by putting on the necks of the disciples a yoke that neither we nor our fathers have been able to bear? ¹¹No! We believe it is through the grace of our Lord Jesus that we are saved, just as they are."

¹²The whole assembly became silent as they listened to Barnabas and Paul telling about the miraculous signs and wonders God had done among the Gentiles through them. ¹³When they finished, James spoke up: "Brothers, listen to me. ¹⁴Simon[b] has described to us how God at first showed his concern by taking from the Gentiles a people for himself. ¹⁵The words of the prophets are in agreement with this, as it is written:

¹⁶" 'After this I will return
and rebuild David's fallen tent.
Its ruins I will rebuild,
and I will restore it,
¹⁷that the remnant of men may seek the
Lord,
and all the Gentiles who bear my
name,
says the Lord, who does these
things'[c]
¹⁸ that have been known for ages.[d]

¹⁹"It is my judgment, therefore, that we should not make it difficult for the Gentiles who are turning to God. ²⁰Instead we should write to them, telling them to abstain from food polluted by idols, from

---

[a] 23 Or *Barnabas ordained elders;* or *Barnabas had elders elected*   [b] 14 Greek *Simeon*, a variant of *Simon;* that is, Peter   [c] 17 Amos 9:11,12   [d] 17,18 Some manuscripts *things'— / ¹⁸known to the Lord for ages is his work*

sexual immorality, from the meat of strangled animals and from blood. ²¹For Moses has been preached in every city from the earliest times and is read in the synagogues on every Sabbath."

The Council's Letter to Gentile Believers

²²Then the apostles and elders, with the whole church, decided to choose some of their own men and send them to Antioch with Paul and Barnabas. They chose Judas (called Barsabbas) and Silas, two men who were leaders among the brothers. ²³With them they sent the following letter:

> The apostles and elders, your brothers,
>
> To the Gentile believers in Antioch, Syria and Cilicia:
>
> Greetings.
>
> ²⁴We have heard that some went out from us without our authorization and disturbed you, troubling your minds by what they said. ²⁵So we all agreed to choose some men and send them to you with our dear friends Barnabas and Paul— ²⁶men who have risked their lives for the name of our Lord Jesus Christ. ²⁷Therefore we are sending Judas and Silas to confirm by word of mouth what we are writing. ²⁸It seemed good to the Holy Spirit and to us not to burden you with anything beyond the following requirements: ²⁹You are to abstain from food sacrificed to idols, from blood, from the meat of strangled animals and from sexual immorality. You will do well to avoid these things.
>
> Farewell.

³⁰The men were sent off and went down to Antioch, where they gathered the church together and delivered the letter. ³¹The people read it and were glad for its encouraging message. ³²Judas and Silas, who themselves were prophets, said much to encourage and strengthen the brothers. ³³After spending some time there, they were sent off by the brothers with the blessing of peace to return to those who had sent them.*ᵃ* ³⁵But Paul and Barnabas remained in Antioch, where they and many others taught and preached the word of the Lord.

Disagreement Between Paul and Barnabas

³⁶Some time later Paul said to Barnabas, "Let us go back and visit the brothers in all the towns where we preached the word of the Lord and see how they are doing." ³⁷Barnabas wanted to take John, also called Mark, with them, ³⁸but Paul did not think it wise to take him, because he had deserted them in Pamphylia and had not continued with them in the work. ³⁹They had such a sharp disagreement that they parted company. Barnabas took Mark and sailed for Cyprus, ⁴⁰but Paul chose Silas and left, commended by the brothers to the grace of the Lord. ⁴¹He went through Syria and Cilicia, strengthening the churches.

Timothy Joins Paul and Silas

16 He came to Derbe and then to Lystra, where a disciple named Timothy lived, whose mother was a Jewess and a believer, but whose father was a Greek. ²The brothers at Lystra and Iconium spoke well of him. ³Paul wanted to take him along on the journey, so he circumcised him because of the Jews who lived in that area, for they all knew that his father was a Greek. ⁴As they traveled from town to town, they delivered the decisions reached by the apostles and elders in Jerusalem for the people to obey. ⁵So the churches were strengthened in the faith and grew daily in numbers.

Paul's Vision of the Man of Macedonia

⁶Paul and his companions traveled throughout the region of Phrygia and Galatia, having been kept by the Holy Spirit from preaching the word in the province of Asia. ⁷When they came to the border of Mysia, they tried to enter Bithynia, but the Spirit of Jesus would not allow them to. ⁸So they passed by Mysia and went down to Troas. ⁹During the night Paul had a vision of a man of Macedonia standing and begging him, "Come over to Macedonia and help us." ¹⁰After Paul had seen the vision, we got ready at once to leave for Macedonia, concluding that God had called us to preach the gospel to them.

ᵃ33 Some manuscripts *them,* ³⁴*but Silas decided to remain there*

Lydia's Conversion in Philippi

[11] From Troas we put out to sea and sailed straight for Samothrace, and the next day on to Neapolis. [12] From there we traveled to Philippi, a Roman colony and the leading city of that district of Macedonia. And we stayed there several days.

[13] On the Sabbath we went outside the city gate to the river, where we expected to find a place of prayer. We sat down and began to speak to the women who had gathered there. [14] One of those listening was a woman named Lydia, a dealer in purple cloth from the city of Thyatira, who was a worshiper of God. The Lord opened her heart to respond to Paul's message. [15] When she and the members of her household were baptized, she invited us to her home. "If you consider me a believer in the Lord," she said, "come and stay at my house." And she persuaded us.

Paul and Silas in Prison

[16] Once when we were going to the place of prayer, we were met by a slave girl who had a spirit by which she predicted the future. She earned a great deal of money for her owners by fortune-telling. [17] This girl followed Paul and the rest of us, shouting, "These men are servants of the Most High God, who are telling you the way to be saved." [18] She kept this up for many days. Finally Paul became so troubled that he turned around and said to the spirit, "In the name of Jesus Christ I command you to come out of her!" At that moment the spirit left her.

[19] When the owners of the slave girl realized that their hope of making money was gone, they seized Paul and Silas and dragged them into the marketplace to face the authorities. [20] They brought them before the magistrates and said, "These men are Jews, and are throwing our city into an uproar [21] by advocating customs unlawful for us Romans to accept or practice."

[22] The crowd joined in the attack against Paul and Silas, and the magistrates ordered them to be stripped and beaten. [23] After they had been severely flogged, they were thrown into prison, and the jailer was commanded to guard them carefully. [24] Upon receiving such orders, he put them in the inner cell and fastened their feet in the stocks.

[25] About midnight Paul and Silas were praying and singing hymns to God, and the other prisoners were listening to them. [26] Suddenly there was such a violent earthquake that the foundations of the prison were shaken. At once all the prison doors flew open, and everybody's chains came loose. [27] The jailer woke up, and when he saw the prison doors open, he drew his sword and was about to kill himself because he thought the prisoners had escaped. [28] But Paul shouted, "Don't harm yourself! We are all here!"

[29] The jailer called for lights, rushed in and fell trembling before Paul and Silas. [30] He then brought them out and asked, "Sirs, what must I do to be saved?"

[31] They replied, "Believe in the Lord Jesus, and you will be saved — you and your household." [32] Then they spoke the word of the Lord to him and to all the others in his house. [33] At that hour of the night the jailer took them and washed their wounds; then immediately he and all his family were baptized. [34] The jailer brought them into his house and set a meal before them; he was filled with joy because he had come to believe in God — he and his whole family.

[35] When it was daylight, the magistrates sent their officers to the jailer with the order: "Release those men." [36] The jailer told Paul, "The magistrates have ordered that you and Silas be released. Now you can leave. Go in peace."

[37] But Paul said to the officers: "They beat us publicly without a trial, even though we are Roman citizens, and threw us into prison. And now do they want to get rid of us quietly? No! Let them come themselves and escort us out."

[38] The officers reported this to the magistrates, and when they heard that Paul and Silas were Roman citizens, they were alarmed. [39] They came to appease them and escorted them from the prison, requesting them to leave the city. [40] After Paul and Silas came out of the prison, they went to Lydia's house, where they met with the brothers and encouraged them. Then they left.

In Thessalonica

17 When they had passed through Amphipolis and Apollonia, they came to Thessalonica, where there was a Jewish synagogue. [2] As his custom was, Paul went into the synagogue, and on three Sabbath days he reasoned with them from the Scriptures, [3] explaining and

proving that the Christ[a] had to suffer and rise from the dead. "This Jesus I am proclaiming to you is the Christ,[a]" he said. ⁴Some of the Jews were persuaded and joined Paul and Silas, as did a large number of God-fearing Greeks and not a few prominent women.

⁵But the Jews were jealous; so they rounded up some bad characters from the marketplace, formed a mob and started a riot in the city. They rushed to Jason's house in search of Paul and Silas in order to bring them out to the crowd.[b] ⁶But when they did not find them, they dragged Jason and some other brothers before the city officials, shouting: "These men who have caused trouble all over the world have now come here, ⁷and Jason has welcomed them into his house. They are all defying Caesar's decrees, saying that there is another king, one called Jesus." ⁸When they heard this, the crowd and the city officials were thrown into turmoil. ⁹Then they made Jason and the others post bond and let them go.

In Berea

¹⁰As soon as it was night, the brothers sent Paul and Silas away to Berea. On arriving there, they went to the Jewish synagogue. ¹¹Now the Bereans were of more noble character than the Thessalonians, for they received the message with great eagerness and examined the Scriptures every day to see if what Paul said was true. ¹²Many of the Jews believed, as did also a number of prominent Greek women and many Greek men.

¹³When the Jews in Thessalonica learned that Paul was preaching the word of God at Berea, they went there too, agitating the crowds and stirring them up. ¹⁴The brothers immediately sent Paul to the coast, but Silas and Timothy stayed at Berea. ¹⁵The men who escorted Paul brought him to Athens and then left with instructions for Silas and Timothy to join him as soon as possible.

In Athens

¹⁶While Paul was waiting for them in Athens, he was greatly distressed to see that the city was full of idols. ¹⁷So he reasoned in the synagogue with the Jews and the God-fearing Greeks, as well as in the marketplace day by day with those who happened to be there. ¹⁸A group of Epicurean and Stoic philosophers began to dispute with him. Some of them asked, "What is this babbler trying to say?" Others remarked, "He seems to be advocating foreign gods." They said this because Paul was preaching the good news about Jesus and the resurrection. ¹⁹Then they took him and brought him to a meeting of the Areopagus, where they said to him, "May we know what this new teaching is that you are presenting? ²⁰You are bringing some strange ideas to our ears, and we want to know what they mean." ²¹(All the Athenians and the foreigners who lived there spent their time doing nothing but talking about and listening to the latest ideas.)

²²Paul then stood up in the meeting of the Areopagus and said: "Men of Athens! I see that in every way you are very religious. ²³For as I walked around and looked carefully at your objects of worship, I even found an altar with this inscription: TO AN UNKNOWN GOD. Now what you worship as something unknown I am going to proclaim to you.

²⁴"The God who made the world and everything in it is the Lord of heaven and earth and does not live in temples built by hands. ²⁵And he is not served by human hands, as if he needed anything, because he himself gives all men life and breath and everything else. ²⁶From one man he made every nation of men, that they should inhabit the whole earth; and he determined the times set for them and the exact places where they should live. ²⁷God did this so that men would seek him and perhaps reach out for him and find him, though he is not far from each one of us. ²⁸'For in him we live and move and have our being.' As some of your own poets have said, 'We are his offspring.'

²⁹"Therefore since we are God's offspring, we should not think that the divine being is like gold or silver or stone—an image made by man's design and skill. ³⁰In the past God overlooked such ignorance, but now he commands all people everywhere to repent. ³¹For he has set a day when he will judge the world with justice by the man he has appointed. He has given proof of this to all men by raising him from the dead."

³²When they heard about the resurrection of the dead, some of them sneered, but others said, "We want to hear you again on this subject." ³³At that, Paul left the Council. ³⁴A few men became follow-

---

[a]3 Or *Messiah*   [b]5 Or *the assembly of the people*

ers of Paul and believed. Among them was Dionysius, a member of the Areopagus, also a woman named Damaris, and a number of others.

In Corinth

18 After this, Paul left Athens and went to Corinth. ²There he met a Jew named Aquila, a native of Pontus, who had recently come from Italy with his wife Priscilla, because Claudius had ordered all the Jews to leave Rome. Paul went to see them, ³and because he was a tentmaker as they were, he stayed and worked with them. ⁴Every Sabbath he reasoned in the synagogue, trying to persuade Jews and Greeks.

⁵When Silas and Timothy came from Macedonia, Paul devoted himself exclusively to preaching, testifying to the Jews that Jesus was the Christ.*a* ⁶But when the Jews opposed Paul and became abusive, he shook out his clothes in protest and said to them, "Your blood be on your own heads! I am clear of my responsibility. From now on I will go to the Gentiles."

⁷Then Paul left the synagogue and went next door to the house of Titius Justus, a worshiper of God. ⁸Crispus, the synagogue ruler, and his entire household believed in the Lord; and many of the Corinthians who heard him believed and were baptized.

⁹One night the Lord spoke to Paul in a vision: "Do not be afraid; keep on speaking, do not be silent. ¹⁰For I am with you,

a 5 Or *Messiah*; also in verse 28

WEDNESDAY

VERSE FOR THE DAY:
Acts 17:11

AUTHOR:
Tom Landry

PASSAGE FOR THE DAY:
Acts 17:10–15

Character Building

HOW do we develop character?

I believe most of a person's character is developed as a child. It's the result of values learned from family and other significant people early in life — which is what makes our role as parents and the role of those who coach kids so important.

We also develop character by going through adversity. Coaches sometimes talk about a losing year being a "character-building season." There's truth to that as I've seen from experience. That strength of character so crucial to the 1970 [Dallas] Cowboys who rallied from almost certain failure to go on to the Super Bowl was forged through those difficult years when we couldn't win the big one.

They were perfect illustrations of what the apostle Paul was saying: "We know that suffering produces perseverance; perseverance, character; and character, hope" [see Romans 5:3–4].

Yet the truth remains, most of our character is established early in life. Adversity can help build it. Coaches can help mold it. But in our adult years, the only thing I've seen that can radically change a person's basic character is a relationship with Jesus Christ.

Additional Scripture Readings:
Proverbs 22:6; 1 Peter 1:3–9

Go to page 185 for your next devotional reading.

and no one is going to attack and harm you, because I have many people in this city." ¹¹So Paul stayed for a year and a half, teaching them the word of God.

¹²While Gallio was proconsul of Achaia, the Jews made a united attack on Paul and brought him into court. ¹³"This man," they charged, "is persuading the people to worship God in ways contrary to the law."

¹⁴Just as Paul was about to speak, Gallio said to the Jews, "If you Jews were making a complaint about some misdemeanor or serious crime, it would be reasonable for me to listen to you. ¹⁵But since it involves questions about words and names and your own law—settle the matter yourselves. I will not be a judge of such things." ¹⁶So he had them ejected from the court. ¹⁷Then they all turned on Sosthenes the synagogue ruler and beat him in front of the court. But Gallio showed no concern whatever.

Priscilla, Aquila and Apollos

¹⁸Paul stayed on in Corinth for some time. Then he left the brothers and sailed for Syria, accompanied by Priscilla and Aquila. Before he sailed, he had his hair cut off at Cenchrea because of a vow he had taken. ¹⁹They arrived at Ephesus, where Paul left Priscilla and Aquila. He himself went into the synagogue and reasoned with the Jews. ²⁰When they asked him to spend more time with them, he declined. ²¹But as he left, he promised, "I will come back if it is God's will." Then he set sail from Ephesus. ²²When he landed at Caesarea, he went up and greeted the church and then went down to Antioch.

²³After spending some time in Antioch, Paul set out from there and traveled from place to place throughout the region of Galatia and Phrygia, strengthening all the disciples.

²⁴Meanwhile a Jew named Apollos, a native of Alexandria, came to Ephesus. He was a learned man, with a thorough knowledge of the Scriptures. ²⁵He had been instructed in the way of the Lord, and he spoke with great fervor[a] and taught about Jesus accurately, though he knew only the baptism of John. ²⁶He began to speak boldly in the synagogue. When Priscilla and Aquila heard him, they invited him to their home and explained to him the way of God more adequately.

²⁷When Apollos wanted to go to Achaia, the brothers encouraged him and wrote to the disciples there to welcome him. On arriving, he was a great help to those who by grace had believed. ²⁸For he vigorously refuted the Jews in public debate, proving from the Scriptures that Jesus was the Christ.

Paul in Ephesus

19 While Apollos was at Corinth, Paul took the road through the interior and arrived at Ephesus. There he found some disciples ²and asked them, "Did you receive the Holy Spirit when[b] you believed?"

They answered, "No, we have not even heard that there is a Holy Spirit."

³So Paul asked, "Then what baptism did you receive?"

"John's baptism," they replied.

⁴Paul said, "John's baptism was a baptism of repentance. He told the people to believe in the one coming after him, that is, in Jesus." ⁵On hearing this, they were baptized into[c] the name of the Lord Jesus. ⁶When Paul placed his hands on them, the Holy Spirit came on them, and they spoke in tongues[d] and prophesied. ⁷There were about twelve men in all.

⁸Paul entered the synagogue and spoke boldly there for three months, arguing persuasively about the kingdom of God. ⁹But some of them became obstinate; they refused to believe and publicly maligned the Way. So Paul left them. He took the disciples with him and had discussions daily in the lecture hall of Tyrannus. ¹⁰This went on for two years, so that all the Jews and Greeks who lived in the province of Asia heard the word of the Lord.

¹¹God did extraordinary miracles through Paul, ¹²so that even handkerchiefs and aprons that had touched him were taken to the sick, and their illnesses were cured and the evil spirits left them.

¹³Some Jews who went around driving out evil spirits tried to invoke the name of the Lord Jesus over those who were demon-possessed. They would say, "In the name of Jesus, whom Paul preaches, I command you to come out." ¹⁴Seven sons of Sceva, a Jewish chief priest, were doing this. ¹⁵One day the evil spirit answered them, "Jesus I know, and I know about Paul, but who are you?" ¹⁶Then the man who had the evil spirit jumped on them and overpowered them all. He gave them

---

a25 Or *with fervor in the Spirit*   *b2* Or *after*   *c5* Or *in*   *d6* Or *other languages*

such a beating that they ran out of the house naked and bleeding.

17 When this became known to the Jews and Greeks living in Ephesus, they were all seized with fear, and the name of the Lord Jesus was held in high honor. 18 Many of those who believed now came and openly confessed their evil deeds. 19 A number who had practiced sorcery brought their scrolls together and burned them publicly. When they calculated the value of the scrolls, the total came to fifty thousand drachmas.*a* 20 In this way the word of the Lord spread widely and grew in power.

21 After all this had happened, Paul decided to go to Jerusalem, passing through Macedonia and Achaia. "After I have been there," he said, "I must visit Rome also." 22 He sent two of his helpers, Timothy and Erastus, to Macedonia, while he stayed in the province of Asia a little longer.

The Riot in Ephesus

23 About that time there arose a great disturbance about the Way. 24 A silversmith named Demetrius, who made silver shrines of Artemis, brought in no little business for the craftsmen. 25 He called them together, along with the workmen in related trades, and said: "Men, you know we receive a good income from this business. 26 And you see and hear how this fellow Paul has convinced and led astray large numbers of people here in Ephesus and in practically the whole province of Asia. He says that man-made gods are no gods at all. 27 There is danger not only that our trade will lose its good name, but also that the temple of the great goddess Artemis will be discredited, and the goddess herself, who is worshiped throughout the province of Asia and the world, will be robbed of her divine majesty."

28 When they heard this, they were furious and began shouting: "Great is Artemis of the Ephesians!" 29 Soon the whole city was in an uproar. The people seized Gaius and Aristarchus, Paul's traveling companions from Macedonia, and rushed as one man into the theater. 30 Paul wanted to appear before the crowd, but the disciples would not let him. 31 Even some of the officials of the province, friends of Paul, sent him a message begging him not to venture into the theater.

32 The assembly was in confusion: Some were shouting one thing, some another. Most of the people did not even know why they were there. 33 The Jews pushed Alexander to the front, and some of the crowd shouted instructions to him. He motioned for silence in order to make a defense before the people. 34 But when they realized he was a Jew, they all shouted in unison for about two hours: "Great is Artemis of the Ephesians!"

35 The city clerk quieted the crowd and said: "Men of Ephesus, doesn't all the world know that the city of Ephesus is the guardian of the temple of the great Artemis and of her image, which fell from heaven? 36 Therefore, since these facts are undeniable, you ought to be quiet and not do anything rash. 37 You have brought these men here, though they have neither robbed temples nor blasphemed our goddess. 38 If, then, Demetrius and his fellow craftsmen have a grievance against anybody, the courts are open and there are proconsuls. They can press charges. 39 If there is anything further you want to bring up, it must be settled in a legal assembly. 40 As it is, we are in danger of being charged with rioting because of today's events. In that case we would not be able to account for this commotion, since there is no reason for it." 41 After he had said this, he dismissed the assembly.

Through Macedonia and Greece

20 When the uproar had ended, Paul sent for the disciples and, after encouraging them, said good-by and set out for Macedonia. 2 He traveled through that area, speaking many words of encouragement to the people, and finally arrived in Greece, 3 where he stayed three months. Because the Jews made a plot against him just as he was about to sail for Syria, he decided to go back through Macedonia. 4 He was accompanied by Sopater son of Pyrrhus from Berea, Aristarchus and Secundus from Thessalonica, Gaius from Derbe, Timothy also, and Tychicus and Trophimus from the province of Asia. 5 These men went on ahead and waited for us at Troas. 6 But we sailed from Philippi after the Feast of Unleavened Bread, and five days later joined the others at Troas, where we stayed seven days.

Eutychus Raised From the Dead at Troas

7 On the first day of the week we came together to break bread. Paul spoke to the

---

a19 A drachma was a silver coin worth about a day's wages.

people and, because he intended to leave the next day, kept on talking until midnight. ⁸There were many lamps in the upstairs room where we were meeting. ⁹Seated in a window was a young man named Eutychus, who was sinking into a deep sleep as Paul talked on and on. When he was sound asleep, he fell to the ground from the third story and was picked up dead. ¹⁰Paul went down, threw himself on the young man and put his arms around him. "Don't be alarmed," he said. "He's alive!" ¹¹Then he went upstairs again and broke bread and ate. After talking until daylight, he left. ¹²The people took the young man home alive and were greatly comforted.

Paul's Farewell to the Ephesian Elders

¹³We went on ahead to the ship and sailed for Assos, where we were going to take Paul aboard. He had made this arrangement because he was going there on foot. ¹⁴When he met us at Assos, we took him aboard and went on to Mitylene. ¹⁵The next day we set sail from there and arrived off Kios. The day after that we crossed over to Samos, and on the following day arrived at Miletus. ¹⁶Paul had decided to sail past Ephesus to avoid spending time in the province of Asia, for he was in a hurry to reach Jerusalem, if possible, by the day of Pentecost.

¹⁷From Miletus, Paul sent to Ephesus for the elders of the church. ¹⁸When they arrived, he said to them: "You know how I lived the whole time I was with you, from the first day I came into the province of Asia. ¹⁹I served the Lord with great humility and with tears, although I was severely tested by the plots of the Jews. ²⁰You know that I have not hesitated to preach anything that would be helpful to you but have taught you publicly and from house to house. ²¹I have declared to both Jews and Greeks that they must turn to God in repentance and have faith in our Lord Jesus.

²²"And now, compelled by the Spirit, I am going to Jerusalem, not knowing what will happen to me there. ²³I only know that in every city the Holy Spirit warns me that prison and hardships are facing me. ²⁴However, I consider my life worth nothing to me, if only I may finish the race and complete the task the Lord Jesus has given me — the task of testifying to the gospel of God's grace.

²⁵"Now I know that none of you among whom I have gone about preaching the kingdom will ever see me again. ²⁶Therefore, I declare to you today that I am innocent of the blood of all men. ²⁷For I have not hesitated to proclaim to you the whole will of God. ²⁸Keep watch over yourselves and all the flock of which the Holy Spirit has made you overseers.ᵃ Be shepherds of the church of God,ᵇ which he bought with his own blood. ²⁹I know that after I leave, savage wolves will come in among you and will not spare the flock. ³⁰Even from your own number men will arise and distort the truth in order to draw away disciples after them. ³¹So be on your guard! Remember that for three years I never stopped warning each of you night and day with tears.

³²"Now I commit you to God and to the word of his grace, which can build you up and give you an inheritance among all those who are sanctified. ³³I have not coveted anyone's silver or gold or clothing. ³⁴You yourselves know that these hands of mine have supplied my own needs and the needs of my companions. ³⁵In everything I did, I showed you that by this kind of hard work we must help the weak, remembering the words the Lord Jesus himself said: 'It is more blessed to give than to receive.' "

³⁶When he had said this, he knelt down with all of them and prayed. ³⁷They all wept as they embraced him and kissed him. ³⁸What grieved them most was his statement that they would never see his face again. Then they accompanied him to the ship.

On to Jerusalem

21 After we had torn ourselves away from them, we put out to sea and sailed straight to Cos. The next day we went to Rhodes and from there to Patara. ²We found a ship crossing over to Phoenicia, went on board and set sail. ³After sighting Cyprus and passing to the south of it, we sailed on to Syria. We landed at Tyre, where our ship was to unload its cargo. ⁴Finding the disciples there, we stayed with them seven days. Through the Spirit they urged Paul not to go on to Jerusalem. ⁵But when our time was up, we left and continued on our way. All the disciples

---

ᵃ28 Traditionally *bishops*   ᵇ28 Many manuscripts *of the Lord*

and their wives and children accompanied us out of the city, and there on the beach we knelt to pray. ⁶After saying good-by to each other, we went aboard the ship, and they returned home.

⁷We continued our voyage from Tyre and landed at Ptolemais, where we greeted the brothers and stayed with them for a day. ⁸Leaving the next day, we reached Caesarea and stayed at the house of Philip the evangelist, one of the Seven. ⁹He had four unmarried daughters who prophesied.

¹⁰After we had been there a number of days, a prophet named Agabus came down from Judea. ¹¹Coming over to us, he took Paul's belt, tied his own hands and feet with it and said, "The Holy Spirit says, 'In this way the Jews of Jerusalem will bind the owner of this belt and will hand him over to the Gentiles.' "

¹²When we heard this, we and the people there pleaded with Paul not to go up to Jerusalem. ¹³Then Paul answered, "Why are you weeping and breaking my heart? I am ready not only to be bound, but also to die in Jerusalem for the name of the Lord Jesus." ¹⁴When he would not be dissuaded, we gave up and said, "The Lord's will be done."

¹⁵After this, we got ready and went up to Jerusalem. ¹⁶Some of the disciples from Caesarea accompanied us and brought us to the home of Mnason, where we were to stay. He was a man from Cyprus and one of the early disciples.

THURSDAY

VERSE FOR THE DAY:
Acts 20:24

AUTHOR:
Patrick Morley

PASSAGE FOR THE DAY:
Acts 20:17–24

Running the Race

WE CAN define the rat race as the pursuit of the beautiful, wrinkle-free life. Since there are no winners, the aftermath of running the race and losing takes a heavy toll . . .

If the pursuit of money and possessions stood alone as an issue, we might be able to rationalize some of our money lust. But every balance sheet has two sides, and the other side of this balance sheet is relationships.

When we choose the rat race, fracture lines soon appear in our relationships, and crumbling is not far behind. Unfortunately, all too often, in pursuit of the good life, *most men leave a trail of broken relationships.*

The way in which we measure our standard of living indicates the race we have decided to run. The American Christian faces a true dilemma. We can choose the rat race, or we can choose to not love this world and "throw off everything that hinders and the sin that so easily entangles, and . . . run with perseverance the race marked out for us" (Hebrews 12:1).

We each make our own choice, but the pressure to make the wrong choice is intense and should not be underestimated. As my first Bible study leader was fond of saying, "You can choose your own way, but you can't choose the result." The cause and effect nature of our choice brands us.

Additional Scripture Readings:
2 Timothy 4:6–8; Hebrews 12:1–3

Go to page 188 for your next devotional reading.

Paul's Arrival at Jerusalem

[17]When we arrived at Jerusalem, the brothers received us warmly. [18]The next day Paul and the rest of us went to see James, and all the elders were present. [19]Paul greeted them and reported in detail what God had done among the Gentiles through his ministry.

[20]When they heard this, they praised God. Then they said to Paul: "You see, brother, how many thousands of Jews have believed, and all of them are zealous for the law. [21]They have been informed that you teach all the Jews who live among the Gentiles to turn away from Moses, telling them not to circumcise their children or live according to our customs. [22]What shall we do? They will certainly hear that you have come, [23]so do what we tell you. There are four men with us who have made a vow. [24]Take these men, join in their purification rites and pay their expenses, so that they can have their heads shaved. Then everybody will know there is no truth in these reports about you, but that you yourself are living in obedience to the law. [25]As for the Gentile believers, we have written to them our decision that they should abstain from food sacrificed to idols, from blood, from the meat of strangled animals and from sexual immorality."

[26]The next day Paul took the men and purified himself along with them. Then he went to the temple to give notice of the date when the days of purification would end and the offering would be made for each of them.

Paul Arrested

[27]When the seven days were nearly over, some Jews from the province of Asia saw Paul at the temple. They stirred up the whole crowd and seized him, [28]shouting, "Men of Israel, help us! This is the man who teaches all men everywhere against our people and our law and this place. And besides, he has brought Greeks into the temple area and defiled this holy place." [29](They had previously seen Trophimus the Ephesian in the city with Paul and assumed that Paul had brought him into the temple area.)

[30]The whole city was aroused, and the people came running from all directions. Seizing Paul, they dragged him from the temple, and immediately the gates were shut. [31]While they were trying to kill him, news reached the commander of the Roman troops that the whole city of Jerusalem was in an uproar. [32]He at once took some officers and soldiers and ran down to the crowd. When the rioters saw the commander and his soldiers, they stopped beating Paul.

[33]The commander came up and arrested him and ordered him to be bound with two chains. Then he asked who he was and what he had done. [34]Some in the crowd shouted one thing and some another, and since the commander could not get at the truth because of the uproar, he ordered that Paul be taken into the barracks. [35]When Paul reached the steps, the violence of the mob was so great he had to be carried by the soldiers. [36]The crowd that followed kept shouting, "Away with him!"

Paul Speaks to the Crowd

[37]As the soldiers were about to take Paul into the barracks, he asked the commander, "May I say something to you?"

"Do you speak Greek?" he replied. [38]"Aren't you the Egyptian who started a revolt and led four thousand terrorists out into the desert some time ago?"

[39]Paul answered, "I am a Jew, from Tarsus in Cilicia, a citizen of no ordinary city. Please let me speak to the people."

[40]Having received the commander's permission, Paul stood on the steps and motioned to the crowd. When they were all silent, he said to them in Aramaic[a]:

22 [1]"Brothers and fathers, listen now to my defense."

[2]When they heard him speak to them in Aramaic, they became very quiet.

Then Paul said: [3]"I am a Jew, born in Tarsus of Cilicia, but brought up in this city. Under Gamaliel I was thoroughly trained in the law of our fathers and was just as zealous for God as any of you are today. [4]I persecuted the followers of this Way to their death, arresting both men and women and throwing them into prison, [5]as also the high priest and all the Council can testify. I even obtained letters from them to their brothers in Damascus, and went there to bring these people as prisoners to Jerusalem to be punished.

[6]"About noon as I came near Damascus, suddenly a bright light from heaven flashed around me. [7]I fell to the ground

---

[a]40 Or possibly *Hebrew*; also in 22:2

and heard a voice say to me, 'Saul! Saul! Why do you persecute me?'

⁸" 'Who are you, Lord?' I asked.

" 'I am Jesus of Nazareth, whom you are persecuting,' he replied. ⁹My companions saw the light, but they did not understand the voice of him who was speaking to me.

¹⁰" 'What shall I do, Lord?' I asked.

" 'Get up,' the Lord said, 'and go into Damascus. There you will be told all that you have been assigned to do.' ¹¹My companions led me by the hand into Damascus, because the brilliance of the light had blinded me.

¹²"A man named Ananias came to see me. He was a devout observer of the law and highly respected by all the Jews living there. ¹³He stood beside me and said, 'Brother Saul, receive your sight!' And at that very moment I was able to see him.

¹⁴"Then he said: 'The God of our fathers has chosen you to know his will and to see the Righteous One and to hear words from his mouth. ¹⁵You will be his witness to all men of what you have seen and heard. ¹⁶And now what are you waiting for? Get up, be baptized and wash your sins away, calling on his name.'

¹⁷"When I returned to Jerusalem and was praying at the temple, I fell into a trance ¹⁸and saw the Lord speaking. 'Quick!' he said to me. 'Leave Jerusalem immediately, because they will not accept your testimony about me.'

¹⁹" 'Lord,' I replied, 'these men know that I went from one synagogue to another to imprison and beat those who believe in you. ²⁰And when the blood of your martyr^a Stephen was shed, I stood there giving my approval and guarding the clothes of those who were killing him.'

²¹"Then the Lord said to me, 'Go; I will send you far away to the Gentiles.' "

Paul the Roman Citizen

²²The crowd listened to Paul until he said this. Then they raised their voices and shouted, "Rid the earth of him! He's not fit to live!"

²³As they were shouting and throwing off their cloaks and flinging dust into the air, ²⁴the commander ordered Paul to be taken into the barracks. He directed that he be flogged and questioned in order to find out why the people were shouting at him like this. ²⁵As they stretched him out to flog him, Paul said to the centurion standing there, "Is it legal for you to flog a Roman citizen who hasn't even been found guilty?"

²⁶When the centurion heard this, he went to the commander and reported it. "What are you going to do?" he asked. "This man is a Roman citizen."

²⁷The commander went to Paul and asked, "Tell me, are you a Roman citizen?"

"Yes, I am," he answered.

²⁸Then the commander said, "I had to pay a big price for my citizenship."

"But I was born a citizen," Paul replied.

²⁹Those who were about to question him withdrew immediately. The commander himself was alarmed when he realized that he had put Paul, a Roman citizen, in chains.

Before the Sanhedrin

³⁰The next day, since the commander wanted to find out exactly why Paul was being accused by the Jews, he released him and ordered the chief priests and all the Sanhedrin to assemble. Then he brought Paul and had him stand before them.

23 Paul looked straight at the Sanhedrin and said, "My brothers, I have fulfilled my duty to God in all good conscience to this day." ²At this the high priest Ananias ordered those standing near Paul to strike him on the mouth. ³Then Paul said to him, "God will strike you, you whitewashed wall! You sit there to judge me according to the law, yet you yourself violate the law by commanding that I be struck!"

⁴Those who were standing near Paul said, "You dare to insult God's high priest?"

⁵Paul replied, "Brothers, I did not realize that he was the high priest; for it is written: 'Do not speak evil about the ruler of your people.'^{b}"

⁶Then Paul, knowing that some of them were Sadducees and the others Pharisees, called out in the Sanhedrin, "My brothers, I am a Pharisee, the son of a Pharisee. I stand on trial because of my hope in the resurrection of the dead." ⁷When he said this, a dispute broke out between the Pharisees and the Sadducees, and the assembly was divided. ⁸(The Sadducees say that there is no resurrection, and that there are neither angels nor spirits, but the Pharisees acknowledge them all.)

---

^{a}20 Or *witness* ^{b}5 Exodus 22:28

⁹There was a great uproar, and some of the teachers of the law who were Pharisees stood up and argued vigorously. "We find nothing wrong with this man," they said. "What if a spirit or an angel has spoken to him?" ¹⁰The dispute became so violent that the commander was afraid Paul would be torn to pieces by them. He ordered the troops to go down and take him away from them by force and bring him into the barracks.

¹¹The following night the Lord stood near Paul and said, "Take courage! As you have testified about me in Jerusalem, so you must also testify in Rome."

The Plot to Kill Paul

¹²The next morning the Jews formed a conspiracy and bound themselves with an oath not to eat or drink until they had killed Paul. ¹³More than forty men were involved in this plot. ¹⁴They went to the chief priests and elders and said, "We have taken a solemn oath not to eat anything until we have killed Paul. ¹⁵Now then, you and the Sanhedrin petition the

---

FRIDAY

VERSE FOR THE DAY:
Acts 22:16

AUTHOR:
Max Lucado

PASSAGE FOR THE DAY:
Acts 22:12–21

Sin Meets Savior

ANANIAS'S instructions to Paul are worth reading: "What are you waiting for? Get up, be baptized and wash your sins away, calling on his name" (Acts 22:16).

He didn't have to be told twice. The legalist Saul was buried, and the liberator Paul was born. He was never the same afterwards. And neither was the world.

Stirring sermons, dedicated disciples, and six thousand miles of trails. If his sandals weren't slapping, his pen was writing. If he wasn't explaining the mystery of grace, he was articulating the theology that would determine the course of Western civilization.

All of his words could be reduced to one sentence. "We preach Christ crucified" (1 Corinthians 1:23). It wasn't that he lacked other sermon outlines; it was just that he couldn't exhaust the first one . . .

Paul never took a course in missions. He never sat in on a committee meeting. He never read a book on church growth. He was just inspired by the Holy Spirit and punch-drunk on the love that makes the impossible possible: salvation.

The message is gripping: Show a man his failures without Jesus, and the result will be found in the roadside gutter. Give a man religion without reminding him of his filth, and the result will be arrogance in a three-piece suit. But get the two in the same heart—get sin to meet Savior and Savior to meet sin—and the result just might be another Pharisee turned preacher who sets the world on fire.

Additional Scripture Readings:
1 Corinthians 1:18–31;
1 Timothy 1:15–17

Go to page 193 for your next devotional reading.

commander to bring him before you on the pretext of wanting more accurate information about his case. We are ready to kill him before he gets here."

¹⁶But when the son of Paul's sister heard of this plot, he went into the barracks and told Paul.

¹⁷Then Paul called one of the centurions and said, "Take this young man to the commander; he has something to tell him." ¹⁸So he took him to the commander. The centurion said, "Paul, the prisoner, sent for me and asked me to bring this young man to you because he has something to tell you."

¹⁹The commander took the young man by the hand, drew him aside and asked, "What is it you want to tell me?"

²⁰He said: "The Jews have agreed to ask you to bring Paul before the Sanhedrin tomorrow on the pretext of wanting more accurate information about him. ²¹Don't give in to them, because more than forty of them are waiting in ambush for him. They have taken an oath not to eat or drink until they have killed him. They are ready now, waiting for your consent to their request."

²²The commander dismissed the young man and cautioned him, "Don't tell anyone that you have reported this to me."

Paul Transferred to Caesarea

²³Then he called two of his centurions and ordered them, "Get ready a detachment of two hundred soldiers, seventy horsemen and two hundred spearmen*ᵃ* to go to Caesarea at nine tonight. ²⁴Provide mounts for Paul so that he may be taken safely to Governor Felix."

²⁵He wrote a letter as follows:

²⁶Claudius Lysias,

To His Excellency, Governor Felix:

Greetings.

²⁷This man was seized by the Jews and they were about to kill him, but I came with my troops and rescued him, for I had learned that he is a Roman citizen. ²⁸I wanted to know why they were accusing him, so I brought him to their Sanhedrin. ²⁹I found that the accusation had to do with questions about their law, but there was no charge against him that deserved death or imprisonment. ³⁰When I was informed of a plot to be carried out against the man, I sent him to you at once. I also ordered his accusers to present to you their case against him.

³¹So the soldiers, carrying out their orders, took Paul with them during the night and brought him as far as Antipatris. ³²The next day they let the cavalry go on with him, while they returned to the barracks. ³³When the cavalry arrived in Caesarea, they delivered the letter to the governor and handed Paul over to him. ³⁴The governor read the letter and asked what province he was from. Learning that he was from Cilicia, ³⁵he said, "I will hear your case when your accusers get here." Then he ordered that Paul be kept under guard in Herod's palace.

The Trial Before Felix

24 Five days later the high priest Ananias went down to Caesarea with some of the elders and a lawyer named Tertullus, and they brought their charges against Paul before the governor. ²When Paul was called in, Tertullus presented his case before Felix: "We have enjoyed a long period of peace under you, and your foresight has brought about reforms in this nation. ³Everywhere and in every way, most excellent Felix, we acknowledge this with profound gratitude. ⁴But in order not to weary you further, I would request that you be kind enough to hear us briefly.

⁵"We have found this man to be a troublemaker, stirring up riots among the Jews all over the world. He is a ringleader of the Nazarene sect ⁶and even tried to desecrate the temple; so we seized him. ⁸By*ᵇ* examining him yourself you will be able to learn the truth about all these charges we are bringing against him."

⁹The Jews joined in the accusation, asserting that these things were true.

¹⁰When the governor motioned for him to speak, Paul replied: "I know that for a number of years you have been a judge over this nation; so I gladly make my defense. ¹¹You can easily verify that no more than twelve days ago I went up to Jerusalem to worship. ¹²My accusers did not find me arguing with anyone at the tem-

---

ᵃ23 The meaning of the Greek for this word is uncertain.   *ᵇ6-8* Some manuscripts *him and wanted to judge him according to our law. ⁷But the commander, Lysias, came and with the use of much force snatched him from our hands ⁸and ordered his accusers to come before you. By*

ple, or stirring up a crowd in the synagogues or anywhere else in the city. ¹³And they cannot prove to you the charges they are now making against me. ¹⁴However, I admit that I worship the God of our fathers as a follower of the Way, which they call a sect. I believe everything that agrees with the Law and that is written in the Prophets, ¹⁵and I have the same hope in God as these men, that there will be a resurrection of both the righteous and the wicked. ¹⁶So I strive always to keep my conscience clear before God and man.

¹⁷"After an absence of several years, I came to Jerusalem to bring my people gifts for the poor and to present offerings. ¹⁸I was ceremonially clean when they found me in the temple courts doing this. There was no crowd with me, nor was I involved in any disturbance. ¹⁹But there are some Jews from the province of Asia, who ought to be here before you and bring charges if they have anything against me. ²⁰Or these who are here should state what crime they found in me when I stood before the Sanhedrin— ²¹unless it was this one thing I shouted as I stood in their presence: 'It is concerning the resurrection of the dead that I am on trial before you today.'"

²²Then Felix, who was well acquainted with the Way, adjourned the proceedings. "When Lysias the commander comes," he said, "I will decide your case." ²³He ordered the centurion to keep Paul under guard but to give him some freedom and permit his friends to take care of his needs.

²⁴Several days later Felix came with his wife Drusilla, who was a Jewess. He sent for Paul and listened to him as he spoke about faith in Christ Jesus. ²⁵As Paul discoursed on righteousness, self-control and the judgment to come, Felix was afraid and said, "That's enough for now! You may leave. When I find it convenient, I will send for you." ²⁶At the same time he was hoping that Paul would offer him a bribe, so he sent for him frequently and talked with him.

²⁷When two years had passed, Felix was succeeded by Porcius Festus, but because Felix wanted to grant a favor to the Jews, he left Paul in prison.

The Trial Before Festus

25 Three days after arriving in the province, Festus went up from Caesarea to Jerusalem, ²where the chief priests and Jewish leaders appeared before him and presented the charges against Paul. ³They urgently requested Festus, as a favor to them, to have Paul transferred to Jerusalem, for they were preparing an ambush to kill him along the way. ⁴Festus answered, "Paul is being held at Caesarea, and I myself am going there soon. ⁵Let some of your leaders come with me and press charges against the man there, if he has done anything wrong."

⁶After spending eight or ten days with them, he went down to Caesarea, and the next day he convened the court and ordered that Paul be brought before him. ⁷When Paul appeared, the Jews who had come down from Jerusalem stood around him, bringing many serious charges against him, which they could not prove.

⁸Then Paul made his defense: "I have done nothing wrong against the law of the Jews or against the temple or against Caesar."

⁹Festus, wishing to do the Jews a favor, said to Paul, "Are you willing to go up to Jerusalem and stand trial before me there on these charges?"

¹⁰Paul answered: "I am now standing before Caesar's court, where I ought to be tried. I have not done any wrong to the Jews, as you yourself know very well. ¹¹If, however, I am guilty of doing anything deserving death, I do not refuse to die. But if the charges brought against me by these Jews are not true, no one has the right to hand me over to them. I appeal to Caesar!"

¹²After Festus had conferred with his council, he declared: "You have appealed to Caesar. To Caesar you will go!"

Festus Consults King Agrippa

¹³A few days later King Agrippa and Bernice arrived at Caesarea to pay their respects to Festus. ¹⁴Since they were spending many days there, Festus discussed Paul's case with the king. He said: "There is a man here whom Felix left as a prisoner. ¹⁵When I went to Jerusalem, the chief priests and elders of the Jews brought charges against him and asked that he be condemned.

¹⁶"I told them that it is not the Roman custom to hand over any man before he has faced his accusers and has had an opportunity to defend himself against their charges. ¹⁷When they came here with me, I did not delay the case, but convened the court the next day and ordered the man to be brought in. ¹⁸When his accusers got up

to speak, they did not charge him with any of the crimes I had expected. ¹⁹Instead, they had some points of dispute with him about their own religion and about a dead man named Jesus who Paul claimed was alive. ²⁰I was at a loss how to investigate such matters; so I asked if he would be willing to go to Jerusalem and stand trial there on these charges. ²¹When Paul made his appeal to be held over for the Emperor's decision, I ordered him held until I could send him to Caesar."

²²Then Agrippa said to Festus, "I would like to hear this man myself."

He replied, "Tomorrow you will hear him."

Paul Before Agrippa

²³The next day Agrippa and Bernice came with great pomp and entered the audience room with the high ranking officers and the leading men of the city. At the command of Festus, Paul was brought in. ²⁴Festus said: "King Agrippa, and all who are present with us, you see this man! The whole Jewish community has petitioned me about him in Jerusalem and here in Caesarea, shouting that he ought not to live any longer. ²⁵I found he had done nothing deserving of death, but because he made his appeal to the Emperor I decided to send him to Rome. ²⁶But I have nothing definite to write to His Majesty about him. Therefore I have brought him before all of you, and especially before you, King Agrippa, so that as a result of this investigation I may have something to write. ²⁷For I think it is unreasonable to send on a prisoner without specifying the charges against him."

26 Then Agrippa said to Paul, "You have permission to speak for yourself."

So Paul motioned with his hand and began his defense: ²"King Agrippa, I consider myself fortunate to stand before you today as I make my defense against all the accusations of the Jews, ³and especially so because you are well acquainted with all the Jewish customs and controversies. Therefore, I beg you to listen to me patiently.

⁴"The Jews all know the way I have lived ever since I was a child, from the beginning of my life in my own country, and also in Jerusalem. ⁵They have known me for a long time and can testify, if they are willing, that according to the strictest sect of our religion, I lived as a Pharisee. ⁶And now it is because of my hope in what God has promised our fathers that I am on trial today. ⁷This is the promise our twelve tribes are hoping to see fulfilled as they earnestly serve God day and night. O king, it is because of this hope that the Jews are accusing me. ⁸Why should any of you consider it incredible that God raises the dead?

⁹"I too was convinced that I ought to do all that was possible to oppose the name of Jesus of Nazareth. ¹⁰And that is just what I did in Jerusalem. On the authority of the chief priests I put many of the saints in prison, and when they were put to death, I cast my vote against them. ¹¹Many a time I went from one synagogue to another to have them punished, and I tried to force them to blaspheme. In my obsession against them, I even went to foreign cities to persecute them.

¹²"On one of these journeys I was going to Damascus with the authority and commission of the chief priests. ¹³About noon, O king, as I was on the road, I saw a light from heaven, brighter than the sun, blazing around me and my companions. ¹⁴We all fell to the ground, and I heard a voice saying to me in Aramaic,*ᵃ* 'Saul, Saul, why do you persecute me? It is hard for you to kick against the goads.'

¹⁵"Then I asked, 'Who are you, Lord?'

" 'I am Jesus, whom you are persecuting,' the Lord replied. ¹⁶'Now get up and stand on your feet. I have appeared to you to appoint you as a servant and as a witness of what you have seen of me and what I will show you. ¹⁷I will rescue you from your own people and from the Gentiles. I am sending you to them ¹⁸to open their eyes and turn them from darkness to light, and from the power of Satan to God, so that they may receive forgiveness of sins and a place among those who are sanctified by faith in me.'

¹⁹"So then, King Agrippa, I was not disobedient to the vision from heaven. ²⁰First to those in Damascus, then to those in Jerusalem and in all Judea, and to the Gentiles also, I preached that they should repent and turn to God and prove their repentance by their deeds. ²¹That is why the Jews seized me in the temple courts and tried to kill me. ²²But I have had God's help to this very day, and so I stand here and testify to small and great alike. I am saying nothing beyond what the prophets

---

ᵃ14 Or Hebrew

and Moses said would happen— ²³that the Christ[a] would suffer and, as the first to rise from the dead, would proclaim light to his own people and to the Gentiles."

²⁴At this point Festus interrupted Paul's defense. "You are out of your mind, Paul!" he shouted. "Your great learning is driving you insane."

²⁵"I am not insane, most excellent Festus," Paul replied. "What I am saying is true and reasonable. ²⁶The king is familiar with these things, and I can speak freely to him. I am convinced that none of this has escaped his notice, because it was not done in a corner. ²⁷King Agrippa, do you believe the prophets? I know you do."

²⁸Then Agrippa said to Paul, "Do you think that in such a short time you can persuade me to be a Christian?"

²⁹Paul replied, "Short time or long—I pray God that not only you but all who are listening to me today may become what I am, except for these chains."

³⁰The king rose, and with him the governor and Bernice and those sitting with them. ³¹They left the room, and while talking with one another, they said, "This man is not doing anything that deserves death or imprisonment."

³²Agrippa said to Festus, "This man could have been set free if he had not appealed to Caesar."

Paul Sails for Rome

27 When it was decided that we would sail for Italy, Paul and some other prisoners were handed over to a centurion named Julius, who belonged to the Imperial Regiment. ²We boarded a ship from Adramyttium about to sail for ports along the coast of Asia, and we put out to sea. Aristarchus, a Macedonian from Thessalonica, was with us.

³The next day we landed at Sidon; and Julius, in kindness to Paul, allowed him to go to his friends so they might provide for his needs. ⁴From there we put out to sea again and passed to the lee of Cyprus because the winds were against us. ⁵When we had sailed across the open sea off the coast of Cilicia and Pamphylia, we landed at Myra in Lycia. ⁶There the centurion found an Alexandrian ship sailing for Italy and put us on board. ⁷We made slow headway for many days and had difficulty arriving off Cnidus. When the wind did not allow us to hold our course, we sailed to the lee of Crete, opposite Salmone. ⁸We moved along the coast with difficulty and came to a place called Fair Havens, near the town of Lasea.

⁹Much time had been lost, and sailing had already become dangerous because by now it was after the Fast.[b] So Paul warned them, ¹⁰"Men, I can see that our voyage is going to be disastrous and bring great loss to ship and cargo, and to our own lives also." ¹¹But the centurion, instead of listening to what Paul said, followed the advice of the pilot and of the owner of the ship. ¹²Since the harbor was unsuitable to winter in, the majority decided that we should sail on, hoping to reach Phoenix and winter there. This was a harbor in Crete, facing both southwest and northwest.

The Storm

¹³When a gentle south wind began to blow, they thought they had obtained what they wanted; so they weighed anchor and sailed along the shore of Crete. ¹⁴Before very long, a wind of hurricane force, called the "northeaster," swept down from the island. ¹⁵The ship was caught by the storm and could not head into the wind; so we gave way to it and were driven along. ¹⁶As we passed to the lee of a small island called Cauda, we were hardly able to make the lifeboat secure. ¹⁷When the men had hoisted it aboard, they passed ropes under the ship itself to hold it together. Fearing that they would run aground on the sandbars of Syrtis, they lowered the sea anchor and let the ship be driven along. ¹⁸We took such a violent battering from the storm that the next day they began to throw the cargo overboard. ¹⁹On the third day, they threw the ship's tackle overboard with their own hands. ²⁰When neither sun nor stars appeared for many days and the storm continued raging, we finally gave up all hope of being saved.

²¹After the men had gone a long time without food, Paul stood up before them and said: "Men, you should have taken my advice not to sail from Crete; then you would have spared yourselves this damage and loss. ²²But now I urge you to keep up your courage, because not one of you will be lost; only the ship will be destroyed. ²³Last night an angel of the God whose I am and whom I serve stood be-

---

[a]23 Or *Messiah* [b]9 That is, the Day of Atonement (Yom Kippur)

WEEKENDING

RECOVER

I have some dreams. It is time for us as men to reject this fragile male ego business. We use it to cover up our failures and avoid looking at ourselves. Thus the women and children in our lives, who presumably have better egos than we do, must pick up the slack and take responsibility for our actions and feelings. Come on guys! Let us at least try to struggle honestly. We need to be confronted by our actions, messages and shortcomings if we expect to learn and grow. No more hiding behind excuses. No blaming others. No hiding behind phrases like, "This is just the way I am." Let us have a look at who we are for that is the best indication of who our sons will become.
– E. James Wilder

REVIVE
Saturday: Romans 12:1–8
Sunday: 2 Corinthians 13:1–10

Go to page 198 for your next devotional reading.

side me ²⁴and said, 'Do not be afraid, Paul. You must stand trial before Caesar; and God has graciously given you the lives of all who sail with you.' ²⁵So keep up your courage, men, for I have faith in God that it will happen just as he told me. ²⁶Nevertheless, we must run aground on some island."

The Shipwreck

²⁷On the fourteenth night we were still being driven across the Adriatic*ᵃ* Sea, when about midnight the sailors sensed they were approaching land. ²⁸They took soundings and found that the water was a hundred and twenty feet*ᵇ* deep. A short time later they took soundings again and found it was ninety feet*ᶜ* deep. ²⁹Fearing that we would be dashed against the rocks, they dropped four anchors from the stern and prayed for daylight. ³⁰In an attempt to escape from the ship, the sailors let the lifeboat down into the sea, pretending they were going to lower some anchors from the bow. ³¹Then Paul said to the centurion and the soldiers, "Unless these men stay with the ship, you cannot be saved." ³²So the soldiers cut the ropes that held the lifeboat and let it fall away.

³³Just before dawn Paul urged them all to eat. "For the last fourteen days," he said, "you have been in constant suspense and have gone without food — you haven't eaten anything. ³⁴Now I urge you to take some food. You need it to survive. Not one of you will lose a single hair from his head." ³⁵After he said this, he took some bread and gave thanks to God in front of them all. Then he broke it and began to eat. ³⁶They were all encouraged and ate some food themselves. ³⁷Altogether there were 276 of us on board. ³⁸When they had eaten as much as they wanted, they lightened the ship by throwing the grain into the sea.

³⁹When daylight came, they did not recognize the land, but they saw a bay with a sandy beach, where they decided to run the ship aground if they could. ⁴⁰Cutting loose the anchors, they left them in the sea and at the same time untied the ropes that held the rudders. Then they hoisted the foresail to the wind and made for the beach. ⁴¹But the ship struck a sandbar and ran aground. The bow stuck fast and would not move, and the stern was broken to pieces by the pounding of the surf. ⁴²The soldiers planned to kill the prisoners to prevent any of them from swimming away and escaping. ⁴³But the centurion wanted to spare Paul's life and kept them from carrying out their plan. He ordered those who could swim to jump overboard first and get to land. ⁴⁴The rest were to get there on planks or on pieces of the ship. In this way everyone reached land in safety.

Ashore on Malta

28 Once safely on shore, we found out that the island was called Malta. ²The islanders showed us unusual kindness. They built a fire and welcomed us all because it was raining and cold. ³Paul gathered a pile of brushwood and, as he put it on the fire, a viper, driven out by the heat, fastened itself on his hand. ⁴When the islanders saw the snake hanging from his hand, they said to each other, "This man must be a murderer; for though he escaped from the sea, Justice has not allowed him to live." ⁵But Paul shook the snake off into the fire and suffered no ill effects. ⁶The people expected him to swell up or suddenly fall dead, but after waiting a long time and seeing nothing unusual happen to him, they changed their minds and said he was a god.

⁷There was an estate nearby that belonged to Publius, the chief official of the island. He welcomed us to his home and for three days entertained us hospitably. ⁸His father was sick in bed, suffering from fever and dysentery. Paul went in to see him and, after prayer, placed his hands on him and healed him. ⁹When this had happened, the rest of the sick on the island came and were cured. ¹⁰They honored us in many ways and when we were ready to sail, they furnished us with the supplies we needed.

Arrival at Rome

¹¹After three months we put out to sea in a ship that had wintered in the island. It was an Alexandrian ship with the figurehead of the twin gods Castor and Pollux. ¹²We put in at Syracuse and stayed there three days. ¹³From there we set sail and arrived at Rhegium. The next day the south wind came up, and on the following day we reached Puteoli. ¹⁴There we found some brothers who invited us to spend a week with them. And so we came to

---

ᵃ27 In ancient times the name referred to an area extending well south of Italy. *ᵇ28* Greek *twenty orguias* (about 37 meters)   *ᶜ28* Greek *fifteen orguias* (about 27 meters)

Rome. ¹⁵The brothers there had heard that we were coming, and they traveled as far as the Forum of Appius and the Three Taverns to meet us. At the sight of these men Paul thanked God and was encouraged. ¹⁶When we got to Rome, Paul was allowed to live by himself, with a soldier to guard him.

Paul Preaches at Rome Under Guard

¹⁷Three days later he called together the leaders of the Jews. When they had assembled, Paul said to them: "My brothers, although I have done nothing against our people or against the customs of our ancestors, I was arrested in Jerusalem and handed over to the Romans. ¹⁸They examined me and wanted to release me, because I was not guilty of any crime deserving death. ¹⁹But when the Jews objected, I was compelled to appeal to Caesar — not that I had any charge to bring against my own people. ²⁰For this reason I have asked to see you and talk with you. It is because of the hope of Israel that I am bound with this chain."

²¹They replied, "We have not received any letters from Judea concerning you, and none of the brothers who have come from there has reported or said anything bad about you. ²²But we want to hear what your views are, for we know that people everywhere are talking against this sect."

²³They arranged to meet Paul on a certain day, and came in even larger numbers to the place where he was staying. From morning till evening he explained and declared to them the kingdom of God and tried to convince them about Jesus from the Law of Moses and from the Prophets. ²⁴Some were convinced by what he said, but others would not believe. ²⁵They disagreed among themselves and began to leave after Paul had made this final statement: "The Holy Spirit spoke the truth to your forefathers when he said through Isaiah the prophet:

²⁶" 'Go to this people and say,
 "You will be ever hearing but never
  understanding;
  you will be ever seeing but never
  perceiving."
²⁷For this people's heart has become
  calloused;
 they hardly hear with their ears,
  and they have closed their eyes.
Otherwise they might see with their
  eyes,
 hear with their ears,
 understand with their hearts
and turn, and I would heal them.'ᵃ

²⁸"Therefore I want you to know that God's salvation has been sent to the Gentiles, and they will listen!"ᵇ

³⁰For two whole years Paul stayed there in his own rented house and welcomed all who came to see him. ³¹Boldly and without hindrance he preached the kingdom of God and taught about the Lord Jesus Christ.

ᵃ27 Isaiah 6:9,10   ᵇ28 Some manuscripts *listen!" ²⁹After he said this, the Jews left, arguing vigorously among themselves.*

Paul, planning a mission trip to Spain (Romans 15:23–29), writes this letter to introduce himself to the church at Rome. In it he summarizes what he has been preaching about sin, Christ, and the way of salvation. Everything you need to know about God's great plan for redemption lies in these sixteen chapters. As you read the book, think about how much God loves you in sending his Son Jesus and how you can say thank you to him by the life you live.

ROMANS

1 Paul, a servant of Christ Jesus, called to be an apostle and set apart for the gospel of God— ²the gospel he promised beforehand through his prophets in the Holy Scriptures ³regarding his Son, who as to his human nature was a descendant of David, ⁴and who through the Spirit[a] of holiness was declared with power to be the Son of God[b] by his resurrection from the dead: Jesus Christ our Lord. ⁵Through him and for his name's sake, we received grace and apostleship to call people from among all the Gentiles to the obedience that comes from faith. ⁶And you also are among those who are called to belong to Jesus Christ.

⁷To all in Rome who are loved by God and called to be saints:

Grace and peace to you from God our Father and from the Lord Jesus Christ.

Paul's Longing to Visit Rome

⁸First, I thank my God through Jesus Christ for all of you, because your faith is being reported all over the world. ⁹God, whom I serve with my whole heart in preaching the gospel of his Son, is my wit-

---

a 4 Or *who as to his spirit* b 4 Or *was appointed to be the Son of God with power* ness how constantly I remember you **10**in my prayers at all times; and I pray that now at last by God's will the way may be opened for me to come to you.

11I long to see you so that I may impart to you some spiritual gift to make you strong— **12**that is, that you and I may be mutually encouraged by each other's faith. **13**I do not want you to be unaware, brothers, that I planned many times to come to you (but have been prevented from doing so until now) in order that I might have a harvest among you, just as I have had among the other Gentiles.

14I am obligated both to Greeks and non-Greeks, both to the wise and the foolish. **15**That is why I am so eager to preach the gospel also to you who are at Rome.

16I am not ashamed of the gospel, because it is the power of God for the salvation of everyone who believes: first for the Jew, then for the Gentile. **17**For in the gospel a righteousness from God is revealed, a righteousness that is by faith from first to last,*a* just as it is written: "The righteous will live by faith."*b*

God's Wrath Against Mankind

18The wrath of God is being revealed from heaven against all the godlessness and wickedness of men who suppress the truth by their wickedness, **19**since what may be known about God is plain to them, because God has made it plain to them. **20**For since the creation of the world God's invisible qualities — his eternal power and divine nature — have been clearly seen, being understood from what has been made, so that men are without excuse.

21For although they knew God, they neither glorified him as God nor gave thanks to him, but their thinking became futile and their foolish hearts were darkened. **22**Although they claimed to be wise, they became fools **23**and exchanged the glory of the immortal God for images made to look like mortal man and birds and animals and reptiles.

24Therefore God gave them over in the sinful desires of their hearts to sexual impurity for the degrading of their bodies with one another. **25**They exchanged the truth of God for a lie, and worshiped and served created things rather than the Creator — who is forever praised. Amen.

26Because of this, God gave them over to shameful lusts. Even their women exchanged natural relations for unnatural ones. **27**In the same way the men also abandoned natural relations with women and were inflamed with lust for one another. Men committed indecent acts with other men, and received in themselves the due penalty for their perversion.

28Furthermore, since they did not think it worthwhile to retain the knowledge of God, he gave them over to a depraved mind, to do what ought not to be done. **29**They have become filled with every kind of wickedness, evil, greed and depravity. They are full of envy, murder, strife, deceit and malice. They are gossips, **30**slanderers, God-haters, insolent, arrogant and boastful; they invent ways of doing evil; they disobey their parents; **31**they are senseless, faithless, heartless, ruthless. **32**Although they know God's righteous decree that those who do such things deserve death, they not only continue to do these very things but also approve of those who practice them.

God's Righteous Judgment

2 You, therefore, have no excuse, you who pass judgment on someone else, for at whatever point you judge the other, you are condemning yourself, because you who pass judgment do the same things. **2**Now we know that God's judgment against those who do such things is based on truth. **3**So when you, a mere man, pass judgment on them and yet do the same things, do you think you will escape God's judgment? **4**Or do you show contempt for the riches of his kindness, tolerance and patience, not realizing that God's kindness leads you toward repentance?

5But because of your stubbornness and your unrepentant heart, you are storing up wrath against yourself for the day of God's wrath, when his righteous judgment will be revealed. **6**God "will give to each person according to what he has done."*c* **7**To those who by persistence in doing good seek glory, honor and immortality, he will give eternal life. **8**But for those who are self-seeking and who reject the truth and follow evil, there will be wrath and anger. **9**There will be trouble and distress for every human being who does evil: first for the Jew, then for the Gentile; **10**but glory, honor and peace for everyone who does good: first for the Jew, then for the Gentile. **11**For God does not show favoritism.

---

a17 Or *is from faith to faith*   *b17* Hab. 2:4   *c6* Psalm 62:12; Prov. 24:12

MONDAY

VERSE FOR THE DAY:
Romans 1:25

AUTHOR:
John Fischer

PASSAGE FOR THE DAY:
Romans 1:18–25

Ask, Seek, Knock

ASKING is a way of life lived with an open hand. To ask is to depend on someone other than yourself. It is very humbling. Asking indicates:

- I don't know.
- I failed.
- I ran out.
- I can't find it.
- I'm not sure.
- I don't understand.
- I forgot.
- I didn't listen.
- I didn't care.
- I was wrong.
- I'm not prepared.
- I need more information.
- I came up short.

There's an interesting dilemma here for Christians. If Christianity is no more than a system that answers all of life's questions, then to admit any of the above shortcomings is to be something less than a good Christian. But in our own attempts to be good Christians, we undermine our need for God. We want Christianity to work. We want it to exist in a closed system where every question has an answer, every problem has a solution. We want to show the world a neat, clean, open-and-shut case for Christianity. But in the process, we unknowingly shut out God.

Claiming to be wise, we become fools; we exchange the truth of God for a lie and worship the created things (our systems, principles and formulas) rather than the Creator—who is forever blessed. Amen (see Romans 1:22–25).

That's why Jesus says we should ask. Asking puts us back on track with God. It assumes a need relationship with him—a hand-to-mouth spiritual existence. A vulnerable daily dependence. In a society that rushes to fill every felt need, that steals away the soul of a person and offers to sell it back at a price, we need to rekindle what it means to ask God.

Additional Scripture Readings:
Matthew 7:7–12; John 16:19–28

Go to page 200 for your next devotional reading.

ROMANS 2–3

¹²All who sin apart from the law will also perish apart from the law, and all who sin under the law will be judged by the law. ¹³For it is not those who hear the law who are righteous in God's sight, but it is those who obey the law who will be declared righteous. ¹⁴(Indeed, when Gentiles, who do not have the law, do by nature things required by the law, they are a law for themselves, even though they do not have the law, ¹⁵since they show that the requirements of the law are written on their hearts, their consciences also bearing witness, and their thoughts now accusing, now even defending them.) ¹⁶This will take place on the day when God will judge men's secrets through Jesus Christ, as my gospel declares.

The Jews and the Law

¹⁷Now you, if you call yourself a Jew; if you rely on the law and brag about your relationship to God; ¹⁸if you know his will and approve of what is superior because you are instructed by the law; ¹⁹if you are convinced that you are a guide for the blind, a light for those who are in the dark, ²⁰an instructor of the foolish, a teacher of infants, because you have in the law the embodiment of knowledge and truth— ²¹you, then, who teach others, do you not teach yourself? You who preach against stealing, do you steal? ²²You who say that people should not commit adultery, do you commit adultery? You who abhor idols, do you rob temples? ²³You who brag about the law, do you dishonor God by breaking the law? ²⁴As it is written: "God's name is blasphemed among the Gentiles because of you."ᵃ

²⁵Circumcision has value if you observe the law, but if you break the law, you have become as though you had not been circumcised. ²⁶If those who are not circumcised keep the law's requirements, will they not be regarded as though they were circumcised? ²⁷The one who is not circumcised physically and yet obeys the law will condemn you who, even though you have theᵇ written code and circumcision, are a lawbreaker.

²⁸A man is not a Jew if he is only one outwardly, nor is circumcision merely outward and physical. ²⁹No, a man is a Jew if he is one inwardly; and circumcision is circumcision of the heart, by the Spirit, not by the written code. Such a man's praise is not from men, but from God.

God's Faithfulness

3 What advantage, then, is there in being a Jew, or what value is there in circumcision? ²Much in every way! First of all, they have been entrusted with the very words of God.

³What if some did not have faith? Will their lack of faith nullify God's faithfulness? ⁴Not at all! Let God be true, and every man a liar. As it is written:

"So that you may be proved right
  when you speak
and prevail when you judge."ᶜ

⁵But if our unrighteousness brings out God's righteousness more clearly, what shall we say? That God is unjust in bringing his wrath on us? (I am using a human argument.) ⁶Certainly not! If that were so, how could God judge the world? ⁷Someone might argue, "If my falsehood enhances God's truthfulness and so increases his glory, why am I still condemned as a sinner?" ⁸Why not say— as we are being slanderously reported as saying and as some claim that we say— "Let us do evil that good may result"? Their condemnation is deserved.

No One Is Righteous

⁹What shall we conclude then? Are we any betterᵈ? Not at all! We have already made the charge that Jews and Gentiles alike are all under sin. ¹⁰As it is written:

"There is no one righteous, not even
    one;
¹¹ there is no one who understands,
    no one who seeks God.
¹²All have turned away,
    they have together become
      worthless;
there is no one who does good,
    not even one."ᵉ
¹³"Their throats are open graves;
    their tongues practice deceit."ᶠ
"The poison of vipers is on their
      lips."ᵍ
¹⁴ "Their mouths are full of cursing
      and bitterness."ʰ
¹⁵"Their feet are swift to shed blood;
¹⁶ ruin and misery mark their ways,

ᵃ24 Isaiah 52:5; Ezek. 36:22   ᵇ27 Or *who, by means of a*   ᶜ4 Psalm 51:4   ᵈ9 Or *worse*
ᵉ12 Psalms 14:1-3; 53:1-3; Eccles. 7:20   ᶠ13 Psalm 5:9   ᵍ13 Psalm 140:3   ʰ14 Psalm 10:7

¹⁷and the way of peace they do not know."ᵃ
¹⁸ "There is no fear of God before their eyes."ᵇ

¹⁹Now we know that whatever the law says, it says to those who are under the law, so that every mouth may be silenced and the whole world held accountable to

ᵃ17 Isaiah 59:7,8   ᵇ18 Psalm 36:1

TUESDAY

VERSE FOR THE DAY:
Romans 2:4

AUTHOR:
Larry Crabb

PASSAGE FOR THE DAY:
Romans 2:1–4

God's Unhurried Ways

IN SPITE of thunderous warnings delivered from well-pounded pulpits, our self-centeredness seems to generate few bad consequences. And every youngster knows that shouting can be easily endured if there are no spankings.

God seems in no hurry to judge. For now, it appears we can live self-centeredly and not pay a price.

But we can interpret God's delay in *two* ways: either our sin doesn't really offend him a great deal or ". . . he is patient with [us], not wanting anyone to perish, but everyone to come to repentance" (2 Peter 3:9).

In our fallen way of thinking, we strongly favor explaining withheld judgment in terms of divine indifference. If God, the ultimate standard of morality who has the power to punish and reward, is not all that bothered by our self-centered ways, then we can carry on with whatever makes us feel good without worrying about punishment for wrongdoing and without giving up our good opinion of ourselves . . .

The truth is we can continue with our everyday failings, at least for a time, without being struck by lightning. And the unpleasant things that happen seem evenly distributed between good people and bad people.

And when we look after ourselves, better things often do come our way. God's unhurried ways can encourage us to think casually about our ongoing struggle with sin . . .

Having dismissed our selfishness as a relatively benign disorder, we are free to keep our focus on what really matters to self-centered people: the immediate quality of our lives. Finding a way to heal our wounds and to restore a sense of personal wholeness continues to be a far more pressing concern than knowing the escape route from judgment and worshiping the One who provided it.

And the disease continues unchecked, ruining relationships and carrying us toward certain judgment.

Additional Scripture Readings:
Galatians 6:7–10; 2 Peter 3:3–10

Go to page 202 for your next devotional reading.

God. **20**Therefore no one will be declared righteous in his sight by observing the law; rather, through the law we become conscious of sin.

Righteousness Through Faith

21But now a righteousness from God, apart from law, has been made known, to which the Law and the Prophets testify. **22**This righteousness from God comes through faith in Jesus Christ to all who believe. There is no difference, **23**for all have sinned and fall short of the glory of God, **24**and are justified freely by his grace through the redemption that came by Christ Jesus. **25**God presented him as a sacrifice of atonement,*a* through faith in his blood. He did this to demonstrate his justice, because in his forbearance he had left the sins committed beforehand unpunished— **26**he did it to demonstrate his justice at the present time, so as to be just and the one who justifies those who have faith in Jesus.

27Where, then, is boasting? It is excluded. On what principle? On that of observing the law? No, but on that of faith. **28**For we maintain that a man is justified by faith apart from observing the law. **29**Is God the God of Jews only? Is he not the God of Gentiles too? Yes, of Gentiles too, **30**since there is only one God, who will justify the circumcised by faith and the uncircumcised through that same faith. **31**Do we, then, nullify the law by this faith? Not at all! Rather, we uphold the law.

Abraham Justified by Faith

4 What then shall we say that Abraham, our forefather, discovered in this matter? **2**If, in fact, Abraham was justified by works, he had something to boast about—but not before God. **3**What does the Scripture say? "Abraham believed God, and it was credited to him as righteousness."*b*

4Now when a man works, his wages are not credited to him as a gift, but as an obligation. **5**However, to the man who does not work but trusts God who justifies the wicked, his faith is credited as righteousness. **6**David says the same thing when he speaks of the blessedness of the man to whom God credits righteousness apart from works:

7"Blessed are they
whose transgressions are forgiven,
whose sins are covered.
8Blessed is the man
whose sin the Lord will never count
against him."*c*

9Is this blessedness only for the circumcised, or also for the uncircumcised? We have been saying that Abraham's faith was credited to him as righteousness. **10**Under what circumstances was it credited? Was it after he was circumcised, or before? It was not after, but before! **11**And he received the sign of circumcision, a seal of the righteousness that he had by faith while he was still uncircumcised. So then, he is the father of all who believe but have not been circumcised, in order that righteousness might be credited to them. **12**And he is also the father of the circumcised who not only are circumcised but who also walk in the footsteps of the faith that our father Abraham had before he was circumcised.

13It was not through law that Abraham and his offspring received the promise that he would be heir of the world, but through the righteousness that comes by faith. **14**For if those who live by law are heirs, faith has no value and the promise is worthless, **15**because law brings wrath. And where there is no law there is no transgression.

16Therefore, the promise comes by faith, so that it may be by grace and may be guaranteed to all Abraham's offspring—not only to those who are of the law but also to those who are of the faith of Abraham. He is the father of us all. **17**As it is written: "I have made you a father of many nations."*d* He is our father in the sight of God, in whom he believed—the God who gives life to the dead and calls things that are not as though they were.

18Against all hope, Abraham in hope believed and so became the father of many nations, just as it had been said to him, "So shall your offspring be."*e* **19**Without weakening in his faith, he faced the fact that his body was as good as dead—since he was about a hundred years old—and that Sarah's womb was also dead. **20**Yet he did not waver through unbelief regarding the promise of God, but was strengthened in his faith and gave glory to God, **21**being

---

a25 Or *as the one who would turn aside his wrath, taking away sin*   *b3* Gen. 15:6; also in verse 22
c8 Psalm 32:1,2   *d17* Gen. 17:5   *e18* Gen. 15:5

fully persuaded that God had power to do what he had promised. ²²This is why "it was credited to him as righteousness." ²³The words "it was credited to him" were written not for him alone, ²⁴but also for us, to whom God will credit righteousness — for us who believe in him who raised Jesus our Lord from the dead. ²⁵He was delivered over to death for our sins and was raised to life for our justification.

Peace and Joy

5 Therefore, since we have been justified through faith, we[a] have peace with God through our Lord Jesus Christ, ²through whom we have gained access by

[a] 1 Or *let us*

WEDNESDAY

VERSE FOR THE DAY:
Romans 3:25

AUTHOR:
C.S. Lewis

PASSAGE FOR THE DAY:
Romans 3:21–26

Nourishment and the Cross

THE central Christian belief is that Christ's death has somehow put us right with God and given us a fresh start. A good many different theories have been held as to how it works; what all Christians are agreed on is that it does work. I will tell you what I think it is like. All sensible people know that if you are tired and hungry a meal will do you good. But the modern theory of nourishment — all about the vitamins and proteins — is a different thing. People ate their dinners and felt better long before the theory of vitamins was ever heard of: and if the theory of vitamins is some day abandoned they will go on eating their dinners just the same. Theories about Christ's death are not Christianity: they are explanations about how it works. Christians would not all agree as to how important these theories are. But I think they will all agree that the thing itself is infinitely more important than any explanations that theologians have produced . . .

We believe that the death of Christ is just that point in history at which something absolutely unimaginable from outside shows through into our own world. And if we cannot picture even the atoms of which our own world is built, of course we are not going to be able to picture this. Indeed, if we found that we could fully understand it, that very fact would show it was not what it professes to be — the inconceivable, the uncreated, the thing from beyond nature, striking down into nature like lightning. You may ask what good it will be to us if we do not understand it. But that is easily answered. A man can eat his dinner without understanding exactly how food nourishes him. A man can accept what Christ has done without knowing how it works: indeed, he certainly would not know how it works until he has accepted it.

Additional Scripture Readings:
Romans 11:33–36; Ephesians 1:3–14

Go to page 204 for your next devotional reading.

faith into this grace in which we now stand. And we[a] rejoice in the hope of the glory of God. ³Not only so, but we[a] also rejoice in our sufferings, because we know that suffering produces perseverance; ⁴perseverance, character; and character, hope. ⁵And hope does not disappoint us, because God has poured out his love into our hearts by the Holy Spirit, whom he has given us.

⁶You see, at just the right time, when we were still powerless, Christ died for the ungodly. ⁷Very rarely will anyone die for a righteous man, though for a good man someone might possibly dare to die. ⁸But God demonstrates his own love for us in this: While we were still sinners, Christ died for us.

⁹Since we have now been justified by his blood, how much more shall we be saved from God's wrath through him! ¹⁰For if, when we were God's enemies, we were reconciled to him through the death of his Son, how much more, having been reconciled, shall we be saved through his life! ¹¹Not only is this so, but we also rejoice in God through our Lord Jesus Christ, through whom we have now received reconciliation.

Death Through Adam, Life Through Christ

¹²Therefore, just as sin entered the world through one man, and death through sin, and in this way death came to all men, because all sinned— ¹³for before the law was given, sin was in the world. But sin is not taken into account when there is no law. ¹⁴Nevertheless, death reigned from the time of Adam to the time of Moses, even over those who did not sin by breaking a command, as did Adam, who was a pattern of the one to come.

¹⁵But the gift is not like the trespass. For if the many died by the trespass of the one man, how much more did God's grace and the gift that came by the grace of the one man, Jesus Christ, overflow to the many! ¹⁶Again, the gift of God is not like the result of the one man's sin: The judgment followed one sin and brought condemnation, but the gift followed many trespasses and brought justification. ¹⁷For if, by the trespass of the one man, death reigned through that one man, how much more will those who receive God's abundant provision of grace and of the gift of righteousness reign in life through the one man, Jesus Christ.

¹⁸Consequently, just as the result of one trespass was condemnation for all men, so also the result of one act of righteousness was justification that brings life for all men. ¹⁹For just as through the disobedience of the one man the many were made sinners, so also through the obedience of the one man the many will be made righteous.

²⁰The law was added so that the trespass might increase. But where sin increased, grace increased all the more, ²¹so that, just as sin reigned in death, so also grace might reign through righteousness to bring eternal life through Jesus Christ our Lord.

Dead to Sin, Alive in Christ

6 What shall we say, then? Shall we go on sinning so that grace may increase? ²By no means! We died to sin; how can we live in it any longer? ³Or don't you know that all of us who were baptized into Christ Jesus were baptized into his death? ⁴We were therefore buried with him through baptism into death in order that, just as Christ was raised from the dead through the glory of the Father, we too may live a new life.

⁵If we have been united with him like this in his death, we will certainly also be united with him in his resurrection. ⁶For we know that our old self was crucified with him so that the body of sin might be done away with,[b] that we should no longer be slaves to sin— ⁷because anyone who has died has been freed from sin.

⁸Now if we died with Christ, we believe that we will also live with him. ⁹For we know that since Christ was raised from the dead, he cannot die again; death no longer has mastery over him. ¹⁰The death he died, he died to sin once for all; but the life he lives, he lives to God.

¹¹In the same way, count yourselves dead to sin but alive to God in Christ Jesus. ¹²Therefore do not let sin reign in your mortal body so that you obey its evil desires. ¹³Do not offer the parts of your body to sin, as instruments of wickedness, but rather offer yourselves to God, as those who have been brought from death to life; and offer the parts of your body to him as instruments of righteousness. ¹⁴For sin shall not be your master, be-

---

[a] 2,3 Or *let us*   [b] 6 Or *be rendered powerless*

cause you are not under law, but under grace.

Slaves to Righteousness

15What then? Shall we sin because we are not under law but under grace? By no means! **16**Don't you know that when you offer yourselves to someone to obey him as slaves, you are slaves to the one whom you obey—whether you are slaves to sin, which leads to death, or to obedience, which leads to righteousness? **17**But thanks be to God that, though you used to be slaves to sin, you wholeheartedly obeyed the form of teaching to which you were entrusted. **18**You have been set free from sin and have become slaves to righteousness.

19I put this in human terms because you are weak in your natural selves. Just as you used to offer the parts of your body in slavery to impurity and to ever-increasing

---

THURSDAY

VERSE FOR THE DAY:
Romans 5:3

AUTHOR:
Gary Smalley and John Trent

PASSAGE FOR THE DAY:
Romans 5:1–11

First Response

OFTEN, the first response by parents can set the tone for how traumatically an event will be taken . . .

When one of my children is hurting, compounding it by reacting with angry words doesn't add to the solution. If anything, such a reaction often freezes things in a problem state.

Responding with initial softness helps the child see that if Dad and Mom aren't panicking, maybe there is a light at the end of the tunnel. If the child sees his parents panicking or moving into anger, he is often barred from responding in any other way . . .

Where does the ability to initiate softness and keep from panicking come from? *From a decision formed in quiet times apart from trials to believe that God works all things unto good* (see Romans 8:28).

In the middle of a fire, there isn't time to think about ways to prevent a fire. Parents who react emotionally in anger or panic to problems instead of having a plan for responding to them can increase the tension in the air. When parents know ahead of time that the very things that have the potential to devalue their children can be used by God to build character into their lives, they are strengthening their grip on their emotions . . .

When a difficulty first happens, don't lecture your children, panic, or become sickeningly pious. Calmly comforting them at the beginning of a trial lays the foundation for them to find value in their experience. Calmness comes from within us when we are confident in God's Word. Painful trials produce maturity, which leads to love!

Additional Scripture Readings:
Hebrews 12:7–11; James 1:2–12

Go to page 206 for your next devotional reading.

wickedness, so now offer them in slavery to righteousness leading to holiness. ²⁰When you were slaves to sin, you were free from the control of righteousness. ²¹What benefit did you reap at that time from the things you are now ashamed of? Those things result in death! ²²But now that you have been set free from sin and have become slaves to God, the benefit you reap leads to holiness, and the result is eternal life. ²³For the wages of sin is death, but the gift of God is eternal life in*ᵃ* Christ Jesus our Lord.

An Illustration From Marriage

7 Do you not know, brothers—for I am speaking to men who know the law—that the law has authority over a man only as long as he lives? ²For example, by law a married woman is bound to her husband as long as he is alive, but if her husband dies, she is released from the law of marriage. ³So then, if she marries another man while her husband is still alive, she is called an adulteress. But if her husband dies, she is released from that law and is not an adulteress, even though she marries another man.

⁴So, my brothers, you also died to the law through the body of Christ, that you might belong to another, to him who was raised from the dead, in order that we might bear fruit to God. ⁵For when we were controlled by the sinful nature,*ᵇ* the sinful passions aroused by the law were at work in our bodies, so that we bore fruit for death. ⁶But now, by dying to what once bound us, we have been released from the law so that we serve in the new way of the Spirit, and not in the old way of the written code.

Struggling With Sin

⁷What shall we say, then? Is the law sin? Certainly not! Indeed I would not have known what sin was except through the law. For I would not have known what coveting really was if the law had not said, "Do not covet."*ᶜ* ⁸But sin, seizing the opportunity afforded by the commandment, produced in me every kind of covetous desire. For apart from law, sin is dead. ⁹Once I was alive apart from law; but when the commandment came, sin sprang to life and I died. ¹⁰I found that the very commandment that was intended to bring life actually brought death. ¹¹For sin, seizing the opportunity afforded by the commandment, deceived me, and through the commandment put me to death. ¹²So then, the law is holy, and the commandment is holy, righteous and good.

¹³Did that which is good, then, become death to me? By no means! But in order that sin might be recognized as sin, it produced death in me through what was good, so that through the commandment sin might become utterly sinful.

¹⁴We know that the law is spiritual; but I am unspiritual, sold as a slave to sin. ¹⁵I do not understand what I do. For what I want to do I do not do, but what I hate I do. ¹⁶And if I do what I do not want to do, I agree that the law is good. ¹⁷As it is, it is no longer I myself who do it, but it is sin living in me. ¹⁸I know that nothing good lives in me, that is, in my sinful nature.*ᵈ* For I have the desire to do what is good, but I cannot carry it out. ¹⁹For what I do is not the good I want to do; no, the evil I do not want to do—this I keep on doing. ²⁰Now if I do what I do not want to do, it is no longer I who do it, but it is sin living in me that does it.

²¹So I find this law at work: When I want to do good, evil is right there with me. ²²For in my inner being I delight in God's law; ²³but I see another law at work in the members of my body, waging war against the law of my mind and making me a prisoner of the law of sin at work within my members. ²⁴What a wretched man I am! Who will rescue me from this body of death? ²⁵Thanks be to God—through Jesus Christ our Lord!

So then, I myself in my mind am a slave to God's law, but in the sinful nature a slave to the law of sin.

Life Through the Spirit

8 Therefore, there is now no condemnation for those who are in Christ Jesus,*ᵉ* ²because through Christ Jesus the law of the Spirit of life set me free from the law of sin and death. ³For what the law was powerless to do in that it was weakened by the sinful nature,*ᶠ* God did by sending his own Son in the likeness of sinful man to be a sin offering.*ᵍ* And so he condemned sin in sinful man,*ʰ* ⁴in order that the righteous requirements of the law

---

ᵃ23 Or *through*   *ᵇ5* Or *the flesh*; also in verse 25   *ᶜ7* Exodus 20:17; Deut. 5:21   *ᵈ18* Or *my flesh*
ᵉ1 Some later manuscripts *Jesus, who do not live according to the sinful nature but according to the Spirit,*
ᶠ3 Or *the flesh*; also in verses 4, 5, 8, 9, 12 and 13   *ᵍ3* Or *man, for sin*   *ʰ3* Or *in the flesh*

might be fully met in us, who do not live according to the sinful nature but according to the Spirit.

⁵Those who live according to the sinful nature have their minds set on what that nature desires; but those who live in accordance with the Spirit have their minds set on what the Spirit desires. ⁶The mind of sinful man*a* is death, but the mind controlled by the Spirit is life and peace; ⁷the sinful mind*b* is hostile to God. It does not submit to God's law, nor can it do so. ⁸Those controlled by the sinful nature cannot please God.

⁹You, however, are controlled not by the sinful nature but by the Spirit, if the Spirit of God lives in you. And if anyone does not have the Spirit of Christ, he does

*a*6 Or *mind set on the flesh*   *b*7 Or *the mind set on the flesh*

FRIDAY

VERSE FOR THE DAY:
Romans 8:17

AUTHOR:
Jerry Bridges

PASSAGE FOR THE DAY:
Romans 8:12–17

Saved from Wrath

ONLY the God-fearing Christian can truly appreciate the love of God. He sees the infinite gulf between a holy God and a sinful creature, and the love that bridged that gulf through the death of the Lord Jesus Christ. God's love for us is many-faceted, but he supremely demonstrated it by sending his Son to die for our sins. All other aspects of his love are secondary, and in fact are made possible for us through the death of Christ . . .

The truly godly person never forgets that he was at one time an object of God's holy and just wrath. He never forgets that Christ Jesus came into the world to save sinners—and he feels along with Paul that he is himself the worst of sinners. But then as he looks to the cross he sees that Jesus was his atoning sacrifice. He sees that Jesus bore his sins in his own body, and that the wrath of God—the wrath which he, a sinner, should have borne—was expended completely and totally upon the holy Son of God. And in this view of Calvary, he sees the love of God.

The love of God has no meaning apart from Calvary. And Calvary has no meaning apart from the holy and just wrath of God. Jesus did not die just to give us peace and a purpose in life; he died to save us from the wrath of God. He died to reconcile us to a holy God who was alienated from us because of our sin. He died to ransom us from the penalty of sin—the punishment of everlasting destruction, shut out from the presence of the Lord. He died that we, the just objects of God's wrath, should become, by his grace, heirs of God and co-heirs with him.

Additional Scripture Readings:
Ephesians 2:1–10;
1 Thessalonians 5:4–11

Go to page 208 for your next devotional reading.

not belong to Christ. [10]But if Christ is in you, your body is dead because of sin, yet your spirit is alive because of righteousness. [11]And if the Spirit of him who raised Jesus from the dead is living in you, he who raised Christ from the dead will also give life to your mortal bodies through his Spirit, who lives in you.

[12]Therefore, brothers, we have an obligation — but it is not to the sinful nature, to live according to it. [13]For if you live according to the sinful nature, you will die; but if by the Spirit you put to death the misdeeds of the body, you will live, [14]because those who are led by the Spirit of God are sons of God. [15]For you did not receive a spirit that makes you a slave again to fear, but you received the Spirit of sonship.[a] And by him we cry, "Abba,[b] Father." [16]The Spirit himself testifies with our spirit that we are God's children. [17]Now if we are children, then we are heirs — heirs of God and co-heirs with Christ, if indeed we share in his sufferings in order that we may also share in his glory.

Future Glory

[18]I consider that our present sufferings are not worth comparing with the glory that will be revealed in us. [19]The creation waits in eager expectation for the sons of God to be revealed. [20]For the creation was subjected to frustration, not by its own choice, but by the will of the one who subjected it, in hope [21]that[c] the creation itself will be liberated from its bondage to decay and brought into the glorious freedom of the children of God.

[22]We know that the whole creation has been groaning as in the pains of childbirth right up to the present time. [23]Not only so, but we ourselves, who have the firstfruits of the Spirit, groan inwardly as we wait eagerly for our adoption as sons, the redemption of our bodies. [24]For in this hope we were saved. But hope that is seen is no hope at all. Who hopes for what he already has? [25]But if we hope for what we do not yet have, we wait for it patiently.

[26]In the same way, the Spirit helps us in our weakness. We do not know what we ought to pray for, but the Spirit himself intercedes for us with groans that words cannot express. [27]And he who searches our hearts knows the mind of the Spirit, because the Spirit intercedes for the saints in accordance with God's will.

More Than Conquerors

[28]And we know that in all things God works for the good of those who love him,[d] who[e] have been called according to his purpose. [29]For those God foreknew he also predestined to be conformed to the likeness of his Son, that he might be the firstborn among many brothers. [30]And those he predestined, he also called; those he called, he also justified; those he justified, he also glorified.

[31]What, then, shall we say in response to this? If God is for us, who can be against us? [32]He who did not spare his own Son, but gave him up for us all — how will he not also, along with him, graciously give us all things? [33]Who will bring any charge against those whom God has chosen? It is God who justifies. [34]Who is he that condemns? Christ Jesus, who died — more than that, who was raised to life — is at the right hand of God and is also interceding for us. [35]Who shall separate us from the love of Christ? Shall trouble or hardship or persecution or famine or nakedness or danger or sword? [36]As it is written:

"For your sake we face death all day long;
we are considered as sheep to be slaughtered."[f]

[37]No, in all these things we are more than conquerors through him who loved us. [38]For I am convinced that neither death nor life, neither angels nor demons,[g] neither the present nor the future, nor any powers, [39]neither height nor depth, nor anything else in all creation, will be able to separate us from the love of God that is in Christ Jesus our Lord.

God's Sovereign Choice

9 I speak the truth in Christ — I am not lying, my conscience confirms it in the Holy Spirit — [2]I have great sorrow and unceasing anguish in my heart. [3]For I could wish that I myself were cursed and cut off from Christ for the sake of my brothers, those of my own race, [4]the people of Israel. Theirs is the adoption as sons; theirs the divine glory, the cov-

---

[a]15 Or *adoption* [b]15 Aramaic for *Father* [c]20,21 Or *subjected it in hope.* [21]*For* [d]28 Some manuscripts *And we know that all things work together for good to those who love God* [e]28 Or *works together with those who love him to bring about what is good — with those who* [f]36 Psalm 44:22 [g]38 Or *nor heavenly rulers*

WEEKENDING

REALIZE

I am personally convinced that this submission, this dying to self, this crucifying of pride [see Philippians 2:1–8] is crucial to our joy. We think of denying self as somber, grim-faced business when it is in truth a prelude to dancing. If you want power, learn to be assertive. If you want joy, learn to be submissive . . .

The reason our death [to self] increases the joy level all around is that it also increases the love level all around. Only when we die to self can we fully love one another. Self is a devilish creature, demanding all of our energy, wanting our constant attention, reaching even into our pocketbooks for favors. How can we be attuned to another's spirit when self is making so much noise? How can we ever hope to love another when self screams for our constant care? When self is alive and well, it offers us an all-or-nothing proposition. We either pacify self, or we crucify it.

– *Judson Edwards*

REVIVE
Saturday: Romans 6:1–14
Sunday: Colossians 3:1–14

Go to page 209 for your next devotional reading.

enants, the receiving of the law, the temple worship and the promises. **5**Theirs are the patriarchs, and from them is traced the human ancestry of Christ, who is God over all, forever praised!*a* Amen.

6It is not as though God's word had failed. For not all who are descended from Israel are Israel. **7**Nor because they are his descendants are they all Abraham's children. On the contrary, "It is through Isaac that your offspring will be reckoned."*b* **8**In other words, it is not the natural children who are God's children, but it is the children of the promise who are regarded as Abraham's offspring. **9**For this was how the promise was stated: "At the appointed time I will return, and Sarah will have a son."*c*

10Not only that, but Rebekah's children had one and the same father, our father Isaac. **11**Yet, before the twins were born or had done anything good or bad—in order that God's purpose in election might stand: **12**not by works but by him who calls—she was told, "The older will serve the younger."*d* **13**Just as it is written: "Jacob I loved, but Esau I hated."*e*

14What then shall we say? Is God unjust? Not at all! **15**For he says to Moses,

"I will have mercy on whom I have mercy,

---

a 5 Or *Christ, who is over all. God be forever praised!* Or *Christ. God who is over all be forever praised!* *b 7* Gen. 21:12   *c 9* Gen. 18:10,14   *d 12* Gen. 25:23   *e 13* Mal. 1:2,3

MONDAY

VERSE FOR THE DAY:
Romans 8:31

AUTHOR:
Michael Card

PASSAGE FOR THE DAY:
Romans 8:31–39

His Cost, Our Gain

JESUS paid a tremendous price to be with us. Certainly the cross was the most obvious cost. But I believe more is in view.

We focus so much on the fact that Jesus died for us, we sometimes forget that he also lived for us and lives for us still. If Jesus had simply come as himself, and not as one of us, the Bible makes it quite clear that we could not have borne the sight of his presence, any more than Moses could have looked directly at the face of God.

Imagine what it would be like to be at the Father's side one moment and struggling to sleep in a cattle trough the next. Imagine what it would be like to go from hearing the praise of angels to suffering the taunts of stupid men. The cost to Jesus is an indication of the incredible value of what he came to give us. And because no one will ever fully know what that cost Jesus, we can only begin to understand the incredible value of his gift to us.

The apostle Paul realized the indescribable gift of Immanuel in a passage which many consider the height of his inspiration. He concludes, "If God is for us, who can be against us?" God is on our side, right or wrong, because even when we are wrong, he still loves us.

Additional Scripture Readings:
John 1:1–14; Hebrews 7:23–28

Go to page 211 for your next devotional reading.

and I will have compassion on whom I have compassion."[a]

[16]It does not, therefore, depend on man's desire or effort, but on God's mercy. [17]For the Scripture says to Pharaoh: "I raised you up for this very purpose, that I might display my power in you and that my name might be proclaimed in all the earth."[b] [18]Therefore God has mercy on whom he wants to have mercy, and he hardens whom he wants to harden.

[19]One of you will say to me: "Then why does God still blame us? For who resists his will?" [20]But who are you, O man, to talk back to God? "Shall what is formed say to him who formed it, 'Why did you make me like this?' "[c] [21]Does not the potter have the right to make out of the same lump of clay some pottery for noble purposes and some for common use?

[22]What if God, choosing to show his wrath and make his power known, bore with great patience the objects of his wrath—prepared for destruction? [23]What if he did this to make the riches of his glory known to the objects of his mercy, whom he prepared in advance for glory— [24]even us, whom he also called, not only from the Jews but also from the Gentiles? [25]As he says in Hosea:

"I will call them 'my people' who are not my people;
and I will call her 'my loved one' who is not my loved one,"[d]

[26]and,

"It will happen that in the very place where it was said to them,
'You are not my people,'
they will be called 'sons of the living God.' "[e]

[27]Isaiah cries out concerning Israel:

"Though the number of the Israelites be like the sand by the sea,
only the remnant will be saved.
[28]For the Lord will carry out his sentence on earth with speed and finality."[f]

[29]It is just as Isaiah said previously:

"Unless the Lord Almighty had left us descendants,
we would have become like Sodom,
we would have been like Gomorrah."[g]

Israel's Unbelief

[30]What then shall we say? That the Gentiles, who did not pursue righteousness, have obtained it, a righteousness that is by faith; [31]but Israel, who pursued a law of righteousness, has not attained it. [32]Why not? Because they pursued it not by faith but as if it were by works. They stumbled over the "stumbling stone." [33]As it is written:

"See, I lay in Zion a stone that causes men to stumble
and a rock that makes them fall,
and the one who trusts in him will never be put to shame."[h]

10 Brothers, my heart's desire and prayer to God for the Israelites is that they may be saved. [2]For I can testify about them that they are zealous for God, but their zeal is not based on knowledge. [3]Since they did not know the righteousness that comes from God and sought to establish their own, they did not submit to God's righteousness. [4]Christ is the end of the law so that there may be righteousness for everyone who believes.

[5]Moses describes in this way the righteousness that is by the law: "The man who does these things will live by them."[i] [6]But the righteousness that is by faith says: "Do not say in your heart, 'Who will ascend into heaven?'[j]" (that is, to bring Christ down) [7]"or 'Who will descend into the deep?'[k]" (that is, to bring Christ up from the dead). [8]But what does it say? "The word is near you; it is in your mouth and in your heart,"[l] that is, the word of faith we are proclaiming: [9]That if you confess with your mouth, "Jesus is Lord," and believe in your heart that God raised him from the dead, you will be saved. [10]For it is with your heart that you believe and are justified, and it is with your mouth that you confess and are saved. [11]As the Scripture says, "Anyone who trusts in him will never be put to shame."[m] [12]For there is no difference between Jew and Gentile—the same Lord is Lord of all and richly blesses all who call on him, [13]for, "Everyone who calls on the name of the Lord will be saved."[n]

[14]How, then, can they call on the one

---

[a]15 Exodus 33:19   [b]17 Exodus 9:16   [c]20 Isaiah 29:16; 45:9   [d]25 Hosea 2:23   [e]26 Hosea 1:10
[f]28 Isaiah 10:22,23   [g]29 Isaiah 1:9   [h]33 Isaiah 8:14; 28:16   [i]5 Lev. 18:5   [j]6 Deut. 30:12
[k]7 Deut. 30:13   [l]8 Deut. 30:14   [m]11 Isaiah 28:16   [n]13 Joel 2:32

TUESDAY

VERSE FOR THE DAY:
Romans 9:21

AUTHOR:
H. Beecher Hicks

PASSAGE FOR THE DAY:
Romans 9:16–21

In the Potter's Hand

LOOK closely here! Paul said that the potter has power over the clay . . . God molds us and makes us and holds us in his hand. It's no news to you that every potter has the job of molding and making and holding . . .

The reason that God is involved in the pottery process is that God needs instruments and not objects. Any potter can make an object to sit on the shelf. Any potter can make an artifact that is a thing of beauty and a joy forever. Any potter can make an item of retail sale that men can purchase or leave alone. But God does not need objects, God needs instruments. Far too many who are engaged in the Christian enterprise are objects, but they're not instruments.

- An instrument says I'm good for something.
- An instrument says I have purpose.
- An instrument says I have value.
- An instrument says I can be used . . .

Always remember that the potter does have power over the clay. The potter has creative power. He brings into being that which was not . . .

The potter has creative power. He can stoop down in the dust of the earth and pick up lumps of clay and breathe the breath of life into it until it walks and talks like a natural man. The potter has creative power.

But more, the potter has re-creative power. Jeremiah says that sometimes the pot is marred in the potter's hand [see Jeremiah 18:1–4]. Sometimes the pot does not do what it was designed to do. But the potter just takes it and breaks it and molds it and makes it what he would have it to be. I'm glad to know that when I'm marred and broken, the Lord is not through with me yet. I want him to re-create me . . .

We end where we began: God molds us and makes us and holds us in his hand. No matter what happens in this life, I'm in his hand. What a mighty God we serve! Right or wrong, up or down, poverty or wealth, sickness or health, come what may, I am in his hand. Hallelujah, I am in his hand.

Additional Scripture Readings:
Psalm 139:1–10; Ephesians 2:1–10

Go to page 215 for your next devotional reading.

they have not believed in? And how can they believe in the one of whom they have not heard? And how can they hear without someone preaching to them? **15**And how can they preach unless they are sent? As it is written, "How beautiful are the feet of those who bring good news!"*a*

16But not all the Israelites accepted the good news. For Isaiah says, "Lord, who has believed our message?"*b* **17**Consequently, faith comes from hearing the message, and the message is heard through the word of Christ. **18**But I ask: Did they not hear? Of course they did:

"Their voice has gone out into all the earth,
 their words to the ends of the world."*c*

19Again I ask: Did Israel not understand? First, Moses says,

"I will make you envious by those who are not a nation;
 I will make you angry by a nation that has no understanding."*d*

20And Isaiah boldly says,

"I was found by those who did not seek me;
 I revealed myself to those who did not ask for me."*e*

21But concerning Israel he says,

"All day long I have held out my hands
 to a disobedient and obstinate people."*f*

The Remnant of Israel

11 I ask then: Did God reject his people? By no means! I am an Israelite myself, a descendant of Abraham, from the tribe of Benjamin. **2**God did not reject his people, whom he foreknew. Don't you know what the Scripture says in the passage about Elijah—how he appealed to God against Israel: **3**"Lord, they have killed your prophets and torn down your altars; I am the only one left, and they are trying to kill me"*g*? **4**And what was God's answer to him? "I have reserved for myself seven thousand who have not bowed the knee to Baal."*h* **5**So too, at the present time there is a remnant chosen by grace. **6**And if by grace, then it is no longer by works; if it were, grace would no longer be grace.*i*

7What then? What Israel sought so earnestly it did not obtain, but the elect did. The others were hardened, **8**as it is written:

"God gave them a spirit of stupor,
 eyes so that they could not see
 and ears so that they could not hear,
to this very day."*j*

9And David says:

"May their table become a snare and a trap,
 a stumbling block and a retribution for them.
10May their eyes be darkened so they cannot see,
 and their backs be bent forever."*k*

Ingrafted Branches

11Again I ask: Did they stumble so as to fall beyond recovery? Not at all! Rather, because of their transgression, salvation has come to the Gentiles to make Israel envious. **12**But if their transgression means riches for the world, and their loss means riches for the Gentiles, how much greater riches will their fullness bring!

13I am talking to you Gentiles. Inasmuch as I am the apostle to the Gentiles, I make much of my ministry **14**in the hope that I may somehow arouse my own people to envy and save some of them. **15**For if their rejection is the reconciliation of the world, what will their acceptance be but life from the dead? **16**If the part of the dough offered as firstfruits is holy, then the whole batch is holy; if the root is holy, so are the branches.

17If some of the branches have been broken off, and you, though a wild olive shoot, have been grafted in among the others and now share in the nourishing sap from the olive root, **18**do not boast over those branches. If you do, consider this: You do not support the root, but the root supports you. **19**You will say then, "Branches were broken off so that I could be grafted in." **20**Granted. But they were broken off because of unbelief, and you stand by faith. Do not be arrogant, but be afraid. **21**For if God did not spare the natural branches, he will not spare you either.

---

a 15 Isaiah 52:7   *b* 16 Isaiah 53:1   *c* 18 Psalm 19:4   *d* 19 Deut. 32:21   *e* 20 Isaiah 65:1
f 21 Isaiah 65:2   *g* 3 1 Kings 19:10,14   *h* 4 1 Kings 19:18   *i* 6 Some manuscripts *by grace. But if by works, then it is no longer grace; if it were, work would no longer be work.*   *j* 8 Deut. 29:4; Isaiah 29:10
k 10 Psalm 69:22,23

²²Consider therefore the kindness and sternness of God: sternness to those who fell, but kindness to you, provided that you continue in his kindness. Otherwise, you also will be cut off. ²³And if they do not persist in unbelief, they will be grafted in, for God is able to graft them in again. ²⁴After all, if you were cut out of an olive tree that is wild by nature, and contrary to nature were grafted into a cultivated olive tree, how much more readily will these, the natural branches, be grafted into their own olive tree!

All Israel Will Be Saved

²⁵I do not want you to be ignorant of this mystery, brothers, so that you may not be conceited: Israel has experienced a hardening in part until the full number of the Gentiles has come in. ²⁶And so all Israel will be saved, as it is written:

"The deliverer will come from Zion;
 he will turn godlessness away from Jacob.
²⁷And this is[a] my covenant with them
 when I take away their sins."[b]

²⁸As far as the gospel is concerned, they are enemies on your account; but as far as election is concerned, they are loved on account of the patriarchs, ²⁹for God's gifts and his call are irrevocable. ³⁰Just as you who were at one time disobedient to God have now received mercy as a result of their disobedience, ³¹so they too have now become disobedient in order that they too may now[c] receive mercy as a result of God's mercy to you. ³²For God has bound all men over to disobedience so that he may have mercy on them all.

Doxology

³³Oh, the depth of the riches of the wisdom and[d] knowledge of God!
 How unsearchable his judgments,
 and his paths beyond tracing out!
³⁴"Who has known the mind of the Lord?
 Or who has been his counselor?"[e]
³⁵"Who has ever given to God,
 that God should repay him?"[f]
³⁶For from him and through him and to him are all things.
 To him be the glory forever! Amen.

Living Sacrifices

12 Therefore, I urge you, brothers, in view of God's mercy, to offer your bodies as living sacrifices, holy and pleasing to God—this is your spiritual[g] act of worship. ²Do not conform any longer to the pattern of this world, but be transformed by the renewing of your mind. Then you will be able to test and approve what God's will is—his good, pleasing and perfect will.

³For by the grace given me I say to every one of you: Do not think of yourself more highly than you ought, but rather think of yourself with sober judgment, in accordance with the measure of faith God has given you. ⁴Just as each of us has one body with many members, and these members do not all have the same function, ⁵so in Christ we who are many form one body, and each member belongs to all the others. ⁶We have different gifts, according to the grace given us. If a man's gift is prophesying, let him use it in proportion to his[h] faith. ⁷If it is serving, let him serve; if it is teaching, let him teach; ⁸if it is encouraging, let him encourage; if it is contributing to the needs of others, let him give generously; if it is leadership, let him govern diligently; if it is showing mercy, let him do it cheerfully.

Love

⁹Love must be sincere. Hate what is evil; cling to what is good. ¹⁰Be devoted to one another in brotherly love. Honor one another above yourselves. ¹¹Never be lacking in zeal, but keep your spiritual fervor, serving the Lord. ¹²Be joyful in hope, patient in affliction, faithful in prayer. ¹³Share with God's people who are in need. Practice hospitality.

¹⁴Bless those who persecute you; bless and do not curse. ¹⁵Rejoice with those who rejoice; mourn with those who mourn. ¹⁶Live in harmony with one another. Do not be proud, but be willing to associate with people of low position.[i] Do not be conceited.

¹⁷Do not repay anyone evil for evil. Be careful to do what is right in the eyes of everybody. ¹⁸If it is possible, as far as it depends on you, live at peace with everyone. ¹⁹Do not take revenge, my friends, but leave room for God's wrath, for it is

---

a27 Or *will be* *b27* Isaiah 59:20,21; 27:9; Jer. 31:33,34 *c31* Some manuscripts do not have *now*.
d33 Or *riches and the wisdom and the* *e34* Isaiah 40:13 *f35* Job 41:11 *g1* Or *reasonable*
h6 Or *in agreement with the* *i16* Or *willing to do menial work*

written: "It is mine to avenge; I will repay,"*a* says the Lord. **20**On the contrary:

"If your enemy is hungry, feed him;
   if he is thirsty, give him something
      to drink.
In doing this, you will heap burning
   coals on his head."*b*

21Do not be overcome by evil, but overcome evil with good.

Submission to the Authorities

13 Everyone must submit himself to the governing authorities, for there is no authority except that which God has established. The authorities that exist have been established by God. **2**Consequently, he who rebels against the authority is rebelling against what God has instituted, and those who do so will bring judgment on themselves. **3**For rulers hold no terror for those who do right, but for those who do wrong. Do you want to be free from fear of the one in authority? Then do what is right and he will commend you. **4**For he is God's servant to do you good. But if you do wrong, be afraid, for he does not bear the sword for nothing. He is God's servant, an agent of wrath to bring punishment on the wrongdoer. **5**Therefore, it is necessary to submit to the authorities, not only because of possible punishment but also because of conscience.

6This is also why you pay taxes, for the authorities are God's servants, who give their full time to governing. **7**Give everyone what you owe him: If you owe taxes, pay taxes; if revenue, then revenue; if respect, then respect; if honor, then honor.

Love, for the Day Is Near

8Let no debt remain outstanding, except the continuing debt to love one another, for he who loves his fellowman has fulfilled the law. **9**The commandments, "Do not commit adultery," "Do not murder," "Do not steal," "Do not covet,"*c* and whatever other commandment there may be, are summed up in this one rule: "Love your neighbor as yourself."*d* **10**Love does no harm to its neighbor. Therefore love is the fulfillment of the law.

11And do this, understanding the present time. The hour has come for you to wake up from your slumber, because our salvation is nearer now than when we first believed. **12**The night is nearly over; the day is almost here. So let us put aside the deeds of darkness and put on the armor of light. **13**Let us behave decently, as in the daytime, not in orgies and drunkenness, not in sexual immorality and debauchery, not in dissension and jealousy. **14**Rather, clothe yourselves with the Lord Jesus Christ, and do not think about how to gratify the desires of the sinful nature.*e*

The Weak and the Strong

14 Accept him whose faith is weak, without passing judgment on disputable matters. **2**One man's faith allows him to eat everything, but another man, whose faith is weak, eats only vegetables. **3**The man who eats everything must not look down on him who does not, and the man who does not eat everything must not condemn the man who does, for God has accepted him. **4**Who are you to judge someone else's servant? To his own master he stands or falls. And he will stand, for the Lord is able to make him stand.

5One man considers one day more sacred than another; another man considers every day alike. Each one should be fully convinced in his own mind. **6**He who regards one day as special, does so to the Lord. He who eats meat, eats to the Lord, for he gives thanks to God; and he who abstains, does so to the Lord and gives thanks to God. **7**For none of us lives to himself alone and none of us dies to himself alone. **8**If we live, we live to the Lord; and if we die, we die to the Lord. So, whether we live or die, we belong to the Lord.

9For this very reason, Christ died and returned to life so that he might be the Lord of both the dead and the living. **10**You, then, why do you judge your brother? Or why do you look down on your brother? For we will all stand before God's judgment seat. **11**It is written:

" 'As surely as I live,' says the Lord,
'every knee will bow before me;
   every tongue will confess to
      God.' "*f*

12So then, each of us will give an account of himself to God.

13Therefore let us stop passing judgment on one another. Instead, make up your mind not to put any stumbling block

---

a 19 Deut. 32:35   *b 20* Prov. 25:21,22   *c 9* Exodus 20:13-15,17; Deut. 5:17-19,21   *d 9* Lev. 19:18
e 14 Or *the flesh*   *f 11* Isaiah 45:23

or obstacle in your brother's way. [14]As one who is in the Lord Jesus, I am fully convinced that no food[a] is unclean in itself. But if anyone regards something as unclean, then for him it is unclean. [15]If your brother is distressed because of what you eat, you are no longer acting in love. Do not by your eating destroy your brother for whom Christ died. [16]Do not allow what you consider good to be spoken of as evil. [17]For the kingdom of God is not a matter of eating and drinking, but of righteousness, peace and joy in the Holy Spirit, [18]because anyone who serves Christ in this way is pleasing to God and approved by men.

[19]Let us therefore make every effort to do what leads to peace and to mutual edification. [20]Do not destroy the work of God for the sake of food. All food is clean, but it is wrong for a man to eat anything that causes someone else to stumble. [21]It is better not to eat meat or drink wine or to do anything else that will cause your brother to fall.

[22]So whatever you believe about these

[a]14 Or *that nothing*

| WEDNESDAY |

VERSE FOR THE DAY:
Romans 14:8

AUTHOR:
Philip W. Williams

PASSAGE FOR THE DAY:
Romans 14:5–8

Out of Sorrow

PAIN and despair are threads that run through us as we move through our journey of bereavement.

In pain and despair we can echo the words of the old spiritual, "Nobody knows the trouble I've seen. Nobody knows my sorrow." We may have been moving through our journey slowly, doing well, when suddenly the reality of our loss, this death, hits again! There is no going back, no recapturing or retrieving what was lost. Our loved one is gone. The pain invades and grips, and the fullness we were beginning to feel seeps out. Emptiness takes over. The wound opens wide and we despair. It's as if all life stops again.

One doesn't have to be married 64 years to feel the pain and despair of death. It is not time, but our closeness to our loved one that increases our vulnerability and opens us to deeper pain and despair. Yet when we confront our pain and despair and begin to accept the loss, surrendering ourselves to God in our powerlessness, then pain and despair can give way to hope. The unwanted pain can be accepted and transformed. When we accept our pain as our own, suffering can grow into compassion. It's as if the heart opens, and out of sorrow come warmth and joy.

The life and death of each of us has influence on others: "If we live, we live to the Lord; and if we die, we die to the Lord. So, whether we live or die, we belong to the Lord" (Romans 14:8).

Additional Scripture Readings:
Psalm 23; Philippians 1:19–26

Go to page 221 for your next devotional reading.

things keep between yourself and God. Blessed is the man who does not condemn himself by what he approves. **23**But the man who has doubts is condemned if he eats, because his eating is not from faith; and everything that does not come from faith is sin.

15 We who are strong ought to bear with the failings of the weak and not to please ourselves. **2**Each of us should please his neighbor for his good, to build him up. **3**For even Christ did not please himself but, as it is written: "The insults of those who insult you have fallen on me."*a* **4**For everything that was written in the past was written to teach us, so that through endurance and the encouragement of the Scriptures we might have hope.

5May the God who gives endurance and encouragement give you a spirit of unity among yourselves as you follow Christ Jesus, **6**so that with one heart and mouth you may glorify the God and Father of our Lord Jesus Christ.

7Accept one another, then, just as Christ accepted you, in order to bring praise to God. **8**For I tell you that Christ has become a servant of the Jews*b* on behalf of God's truth, to confirm the promises made to the patriarchs **9**so that the Gentiles may glorify God for his mercy, as it is written:

"Therefore I will praise you among the
    Gentiles;
I will sing hymns to your name."*c*

10Again, it says,

"Rejoice, O Gentiles, with his
    people."*d*

11And again,

"Praise the Lord, all you Gentiles,
and sing praises to him, all you
    peoples."*e*

12And again, Isaiah says,

"The Root of Jesse will spring up,
    one who will arise to rule over the
        nations;
the Gentiles will hope in him."*f*

13May the God of hope fill you with all joy and peace as you trust in him, so that you may overflow with hope by the power of the Holy Spirit.

Paul the Minister to the Gentiles

14I myself am convinced, my brothers, that you yourselves are full of goodness, complete in knowledge and competent to instruct one another. **15**I have written you quite boldly on some points, as if to remind you of them again, because of the grace God gave me **16**to be a minister of Christ Jesus to the Gentiles with the priestly duty of proclaiming the gospel of God, so that the Gentiles might become an offering acceptable to God, sanctified by the Holy Spirit.

17Therefore I glory in Christ Jesus in my service to God. **18**I will not venture to speak of anything except what Christ has accomplished through me in leading the Gentiles to obey God by what I have said and done— **19**by the power of signs and miracles, through the power of the Spirit. So from Jerusalem all the way around to Illyricum, I have fully proclaimed the gospel of Christ. **20**It has always been my ambition to preach the gospel where Christ was not known, so that I would not be building on someone else's foundation. **21**Rather, as it is written:

"Those who were not told about him
    will see,
and those who have not heard will
    understand."*g*

22This is why I have often been hindered from coming to you.

Paul's Plan to Visit Rome

23But now that there is no more place for me to work in these regions, and since I have been longing for many years to see you, **24**I plan to do so when I go to Spain. I hope to visit you while passing through and to have you assist me on my journey there, after I have enjoyed your company for a while. **25**Now, however, I am on my way to Jerusalem in the service of the saints there. **26**For Macedonia and Achaia were pleased to make a contribution for the poor among the saints in Jerusalem. **27**They were pleased to do it, and indeed they owe it to them. For if the Gentiles have shared in the Jews' spiritual blessings, they owe it to the Jews to share with them their material blessings. **28**So after I have completed this task and have made sure that they have received this fruit, I will go to Spain and visit you on the way.

---

a3 Psalm 69:9   *b8* Greek *circumcision*   *c9* 2 Samuel 22:50; Psalm 18:49   *d10* Deut. 32:43
e11 Psalm 117:1   *f12* Isaiah 11:10   *g21* Isaiah 52:15

²⁹I know that when I come to you, I will come in the full measure of the blessing of Christ.
³⁰I urge you, brothers, by our Lord Jesus Christ and by the love of the Spirit, to join me in my struggle by praying to God for me. ³¹Pray that I may be rescued from the unbelievers in Judea and that my service in Jerusalem may be acceptable to the saints there, ³²so that by God's will I may come to you with joy and together with you be refreshed. ³³The God of peace be with you all. Amen.

Personal Greetings

16 I commend to you our sister Phoebe, a servant[a] of the church in Cenchrea. ²I ask you to receive her in the Lord in a way worthy of the saints and to give her any help she may need from you, for she has been a great help to many people, including me.

³Greet Priscilla[b] and Aquila, my fellow workers in Christ Jesus. ⁴They risked their lives for me. Not only I but all the churches of the Gentiles are grateful to them.

⁵Greet also the church that meets at their house.

Greet my dear friend Epenetus, who was the first convert to Christ in the province of Asia.

⁶Greet Mary, who worked very hard for you.

⁷Greet Andronicus and Junias, my relatives who have been in prison with me. They are outstanding among the apostles, and they were in Christ before I was.

⁸Greet Ampliatus, whom I love in the Lord.

⁹Greet Urbanus, our fellow worker in Christ, and my dear friend Stachys.

¹⁰Greet Apelles, tested and approved in Christ.

Greet those who belong to the household of Aristobulus.

¹¹Greet Herodion, my relative.

Greet those in the household of Narcissus who are in the Lord.

¹²Greet Tryphena and Tryphosa, those women who work hard in the Lord.

Greet my dear friend Persis, another woman who has worked very hard in the Lord.

¹³Greet Rufus, chosen in the Lord, and his mother, who has been a mother to me, too.

¹⁴Greet Asyncritus, Phlegon, Hermes, Patrobas, Hermas and the brothers with them.

¹⁵Greet Philologus, Julia, Nereus and his sister, and Olympas and all the saints with them.

¹⁶Greet one another with a holy kiss.

All the churches of Christ send greetings.

¹⁷I urge you, brothers, to watch out for those who cause divisions and put obstacles in your way that are contrary to the teaching you have learned. Keep away from them. ¹⁸For such people are not serving our Lord Christ, but their own appetites. By smooth talk and flattery they deceive the minds of naive people. ¹⁹Everyone has heard about your obedience, so I am full of joy over you; but I want you to be wise about what is good, and innocent about what is evil.

²⁰The God of peace will soon crush Satan under your feet.

The grace of our Lord Jesus be with you.

²¹Timothy, my fellow worker, sends his greetings to you, as do Lucius, Jason and Sosipater, my relatives.

²²I, Tertius, who wrote down this letter, greet you in the Lord.

²³Gaius, whose hospitality I and the whole church here enjoy, sends you his greetings.

Erastus, who is the city's director of public works, and our brother Quartus send you their greetings.[c]

²⁵Now to him who is able to establish you by my gospel and the proclamation of Jesus Christ, according to the revelation of the mystery hidden for long ages past, ²⁶but now revealed and made known through the prophetic writings by the command of the eternal God, so that all nations might believe and obey him— ²⁷to the only wise God be glory forever through Jesus Christ! Amen.

---

[a]1 Or *deaconess* [b]3 Greek *Prisca*, a variant of *Priscilla* [c]23 Some manuscripts *their greetings.* ²⁴*May the grace of our Lord Jesus Christ be with all of you. Amen.*

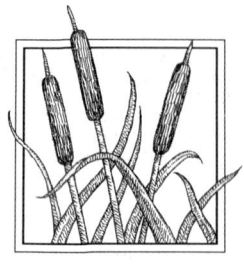

*P*AUL, *while staying in Ephesus (Acts 19), writes this letter to the church he started in Corinth (Acts 18:1–17). He addresses various problems he has heard about and answers questions they have asked of him in a letter (see 1 Corinthians 7:1). He places a high priority on being obedient to Christ and on striving for unity, humility and love in the church. As you read this book, make a decision to seek the Lord's will in everything you do and to work hard to be humble, to love others, and to become one in spirit with your fellow believers.*

1 CORINTHIANS

1 Paul, called to be an apostle of Christ Jesus by the will of God, and our brother Sosthenes,

²To the church of God in Corinth, to those sanctified in Christ Jesus and called to be holy, together with all those everywhere who call on the name of our Lord Jesus Christ—their Lord and ours:

³Grace and peace to you from God our Father and the Lord Jesus Christ.

Thanksgiving

⁴I always thank God for you because of his grace given you in Christ Jesus. ⁵For in him you have been enriched in every way—in all your speaking and in all your knowledge— ⁶because our testimony about Christ was confirmed in you. ⁷Therefore you do not lack any spiritual gift as you eagerly wait for our Lord Jesus Christ to be revealed. ⁸He will keep you strong to the end, so that you will be blameless on the day of our Lord Jesus

Christ. **9**God, who has called you into fellowship with his Son Jesus Christ our Lord, is faithful.

Divisions in the Church

10I appeal to you, brothers, in the name of our Lord Jesus Christ, that all of you agree with one another so that there may be no divisions among you and that you may be perfectly united in mind and thought. **11**My brothers, some from Chloe's household have informed me that there are quarrels among you. **12**What I mean is this: One of you says, "I follow Paul"; another, "I follow Apollos"; another, "I follow Cephas[a]"; still another, "I follow Christ."

13Is Christ divided? Was Paul crucified for you? Were you baptized into[b] the name of Paul? **14**I am thankful that I did not baptize any of you except Crispus and Gaius, **15**so no one can say that you were baptized into my name. **16**(Yes, I also baptized the household of Stephanas; beyond that, I don't remember if I baptized anyone else.) **17**For Christ did not send me to baptize, but to preach the gospel — not with words of human wisdom, lest the cross of Christ be emptied of its power.

Christ the Wisdom and Power of God

18For the message of the cross is foolishness to those who are perishing, but to us who are being saved it is the power of God. **19**For it is written:

"I will destroy the wisdom of the wise;
 the intelligence of the intelligent I
  will frustrate."[c]

20Where is the wise man? Where is the scholar? Where is the philosopher of this age? Has not God made foolish the wisdom of the world? **21**For since in the wisdom of God the world through its wisdom did not know him, God was pleased through the foolishness of what was preached to save those who believe. **22**Jews demand miraculous signs and Greeks look for wisdom, **23**but we preach Christ crucified: a stumbling block to Jews and foolishness to Gentiles, **24**but to those whom God has called, both Jews and Greeks, Christ the power of God and the wisdom of God. **25**For the foolishness of God is wiser than man's wisdom, and the weakness of God is stronger than man's strength.

26Brothers, think of what you were when you were called. Not many of you were wise by human standards; not many were influential; not many were of noble birth. **27**But God chose the foolish things of the world to shame the wise; God chose the weak things of the world to shame the strong. **28**He chose the lowly things of this world and the despised things — and the things that are not — to nullify the things that are, **29**so that no one may boast before him. **30**It is because of him that you are in Christ Jesus, who has become for us wisdom from God — that is, our righteousness, holiness and redemption. **31**Therefore, as it is written: "Let him who boasts boast in the Lord."[d]

2 When I came to you, brothers, I did not come with eloquence or superior wisdom as I proclaimed to you the testimony about God.[e] **2**For I resolved to know nothing while I was with you except Jesus Christ and him crucified. **3**I came to you in weakness and fear, and with much trembling. **4**My message and my preaching were not with wise and persuasive words, but with a demonstration of the Spirit's power, **5**so that your faith might not rest on men's wisdom, but on God's power.

Wisdom From the Spirit

6We do, however, speak a message of wisdom among the mature, but not the wisdom of this age or of the rulers of this age, who are coming to nothing. **7**No, we speak of God's secret wisdom, a wisdom that has been hidden and that God destined for our glory before time began. **8**None of the rulers of this age understood it, for if they had, they would not have crucified the Lord of glory. **9**However, as it is written:

"No eye has seen,
 no ear has heard,
no mind has conceived
 what God has prepared for those
  who love him"[f] —

10but God has revealed it to us by his Spirit.

The Spirit searches all things, even the deep things of God. **11**For who among men knows the thoughts of a man except the man's spirit within him? In the same way no one knows the thoughts of God except the Spirit of God. **12**We have not received

---

[a]12 That is, Peter   [b]13 Or in; also in verse 15 manuscripts as I proclaimed to you God's mystery   [c]19 Isaiah 29:14   [d]31 Jer. 9:24   [e]1 Some   [f]9 Isaiah 64:4

the spirit of the world but the Spirit who is from God, that we may understand what God has freely given us. ¹³This is what we speak, not in words taught us by human wisdom but in words taught by the Spirit, expressing spiritual truths in spiritual words.*a* ¹⁴The man without the Spirit does not accept the things that come from the Spirit of God, for they are foolishness to him, and he cannot understand them, because they are spiritually discerned. ¹⁵The spiritual man makes judgments about all things, but he himself is not subject to any man's judgment:

¹⁶"For who has known the mind of the Lord
that he may instruct him?"*b*

But we have the mind of Christ.

On Divisions in the Church

3 Brothers, I could not address you as spiritual but as worldly—mere infants in Christ. ²I gave you milk, not solid food, for you were not yet ready for it. Indeed, you are still not ready. ³You are still worldly. For since there is jealousy and quarreling among you, are you not worldly? Are you not acting like mere men? ⁴For when one says, "I follow Paul," and another, "I follow Apollos," are you not mere men?

⁵What, after all, is Apollos? And what is Paul? Only servants, through whom you came to believe—as the Lord has assigned to each his task. ⁶I planted the seed, Apollos watered it, but God made it grow. ⁷So neither he who plants nor he who waters is anything, but only God, who makes things grow. ⁸The man who plants and the man who waters have one purpose, and each will be rewarded according to his own labor. ⁹For we are God's fellow workers; you are God's field, God's building.

¹⁰By the grace God has given me, I laid a foundation as an expert builder, and someone else is building on it. But each one should be careful how he builds. ¹¹For no one can lay any foundation other than the one already laid, which is Jesus Christ. ¹²If any man builds on this foundation using gold, silver, costly stones, wood, hay or straw, ¹³his work will be shown for what it is, because the Day will bring it to light. It will be revealed with fire, and the fire will test the quality of each man's work. ¹⁴If what he has built survives, he will receive his reward. ¹⁵If it is burned up, he will suffer loss; he himself will be saved, but only as one escaping through the flames.

¹⁶Don't you know that you yourselves are God's temple and that God's Spirit lives in you? ¹⁷If anyone destroys God's temple, God will destroy him; for God's temple is sacred, and you are that temple.

¹⁸Do not deceive yourselves. If any one of you thinks he is wise by the standards of this age, he should become a "fool" so that he may become wise. ¹⁹For the wisdom of this world is foolishness in God's sight. As it is written: "He catches the wise in their craftiness"*c*; ²⁰and again, "The Lord knows that the thoughts of the wise are futile."*d* ²¹So then, no more boasting about men! All things are yours, ²²whether Paul or Apollos or Cephas*e* or the world or life or death or the present or the future—all are yours, ²³and you are of Christ, and Christ is of God.

Apostles of Christ

4 So then, men ought to regard us as servants of Christ and as those entrusted with the secret things of God. ²Now it is required that those who have been given a trust must prove faithful. ³I care very little if I am judged by you or by any human court; indeed, I do not even judge myself. ⁴My conscience is clear, but that does not make me innocent. It is the Lord who judges me. ⁵Therefore judge nothing before the appointed time; wait till the Lord comes. He will bring to light what is hidden in darkness and will expose the motives of men's hearts. At that time each will receive his praise from God.

⁶Now, brothers, I have applied these things to myself and Apollos for your benefit, so that you may learn from us the meaning of the saying, "Do not go beyond what is written." Then you will not take pride in one man over against another. ⁷For who makes you different from anyone else? What do you have that you did not receive? And if you did receive it, why do you boast as though you did not?

⁸Already you have all you want! Already you have become rich! You have become kings—and that without us! How I wish that you really had become kings so that we might be kings with you! ⁹For it seems to me that God has put us apostles

---

a 13 Or *Spirit, interpreting spiritual truths to spiritual men*   *b* 16 Isaiah 40:13   *c* 19 Job 5:13
d 20 Psalm 94:11   *e* 22 That is, Peter

on display at the end of the procession, like men condemned to die in the arena. We have been made a spectacle to the whole universe, to angels as well as to men. ¹⁰We are fools for Christ, but you are so wise in Christ! We are weak, but you are strong! You are honored, we are dishonored! ¹¹To this very hour we go hungry and thirsty, we are in rags, we are brutally treated, we are homeless. ¹²We work hard with our own hands. When we are cursed, we bless; when we are persecuted, we endure it; ¹³when we are slandered, we answer kindly. Up to this moment we have become the scum of the earth, the refuse of the world.

¹⁴I am not writing this to shame you, but to warn you, as my dear children. ¹⁵Even though you have ten thousand guardians in Christ, you do not have many fathers, for in Christ Jesus I became your father through the gospel. ¹⁶Therefore I urge you to imitate me. ¹⁷For this reason I am sending to you Timothy, my son whom I love, who is faithful in the Lord. He will remind you of my way of life in

---

THURSDAY

VERSE FOR THE DAY:
1 Corinthians 4:2

AUTHOR:
Steve Farrar

PASSAGE FOR THE DAY:
1 Corinthians 4:1–5

The Spirit of Our Age

WE LIVE in an era where commitment is cheap. It's cheap in marriage, business, politics, and even athletics. Commitment is cheap in professional sports when a running back will sign a six-year, multi-million dollar contract, and then stay out of training camp in his third year because the team won't renegotiate his contract. Why does he want to renegotiate? Because some other backs in the league recently signed new contracts worth more than his. He wants to renegotiate because his contract is no longer personally convenient, and he refuses to keep his commitment until he gets his way. One player recently hinted that if his contract wasn't renegotiated, he wouldn't be able to give 100 percent on the field. Can you blame him? He was only making $685,000 a year.

The spirit of our age, whether expressed in athletics, business, politics or marriage, maintains that commitments should be honored only while convenient. When a commitment becomes inconvenient, bag it. Burton Hillis once said, "There's a mighty big difference between good, sound reasons, and reasons that sound good." Generally speaking, our society believes that only one commitment sounds good: The right to be happy . . .

A boy who has a father who is committed to his mother will have a tremendous advantage when he becomes a husband. He will have an intuitive understanding that his commitment in marriage is not a right to be happy, but to demonstrate a willingness to be responsible. Even when it's inconvenient. Even when it crowds out his personal happiness.

Additional Scripture Readings:
Philippians 3:7–16; Titus 2:11–14

Go to page 223 for your next devotional reading.

Christ Jesus, which agrees with what I teach everywhere in every church.

18Some of you have become arrogant, as if I were not coming to you. **19**But I will come to you very soon, if the Lord is willing, and then I will find out not only how these arrogant people are talking, but what power they have. **20**For the kingdom of God is not a matter of talk but of power. **21**What do you prefer? Shall I come to you with a whip, or in love and with a gentle spirit?

Expel the Immoral Brother!

5 It is actually reported that there is sexual immorality among you, and of a kind that does not occur even among pagans: A man has his father's wife. **2**And you are proud! Shouldn't you rather have been filled with grief and have put out of your fellowship the man who did this? **3**Even though I am not physically present, I am with you in spirit. And I have already passed judgment on the one who did this, just as if I were present. **4**When you are assembled in the name of our Lord Jesus and I am with you in spirit, and the power of our Lord Jesus is present, **5**hand this man over to Satan, so that the sinful nature[a] may be destroyed and his spirit saved on the day of the Lord.

6Your boasting is not good. Don't you know that a little yeast works through the whole batch of dough? **7**Get rid of the old yeast that you may be a new batch without yeast—as you really are. For Christ, our Passover lamb, has been sacrificed. **8**Therefore let us keep the Festival, not with the old yeast, the yeast of malice and wickedness, but with bread without yeast, the bread of sincerity and truth.

9I have written you in my letter not to associate with sexually immoral people— **10**not at all meaning the people of this world who are immoral, or the greedy and swindlers, or idolaters. In that case you would have to leave this world. **11**But now I am writing you that you must not associate with anyone who calls himself a brother but is sexually immoral or greedy, an idolater or a slanderer, a drunkard or a swindler. With such a man do not even eat.

12What business is it of mine to judge those outside the church? Are you not to judge those inside? **13**God will judge those outside. "Expel the wicked man from among you."[b]

Lawsuits Among Believers

6 If any of you has a dispute with another, dare he take it before the ungodly for judgment instead of before the saints? **2**Do you not know that the saints will judge the world? And if you are to judge the world, are you not competent to judge trivial cases? **3**Do you not know that we will judge angels? How much more the things of this life! **4**Therefore, if you have disputes about such matters, appoint as judges even men of little account in the church![c] **5**I say this to shame you. Is it possible that there is nobody among you wise enough to judge a dispute between believers? **6**But instead, one brother goes to law against another—and this in front of unbelievers!

7The very fact that you have lawsuits among you means you have been completely defeated already. Why not rather be wronged? Why not rather be cheated? **8**Instead, you yourselves cheat and do wrong, and you do this to your brothers.

9Do you not know that the wicked will not inherit the kingdom of God? Do not be deceived: Neither the sexually immoral nor idolaters nor adulterers nor male prostitutes nor homosexual offenders **10**nor thieves nor the greedy nor drunkards nor slanderers nor swindlers will inherit the kingdom of God. **11**And that is what some of you were. But you were washed, you were sanctified, you were justified in the name of the Lord Jesus Christ and by the Spirit of our God.

Sexual Immorality

12"Everything is permissible for me"— but not everything is beneficial. "Everything is permissible for me"—but I will not be mastered by anything. **13**"Food for the stomach and the stomach for food"— but God will destroy them both. The body is not meant for sexual immorality, but for the Lord, and the Lord for the body. **14**By his power God raised the Lord from the dead, and he will raise us also. **15**Do you not know that your bodies are members of Christ himself? Shall I then take the members of Christ and unite them with a prostitute? Never! **16**Do you not know that he who unites himself with a prostitute is one with her in body? For it is said, "The

---

[a]5 Or *that his body;* or *that the flesh*   [b]13 Deut. 17:7; 19:19; 21:21; 22:21,24; 24:7   [c]4 Or *matters, do you appoint as judges men of little account in the church?*

two will become one flesh."*a* **17**But he who unites himself with the Lord is one with him in spirit.

18Flee from sexual immorality. All other sins a man commits are outside his body, but he who sins sexually sins against his own body. **19**Do you not know that your body is a temple of the Holy Spirit, who is in you, whom you have received from God? You are not your own; **20**you were bought at a price. Therefore honor God with your body.

Marriage

7 Now for the matters you wrote about: It is good for a man not to marry.*b* **2**But since there is so much immorality, each man should have his own wife, and each woman her own husband. **3**The husband should fulfill his marital duty to his

---

a 16 Gen. 2:24 *b 1* Or "*It is good for a man not to have sexual relations with a woman.*"

FRIDAY

VERSE FOR THE DAY:
1 Corinthians 6:19

AUTHOR:
Thomas Merton

PASSAGE FOR THE DAY:
1 Corinthians 6:18–20

Sons of God

EVERY baptized Christian is obliged by his baptismal promises to renounce sin and to give himself completely, without compromise, to Christ, in order that he may fulfill his vocation, save his soul, enter into the mystery of God, and there find himself perfectly in the light of Christ.

As Saint Paul reminds us, we are not our own (1 Corinthians 6:19). We belong entirely to Christ. His Spirit has taken possession of us at baptism. We are the temples of the Holy Spirit. Our thoughts, our actions, our desires, are by rights more his than our own. But we have to struggle to ensure that God always receives from us what we owe him by right. If we do not labor to overcome our natural weakness, our disordered and selfish passions, what belongs to God in us will be withdrawn from the sanctifying power of his love and will be corrupted by selfishness, blinded by irrational desire, hardened by pride, and will eventually plunge into the abyss of moral nonentity which is called sin.

Sin is the refusal of spiritual life, the rejection of the inner order and peace that come from our union with the divine will. In a word, sin is the refusal of God's will and of his love. It is not only a refusal to "do" this or that thing willed by God, or a determination to do what he forbids. It is more radically a refusal to be what we are, a rejection of our mysterious, contingent, spiritual reality hidden in the very mystery of God. Sin is our refusal to be what we were created to be—sons of God, images of God. Ultimately sin, while seeming to be an assertion of freedom, is a flight from the freedom and the responsibility of divine sonship.

Additional Scripture Readings:
Romans 8:12–17;
Galatians 3:26—4:7

Go to page 225 for your next devotional reading.

wife, and likewise the wife to her husband. ⁴The wife's body does not belong to her alone but also to her husband. In the same way, the husband's body does not belong to him alone but also to his wife. ⁵Do not deprive each other except by mutual consent and for a time, so that you may devote yourselves to prayer. Then come together again so that Satan will not tempt you because of your lack of self-control. ⁶I say this as a concession, not as a command. ⁷I wish that all men were as I am. But each man has his own gift from God; one has this gift, another has that.

⁸Now to the unmarried and the widows I say: It is good for them to stay unmarried, as I am. ⁹But if they cannot control themselves, they should marry, for it is better to marry than to burn with passion.

¹⁰To the married I give this command (not I, but the Lord): A wife must not separate from her husband. ¹¹But if she does, she must remain unmarried or else be reconciled to her husband. And a husband must not divorce his wife.

¹²To the rest I say this (I, not the Lord): If any brother has a wife who is not a believer and she is willing to live with him, he must not divorce her. ¹³And if a woman has a husband who is not a believer and he is willing to live with her, she must not divorce him. ¹⁴For the unbelieving husband has been sanctified through his wife, and the unbelieving wife has been sanctified through her believing husband. Otherwise your children would be unclean, but as it is, they are holy.

¹⁵But if the unbeliever leaves, let him do so. A believing man or woman is not bound in such circumstances; God has called us to live in peace. ¹⁶How do you know, wife, whether you will save your husband? Or, how do you know, husband, whether you will save your wife?

¹⁷Nevertheless, each one should retain the place in life that the Lord assigned to him and to which God has called him. This is the rule I lay down in all the churches. ¹⁸Was a man already circumcised when he was called? He should not become uncircumcised. Was a man uncircumcised when he was called? He should not be circumcised. ¹⁹Circumcision is nothing and uncircumcision is nothing. Keeping God's commands is what counts. ²⁰Each one should remain in the situation which he was in when God called him. ²¹Were you a slave when you were called? Don't let it trouble you—although if you can gain your freedom, do so. ²²For he who was a slave when he was called by the Lord is the Lord's freedman; similarly, he who was a free man when he was called is Christ's slave. ²³You were bought at a price; do not become slaves of men. ²⁴Brothers, each man, as responsible to God, should remain in the situation God called him to.

²⁵Now about virgins: I have no command from the Lord, but I give a judgment as one who by the Lord's mercy is trustworthy. ²⁶Because of the present crisis, I think that it is good for you to remain as you are. ²⁷Are you married? Do not seek a divorce. Are you unmarried? Do not look for a wife. ²⁸But if you do marry, you have not sinned; and if a virgin marries, she has not sinned. But those who marry will face many troubles in this life, and I want to spare you this.

²⁹What I mean, brothers, is that the time is short. From now on those who have wives should live as if they had none; ³⁰those who mourn, as if they did not; those who are happy, as if they were not; those who buy something, as if it were not theirs to keep; ³¹those who use the things of the world, as if not engrossed in them. For this world in its present form is passing away.

³²I would like you to be free from concern. An unmarried man is concerned about the Lord's affairs—how he can please the Lord. ³³But a married man is concerned about the affairs of this world—how he can please his wife— ³⁴and his interests are divided. An unmarried woman or virgin is concerned about the Lord's affairs: Her aim is to be devoted to the Lord in both body and spirit. But a married woman is concerned about the affairs of this world—how she can please her husband. ³⁵I am saying this for your own good, not to restrict you, but that you may live in a right way in undivided devotion to the Lord.

³⁶If anyone thinks he is acting improperly toward the virgin he is engaged to, and if she is getting along in years and he feels he ought to marry, he should do as he wants. He is not sinning. They should get married. ³⁷But the man who has settled the matter in his own mind, who is under no compulsion but has control over his own will, and who has made up his mind not to marry the virgin—this man also does the right thing. ³⁸So then, he

WEEKENDING

RECOGNIZE

Everyone who comes to know Jesus stumbles because of him. He fails to meet our wrong expectations. He calls us to do impossible things or to become something we think we could never become. This is his way of teaching us how much we need him. He breaks us to pieces so that he can put us back together in his image.

– *Michael Card*

RENEW

The rule is this: Christians are people who remember their own weaknesses and failure. They are under reconstruction. So they offer hope and forgiveness to people who fall and who need Jesus' healing grace and hope.

– *Donald M. Joy*

REVIVE

Saturday: 1 Corinthians 1:20–31
Sunday: 2 Corinthians 4:1–12

Go to page 226 for your next devotional reading.

who marries the virgin does right, but he who does not marry her does even better.[a]

39 A woman is bound to her husband as long as he lives. But if her husband dies, she is free to marry anyone she wishes, but he must belong to the Lord. **40** In my judgment, she is happier if she stays as she is—and I think that I too have the Spirit of God.

[a] 36-38 Or ³⁶*If anyone thinks he is not treating his daughter properly, and if she is getting along in years, and he feels she ought to marry, he should do as he wants. He is not sinning. He should let her get married.* ³⁷*But the man who has settled the matter in his own mind, who is under no compulsion but has control over his own will, and who has made up his mind to keep the virgin unmarried—this man also does the right thing.* ³⁸*So then, he who gives his virgin in marriage does right, but he who does not give her in marriage does even better.*

MONDAY

VERSE FOR THE DAY:
1 Corinthians 7:32

AUTHOR:
Leonard LeSourd

PASSAGE FOR THE DAY:
1 Corinthians 7:32–38

Dynamic Celibacy

THE key to a dynamic celibacy is to live a selfless life. When a man's life is centered on serving God and helping others, his energies are directed outward and there's no time to dwell on sexual hang-ups.

The apostle Paul discovered this secret. "An unmarried man is concerned about the Lord's affairs—how he can please the Lord . . . The man who . . . has control over his own will, and who has made up his mind not to marry the virgin—this man also does the right thing. So then, he who marries the virgin does right, but he who does not marry her does even better" (1 Corinthians 7:32,37–38).

Is Paul putting down marriage?

Not at all. He is simply holding up another commitment—an even more demanding and absorbing one: one hundred percent, all-out devotion to God. In his ministry to men, Paul is continually exhorting them to find "the best" through self-discipline, whatever their marital status: "Flee the evil desires of youth" (2 Timothy 2:22). "It is God's will that you should be sanctified: that you should avoid sexual immorality . . . For God did not call us to be impure, but to live a holy life" (1 Thessalonians 4:3,7).

Celibacy in no way implies withdrawal from people or a life of seclusion. In fact, because the single person usually has fewer family responsibilities, he is freer to reach out to those around him who need his love. If I were young and single again in today's hurting world, I would opt to learn more about holy living.

Additional Scripture Readings:
1 Thessalonians 4:3–8;
1 Peter 1:13–25

Go to page 230 for your next devotional reading.

Food Sacrificed to Idols

8 Now about food sacrificed to idols: We know that we all possess knowledge.[a] Knowledge puffs up, but love builds up. ²The man who thinks he knows something does not yet know as he ought to know. ³But the man who loves God is known by God.

⁴So then, about eating food sacrificed to idols: We know that an idol is nothing at all in the world and that there is no God but one. ⁵For even if there are so-called gods, whether in heaven or on earth (as indeed there are many "gods" and many "lords"), ⁶yet for us there is but one God, the Father, from whom all things came and for whom we live; and there is but one Lord, Jesus Christ, through whom all things came and through whom we live.

⁷But not everyone knows this. Some people are still so accustomed to idols that when they eat such food they think of it as having been sacrificed to an idol, and since their conscience is weak, it is defiled. ⁸But food does not bring us near to God; we are no worse if we do not eat, and no better if we do.

⁹Be careful, however, that the exercise of your freedom does not become a stumbling block to the weak. ¹⁰For if anyone with a weak conscience sees you who have this knowledge eating in an idol's temple, won't he be emboldened to eat what has been sacrificed to idols? ¹¹So this weak brother, for whom Christ died, is destroyed by your knowledge. ¹²When you sin against your brothers in this way and wound their weak conscience, you sin against Christ. ¹³Therefore, if what I eat causes my brother to fall into sin, I will never eat meat again, so that I will not cause him to fall.

The Rights of an Apostle

9 Am I not free? Am I not an apostle? Have I not seen Jesus our Lord? Are you not the result of my work in the Lord? ²Even though I may not be an apostle to others, surely I am to you! For you are the seal of my apostleship in the Lord.

³This is my defense to those who sit in judgment on me. ⁴Don't we have the right to food and drink? ⁵Don't we have the right to take a believing wife along with us, as do the other apostles and the Lord's brothers and Cephas[b]? ⁶Or is it only I and Barnabas who must work for a living?

⁷Who serves as a soldier at his own expense? Who plants a vineyard and does not eat of its grapes? Who tends a flock and does not drink of the milk? ⁸Do I say this merely from a human point of view? Doesn't the Law say the same thing? ⁹For it is written in the Law of Moses: "Do not muzzle an ox while it is treading out the grain."[c] Is it about oxen that God is concerned? ¹⁰Surely he says this for us, doesn't he? Yes, this was written for us, because when the plowman plows and the thresher threshes, they ought to do so in the hope of sharing in the harvest. ¹¹If we have sown spiritual seed among you, is it too much if we reap a material harvest from you? ¹²If others have this right of support from you, shouldn't we have it all the more?

But we did not use this right. On the contrary, we put up with anything rather than hinder the gospel of Christ. ¹³Don't you know that those who work in the temple get their food from the temple, and those who serve at the altar share in what is offered on the altar? ¹⁴In the same way, the Lord has commanded that those who preach the gospel should receive their living from the gospel.

¹⁵But I have not used any of these rights. And I am not writing this in the hope that you will do such things for me. I would rather die than have anyone deprive me of this boast. ¹⁶Yet when I preach the gospel, I cannot boast, for I am compelled to preach. Woe to me if I do not preach the gospel! ¹⁷If I preach voluntarily, I have a reward; if not voluntarily, I am simply discharging the trust committed to me. ¹⁸What then is my reward? Just this: that in preaching the gospel I may offer it free of charge, and so not make use of my rights in preaching it.

¹⁹Though I am free and belong to no man, I make myself a slave to everyone, to win as many as possible. ²⁰To the Jews I became like a Jew, to win the Jews. To those under the law I became like one under the law (though I myself am not under the law), so as to win those under the law. ²¹To those not having the law I became like one not having the law (though I am not free from God's law but am under Christ's law), so as to win those not having the law. ²²To the weak I became weak, to win the weak. I have become all things to all men so that by all possible means I might save some. ²³I do all this for the

---

[a] 1 Or "We all possess knowledge," as you say [b] 5 That is, Peter [c] 9 Deut. 25:4

sake of the gospel, that I may share in its blessings.

²⁴Do you not know that in a race all the runners run, but only one gets the prize? Run in such a way as to get the prize. ²⁵Everyone who competes in the games goes into strict training. They do it to get a crown that will not last; but we do it to get a crown that will last forever. ²⁶Therefore I do not run like a man running aimlessly; I do not fight like a man beating the air. ²⁷No, I beat my body and make it my slave so that after I have preached to others, I myself will not be disqualified for the prize.

Warnings From Israel's History

10 For I do not want you to be ignorant of the fact, brothers, that our forefathers were all under the cloud and that they all passed through the sea. ²They were all baptized into Moses in the cloud and in the sea. ³They all ate the same spiritual food ⁴and drank the same spiritual drink; for they drank from the spiritual rock that accompanied them, and that rock was Christ. ⁵Nevertheless, God was not pleased with most of them; their bodies were scattered over the desert.

⁶Now these things occurred as examples*ᵃ* to keep us from setting our hearts on evil things as they did. ⁷Do not be idolaters, as some of them were; as it is written: "The people sat down to eat and drink and got up to indulge in pagan revelry."*ᵇ* ⁸We should not commit sexual immorality, as some of them did—and in one day twenty-three thousand of them died. ⁹We should not test the Lord, as some of them did—and were killed by snakes. ¹⁰And do not grumble, as some of them did—and were killed by the destroying angel.

¹¹These things happened to them as examples and were written down as warnings for us, on whom the fulfillment of the ages has come. ¹²So, if you think you are standing firm, be careful that you don't fall! ¹³No temptation has seized you except what is common to man. And God is faithful; he will not let you be tempted beyond what you can bear. But when you are tempted, he will also provide a way out so that you can stand up under it.

Idol Feasts and the Lord's Supper

¹⁴Therefore, my dear friends, flee from idolatry. ¹⁵I speak to sensible people; judge for yourselves what I say. ¹⁶Is not the cup of thanksgiving for which we give thanks a participation in the blood of Christ? And is not the bread that we break a participation in the body of Christ? ¹⁷Because there is one loaf, we, who are many, are one body, for we all partake of the one loaf.

¹⁸Consider the people of Israel: Do not those who eat the sacrifices participate in the altar? ¹⁹Do I mean then that a sacrifice offered to an idol is anything, or that an idol is anything? ²⁰No, but the sacrifices of pagans are offered to demons, not to God, and I do not want you to be participants with demons. ²¹You cannot drink the cup of the Lord and the cup of demons too; you cannot have a part in both the Lord's table and the table of demons. ²²Are we trying to arouse the Lord's jealousy? Are we stronger than he?

The Believer's Freedom

²³"Everything is permissible"—but not everything is beneficial. "Everything is permissible"—but not everything is constructive. ²⁴Nobody should seek his own good, but the good of others.

²⁵Eat anything sold in the meat market without raising questions of conscience, ²⁶for, "The earth is the Lord's, and everything in it."*ᶜ*

²⁷If some unbeliever invites you to a meal and you want to go, eat whatever is put before you without raising questions of conscience. ²⁸But if anyone says to you, "This has been offered in sacrifice," then do not eat it, both for the sake of the man who told you and for conscience' sake*ᵈ*— ²⁹the other man's conscience, I mean, not yours. For why should my freedom be judged by another's conscience? ³⁰If I take part in the meal with thankfulness, why am I denounced because of something I thank God for?

³¹So whether you eat or drink or whatever you do, do it all for the glory of God. ³²Do not cause anyone to stumble, whether Jews, Greeks or the church of God— ³³even as I try to please everybody in every way. For I am not seeking my own good but the good of many, so that they may be saved. **11** ¹Follow my example, as I follow the example of Christ.

ᵃ6 Or *types*; also in verse 11   *ᵇ7* Exodus 32:6   *ᶜ26* Psalm 24:1   *ᵈ28* Some manuscripts *conscience' sake, for "the earth is the Lord's and everything in it"*

Propriety in Worship

²I praise you for remembering me in everything and for holding to the teachings,*a* just as I passed them on to you. ³Now I want you to realize that the head of every man is Christ, and the head of the woman is man, and the head of Christ is God. ⁴Every man who prays or prophesies with his head covered dishonors his head. ⁵And every woman who prays or prophesies with her head uncovered dishonors her head—it is just as though her head were shaved. ⁶If a woman does not cover her head, she should have her hair cut off; and if it is a disgrace for a woman to have her hair cut or shaved off, she should cover her head. ⁷A man ought not to cover his head,*b* since he is the image and glory of God; but the woman is the glory of man. ⁸For man did not come from woman, but woman from man; ⁹neither was man created for woman, but woman for man. ¹⁰For this reason, and because of the angels, the woman ought to have a sign of authority on her head.

¹¹In the Lord, however, woman is not independent of man, nor is man independent of woman. ¹²For as woman came from man, so also man is born of woman. But everything comes from God. ¹³Judge for yourselves: Is it proper for a woman to pray to God with her head uncovered? ¹⁴Does not the very nature of things teach you that if a man has long hair, it is a disgrace to him, ¹⁵but that if a woman has long hair, it is her glory? For long hair is given to her as a covering. ¹⁶If anyone wants to be contentious about this, we have no other practice—nor do the churches of God.

The Lord's Supper

¹⁷In the following directives I have no praise for you, for your meetings do more harm than good. ¹⁸In the first place, I hear that when you come together as a church, there are divisions among you, and to some extent I believe it. ¹⁹No doubt there have to be differences among you to show which of you have God's approval. ²⁰When you come together, it is not the Lord's Supper you eat, ²¹for as you eat, each of you goes ahead without waiting for anybody else. One remains hungry, another gets drunk. ²²Don't you have homes to eat and drink in? Or do you despise the church of God and humiliate those who have nothing? What shall I say to you? Shall I praise you for this? Certainly not!

²³For I received from the Lord what I also passed on to you: The Lord Jesus, on the night he was betrayed, took bread, ²⁴and when he had given thanks, he broke it and said, "This is my body, which is for you; do this in remembrance of me." ²⁵In the same way, after supper he took the cup, saying, "This cup is the new covenant in my blood; do this, whenever you drink it, in remembrance of me." ²⁶For whenever you eat this bread and drink this cup, you proclaim the Lord's death until he comes.

²⁷Therefore, whoever eats the bread or drinks the cup of the Lord in an unworthy manner will be guilty of sinning against the body and blood of the Lord. ²⁸A man ought to examine himself before he eats of the bread and drinks of the cup. ²⁹For anyone who eats and drinks without recognizing the body of the Lord eats and drinks judgment on himself. ³⁰That is why many among you are weak and sick, and a number of you have fallen asleep. ³¹But if we judged ourselves, we would not come under judgment. ³²When we are judged by the Lord, we are being disciplined so that we will not be condemned with the world.

³³So then, my brothers, when you come together to eat, wait for each other. ³⁴If anyone is hungry, he should eat at home, so that when you meet together it may not result in judgment.

And when I come I will give further directions.

Spiritual Gifts

12 Now about spiritual gifts, brothers, I do not want you to be ignorant. ²You know that when you were pagans, somehow or other you were influenced and led astray to mute idols. ³Therefore I tell you that no one who is speaking by the Spirit of God says, "Jesus be cursed," and no one can say, "Jesus is Lord," except by the Holy Spirit.

⁴There are different kinds of gifts, but

---

*a*2 Or *traditions*   *b*4-7 Or *Every man who prays or prophesies with long hair dishonors his head. ⁵And every woman who prays or prophesies with no covering ₀of hair₎ on her head dishonors her head—she is just like one of the "shorn women." ⁶If a woman has no covering, let her be for now with short hair, but since it is a disgrace for a woman to have her hair shorn or shaved, she should grow it again. ⁷A man ought not to have long hair*

the same Spirit. ⁵There are different kinds of service, but the same Lord. ⁶There are different kinds of working, but the same God works all of them in all men.

⁷Now to each one the manifestation of the Spirit is given for the common good. ⁸To one there is given through the Spirit the message of wisdom, to another the message of knowledge by means of the same Spirit, ⁹to another faith by the same Spirit, to another gifts of healing by that one Spirit, ¹⁰to another miraculous powers, to another prophecy, to another distinguishing between spirits, to another speaking in different kinds of tongues,ᵃ and to still another the interpretation of

ᵃ10 Or *languages*; also in verse 28

TUESDAY

VERSE FOR THE DAY:
1 Corinthians 11:3

AUTHOR:
David Augsburger

PASSAGE FOR THE DAY:
1 Corinthians 11:2–10

Headship's New Meaning

DOES the Biblical recognition of man as "head" in marriage endow him with authority and right-to-dominate? Some have thought that Paul's patterning of man's role as "head" after Christ's position as "head-of-the-church" gives great weight to the husband's role.

Does the husband, like Christ, become lord and master? The ultimate word? Since the two, man and Christ, are compared, does that give man all the rights and roles of lord in the home? On the contrary, the purposes of the comparison are specifically stated (in both 1 Corinthians 11:2–10 and Ephesians 5:21–33). Headship means responsibility and initiative: responsibility to act in love; initiative to act in service. As Christ acted in self-giving love and self-humbling service (giving us a whole new meaning to "headship"), so husbands take the initiative in building an atmosphere of loving, self-sacrificing service.

Headmanship is only part of leadership, one facet of one kind of leadership.

Christ cut through our contorted ideas of headship with surgical words: "The kings of the Gentiles lord it over them; and those who exercise authority over them call themselves Benefactors. But you are not to be like that. Instead, the greatest among you should be like the youngest, and the one who rules like the one who serves. For who is greater, the one who is at the table or the one who serves? Is it not the one who is at the table? But I am among you as one who serves" (Luke 22:25–27).

Leadership is accepting responsibilities and performing certain functions in a marriage relationship in a way that advances both together toward their goals.

Additional Scripture Readings:
Matthew 20:20–28;
Ephesians 5:21–33

Go to page 232 for your next devotional reading.

tongues.[a] ¹¹All these are the work of one and the same Spirit, and he gives them to each one, just as he determines.

One Body, Many Parts

¹²The body is a unit, though it is made up of many parts; and though all its parts are many, they form one body. So it is with Christ. ¹³For we were all baptized by[b] one Spirit into one body—whether Jews or Greeks, slave or free—and we were all given the one Spirit to drink.

¹⁴Now the body is not made up of one part but of many. ¹⁵If the foot should say, "Because I am not a hand, I do not belong to the body," it would not for that reason cease to be part of the body. ¹⁶And if the ear should say, "Because I am not an eye, I do not belong to the body," it would not for that reason cease to be part of the body. ¹⁷If the whole body were an eye, where would the sense of hearing be? If the whole body were an ear, where would the sense of smell be? ¹⁸But in fact God has arranged the parts in the body, every one of them, just as he wanted them to be. ¹⁹If they were all one part, where would the body be? ²⁰As it is, there are many parts, but one body.

²¹The eye cannot say to the hand, "I don't need you!" And the head cannot say to the feet, "I don't need you!" ²²On the contrary, those parts of the body that seem to be weaker are indispensable, ²³and the parts that we think are less honorable we treat with special honor. And the parts that are unpresentable are treated with special modesty, ²⁴while our presentable parts need no special treatment. But God has combined the members of the body and has given greater honor to the parts that lacked it, ²⁵so that there should be no division in the body, but that its parts should have equal concern for each other. ²⁶If one part suffers, every part suffers with it; if one part is honored, every part rejoices with it.

²⁷Now you are the body of Christ, and each one of you is a part of it. ²⁸And in the church God has appointed first of all apostles, second prophets, third teachers, then workers of miracles, also those having gifts of healing, those able to help others, those with gifts of administration, and those speaking in different kinds of tongues. ²⁹Are all apostles? Are all prophets? Are all teachers? Do all work miracles? ³⁰Do all have gifts of healing? Do all speak in tongues[c]? Do all interpret? ³¹But eagerly desire[d] the greater gifts.

Love

And now I will show you the most excellent way.

13 If I speak in the tongues[e] of men and of angels, but have not love, I am only a resounding gong or a clanging cymbal. ²If I have the gift of prophecy and can fathom all mysteries and all knowledge, and if I have a faith that can move mountains, but have not love, I am nothing. ³If I give all I possess to the poor and surrender my body to the flames,[f] but have not love, I gain nothing.

⁴Love is patient, love is kind. It does not envy, it does not boast, it is not proud. ⁵It is not rude, it is not self-seeking, it is not easily angered, it keeps no record of wrongs. ⁶Love does not delight in evil but rejoices with the truth. ⁷It always protects, always trusts, always hopes, always perseveres.

⁸Love never fails. But where there are prophecies, they will cease; where there are tongues, they will be stilled; where there is knowledge, it will pass away. ⁹For we know in part and we prophesy in part, ¹⁰but when perfection comes, the imperfect disappears. ¹¹When I was a child, I talked like a child, I thought like a child, I reasoned like a child. When I became a man, I put childish ways behind me. ¹²Now we see but a poor reflection as in a mirror; then we shall see face to face. Now I know in part; then I shall know fully, even as I am fully known.

¹³And now these three remain: faith, hope and love. But the greatest of these is love.

Gifts of Prophecy and Tongues

14 Follow the way of love and eagerly desire spiritual gifts, especially the gift of prophecy. ²For anyone who speaks in a tongue[g] does not speak to men but to God. Indeed, no one understands him; he utters mysteries with his spirit.[h] ³But everyone who prophesies speaks to men for their strengthening, encouragement and comfort. ⁴He who speaks in a tongue edifies himself, but he who prophesies edifies the church. ⁵I would like every one of

---

[a]10 Or languages; also in verse 28   [b]13 Or with; or in   [c]30 Or other languages   [d]31 Or But you are eagerly desiring   [e]1 Or languages   [f]3 Some early manuscripts body that I may boast   [g]2 Or another language; also in verses 4, 13, 14, 19, 26 and 27   [h]2 Or by the Spirit

you to speak in tongues,[a] but I would rather have you prophesy. He who prophesies is greater than one who speaks in tongues,[a] unless he interprets, so that the church may be edified.

⁶Now, brothers, if I come to you and speak in tongues, what good will I be to you, unless I bring you some revelation or knowledge or prophecy or word of instruction? ⁷Even in the case of lifeless things that make sounds, such as the flute or harp, how will anyone know what tune is being played unless there is a distinction in the notes? ⁸Again, if the trumpet does not sound a clear call, who will get ready for battle? ⁹So it is with you. Unless

[a]5 Or *other languages*; also in verses 6, 18, 22, 23 and 39

WEDNESDAY

VERSE FOR THE DAY:
1 Corinthians 12:12

AUTHOR:
Paul Brand

PASSAGE FOR THE DAY:
1 Corinthians 12:12–31

Body Life

I SOMETIMES think of the human body as a community, and then of its individual cells such as the white cell. The cell is the basic unit of an organism; it can live for itself, or it can help form and sustain the larger organism. I recall the apostle Paul's use of analogy in 1 Corinthians 12 where he compares the church of Christ to the human body. That inspired analogy takes on even more meaning to me because of the expanded vistas allowed by the invention of microscopes. Since Paul's analogy renders a basic principle of God's creation, I can augment it like this:

The body is one unit, though it is made up of many cells, and though all of its cells are many, they form one body . . . If the white cell should say, because I am not a brain cell, I do not belong to the body, it would not for that reason cease to be part of the body. And if the muscle cell should say to the optic nerve cell, because I am not an optic nerve, I do not belong to the body, it would not for that reason cease to be part of the body. If the whole body were an optic nerve cell, where would be the ability to walk? If the whole body were an auditory nerve, where would be the sense of sight? But in fact God has arranged the cells in the body, every one of them, just as he wanted them to be. If all cells were the same, where would the body be? As it is, there are many cells, but one body.

That analogy conveys a more precise meaning to me because though a hand or foot or ear cannot have a life separate from the body, a cell does have that potential. It can be part of the body as a loyalist, or it can cling to its own life. Some cells do choose to live in the body, sharing its benefits while maintaining complete independence—they become parasites or cancer cells.

Additional Scripture Readings:
Romans 12:3–8; Ephesians 4:1–16

Go to page 233 for your next devotional reading.

you speak intelligible words with your tongue, how will anyone know what you are saying? You will just be speaking into the air. ¹⁰Undoubtedly there are all sorts of languages in the world, yet none of them is without meaning. ¹¹If then I do not grasp the meaning of what someone is saying, I am a foreigner to the speaker, and he is a foreigner to me. ¹²So it is with you. Since you are eager to have spiritual gifts, try to excel in gifts that build up the church.

¹³For this reason anyone who speaks in a tongue should pray that he may interpret what he says. ¹⁴For if I pray in a tongue, my spirit prays, but my mind is

---

THURSDAY

VERSE FOR THE DAY:
1 Corinthians 13:4

AUTHOR:
Larry Crabb

PASSAGE FOR THE DAY:
1 Corinthians 13:1–13

Real Love

I WAS sitting on an old worn-velvet loveseat in the preacher's living room. Nestled close beside me was Rachael, my beautiful bride-to-be. It would have been difficult to slide even a thin book between us.

Across from us, in separate chairs perhaps ten feet apart, sat the preacher and his wife, both in their late seventies. She nodded her gray head and smiled and listened and rocked as her hands worked a rapid rhythm with yarn and knitting needles. He was relaxed into an old stuffed recliner, busily jotting notes in a small, well-used black notebook.

As we discussed the details of our wedding ceremony, I found myself watching the old couple, not as preacher and preacher's wife, but as husband and wife. Suddenly something struck me. Those two, sitting in separate chairs with more than three yards between them, conveyed more love with a single meeting of their eyes than my fiancée and I were exchanging with all our snuggling, grinning and whispered endearments.

I still remember thinking, "How do we get from here to there, from where we are in our eager young love to where they are in their loving maturity?"

Marriage is a stage on which real love—the kind the apostle Paul described as the greatest virtue—can be enacted for the world to see: the kind of love that enables us to endure wrong with patience, to resist evil with conviction, to enjoy the good things with gusto, to give richly of ourselves with humility, and to nourish another's soul with long-suffering.

When all these virtues are present, not only is each marriage partner incomparably blessed, but sometimes a couple of young apprentices about to take their place on this same stage can catch a glimpse of what the marriage relationship *could* be—a glimpse that won't let them settle for anything less.

Additional Scripture Readings:
1 Peter 4:7–11; 1 John 4:7–21

Go to page 235 for your next devotional reading.

unfruitful. **15**So what shall I do? I will pray with my spirit, but I will also pray with my mind; I will sing with my spirit, but I will also sing with my mind. **16**If you are praising God with your spirit, how can one who finds himself among those who do not understand[a] say "Amen" to your thanksgiving, since he does not know what you are saying? **17**You may be giving thanks well enough, but the other man is not edified.

18I thank God that I speak in tongues more than all of you. **19**But in the church I would rather speak five intelligible words to instruct others than ten thousand words in a tongue.

20Brothers, stop thinking like children. In regard to evil be infants, but in your thinking be adults. **21**In the Law it is written:

"Through men of strange tongues
 and through the lips of foreigners
I will speak to this people,
 but even then they will not listen to me,"[b]
says the Lord.

22Tongues, then, are a sign, not for believers but for unbelievers; prophecy, however, is for believers, not for unbelievers. **23**So if the whole church comes together and everyone speaks in tongues, and some who do not understand[c] or some unbelievers come in, will they not say that you are out of your mind? **24**But if an unbeliever or someone who does not understand[d] comes in while everybody is prophesying, he will be convinced by all that he is a sinner and will be judged by all, **25**and the secrets of his heart will be laid bare. So he will fall down and worship God, exclaiming, "God is really among you!"

Orderly Worship

26What then shall we say, brothers? When you come together, everyone has a hymn, or a word of instruction, a revelation, a tongue or an interpretation. All of these must be done for the strengthening of the church. **27**If anyone speaks in a tongue, two—or at the most three—should speak, one at a time, and someone must interpret. **28**If there is no interpreter, the speaker should keep quiet in the church and speak to himself and God.

29Two or three prophets should speak, and the others should weigh carefully what is said. **30**And if a revelation comes to someone who is sitting down, the first speaker should stop. **31**For you can all prophesy in turn so that everyone may be instructed and encouraged. **32**The spirits of prophets are subject to the control of prophets. **33**For God is not a God of disorder but of peace.

As in all the congregations of the saints, **34**women should remain silent in the churches. They are not allowed to speak, but must be in submission, as the Law says. **35**If they want to inquire about something, they should ask their own husbands at home; for it is disgraceful for a woman to speak in the church.

36Did the word of God originate with you? Or are you the only people it has reached? **37**If anybody thinks he is a prophet or spiritually gifted, let him acknowledge that what I am writing to you is the Lord's command. **38**If he ignores this, he himself will be ignored.[e]

39Therefore, my brothers, be eager to prophesy, and do not forbid speaking in tongues. **40**But everything should be done in a fitting and orderly way.

The Resurrection of Christ

15 Now, brothers, I want to remind you of the gospel I preached to you, which you received and on which you have taken your stand. **2**By this gospel you are saved, if you hold firmly to the word I preached to you. Otherwise, you have believed in vain.

3For what I received I passed on to you as of first importance[f]: that Christ died for our sins according to the Scriptures, **4**that he was buried, that he was raised on the third day according to the Scriptures, **5**and that he appeared to Peter,[g] and then to the Twelve. **6**After that, he appeared to more than five hundred of the brothers at the same time, most of whom are still living, though some have fallen asleep. **7**Then he appeared to James, then to all the apostles, **8**and last of all he appeared to me also, as to one abnormally born.

9For I am the least of the apostles and do not even deserve to be called an apostle, because I persecuted the church of God. **10**But by the grace of God I am what I am, and his grace to me was not without

---

*a*16 Or *among the inquirers*   *b*21 Isaiah 28:11,12   *c*23 Or *some inquirers*   *d*24 Or *or some inquirer*   *e*38 Some manuscripts *If he is ignorant of this, let him be ignorant*   *f*3 Or *you at the first*   *g*5 Greek *Cephas*

effect. No, I worked harder than all of them—yet not I, but the grace of God that was with me. **11**Whether, then, it was I or they, this is what we preach, and this is what you believed.

The Resurrection of the Dead

12But if it is preached that Christ has been raised from the dead, how can some of you say that there is no resurrection of the dead? **13**If there is no resurrection of the dead, then not even Christ has been raised. **14**And if Christ has not been raised, our preaching is useless and so is your faith. **15**More than that, we are then found to be false witnesses about God, for we have testified about God that he raised Christ from the dead. But he did not raise him if in fact the dead are not raised. **16**For if the dead are not raised, then Christ has not been raised either. **17**And if Christ has not been raised, your faith is futile; you are still in your sins. **18**Then those also who have fallen asleep in Christ are lost. **19**If only for this life we have hope in Christ, we are to be pitied more than all men.

20But Christ has indeed been raised from the dead, the firstfruits of those who have fallen asleep. **21**For since death came through a man, the resurrection of the dead comes also through a man. **22**For as in Adam all die, so in Christ all will be made alive. **23**But each in his own turn: Christ, the firstfruits; then, when he comes, those who belong to him. **24**Then the end will come, when he hands over the kingdom to God the Father after he

---

FRIDAY

VERSE FOR THE DAY:
1 Corinthians 15:57

AUTHOR:
Philip W. Williams

PASSAGE FOR THE DAY:
1 Corinthians 15:51–58

A Defeated Enemy

IN THE Old Testament it is death that the man of faith sees as a threat to his relationship with God. It was life that was to be felt and experienced in relationship with God. The stranger, death, was the mysterious visitor that could bring this meaningful, covenanted relationship with God to an end.

Jesus did little preaching or teaching about death. He didn't see death as a roadblock to our relationship with God. Jesus emphasized life and its fulfillment. His own death was overcome by his victorious resurrection. Jesus didn't say much about what happened to people after they died, but he promised everlasting life to all who believed in him.

Paul saw death as the enemy, but an enemy defeated by Christ. Death is our foe, but "thanks be to God! He gives us the victory through our Lord Jesus Christ." We take heart and hope in this resurrection victory . . .

Dear Father, my death and the deaths of people I love are a mystery. Although I may not give up searching out the mystery, I do not want to torture myself to know the unknowable. You have penetrated and conquered it. My hope is in you; I need no more. Your saving grace is enough. Thank you, through Christ my Lord. Amen.

Additional Scripture Readings:
Romans 8:31–39; Hebrews 2:14–18

Go to page 237 for your next devotional reading.

has destroyed all dominion, authority and power. ²⁵For he must reign until he has put all his enemies under his feet. ²⁶The last enemy to be destroyed is death. ²⁷For he "has put everything under his feet."ᵃ Now when it says that "everything" has been put under him, it is clear that this does not include God himself, who put everything under Christ. ²⁸When he has done this, then the Son himself will be made subject to him who put everything under him, so that God may be all in all.

²⁹Now if there is no resurrection, what will those do who are baptized for the dead? If the dead are not raised at all, why are people baptized for them? ³⁰And as for us, why do we endanger ourselves every hour? ³¹I die every day—I mean that, brothers—just as surely as I glory over you in Christ Jesus our Lord. ³²If I fought wild beasts in Ephesus for merely human reasons, what have I gained? If the dead are not raised,

"Let us eat and drink,
 for tomorrow we die."ᵇ

³³Do not be misled: "Bad company corrupts good character." ³⁴Come back to your senses as you ought, and stop sinning; for there are some who are ignorant of God—I say this to your shame.

The Resurrection Body

³⁵But someone may ask, "How are the dead raised? With what kind of body will they come?" ³⁶How foolish! What you sow does not come to life unless it dies. ³⁷When you sow, you do not plant the body that will be, but just a seed, perhaps of wheat or of something else. ³⁸But God gives it a body as he has determined, and to each kind of seed he gives its own body. ³⁹All flesh is not the same: Men have one kind of flesh, animals have another, birds another and fish another. ⁴⁰There are also heavenly bodies and there are earthly bodies; but the splendor of the heavenly bodies is one kind, and the splendor of the earthly bodies is another. ⁴¹The sun has one kind of splendor, the moon another and the stars another; and star differs from star in splendor.

⁴²So will it be with the resurrection of the dead. The body that is sown is perishable, it is raised imperishable; ⁴³it is sown in dishonor, it is raised in glory; it is sown in weakness, it is raised in power; ⁴⁴it is sown a natural body, it is raised a spiritual body.

If there is a natural body, there is also a spiritual body. ⁴⁵So it is written: "The first man Adam became a living being"ᶜ; the last Adam, a life-giving spirit. ⁴⁶The spiritual did not come first, but the natural, and after that the spiritual. ⁴⁷The first man was of the dust of the earth, the second man from heaven. ⁴⁸As was the earthly man, so are those who are of the earth; and as is the man from heaven, so also are those who are of heaven. ⁴⁹And just as we have borne the likeness of the earthly man, so shall weᵈ bear the likeness of the man from heaven.

⁵⁰I declare to you, brothers, that flesh and blood cannot inherit the kingdom of God, nor does the perishable inherit the imperishable. ⁵¹Listen, I tell you a mystery: We will not all sleep, but we will all be changed— ⁵²in a flash, in the twinkling of an eye, at the last trumpet. For the trumpet will sound, the dead will be raised imperishable, and we will be changed. ⁵³For the perishable must clothe itself with the imperishable, and the mortal with immortality. ⁵⁴When the perishable has been clothed with the imperishable, and the mortal with immortality, then the saying that is written will come true: "Death has been swallowed up in victory."ᵉ

⁵⁵"Where, O death, is your victory?
 Where, O death, is your sting?"ᶠ

⁵⁶The sting of death is sin, and the power of sin is the law. ⁵⁷But thanks be to God! He gives us the victory through our Lord Jesus Christ.

⁵⁸Therefore, my dear brothers, stand firm. Let nothing move you. Always give yourselves fully to the work of the Lord, because you know that your labor in the Lord is not in vain.

The Collection for God's People

16 Now about the collection for God's people: Do what I told the Galatian churches to do. ²On the first day of every week, each one of you should set aside a sum of money in keeping with his income, saving it up, so that when I come no collections will have to be made. ³Then, when I arrive, I will give letters of introduction to the men you approve and send them with your gift to Jerusalem. ⁴If it

---

ᵃ27 Psalm 8:6   ᵇ32 Isaiah 22:13   ᶜ45 Gen. 2:7   ᵈ49 Some early manuscripts *so let us*
ᵉ54 Isaiah 25:8   ᶠ55 Hosea 13:14

WEEKENDING

RESOLVE

More than anything else in heaven or on
   earth,
  I pray for the power to love my fellow
   person,
  to break through the damning bigotry,
  the crippling prejudice,
  the stifling self-centeredness
  that smothers God's Spirit within me,
  and to channel and communicate divine
   love
  to lonely, loveless people about me.
And I pray as well for the ability to translate
  the message of God's eternal love into
   words
  that will pierce the benumbed minds of
   busy men
  and move their hearts to faith and
   obedience.

– Leslie Brandt

REVIVE
Saturday: 1 Corinthians 14:1–5
Sunday: 1 Peter 4:7–11

Go to page 238 for your next devotional reading.

seems advisable for me to go also, they will accompany me.

Personal Requests

⁵After I go through Macedonia, I will come to you—for I will be going through Macedonia. ⁶Perhaps I will stay with you awhile, or even spend the winter, so that you can help me on my journey, wherever I go. ⁷I do not want to see you now and make only a passing visit; I hope to spend some time with you, if the Lord permits. ⁸But I will stay on at Ephesus until Pentecost, ⁹because a great door for effective work has opened to me, and there are many who oppose me.

¹⁰If Timothy comes, see to it that he has nothing to fear while he is with you, for he is carrying on the work of the Lord, just as I am. ¹¹No one, then, should refuse to accept him. Send him on his way in peace so

---

MONDAY

| VERSE FOR THE DAY: | AUTHOR: | PASSAGE FOR THE DAY: |
| 1 Corinthians 16:13 | Bill Hybels | 1 Corinthians 16:13–14 |

Be Men of Courage

FOR a marriage relationship to flourish, there must be intimacy. It takes an enormous amount of courage to say to your spouse, "This is me. I'm not proud of it—in fact, I'm a little embarrassed by it—but this is who I am." It also takes courage to look your spouse in the eye and say, "Our marriage is in serious trouble, and we've got to do something about it." What do most people do? They put their problems on the back burner and go their own directions. While they pursue their own careers and their own recreations, the marriage disintegrates from lack of courage. They did not have the courage to put on the gloves and say, "Let's fight for this marriage. Let's go to a marriage retreat. Let's see a marriage counselor. Let's get together with another couple we respect. Let's lay it out on the table and solve these problems instead of running from them." It takes courage to fight off the "greener grass" temptations, to work through layer after layer of masks, cover-ups, and defense mechanisms, to keep working on that marriage year after year. Relational courage does not apply only to the husband-wife relationship . . .

It also takes relational courage to build significant relationships with friends, to look another person in the eye and say, "Isn't it time we stopped talking about the weather and the stock market and started talking about what's going on in your life and mine? Isn't it time we became brothers?" Not many men have the courage to challenge each other, to fight for each other's spiritual and relational growth. But I have learned over the years that I will never be a success in my marriage, with my kids or with my friends, without courage.

Additional Scripture Readings: Ephesians 6:10–18; Hebrews 3:1–6

Go to page 241 for your next devotional reading.

that he may return to me. I am expecting him along with the brothers.

¹²Now about our brother Apollos: I strongly urged him to go to you with the brothers. He was quite unwilling to go now, but he will go when he has the opportunity.

¹³Be on your guard; stand firm in the faith; be men of courage; be strong. ¹⁴Do everything in love.

¹⁵You know that the household of Stephanas were the first converts in Achaia, and they have devoted themselves to the service of the saints. I urge you, brothers, ¹⁶to submit to such as these and to everyone who joins in the work, and labors at it. ¹⁷I was glad when Stephanas, Fortunatus and Achaicus arrived, because they have supplied what was lacking from you. ¹⁸For they refreshed my spirit and yours also. Such men deserve recognition.

Final Greetings

¹⁹The churches in the province of Asia send you greetings. Aquila and Priscilla[a] greet you warmly in the Lord, and so does the church that meets at their house. ²⁰All the brothers here send you greetings. Greet one another with a holy kiss.

²¹I, Paul, write this greeting in my own hand.

²²If anyone does not love the Lord—a curse be on him. Come, O Lord[b]!

²³The grace of the Lord Jesus be with you.

²⁴My love to all of you in Christ Jesus. Amen.[c]

---

[a]19 Greek *Prisca*, a variant of *Priscilla* [b]22 In Aramaic the expression *Come, O Lord* is *Marana tha*.
[c]24 Some manuscripts do not have *Amen*.

*P*AUL *writes this second letter to the church in Corinth from Macedonia (Acts 20:1; 2 Corinthians 7:5), while on his way to Corinth (2 Corinthians 13:1). As the most personal of all his letters, he expresses both how exciting and how painful his life as a missionary has been. He also finds it necessary to defend himself against those who are criticizing him. As you read this letter, think about how exciting it can be to serve the Lord, but realize too that being a Christian can sometimes lead to pain and suffering.*

2 CORINTHIANS

1 Paul, an apostle of Christ Jesus by the will of God, and Timothy our brother,

To the church of God in Corinth, together with all the saints throughout Achaia:

²Grace and peace to you from God our Father and the Lord Jesus Christ.

The God of All Comfort

³Praise be to the God and Father of our Lord Jesus Christ, the Father of compassion and the God of all comfort, ⁴who comforts us in all our troubles, so that we can comfort those in any trouble with the comfort we ourselves have received from God. ⁵For just as the sufferings of Christ flow over into our lives, so also through Christ our comfort overflows. ⁶If we are distressed, it is for your comfort and salvation; if we are comforted, it is for your comfort, which produces in you patient endurance of the same sufferings we suffer. ⁷And our hope for you is firm, because we know that just as you share in our sufferings, so also you share in our comfort.

⁸We do not want you to be uninformed, brothers, about the hardships we suffered in the province of Asia. We were under great pressure, far beyond our ability to endure, so that we despaired even of life.

2 CORINTHIANS 1

⁹Indeed, in our hearts we felt the sentence of death. But this happened that we might not rely on ourselves but on God, who raises the dead. ¹⁰He has delivered us from such a deadly peril, and he will deliver us. On him we have set our hope that he will continue to deliver us, ¹¹as you help us by your prayers. Then many will give thanks on our*a* behalf for the gracious favor granted us in answer to the prayers of many.

Paul's Change of Plans

¹²Now this is our boast: Our conscience testifies that we have conducted ourselves in the world, and especially in our relations with you, in the holiness and sincerity that are from God. We have done so not according to worldly wisdom but according to God's grace. ¹³For we do not write you anything you cannot read or understand. And I hope that, ¹⁴as you have understood us in part, you will come to

a11 Many manuscripts *your*

TUESDAY

VERSE FOR THE DAY:
2 Corinthians 1:9

AUTHOR:
C.S. Lewis

PASSAGE FOR THE DAY:
2 Corinthians 1:8–11

He Stoops to Conquer

GOD, who has made us, knows what we are and that our happiness lies in him. Yet we will not seek it in him as long as he leaves us any other resort where it can even plausibly be looked for. While what we call "our own life" remains agreeable we will not surrender it to him . . . We are perplexed to see misfortune falling upon decent, inoffensive, worthy people—on capable, hard-working mothers of families or diligent, thrifty little tradespeople, on those who have worked so hard, and so honestly, for their modest stock of happiness and now seem to be entering on the enjoyment of it with the fullest right . . .

Let me implore the reader to try to believe, if only for the moment, that God, who made these deserving people, may really be right when he thinks that their modest prosperity and the happiness of their children are not enough to make them blessed: that all this must fall from them in the end, and that if they have not learned to know him they will be wretched. And therefore he troubles them, warning them in advance on an insufficiency that one day they will have to discover . . . I call this a Divine humility because it is a poor thing to strike our colors to God when the ship is going down under us; a poor thing to come to him as a last resort, to offer up "our own" when it is no longer worth keeping. If God were proud he would hardly have us on such terms: but he is not proud, he stoops to conquer, he will have us even though we have shown that we prefer everything else to him, and come to him because there is "nothing better" now to be had.

Additional Scripture Readings:
Psalm 146; Hebrews 12:7–11

Go to page 245 for your next devotional reading.

understand fully that you can boast of us just as we will boast of you in the day of the Lord Jesus.

¹⁵Because I was confident of this, I planned to visit you first so that you might benefit twice. ¹⁶I planned to visit you on my way to Macedonia and to come back to you from Macedonia, and then to have you send me on my way to Judea. ¹⁷When I planned this, did I do it lightly? Or do I make my plans in a worldly manner so that in the same breath I say, "Yes, yes" and "No, no"?

¹⁸But as surely as God is faithful, our message to you is not "Yes" and "No." ¹⁹For the Son of God, Jesus Christ, who was preached among you by me and Silas[a] and Timothy, was not "Yes" and "No," but in him it has always been "Yes." ²⁰For no matter how many promises God has made, they are "Yes" in Christ. And so through him the "Amen" is spoken by us to the glory of God. ²¹Now it is God who makes both us and you stand firm in Christ. He anointed us, ²²set his seal of ownership on us, and put his Spirit in our hearts as a deposit, guaranteeing what is to come.

²³I call God as my witness that it was in order to spare you that I did not return to Corinth. ²⁴Not that we lord it over your faith, but we work with you for your joy, because it is by faith you stand firm.

2 ¹So I made up my mind that I would not make another painful visit to you. ²For if I grieve you, who is left to make me glad but you whom I have grieved? ³I wrote as I did so that when I came I should not be distressed by those who ought to make me rejoice. I had confidence in all of you, that you would all share my joy. ⁴For I wrote you out of great distress and anguish of heart and with many tears, not to grieve you but to let you know the depth of my love for you.

Forgiveness for the Sinner

⁵If anyone has caused grief, he has not so much grieved me as he has grieved all of you, to some extent—not to put it too severely. ⁶The punishment inflicted on him by the majority is sufficient for him. ⁷Now instead, you ought to forgive and comfort him, so that he will not be overwhelmed by excessive sorrow. ⁸I urge you, therefore, to reaffirm your love for him. ⁹The reason I wrote you was to see if you would stand the test and be obedient in everything. ¹⁰If you forgive anyone, I also forgive him. And what I have forgiven—if there was anything to forgive—I have forgiven in the sight of Christ for your sake, ¹¹in order that Satan might not outwit us. For we are not unaware of his schemes.

Ministers of the New Covenant

¹²Now when I went to Troas to preach the gospel of Christ and found that the Lord had opened a door for me, ¹³I still had no peace of mind, because I did not find my brother Titus there. So I said good-by to them and went on to Macedonia.

¹⁴But thanks be to God, who always leads us in triumphal procession in Christ and through us spreads everywhere the fragrance of the knowledge of him. ¹⁵For we are to God the aroma of Christ among those who are being saved and those who are perishing. ¹⁶To the one we are the smell of death; to the other, the fragrance of life. And who is equal to such a task? ¹⁷Unlike so many, we do not peddle the word of God for profit. On the contrary, in Christ we speak before God with sincerity, like men sent from God.

3 ¹Are we beginning to commend ourselves again? Or do we need, like some people, letters of recommendation to you or from you? ²You yourselves are our letter, written on our hearts, known and read by everybody. ³You show that you are a letter from Christ, the result of our ministry, written not with ink but with the Spirit of the living God, not on tablets of stone but on tablets of human hearts.

⁴Such confidence as this is ours through Christ before God. ⁵Not that we are competent in ourselves to claim anything for ourselves, but our competence comes from God. ⁶He has made us competent as ministers of a new covenant—not of the letter but of the Spirit; for the letter kills, but the Spirit gives life.

The Glory of the New Covenant

⁷Now if the ministry that brought death, which was engraved in letters on stone, came with glory, so that the Israelites could not look steadily at the face of Moses because of its glory, fading though it was, ⁸will not the ministry of the Spirit be even more glorious? ⁹If the ministry that condemns men is glorious, how much

---

[a] 19 Greek *Silvanus*, a variant of *Silas*

more glorious is the ministry that brings righteousness! ¹⁰For what was glorious has no glory now in comparison with the surpassing glory. ¹¹And if what was fading away came with glory, how much greater is the glory of that which lasts!

¹²Therefore, since we have such a hope, we are very bold. ¹³We are not like Moses, who would put a veil over his face to keep the Israelites from gazing at it while the radiance was fading away. ¹⁴But their minds were made dull, for to this day the same veil remains when the old covenant is read. It has not been removed, because only in Christ is it taken away. ¹⁵Even to this day when Moses is read, a veil covers their hearts. ¹⁶But whenever anyone turns to the Lord, the veil is taken away. ¹⁷Now the Lord is the Spirit, and where the Spirit of the Lord is, there is freedom. ¹⁸And we, who with unveiled faces all reflect^a the Lord's glory, are being transformed into his likeness with ever-increasing glory, which comes from the Lord, who is the Spirit.

Treasures in Jars of Clay

4 Therefore, since through God's mercy we have this ministry, we do not lose heart. ²Rather, we have renounced secret and shameful ways; we do not use deception, nor do we distort the word of God. On the contrary, by setting forth the truth plainly we commend ourselves to every man's conscience in the sight of God. ³And even if our gospel is veiled, it is veiled to those who are perishing. ⁴The god of this age has blinded the minds of unbelievers, so that they cannot see the light of the gospel of the glory of Christ, who is the image of God. ⁵For we do not preach ourselves, but Jesus Christ as Lord, and ourselves as your servants for Jesus' sake. ⁶For God, who said, "Let light shine out of darkness,"^{b} made his light shine in our hearts to give us the light of the knowledge of the glory of God in the face of Christ.

⁷But we have this treasure in jars of clay to show that this all-surpassing power is from God and not from us. ⁸We are hard pressed on every side, but not crushed; perplexed, but not in despair; ⁹persecuted, but not abandoned; struck down, but not destroyed. ¹⁰We always carry around in our body the death of Jesus, so that the life of Jesus may also be revealed in our body. ¹¹For we who are alive are always being given over to death for Jesus' sake, so that his life may be revealed in our mortal body. ¹²So then, death is at work in us, but life is at work in you.

¹³It is written: "I believed; therefore I have spoken."^{c} With that same spirit of faith we also believe and therefore speak, ¹⁴because we know that the one who raised the Lord Jesus from the dead will also raise us with Jesus and present us with you in his presence. ¹⁵All this is for your benefit, so that the grace that is reaching more and more people may cause thanksgiving to overflow to the glory of God.

¹⁶Therefore we do not lose heart. Though outwardly we are wasting away, yet inwardly we are being renewed day by day. ¹⁷For our light and momentary troubles are achieving for us an eternal glory that far outweighs them all. ¹⁸So we fix our eyes not on what is seen, but on what is unseen. For what is seen is temporary, but what is unseen is eternal.

Our Heavenly Dwelling

5 Now we know that if the earthly tent we live in is destroyed, we have a building from God, an eternal house in heaven, not built by human hands. ²Meanwhile we groan, longing to be clothed with our heavenly dwelling, ³because when we are clothed, we will not be found naked. ⁴For while we are in this tent, we groan and are burdened, because we do not wish to be unclothed but to be clothed with our heavenly dwelling, so that what is mortal may be swallowed up by life. ⁵Now it is God who has made us for this very purpose and has given us the Spirit as a deposit, guaranteeing what is to come.

⁶Therefore we are always confident and know that as long as we are at home in the body we are away from the Lord. ⁷We live by faith, not by sight. ⁸We are confident, I say, and would prefer to be away from the body and at home with the Lord. ⁹So we make it our goal to please him, whether we are at home in the body or away from it. ¹⁰For we must all appear before the judgment seat of Christ, that each one may receive what is due him for the things done while in the body, whether good or bad.

The Ministry of Reconciliation

¹¹Since, then, we know what it is to fear

---

^{a}18 Or *contemplate* ^{b}6 Gen. 1:3 ^{c}13 Psalm 116:10

the Lord, we try to persuade men. What we are is plain to God, and I hope it is also plain to your conscience. ¹²We are not trying to commend ourselves to you again, but are giving you an opportunity to take pride in us, so that you can answer those who take pride in what is seen rather than in what is in the heart. ¹³If we are out of our mind, it is for the sake of God; if we are in our right mind, it is for you. ¹⁴For Christ's love compels us, because we are convinced that one died for all, and therefore all died. ¹⁵And he died for all, that those who live should no longer live for themselves but for him who died for them and was raised again.

¹⁶So from now on we regard no one from a worldly point of view. Though we once regarded Christ in this way, we do so no longer. ¹⁷Therefore, if anyone is in Christ, he is a new creation; the old has gone, the new has come! ¹⁸All this is from God, who reconciled us to himself through Christ and gave us the ministry of reconciliation: ¹⁹that God was reconciling the world to himself in Christ, not counting men's sins against them. And he has committed to us the message of reconciliation. ²⁰We are therefore Christ's ambassadors, as though God were making his appeal through us. We implore you on Christ's behalf: Be reconciled to God. ²¹God made him who had no sin to be sin*a* for us, so that in him we might become the righteousness of God.

6 As God's fellow workers we urge you not to receive God's grace in vain. ²For he says,

"In the time of my favor I heard you,
 and in the day of salvation I helped
  you."*b*

I tell you, now is the time of God's favor, now is the day of salvation.

Paul's Hardships

³We put no stumbling block in anyone's path, so that our ministry will not be discredited. ⁴Rather, as servants of God we commend ourselves in every way: in great endurance; in troubles, hardships and distresses; ⁵in beatings, imprisonments and riots; in hard work, sleepless nights and hunger; ⁶in purity, understanding, patience and kindness; in the Holy Spirit and in sincere love; ⁷in truthful speech and in the power of God; with weapons of righteousness in the right hand and in the left; ⁸through glory and dishonor, bad report and good report; genuine, yet regarded as impostors; ⁹known, yet regarded as unknown; dying, and yet we live on; beaten, and yet not killed; ¹⁰sorrowful, yet always rejoicing; poor, yet making many rich; having nothing, and yet possessing everything.

¹¹We have spoken freely to you, Corinthians, and opened wide our hearts to you. ¹²We are not withholding our affection from you, but you are withholding yours from us. ¹³As a fair exchange—I speak as to my children—open wide your hearts also.

Do Not Be Yoked With Unbelievers

¹⁴Do not be yoked together with unbelievers. For what do righteousness and wickedness have in common? Or what fellowship can light have with darkness? ¹⁵What harmony is there between Christ and Belial*c*? What does a believer have in common with an unbeliever? ¹⁶What agreement is there between the temple of God and idols? For we are the temple of the living God. As God has said: "I will live with them and walk among them, and I will be their God, and they will be my people."*d*

¹⁷"Therefore come out from them
  and be separate,
                              says the Lord.
 Touch no unclean thing,
  and I will receive you."*e*
¹⁸"I will be a Father to you,
  and you will be my sons and
    daughters,
                says the Lord Almighty."*f*

7 Since we have these promises, dear friends, let us purify ourselves from everything that contaminates body and spirit, perfecting holiness out of reverence for God.

Paul's Joy

²Make room for us in your hearts. We have wronged no one, we have corrupted no one, we have exploited no one. ³I do not say this to condemn you; I have said before that you have such a place in our hearts that we would live or die with you. ⁴I have great confidence in you; I take great pride in you. I am greatly encour-

---

*a*21 Or *be a sin offering*   *b*2 Isaiah 49:8   *c*15 Greek *Beliar,* a variant of *Belial*   *d*16 Lev. 26:12; Jer. 32:38; Ezek. 37:27   *e*17 Isaiah 52:11; Ezek. 20:34,41   *f*18 2 Samuel 7:14; 7:8

aged; in all our troubles my joy knows no bounds. ⁵For when we came into Macedonia, this body of ours had no rest, but we were harassed at every turn—conflicts on the outside, fears within. ⁶But God, who comforts the downcast, comforted us by the coming of Titus, ⁷and not only by his coming but also by the comfort you had given him. He told us about your longing for me, your deep sorrow, your ardent concern for me, so that my joy was greater than ever.

⁸Even if I caused you sorrow by my letter, I do not regret it. Though I did regret it—I see that my letter hurt you, but only for a little while— ⁹yet now I am happy, not because you were made sorry, but because your sorrow led you to repentance. For you became sorrowful as God intended and so were not harmed in any way by us. ¹⁰Godly sorrow brings repentance that leads to salvation and leaves no regret, but worldly sorrow brings death. ¹¹See what this godly sorrow has produced in you: what earnestness, what eagerness to clear

---

WEDNESDAY

VERSE FOR THE DAY:
2 Corinthians 5:17

AUTHOR:
Paul Brand

PASSAGE FOR THE DAY:
2 Corinthians 5:16–21

We in Him, He in Us

[THE] unfathomable idea of an actual identity exchange is implicit in conversion. Jesus described the process in terms his hearers could understand. To Nicodemus he called it being "born again" or "born from above," indicating that spiritual life requires an identity change as drastic as a person's first entrance into the world.

As a result of this stuff-exchange, we carry within us not just the image of, or the philosophy of, or faith in, but the actual substance of God. One staggering consequence credits us with the spiritual genes of Christ; as we stand before God, we are judged on the basis of Christ's perfection, not our unworthiness. "If anyone is in Christ, he is a new creation; the old has gone, the new has come! . . . God made him who had no sin to be sin for us, so that in him we might become the righteousness of God" (2 Corinthians 5:17,21). Elsewhere, Paul underscored, "Your life is now hidden with Christ in God" (Colossians 3:3). We are "in him" and he is "in us."

Just as the complete identity code of my body inheres in each individual cell, so also the reality of God permeates every cell in his Body, linking us members with a true, organic bond. I sense that bond when I meet strangers in India or Africa or California who share my loyalty to the Head: instantly we become brothers and sisters, fellow cells in Christ's Body. I share the ecstasy of community in a universal Body that includes every man and woman in whom God resides.

Additional Scripture Readings:
Ephesians 1:15–23;
Colossians 3:1–11

Go to page 247 for your next devotional reading.

yourselves, what indignation, what alarm, what longing, what concern, what readiness to see justice done. At every point you have proved yourselves to be innocent in this matter. **12**So even though I wrote to you, it was not on account of the one who did the wrong or of the injured party, but rather that before God you could see for yourselves how devoted to us you are. **13**By all this we are encouraged.

In addition to our own encouragement, we were especially delighted to see how happy Titus was, because his spirit has been refreshed by all of you. **14**I had boasted to him about you, and you have not embarrassed me. But just as everything we said to you was true, so our boasting about you to Titus has proved to be true as well. **15**And his affection for you is all the greater when he remembers that you were all obedient, receiving him with fear and trembling. **16**I am glad I can have complete confidence in you.

Generosity Encouraged

8 And now, brothers, we want you to know about the grace that God has given the Macedonian churches. **2**Out of the most severe trial, their overflowing joy and their extreme poverty welled up in rich generosity. **3**For I testify that they gave as much as they were able, and even beyond their ability. Entirely on their own, **4**they urgently pleaded with us for the privilege of sharing in this service to the saints. **5**And they did not do as we expected, but they gave themselves first to the Lord and then to us in keeping with God's will. **6**So we urged Titus, since he had earlier made a beginning, to bring also to completion this act of grace on your part. **7**But just as you excel in everything—in faith, in speech, in knowledge, in complete earnestness and in your love for us^a—see that you also excel in this grace of giving.

8I am not commanding you, but I want to test the sincerity of your love by comparing it with the earnestness of others. **9**For you know the grace of our Lord Jesus Christ, that though he was rich, yet for your sakes he became poor, so that you through his poverty might become rich.

10And here is my advice about what is best for you in this matter: Last year you were the first not only to give but also to have the desire to do so. **11**Now finish the work, so that your eager willingness to do it may be matched by your completion of it, according to your means. **12**For if the willingness is there, the gift is acceptable according to what one has, not according to what he does not have.

13Our desire is not that others might be relieved while you are hard pressed, but that there might be equality. **14**At the present time your plenty will supply what they need, so that in turn their plenty will supply what you need. Then there will be equality, **15**as it is written: "He who gathered much did not have too much, and he who gathered little did not have too little."^{b}

Titus Sent to Corinth

16I thank God, who put into the heart of Titus the same concern I have for you. **17**For Titus not only welcomed our appeal, but he is coming to you with much enthusiasm and on his own initiative. **18**And we are sending along with him the brother who is praised by all the churches for his service to the gospel. **19**What is more, he was chosen by the churches to accompany us as we carry the offering, which we administer in order to honor the Lord himself and to show our eagerness to help. **20**We want to avoid any criticism of the way we administer this liberal gift. **21**For we are taking pains to do what is right, not only in the eyes of the Lord but also in the eyes of men.

22In addition, we are sending with them our brother who has often proved to us in many ways that he is zealous, and now even more so because of his great confidence in you. **23**As for Titus, he is my partner and fellow worker among you; as for our brothers, they are representatives of the churches and an honor to Christ. **24**Therefore show these men the proof of your love and the reason for our pride in you, so that the churches can see it.

9 There is no need for me to write to you about this service to the saints. **2**For I know your eagerness to help, and I have been boasting about it to the Macedonians, telling them that since last year you in Achaia were ready to give; and your enthusiasm has stirred most of them to action. **3**But I am sending the brothers in order that our boasting about you in this matter should not prove hollow, but that you may be ready, as I said you would be. **4**For if any Macedonians come with

---

^{a}7 Some manuscripts *in our love for you* ^{b}15 Exodus 16:18

me and find you unprepared, we — not to say anything about you — would be ashamed of having been so confident. **⁵**So I thought it necessary to urge the brothers to visit you in advance and finish the arrangements for the generous gift you had promised. Then it will be ready as a generous gift, not as one grudgingly given.

Sowing Generously

⁶Remember this: Whoever sows sparingly will also reap sparingly, and whoev-

---

THURSDAY

VERSE FOR THE DAY:
2 Corinthians 8:7

AUTHOR:
Daniel Taylor

PASSAGE FOR THE DAY:
2 Corinthians 8:1–9

Your Giving Muscles

WE SHOULD give for the same reason that we should exercise our bodies. Our muscles are made so that they are best off when forced to work. If you "save" your muscles by never making them do anything, you actually are hurting them and yourself. You haven't "spent" any energy, but, strangely, the result is you have less strength and energy than if you had. Eventually you become like a jellyfish plopped helplessly on the beach.

Something like this is true of your giving muscles as well. God has made us to be givers. It isn't something we *have* to do in order to please him so much as it's something we need to do to keep ourselves working properly. We are healthy and whole when we are both giving and receiving . . .

Giving is really more an attitude toward life than it is a specific act at one time or another. Giving people offer friendship easily; they are openhanded not only with their money but with emotions. They are quick to encourage and console. They take genuine delight in the good fortune of others. They think of strangers only as people whom they haven't happened yet to meet.

Givers have a certain openness about them. They are not aggressively competitive. They do not speak a lot about their "rights." They generally laugh a lot and have very little self-pity. They do not run constant cost-benefit analyses to see if an opportunity for generosity is to their advantage. They are not attached like lampreys to the things in their lives.

As it happens, giving is to your benefit. It doesn't make you a saint or martyr to give. In giving you are simply reflecting God's image — he who gave everything. Miserliness in all forms — monetary and emotional — diminishes us. The more we keep the less we have. And the less we are.

This is one of life's interesting paradoxes.

Additional Scripture Readings:
2 Corinthians 9:6–15;
Ephesians 4:25 — 5:2

Go to page 249 for your next devotional reading.

er sows generously will also reap generously. ⁷Each man should give what he has decided in his heart to give, not reluctantly or under compulsion, for God loves a cheerful giver. ⁸And God is able to make all grace abound to you, so that in all things at all times, having all that you need, you will abound in every good work. ⁹As it is written:

"He has scattered abroad his gifts to
    the poor;
his righteousness endures
    forever."ᵃ

¹⁰Now he who supplies seed to the sower and bread for food will also supply and increase your store of seed and will enlarge the harvest of your righteousness. ¹¹You will be made rich in every way so that you can be generous on every occasion, and through us your generosity will result in thanksgiving to God.

¹²This service that you perform is not only supplying the needs of God's people but is also overflowing in many expressions of thanks to God. ¹³Because of the service by which you have proved yourselves, men will praise God for the obedience that accompanies your confession of the gospel of Christ, and for your generosity in sharing with them and with everyone else. ¹⁴And in their prayers for you their hearts will go out to you, because of the surpassing grace God has given you. ¹⁵Thanks be to God for his indescribable gift!

Paul's Defense of His Ministry

10 By the meekness and gentleness of Christ, I appeal to you—I, Paul, who am "timid" when face to face with you, but "bold" when away! ²I beg you that when I come I may not have to be as bold as I expect to be toward some people who think that we live by the standards of this world. ³For though we live in the world, we do not wage war as the world does. ⁴The weapons we fight with are not the weapons of the world. On the contrary, they have divine power to demolish strongholds. ⁵We demolish arguments and every pretension that sets itself up against the knowledge of God, and we take captive every thought to make it obedient to Christ. ⁶And we will be ready to punish every act of disobedience, once your obedience is complete.

⁷You are looking only on the surface of things.ᵇ If anyone is confident that he belongs to Christ, he should consider again that we belong to Christ just as much as he. ⁸For even if I boast somewhat freely about the authority the Lord gave us for building you up rather than pulling you down, I will not be ashamed of it. ⁹I do not want to seem to be trying to frighten you with my letters. ¹⁰For some say, "His letters are weighty and forceful, but in person he is unimpressive and his speaking amounts to nothing." ¹¹Such people should realize that what we are in our letters when we are absent, we will be in our actions when we are present.

¹²We do not dare to classify or compare ourselves with some who commend themselves. When they measure themselves by themselves and compare themselves with themselves, they are not wise. ¹³We, however, will not boast beyond proper limits, but will confine our boasting to the field God has assigned to us, a field that reaches even to you. ¹⁴We are not going too far in our boasting, as would be the case if we had not come to you, for we did get as far as you with the gospel of Christ. ¹⁵Neither do we go beyond our limits by boasting of work done by others.ᶜ Our hope is that, as your faith continues to grow, our area of activity among you will greatly expand, ¹⁶so that we can preach the gospel in the regions beyond you. For we do not want to boast about work already done in another man's territory. ¹⁷But, "Let him who boasts boast in the Lord."ᵈ ¹⁸For it is not the one who commends himself who is approved, but the one whom the Lord commends.

Paul and the False Apostles

11 I hope you will put up with a little of my foolishness; but you are already doing that. ²I am jealous for you with a godly jealousy. I promised you to one husband, to Christ, so that I might present you as a pure virgin to him. ³But I am afraid that just as Eve was deceived by the serpent's cunning, your minds may somehow be led astray from your sincere and pure devotion to Christ. ⁴For if someone comes to you and preaches a Jesus

---

ᵃ9 Psalm 112:9   ᵇ7 Or *Look at the obvious facts*   ᶜ13-15 Or ¹³*We, however, will not boast about things that cannot be measured, but we will boast according to the standard of measurement that the God of measure has assigned us—a measurement that relates even to you.* ¹⁴ . . . . ¹⁵*Neither do we boast about things that cannot be measured in regard to the work done by others.*   ᵈ17 Jer. 9:24

other than the Jesus we preached, or if you receive a different spirit from the one you received, or a different gospel from the one you accepted, you put up with it easily enough. ⁵But I do not think I am in the least inferior to those "super-apostles." ⁶I may not be a trained speaker, but I do have knowledge. We have made this perfectly clear to you in every way.

⁷Was it a sin for me to lower myself in order to elevate you by preaching the gospel of God to you free of charge? ⁸I robbed other churches by receiving support from them so as to serve you. ⁹And when I was with you and needed something, I was not a burden to anyone, for the brothers who came from Macedonia supplied what I needed. I have kept myself from being a burden to you in any way, and will continue to do so. ¹⁰As surely as the truth of Christ is in me, nobody in the regions of Achaia will stop this boasting of mine. ¹¹Why? Because I do not love you? God knows I do! ¹²And I will keep on doing what I am doing in order to cut the ground from under those who want an opportunity to be considered equal with us in the things they boast about.

¹³For such men are false apostles, deceitful workmen, masquerading as apostles of Christ. ¹⁴And no wonder, for Satan himself masquerades as an angel of light.

FRIDAY

VERSE FOR THE DAY:
2 Corinthians 10:4

AUTHOR:
Leonard LeSourd

PASSAGE FOR THE DAY:
2 Corinthians 10:1–6

Under Enemy Attack

HUSBANDS, *accept the fact that you are under attack by forces you cannot see, that you have a very real enemy in Satan who wants to destroy your marriage.*

The fact that a dark force out there wants to break up your marriage should arouse your fighting spirit. "How dare he single me out!" Your home suddenly becomes a place you will go all-out to protect.

As a husband you need to understand exactly what spiritual warfare is. This is not difficult. There are many books on the subject. More and more churches are dealing with it.

Most important for every husband is to accept the authority the Lord gives him when he becomes the spiritual head of his home.

With this authority a husband can pray against the dark forces he may feel pressing in on him and his family. He prays this way against sickness, against temptations, against forces in his community that would corrupt his children. The prayer for his home could go like this: Lord, with the authority you gave me as the head of this household, I come against all perverse spirits, against principalities and the forces of darkness that are trying to upset the peace and order of our home. In the name of Jesus I rebuke these spirits and cast them out. They have no ground in this house. I pray now that you would fill this place with your Spirit, your love, your peace, your joy.

Additional Scripture Readings:
Ephesians 6:10–18;
Hebrews 2:14–18

Go to page 251 for your next devotional reading.

¹⁵It is not surprising, then, if his servants masquerade as servants of righteousness. Their end will be what their actions deserve.

Paul Boasts About His Sufferings

¹⁶I repeat: Let no one take me for a fool. But if you do, then receive me just as you would a fool, so that I may do a little boasting. ¹⁷In this self-confident boasting I am not talking as the Lord would, but as a fool. ¹⁸Since many are boasting in the way the world does, I too will boast. ¹⁹You gladly put up with fools since you are so wise! ²⁰In fact, you even put up with anyone who enslaves you or exploits you or takes advantage of you or pushes himself forward or slaps you in the face. ²¹To my shame I admit that we were too weak for that!

What anyone else dares to boast about—I am speaking as a fool—I also dare to boast about. ²²Are they Hebrews? So am I. Are they Israelites? So am I. Are they Abraham's descendants? So am I. ²³Are they servants of Christ? (I am out of my mind to talk like this.) I am more. I have worked much harder, been in prison more frequently, been flogged more severely, and been exposed to death again and again. ²⁴Five times I received from the Jews the forty lashes minus one. ²⁵Three times I was beaten with rods, once I was stoned, three times I was shipwrecked, I spent a night and a day in the open sea, ²⁶I have been constantly on the move. I have been in danger from rivers, in danger from bandits, in danger from my own countrymen, in danger from Gentiles; in danger in the city, in danger in the country, in danger at sea; and in danger from false brothers. ²⁷I have labored and toiled and have often gone without sleep; I have known hunger and thirst and have often gone without food; I have been cold and naked. ²⁸Besides everything else, I face daily the pressure of my concern for all the churches. ²⁹Who is weak, and I do not feel weak? Who is led into sin, and I do not inwardly burn?

³⁰If I must boast, I will boast of the things that show my weakness. ³¹The God and Father of the Lord Jesus, who is to be praised forever, knows that I am not lying. ³²In Damascus the governor under King Aretas had the city of the Damascenes guarded in order to arrest me. ³³But I was lowered in a basket from a window in the wall and slipped through his hands.

Paul's Vision and His Thorn

12 I must go on boasting. Although there is nothing to be gained, I will go on to visions and revelations from the Lord. ²I know a man in Christ who fourteen years ago was caught up to the third heaven. Whether it was in the body or out of the body I do not know—God knows. ³And I know that this man—whether in the body or apart from the body I do not know, but God knows— ⁴was caught up to paradise. He heard inexpressible things, things that man is not permitted to tell. ⁵I will boast about a man like that, but I will not boast about myself, except about my weaknesses. ⁶Even if I should choose to boast, I would not be a fool, because I would be speaking the truth. But I refrain, so no one will think more of me than is warranted by what I do or say.

⁷To keep me from becoming conceited because of these surpassingly great revelations, there was given me a thorn in my flesh, a messenger of Satan, to torment me. ⁸Three times I pleaded with the Lord to take it away from me. ⁹But he said to me, "My grace is sufficient for you, for my power is made perfect in weakness." Therefore I will boast all the more gladly about my weaknesses, so that Christ's power may rest on me. ¹⁰That is why, for Christ's sake, I delight in weaknesses, in insults, in hardships, in persecutions, in difficulties. For when I am weak, then I am strong.

Paul's Concern for the Corinthians

¹¹I have made a fool of myself, but you drove me to it. I ought to have been commended by you, for I am not in the least inferior to the "super-apostles," even though I am nothing. ¹²The things that mark an apostle—signs, wonders and miracles—were done among you with great perseverance. ¹³How were you inferior to the other churches, except that I was never a burden to you? Forgive me this wrong!

¹⁴Now I am ready to visit you for the third time, and I will not be a burden to you, because what I want is not your possessions but you. After all, children should not have to save up for their parents, but parents for their children. ¹⁵So I will very gladly spend for you everything I have and expend myself as well. If I love you more, will you love me less? ¹⁶Be that as it may, I have not been a burden to you. Yet, crafty fellow that I am, I caught you

WEEKENDING

REALIZE

Persistent, faithful, plodding belief and hope are necessary if we are to remain free to give.
Despair, which descends by dungeon steps to depression, is one of the major afflictions in our society. People seek relief from it sometimes in entertainment, sometimes in violence.
Christians make their way out of it step by step, sometimes with great effort, on hardly visible footholds of sharing. The besetting temptation of the life of the Spirit is simply to quit.
– *Eugene H. Peterson*

REJOICE

Giving and gratitude go together like humor and laughter, like having one's back rubbed and the sigh that follows, like a blowing wind and the murmur of wind chimes. Gratitude keeps alive the rhythm of grace given and grace grateful, a lively lilt that lightens a heavy world.
– *Lewis B. Smedes*

REVIVE

Saturday: 2 Corinthians 9:6–15
Sunday: Galatians 6:7–10

Go to page 252 for your next devotional reading.

by trickery! **17**Did I exploit you through any of the men I sent you? **18**I urged Titus to go to you and I sent our brother with him. Titus did not exploit you, did he? Did we not act in the same spirit and follow the same course?

19Have you been thinking all along that we have been defending ourselves to you? We have been speaking in the sight of God as those in Christ; and everything we do, dear friends, is for your strengthening. **20**For I am afraid that when I come I may not find you as I want you to be, and you may not find me as you want me to be. I fear that there may be quarreling, jealousy, outbursts of anger, factions, slander, gossip, arrogance and disorder. **21**I am afraid that when I come again my God will humble me before you, and I will be grieved over many who have sinned earlier and have not repented of the impurity, sexual sin and debauchery in which they have indulged.

Final Warnings

13 This will be my third visit to you. "Every matter must be established by the testimony of two or three witnesses."*a* **2**I already gave you a warning when I was with you the second time. I

a1 Deut. 19:15

MONDAY

VERSE FOR THE DAY:
2 Corinthians 12:14

AUTHOR:
D. Bruce Lockerbie

PASSAGE FOR THE DAY:
2 Corinthians 12:14–18

Here to Stay

THE main reason why a father's task, no less than a mother's, is the toughest job in the world is that it never ends. The challenges are daily, weekly, monthly, year after year. Being a parent is a full-time job with no reprieve, no time off even for illness and recuperation. Children, we soon discover, are *here to stay* for at least a score of years. They don't appear like robins in the spring, then fly away at summer's end; or if, as it sometimes seems, they do come and go during high school and college years, their absence in no way lessens our burden of responsibility. In fact, as our children get older, instead of relaxing, our task seemingly intensifies.

"It's the only job I know," says Ted Hutchens, a father with two daughters still at home and a son away at college, "that never seems to get any easier, in spite of all those years of experience". . .

The point is clear: Once a parent, always a parent. Fathers and mothers alike, we don't stop caring just because we're no longer the main providers of shelter, food and the comforts of home. It's not merely our bounden duty, as *The Book of Common Prayer* says, as biological parents of these children; it's also our joyful pleasure to care for them, even after they no longer seem to need us.

Additional Scripture Readings:
Philippians 2:14–18;
1 Thessalonians 2:1–12

Go to page 255 for your next devotional reading.

now repeat it while absent: On my return I will not spare those who sinned earlier or any of the others, ³since you are demanding proof that Christ is speaking through me. He is not weak in dealing with you, but is powerful among you. ⁴For to be sure, he was crucified in weakness, yet he lives by God's power. Likewise, we are weak in him, yet by God's power we will live with him to serve you.

⁵Examine yourselves to see whether you are in the faith; test yourselves. Do you not realize that Christ Jesus is in you—unless, of course, you fail the test? ⁶And I trust that you will discover that we have not failed the test. ⁷Now we pray to God that you will not do anything wrong. Not that people will see that we have stood the test but that you will do what is right even though we may seem to have failed. ⁸For we cannot do anything against the truth, but only for the truth. ⁹We are glad whenever we are weak but you are strong; and our prayer is for your perfection. ¹⁰This is why I write these things when I am absent, that when I come I may not have to be harsh in my use of authority—the authority the Lord gave me for building you up, not for tearing you down.

Final Greetings

¹¹Finally, brothers, good-by. Aim for perfection, listen to my appeal, be of one mind, live in peace. And the God of love and peace will be with you.

¹²Greet one another with a holy kiss. ¹³All the saints send their greetings.

¹⁴May the grace of the Lord Jesus Christ, and the love of God, and the fellowship of the Holy Spirit be with you all.

PAUL writes this letter to the churches he founded in Galatia (Acts 13:13–14:28), warning them against certain false teachers. He reminds them of the simple message of salvation by faith alone, which he and other church leaders teach, and concludes with advice on how to live a Spirit-filled life. As you read this book, be sure that you are saved by a personal faith in Jesus, and ask God's Spirit to help you walk in Christian love and peace.

GALATIANS

1 Paul, an apostle—sent not from men nor by man, but by Jesus Christ and God the Father, who raised him from the dead— ²and all the brothers with me,

To the churches in Galatia:

³Grace and peace to you from God our Father and the Lord Jesus Christ, ⁴who gave himself for our sins to rescue us from the present evil age, according to the will of our God and Father, ⁵to whom be glory for ever and ever. Amen.

No Other Gospel

⁶I am astonished that you are so quickly deserting the one who called you by the grace of Christ and are turning to a different gospel— ⁷which is really no gospel at all. Evidently some people are throwing you into confusion and are trying to pervert the gospel of Christ. ⁸But even if we or an angel from heaven should preach a gospel other than the one we preached to you, let him be eternally condemned! ⁹As we have already said, so now I say again: If anybody is preaching to you a gospel other than what you accepted, let him be eternally condemned!

¹⁰Am I now trying to win the approval of men, or of God? Or am I trying to please men? If I were still trying to please men, I would not be a servant of Christ.

Paul Called by God

¹¹I want you to know, brothers, that the gospel I preached is not something that man made up. ¹²I did not receive it from any man, nor was I taught it; rather, I received it by revelation from Jesus Christ. ¹³For you have heard of my previous way of life in Judaism, how intensely I persecuted the church of God and tried to destroy it. ¹⁴I was advancing in Judaism beyond many Jews of my own age and was extremely zealous for the traditions of my fathers. ¹⁵But when God, who set

---

TUESDAY

VERSE FOR THE DAY:
Galatians 1:4

AUTHOR:
W. Phillip Keller

PASSAGE FOR THE DAY:
Galatians 1:1–5

Friend, Not Foe

SO MANY people are of the opinion that because God is an infinite being he is beyond our human comprehension. They have the notion he is someone distant, far removed from us, who may be appealed to only in great extremity across spans of space.

The truth is just the opposite. He is our Father, our Friend, and can be our Companion on the path of life. Such an association becomes the most cherished relationship in the world. But it can only become such if we begin to understand God's character and the wondrous ways in which he deals with us . . .

Most human beings have despised and rejected God simply because they never grasped *who he was* and *what he was like.* They saw him as a foe, not a friend.

This explains why Christ called out in profound pathos —while the iron spikes tore through his hands and his feet —*"Father, forgive them, for they do not know what they are doing"* [Luke 23:34, italics added]. It was the intense heart-cry of our compassionate, caring God giving us himself, sharing with us his own life, in a superb act of selfless self-sacrifice.

This caliber of divine love eludes us mortals. We are, for the most part, so selfish, so self-centered, so self-preoccupied, we recoil from those spike-torn hands extended to us in mercy, compassion and deep longing. We simply refuse to believe anyone truly can care for us with such pure motives.

Yes, across the terrible, tortured, tragic centuries of our human history mankind has rejected God. They have assumed always that like themselves he was at heart a tyrant—a stern and unjust judge, a formidable potentate to be feared. All because they seldom understood him. They knew nothing of him in intimate, firsthand communion.

Additional Scripture Readings:
John 15:9–17; Romans 5:1–11

Go to page 257 for your next devotional reading.

me apart from birth[a] and called me by his grace, was pleased [16]to reveal his Son in me so that I might preach him among the Gentiles, I did not consult any man, [17]nor did I go up to Jerusalem to see those who were apostles before I was, but I went immediately into Arabia and later returned to Damascus.

[18]Then after three years, I went up to Jerusalem to get acquainted with Peter[b] and stayed with him fifteen days. [19]I saw none of the other apostles — only James, the Lord's brother. [20]I assure you before God that what I am writing you is no lie. [21]Later I went to Syria and Cilicia. [22]I was personally unknown to the churches of Judea that are in Christ. [23]They only heard the report: "The man who formerly persecuted us is now preaching the faith he once tried to destroy." [24]And they praised God because of me.

Paul Accepted by the Apostles

2 Fourteen years later I went up again to Jerusalem, this time with Barnabas. I took Titus along also. [2]I went in response to a revelation and set before them the gospel that I preach among the Gentiles. But I did this privately to those who seemed to be leaders, for fear that I was running or had run my race in vain. [3]Yet not even Titus, who was with me, was compelled to be circumcised, even though he was a Greek. [4]This matter arose, because some false brothers had infiltrated our ranks to spy on the freedom we have in Christ Jesus and to make us slaves. [5]We did not give in to them for a moment, so that the truth of the gospel might remain with you.

[6]As for those who seemed to be important — whatever they were makes no difference to me; God does not judge by external appearance — those men added nothing to my message. [7]On the contrary, they saw that I had been entrusted with the task of preaching the gospel to the Gentiles,[c] just as Peter had been to the Jews.[d] [8]For God, who was at work in the ministry of Peter as an apostle to the Jews, was also at work in my ministry as an apostle to the Gentiles. [9]James, Peter[e] and John, those reputed to be pillars, gave me and Barnabas the right hand of fellowship when they recognized the grace given to me. They agreed that we should go to the Gentiles, and they to the Jews. [10]All they asked was that we should continue to remember the poor, the very thing I was eager to do.

Paul Opposes Peter

[11]When Peter came to Antioch, I opposed him to his face, because he was clearly in the wrong. [12]Before certain men came from James, he used to eat with the Gentiles. But when they arrived, he began to draw back and separate himself from the Gentiles because he was afraid of those who belonged to the circumcision group. [13]The other Jews joined him in his hypocrisy, so that by their hypocrisy even Barnabas was led astray.

[14]When I saw that they were not acting in line with the truth of the gospel, I said to Peter in front of them all, "You are a Jew, yet you live like a Gentile and not like a Jew. How is it, then, that you force Gentiles to follow Jewish customs?

[15]"We who are Jews by birth and not 'Gentile sinners' [16]know that a man is not justified by observing the law, but by faith in Jesus Christ. So we, too, have put our faith in Christ Jesus that we may be justified by faith in Christ and not by observing the law, because by observing the law no one will be justified.

[17]"If, while we seek to be justified in Christ, it becomes evident that we ourselves are sinners, does that mean that Christ promotes sin? Absolutely not! [18]If I rebuild what I destroyed, I prove that I am a lawbreaker. [19]For through the law I died to the law so that I might live for God. [20]I have been crucified with Christ and I no longer live, but Christ lives in me. The life I live in the body, I live by faith in the Son of God, who loved me and gave himself for me. [21]I do not set aside the grace of God, for if righteousness could be gained through the law, Christ died for nothing!"[f]

Faith or Observance of the Law

3 You foolish Galatians! Who has bewitched you? Before your very eyes Jesus Christ was clearly portrayed as crucified. [2]I would like to learn just one thing from you: Did you receive the Spirit by observing the law, or by believing what you heard? [3]Are you so foolish? After beginning with the Spirit, are you now trying to

---

[a]15 Or *from my mother's womb* [b]18 Greek *Cephas* [c]7 Greek *uncircumcised* [d]7 Greek *circumcised*; also in verses 8 and 9 [e]9 Greek *Cephas*; also in verses 11 and 14 [f]21 Some interpreters end the quotation after verse 14.

attain your goal by human effort? **4**Have you suffered so much for nothing—if it really was for nothing? **5**Does God give you his Spirit and work miracles among you because you observe the law, or because you believe what you heard?

6Consider Abraham: "He believed God, and it was credited to him as righteousness."*a* **7**Understand, then, that those who believe are children of Abraham. **8**The Scripture foresaw that God would justify the Gentiles by faith, and announced the gospel in advance to Abraham: "All nations will be blessed through you."*b* **9**So those who have faith are blessed along with Abraham, the man of faith.

10All who rely on observing the law are under a curse, for it is written: "Cursed is everyone who does not continue to do everything written in the Book of the Law."*c* **11**Clearly no one is justified before

a6 Gen. 15:6   *b8* Gen. 12:3; 18:18; 22:18   *c10* Deut. 27:26

WEDNESDAY

VERSE FOR THE DAY:
Galatians 2:10

AUTHOR:
Doug Sherman and
William Hendricks

PASSAGE FOR THE DAY:
Galatians 2:6–10

Remember the Poor

THROUGH our work we can love others and love ourselves. We can love others by serving their needs through the goods we help produce or distribute, or through the services we help provide. And we can love ourselves by gaining an income to provide for our needs and the needs of our families.

But Scripture adds a purely benevolent purpose to work: to earn money in order to give it away to others. In fact, the overwhelming thrust of the Scriptures is that as God sees fit to prosper us, our abundance should begin to spill over and start benefiting others who, for a variety of reasons, are in need. For example, in Psalm 37:25–26, the writer looks back on his life and says: "I was young and now I am old, yet I have never seen the righteous forsaken or their children begging bread. They are always generous and lend freely; their children will be blessed." In other words, as God has prospered the righteous person and his family, it results in generosity toward others . . .

Giving some portion of your income away is a discipline and a privilege taught by Scripture. I believe every Christian, no matter what his level of lifestyle, should use part of his money to meet the financial and material needs of others . . .

God is deeply concerned to see us meet their [the poor's] needs. His concern does not arise because the poor are inherently better but because they are needy. And from the beginning of creation, he has desired to meet human needs. He wants to meet some of them through you and me.

Additional Scripture Readings:
Psalm 72:1-14; 1 Timothy 6:17-19

Go to page 259 for your next devotional reading.

God by the law, because, "The righteous will live by faith."*a* ¹²The law is not based on faith; on the contrary, "The man who does these things will live by them."*b* ¹³Christ redeemed us from the curse of the law by becoming a curse for us, for it is written: "Cursed is everyone who is hung on a tree."*c* ¹⁴He redeemed us in order that the blessing given to Abraham might come to the Gentiles through Christ Jesus, so that by faith we might receive the promise of the Spirit.

The Law and the Promise

¹⁵Brothers, let me take an example from everyday life. Just as no one can set aside or add to a human covenant that has been duly established, so it is in this case. ¹⁶The promises were spoken to Abraham and to his seed. The Scripture does not say "and to seeds," meaning many people, but "and to your seed,"*d* meaning one person, who is Christ. ¹⁷What I mean is this: The law, introduced 430 years later, does not set aside the covenant previously established by God and thus do away with the promise. ¹⁸For if the inheritance depends on the law, then it no longer depends on a promise; but God in his grace gave it to Abraham through a promise.

¹⁹What, then, was the purpose of the law? It was added because of transgressions until the Seed to whom the promise referred had come. The law was put into effect through angels by a mediator. ²⁰A mediator, however, does not represent just one party; but God is one.

²¹Is the law, therefore, opposed to the promises of God? Absolutely not! For if a law had been given that could impart life, then righteousness would certainly have come by the law. ²²But the Scripture declares that the whole world is a prisoner of sin, so that what was promised, being given through faith in Jesus Christ, might be given to those who believe.

²³Before this faith came, we were held prisoners by the law, locked up until faith should be revealed. ²⁴So the law was put in charge to lead us to Christ*e* that we might be justified by faith. ²⁵Now that faith has come, we are no longer under the supervision of the law.

Sons of God

²⁶You are all sons of God through faith in Christ Jesus, ²⁷for all of you who were baptized into Christ have clothed yourselves with Christ. ²⁸There is neither Jew nor Greek, slave nor free, male nor female, for you are all one in Christ Jesus. ²⁹If you belong to Christ, then you are Abraham's seed, and heirs according to the promise.

4 What I am saying is that as long as the heir is a child, he is no different from a slave, although he owns the whole estate. ²He is subject to guardians and trustees until the time set by his father. ³So also, when we were children, we were in slavery under the basic principles of the world. ⁴But when the time had fully come, God sent his Son, born of a woman, born under law, ⁵to redeem those under law, that we might receive the full rights of sons. ⁶Because you are sons, God sent the Spirit of his Son into our hearts, the Spirit who calls out, "Abba,*f* Father." ⁷So you are no longer a slave, but a son; and since you are a son, God has made you also an heir.

Paul's Concern for the Galatians

⁸Formerly, when you did not know God, you were slaves to those who by nature are not gods. ⁹But now that you know God — or rather are known by God — how is it that you are turning back to those weak and miserable principles? Do you wish to be enslaved by them all over again? ¹⁰You are observing special days and months and seasons and years! ¹¹I fear for you, that somehow I have wasted my efforts on you.

¹²I plead with you, brothers, become like me, for I became like you. You have done me no wrong. ¹³As you know, it was because of an illness that I first preached the gospel to you. ¹⁴Even though my illness was a trial to you, you did not treat me with contempt or scorn. Instead, you welcomed me as if I were an angel of God, as if I were Christ Jesus himself. ¹⁵What has happened to all your joy? I can testify that, if you could have done so, you would have torn out your eyes and given them to me. ¹⁶Have I now become your enemy by telling you the truth?

¹⁷Those people are zealous to win you over, but for no good. What they want is to alienate you ⌊from us⌋, so that you may be zealous for them. ¹⁸It is fine to be zealous, provided the purpose is good, and to

---

a 11 Hab. 2:4   *b* 12 Lev. 18:5   *c* 13 Deut. 21:23   *d* 16 Gen. 12:7; 13:15; 24:7   *e* 24 Or *charge until Christ came*   *f* 6 Aramaic for *Father*

be so always and not just when I am with you. **19**My dear children, for whom I am again in the pains of childbirth until Christ is formed in you, **20**how I wish I could be with you now and change my tone, because I am perplexed about you!

Hagar and Sarah

21Tell me, you who want to be under the law, are you not aware of what the law says? **22**For it is written that Abraham had two sons, one by the slave woman and the other by the free woman. **23**His son by the

---

THURSDAY

VERSE FOR THE DAY:
Galatians 4:19

AUTHOR:
David Augsburger

PASSAGE FOR THE DAY:
Galatians 4:12–20

To Be a Man

MARRIAGE partners tend to become like each other, taking on the other's qualities, or developing the opposite characteristics in negative reaction to the other.

Leadership shared in mutual respect can establish a climate of dignity, freedom and responsibility, creating an atmosphere which is both comforting and stimulating to both—a Christian atmosphere. In it, each is free to grow toward personal maturity and each is eager to see the shape of Christ forming in the other (see Galatians 4:19–20).

But where one seizes power, or both struggle for control, an atmosphere of competition and conflict chokes communication and understanding. Even the unconscious assuming of power by one partner or the other will mold the relationship, perhaps in ways neither desire.

Leadership is a function which should always be shared.

Authority in one area or another is a responsibility which is mutually designated to one or the other through honest negotiation. It can be renegotiated at any time.

Life together is life shared. Shared love, shared work, shared opportunities, shared leadership, even shared initiative. Man, the nominal head, may function officially for both in public matters of leadership. Woman, recognized as his equal in partnership, leads with, and not against, him. Together, they choose to grow.

To be a man—is to possess the strength to love another, not the need to dominate over others.

To be a man—is to experience the courage to accept another, not the compulsion to be an aggressor.

To be a man—is to keep faith with human values in relationships, not to value oneself by position or possessions.

To be a man—is to be free to give love and to be free to accept love in return.

Additional Scripture Readings:
Galatians 5:13–18;
Ephesians 5:21–33

Go to page 264 for your next devotional reading.

slave woman was born in the ordinary way; but his son by the free woman was born as the result of a promise.

24These things may be taken figuratively, for the women represent two covenants. One covenant is from Mount Sinai and bears children who are to be slaves: This is Hagar. 25Now Hagar stands for Mount Sinai in Arabia and corresponds to the present city of Jerusalem, because she is in slavery with her children. 26But the Jerusalem that is above is free, and she is our mother. 27For it is written:

"Be glad, O barren woman,
 who bears no children;
break forth and cry aloud,
 you who have no labor pains;
because more are the children of the
  desolate woman
 than of her who has a husband."*a*

28Now you, brothers, like Isaac, are children of promise. 29At that time the son born in the ordinary way persecuted the son born by the power of the Spirit. It is the same now. 30But what does the Scripture say? "Get rid of the slave woman and her son, for the slave woman's son will never share in the inheritance with the free woman's son."*b* 31Therefore, brothers, we are not children of the slave woman, but of the free woman.

Freedom in Christ

5 It is for freedom that Christ has set us free. Stand firm, then, and do not let yourselves be burdened again by a yoke of slavery.

2Mark my words! I, Paul, tell you that if you let yourselves be circumcised, Christ will be of no value to you at all. 3Again I declare to every man who lets himself be circumcised that he is obligated to obey the whole law. 4You who are trying to be justified by law have been alienated from Christ; you have fallen away from grace. 5But by faith we eagerly await through the Spirit the righteousness for which we hope. 6For in Christ Jesus neither circumcision nor uncircumcision has any value. The only thing that counts is faith expressing itself through love.

7You were running a good race. Who cut in on you and kept you from obeying the truth? 8That kind of persuasion does not come from the one who calls you. 9"A little yeast works through the whole batch of dough." 10I am confident in the Lord that you will take no other view. The one who is throwing you into confusion will pay the penalty, whoever he may be. 11Brothers, if I am still preaching circumcision, why am I still being persecuted? In that case the offense of the cross has been abolished. 12As for those agitators, I wish they would go the whole way and emasculate themselves!

13You, my brothers, were called to be free. But do not use your freedom to indulge the sinful nature*c*; rather, serve one another in love. 14The entire law is summed up in a single command: "Love your neighbor as yourself."*d* 15If you keep on biting and devouring each other, watch out or you will be destroyed by each other.

Life by the Spirit

16So I say, live by the Spirit, and you will not gratify the desires of the sinful nature. 17For the sinful nature desires what is contrary to the Spirit, and the Spirit what is contrary to the sinful nature. They are in conflict with each other, so that you do not do what you want. 18But if you are led by the Spirit, you are not under law.

19The acts of the sinful nature are obvious: sexual immorality, impurity and debauchery; 20idolatry and witchcraft; hatred, discord, jealousy, fits of rage, selfish ambition, dissensions, factions 21and envy; drunkenness, orgies, and the like. I warn you, as I did before, that those who live like this will not inherit the kingdom of God.

22But the fruit of the Spirit is love, joy, peace, patience, kindness, goodness, faithfulness, 23gentleness and self-control. Against such things there is no law. 24Those who belong to Christ Jesus have crucified the sinful nature with its passions and desires. 25Since we live by the Spirit, let us keep in step with the Spirit. 26Let us not become conceited, provoking and envying each other.

Doing Good to All

6 Brothers, if someone is caught in a sin, you who are spiritual should restore him gently. But watch yourself, or

a27 Isaiah 54:1   *b30* Gen. 21:10   *c13* Or *the flesh*; also in verses 16, 17, 19 and 24   *d14* Lev. 19:18

you also may be tempted. ²Carry each other's burdens, and in this way you will fulfill the law of Christ. ³If anyone thinks he is something when he is nothing, he deceives himself. ⁴Each one should test his own actions. Then he can take pride in himself, without comparing himself to somebody else, ⁵for each one should carry his own load.

⁶Anyone who receives instruction in the word must share all good things with his instructor.

⁷Do not be deceived: God cannot be mocked. A man reaps what he sows. ⁸The one who sows to please his sinful nature, from that nature^a will reap destruction; the one who sows to please the Spirit, from the Spirit will reap eternal life. ⁹Let us not become weary in doing good, for at the proper time we will reap a harvest if we do not give up. ¹⁰Therefore, as we have opportunity, let us do good to all people, especially to those who belong to the family of believers.

Not Circumcision but a New Creation

¹¹See what large letters I use as I write to you with my own hand!

¹²Those who want to make a good impression outwardly are trying to compel you to be circumcised. The only reason they do this is to avoid being persecuted for the cross of Christ. ¹³Not even those who are circumcised obey the law, yet they want you to be circumcised that they may boast about your flesh. ¹⁴May I never boast except in the cross of our Lord Jesus Christ, through which^b the world has been crucified to me, and I to the world. ¹⁵Neither circumcision nor uncircumcision means anything; what counts is a new creation. ¹⁶Peace and mercy to all who follow this rule, even to the Israel of God.

¹⁷Finally, let no one cause me trouble, for I bear on my body the marks of Jesus.

¹⁸The grace of our Lord Jesus Christ be with your spirit, brothers. Amen.

---

a 8 Or *his flesh, from the flesh* b 14 Or *whom*

*P*AUL *writes this letter from prison (Ephesians 4:1; probably in Rome, see Acts 28:30–31) to the church he started in Ephesus (Acts 19). In the first half he explains God's great plan to redeem the world through Christ, showing what this means for individual Christians and for the whole church. In the second half he gives practical advice on how to live the Christian life. As you read this book, first examine yourself to be sure that you are saved. Then move on to fight against Satan and show your love to your family, your church and your community.*

EPHESIANS

1 Paul, an apostle of Christ Jesus by the will of God,

To the saints in Ephesus,*a* the faithful*b* in Christ Jesus:

2Grace and peace to you from God our Father and the Lord Jesus Christ.

Spiritual Blessings in Christ

3Praise be to the God and Father of our Lord Jesus Christ, who has blessed us in the heavenly realms with every spiritual blessing in Christ. **4**For he chose us in him before the creation of the world to be holy and blameless in his sight. In love **5**he*c* predestined us to be adopted as his sons through Jesus Christ, in accordance with his pleasure and will— **6**to the praise of his glorious grace, which he has freely given us in the One he loves. **7**In him we have

---

a 1 Some early manuscripts do not have *in Ephesus.* *b 1* Or *believers who are* *c 4,5* Or *sight in love. 5He*

redemption through his blood, the forgiveness of sins, in accordance with the riches of God's grace ⁸that he lavished on us with all wisdom and understanding. ⁹And he[a] made known to us the mystery of his will according to his good pleasure, which he purposed in Christ, ¹⁰to be put into effect when the times will have reached their fulfillment — to bring all things in heaven and on earth together under one head, even Christ.

¹¹In him we were also chosen,[b] having been predestined according to the plan of him who works out everything in conformity with the purpose of his will, ¹²in order that we, who were the first to hope in Christ, might be for the praise of his glory. ¹³And you also were included in Christ when you heard the word of truth, the gospel of your salvation. Having believed, you were marked in him with a seal, the promised Holy Spirit, ¹⁴who is a deposit guaranteeing our inheritance until the redemption of those who are God's possession — to the praise of his glory.

Thanksgiving and Prayer

¹⁵For this reason, ever since I heard about your faith in the Lord Jesus and your love for all the saints, ¹⁶I have not stopped giving thanks for you, remembering you in my prayers. ¹⁷I keep asking that the God of our Lord Jesus Christ, the glorious Father, may give you the Spirit[c] of wisdom and revelation, so that you may know him better. ¹⁸I pray also that the eyes of your heart may be enlightened in order that you may know the hope to which he has called you, the riches of his glorious inheritance in the saints, ¹⁹and his incomparably great power for us who believe. That power is like the working of his mighty strength, ²⁰which he exerted in Christ when he raised him from the dead and seated him at his right hand in the heavenly realms, ²¹far above all rule and authority, power and dominion, and every title that can be given, not only in the present age but also in the one to come. ²²And God placed all things under his feet and appointed him to be head over everything for the church, ²³which is his body, the fullness of him who fills everything in every way.

Made Alive in Christ

2 As for you, you were dead in your transgressions and sins, ²in which you used to live when you followed the ways of this world and of the ruler of the kingdom of the air, the spirit who is now at work in those who are disobedient. ³All of us also lived among them at one time, gratifying the cravings of our sinful nature[d] and following its desires and thoughts. Like the rest, we were by nature objects of wrath. ⁴But because of his great love for us, God, who is rich in mercy, ⁵made us alive with Christ even when we were dead in transgressions — it is by grace you have been saved. ⁶And God raised us up with Christ and seated us with him in the heavenly realms in Christ Jesus, ⁷in order that in the coming ages he might show the incomparable riches of his grace, expressed in his kindness to us in Christ Jesus. ⁸For it is by grace you have been saved, through faith — and this not from yourselves, it is the gift of God — ⁹not by works, so that no one can boast. ¹⁰For we are God's workmanship, created in Christ Jesus to do good works, which God prepared in advance for us to do.

One in Christ

¹¹Therefore, remember that formerly you who are Gentiles by birth and called "uncircumcised" by those who call themselves "the circumcision" (that done in the body by the hands of men) — ¹²remember that at that time you were separate from Christ, excluded from citizenship in Israel and foreigners to the covenants of the promise, without hope and without God in the world. ¹³But now in Christ Jesus you who once were far away have been brought near through the blood of Christ.

¹⁴For he himself is our peace, who has made the two one and has destroyed the barrier, the dividing wall of hostility, ¹⁵by abolishing in his flesh the law with its commandments and regulations. His purpose was to create in himself one new man out of the two, thus making peace, ¹⁶and in this one body to reconcile both of them to God through the cross, by which he put to death their hostility. ¹⁷He came and preached peace to you who were far away and peace to those who were near.

---

[a] 8,9 Or us. With all wisdom and understanding, ⁹he [b] 11 Or were made heirs [c] 17 Or a spirit
[d] 3 Or our flesh

FRIDAY

VERSE FOR THE DAY:
Ephesians 2:8

AUTHOR:
Mark Ritchie

PASSAGE FOR THE DAY:
Ephesians 2:1–10

Saved by Grace

WHILE *working as an engineer in Afghanistan, Mark Ritchie's father had found an opportunity, despite a ban on proselytizing, to teach a new believer from the Bible.*

It was strictly forbidden for any foreigner in Afghanistan to do anything to "Christianize" an Afghan. [The Muslim passenger in our car] told me how, as a student of Western civilization, he had read about the Reformation and the arguments put forward by Erasmus and Luther on the issue of justification by faith in Jesus Christ—not by the Church's system of works.

"When I read it," he said, "I knew that this was the true way. Doing good works is one of the main tenets of Islam; without good works a person could never get to heaven. But anyone who has really tried to be good knows himself well enough to know he could never be good enough. So I became a believer in Jesus Christ. And I asked your father to help me understand more about it."

I had to admit, this was a new one on me. I had never before heard of anyone being converted to Christianity by reading a history textbook. Just wait till the publishers hear about this, I thought, while our Travelall bounced through the narrow side streets of Herat. I could just see the headlines: MUSLIM READS HISTORY BOOK—CONVERTS—DIPLOMATIC SCANDAL BREWS. This could make a textbook writer's head roll.

Once again I found myself surprised. The remote carpenter from Galilee had written his signature so powerfully across history that I found a Muslim in the farthest corner of the globe who came to the same conclusion about him as I had. It had taken me years of study to become convinced that the carpenter was God. Meanwhile, this man, raised in a Muslim home, saw it after one chapter in a Western civilization textbook.

On reflection, I wondered why I should be so surprised. Isn't this what one might expect to find if the itinerant preacher from Nazareth was as he claimed to be, the creator of the universe?

Additional Scripture Readings:
John 1:1–14; Romans 10:8–18

Go to page 266 for your next devotional reading.

¹⁸For through him we both have access to the Father by one Spirit.

¹⁹Consequently, you are no longer foreigners and aliens, but fellow citizens with God's people and members of God's household, ²⁰built on the foundation of the apostles and prophets, with Christ Jesus himself as the chief cornerstone. ²¹In him the whole building is joined together and rises to become a holy temple in the Lord. ²²And in him you too are being built together to become a dwelling in which God lives by his Spirit.

Paul the Preacher to the Gentiles

3 For this reason I, Paul, the prisoner of Christ Jesus for the sake of you Gentiles—

²Surely you have heard about the administration of God's grace that was given to me for you, ³that is, the mystery made known to me by revelation, as I have already written briefly. ⁴In reading this, then, you will be able to understand my insight into the mystery of Christ, ⁵which was not made known to men in other generations as it has now been revealed by the Spirit to God's holy apostles and prophets. ⁶This mystery is that through the gospel the Gentiles are heirs together with Israel, members together of one body, and sharers together in the promise in Christ Jesus.

⁷I became a servant of this gospel by the gift of God's grace given me through the working of his power. ⁸Although I am less than the least of all God's people, this grace was given me: to preach to the Gentiles the unsearchable riches of Christ, ⁹and to make plain to everyone the administration of this mystery, which for ages past was kept hidden in God, who created all things. ¹⁰His intent was that now, through the church, the manifold wisdom of God should be made known to the rulers and authorities in the heavenly realms, ¹¹according to his eternal purpose which he accomplished in Christ Jesus our Lord. ¹²In him and through faith in him we may approach God with freedom and confidence. ¹³I ask you, therefore, not to be discouraged because of my sufferings for you, which are your glory.

A Prayer for the Ephesians

¹⁴For this reason I kneel before the Father, ¹⁵from whom his whole family*ᵃ* in heaven and on earth derives its name. ¹⁶I pray that out of his glorious riches he may strengthen you with power through his Spirit in your inner being, ¹⁷so that Christ may dwell in your hearts through faith. And I pray that you, being rooted and established in love, ¹⁸may have power, together with all the saints, to grasp how wide and long and high and deep is the love of Christ, ¹⁹and to know this love that surpasses knowledge—that you may be filled to the measure of all the fullness of God.

²⁰Now to him who is able to do immeasurably more than all we ask or imagine, according to his power that is at work within us, ²¹to him be glory in the church and in Christ Jesus throughout all generations, for ever and ever! Amen.

Unity in the Body of Christ

4 As a prisoner for the Lord, then, I urge you to live a life worthy of the calling you have received. ²Be completely humble and gentle; be patient, bearing with one another in love. ³Make every effort to keep the unity of the Spirit through the bond of peace. ⁴There is one body and one Spirit— just as you were called to one hope when you were called— ⁵one Lord, one faith, one baptism; ⁶one God and Father of all, who is over all and through all and in all.

⁷But to each one of us grace has been given as Christ apportioned it. ⁸This is why it*ᵇ* says:

"When he ascended on high,
he led captives in his train
and gave gifts to men."*ᶜ*

⁹(What does "he ascended" mean except that he also descended to the lower, earthly regions*ᵈ*? ¹⁰He who descended is the very one who ascended higher than all the heavens, in order to fill the whole universe.) ¹¹It was he who gave some to be apostles, some to be prophets, some to be evangelists, and some to be pastors and teachers, ¹²to prepare God's people for works of service, so that the body of Christ may be built up ¹³until we all reach unity in the faith and in the knowledge of the Son of God and become mature, attaining to the whole measure of the fullness of Christ.

¹⁴Then we will no longer be infants, tossed back and forth by the waves, and blown here and there by every wind of teaching and by the cunning and crafti-

---

ᵃ15 Or *whom all fatherhood*   *ᵇ8* Or *God*   *ᶜ8* Psalm 68:18   *ᵈ9* Or *the depths of the earth*

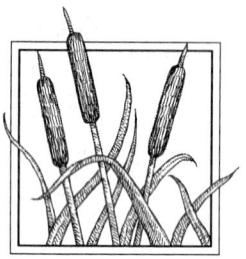

WEEKENDING

RETHINK

The right kind of toughness—strength of character—ought to mark the man of today . . . but not only that. Tenderness—gentleness—is equally important.

God considers it so important he places it on the list of nine qualities he feels should mark the life of his children . . .

Our goal is balance . . . always balance. Not either-or, but both-and. Not just *tough*. That alone makes a man cold, distant, intolerant, unbearable. But tough *and* tender . . . gentle, thoughtful, teachable, considerate.

– Charles Swindoll

REVIVE
Saturday: Galatians 5:22–23
Sunday: Ephesians 4:1–6

Go to page 267 for your next devotional reading.

ness of men in their deceitful scheming. ⁱ⁵Instead, speaking the truth in love, we will in all things grow up into him who is the Head, that is, Christ. ¹⁶From him the whole body, joined and held together by every supporting ligament, grows and builds itself up in love, as each part does its work.

Living as Children of Light

¹⁷So I tell you this, and insist on it in the Lord, that you must no longer live as the Gentiles do, in the futility of their thinking. ¹⁸They are darkened in their understanding and separated from the life of God because of the ignorance that is in them due to the hardening of their hearts. ¹⁹Having lost all sensitivity, they have given themselves over to sensuality so as to indulge in every kind of impurity, with a continual lust for more.

²⁰You, however, did not come to know Christ that way. ²¹Surely you heard of him and were taught in him in accordance with the truth that is in Jesus. ²²You were taught, with regard to your former way of life, to put off your old self, which is being corrupted by its deceitful desires; ²³to be

MONDAY

VERSE FOR THE DAY: *AUTHOR:* *PASSAGE FOR THE DAY:*
Ephesians 4:16 *Paul Brand* *Ephesians 4:1–16*

A Luxuriant Body

WHENEVER I travel overseas, I am struck anew by the world's incredible diversity, and the churches overseas are now beginning to show that cultural self-expression. For too long they were bound up in Western ways (as the early church had been bound in Jewish ways) so that hymns, dress, architecture and church names were the same around the world. Now indigenous churches are bursting out with their own spontaneous expressions of worship to God. I must guard against picturing the Body of Christ as composed only of American or British cells; it is far grander and more luxuriant than that . . .

I have learned that when God looks upon his Body, spread like an archipelago throughout the world, he sees the whole thing. And I think he, understanding the cultural backgrounds and true intent of the worshipers, likes the variety he sees.

Blacks in Murphy, North Carolina, shout their praises to God. Believers in Austria intone them, accompanied by magnificent organs and illuminated by stained glass. Some Africans dance their praise to God, following the beat of a skilled drummer. Sedate Japanese Christians express their gratitude by creating objects of beauty . . .

The Body of Christ, like our own bodies, is composed of individual, unlike cells that are knit together to form one Body. He is the whole thing, and the joy of the Body increases as individual cells realize they can be diverse without becoming isolated outposts.

Additional Scripture Readings:
Romans 12:3–8;
1 Corinthians 12:12–27

Go to page 269 for your next devotional reading.

made new in the attitude of your minds; ²⁴and to put on the new self, created to be like God in true righteousness and holiness.

²⁵Therefore each of you must put off falsehood and speak truthfully to his neighbor, for we are all members of one body. ²⁶"In your anger do not sin"[a]: Do not let the sun go down while you are still angry, ²⁷and do not give the devil a foothold. ²⁸He who has been stealing must steal no longer, but must work, doing something useful with his own hands, that he may have something to share with those in need.

²⁹Do not let any unwholesome talk come out of your mouths, but only what is helpful for building others up according to their needs, that it may benefit those who listen. ³⁰And do not grieve the Holy Spirit of God, with whom you were sealed for the day of redemption. ³¹Get rid of all bitterness, rage and anger, brawling and slander, along with every form of malice. ³²Be kind and compassionate to one another, forgiving each other, just as in Christ God forgave you.

5 Be imitators of God, therefore, as dearly loved children ²and live a life of love, just as Christ loved us and gave himself up for us as a fragrant offering and sacrifice to God.

³But among you there must not be even a hint of sexual immorality, or of any kind of impurity, or of greed, because these are improper for God's holy people. ⁴Nor should there be obscenity, foolish talk or coarse joking, which are out of place, but rather thanksgiving. ⁵For of this you can be sure: No immoral, impure or greedy person—such a man is an idolater—has any inheritance in the kingdom of Christ and of God.[b] ⁶Let no one deceive you with empty words, for because of such things God's wrath comes on those who are disobedient. ⁷Therefore do not be partners with them.

⁸For you were once darkness, but now you are light in the Lord. Live as children of light ⁹(for the fruit of the light consists in all goodness, righteousness and truth) ¹⁰and find out what pleases the Lord. ¹¹Have nothing to do with the fruitless deeds of darkness, but rather expose them. ¹²For it is shameful even to mention what the disobedient do in secret. ¹³But everything exposed by the light becomes visible, ¹⁴for it is light that makes everything visible. This is why it is said:

"Wake up, O sleeper,
 rise from the dead,
and Christ will shine on you."

¹⁵Be very careful, then, how you live—not as unwise but as wise, ¹⁶making the most of every opportunity, because the days are evil. ¹⁷Therefore do not be foolish, but understand what the Lord's will is. ¹⁸Do not get drunk on wine, which leads to debauchery. Instead, be filled with the Spirit. ¹⁹Speak to one another with psalms, hymns and spiritual songs. Sing and make music in your heart to the Lord, ²⁰always giving thanks to God the Father for everything, in the name of our Lord Jesus Christ.

²¹Submit to one another out of reverence for Christ.

Wives and Husbands

²²Wives, submit to your husbands as to the Lord. ²³For the husband is the head of the wife as Christ is the head of the church, his body, of which he is the Savior. ²⁴Now as the church submits to Christ, so also wives should submit to their husbands in everything.

²⁵Husbands, love your wives, just as Christ loved the church and gave himself up for her ²⁶to make her holy, cleansing[c] her by the washing with water through the word, ²⁷and to present her to himself as a radiant church, without stain or wrinkle or any other blemish, but holy and blameless. ²⁸In this same way, husbands ought to love their wives as their own bodies. He who loves his wife loves himself. ²⁹After all, no one ever hated his own body, but he feeds and cares for it, just as Christ does the church— ³⁰for we are members of his body. ³¹"For this reason a man will leave his father and mother and be united to his wife, and the two will become one flesh."[d] ³²This is a profound mystery—but I am talking about Christ and the church. ³³However, each one of you also must love his wife as he loves himself, and the wife must respect her husband.

Children and Parents

6 Children, obey your parents in the Lord, for this is right. ²"Honor your father and mother"—which is the first commandment with a promise— ³"that it may

---

[a]26 Psalm 4:4   [b]5 Or *kingdom of the Christ and God*   [c]26 Or *having cleansed*   [d]31 Gen. 2:24

go well with you and that you may enjoy long life on the earth."[a]

4Fathers, do not exasperate your children; instead, bring them up in the training and instruction of the Lord.

Slaves and Masters

5Slaves, obey your earthly masters with respect and fear, and with sincerity of heart, just as you would obey Christ. **6**Obey them not only to win their favor when their eye is on you, but like slaves of Christ, doing the will of God from your heart. **7**Serve wholeheartedly, as if you were serving the Lord, not men, **8**because you know that the Lord will reward everyone for whatever good he does, whether he is slave or free.

9And masters, treat your slaves in the same way. Do not threaten them, since you know that he who is both their Master and yours is in heaven, and there is no favoritism with him.

*a*3 Deut. 5:16

TUESDAY

VERSE FOR THE DAY:	AUTHOR:	PASSAGE FOR THE DAY:
Ephesians 5:22	Mike Singletary	Ephesians 5:21–33

Servant Leadership

MEN took the Scriptures and went too far. They took a man's role of headship and took it as license to rule as a superior. But man's headship was supposed to be patterned after Jesus' style of leadership: servanthood. He said that he who would be the leader should be the servant of all. He never said to keep your wife barefoot, pregnant, and in the kitchen. The Word of God is the same yesterday, today and forever. It teaches that a man is supposed to love his wife as Christ loved the church.

Too many men read the verse about wives submitting to their husbands and misread it to say that a man has the right to subject his wife. It doesn't say that. The whole passage implies that if a man loves his wife in a godly, selfless, servant-like way, she will *want* to submit to his authority. I know that very word *authority* jars the feminist and she asks, "Why should any man be in authority over me?"

If a man exercised his authority in the way it is outlined in the Bible, a woman would not resent it. She would find herself served. She would find her needs met. She would have her say, be able to exercise her gifts, not be pushed back and ignored and treated like a second-class citizen. God's design for marriage is for husbands to love their wives as Christ loved the church and for wives to respect their husbands. Christ loved the church enough to die for it, and that kind of love is worthy of respect.

Additional Scripture Readings: Mark 10:35–45; John 13:1–17

Go to page 270 for your next devotional reading.

EPHESIANS 6

The Armor of God

10Finally, be strong in the Lord and in his mighty power. **11**Put on the full armor of God so that you can take your stand against the devil's schemes. **12**For our struggle is not against flesh and blood, but against the rulers, against the authorities, against the powers of this dark world and against the spiritual forces of evil in the heavenly realms. **13**Therefore put on the full armor of God, so that when the day of evil comes, you may be able to stand your ground, and after you have done everything, to stand. **14**Stand firm then, with the belt of truth buckled around your waist, with the breastplate of righteousness in place, **15**and with your feet fitted with the readiness that comes from the gospel of peace. **16**In addition to all this, take up the shield of faith, with which you can extinguish all the flaming arrows of the evil one. **17**Take the helmet of salvation and the sword of the Spirit, which is the word of God. **18**And pray in the Spirit on all occasions with all kinds of prayers and requests. With this in mind, be alert and always keep on praying for all the saints.

19Pray also for me, that whenever I open my mouth, words may be given me so that I will fearlessly make known the mystery of the gospel, **20**for which I am an ambassador in chains. Pray that I may declare it fearlessly, as I should.

Final Greetings

21Tychicus, the dear brother and faithful servant in the Lord, will tell you everything, so that you also may know how I

WEDNESDAY

VERSE FOR THE DAY:
Ephesians 6:4

AUTHOR:
Stephen Arterburn and David Stoop

PASSAGE FOR THE DAY:
Ephesians 6:1–4

Fathers Who Nurture

EXPERIENCE has shown us that the men who are happiest and most content in the masculine role today are those whose fathers invested a great deal of time and energy in their lives. These dads may have worked outside the home, as the vast majority of fathers in our society today do. But they were committed to maintaining a positive, nurturing relationship with their sons. These fathers supported their sons in their chosen careers, attempted to understand their ambitions (even when they differed from their own), and appreciated their achievements. As a result of their investment, their sons are among the most well-adjusted and peaceful husbands and fathers in our society.

However, men with these kinds of fathers are in the minority today. Most men are struggling to recover from relationships with fathers who failed to nurture, affirm and validate them at some level. These fathers have left their sons a legacy of pain, confusion, frustration, anxiety, bitterness, fear and anger. These adult sons are the angry men of our society.

Additional Scripture Readings:
Psalm 103:7–18;
1 Thessalonians 2:7–12

Go to page 273 for your next devotional reading.

am and what I am doing. ²²I am sending him to you for this very purpose, that you may know how we are, and that he may encourage you.

²³Peace to the brothers, and love with faith from God the Father and the Lord Jesus Christ. ²⁴Grace to all who love our Lord Jesus Christ with an undying love.

*P*AUL *writes this letter to the church he started in Philippi (Acts 16:11–40). Even though he is in prison, he feels happy when he thinks of what Christ means to him and of what the Philippians are doing for him. He gives some very practical advice on how to live the Christian life. As you read this book, remember always to rejoice in the Lord and to be content, whatever the circumstances.*

PHILIPPIANS

1 Paul and Timothy, servants of Christ Jesus,

To all the saints in Christ Jesus at Philippi, together with the overseers[a] and deacons:

2Grace and peace to you from God our Father and the Lord Jesus Christ.

Thanksgiving and Prayer

3I thank my God every time I remember you. **4**In all my prayers for all of you, I always pray with joy **5**because of your partnership in the gospel from the first day until now, **6**being confident of this, that he who began a good work in you will carry it on to completion until the day of Christ Jesus.

7It is right for me to feel this way about all of you, since I have you in my heart; for whether I am in chains or defending and confirming the gospel, all of you share in God's grace with me. **8**God can testify how I long for all of you with the affection of Christ Jesus.

9And this is my prayer: that your love may abound more and more in knowledge and depth of insight, **10**so that you may be able to discern what is best and may be pure and blameless until the day of Christ, **11**filled with the fruit of righteousness that

---

[a] 1 Traditionally *bishops*

comes through Jesus Christ — to the glory and praise of God.

Paul's Chains Advance the Gospel

12Now I want you to know, brothers, that what has happened to me has really served to advance the gospel. **13**As a result, it has become clear throughout the whole palace guard[a] and to everyone else that I am in chains for Christ. **14**Because of my chains, most of the brothers in the Lord have been encouraged to speak the word of God more courageously and fearlessly.

15It is true that some preach Christ out of envy and rivalry, but others out of goodwill. **16**The latter do so in love, knowing that I am put here for the defense of the gospel. **17**The former preach Christ out of selfish ambition, not sincerely, supposing that they can stir up trouble for me while I am in chains.[b] **18**But what does it matter? The important thing is that in every way, whether from false motives or

a13 Or *whole palace*   *b16,17* Some late manuscripts have verses 16 and 17 in reverse order.

THURSDAY

VERSE FOR THE DAY:
Philippians 1:21

AUTHOR:
Daniel Taylor

PASSAGE FOR THE DAY:
Philippians 1:18–26

Dying to Live

AH, PHYLLIS! . . .

Phyllis had had a tough life, partly of her own doing, and now she was laced with cancer, sleeping in a chair, wearing a wig and waiting to die . . .

Phyllis knew God. She had seen the first and the last, the beginning and the end. She knew who had made her, who had redeemed her, and who (her broken body notwithstanding) was ready to take her back to himself . . .

Phyllis had no money; she was divorced and living alone; she was in constant physical pain; her precious teenage daughter had been killed a few years earlier. It is very odd, by the world's standards, that this woman should be the most contented person I have ever known. Some people would say she had lost touch with reality in order to protect herself against its pain. I think, rather, she had gotten *in touch* with reality in a way that few of us ever do, and had seen its beauty.

So what does this say about dying? I don't know. Maybe it says that dying is one of the things that helps us know what living is. It says that dying hurts, both those who die and those who are left behind, who will die when their turn comes. It also suggests, however, that dying may be the beginning of something rather than the end . . .

We die because we have lived. We live in order to know and love the God who made us. In dying we become more real than we ever can be while part of this sorrowful world.

I will die someday, and so will you. And that is a good thing.

Additional Scripture Readings:
John 12:23–26; Romans 14:8–9

Go to page 275 for your next devotional reading.

true, Christ is preached. And because of this I rejoice.

Yes, and I will continue to rejoice, ¹⁹for I know that through your prayers and the help given by the Spirit of Jesus Christ, what has happened to me will turn out for my deliverance.ᵃ ²⁰I eagerly expect and hope that I will in no way be ashamed, but will have sufficient courage so that now as always Christ will be exalted in my body, whether by life or by death. ²¹For to me, to live is Christ and to die is gain. ²²If I am to go on living in the body, this will mean fruitful labor for me. Yet what shall I choose? I do not know! ²³I am torn between the two: I desire to depart and be with Christ, which is better by far; ²⁴but it is more necessary for you that I remain in the body. ²⁵Convinced of this, I know that I will remain, and I will continue with all of you for your progress and joy in the faith, ²⁶so that through my being with you again your joy in Christ Jesus will overflow on account of me.

²⁷Whatever happens, conduct yourselves in a manner worthy of the gospel of Christ. Then, whether I come and see you or only hear about you in my absence, I will know that you stand firm in one spirit, contending as one man for the faith of the gospel ²⁸without being frightened in any way by those who oppose you. This is a sign to them that they will be destroyed, but that you will be saved—and that by God. ²⁹For it has been granted to you on behalf of Christ not only to believe on him, but also to suffer for him, ³⁰since you are going through the same struggle you saw I had, and now hear that I still have.

Imitating Christ's Humility

2 If you have any encouragement from being united with Christ, if any comfort from his love, if any fellowship with the Spirit, if any tenderness and compassion, ²then make my joy complete by being like-minded, having the same love, being one in spirit and purpose. ³Do nothing out of selfish ambition or vain conceit, but in humility consider others better than yourselves. ⁴Each of you should look not only to your own interests, but also to the interests of others.

⁵Your attitude should be the same as that of Christ Jesus:

⁶Who, being in very natureᵇ God,
did not consider equality with God
   something to be grasped,
⁷but made himself nothing,
   taking the very natureᶜ of a
      servant,
   being made in human likeness.
⁸And being found in appearance as a
      man,
   he humbled himself
   and became obedient to death—
      even death on a cross!
⁹Therefore God exalted him to the
      highest place
   and gave him the name that is
      above every name,
¹⁰that at the name of Jesus every knee
      should bow,
   in heaven and on earth and under
      the earth,
¹¹and every tongue confess that Jesus
      Christ is Lord,
   to the glory of God the Father.

Shining as Stars

¹²Therefore, my dear friends, as you have always obeyed—not only in my presence, but now much more in my absence—continue to work out your salvation with fear and trembling, ¹³for it is God who works in you to will and to act according to his good purpose.

¹⁴Do everything without complaining or arguing, ¹⁵so that you may become blameless and pure, children of God without fault in a crooked and depraved generation, in which you shine like stars in the universe ¹⁶as you hold outᵈ the word of life—in order that I may boast on the day of Christ that I did not run or labor for nothing. ¹⁷But even if I am being poured out like a drink offering on the sacrifice and service coming from your faith, I am glad and rejoice with all of you. ¹⁸So you too should be glad and rejoice with me.

Timothy and Epaphroditus

¹⁹I hope in the Lord Jesus to send Timothy to you soon, that I also may be cheered when I receive news about you. ²⁰I have no one else like him, who takes a genuine interest in your welfare. ²¹For everyone looks out for his own interests, not those of Jesus Christ. ²²But you know that Timothy has proved himself, because as a son with his father he has served with me in the work of the gospel. ²³I hope, therefore, to send him as soon as I see how

---

ᵃ19 Or *salvation*   ᵇ6 Or *in the form of*   ᶜ7 Or *the form*   ᵈ16 Or *hold on to*

things go with me. **24**And I am confident in the Lord that I myself will come soon.

25But I think it is necessary to send back to you Epaphroditus, my brother, fellow worker and fellow soldier, who is also your messenger, whom you sent to take care of my needs. **26**For he longs for all of you and is distressed because you heard he was ill. **27**Indeed he was ill, and almost died. But God had mercy on him, and not on him only but also on me, to spare me sorrow upon sorrow. **28**Therefore I am all the more eager to send him, so that when you see him again you may be glad and I may have less anxiety. **29**Welcome him in the Lord with great joy, and honor men like him, **30**because he almost died for the work of Christ, risking his life to make up for the help you could not give me.

No Confidence in the Flesh

3 Finally, my brothers, rejoice in the Lord! It is no trouble for me to write

---

FRIDAY

VERSE FOR THE DAY:
Philippians 2:3

AUTHOR:
James Dobson

PASSAGE FOR THE DAY:
Philippians 2:1–11

Divine Perspective

TWO people are not compatible simply because they love each other and are both professing Christians. Many young couples assume that the sunshine and flowers that characterized their courtship will continue for the rest of their lives. No way, José. It is naive to expect two unique and strong-willed individuals to mesh together like a couple of machines. Even gears have multiple cogs with rough edges to be honed before they will work in concert.

That honing process usually occurs in the first year or two of marriage. The foundation for all that is to follow is laid in those critical months. What often occurs at this time is a dramatic struggle for power in the relationship. Who will lead? Who will follow? Who will determine how the money is spent? Who will get his or her way in times of disagreement? Everything is up for grabs in the beginning, and the way these early decisions are made will set the stage for the future.

Therein lies the danger. Abraham Lincoln said, "A house divided against itself cannot stand" [see Matthew 12:25]. If both partners come into the relationship prepared to battle in those first two years, the foundation will begin to crumble. The apostle Paul gave us the divine perspective on human relationships —not only in marriage but in every dimension of life. He wrote, "Do nothing out of selfish ambition or vain conceit, but in humility consider others better than yourselves" (Philippians 2:3).

That one verse contains more wisdom than most marriage manuals combined. If heeded, it could virtually eliminate divorce from the catalog of human experience.

Additional Scripture Readings:
Romans 12:9–13; 1 Peter 5:5–7

Go to page 276 for your next devotional reading.

WEEKENDING

RECEIVE

God has chosen to be closer to each of us than anyone else can be. He wants us to have an intimate personal relationship to him that allows us to enter into him and he into each of us. Many people who believe in Jesus have never come to know God that way. They have not grasped the wonder and ecstasy of being personally loved by God. They are impressed by his creative power, but they do not know that he lays aside the garments of his station and humbly presents himself in love . . .

For me, the good news is that the great One who is totally other and past finding out has humbled himself and presented himself to us not in power but in love.

– *Tony Campolo*

REVIVE
Saturday: John 13:1–17
Sunday: Philippians 2:1–11

Go to page 277 for your next devotional reading.

the same things to you again, and it is a safeguard for you.

2Watch out for those dogs, those men who do evil, those mutilators of the flesh. **3**For it is we who are the circumcision, we who worship by the Spirit of God, who glory in Christ Jesus, and who put no confidence in the flesh— **4**though I myself have reasons for such confidence.

If anyone else thinks he has reasons to put confidence in the flesh, I have more: **5**circumcised on the eighth day, of the people of Israel, of the tribe of Benjamin, a Hebrew of Hebrews; in regard to the law, a Pharisee; **6**as for zeal, persecuting the church; as for legalistic righteousness, faultless.

7But whatever was to my profit I now consider loss for the sake of Christ. **8**What is more, I consider everything a loss compared to the surpassing greatness of knowing Christ Jesus my Lord, for whose sake I have lost all things. I consider them rubbish, that I may gain Christ **9**and be found in him, not having a righteousness of my own that comes from the law, but that which is through faith in Christ—the righteousness that comes from God and is by faith. **10**I want to know Christ and the power of his resurrection and the fellow-

---

MONDAY

VERSE FOR THE DAY:
Philippians 3:14

AUTHOR:
Philip W. Williams

PASSAGE FOR THE DAY:
Philippians 3:12–16

Press On

IN CHRIST, life is intended to have purpose. Perhaps we all too easily become worshipers of life. We may make life itself into an idol. If all our marbles are in a basket called *life*, death may indeed be the unwanted, purposeless intruder. This is not to say we shouldn't "have life, and have it to the full" [John 10:10], as Jesus said. But to make anything, including life, into the "be all and end all," squeezes God out of the picture. It is our relationship with God in life that enables us to make sense out of seeming nonsense. Even when sense and purpose seem to escape us, we trust that one day we will understand. On that day we will come face to face with the author of life.

A courageous statement was made by a person who, in struggling to understand the death of his beloved, said, "I still do not see the purpose. I struggle, but I don't give up. Somehow I feel that in my very struggle with this I am choosing to say that there is meaning and purpose." Giving up may mean the quiet desperation of despair. There is wisdom in the search and struggle.

When Jesus met Martha, she said to him, "If you had been here, my brother would not have died." Jesus answered, "I am the resurrection and the life. He who believes in me will live, even though he dies; and whoever lives and believes in me will never die. Do you believe this?" [John 11:25–26].

Additional Scripture Readings:
2 Corinthians 4:7–18;
Colossians 3:1–4

Go to page 279 for your next devotional reading.

ship of sharing in his sufferings, becoming like him in his death, ⁱ¹and so, somehow, to attain to the resurrection from the dead.

Pressing on Toward the Goal

¹²Not that I have already obtained all this, or have already been made perfect, but I press on to take hold of that for which Christ Jesus took hold of me. ¹³Brothers, I do not consider myself yet to have taken hold of it. But one thing I do: Forgetting what is behind and straining toward what is ahead, ¹⁴I press on toward the goal to win the prize for which God has called me heavenward in Christ Jesus.

¹⁵All of us who are mature should take such a view of things. And if on some point you think differently, that too God will make clear to you. ¹⁶Only let us live up to what we have already attained.

¹⁷Join with others in following my example, brothers, and take note of those who live according to the pattern we gave you. ¹⁸For, as I have often told you before and now say again even with tears, many live as enemies of the cross of Christ. ¹⁹Their destiny is destruction, their god is their stomach, and their glory is in their shame. Their mind is on earthly things. ²⁰But our citizenship is in heaven. And we eagerly await a Savior from there, the Lord Jesus Christ, ²¹who, by the power that enables him to bring everything under his control, will transform our lowly bodies so that they will be like his glorious body.

4 Therefore, my brothers, you whom I love and long for, my joy and crown, that is how you should stand firm in the Lord, dear friends!

Exhortations

²I plead with Euodia and I plead with Syntyche to agree with each other in the Lord. ³Yes, and I ask you, loyal yokefellow,[a] help these women who have contended at my side in the cause of the gospel, along with Clement and the rest of my fellow workers, whose names are in the book of life.

⁴Rejoice in the Lord always. I will say it again: Rejoice! ⁵Let your gentleness be evident to all. The Lord is near. ⁶Do not be anxious about anything, but in everything, by prayer and petition, with thanksgiving, present your requests to God. ⁷And the peace of God, which transcends all understanding, will guard your hearts and your minds in Christ Jesus.

⁸Finally, brothers, whatever is true, whatever is noble, whatever is right, whatever is pure, whatever is lovely, whatever is admirable — if anything is excellent or praiseworthy — think about such things. ⁹Whatever you have learned or received or heard from me, or seen in me — put it into practice. And the God of peace will be with you.

Thanks for Their Gifts

¹⁰I rejoice greatly in the Lord that at last you have renewed your concern for me. Indeed, you have been concerned, but you had no opportunity to show it. ¹¹I am not saying this because I am in need, for I have learned to be content whatever the circumstances. ¹²I know what it is to be in need, and I know what it is to have plenty. I have learned the secret of being content in any and every situation, whether well fed or hungry, whether living in plenty or in want. ¹³I can do everything through him who gives me strength.

¹⁴Yet it was good of you to share in my troubles. ¹⁵Moreover, as you Philippians know, in the early days of your acquaintance with the gospel, when I set out from Macedonia, not one church shared with me in the matter of giving and receiving, except you only; ¹⁶for even when I was in Thessalonica, you sent me aid again and again when I was in need. ¹⁷Not that I am looking for a gift, but I am looking for what may be credited to your account. ¹⁸I have received full payment and even more; I am amply supplied, now that I have received from Epaphroditus the gifts you sent. They are a fragrant offering, an acceptable sacrifice, pleasing to God. ¹⁹And my God will meet all your needs according to his glorious riches in Christ Jesus.

²⁰To our God and Father be glory for ever and ever. Amen.

Final Greetings

²¹Greet all the saints in Christ Jesus. The brothers who are with me send greetings. ²²All the saints send you greetings, especially those who belong to Caesar's household.

²³The grace of the Lord Jesus Christ be with your spirit. Amen.[b]

---

[a]3 Or *loyal Syzygus*   [b]23 Some manuscripts do not have *Amen.*

TUESDAY

VERSE FOR THE DAY:
Philippians 4:6

AUTHOR:
Frederick Buechner

PASSAGE FOR THE DAY:
Philippians 4:2–9

Visions of the Worst

"DO NOT be anxious about anything," Paul writes to the Philippians. In one sense it is like telling a woman with a bad head cold not to sniffle and sneeze so much or a lame man to stop dragging his feet. Or maybe it is more like telling a wino to lay off the booze or a compulsive gambler to stay away from the track.

Is anxiety a disease or an addiction? Perhaps it is something of both. Partly, perhaps, because you can't help it, and partly because for some dark reason you choose not to help it, you torment yourself with detailed visions of the worst that can possibly happen. The nagging headache turns out to be a malignant brain tumor. When your teenage son fails to get off the plane you've gone to meet, you see his picture being tacked up in the post office among the missing and his disappearance never accounted for . . .

Does the terrible fear of disaster conceal an even more terrible hankering for it? Do the accelerated pulse and the knot in the stomach mean that beneath whatever their immediate cause, you are acting out some ancient and unresolved drama of childhood? . . .

But answer or no answer, the worst things will happen at last even so . . . Sorrow, loss, death await us all and everybody we love. Yet "The Lord is near. Do not be anxious about anything," Paul writes, who was evidently in prison at the time and with good reason to be anxious about everything, "but in everything, by prayer and petition, with thanksgiving, present your requests to God."

He does not deny that the worst things will happen finally to all of us, as indeed he must have had a strong suspicion they were soon to happen to him. He does not try to minimize them. He does not try to explain them away as God's will or God's judgment or God's method of testing our spiritual fiber. He simply tells the Philippians that in spite of them—even in the thick of them—they are to keep in constant touch with the One who unimaginably transcends the worst things as he also unimaginably transcends the best.

Additional Scripture Readings:
Matthew 6:25–31; Ephesians 3:14–21

Go to page 281 for your next devotional reading.

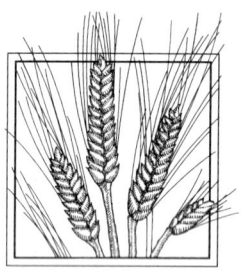

PAUL writes this letter to the church in Colosse at about the same time as he writes Ephesians. False teachers are deceiving some of those to whom he writes (Colossians 2:4). Therefore, Paul stresses the power and glory of Christ and instructs his readers on how to live as Christians. As you read this book, put your faith in this glorious Savior who died for you, and promise him that you will show Christian love and compassion to others.

COLOSSIANS

1 Paul, an apostle of Christ Jesus by the will of God, and Timothy our brother,

²To the holy and faithful*a* brothers in Christ at Colosse:

Grace and peace to you from God our Father.*b*

Thanksgiving and Prayer

³We always thank God, the Father of our Lord Jesus Christ, when we pray for you, ⁴because we have heard of your faith in Christ Jesus and of the love you have for all the saints — ⁵the faith and love that spring from the hope that is stored up for you in heaven and that you have already heard about in the word of truth, the gospel ⁶that has come to you. All over the world this gospel is bearing fruit and growing, just as it has been doing among you since the day you heard it and understood God's grace in all its truth. ⁷You learned it from Epaphras, our dear fellow servant, who is a faithful minister of Christ on our*c* behalf, ⁸and who also told us of your love in the Spirit.

⁹For this reason, since the day we heard about you, we have not stopped praying for you and asking God to fill you with the knowledge of his will through all spiritual

---

*a*2 Or *believing*   *b*2 Some manuscripts *Father and the Lord Jesus Christ*   *c*7 Some manuscripts *your*

wisdom and understanding. **10**And we pray this in order that you may live a life worthy of the Lord and may please him in every way: bearing fruit in every good work, growing in the knowledge of God, **11**being strengthened with all power according to his glorious might so that you may have great endurance and patience, and joyfully **12**giving thanks to the Father, who has qualified you[a] to share in the inheritance of the saints in the kingdom of light. **13**For he has rescued us from the dominion of darkness and brought us into the kingdom of the Son he loves, **14**in whom we have redemption,[b] the forgiveness of sins.

[a]12 Some manuscripts *us*   [b]14 A few late manuscripts *redemption through his blood*

WEDNESDAY

VERSE FOR THE DAY:
Colossians 2:6

AUTHOR:
John Fischer

PASSAGE FOR THE DAY:
Colossians 2:6–12

The Hourglass of Life

JESUS never closes a mind; he opens it. Jesus is never threatened by a question; he welcomes it. He knows all questions will ultimately end up with him, so fire away!

Jesus is the answer, and when he walks through a question, he always leaves the door open so anyone can get to it from either side. Modern Christians keep wanting to shut the door (once they've passed through, of course).

For many Christians, the experience of truth has been a narrowing experience, and in one sense this is right. All those questions—religions, sins, frustrations, explorations—finally ended up with Jesus. Like following the inside of a cone, all experiences funneled to a point, and at that point was Jesus on the cross for my sin.

The error, however, is when we stop here and move no further. For our experience of truth to grow, we must move through the cross back out into the same reality—the same questions, the same world—with a different perspective.

It's like an hourglass with the cross at the center. All my preconversion experiences narrowed me toward a personal encounter with Christ; but once through, he leads me back out into the world I came from where the lines now, instead of converging, open up into an ever-widening reality. The sands of truth always move this way—in toward the center and out again.

Yes, Jesus is the answer, and it's precisely *because* he is the answer that we can venture out. Because he is Lord of all, we can walk into all and find him Lord. This is not only a privilege, it's a mandate. It's what Christians are called to do in the world.

Additional Scripture Readings:
Romans 12:1–2;
2 Corinthians 3:12—4:6

Go to page 283 for your next devotional reading.

The Supremacy of Christ

15He is the image of the invisible God, the firstborn over all creation. **16**For by him all things were created: things in heaven and on earth, visible and invisible, whether thrones or powers or rulers or authorities; all things were created by him and for him. **17**He is before all things, and in him all things hold together. **18**And he is the head of the body, the church; he is the beginning and the firstborn from among the dead, so that in everything he might have the supremacy. **19**For God was pleased to have all his fullness dwell in him, **20**and through him to reconcile to himself all things, whether things on earth or things in heaven, by making peace through his blood, shed on the cross.

21Once you were alienated from God and were enemies in your minds because of*a* your evil behavior. **22**But now he has reconciled you by Christ's physical body through death to present you holy in his sight, without blemish and free from accusation— **23**if you continue in your faith, established and firm, not moved from the hope held out in the gospel. This is the gospel that you heard and that has been proclaimed to every creature under heaven, and of which I, Paul, have become a servant.

Paul's Labor for the Church

24Now I rejoice in what was suffered for you, and I fill up in my flesh what is still lacking in regard to Christ's afflictions, for the sake of his body, which is the church. **25**I have become its servant by the commission God gave me to present to you the word of God in its fullness— **26**the mystery that has been kept hidden for ages and generations, but is now disclosed to the saints. **27**To them God has chosen to make known among the Gentiles the glorious riches of this mystery, which is Christ in you, the hope of glory.

28We proclaim him, admonishing and teaching everyone with all wisdom, so that we may present everyone perfect in Christ. **29**To this end I labor, struggling with all his energy, which so powerfully works in me.

2 I want you to know how much I am struggling for you and for those at Laodicea, and for all who have not met me personally. **2**My purpose is that they may be encouraged in heart and united in love, so that they may have the full riches of complete understanding, in order that they may know the mystery of God, namely, Christ, **3**in whom are hidden all the treasures of wisdom and knowledge. **4**I tell you this so that no one may deceive you by fine-sounding arguments. **5**For though I am absent from you in body, I am present with you in spirit and delight to see how orderly you are and how firm your faith in Christ is.

Freedom From Human Regulations Through Life With Christ

6So then, just as you received Christ Jesus as Lord, continue to live in him, **7**rooted and built up in him, strengthened in the faith as you were taught, and overflowing with thankfulness.

8See to it that no one takes you captive through hollow and deceptive philosophy, which depends on human tradition and the basic principles of this world rather than on Christ.

9For in Christ all the fullness of the Deity lives in bodily form, **10**and you have been given fullness in Christ, who is the head over every power and authority. **11**In him you were also circumcised, in the putting off of the sinful nature,*b* not with a circumcision done by the hands of men but with the circumcision done by Christ, **12**having been buried with him in baptism and raised with him through your faith in the power of God, who raised him from the dead.

13When you were dead in your sins and in the uncircumcision of your sinful nature,*c* God made you*d* alive with Christ. He forgave us all our sins, **14**having canceled the written code, with its regulations, that was against us and that stood opposed to us; he took it away, nailing it to the cross. **15**And having disarmed the powers and authorities, he made a public spectacle of them, triumphing over them by the cross.*e*

16Therefore do not let anyone judge you by what you eat or drink, or with regard to a religious festival, a New Moon celebration or a Sabbath day. **17**These are a shadow of the things that were to come; the reality, however, is found in Christ. **18**Do

---

*a*21 Or *minds, as shown by*   *b*11 Or *the flesh*   *c*13 Or *your flesh*   *d*13 Some manuscripts *us*
*e*15 Or *them in him*

not let anyone who delights in false humility and the worship of angels disqualify you for the prize. Such a person goes into great detail about what he has seen, and his unspiritual mind puffs him up with idle notions. [19]He has lost connection with the Head, from whom the whole body, supported and held together by its ligaments and sinews, grows as God causes it to grow.

[20]Since you died with Christ to the basic principles of this world, why, as though you still belonged to it, do you submit to its rules: [21]"Do not handle! Do not taste! Do not touch!"? [22]These are all destined to perish with use, because they are based

---

THURSDAY

VERSE FOR THE DAY:
Colossians 3:5

AUTHOR:
Charles Swindoll

PASSAGE FOR THE DAY:
Colossians 3:5–11

Lust Is Lurking

I THINK of the gentleman I met several years ago—a fine itinerant Bible teacher. He said he had been keeping a confidential list of men who were once outstanding expositors of the Scripture, capable and respected men of God . . . who have shipwrecked their faith on the shoals of moral defilement. During the previous week, he said, he had entered the name of *number forty-two* in his book. This sad, sordid statistic, he claims, caused him to be extra cautious and discreet in his own life. Perhaps, by now, he has added a couple dozen more.

A chill ran down my spine when he told that story. No one is immune. You're not. I'm not. Lust is no respecter of persons . . . Its alluring voice can infiltrate the most intelligent mind and cause its victim to believe its lies and respond to its appeal. And beware—it never gives up . . . it never runs out of ideas. Bolt your front door and it'll rattle at the bedroom window, crawl into the living room through the TV screen, or wink at you out of a magazine in the den . . .

Lust is persistent. If it's knocked on your door once, it'll knock again. And again. You are safe just so long as you draw upon your Savior's strength. Try to handle it yourself and you'll lose—every time. This is why we are warned again and again in the New Testament to *flee* sexual temptations. Remember, lust is committed to wage *war* against your soul—in a life-and-death struggle—in hand-to-hand combat. Don't stand before this mortal enemy and argue or fight in your own strength—run for cover . . . If you get yourself into a situation that leaves you defenseless and weak, if your door is left even slightly ajar, you may be sure that this ancient enemy will kick it open with six-guns blazing. So don't leave it open. Don't give lust a foothold—or even a toehold.

Additional Scripture Readings:
1 Corinthians 6:12–20;
1 Thessalonians 4:3–8

Go to page 284 for your next devotional reading.

on human commands and teachings. ²³Such regulations indeed have an appearance of wisdom, with their self-imposed worship, their false humility and their harsh treatment of the body, but they lack any value in restraining sensual indulgence.

Rules for Holy Living

3 Since, then, you have been raised with Christ, set your hearts on things above, where Christ is seated at the right hand of God. ²Set your minds on things above, not on earthly things. ³For you died, and your life is now hidden

---

FRIDAY

VERSE FOR THE DAY:
Colossians 3:14

AUTHOR:
G.R. Slater

PASSAGE FOR THE DAY:
Colossians 3:12–14

Great Expectations

WE ARE seeking too much from marriage today. Life has become impersonal. Our circle of friends changes often, and there are few long-time friendships. The family has cut itself adrift from formerly close kinship bonds. Now all the closeness and intimacy previously shared in these other ways among many people is being focused on one person, and the whole load is placed on one pair of shoulders—the husband's or the wife's. It is only realistic to recognize the strain that this excessive closeness and extreme demand places upon both husband and wife. One cannot be expected to be mate, brother, father, friend and psychiatrist all rolled up in one . . .

Conflict can be creative, and the love which is "patient and kind" is able to embrace tensions creatively in at least two ways:

First, it makes possible an openness and honesty about one's disappointments. Often a person feels that his faith forbids him to be honest or critical with his mate, but you owe it to your marriage partner to let her know how you feel. Such openness, within the setting of love and acceptance, can be the basis of a new beginning and partnership at a deeper level . . .

Second, this love that is at liberty to be realistic calls us to recognize that marriage is something that must be worked out. It is not like a coat that is put on, but like a flower that grows. As one elderly lady testified, "Love is what you go through together." It is the recognition, therefore, that you have some needs which are not going to be met by the other person, and that there are some things upon which you will never totally agree. Realism demands patience and a willingness to adjust. The art of marriage, it has been said, is in maintaining equilibrium through the various changes and adjustments of life together.

Additional Scripture Readings:
1 Corinthians 13:1–13;
Ephesians 5:21–33

Go to page 286 for your next devotional reading.

with Christ in God. ⁴When Christ, who is your[a] life, appears, then you also will appear with him in glory.

⁵Put to death, therefore, whatever belongs to your earthly nature: sexual immorality, impurity, lust, evil desires and greed, which is idolatry. ⁶Because of these, the wrath of God is coming.[b] ⁷You used to walk in these ways, in the life you once lived. ⁸But now you must rid yourselves of all such things as these: anger, rage, malice, slander, and filthy language from your lips. ⁹Do not lie to each other, since you have taken off your old self with its practices ¹⁰and have put on the new self, which is being renewed in knowledge in the image of its Creator. ¹¹Here there is no Greek or Jew, circumcised or uncircumcised, barbarian, Scythian, slave or free, but Christ is all, and is in all.

¹²Therefore, as God's chosen people, holy and dearly loved, clothe yourselves with compassion, kindness, humility, gentleness and patience. ¹³Bear with each other and forgive whatever grievances you may have against one another. Forgive as the Lord forgave you. ¹⁴And over all these virtues put on love, which binds them all together in perfect unity.

¹⁵Let the peace of Christ rule in your hearts, since as members of one body you were called to peace. And be thankful. ¹⁶Let the word of Christ dwell in you richly as you teach and admonish one another with all wisdom, and as you sing psalms, hymns and spiritual songs with gratitude in your hearts to God. ¹⁷And whatever you do, whether in word or deed, do it all in the name of the Lord Jesus, giving thanks to God the Father through him.

Rules for Christian Households

¹⁸Wives, submit to your husbands, as is fitting in the Lord.

¹⁹Husbands, love your wives and do not be harsh with them.

²⁰Children, obey your parents in everything, for this pleases the Lord.

²¹Fathers, do not embitter your children, or they will become discouraged.

²²Slaves, obey your earthly masters in everything; and do it, not only when their eye is on you and to win their favor, but with sincerity of heart and reverence for the Lord. ²³Whatever you do, work at it with all your heart, as working for the Lord, not for men, ²⁴since you know that you will receive an inheritance from the Lord as a reward. It is the Lord Christ you are serving. ²⁵Anyone who does wrong will be repaid for his wrong, and there is no favoritism.

4 Masters, provide your slaves with what is right and fair, because you know that you also have a Master in heaven.

Further Instructions

²Devote yourselves to prayer, being watchful and thankful. ³And pray for us, too, that God may open a door for our message, so that we may proclaim the mystery of Christ, for which I am in chains. ⁴Pray that I may proclaim it clearly, as I should. ⁵Be wise in the way you act toward outsiders; make the most of every opportunity. ⁶Let your conversation be always full of grace, seasoned with salt, so that you may know how to answer everyone.

Final Greetings

⁷Tychicus will tell you all the news about me. He is a dear brother, a faithful minister and fellow servant in the Lord. ⁸I am sending him to you for the express purpose that you may know about our[c] circumstances and that he may encourage your hearts. ⁹He is coming with Onesimus, our faithful and dear brother, who is one of you. They will tell you everything that is happening here.

¹⁰My fellow prisoner Aristarchus sends you his greetings, as does Mark, the cousin of Barnabas. (You have received instructions about him; if he comes to you, welcome him.) ¹¹Jesus, who is called Justus, also sends greetings. These are the only Jews among my fellow workers for the kingdom of God, and they have proved a comfort to me. ¹²Epaphras, who is one of you and a servant of Christ Jesus, sends greetings. He is always wrestling in prayer for you, that you may stand firm in all the will of God, mature and fully assured. ¹³I vouch for him that he is working hard for you and for those at Laodicea and Hierapolis. ¹⁴Our dear friend Luke, the doctor, and Demas send greetings. ¹⁵Give my greetings to the brothers at Laodicea, and to Nympha and the church in her house.

---

[a] 4 Some manuscripts *our* [b] 6 Some early manuscripts *coming on those who are disobedient*
[c] 8 Some manuscripts *that he may know about your*

WEEKENDING

REFLECT

The magic of a thankful spirit is that it has the power to replace anger with love, resentment with happiness, fear with faith, worry with peace, the desire to dominate with the wish to play on a team, self-preoccupation with concern for the needs of others, guilt with an open door to forgiveness, sexual impurity with honor and respect, jealousy with joy at another's success, lack of creativity with inspired productivity, inferiorities with dignity, a lack of love with an abundance of self-sharing.

– Donald E. Demaray

REVIVE
Saturday: Psalm 100
Sunday: Colossians 3:15–17

Go to page 287 for your next devotional reading.

¹⁶After this letter has been read to you, see that it is also read in the church of the Laodiceans and that you in turn read the letter from Laodicea.

¹⁷Tell Archippus: "See to it that you complete the work you have received in the Lord."

¹⁸I, Paul, write this greeting in my own hand. Remember my chains. Grace be with you.

MONDAY

VERSE FOR THE DAY:
Colossians 4:3

AUTHOR:
Reggie White

PASSAGE FOR THE DAY:
Colossians 4:2–6

An Open Door

WE ARE walking witnesses for Jesus Christ wherever we go. How can we do less than witness with all our heart. Our styles may be different, but the intensity shouldn't be. I know all Christians can't do it in the same manner as I do, but I have no choice but to do it with all my heart.

A.C. Green is a Christian brother who plays for the Los Angeles Lakers basketball team. He told me that a reporter once asked him how a Christian could play a game like NBA basketball, a game with so much physical contact. A.C.'s response was that his life on the basketball court is the same as his life off the hardwood. He's going to be aggressive and give it all he's got both on and off the court—on, to win the game for his team; off, to win people for Christ.

God has given me an incredible platform as an NFL professional football player. The reason I'm in Philadelphia today is that that's exactly where God wants me to serve him right now. And any time I have a chance to proclaim Jesus Christ as Lord, I'm going to do it. Period!

Additional Scripture Readings:
Matthew 28:16–20; 1 Peter 3:13–16

Go to page 289 for your next devotional reading.

*P*AUL *writes this letter to the church he began in Thessalonica (Acts 17:1–9), shortly after leaving them and being unable to return (1 Thessalonians 2:17–18). He is excited about their Christian faith, reminds them of his intense love for them, and answers questions about what death means for a Christian. As you read this book, find comfort as a believer that when you die you will still be under God's care and will "be with the Lord forever" (1 Thessalonians 4:17).*

1 THESSALONIANS

1 Paul, Silas[a] and Timothy,

To the church of the Thessalonians in God the Father and the Lord Jesus Christ:

Grace and peace to you.[b]

Thanksgiving for the Thessalonians' Faith

2We always thank God for all of you, mentioning you in our prayers. **3**We continually remember before our God and Father your work produced by faith, your labor prompted by love, and your endurance inspired by hope in our Lord Jesus Christ.

4For we know, brothers loved by God, that he has chosen you, **5**because our gospel came to you not simply with words, but also with power, with the Holy Spirit and with deep conviction. You know how we lived among you for your sake. **6**You became imitators of us and of the Lord; in

---

[a] 1 Greek *Silvanus*, a variant of *Silas* [b] 1 Some early manuscripts *you from God our Father and the Lord Jesus Christ*

spite of severe suffering, you welcomed the message with the joy given by the Holy Spirit. ⁷And so you became a model to all the believers in Macedonia and Achaia. ⁸The Lord's message rang out from you not only in Macedonia and Achaia—your faith in God has become known everywhere. Therefore we do not need to say anything about it, ⁹for they themselves report what kind of reception you gave us. They tell how you turned to God from idols to serve the living and true God, ¹⁰and to wait for his Son from heaven, whom he raised from the dead—Jesus, who rescues us from the coming wrath.

Paul's Ministry in Thessalonica

2 You know, brothers, that our visit to you was not a failure. ²We had previously suffered and been insulted in Philippi, as you know, but with the help of our God we dared to tell you his gospel in spite of strong opposition. ³For the appeal we make does not spring from error or impure motives, nor are we trying to trick you. ⁴On the contrary, we speak as men approved by God to be entrusted with the gospel. We are not trying to please men but God, who tests our hearts. ⁵You know we never used flattery, nor did we put on a mask to cover up greed—God is our witness. ⁶We were not looking for praise

TUESDAY

VERSE FOR THE DAY:
1 Thessalonians 1:6

AUTHOR:
Mike Singletary

PASSAGE FOR THE DAY:
1 Thessalonians 1:2–10

Set Them an Example

I DON'T mind being a role model. I'm flattered when people say they'd like their kids to be like me. To me, being a role model is a heavy responsibility and a gift from God. I accept it openheartedly. But at the same time, I don't feel I should become more important in a kid's life than his father and mother. Very few kids ever actually emulate their heroes. They do what their parents did. Parents are the most important role models in their children's lives, for good or bad.

I may be signing autographs somewhere and a single mom will come up with her son. She'll say, "I'm so glad he got to meet you because you're his hero, and he'll do what you say. If you tell him to listen to his mother and do what I tell him, he'll do it."

That's sad. I often give them both a little encouragement, but I'd rather that kid know that I'm human too. I came from a broken home too. I knew what it was to be disappointed in my father and to be raised by my mother. That mom has the toughest job because she will serve as both the father and the mother role model for that child. He may admire me and look up to me or some other celebrity, but when the chips are down, he'll pattern his life after his parents. If we've got a role model crisis in this country, it's because parents are not good ones.

Additional Scripture Readings:
Philippians 3:17—4:1; Titus 2:6–8

Go to page 291 for your next devotional reading.

from men, not from you or anyone else. As apostles of Christ we could have been a burden to you, ⁷but we were gentle among you, like a mother caring for her little children. ⁸We loved you so much that we were delighted to share with you not only the gospel of God but our lives as well, because you had become so dear to us. ⁹Surely you remember, brothers, our toil and hardship; we worked night and day in order not to be a burden to anyone while we preached the gospel of God to you.

¹⁰You are witnesses, and so is God, of how holy, righteous and blameless we were among you who believed. ¹¹For you know that we dealt with each of you as a father deals with his own children, ¹²encouraging, comforting and urging you to live lives worthy of God, who calls you into his kingdom and glory.

¹³And we also thank God continually because, when you received the word of God, which you heard from us, you accepted it not as the word of men, but as it actually is, the word of God, which is at work in you who believe. ¹⁴For you, brothers, became imitators of God's churches in Judea, which are in Christ Jesus: You suffered from your own countrymen the same things those churches suffered from the Jews, ¹⁵who killed the Lord Jesus and the prophets and also drove us out. They displease God and are hostile to all men ¹⁶in their effort to keep us from speaking to the Gentiles so that they may be saved. In this way they always heap up their sins to the limit. The wrath of God has come upon them at last.*ᵃ*

Paul's Longing to See the Thessalonians

¹⁷But, brothers, when we were torn away from you for a short time (in person, not in thought), out of our intense longing we made every effort to see you. ¹⁸For we wanted to come to you—certainly I, Paul, did, again and again—but Satan stopped us. ¹⁹For what is our hope, our joy, or the crown in which we will glory in the presence of our Lord Jesus when he comes? Is it not you? ²⁰Indeed, you are our glory and joy.

3 So when we could stand it no longer, we thought it best to be left by ourselves in Athens. ²We sent Timothy, who is our brother and God's fellow worker*ᵇ* in spreading the gospel of Christ, to strengthen and encourage you in your faith, ³so that no one would be unsettled by these trials. You know quite well that we were destined for them. ⁴In fact, when we were with you, we kept telling you that we would be persecuted. And it turned out that way, as you well know. ⁵For this reason, when I could stand it no longer, I sent to find out about your faith. I was afraid that in some way the tempter might have tempted you and our efforts might have been useless.

Timothy's Encouraging Report

⁶But Timothy has just now come to us from you and has brought good news about your faith and love. He has told us that you always have pleasant memories of us and that you long to see us, just as we also long to see you. ⁷Therefore, brothers, in all our distress and persecution we were encouraged about you because of your faith. ⁸For now we really live, since you are standing firm in the Lord. ⁹How can we thank God enough for you in return for all the joy we have in the presence of our God because of you? ¹⁰Night and day we pray most earnestly that we may see you again and supply what is lacking in your faith.

¹¹Now may our God and Father himself and our Lord Jesus clear the way for us to come to you. ¹²May the Lord make your love increase and overflow for each other and for everyone else, just as ours does for you. ¹³May he strengthen your hearts so that you will be blameless and holy in the presence of our God and Father when our Lord Jesus comes with all his holy ones.

Living to Please God

4 Finally, brothers, we instructed you how to live in order to please God, as in fact you are living. Now we ask you and urge you in the Lord Jesus to do this more and more. ²For you know what instructions we gave you by the authority of the Lord Jesus.

³It is God's will that you should be sanctified: that you should avoid sexual immorality; ⁴that each of you should learn to control his own body*ᶜ* in a way that is holy and honorable, ⁵not in passionate lust like the heathen, who do not know

---

*ᵃ*16 Or *them fully* *ᵇ*2 Some manuscripts *brother and fellow worker*; other manuscripts *brother and God's servant* *ᶜ*4 Or *learn to live with his own wife*; or *learn to acquire a wife*

God; **6**and that in this matter no one should wrong his brother or take advantage of him. The Lord will punish men for all such sins, as we have already told you and warned you. **7**For God did not call us to be impure, but to live a holy life. **8**Therefore, he who rejects this instruction does not reject man but God, who gives you his Holy Spirit.

9Now about brotherly love we do not need to write to you, for you yourselves have been taught by God to love each other. **10**And in fact, you do love all the brothers throughout Macedonia. Yet we urge you, brothers, to do so more and more. **11**Make it your ambition to lead a quiet life, to mind your own business and to work with your hands, just as we told you, **12**so that your daily life may win the respect of outsiders and so that you will not be dependent on anybody.

The Coming of the Lord

13Brothers, we do not want you to be ignorant about those who fall asleep, or to grieve like the rest of men, who have no hope. **14**We believe that Jesus died and rose again and so we believe that God will

---

WEDNESDAY

VERSE FOR THE DAY:
1 Thessalonians 4:3

AUTHOR:
James Dobson

PASSAGE FOR THE DAY:
1 Thessalonians 4:3–8

A "New" Recipe

EVEN those outside the Christian faith are now agreeing that the sexual revolution was an unmitigated disaster. As it turns out, abstinence before marriage, and lifelong fidelity were pretty good ideas after all. Some sociologists are all rediscovering the benefits of sexual restraint—as though they had stumbled onto a brand new concept . . .

What I am recommending to my unmarried readers is this: *stay out of bed unless you go there alone*! Not only is virginity the only way to avoid disease, it is also the best foundation for a healthy marriage. That's the way the system was designed by the Creator and no one has yet devised a way to improve on his plan. We are sexual creatures, both physically and psychologically. Our very identity ("Who am I?") begins with gender assignment and the implications of masculinity versus femininity. Virtually every aspect of life is influenced by this biological foundation. Who can deny the hormonal and reproductive forces that shape the way we think and behave? Given this nature and the vast significance it carries, even an atheist should have recognized the dangers of the sexual revolution and the changes it portended. Any upheaval of such proportion was certain to have far-reaching consequences for the stability of the family. How could we have *expected* to preserve symbiotic relationships between men and women when the rules governing our sexual behavior turned upside down? Family disintegration was inevitable.

Additional Scripture Readings:
1 Corinthians 6:12–20;
Colossians 3:5–11

Go to page 292 for your next devotional reading.

bring with Jesus those who have fallen asleep in him. ¹⁵According to the Lord's own word, we tell you that we who are still alive, who are left till the coming of the Lord, will certainly not precede those who have fallen asleep. ¹⁶For the Lord himself will come down from heaven, with a loud command, with the voice of the archangel and with the trumpet call of God, and the dead in Christ will rise first. ¹⁷After that, we who are still alive and are left will be caught up together with them in the clouds to meet the Lord in the air. And so we will be with the Lord forever. ¹⁸Therefore encourage each other with these words.

5 Now, brothers, about times and dates we do not need to write to you, ²for you know very well that the day of the Lord will come like a thief in the night. ³While people are saying, "Peace and safety," destruction will come on them sud-

THURSDAY

VERSE FOR THE DAY:
1 Thessalonians 5:17

AUTHOR:
Daniel Taylor

PASSAGE FOR THE DAY:
1 Thessalonians 5:16–18

Prayer Matters to God

DOES prayer "work"? Julie Taylor asked, and her father replied:

How does God decide what to do when we ask him for something? Does it really do any good to ask? Isn't he going to do whatever he wants anyway?

The short answer is, we don't know—or at least I don't. God didn't tell us how these things work. But he has told us one very important thing—we *are* supposed to pray. He says it *does* matter. He says, "Tell me what you want, how you feel. I want to know. I want to hear it from you. It matters to me."

And if God says to do something, it has always been my experience that the best thing is to do it. I have a guess as to why maybe God hasn't told us how this works. (This is only a guess.) I think maybe if we knew how it worked we would stop *talking*. If we thought we had it worked out how prayer got answered, we would keep asking, even demanding, but would stop really talking. We'd put in our orders, you might say, and not really talk with the One who made us. We do that quite a bit even as it is.

So why when we prayed for [our friend] Mr. Cuendet did he get well, but when we prayed for Uncle Clinton, God took him to heaven instead? I don't know. God never promised to tell me why everything happens the way it does. But he did promise me that anytime I wanted to talk, he would be happy to listen. And in a world where so many people feel they are all alone, that's a pretty great thing to know.

One more thing. God not only listens, he talks too. So when you are praying, *keep your ears open!*

Additional Scripture Readings:
Luke 18:1–8; Philippians 4:4–9

Go to page 295 for your next devotional reading.

denly, as labor pains on a pregnant woman, and they will not escape.

⁴But you, brothers, are not in darkness so that this day should surprise you like a thief. ⁵You are all sons of the light and sons of the day. We do not belong to the night or to the darkness. ⁶So then, let us not be like others, who are asleep, but let us be alert and self-controlled. ⁷For those who sleep, sleep at night, and those who get drunk, get drunk at night. ⁸But since we belong to the day, let us be self-controlled, putting on faith and love as a breastplate, and the hope of salvation as a helmet. ⁹For God did not appoint us to suffer wrath but to receive salvation through our Lord Jesus Christ. ¹⁰He died for us so that, whether we are awake or asleep, we may live together with him. ¹¹Therefore encourage one another and build each other up, just as in fact you are doing.

Final Instructions

¹²Now we ask you, brothers, to respect those who work hard among you, who are over you in the Lord and who admonish you. ¹³Hold them in the highest regard in love because of their work. Live in peace with each other. ¹⁴And we urge you, brothers, warn those who are idle, encourage the timid, help the weak, be patient with everyone. ¹⁵Make sure that nobody pays back wrong for wrong, but always try to be kind to each other and to everyone else.

¹⁶Be joyful always; ¹⁷pray continually; ¹⁸give thanks in all circumstances, for this is God's will for you in Christ Jesus.

¹⁹Do not put out the Spirit's fire; ²⁰do not treat prophecies with contempt. ²¹Test everything. Hold on to the good. ²²Avoid every kind of evil.

²³May God himself, the God of peace, sanctify you through and through. May your whole spirit, soul and body be kept blameless at the coming of our Lord Jesus Christ. ²⁴The one who calls you is faithful and he will do it.

²⁵Brothers, pray for us. ²⁶Greet all the brothers with a holy kiss. ²⁷I charge you before the Lord to have this letter read to all the brothers.

²⁸The grace of our Lord Jesus Christ be with you.

*P*AUL *writes this letter shortly after 1 Thessalonians to clarify some things that the church failed to understand in his first letter. He tells them that the antichrist is coming, but they must continue with their regular schedules until Jesus returns. As you read this book, remember that God wants you to look forward to Christ's return as well as to continue doing your daily work.*

2 THESSALONIANS

1 Paul, Silas*a* and Timothy,

To the church of the Thessalonians in God our Father and the Lord Jesus Christ:

2Grace and peace to you from God the Father and the Lord Jesus Christ.

Thanksgiving and Prayer

3We ought always to thank God for you, brothers, and rightly so, because your faith is growing more and more, and the love every one of you has for each other is increasing. **4**Therefore, among God's churches we boast about your perseverance and faith in all the persecutions and trials you are enduring.

5All this is evidence that God's judgment is right, and as a result you will be counted worthy of the kingdom of God, for which you are suffering. **6**God is just: He will pay back trouble to those who trouble you **7**and give relief to you who are troubled, and to us as well. This will happen when the Lord Jesus is revealed from heaven in blazing fire with his powerful angels. **8**He will punish those who do not know God and do not obey the gospel of our Lord Jesus. **9**They will be punished with everlasting destruction and shut out from the presence of the Lord and from the majesty of his power **10**on the day he comes to be glorified in his holy people and to be marveled at among all those who have believed. This includes you, because you believed our testimony to you.

11With this in mind, we constantly pray

---

a 1 Greek *Silvanus*, a variant of *Silas*

for you, that our God may count you worthy of his calling, and that by his power he may fulfill every good purpose of yours and every act prompted by your faith. **12**We pray this so that the name of our Lord Jesus may be glorified in you, and you in him, according to the grace of our God and the Lord Jesus Christ.*a*

The Man of Lawlessness

2 Concerning the coming of our Lord Jesus Christ and our being gathered to him, we ask you, brothers, **2**not to become easily unsettled or alarmed by some prophecy, report or letter supposed to have come from us, saying that the day of the Lord has already come. **3**Don't let anyone deceive you in any way, for that day will not come, until the rebellion occurs and the man of lawlessness*b* is revealed, the man doomed to destruction. **4**He will oppose and will exalt himself over everything that is called God or is worshiped, so that he sets himself up in God's temple, proclaiming himself to be God.

5Don't you remember that when I was with you I used to tell you these things? **6**And now you know what is holding him back, so that he may be revealed at the proper time. **7**For the secret power of lawlessness is already at work; but the one who now holds it back will continue to do

a12 Or *God and Lord, Jesus Christ*   *b3* Some manuscripts *sin*

FRIDAY

VERSE FOR THE DAY:
2 Thessalonians 1:11

AUTHOR:
Frederick Buechner

PASSAGE FOR THE DAY:
2 Thessalonians 1:3–12

All Sorts of Voices

IN THE year that King Uzziah died [see Isaiah 6], or in the year that John F. Kennedy died, or in the year that somebody you loved died, you go into the temple if that is your taste, or you hide your face in the little padded temple of your hands, and a voice says, "Whom shall I send into the pain of a world where people die?" and if you are not careful, you may find yourself answering, "Send me." You may hear the voice say, "Go." Just *go*.

Like "duty," "law," "religion," the word "vocation" has a dull ring to it, but in terms of what it means, it is really not dull at all. *Vocare*, to call, of course, and a man's vocation is a man's calling. It is the work that he is called to in this world, the thing that he is summoned to spend his life doing. We can speak of a man's choosing his vocation, but perhaps it is at least as accurate to speak of a vocation's choosing the man, of a call's being given and a man's hearing it, or not hearing it. And maybe that is the place to start: the business of listening and hearing. A man's life is full of all sorts of voices calling him in all sorts of directions. Some of them are voices from inside and some of them are voices from outside. The more alive and alert we are, the more clamorous our lives are. Which do we listen to? What kind of voice do we listen for?

Additional Scripture Readings:
Acts 26:12–20; James 1:19–27

Go to page 296 for your next devotional reading.

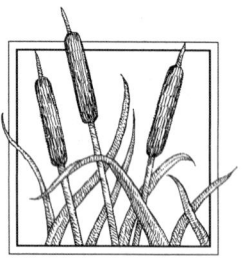

Weekending

RECALL

To believe in Christ's rising and death's dying is also to live with the power and the challenge to rise up now from all our dark graves of suffering love. If sympathy for the world's wounds is not enlarged by our anguish, if love for those around us is not expanded, if gratitude for what is good does not flame up, if insight is not deepened, if commitment to what is important is not strengthened, if aching for a new day is not intensified, if hope is weakened and faith diminished, if from the experience of death comes nothing good, then death has won. Then death, be proud.

So I shall struggle to live the reality of Christ's rising and death's dying. In my living, my son's dying will not be the last word. But as I rise up, I bear the wounds of his death. My rising does not remove them. They mark me. If you want to know who I am, put your hand in.
– *Nicholas Wolterstorff*

REVIVE
Saturday: John 21:24–31
Sunday: 1 Corinthians 15:54–57

Go to page 297 for your next devotional reading.

so till he is taken out of the way. **8**And then the lawless one will be revealed, whom the Lord Jesus will overthrow with the breath of his mouth and destroy by the splendor of his coming. **9**The coming of the lawless one will be in accordance with the work of Satan displayed in all kinds of counterfeit miracles, signs and wonders, **10**and in every sort of evil that deceives those who are perishing. They perish because they refused to love the truth and so be saved. **11**For this reason God sends them a powerful delusion so that they will believe the lie **12**and so that all will be condemned who have not believed the truth but have delighted in wickedness.

Stand Firm

13But we ought always to thank God for you, brothers loved by the Lord, because from the beginning God chose you*a* to be saved through the sanctifying work of the Spirit and through belief in the truth. **14**He called you to this through our gospel, that you might share in the glory of our Lord

a13 Some manuscripts *because God chose you as his firstfruits*

| MONDAY |

| VERSE FOR THE DAY: | AUTHOR: | PASSAGE FOR THE DAY: |
| 2 Thessalonians 3:10 | Thomas Merton | 2 Thessalonians 3:6–15 |

Work and the Spiritual Life

AN ACTIVITY that is based on the frenzies and impulsions of human ambition is a delusion and an obstacle to grace. It gets in the way of God's will, and it creates more problems than it solves. We must learn to distinguish between the pseudo spirituality of activism and the true vitality and energy of Christian action guided by the Spirit. At the same time we must not create a split in the Christian life by assuming that all activity is somehow dangerous to the spiritual life. The spiritual life is not a life of quiet withdrawal, a hothouse of growth of artificial ascetic practices beyond the reach of people living ordinary lives. It is in the ordinary duties and labors of life that the Christian can and should develop his spiritual union with God.

This is no new principle. But it is perhaps not often easy to apply in practice. A writer or preacher who assumes that it is very easy may seriously mislead those who try to follow his advice. Work in a normal, healthy human context, work with a sane and moderate human measure, integrated in a productive social milieu, is by itself capable of contributing much to the spiritual life. But work that is disordered, irrational, unproductive, dominated by the exhausting frenzies and wastefulness of a worldwide struggle for power and wealth, is not necessarily going to make a valid contribution to the spiritual lives of all those engaged in it.

Additional Scripture Readings:
Ephesians 4:25–32;
1 Thessalonians 4:3–12

Go to page 300 for your next devotional reading.

Jesus Christ. ¹⁵So then, brothers, stand firm and hold to the teachings*a* we passed on to you, whether by word of mouth or by letter.

¹⁶May our Lord Jesus Christ himself and God our Father, who loved us and by his grace gave us eternal encouragement and good hope, ¹⁷encourage your hearts and strengthen you in every good deed and word.

Request for Prayer

3 Finally, brothers, pray for us that the message of the Lord may spread rapidly and be honored, just as it was with you. ²And pray that we may be delivered from wicked and evil men, for not everyone has faith. ³But the Lord is faithful, and he will strengthen and protect you from the evil one. ⁴We have confidence in the Lord that you are doing and will continue to do the things we command. ⁵May the Lord direct your hearts into God's love and Christ's perseverance.

Warning Against Idleness

⁶In the name of the Lord Jesus Christ, we command you, brothers, to keep away from every brother who is idle and does not live according to the teaching*b* you received from us. ⁷For you yourselves know how you ought to follow our example. We were not idle when we were with you, ⁸nor did we eat anyone's food without paying for it. On the contrary, we worked night and day, laboring and toiling so that we would not be a burden to any of you. ⁹We did this, not because we do not have the right to such help, but in order to make ourselves a model for you to follow. ¹⁰For even when we were with you, we gave you this rule: "If a man will not work, he shall not eat."

¹¹We hear that some among you are idle. They are not busy; they are busybodies. ¹²Such people we command and urge in the Lord Jesus Christ to settle down and earn the bread they eat. ¹³And as for you, brothers, never tire of doing what is right.

¹⁴If anyone does not obey our instruction in this letter, take special note of him. Do not associate with him, in order that he may feel ashamed. ¹⁵Yet do not regard him as an enemy, but warn him as a brother.

Final Greetings

¹⁶Now may the Lord of peace himself give you peace at all times and in every way. The Lord be with all of you.

¹⁷I, Paul, write this greeting in my own hand, which is the distinguishing mark in all my letters. This is how I write.

¹⁸The grace of our Lord Jesus Christ be with you all.

---

a 15 Or *traditions*   *b* 6 Or *tradition*

*P*AUL *writes this letter to young Timothy, who is serving as a pastor in Ephesus. He instructs him how to organize and run the church and how to deal with false teachers and refute what they say. As you read this book, promise God that you will not stray from true faith.*

1 TIMOTHY

1 Paul, an apostle of Christ Jesus by the command of God our Savior and of Christ Jesus our hope,

²To Timothy my true son in the faith:

Grace, mercy and peace from God the Father and Christ Jesus our Lord.

Warning Against False Teachers of the Law

³As I urged you when I went into Macedonia, stay there in Ephesus so that you may command certain men not to teach false doctrines any longer ⁴nor to devote themselves to myths and endless genealogies. These promote controversies rather than God's work—which is by faith. ⁵The goal of this command is love, which comes from a pure heart and a good conscience and a sincere faith. ⁶Some have wandered away from these and turned to meaningless talk. ⁷They want to be teachers of the law, but they do not know what they are talking about or what they so confidently affirm.

⁸We know that the law is good if one uses it properly. ⁹We also know that law*a* is made not for the righteous but for lawbreakers and rebels, the ungodly and sinful, the unholy and irreligious; for those who kill their fathers or mothers, for murderers, ¹⁰for adulterers and perverts, for slave traders and liars and perjurers—and for whatever else is contrary to the sound doctrine ¹¹that conforms to the glorious gospel of the blessed God, which he entrusted to me.

The Lord's Grace to Paul

¹²I thank Christ Jesus our Lord, who has given me strength, that he considered me faithful, appointing me to his service. ¹³Even though I was once a blasphemer and a persecutor and a violent man, I was shown mercy because I acted in ignorance

a9 Or that the law

and unbelief. **14**The grace of our Lord was poured out on me abundantly, along with the faith and love that are in Christ Jesus.

15Here is a trustworthy saying that deserves full acceptance: Christ Jesus came into the world to save sinners—of whom I am the worst. **16**But for that very reason I was shown mercy so that in me, the worst of sinners, Christ Jesus might display his unlimited patience as an example for those who would believe on him and receive eternal life. **17**Now to the King eternal, immortal, invisible, the only God, be honor and glory for ever and ever. Amen.

18Timothy, my son, I give you this instruction in keeping with the prophecies once made about you, so that by following them you may fight the good fight, **19**holding on to faith and a good conscience. Some have rejected these and so have shipwrecked their faith. **20**Among them are Hymenaeus and Alexander, whom I have handed over to Satan to be taught not to blaspheme.

TUESDAY

VERSE FOR THE DAY:
1 Timothy 1:15

AUTHOR:
Jim Conway

PASSAGE FOR THE DAY:
1 Timothy 1:12–17

Overcoming Perfectionism

IT MAY sound strange, but frequently a person with a poor self-image tends to be a perfectionist. If you feel inadequate, unsure of other people's love, then you start saying to yourself, "If only I try harder, if I achieve more, if I'm a better person, then I'll feel better about myself and other people will love me."

Perfectionism, however, is never satisfied! If you can't accept any good things that people say of you, then even if you do great things, your accomplishments will not satisfy that insatiable, gulping appetite of perfectionism.

The perfectionist never asks the question, "How much is enough? At what point can I stop? How much perfection will I have to accomplish to receive the love from people that I really want?" There never is an end; only God is perfect.

The perfectionism also fails to realize that God loves unconditionally. God doesn't withhold love until we arrive at perfection. He loves us while we are growing and even while we are his enemies. His love enables us to change and mature.

Tragically, perfectionists think other people will like them better for their perfection. But truthfully, it is just the opposite. People like to be around flexible, tolerant, imperfect people —like themselves. Perfect people frighten them and cause them to withdraw.

Perfectionists are always paying a debt. The irony is that no one is asking that any debt be paid. Perfectionists do all of this because their poor self-images manipulate them into doing it.

Additional Scripture Readings:
Romans 5:1–11; Romans 8:31–39

Go to page 302 for your next devotional reading.

Instructions on Worship

2 I urge, then, first of all, that requests, prayers, intercession and thanksgiving be made for everyone — ²for kings and all those in authority, that we may live peaceful and quiet lives in all godliness and holiness. ³This is good, and pleases God our Savior, ⁴who wants all men to be saved and to come to a knowledge of the truth. ⁵For there is one God and one mediator between God and men, the man Christ Jesus, ⁶who gave himself as a ransom for all men — the testimony given in its proper time. ⁷And for this purpose I was appointed a herald and an apostle — I am telling the truth, I am not lying — and a teacher of the true faith to the Gentiles.

⁸I want men everywhere to lift up holy hands in prayer, without anger or disputing.

⁹I also want women to dress modestly, with decency and propriety, not with braided hair or gold or pearls or expensive clothes, ¹⁰but with good deeds, appropriate for women who profess to worship God.

¹¹A woman should learn in quietness and full submission. ¹²I do not permit a woman to teach or to have authority over a man; she must be silent. ¹³For Adam was formed first, then Eve. ¹⁴And Adam was not the one deceived; it was the woman who was deceived and became a sinner. ¹⁵But women[a] will be saved[b] through childbearing — if they continue in faith, love and holiness with propriety.

Overseers and Deacons

3 Here is a trustworthy saying: If anyone sets his heart on being an overseer,[c] he desires a noble task. ²Now the overseer must be above reproach, the husband of but one wife, temperate, self-controlled, respectable, hospitable, able to teach, ³not given to drunkenness, not violent but gentle, not quarrelsome, not a lover of money. ⁴He must manage his own family well and see that his children obey him with proper respect. ⁵(If anyone does not know how to manage his own family, how can he take care of God's church?) ⁶He must not be a recent convert, or he may become conceited and fall under the same judgment as the devil. ⁷He must also have a good reputation with outsiders, so that he will not fall into disgrace and into the devil's trap.

⁸Deacons, likewise, are to be men worthy of respect, sincere, not indulging in much wine, and not pursuing dishonest gain. ⁹They must keep hold of the deep truths of the faith with a clear conscience. ¹⁰They must first be tested; and then if there is nothing against them, let them serve as deacons.

¹¹In the same way, their wives[d] are to be women worthy of respect, not malicious talkers but temperate and trustworthy in everything.

¹²A deacon must be the husband of but one wife and must manage his children and his household well. ¹³Those who have served well gain an excellent standing and great assurance in their faith in Christ Jesus.

¹⁴Although I hope to come to you soon, I am writing you these instructions so that, ¹⁵if I am delayed, you will know how people ought to conduct themselves in God's household, which is the church of the living God, the pillar and foundation of the truth. ¹⁶Beyond all question, the mystery of godliness is great:

> He[e] appeared in a body,[f]
> was vindicated by the Spirit,
> was seen by angels,
> was preached among the nations,
> was believed on in the world,
> was taken up in glory.

Instructions to Timothy

4 The Spirit clearly says that in later times some will abandon the faith and follow deceiving spirits and things taught by demons. ²Such teachings come through hypocritical liars, whose consciences have been seared as with a hot iron. ³They forbid people to marry and order them to abstain from certain foods, which God created to be received with thanksgiving by those who believe and who know the truth. ⁴For everything God created is good, and nothing is to be rejected if it is received with thanksgiving, ⁵because it is consecrated by the word of God and prayer.

⁶If you point these things out to the brothers, you will be a good minister of Christ Jesus, brought up in the truths of the faith and of the good teaching that you have followed. ⁷Have nothing to do with

---

[a]15 Greek *she* [b]15 Or *restored* [c]1 Traditionally *bishop*; also in verse 2 [d]11 Or *way*, *deaconesses* [e]16 Some manuscripts *God* [f]16 Or *in the flesh*

godless myths and old wives' tales; rather, train yourself to be godly. **⁸**For physical training is of some value, but godliness has value for all things, holding promise for both the present life and the life to come.

⁹This is a trustworthy saying that deserves full acceptance **¹⁰**(and for this we labor and strive), that we have put our hope in the living God, who is the Savior of all men, and especially of those who believe.

¹¹Command and teach these things. **¹²**Don't let anyone look down on you because you are young, but set an example for the believers in speech, in life, in love, in faith and in purity. **¹³**Until I come, devote yourself to the public reading of Scripture, to preaching and to teaching. **¹⁴**Do not neglect your gift, which was given you through a prophetic message when the body of elders laid their hands on you.

¹⁵Be diligent in these matters; give yourself wholly to them, so that everyone may see your progress. **¹⁶**Watch your life and doctrine closely. Persevere in them, because if you do, you will save both yourself and your hearers.

WEDNESDAY

VERSE FOR THE DAY:
1 Timothy 3:4

AUTHOR:
J.H. Waterink

PASSAGE FOR THE DAY:
1 Timothy 3:1–7

On Rights and Duties

PERMIT me to make this observation: we must be very careful in speaking of our rights. People who constantly refer to their rights tread on dangerous ground. Is it true that you have the unqualified right to the respect of your children, and that you have every right to exercise authority over your children? No, you certainly do not have an "unqualified right." You can never sever that right from your parental duty before God. [Reformation leader John] Calvin states it beautifully: "Does a person demand his rights? Certainly, I am prepared to grant him his rights, but in so doing I shall say that he has no other rights than the rights to fulfill his duties" . . .

Parents, perform your parental duty toward God and toward your children. Then, and then only, can you speak of your parental rights . . .

Much is being said about the rebellious spirit of children and young people. On the one hand, this spirit of rebellion has come about because children have never learned respect for authority as their parents did not exercise authority; on the other hand, it is also possible that they did not learn respect for authority because the parents misused it. Both are equally dangerous. It is no wonder that there are so many pitfalls in the exercising of authority: he who wields authority wields a God-given weapon, and he must constantly be on guard lest he misuse it for selfish ends. Authority must never be exercised in an arbitrary, unreasonable manner.

Additional Scripture Readings:
Proverbs 22:6; Romans 12:9–16

Go to page 303 for your next devotional reading.

Advice About Widows, Elders and Slaves

5 Do not rebuke an older man harshly, but exhort him as if he were your father. Treat younger men as brothers, ²older women as mothers, and younger women as sisters, with absolute purity.

³Give proper recognition to those widows who are really in need. ⁴But if a widow has children or grandchildren, these should learn first of all to put their religion into practice by caring for their own family and so repaying their parents and grandparents, for this is pleasing to God. ⁵The widow who is really in need and left all alone puts her hope in God and continues night and day to pray and to ask God for help. ⁶But the widow who lives for pleasure is dead even while she lives. ⁷Give the people these instructions, too, so that no one may be open to blame. ⁸If

---

THURSDAY

VERSE FOR THE DAY:
1 Timothy 5:8

AUTHOR:
Doug Sherman and
William Hendricks

PASSAGE FOR THE DAY:
1 Timothy 5:1–8

A God-given Motive

IT IS not always noticed, but the Great Commandments include a legitimate self-interest: "Love your neighbor *as yourself*" [Mark 12:31, italics added]. The idea is that each of us has a responsibility before God to care for himself as God's person. Not just physically, but spiritually, emotionally, relationally, morally, intellectually, and so forth.

Work is an important means toward fulfilling this responsibility. In 2 Thessalonians 3, Paul says that we should pursue gainful employment in order to provide for our needs . . .

So we are actually commanded to work. Furthermore, we are to work in order to provide for our families: "If anyone does not provide for his relatives, and especially for his immediate family, he has denied the faith and is worse than an unbeliever" (1 Timothy 5:8).

This is remarkably strong language! Failing to try to meet even the basic needs of one's family is denying the faith. Why? Because it directly opposes God's command to love those who are our own. In fact, it is to act worse than an unbeliever, because even pagans have the sense and decency to provide a livelihood for their families.

Fortunately, I find that providing for the family is one of the most important reasons why people go to work, as they explain it to me. In fact, because this motive is so common, many people fail to see it as a God-given reason for work. But that won't do. If you work to meet the legitimate needs of your family, then you are fulfilling something important that God wants done in the world.

Additional Scripture Readings:
Ephesians 4:25–28;
2 Thessalonians 3:6–15

Go to page 305 for your next devotional reading.

anyone does not provide for his relatives, and especially for his immediate family, he has denied the faith and is worse than an unbeliever.

⁹No widow may be put on the list of widows unless she is over sixty, has been faithful to her husband,*ᵃ* ¹⁰and is well known for her good deeds, such as bringing up children, showing hospitality, washing the feet of the saints, helping those in trouble and devoting herself to all kinds of good deeds.

¹¹As for younger widows, do not put them on such a list. For when their sensual desires overcome their dedication to Christ, they want to marry. ¹²Thus they bring judgment on themselves, because they have broken their first pledge. ¹³Besides, they get into the habit of being idle and going about from house to house. And not only do they become idlers, but also gossips and busybodies, saying things they ought not to. ¹⁴So I counsel younger widows to marry, to have children, to manage their homes and to give the enemy no opportunity for slander. ¹⁵Some have in fact already turned away to follow Satan.

¹⁶If any woman who is a believer has widows in her family, she should help them and not let the church be burdened with them, so that the church can help those widows who are really in need.

¹⁷The elders who direct the affairs of the church well are worthy of double honor, especially those whose work is preaching and teaching. ¹⁸For the Scripture says, "Do not muzzle the ox while it is treading out the grain,"*ᵇ* and "The worker deserves his wages."*ᶜ* ¹⁹Do not entertain an accusation against an elder unless it is brought by two or three witnesses. ²⁰Those who sin are to be rebuked publicly, so that the others may take warning.

²¹I charge you, in the sight of God and Christ Jesus and the elect angels, to keep these instructions without partiality, and to do nothing out of favoritism.

²²Do not be hasty in the laying on of hands, and do not share in the sins of others. Keep yourself pure.

²³Stop drinking only water, and use a little wine because of your stomach and your frequent illnesses.

²⁴The sins of some men are obvious, reaching the place of judgment ahead of them; the sins of others trail behind them. ²⁵In the same way, good deeds are obvious, and even those that are not cannot be hidden.

6 All who are under the yoke of slavery should consider their masters worthy of full respect, so that God's name and our teaching may not be slandered. ²Those who have believing masters are not to show less respect for them because they are brothers. Instead, they are to serve them even better, because those who benefit from their service are believers, and dear to them. These are the things you are to teach and urge on them.

Love of Money

³If anyone teaches false doctrines and does not agree to the sound instruction of our Lord Jesus Christ and to godly teaching, ⁴he is conceited and understands nothing. He has an unhealthy interest in controversies and quarrels about words that result in envy, strife, malicious talk, evil suspicions ⁵and constant friction between men of corrupt mind, who have been robbed of the truth and who think that godliness is a means to financial gain.

⁶But godliness with contentment is great gain. ⁷For we brought nothing into the world, and we can take nothing out of it. ⁸But if we have food and clothing, we will be content with that. ⁹People who want to get rich fall into temptation and a trap and into many foolish and harmful desires that plunge men into ruin and destruction. ¹⁰For the love of money is a root of all kinds of evil. Some people, eager for money, have wandered from the faith and pierced themselves with many griefs.

Paul's Charge to Timothy

¹¹But you, man of God, flee from all this, and pursue righteousness, godliness, faith, love, endurance and gentleness. ¹²Fight the good fight of the faith. Take hold of the eternal life to which you were called when you made your good confession in the presence of many witnesses. ¹³In the sight of God, who gives life to everything, and of Christ Jesus, who while testifying before Pontius Pilate made the good confession, I charge you ¹⁴to keep this command without spot or blame until

---

*ᵃ*9 Or *has had but one husband*   *ᵇ*18 Deut. 25:4   *ᶜ*18 Luke 10:7

the appearing of our Lord Jesus Christ, **15**which God will bring about in his own time—God, the blessed and only Ruler, the King of kings and Lord of lords, **16**who alone is immortal and who lives in unapproachable light, whom no one has seen or can see. To him be honor and might forever. Amen.

17Command those who are rich in this present world not to be arrogant nor to put their hope in wealth, which is so uncertain, but to put their hope in God, who richly provides us with everything for our enjoyment. **18**Command them to do good, to be rich in good deeds, and to be generous and willing to share. **19**In this way they will lay up treasure for themselves as a firm foundation for the coming age, so that they may take hold of the life that is truly life.

20Timothy, guard what has been entrusted to your care. Turn away from godless chatter and the opposing ideas of what is falsely called knowledge, **21**which some have professed and in so doing have wandered from the faith.

Grace be with you.

FRIDAY

VERSE FOR THE DAY:
1 Timothy 6:12

AUTHOR:
Orel Hershiser

PASSAGE FOR THE DAY:
1 Timothy 6:11–16

No Excuse for Mediocrity

LOS Angeles Dodgers pitcher and World Series Most Valuable Player award winner Orel Hershiser is competitive. Even so, he has discovered that failure need not be devastating.

I don't like to fail, but I can handle it. That hasn't always been true, but as a Christian of ten years, I know where my strength comes from. I know that even if I give up a home run that makes me a goat, I'll survive. My wife and kids will still love me. God is still in his heaven. The world will not come to an end, regardless of my performance.

It's that same faith, though, that makes me determined to be a good steward of the mind and body I've been blessed with. If my faith merely made me accept defeat and failure, it would be a crutch—a weak, sad alibi. People who criticize Christians for being less competitive—and Christians who *are* less competitive—have missed the point of the faith.

It's my faith that lifts me up when I've failed. It's my faith that reminds me of my true insignificance when the world has been laid at my feet because of my success throwing a ball. To call myself a Christian and then not strive to be the best I can be and do the most I can with what has been given me would be the height of hypocrisy. Being a Christian is no excuse for mediocrity or passive acceptance of defeat. If anything, Christianity demands a higher standard, more devotion to the task.

Additional Scripture Readings:
Psalm 86:1–13;
1 Corinthians 16:13–18

Go to page 306 for your next devotional reading.

WEEKENDING

REVIEW

Nothing prohibits Christians from obeying God more than the tug of material comforts. Once we have adjusted to a lifestyle that includes many comforts, it is very difficult to surrender them to serve God. Obviously, God doesn't call everyone to leave his vocation and go into what is traditionally called "Christian work." God can and does use Christians everywhere. But in order to be used by God in any capacity, a Christian must be willing to serve God no matter what the costs . . .

Whenever someone asked Christ about what would be expected of him as a follower, he always tested their willingness to surrender everything for God's sake. Without that attitude, we can't even be trusted with material riches because we would spend them on our own indulgences or build bigger barns to store them in.

– *Larry Burkett*

REVIVE
Saturday: Luke 12:13–21
Sunday: 1 Timothy 6:3–10

Go to page 308 for your next devotional reading.

THIS second letter to Timothy is written by Paul shortly before Paul dies (2 Timothy 4:6–8). Times are difficult, both morally and spiritually, and Paul wants to encourage Timothy to persevere in his Christian faith and life. As you read this book, be sure to find your daily strength in Jesus Christ and in God's inspired word.

2 TIMOTHY

1 Paul, an apostle of Christ Jesus by the will of God, according to the promise of life that is in Christ Jesus,

²To Timothy, my dear son:

Grace, mercy and peace from God the Father and Christ Jesus our Lord.

Encouragement to Be Faithful

³I thank God, whom I serve, as my forefathers did, with a clear conscience, as night and day I constantly remember you in my prayers. ⁴Recalling your tears, I long to see you, so that I may be filled with joy. ⁵I have been reminded of your sincere faith, which first lived in your grandmother Lois and in your mother Eunice and, I am persuaded, now lives in you also. ⁶For this reason I remind you to fan into flame the gift of God, which is in you through the laying on of my hands. ⁷For God did not give us a spirit of timidity, but a spirit of power, of love and of self-discipline.

⁸So do not be ashamed to testify about our Lord, or ashamed of me his prisoner. But join with me in suffering for the gospel, by the power of God, ⁹who has saved us and called us to a holy life—not because of anything we have done but because of his own purpose and grace. This grace was given us in Christ Jesus before the beginning of time, ¹⁰but it has now been revealed through the appearing of our Savior, Christ Jesus, who has destroyed death and has brought life and immortality to light through the gospel. ¹¹And of this gospel I was appointed a herald and an apostle and a teacher. ¹²That is why I am suffering as I am. Yet I am not ashamed, because I know whom I have

believed, and am convinced that he is able to guard what I have entrusted to him for that day.

13What you heard from me, keep as the pattern of sound teaching, with faith and love in Christ Jesus. **14**Guard the good deposit that was entrusted to you—guard it with the help of the Holy Spirit who lives in us.

15You know that everyone in the province of Asia has deserted me, including Phygelus and Hermogenes.

16May the Lord show mercy to the household of Onesiphorus, because he often refreshed me and was not ashamed of my chains. **17**On the contrary, when he was in Rome, he searched hard for me until he found me. **18**May the Lord grant that he will find mercy from the Lord on that day! You know very well in how many ways he helped me in Ephesus.

2 You then, my son, be strong in the grace that is in Christ Jesus. **2**And the things you have heard me say in the presence of many witnesses entrust to reliable men who will also be qualified to teach others. **3**Endure hardship with us like a good soldier of Christ Jesus. **4**No one serving as a soldier gets involved in civilian affairs—he wants to please his commanding officer. **5**Similarly, if anyone competes as an athlete, he does not receive the victor's crown unless he competes according to the rules. **6**The hardworking farmer should be the first to receive a share of the crops. **7**Reflect on what I am saying, for the Lord will give you insight into all this.

8Remember Jesus Christ, raised from

MONDAY

VERSE FOR THE DAY:
2 Timothy 1:8

AUTHOR:
Orel Hershiser

PASSAGE FOR THE DAY:
2 Timothy 1:8–12

Show and Tell

I'M NOT one to wear my faith on my sleeve. Christians can do a disservice to unbelievers by being obnoxious or judgmental. I'm a chapel leader and have been since my second year in the minors. People know where I'm coming from without my having to harp on it all the time. I know that the message of Christ offends because it calls sin sin and says we are all sinners. There's no way to soften that truth. It's jarring and can alienate people until they begin to realize that it's true. My pushing it down everyone's throat will not make it any easier for them to investigate what it's all about.

I just tell people about God naturally, when opportunities arise or when I'm asked. It's amazing how many people notice when you tend to be straight. If you're not a carouser, not a womanizer, not foul-mouthed, not a gossip, it gets around! . . .

We're far from perfect. We fail. There are people who may think we are insincere or who think we're judgmental. I can't defend myself against people who say I'm phony. Only my family, my true friends and I know who I really am inside. I'll have to answer for that someday. I can only do and be what I think God wants me to do and be. I never want to embarrass him or bring him shame.

Additional Scripture Readings:
Romans 1:11–17; 1 Peter 3:13–17

Go to page 309 for your next devotional reading.

the dead, descended from David. This is my gospel, **9**for which I am suffering even to the point of being chained like a criminal. But God's word is not chained. **10**Therefore I endure everything for the sake of the elect, that they too may obtain the salvation that is in Christ Jesus, with eternal glory.

11Here is a trustworthy saying:

If we died with him,
  we will also live with him;
12if we endure,
  we will also reign with him.
If we disown him,
  he will also disown us;
13if we are faithless,
  he will remain faithful,
  for he cannot disown himself.

A Workman Approved by God

14Keep reminding them of these things. Warn them before God against quarreling about words; it is of no value, and only ruins those who listen. **15**Do your best to present yourself to God as one approved, a workman who does not need to be ashamed and who correctly handles the word of truth. **16**Avoid godless chatter, because those who indulge in it will become more and more ungodly. **17**Their teaching will spread like gangrene. Among them are Hymenaeus and Philetus, **18**who have wandered away from the truth. They say that the resurrection has already taken place, and they destroy the faith of some. **19**Nevertheless, God's solid foundation stands firm, sealed with this inscription:

TUESDAY

VERSE FOR THE DAY:
2 Timothy 2:15

AUTHOR:
Orel Hershiser

PASSAGE FOR THE DAY:
2 Timothy 2:14–19

Life's Balancing Agent

MY FAITH has been a balancing agent in my life. Christ thrills me with who I am in him, and reminds me gently who I am not. When I suffer, I know I'm still loved. When I'm on top of the world, I remember that my accomplishments mean nothing in light of eternity. The biggest surprise to me was to discover that Christ is real. He's not some nebulous concept, some idea or system or approach or philosophy. He's a Person, someone I can know.

And he knows me. How do I know? Because while he changed me from sinner to forgiven-sinner, he also realigned my motives. I still had the same character and personality, but my mind was renewed because I now wanted to do what he wanted me to do. The obsession and perfectionism I had used to promote myself was now redirected. I wanted to be the best baseball player I could be, and now that my motives were right, I was free to enjoy my pursuit rather than be frustrated by it. I've seen players worry so much about how they're doing that they are no longer effective.

If anything, I became more dedicated to paying the price, to working out, to listening, to learning. I wanted to soak up all the baseball knowledge I could.

Additional Scripture Readings:
John 10:11–18; Romans 12:1–2

Go to page 311 for your next devotional reading.

"The Lord knows those who are his,"[a] and, "Everyone who confesses the name of the Lord must turn away from wickedness."

20In a large house there are articles not only of gold and silver, but also of wood and clay; some are for noble purposes and some for ignoble. **21**If a man cleanses himself from the latter, he will be an instrument for noble purposes, made holy, useful to the Master and prepared to do any good work.

22Flee the evil desires of youth, and pursue righteousness, faith, love and peace, along with those who call on the Lord out of a pure heart. **23**Don't have anything to do with foolish and stupid arguments, because you know they produce quarrels. **24**And the Lord's servant must not quarrel; instead, he must be kind to everyone, able to teach, not resentful. **25**Those who oppose him he must gently instruct, in the hope that God will grant them repentance leading them to a knowledge of the truth, **26**and that they will come to their senses and escape from the trap of the devil, who has taken them captive to do his will.

Godlessness in the Last Days

3 But mark this: There will be terrible times in the last days. **2**People will be lovers of themselves, lovers of money, boastful, proud, abusive, disobedient to their parents, ungrateful, unholy, **3**without love, unforgiving, slanderous, without self-control, brutal, not lovers of the good, **4**treacherous, rash, conceited, lovers of pleasure rather than lovers of God— **5**having a form of godliness but denying its power. Have nothing to do with them.

6They are the kind who worm their way into homes and gain control over weak-willed women, who are loaded down with sins and are swayed by all kinds of evil desires, **7**always learning but never able to acknowledge the truth. **8**Just as Jannes and Jambres opposed Moses, so also these men oppose the truth—men of depraved minds, who, as far as the faith is concerned, are rejected. **9**But they will not get very far because, as in the case of those men, their folly will be clear to everyone.

Paul's Charge to Timothy

10You, however, know all about my teaching, my way of life, my purpose, faith, patience, love, endurance, **11**persecutions, sufferings—what kinds of things happened to me in Antioch, Iconium and Lystra, the persecutions I endured. Yet the Lord rescued me from all of them. **12**In fact, everyone who wants to live a godly life in Christ Jesus will be persecuted, **13**while evil men and impostors will go from bad to worse, deceiving and being deceived. **14**But as for you, continue in what you have learned and have become convinced of, because you know those from whom you learned it, **15**and how from infancy you have known the holy Scriptures, which are able to make you wise for salvation through faith in Christ Jesus. **16**All Scripture is God-breathed and is useful for teaching, rebuking, correcting and training in righteousness, **17**so that the man of God may be thoroughly equipped for every good work.

4 In the presence of God and of Christ Jesus, who will judge the living and the dead, and in view of his appearing and his kingdom, I give you this charge: **2**Preach the Word; be prepared in season and out of season; correct, rebuke and encourage—with great patience and careful instruction. **3**For the time will come when men will not put up with sound doctrine. Instead, to suit their own desires, they will gather around them a great number of teachers to say what their itching ears want to hear. **4**They will turn their ears away from the truth and turn aside to myths. **5**But you, keep your head in all situations, endure hardship, do the work of an evangelist, discharge all the duties of your ministry.

6For I am already being poured out like a drink offering, and the time has come for my departure. **7**I have fought the good fight, I have finished the race, I have kept the faith. **8**Now there is in store for me the crown of righteousness, which the Lord, the righteous Judge, will award to me on that day—and not only to me, but also to all who have longed for his appearing.

Personal Remarks

9Do your best to come to me quickly, **10**for Demas, because he loved this world, has deserted me and has gone to Thessalonica. Crescens has gone to Galatia, and Titus to Dalmatia. **11**Only Luke is with me. Get Mark and bring him with you, because he is helpful to me in my ministry. **12**I sent Tychicus to Ephesus. **13**When you come, bring the cloak that I left with Car-

---

[a] 19 Num. 16:5 (see Septuagint)

pus at Troas, and my scrolls, especially the parchments. ¹⁴Alexander the metalworker did me a great deal of harm. The Lord will repay him for what he has done. ¹⁵You too should be on your guard against him, because he strongly opposed our message.

¹⁶At my first defense, no one came to my support, but everyone deserted me. May it not be held against them. ¹⁷But the Lord stood at my side and gave me strength, so that through me the message might be fully proclaimed and all the Gentiles might hear it. And I was delivered from the lion's mouth. ¹⁸The Lord will rescue me from every evil attack and will bring me safely to his heavenly kingdom. To him be glory for ever and ever. Amen.

Final Greetings

¹⁹Greet Priscilla*ᵃ* and Aquila and the

ᵃ19 Greek *Prisca*, a variant of *Priscilla*

WEDNESDAY

VERSE FOR THE DAY:
2 Timothy 4:2

AUTHOR:
Dietrich Bonhoeffer

PASSAGE FOR THE DAY:
2 Timothy 3:14—4:5

Preach the Word

WHEN we go to church and listen to the sermon, what we want to hear is his Word—and that not merely for selfish reasons, but for the sake of the many for whom the church and her message are foreign. We have a strange feeling that if Jesus himself—Jesus alone with his Word—could come into our midst at sermon time, we should find quite a different set of men hearing the Word, and quite a different set rejecting it. That is not to deny that the Word of God is to be heard in the preaching that goes on in our church. The real trouble is that the pure Word of Jesus has been overlaid with so much human ballast—burdensome rules and regulations, false hopes and consolations—that it has become extremely difficult to make a genuine decision for Christ.

Of course it is our aim to preach Christ and Christ alone, but, when all is said and done, it is not the fault of our critics that they find our preaching so hard to understand, so overburdened with ideas and expressions that are hopelessly out of touch with the mental climate in which they live . . . Perhaps it would be just as well to ask ourselves whether we do not in fact often act as obstacles to Jesus and his Word . . . Are we not constantly harping on certain ideas at the expense of others that are just as important? Does not our preaching contain too much of our own opinions and convictions, and too little of Jesus Christ? . . . Let us try to get away from the poverty and pettiness of our own little convictions and problems, and seek the wealth and splendor that are vouchsafed to us in Jesus Christ.

Additional Scripture Readings:
1 Corinthians 15:1–11;
Hebrews 4:12–13

Go to page 314 for your next devotional reading.

household of Onesiphorus. ²⁰Erastus stayed in Corinth, and I left Trophimus sick in Miletus. ²¹Do your best to get here before winter. Eubulus greets you, and so do Pudens, Linus, Claudia and all the brothers.

²²The Lord be with your spirit. Grace be with you.

*P*AUL *writes to Titus, a pastor serving in Crete, to advise him both on what to teach the churches and on how to organize them, especially with false teachers around. As you read this book, note God's concern for proper order in the church and for true teaching about Christ.*

TITUS

1 Paul, a servant of God and an apostle of Jesus Christ for the faith of God's elect and the knowledge of the truth that leads to godliness— ²a faith and knowledge resting on the hope of eternal life, which God, who does not lie, promised before the beginning of time, ³and at his appointed season he brought his word to light through the preaching entrusted to me by the command of God our Savior,

⁴To Titus, my true son in our common faith:

Grace and peace from God the Father and Christ Jesus our Savior.

Titus' Task on Crete

⁵The reason I left you in Crete was that you might straighten out what was left unfinished and appoint*a* elders in every town, as I directed you. ⁶An elder must be blameless, the husband of but one wife, a man whose children believe and are not open to the charge of being wild and disobedient. ⁷Since an overseer*b* is entrusted with God's work, he must be blameless—not overbearing, not quick-tempered, not given to drunkenness, not violent, not pursuing dishonest gain. ⁸Rather he must be hospitable, one who loves what is good, who is self-controlled, upright, holy and disciplined. ⁹He must hold firmly to the trustworthy message as it has been taught, so that he can encourage others by sound doctrine and refute those who oppose it.

¹⁰For there are many rebellious people, mere talkers and deceivers, especially those of the circumcision group. ¹¹They

a 5 Or *ordain* *b 7* Traditionally *bishop*

must be silenced, because they are ruining whole households by teaching things they ought not to teach—and that for the sake of dishonest gain. ¹²Even one of their own prophets has said, "Cretans are always liars, evil brutes, lazy gluttons." ¹³This testimony is true. Therefore, rebuke them sharply, so that they will be sound in the faith ¹⁴and will pay no attention to Jewish myths or to the commands of those who reject the truth. ¹⁵To the pure, all things are pure, but to those who are corrupted and do not believe, nothing is pure. In fact, both their minds and consciences are corrupted. ¹⁶They claim to know God, but by their actions they deny him. They are detestable, disobedient and unfit for doing anything good.

THURSDAY

VERSE FOR THE DAY:
Titus 2:11

AUTHOR:
Orel Hershiser

PASSAGE FOR THE DAY:
Titus 2:11–15

From Skepticism to Belief

[A FELLOW minor league baseball player named] Butch said God loved me and wanted a relationship with me. What could *that* mean? I could know God? God could know me? God was perfect and I wasn't. I was just a guy, and he was, well, God. How could I relate to him? Butch said Jesus was the answer. I could relate to him because even though he was perfect, he had also become a man. He was the bridge. He paid for my sin. If I could accept that and believe in Christ, then I could be forgiven and know I was going to heaven.

One September night . . . I pulled out the Gideon Bible and was reading the book of John. My mind was racing. Do I believe in God? Yes. Do I believe the Bible is God's message to man? Yes. Do I believe what the Bible says? Yes. That all have sinned? Yes. That nothing I can do can save me from my sin? Yes. That Jesus already did it for me and that he is the only way to God? Yes. Do I want Christ in my life? Do I want to become a Christian?

I slipped off the bed and knelt beside it. How does one go about praying? I didn't know. I figured if God was God, he would understand if I just told him what was on my mind. I said, "God, I don't know everything about you. I don't think I ever will. But I know I'm a sinner and I know I want to be forgiven. I know I want Christ in my life, and I want to go to heaven. I want to become a Christian. With that, I accept you. Amen."

No tears, no lightning, no wind, no visions. I just got back on the bed and continued to read the Bible. What a relief! I knew I had done the right thing. I had stepped from skepticism to belief.

Additional Scripture Readings:
John 14:1–14; Romans 5:1–11

Go to page 315 for your next devotional reading.

TITUS 2

What Must Be Taught to Various Groups

2 You must teach what is in accord with sound doctrine. ²Teach the older men to be temperate, worthy of respect, self-controlled, and sound in faith, in love and in endurance.

³Likewise, teach the older women to be reverent in the way they live, not to be slanderers or addicted to much wine, but to teach what is good. ⁴Then they can train the younger women to love their husbands and children, ⁵to be self-controlled and pure, to be busy at home, to be kind, and to be subject to their husbands, so that no one will malign the word of God.

⁶Similarly, encourage the young men to be self-controlled. ⁷In everything set them an example by doing what is good. In your teaching show integrity, seriousness ⁸and soundness of speech that cannot be condemned, so that those who oppose you may be ashamed because they have nothing bad to say about us.

⁹Teach slaves to be subject to their masters in everything, to try to please them,

---

FRIDAY

VERSE FOR THE DAY:
Titus 3:7

AUTHOR:
Dave Dravecky

PASSAGE FOR THE DAY:
Titus 3:1–8

A Deep Well of Hope

GOD is personal. That lesson, learned [while on an Amarillo Double-A baseball team], changed our lives forever. It transformed our response to the news [of a tumor in my pitching arm] we heard seven years later at the Cleveland Clinic.

It prevented us from responding to the tumor with bitterness and anger. If I'd still had an image of God as a distant Keeper of the Rules, then it would have seemed very unfair to me that I was getting a tougher deal than a lot of other ballplayers. What was happening wasn't fair, and a Rulekeeper God either didn't exist, or I had good reason for being very angry at him.

But that's not my image of God any longer. He's not the Cosmic Bookkeeper, the one to blame if things don't work out the way you think they should. Life isn't always fair, at least in the short run, but the Bible taught me not to confuse life with God. When you're confronted with trouble you don't ask, "Why me?" You ask God, "What do you want me to do in this situation?"

Because the God who revealed himself in Jesus is full of love. He never deserts his children. Janice and I entered this difficult period, when life was often beyond our control, with a deep conviction that God was for us. Jesus had given his life for us. There was nothing else—no other good thing—he would withhold. We expected to see God's love in whatever came—however strange the twists and turns of the road might be. That fundamental belief gave us a deep well of hope to draw from.

Additional Scripture Readings:
Colossians 1:3–14; 1 Peter 1:3–9

Go to page 318 for your next devotional reading.

not to talk back to them, ¹⁰and not to steal from them, but to show that they can be fully trusted, so that in every way they will make the teaching about God our Savior attractive.

¹¹For the grace of God that brings salvation has appeared to all men. ¹²It teaches us to say "No" to ungodliness and worldly passions, and to live self-controlled, upright and godly lives in this present age, ¹³while we wait for the blessed hope — the glorious appearing of our great God and Savior, Jesus Christ, ¹⁴who gave himself for us to redeem us from all wickedness and to purify for himself a people that are his very own, eager to do what is good.

¹⁵These, then, are the things you should teach. Encourage and rebuke with all authority. Do not let anyone despise you.

Doing What Is Good

3 Remind the people to be subject to rulers and authorities, to be obedient, to be ready to do whatever is good, ²to slander no one, to be peaceable and considerate, and to show true humility toward all men.

³At one time we too were foolish, disobedient, deceived and enslaved by all kinds of passions and pleasures. We lived in malice and envy, being hated and hating one another. ⁴But when the kindness and love of God our Savior appeared, ⁵he saved us, not because of righteous things we had done, but because of his mercy. He saved us through the washing of rebirth and renewal by the Holy Spirit, ⁶whom he poured out on us generously through Jesus Christ our Savior, ⁷so that, having been justified by his grace, we might become heirs having the hope of eternal life. ⁸This is a trustworthy saying. And I want you to stress these things, so that those who have trusted in God may be careful to devote themselves to doing what is good. These things are excellent and profitable for everyone.

⁹But avoid foolish controversies and genealogies and arguments and quarrels about the law, because these are unprofitable and useless. ¹⁰Warn a divisive person once, and then warn him a second time. After that, have nothing to do with him. ¹¹You may be sure that such a man is warped and sinful; he is self-condemned.

Final Remarks

¹²As soon as I send Artemas or Tychicus to you, do your best to come to me at Nicopolis, because I have decided to winter there. ¹³Do everything you can to help Zenas the lawyer and Apollos on their way and see that they have everything they need. ¹⁴Our people must learn to devote themselves to doing what is good, in order that they may provide for daily necessities and not live unproductive lives.

¹⁵Everyone with me sends you greetings. Greet those who love us in the faith.

Grace be with you all.

*P*AUL *writes this brief letter to ask Philemon, a Christian brother living (probably) in Colosse, to forgive and take back Onesimus, a runaway slave who has become a Christian and is helping Paul in prison. As you read this book, be willing to forgive others, no matter what they do to you.*

PHILEMON

¹Paul, a prisoner of Christ Jesus, and Timothy our brother,

To Philemon our dear friend and fellow worker, ²to Apphia our sister, to Archippus our fellow soldier and to the church that meets in your home:

³Grace to you and peace from God our Father and the Lord Jesus Christ.

Thanksgiving and Prayer

⁴I always thank my God as I remember you in my prayers, ⁵because I hear about your faith in the Lord Jesus and your love for all the saints. ⁶I pray that you may be active in sharing your faith, so that you will have a full understanding of every good thing we have in Christ. ⁷Your love has given me great joy and encouragement, because you, brother, have refreshed the hearts of the saints.

Paul's Plea for Onesimus

⁸Therefore, although in Christ I could be bold and order you to do what you ought to do, ⁹yet I appeal to you on the basis of love. I then, as Paul—an old man and now also a prisoner of Christ Jesus— ¹⁰I appeal to you for my son Onesimus,[a] who became my son while I was in chains. ¹¹Formerly he was useless to you, but now he has become useful both to you and to me.

¹²I am sending him—who is my very heart—back to you. ¹³I would have liked to keep him with me so that he could take your place in helping me while I am in chains for the gospel. ¹⁴But I did not want to do anything without your consent, so that any favor you do will be spontaneous and not forced. ¹⁵Perhaps the reason he was separated from you for a little while was that you might have him back for

---

[a] 10 *Onesimus* means *useful.*

WEEKENDING

RELAX

The little child says
Here I am daddy
as he bursts
on father's sight
from behind the chair
where he's been hiding.
He doesn't say
What can I do for you?
How can I help you?
I want to serve you
seeking somehow
to work and gain
the father's favor
and delight.
He knows they are his
without exhausting effort
to achieve.
They are his always.
Here I am daddy
—Abba Father—
not working
just being
your eternal son.

– *Joseph Bayly*

REVIVE
Saturday: John 1:10–13
Sunday: Romans 8:12–17

Go to page 319 for your next devotional reading.

good— ¹⁶no longer as a slave, but better than a slave, as a dear brother. He is very dear to me but even dearer to you, both as a man and as a brother in the Lord.

¹⁷So if you consider me a partner, welcome him as you would welcome me. ¹⁸If he has done you any wrong or owes you anything, charge it to me. ¹⁹I, Paul, am writing this with my own hand. I will pay it back—not to mention that you owe me your very self. ²⁰I do wish, brother, that I may have some benefit from you in the Lord; refresh my heart in Christ. ²¹Confident of your obedience, I write to you, knowing that you will do even more than I ask.

²²And one thing more: Prepare a guest room for me, because I hope to be restored to you in answer to your prayers.

²³Epaphras, my fellow prisoner in Christ Jesus, sends you greetings. ²⁴And so do Mark, Aristarchus, Demas and Luke, my fellow workers.

²⁵The grace of the Lord Jesus Christ be with your spirit.

MONDAY

VERSE FOR THE DAY:
Philemon 16

AUTHOR:
Charles Stanley

PASSAGE FOR THE DAY:
Philemon 12–18

Grabbing Rattlesnakes

A PERSON who harbors unforgiveness always loses. Regardless of how wrong the other person may have been, refusing to forgive means reaping corruption in life. And that corruption begins in one relationship including the relationship with God, and works its way into all the rest.

Holding on to hurt is like grabbing a rattlesnake by the tail; you are going to be bitten. As the poison of bitterness works its way through the many facets of your personality, death will occur—death that is more far-reaching than your physical death, for it has the potential to destroy those around you as well.

Have you been hurt? Has somebody, somewhere in your past, rejected you in such a way that you still hurt when you think about it? Do you become critical of people in your past the minute their names are mentioned? Did you leave home as a child or a college student with great relief that you were leaving, swearing you would never return? . . .

Whatever your situation, whatever has happened in your past, remember that you are the loser if you do not deal with an unforgiving spirit. And the people around you suffer, too.

Additional Scripture Readings:
Matthew 18:21–35;
Ephesians 4:25–32

Go to page 322 for your next devotional reading.

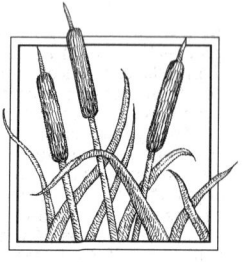

THE author of this letter encourages Christians who are being persecuted for their faith by pointing them to the greatness of the Son of God who became man. Christ is the full expression of God's revelation, better than anything in the Old Testament; the author warns his readers to depend on Christ alone. As you read this book, commit yourself firmly to Jesus your Intercessor, and be sure to persevere and grow daily in your Christian faith and life.

HEBREWS

The Son Superior to Angels

1 In the past God spoke to our forefathers through the prophets at many times and in various ways, **2**but in these last days he has spoken to us by his Son, whom he appointed heir of all things, and through whom he made the universe. **3**The Son is the radiance of God's glory and the exact representation of his being, sustaining all things by his powerful word. After he had provided purification for sins, he sat down at the right hand of the Majesty in heaven. **4**So he became as much superior to the angels as the name he has inherited is superior to theirs.

5For to which of the angels did God ever say,

"You are my Son;
today I have become your Father[a]"[b]?

Or again,

"I will be his Father,
and he will be my Son"[c]?

6And again, when God brings his firstborn into the world, he says,

---

[a]5 Or *have begotten you*   [b]5 Psalm 2:7   [c]5 2 Samuel 7:14; 1 Chron. 17:13

"Let all God's angels worship him."*a*

⁷In speaking of the angels he says,

"He makes his angels winds,
  his servants flames of fire."*b*

⁸But about the Son he says,

"Your throne, O God, will last for ever
    and ever,
  and righteousness will be the
    scepter of your kingdom.
⁹You have loved righteousness and
    hated wickedness;
  therefore God, your God, has set
    you above your companions
  by anointing you with the oil of
    joy."*c*

¹⁰He also says,

"In the beginning, O Lord, you laid
    the foundations of the earth,
  and the heavens are the work of
    your hands.
¹¹They will perish, but you remain;
  they will all wear out like a
    garment.
¹²You will roll them up like a robe;
  like a garment they will be changed.
But you remain the same,
  and your years will never end."*d*

¹³To which of the angels did God ever say,

"Sit at my right hand
until I make your enemies
  a footstool for your feet"*e*?

¹⁴Are not all angels ministering spirits sent to serve those who will inherit salvation?

Warning to Pay Attention

2 We must pay more careful attention, therefore, to what we have heard, so that we do not drift away. ²For if the message spoken by angels was binding, and every violation and disobedience received its just punishment, ³how shall we escape if we ignore such a great salvation? This salvation, which was first announced by the Lord, was confirmed to us by those who heard him. ⁴God also testified to it by signs, wonders and various miracles, and gifts of the Holy Spirit distributed according to his will.

Jesus Made Like His Brothers

⁵It is not to angels that he has subjected the world to come, about which we are speaking. ⁶But there is a place where someone has testified:

"What is man that you are mindful of
    him,
  the son of man that you care for
    him?
⁷You made him a little*f* lower than
    the angels;
  you crowned him with glory and
    honor
⁸ and put everything under his
    feet."*g*

In putting everything under him, God left nothing that is not subject to him. Yet at present we do not see everything subject to him. ⁹But we see Jesus, who was made a little lower than the angels, now crowned with glory and honor because he suffered death, so that by the grace of God he might taste death for everyone.

¹⁰In bringing many sons to glory, it was fitting that God, for whom and through whom everything exists, should make the author of their salvation perfect through suffering. ¹¹Both the one who makes men holy and those who are made holy are of the same family. So Jesus is not ashamed to call them brothers. ¹²He says,

"I will declare your name to my
    brothers;
  in the presence of the congregation
    I will sing your praises."*h*

¹³And again,

"I will put my trust in him."*i*

And again he says,

"Here am I, and the children God has
    given me."*j*

¹⁴Since the children have flesh and blood, he too shared in their humanity so that by his death he might destroy him who holds the power of death—that is, the devil— ¹⁵and free those who all their lives were held in slavery by their fear of death. ¹⁶For surely it is not angels he helps, but Abraham's descendants. ¹⁷For this reason he had to be made like his brothers in every way, in order that he might become a merciful and faithful high

---

*a*6 Deut. 32:43 (see Dead Sea Scrolls and Septuagint)   *b*7 Psalm 104:4   *c*9 Psalm 45:6,7
*d*12 Psalm 102:25-27   *e*13 Psalm 110:1   *f*7 Or *him for a little while*; also in verse 9
*g*8 Psalm 8:4-6   *h*12 Psalm 22:22   *i*13 Isaiah 8:17   *j*13 Isaiah 8:18

TUESDAY

VERSE FOR THE DAY:
Hebrews 2:11

AUTHOR:
Reuben R. Welch

PASSAGE FOR THE DAY:
Hebrews 2:5–18

He Calls Us Brothers

THE warnings at the beginning of chapter 2 [of Hebrews] called the Hebrews to renewed attentiveness, renewed grip and spirit, new heart and enthusiasm, and recovery of the joy of first love.

Perhaps the writer knew that underneath their drift and loss of nerve were secret hurts and failures, hidden burdens and defeats. Very few believers choose to drift; seldom do Christians plan to be lukewarm. But poor performance undermines confidence and failure causes discouragement. Temptation, even when overcome, leaves us battle-scarred and weary. It is sometimes difficult to tell the difference between victory and defeat because issues are never clear-cut and our successes never total. When one has struggled through the testing time and finally endured, it seldom feels like triumph.

At such times . . . we desperately need to know that Jesus is our brother, with us as we struggle on the way, having the compassion that can only come through his shared experience of suffering and temptation. Our approach to the throne of grace (4:16) is not on the basis of our victories. We are not invited because we are worthy. Jesus our brother opens up the way for us to come in our weaknesses, temptations and failures. He is with us in sympathy and help, not at the end of our struggle, but all the way through.

This is the only way, I believe, that we can maintain vitality and energy and joy in the long haul of the Christian life. Someone has to help us *at the time of our struggle*; we need help *while we are trying*; we need a brother *in the hour of trial*, and especially when we fail. Otherwise we fall into the discouragement of trying harder or of never quite measuring up. The subtle shift from trust in Christ to our own self-efforts robs us of hope and joy. We begin to tally hurts, count disappointments and weigh sacrifices. And already the drift has set in. We need the warning, but more than that, we need to know that we are known, understood and loved by someone who has marked out the path, has won the victory and is with us on the way. That someone is Jesus.

Additional Scripture Readings:
Matthew 11:25–30; Hebrews 4:14–16

Go to page 324 for your next devotional reading.

priest in service to God, and that he might make atonement for[a] the sins of the people. ¹⁸Because he himself suffered when he was tempted, he is able to help those who are being tempted.

Jesus Greater Than Moses

3 Therefore, holy brothers, who share in the heavenly calling, fix your thoughts on Jesus, the apostle and high priest whom we confess. ²He was faithful to the one who appointed him, just as Moses was faithful in all God's house. ³Jesus has been found worthy of greater honor than Moses, just as the builder of a house has greater honor than the house itself. ⁴For every house is built by someone, but God is the builder of everything. ⁵Moses was faithful as a servant in all God's house, testifying to what would be said in the future. ⁶But Christ is faithful as a son over God's house. And we are his house, if we hold on to our courage and the hope of which we boast.

Warning Against Unbelief

⁷So, as the Holy Spirit says:

"Today, if you hear his voice,
⁸ do not harden your hearts
 as you did in the rebellion,
  during the time of testing in the desert,
⁹where your fathers tested and tried me
 and for forty years saw what I did.
¹⁰That is why I was angry with that generation,
 and I said, 'Their hearts are always going astray,
 and they have not known my ways.'
¹¹So I declared on oath in my anger,
 'They shall never enter my rest.' "[b]

¹²See to it, brothers, that none of you has a sinful, unbelieving heart that turns away from the living God. ¹³But encourage one another daily, as long as it is called Today, so that none of you may be hardened by sin's deceitfulness. ¹⁴We have come to share in Christ if we hold firmly till the end the confidence we had at first. ¹⁵As has just been said:

"Today, if you hear his voice,
 do not harden your hearts
 as you did in the rebellion."[c]

¹⁶Who were they who heard and rebelled? Were they not all those Moses led out of Egypt? ¹⁷And with whom was he angry for forty years? Was it not with those who sinned, whose bodies fell in the desert? ¹⁸And to whom did God swear that they would never enter his rest if not to those who disobeyed[d]? ¹⁹So we see that they were not able to enter, because of their unbelief.

A Sabbath-Rest for the People of God

4 Therefore, since the promise of entering his rest still stands, let us be careful that none of you be found to have fallen short of it. ²For we also have had the gospel preached to us, just as they did; but the message they heard was of no value to them, because those who heard did not combine it with faith.[e] ³Now we who have believed enter that rest, just as God has said,

"So I declared on oath in my anger,
 'They shall never enter my rest.' "[f]

And yet his work has been finished since the creation of the world. ⁴For somewhere he has spoken about the seventh day in these words: "And on the seventh day God rested from all his work."[g] ⁵And again in the passage above he says, "They shall never enter my rest."

⁶It still remains that some will enter that rest, and those who formerly had the gospel preached to them did not go in, because of their disobedience. ⁷Therefore God again set a certain day, calling it Today, when a long time later he spoke through David, as was said before:

"Today, if you hear his voice,
 do not harden your hearts."[c]

⁸For if Joshua had given them rest, God would not have spoken later about another day. ⁹There remains, then, a Sabbath-rest for the people of God; ¹⁰for anyone who enters God's rest also rests from his own work, just as God did from his. ¹¹Let us, therefore, make every effort to enter that rest, so that no one will fall by following their example of disobedience.

¹²For the word of God is living and active. Sharper than any double-edged sword, it penetrates even to dividing soul and spirit, joints and marrow; it judges the thoughts and attitudes of the heart.

---

[a]17 Or *and that he might turn aside God's wrath, taking away* [b]11 Psalm 95:7-11
[c]15,7 Psalm 95:7,8 [d]18 Or *disbelieved* [e]2 Many manuscripts *because they did not share in the faith of those who obeyed* [f]3 Psalm 95:11; also in verse 5 [g]4 Gen. 2:2

¹³Nothing in all creation is hidden from God's sight. Everything is uncovered and laid bare before the eyes of him to whom we must give account.

Jesus the Great High Priest

¹⁴Therefore, since we have a great high priest who has gone through the heavens,*a* Jesus the Son of God, let us hold firmly to the faith we profess. ¹⁵For we do not have a high priest who is unable to sympathize with our weaknesses, but we have one who has been tempted in every way, just as we are—yet was without sin. ¹⁶Let us then approach the throne of grace with confidence, so that we may receive mercy and find grace to help us in our time of need.

5 Every high priest is selected from among men and is appointed to represent them in matters related to God, to offer gifts and sacrifices for sins. ²He is able to deal gently with those who are ignorant and are going astray, since he himself is

a 14 Or gone into heaven

WEDNESDAY

VERSE FOR THE DAY:
Hebrews 4:16

AUTHOR:
Jim Conway

PASSAGE FOR THE DAY:
Hebrews 4:14–16

Great Physician and Friend

WHY have people been so attracted to Jesus down through the centuries? The Bible answers that question in a simple phrase, "We love because he first loved us" (1 John 4:19).

As you look at the special relationship Jesus had with so many people, you must be convinced that Jesus is on the side of common people. Anybody who was hurt, sick, mistreated, lonely, disenfranchised or condemned—people like you and me—were the ones Jesus came to help.

Matthew wrote, "When the Pharisees saw this, they asked his disciples, 'Why does your teacher eat with tax collectors and "sinners"?' On hearing this, Jesus said, 'It is not the healthy who need a doctor, but the sick'" (Matthew 9:11–12). In essence, Jesus was saying, "My job here on earth is to get sinners back to God, not to worry about the good people."

Jesus does not present himself to us as "holier than thou," but rather as a friend. He said, "I no longer call you servants, because a servant does not know his master's business. Instead, I have called you friends, for everything that I learned from my Father I have made known to you" (John 15:15).

We are not second-class citizens. The Bible says we are part of God's family. Hebrews 4 records that Jesus, who is now in heaven, intercedes for us and that he understands our weaknesses. We are encouraged to "approach the throne of grace with confidence, so that we may receive mercy and find grace to help us in our time of need" (Hebrews 4:16).

Additional Scripture Readings:
Matthew 9:9–13; John 15:9–17

Go to page 326 for your next devotional reading.

subject to weakness. ³This is why he has to offer sacrifices for his own sins, as well as for the sins of the people.

⁴No one takes this honor upon himself; he must be called by God, just as Aaron was. ⁵So Christ also did not take upon himself the glory of becoming a high priest. But God said to him,

"You are my Son;
today I have become your
Father."ᵃ "ᵇ

⁶And he says in another place,

"You are a priest forever,
in the order of Melchizedek."ᶜ

⁷During the days of Jesus' life on earth, he offered up prayers and petitions with loud cries and tears to the one who could save him from death, and he was heard because of his reverent submission. ⁸Although he was a son, he learned obedience from what he suffered ⁹and, once made perfect, he became the source of eternal salvation for all who obey him ¹⁰and was designated by God to be high priest in the order of Melchizedek.

Warning Against Falling Away

¹¹We have much to say about this, but it is hard to explain because you are slow to learn. ¹²In fact, though by this time you ought to be teachers, you need someone to teach you the elementary truths of God's word all over again. You need milk, not solid food! ¹³Anyone who lives on milk, being still an infant, is not acquainted with the teaching about righteousness. ¹⁴But solid food is for the mature, who by constant use have trained themselves to distinguish good from evil.

6 Therefore let us leave the elementary teachings about Christ and go on to maturity, not laying again the foundation of repentance from acts that lead to death,ᵈ and of faith in God, ²instruction about baptisms, the laying on of hands, the resurrection of the dead, and eternal judgment. ³And God permitting, we will do so.

⁴It is impossible for those who have once been enlightened, who have tasted the heavenly gift, who have shared in the Holy Spirit, ⁵who have tasted the goodness of the word of God and the powers of the coming age, ⁶if they fall away, to be brought back to repentance, becauseᵉ to their loss they are crucifying the Son of God all over again and subjecting him to public disgrace.

⁷Land that drinks in the rain often falling on it and that produces a crop useful to those for whom it is farmed receives the blessing of God. ⁸But land that produces thorns and thistles is worthless and is in danger of being cursed. In the end it will be burned.

⁹Even though we speak like this, dear friends, we are confident of better things in your case — things that accompany salvation. ¹⁰God is not unjust; he will not forget your work and the love you have shown him as you have helped his people and continue to help them. ¹¹We want each of you to show this same diligence to the very end, in order to make your hope sure. ¹²We do not want you to become lazy, but to imitate those who through faith and patience inherit what has been promised.

The Certainty of God's Promise

¹³When God made his promise to Abraham, since there was no one greater for him to swear by, he swore by himself, ¹⁴saying, "I will surely bless you and give you many descendants."ᶠ ¹⁵And so after waiting patiently, Abraham received what was promised.

¹⁶Men swear by someone greater than themselves, and the oath confirms what is said and puts an end to all argument. ¹⁷Because God wanted to make the unchanging nature of his purpose very clear to the heirs of what was promised, he confirmed it with an oath. ¹⁸God did this so that, by two unchangeable things in which it is impossible for God to lie, we who have fled to take hold of the hope offered to us may be greatly encouraged. ¹⁹We have this hope as an anchor for the soul, firm and secure. It enters the inner sanctuary behind the curtain, ²⁰where Jesus, who went before us, has entered on our behalf. He has become a high priest forever, in the order of Melchizedek.

Melchizedek the Priest

7 This Melchizedek was king of Salem and priest of God Most High. He met Abraham returning from the defeat of the kings and blessed him, ²and Abraham gave him a tenth of everything. First, his name means "king of righteousness"; then

---

ᵃ5 Or *have begotten you*   ᵇ5 Psalm 2:7   ᶜ6 Psalm 110:4   ᵈ1 Or *from useless rituals*   ᵉ6 Or *repentance while*   ᶠ14 Gen. 22:17

THURSDAY

VERSE FOR THE DAY:
Hebrews 5:14

AUTHOR:
Reggie White

PASSAGE FOR THE DAY:
Hebrews 5:11—6:3

A Good Defense

YOU know, as a Christian, I run into the very same problems on a spiritual level that I do on the football field. I can get blindsided by friends or other people who don't understand me and what I stand for. I probably trust too many persons and when I'm not looking, I have received a crackback block mentally and sometimes physically. I've also been attacked for my beliefs by a double-team and a triple-team.

How do I handle these threats to my faith? The same way I do as a football player.

The first step is training. I must study God's Word on a daily basis. Paul wrote to Timothy: "Do your best to present yourself to God as one approved, a workman who does not need to be ashamed and who correctly handles the word of truth" (2 Timothy 2:15).

There is no way I will ever be able to deal with all that life has to offer without daily and diligently delving into God's Word . . .

The second focus is on my surroundings. I must also be careful not to surround myself too closely with those who don't believe in God's Word. I have many friends who are not Christians and I sure do love them. But we have a different relationship. Unbelievers just don't have as much in common as believers do. They don't have the same goals, morals or social life that believers in Christ have.

It doesn't take too much sense to realize that you become like those with whom you spend the most time. Know your surroundings and control them; don't let your surroundings control you.

Finally, practice what you know is right. Too often we focus on doing what we've always done. We don't progress, keep in shape, work out daily. The warning is clear: "Solid food is for the mature, who by constant use have trained themselves to distinguish good from evil. Therefore let us leave the elementary teachings about Christ and go on to maturity" (Hebrews 5:14—6:1).

Additional Scripture Readings:
2 Corinthians 6:14–18;
1 Timothy 4:6–8

Go to page 329 for your next devotional reading.

also, "king of Salem" means "king of peace." **3**Without father or mother, without genealogy, without beginning of days or end of life, like the Son of God he remains a priest forever.

4Just think how great he was: Even the patriarch Abraham gave him a tenth of the plunder! **5**Now the law requires the descendants of Levi who become priests to collect a tenth from the people — that is, their brothers — even though their brothers are descended from Abraham. **6**This man, however, did not trace his descent from Levi, yet he collected a tenth from Abraham and blessed him who had the promises. **7**And without doubt the lesser person is blessed by the greater. **8**In the one case, the tenth is collected by men who die; but in the other case, by him who is declared to be living. **9**One might even say that Levi, who collects the tenth, paid the tenth through Abraham, **10**because when Melchizedek met Abraham, Levi was still in the body of his ancestor.

Jesus Like Melchizedek

11If perfection could have been attained through the Levitical priesthood (for on the basis of it the law was given to the people), why was there still need for another priest to come — one in the order of Melchizedek, not in the order of Aaron? **12**For when there is a change of the priesthood, there must also be a change of the law. **13**He of whom these things are said belonged to a different tribe, and no one from that tribe has ever served at the altar. **14**For it is clear that our Lord descended from Judah, and in regard to that tribe Moses said nothing about priests. **15**And what we have said is even more clear if another priest like Melchizedek appears, **16**one who has become a priest not on the basis of a regulation as to his ancestry but on the basis of the power of an indestructible life. **17**For it is declared:

"You are a priest forever,
 in the order of Melchizedek."[a]

18The former regulation is set aside because it was weak and useless **19**(for the law made nothing perfect), and a better hope is introduced, by which we draw near to God.

20And it was not without an oath! Others became priests without any oath, **21**but he became a priest with an oath when God said to him:

"The Lord has sworn
 and will not change his mind:
'You are a priest forever.' "[a]

22Because of this oath, Jesus has become the guarantee of a better covenant.

23Now there have been many of those priests, since death prevented them from continuing in office; **24**but because Jesus lives forever, he has a permanent priesthood. **25**Therefore he is able to save completely[b] those who come to God through him, because he always lives to intercede for them.

26Such a high priest meets our need — one who is holy, blameless, pure, set apart from sinners, exalted above the heavens. **27**Unlike the other high priests, he does not need to offer sacrifices day after day, first for his own sins, and then for the sins of the people. He sacrificed for their sins once for all when he offered himself. **28**For the law appoints as high priests men who are weak; but the oath, which came after the law, appointed the Son, who has been made perfect forever.

The High Priest of a New Covenant

8 The point of what we are saying is this: We do have such a high priest, who sat down at the right hand of the throne of the Majesty in heaven, **2**and who serves in the sanctuary, the true tabernacle set up by the Lord, not by man.

3Every high priest is appointed to offer both gifts and sacrifices, and so it was necessary for this one also to have something to offer. **4**If he were on earth, he would not be a priest, for there are already men who offer the gifts prescribed by the law. **5**They serve at a sanctuary that is a copy and shadow of what is in heaven. This is why Moses was warned when he was about to build the tabernacle: "See to it that you make everything according to the pattern shown you on the mountain."[c] **6**But the ministry Jesus has received is as superior to theirs as the covenant of which he is mediator is superior to the old one, and it is founded on better promises.

7For if there had been nothing wrong with that first covenant, no place would have been sought for another. **8**But God found fault with the people and said[d]:

---

[a] 17,21 Psalm 110:4   [b] 25 Or *forever*   [c] 5 Exodus 25:40   [d] 8 Some manuscripts may be translated *fault and said to the people.*

"The time is coming, declares the Lord,
when I will make a new covenant
with the house of Israel
and with the house of Judah.
⁹It will not be like the covenant
I made with their forefathers
when I took them by the hand
to lead them out of Egypt,
because they did not remain faithful
to my covenant,
and I turned away from them,
declares the Lord.
¹⁰This is the covenant I will make with
the house of Israel
after that time, declares the Lord.
I will put my laws in their minds
and write them on their hearts.
I will be their God,
and they will be my people.
¹¹No longer will a man teach his
neighbor,
or a man his brother, saying, 'Know
the Lord,'
because they will all know me,
from the least of them to the
greatest.
¹²For I will forgive their wickedness
and will remember their sins no
more."ᵃ

¹³By calling this covenant "new," he has made the first one obsolete; and what is obsolete and aging will soon disappear.

Worship in the Earthly Tabernacle

9 Now the first covenant had regulations for worship and also an earthly sanctuary. ²A tabernacle was set up. In its first room were the lampstand, the table and the consecrated bread; this was called the Holy Place. ³Behind the second curtain was a room called the Most Holy Place, ⁴which had the golden altar of incense and the gold-covered ark of the covenant. This ark contained the gold jar of manna, Aaron's staff that had budded, and the stone tablets of the covenant. ⁵Above the ark were the cherubim of the Glory, overshadowing the atonement cover.ᵇ But we cannot discuss these things in detail now.

⁶When everything had been arranged like this, the priests entered regularly into the outer room to carry on their ministry. ⁷But only the high priest entered the inner room, and that only once a year, and never without blood, which he offered for himself and for the sins the people had committed in ignorance. ⁸The Holy Spirit was showing by this that the way into the Most Holy Place had not yet been disclosed as long as the first tabernacle was still standing. ⁹This is an illustration for the present time, indicating that the gifts and sacrifices being offered were not able to clear the conscience of the worshiper. ¹⁰They are only a matter of food and drink and various ceremonial washings—external regulations applying until the time of the new order.

The Blood of Christ

¹¹When Christ came as high priest of the good things that are already here,ᶜ he went through the greater and more perfect tabernacle that is not man-made, that is to say, not a part of this creation. ¹²He did not enter by means of the blood of goats and calves; but he entered the Most Holy Place once for all by his own blood, having obtained eternal redemption. ¹³The blood of goats and bulls and the ashes of a heifer sprinkled on those who are ceremonially unclean sanctify them so that they are outwardly clean. ¹⁴How much more, then, will the blood of Christ, who through the eternal Spirit offered himself unblemished to God, cleanse our consciences from acts that lead to death,ᵈ so that we may serve the living God!

¹⁵For this reason Christ is the mediator of a new covenant, that those who are called may receive the promised eternal inheritance—now that he has died as a ransom to set them free from the sins committed under the first covenant.

¹⁶In the case of a will,ᵉ it is necessary to prove the death of the one who made it, ¹⁷because a will is in force only when somebody has died; it never takes effect while the one who made it is living. ¹⁸This is why even the first covenant was not put into effect without blood. ¹⁹When Moses had proclaimed every commandment of the law to all the people, he took the blood of calves, together with water, scarlet wool and branches of hyssop, and sprinkled the scroll and all the people. ²⁰He said, "This is the blood of the covenant, which God has commanded you to keep."ᶠ ²¹In the same way, he sprinkled with the blood both the tabernacle and everything used in its ceremonies. ²²In fact,

---

ᵃ12 Jer. 31:31-34   ᵇ5 Traditionally *the mercy seat*   ᶜ11 Some early manuscripts *are to come*
ᵈ14 Or *from useless rituals*   ᵉ16 Same Greek word as *covenant*; also in verse 17   ᶠ20 Exodus 24:8

the law requires that nearly everything be cleansed with blood, and without the shedding of blood there is no forgiveness. ²³It was necessary, then, for the copies of the heavenly things to be purified with these sacrifices, but the heavenly things themselves with better sacrifices than these. ²⁴For Christ did not enter a man-made sanctuary that was only a copy of the true one; he entered heaven itself, now to appear for us in God's presence. ²⁵Nor did he enter heaven to offer himself again and again, the way the high priest enters the Most Holy Place every year with blood that is not his own. ²⁶Then Christ would have had to suffer many times since the creation of the world. But now he has appeared once for all at the end of the ages to do away with sin by the sacrifice of himself. ²⁷Just as man is destined to die once, and after that to face judgment, ²⁸so Christ was sacrificed once to take away the sins of many people; and he will appear a second time, not to bear sin, but to bring salvation to those who are waiting for him.

Christ's Sacrifice Once for All

10 The law is only a shadow of the good things that are coming—not the realities themselves. For this reason it can never, by the same sacrifices repeated

---

FRIDAY

VERSE FOR THE DAY:
Hebrews 9:15

AUTHOR:
Dietrich Bonhoeffer

PASSAGE FOR THE DAY:
Hebrews 9:11–15

Christianity Without Christ

DISCIPLESHIP means adherence to Christ, and, because Christ is the object of that adherence, it must take the form of discipleship. An abstract Christology, a doctrinal system, a general religious knowledge on the subject of grace or on the forgiveness of sins, render discipleship superfluous, and in fact they positively exclude any idea of discipleship whatever, and are essentially inimical to the whole conception of following Christ. With an abstract idea it is possible to enter into a relation of formal knowledge, to become enthusiastic about it, and perhaps even to put it into practice; but it can never be followed in personal obedience.

Christianity without the living Christ is inevitably Christianity without discipleship, and Christianity without discipleship is always Christianity without Christ. It remains an abstract idea, a myth that has a place for the Fatherhood of God, but omits Christ as the living Son. And a Christianity of that kind is nothing more or less than the end of discipleship. In such a religion there is trust in God, but no following of Christ. Because the Son of God became Man, because he is the Mediator, for that reason alone the only true relation we can have with him is to follow him. Discipleship is bound to Christ as the Mediator, and where it is properly understood, it necessarily implies faith in the Son of God as the Mediator. Only the Mediator, the God-Man, can call men to follow him.

Additional Scripture Readings:
John 10:7–18; 1 Timothy 2:1–7

Go to page 331 for your next devotional reading.

endlessly year after year, make perfect those who draw near to worship. **2**If it could, would they not have stopped being offered? For the worshipers would have been cleansed once for all, and would no longer have felt guilty for their sins. **3**But those sacrifices are an annual reminder of sins, **4**because it is impossible for the blood of bulls and goats to take away sins.

5Therefore, when Christ came into the world, he said:

"Sacrifice and offering you did not
 desire,
 but a body you prepared for me;
6with burnt offerings and sin offerings
 you were not pleased.
7Then I said, 'Here I am—it is written
 about me in the scroll—
 I have come to do your will,
 O God.'" *a*

8First he said, "Sacrifices and offerings, burnt offerings and sin offerings you did not desire, nor were you pleased with them" (although the law required them to be made). **9**Then he said, "Here I am, I have come to do your will." He sets aside the first to establish the second. **10**And by that will, we have been made holy through the sacrifice of the body of Jesus Christ once for all.

11Day after day every priest stands and performs his religious duties; again and again he offers the same sacrifices, which can never take away sins. **12**But when this priest had offered for all time one sacrifice for sins, he sat down at the right hand of God. **13**Since that time he waits for his enemies to be made his footstool, **14**because by one sacrifice he has made perfect forever those who are being made holy.

15The Holy Spirit also testifies to us about this. First he says:

16"This is the covenant I will make with
 them
 after that time, says the Lord.
 I will put my laws in their hearts,
 and I will write them on their
 minds." *b*

17Then he adds:

"Their sins and lawless acts
 I will remember no more." *c*

18And where these have been forgiven, there is no longer any sacrifice for sin.

A Call to Persevere

19Therefore, brothers, since we have confidence to enter the Most Holy Place by the blood of Jesus, **20**by a new and living way opened for us through the curtain, that is, his body, **21**and since we have a great priest over the house of God, **22**let us draw near to God with a sincere heart in full assurance of faith, having our hearts sprinkled to cleanse us from a guilty conscience and having our bodies washed with pure water. **23**Let us hold unswervingly to the hope we profess, for he who promised is faithful. **24**And let us consider how we may spur one another on toward love and good deeds. **25**Let us not give up meeting together, as some are in the habit of doing, but let us encourage one another—and all the more as you see the Day approaching.

26If we deliberately keep on sinning after we have received the knowledge of the truth, no sacrifice for sins is left, **27**but only a fearful expectation of judgment and of raging fire that will consume the enemies of God. **28**Anyone who rejected the law of Moses died without mercy on the testimony of two or three witnesses. **29**How much more severely do you think a man deserves to be punished who has trampled the Son of God under foot, who has treated as an unholy thing the blood of the covenant that sanctified him, and who has insulted the Spirit of grace? **30**For we know him who said, "It is mine to avenge; I will repay," *d* and again, "The Lord will judge his people." *e* **31**It is a dreadful thing to fall into the hands of the living God.

32Remember those earlier days after you had received the light, when you stood your ground in a great contest in the face of suffering. **33**Sometimes you were publicly exposed to insult and persecution; at other times you stood side by side with those who were so treated. **34**You sympathized with those in prison and joyfully accepted the confiscation of your property, because you knew that you yourselves had better and lasting possessions.

35So do not throw away your confidence; it will be richly rewarded. **36**You need to persevere so that when you have done the will of God, you will receive

---

*a*7 Psalm 40:6-8 (see Septuagint)   *b*16 Jer. 31:33   *c*17 Jer. 31:34   *d*30 Deut. 32:35   *e*30 Deut. 32:36; Psalm 135:14

WEEKENDING

RECEIVE

Prayer is one of the unlimited resources available to each of us. In this bound-up world, prayer may be a lost art, but it is always the starting point when we move toward God. In prayer we set aside our agendas, letting God's priorities become our priorities, and we receive his resources.

– *John F. Westfall*

RESOLVE

You don't have to learn some special prayer jargon to start a conversation with God. Honesty and a willingness to establish a personal relationship with him are the only initial requirements. God is looking for an opportunity to reveal himself to you, so if you put him to the test and then watch for an answer without too many preconceptions about how that answer will come, *I can guarantee you that you'll be in for some exciting surprises.*

– *Pat Boone*

REVIVE
Saturday: Philippians 4:4–9
Sunday: Hebrews 4:14–16

Go to page 333 for your next devotional reading.

what he has promised. ³⁷For in just a very little while,

"He who is coming will come and will not delay.
³⁸ But my righteous one[a] will live by faith.
And if he shrinks back,
I will not be pleased with him."[b]

³⁹But we are not of those who shrink back and are destroyed, but of those who believe and are saved.

By Faith

11 Now faith is being sure of what we hope for and certain of what we do not see. ²This is what the ancients were commended for.

³By faith we understand that the universe was formed at God's command, so that what is seen was not made out of what was visible.

⁴By faith Abel offered God a better sacrifice than Cain did. By faith he was commended as a righteous man, when God spoke well of his offerings. And by faith he still speaks, even though he is dead.

⁵By faith Enoch was taken from this life, so that he did not experience death; he could not be found, because God had taken him away. For before he was taken, he was commended as one who pleased God. ⁶And without faith it is impossible to please God, because anyone who comes to him must believe that he exists and that he rewards those who earnestly seek him.

⁷By faith Noah, when warned about things not yet seen, in holy fear built an ark to save his family. By his faith he condemned the world and became heir of the righteousness that comes by faith.

⁸By faith Abraham, when called to go to a place he would later receive as his inheritance, obeyed and went, even though he did not know where he was going. ⁹By faith he made his home in the promised land like a stranger in a foreign country; he lived in tents, as did Isaac and Jacob, who were heirs with him of the same promise. ¹⁰For he was looking forward to the city with foundations, whose architect and builder is God.

¹¹By faith Abraham, even though he was past age — and Sarah herself was barren — was enabled to become a father because he[c] considered him faithful who had made the promise. ¹²And so from this one man, and he as good as dead, came descendants as numerous as the stars in the sky and as countless as the sand on the seashore.

¹³All these people were still living by faith when they died. They did not receive the things promised; they only saw them and welcomed them from a distance. And they admitted that they were aliens and strangers on earth. ¹⁴People who say such things show that they are looking for a country of their own. ¹⁵If they had been thinking of the country they had left, they would have had opportunity to return. ¹⁶Instead, they were longing for a better country — a heavenly one. Therefore God is not ashamed to be called their God, for he has prepared a city for them.

¹⁷By faith Abraham, when God tested him, offered Isaac as a sacrifice. He who had received the promises was about to sacrifice his one and only son, ¹⁸even though God had said to him, "It is through Isaac that your offspring[d] will be reckoned."[e] ¹⁹Abraham reasoned that God could raise the dead, and figuratively speaking, he did receive Isaac back from death.

²⁰By faith Isaac blessed Jacob and Esau in regard to their future.

²¹By faith Jacob, when he was dying, blessed each of Joseph's sons, and worshiped as he leaned on the top of his staff.

²²By faith Joseph, when his end was near, spoke about the exodus of the Israelites from Egypt and gave instructions about his bones.

²³By faith Moses' parents hid him for three months after he was born, because they saw he was no ordinary child, and they were not afraid of the king's edict.

²⁴By faith Moses, when he had grown up, refused to be known as the son of Pharaoh's daughter. ²⁵He chose to be mistreated along with the people of God rather than to enjoy the pleasures of sin for a short time. ²⁶He regarded disgrace for the sake of Christ as of greater value than the treasures of Egypt, because he was looking ahead to his reward. ²⁷By faith he left Egypt, not fearing the king's anger; he persevered because he saw him who is invisible. ²⁸By faith he kept the Passover and the sprinkling of blood, so that the destroyer of the firstborn would not touch the firstborn of Israel.

²⁹By faith the people passed through

---

[a]38 One early manuscript *But the righteous past age, was enabled to bear children because she*   [b]38 Hab. 2:3,4   [c]11 Or *By faith even Sarah, who was*   [d]18 Greek *seed*   [e]18 Gen. 21:12

the Red Sea[a] as on dry land; but when the Egyptians tried to do so, they were drowned.

30By faith the walls of Jericho fell, after the people had marched around them for seven days.

31By faith the prostitute Rahab, because she welcomed the spies, was not killed with those who were disobedient.[b]

32And what more shall I say? I do not have time to tell about Gideon, Barak, Samson, Jephthah, David, Samuel and the prophets, **33**who through faith conquered kingdoms, administered justice, and gained what was promised; who shut the mouths of lions, **34**quenched the fury of the flames, and escaped the edge of the sword; whose weakness was turned to strength; and who became powerful in battle and routed foreign armies. **35**Women received back their dead, raised to life again. Others were tortured and refused to

[a]29 That is, Sea of Reeds   [b]31 Or *unbelieving*

MONDAY

VERSE FOR THE DAY:
Hebrews 10:22

AUTHOR:
Reggie White

PASSAGE FOR THE DAY:
Hebrews 10:19–25

The Way to Success

YOU cannot be a complete human being without filling the spiritual void that is inside every person. Training camp Christians [those who attempt to barter with God to achieve success] try to fill that void with religion, money, success, sex, drugs, and the list could go on and on. This void can only be filled with a relationship and continued walking with God through his Son, Jesus Christ.

A well-known national television talk-show host once invited a minister of the gospel on his program. To win the sympathy of the TV audience, he tried to embarrass the minister with question after question. To the talk-show host's chagrin, the minister never gave one answer or opinion of his own. He only quoted Scripture.

At one point the talk-show host asked the man of God why Christians were so narrow-minded in thinking that they were the only people in the whole world who knew God and who knew they were going to heaven.

The minister again quoted Scripture, this time from the New Testament: "I am the way and the truth and the life. No one comes to the Father except through me" (John 14:6).

The preacher then stated, "I didn't say that, God did. If you don't agree with it, tell him, not me."

And that's the answer for training camp Christians also. The promises made, but not kept; the functions attended, but not experienced; the hopes dreamed, but not put into action—commitment matters. There is no success for a football player—or a Christian—without it.

Additional Scripture Readings:
John 14:5–14; John 15:1–8

Go to page 335 for your next devotional reading.

be released, so that they might gain a better resurrection. ³⁶Some faced jeers and flogging, while still others were chained and put in prison. ³⁷They were stoned*ᵃ*; they were sawed in two; they were put to death by the sword. They went about in sheepskins and goatskins, destitute, persecuted and mistreated— ³⁸the world was not worthy of them. They wandered in deserts and mountains, and in caves and holes in the ground.

³⁹These were all commended for their faith, yet none of them received what had been promised. ⁴⁰God had planned something better for us so that only together with us would they be made perfect.

God Disciplines His Sons

12 Therefore, since we are surrounded by such a great cloud of witnesses, let us throw off everything that hinders and the sin that so easily entangles, and let us run with perseverance the race marked out for us. ²Let us fix our eyes on Jesus, the author and perfecter of our faith, who for the joy set before him endured the cross, scorning its shame, and sat down at the right hand of the throne of God. ³Consider him who endured such opposition from sinful men, so that you will not grow weary and lose heart.

⁴In your struggle against sin, you have not yet resisted to the point of shedding your blood. ⁵And you have forgotten that word of encouragement that addresses you as sons:

"My son, do not make light of the
  Lord's discipline,
and do not lose heart when he
  rebukes you,
⁶because the Lord disciplines those he
  loves,
and he punishes everyone he
  accepts as a son."*ᵇ*

⁷Endure hardship as discipline; God is treating you as sons. For what son is not disciplined by his father? ⁸If you are not disciplined (and everyone undergoes discipline), then you are illegitimate children and not true sons. ⁹Moreover, we have all had human fathers who disciplined us and we respected them for it. How much more should we submit to the Father of our spirits and live! ¹⁰Our fathers disciplined us for a little while as they thought best; but God disciplines us for our good, that we may share in his holiness. ¹¹No discipline seems pleasant at the time, but painful. Later on, however, it produces a harvest of righteousness and peace for those who have been trained by it.

¹²Therefore, strengthen your feeble arms and weak knees. ¹³"Make level paths for your feet,"*ᶜ* so that the lame may not be disabled, but rather healed.

Warning Against Refusing God

¹⁴Make every effort to live in peace with all men and to be holy; without holiness no one will see the Lord. ¹⁵See to it that no one misses the grace of God and that no bitter root grows up to cause trouble and defile many. ¹⁶See that no one is sexually immoral, or is godless like Esau, who for a single meal sold his inheritance rights as the oldest son. ¹⁷Afterward, as you know, when he wanted to inherit this blessing, he was rejected. He could bring about no change of mind, though he sought the blessing with tears.

¹⁸You have not come to a mountain that can be touched and that is burning with fire; to darkness, gloom and storm; ¹⁹to a trumpet blast or to such a voice speaking words that those who heard it begged that no further word be spoken to them, ²⁰because they could not bear what was commanded: "If even an animal touches the mountain, it must be stoned."*ᵈ* ²¹The sight was so terrifying that Moses said, "I am trembling with fear."*ᵉ*

²²But you have come to Mount Zion, to the heavenly Jerusalem, the city of the living God. You have come to thousands upon thousands of angels in joyful assembly, ²³to the church of the firstborn, whose names are written in heaven. You have come to God, the judge of all men, to the spirits of righteous men made perfect, ²⁴to Jesus the mediator of a new covenant, and to the sprinkled blood that speaks a better word than the blood of Abel.

²⁵See to it that you do not refuse him who speaks. If they did not escape when they refused him who warned them on earth, how much less will we, if we turn away from him who warns us from heaven? ²⁶At that time his voice shook the earth, but now he has promised, "Once more I will shake not only the earth but also the heavens."*ᶠ* ²⁷The words "once

---

ᵃ37 Some early manuscripts *stoned; they were put to the test;*   *ᵇ6* Prov. 3:11,12   *ᶜ13* Prov. 4:26
ᵈ20 Exodus 19:12,13   *ᵉ21* Deut. 9:19   *ᶠ26* Haggai 2:6

more" indicate the removing of what can be shaken—that is, created things—so that what cannot be shaken may remain. **28**Therefore, since we are receiving a kingdom that cannot be shaken, let us be thankful, and so worship God acceptably with reverence and awe, **29**for our "God is a consuming fire."*a*

Concluding Exhortations

13 Keep on loving each other as brothers. **2**Do not forget to entertain strangers, for by so doing some people have entertained angels without knowing it. **3**Remember those in prison as if you were their fellow prisoners, and those who are mistreated as if you yourselves were suffering.

4Marriage should be honored by all, and the marriage bed kept pure, for God will judge the adulterer and all the sexually immoral. **5**Keep your lives free from the love of money and be content with what you have, because God has said,

a29 Deut. 4:24

TUESDAY

VERSE FOR THE DAY:
Hebrews 12:28

AUTHOR:
Jerry Bridges

PASSAGE FOR THE DAY:
Hebrews 12:18–29

With Reverence and Awe

ONE of the more serious sins of Christians today may well be the almost flippant familiarity with which we often address God in prayer. None of the godly men of the Bible ever adopted the casual manner we often do. They always addressed God with reverence. The same writer who tells us that we have confidence to enter the Most Holy Place, the throne room of God, also tells us that we should worship God acceptably with reverence and awe, "for our 'God is a consuming fire'" (Hebrews 10:19 and 12:28–29). The same Paul who tells us that the Holy Spirit dwelling within us causes us to cry, "*Abba*, Father," also tells us that this same God lives in "unapproachable light" (Romans 8:15 and 1 Timothy 6:16).

In our day we must begin to recover a sense of awe and profound reverence for God. We must begin to view him once again in the infinite majesty that alone belongs to him who is the Creator and Supreme Ruler of the entire universe. There is an infinite gap in worth and dignity between God the Creator and man the creature, even though man has been created in the image of God. The fear of God is a heartfelt recognition of this gap—not a put-down of man, but an exaltation of God . . .

We seem to have magnified the love of God almost to the exclusion of the fear of God. Because of this preoccupation we are not honoring God and reverencing him as we should. We should magnify the love of God; but although we revel in his love and mercy, we must never lose sight of his majesty and his holiness.

Additional Scripture Readings:
Psalm 34:8–14; 1 Peter 1:17–21

Go to page 336 for your next devotional reading.

"Never will I leave you;
never will I forsake you."[a]

[6] So we say with confidence,

"The Lord is my helper; I will not be afraid.
What can man do to me?"[b]

[7] Remember your leaders, who spoke the word of God to you. Consider the outcome of their way of life and imitate their faith. [8] Jesus Christ is the same yesterday and today and forever.

[9] Do not be carried away by all kinds of strange teachings. It is good for our hearts

[a] 5 Deut. 31:6 [b] 6 Psalm 118:6,7

WEDNESDAY

VERSE FOR THE DAY:
Hebrews 13:6

AUTHOR:
Dave Dravecky

PASSAGE FOR THE DAY:
Hebrews 13:5–8

Your Only Audience

DAVE Dravecky's first weeks as a major league baseball pitcher were anxious ones because he was pitching poorly. He was frightened.

"Are you forgetting what you've always said?" [my wife] Janice asked. "Remember? You and Byron used to say you should pitch as though Jesus Christ is your only audience."

That took me back to wonderful, hot Texas days, when I'd been just a scrambling Double-A ballplayer. I'd been with some of my closest friends, playing baseball, enjoying the game, and knowing that a loving God had the only opinion of me that really mattered. Those days in Amarillo had been the happiest of my life. The reason had been, above all, that I knew who I was living for. I knew my audience.

To everybody else, you were only as good as your last performance. The pressure was relentless from the crowd, from the manager, even from the expectations of your friends and family back home. Heck, the pressure could be relentless from inside yourself. But God was concerned only that you did your best. And he was bigger than all the rest combined.

Growing up, I had always been at the center of attention. That was exactly how I had wanted it. My performance had been for me, and no one else. I had to be the star.

That kind of motivation can keep you going strong, so long as you succeed. But it's not so good for dealing with failure, or with forces beyond your control. Seeing Jesus Christ as your audience shifted the pressure off yourself. You did your best to bring glory to God, not yourself. If you lost, the loss would hurt, but it wouldn't change anything fundamental. God would still be there.

Additional Scripture Readings:
Colossians 3:22–25;
1 Corinthians 10:31—11:1

Go to page 339 for your next devotional reading.

to be strengthened by grace, not by ceremonial foods, which are of no value to those who eat them. **10**We have an altar from which those who minister at the tabernacle have no right to eat.

11The high priest carries the blood of animals into the Most Holy Place as a sin offering, but the bodies are burned outside the camp. **12**And so Jesus also suffered outside the city gate to make the people holy through his own blood. **13**Let us, then, go to him outside the camp, bearing the disgrace he bore. **14**For here we do not have an enduring city, but we are looking for the city that is to come.

15Through Jesus, therefore, let us continually offer to God a sacrifice of praise — the fruit of lips that confess his name. **16**And do not forget to do good and to share with others, for with such sacrifices God is pleased.

17Obey your leaders and submit to their authority. They keep watch over you as men who must give an account. Obey them so that their work will be a joy, not a burden, for that would be of no advantage to you.

18Pray for us. We are sure that we have a clear conscience and desire to live honorably in every way. **19**I particularly urge you to pray so that I may be restored to you soon.

20May the God of peace, who through the blood of the eternal covenant brought back from the dead our Lord Jesus, that great Shepherd of the sheep, **21**equip you with everything good for doing his will, and may he work in us what is pleasing to him, through Jesus Christ, to whom be glory for ever and ever. Amen.

22Brothers, I urge you to bear with my word of exhortation, for I have written you only a short letter.

23I want you to know that our brother Timothy has been released. If he arrives soon, I will come with him to see you.

24Greet all your leaders and all God's people. Those from Italy send you their greetings.

25Grace be with you all.

*J*AMES *(a brother of Jesus) writes this letter to urge Christians to express their faith in daily living. He reminds them of what Jesus said, especially in the Sermon on the Mount (Matthew 5–7). As you read this book, ask yourself whether others can see by what you do and say that you believe in Jesus.*

JAMES

1 James, a servant of God and of the Lord Jesus Christ,

To the twelve tribes scattered among the nations:

Greetings.

Trials and Temptations

²Consider it pure joy, my brothers, whenever you face trials of many kinds, ³because you know that the testing of your faith develops perseverance. ⁴Perseverance must finish its work so that you may be mature and complete, not lacking anything. ⁵If any of you lacks wisdom, he should ask God, who gives generously to all without finding fault, and it will be given to him. ⁶But when he asks, he must believe and not doubt, because he who doubts is like a wave of the sea, blown and tossed by the wind. ⁷That man should not think he will receive anything from the Lord; ⁸he is a double-minded man, unstable in all he does.

⁹The brother in humble circumstances ought to take pride in his high position. ¹⁰But the one who is rich should take pride in his low position, because he will pass away like a wild flower. ¹¹For the sun rises with scorching heat and withers the plant; its blossom falls and its beauty is destroyed. In the same way, the rich man will fade away even while he goes about his business.

¹²Blessed is the man who perseveres under trial, because when he has stood the test, he will receive the crown of life that God has promised to those who love him.

¹³When tempted, no one should say, "God is tempting me." For God cannot be tempted by evil, nor does he tempt anyone; ¹⁴but each one is tempted when, by his own evil desire, he is dragged away and enticed. ¹⁵Then, after desire has con-

ceived, it gives birth to sin; and sin, when it is full-grown, gives birth to death.

[16] Don't be deceived, my dear brothers. [17] Every good and perfect gift is from above, coming down from the Father of the heavenly lights, who does not change like shifting shadows. [18] He chose to give us birth through the word of truth, that we might be a kind of firstfruits of all he created.

Listening and Doing

[19] My dear brothers, take note of this: Everyone should be quick to listen, slow to speak and slow to become angry, [20] for man's anger does not bring about the righteous life that God desires. [21] Therefore, get rid of all moral filth and the evil that is so prevalent and humbly accept the word planted in you, which can save you.

[22] Do not merely listen to the word, and so deceive yourselves. Do what it says. [23] Anyone who listens to the word but does not do what it says is like a man who looks at his face in a mirror [24] and, after looking at himself, goes away and immediately forgets what he looks like. [25] But the man who looks intently into the perfect law that gives freedom, and continues

---

THURSDAY

VERSE FOR THE DAY:
James 1:2

AUTHOR:
Gary Smalley and John Trent

PASSAGE FOR THE DAY:
James 1:2–8

Consider It Pure Joy?

AS LOVING parents, one way we can honor our children and build value into their lives is to help them see the positive gain in troubled times. Whether we like it or not, before they leave our homes, our sons or daughters may experience moments or even days of doubt, discouragement, loneliness, disappointment or depression.

They may be betrayed by a friend, fail to get into the college or the profession of their choice, be dumped later in life by a spouse, or perhaps experience the disabling results of experimenting with drugs or alcohol. And with each painful experience their child suffers, Mom and Dad feel the aftershocks in their hearts . . .

It is certainly not wrong to avoid pain when we can. But it is wrong to deny problems, ignore them or try to explain them away. One of the all-time great truths is that life is difficult and often unfair. The better we are at seeing through trials to what they can produce in our lives and our children's lives, the better able we'll be to provide calmness, assurance and genuine love to our children, even in the midst of trying times. In fact, trials have the capacity to bring strength, maturity, courage, genuine love, righteousness and perseverance to those who are willing to be trained by them. The very things we fear might happen to our children can make them stronger people, depending on their response and our response to their difficulties.

Additional Scripture Readings:
Hebrews 12:7-13; 1 Peter 1:3–9

Go to page 340 for your next devotional reading.

to do this, not forgetting what he has heard, but doing it—he will be blessed in what he does.

²⁶If anyone considers himself religious and yet does not keep a tight rein on his tongue, he deceives himself and his religion is worthless. ²⁷Religion that God our Father accepts as pure and faultless is this: to look after orphans and widows in their distress and to keep oneself from being polluted by the world.

Favoritism Forbidden

2 My brothers, as believers in our glorious Lord Jesus Christ, don't show favoritism. ²Suppose a man comes into your meeting wearing a gold ring and fine clothes, and a poor man in shabby clothes also comes in. ³If you show special attention to the man wearing fine clothes and say, "Here's a good seat for you," but say to the poor man, "You stand there" or "Sit on the floor by my feet," ⁴have you not

---

FRIDAY

VERSE FOR THE DAY:
James 1:22

AUTHOR:
John E. Crawford

PASSAGE FOR THE DAY:
James 1:19–25

Building Lofty Cathedrals

EVERY experienced parent knows that bad behavior in a child rarely happens with no previous signals and no past incidents of disobedience or defiance. There are always signals of trouble ahead. Alert fathers and mothers notice such signals in time to intervene and prevent the youngster from skidding into serious mistakes . . .

Your wisdom in controlling your youngster is one of the best measures of how much you really love and value her. She knows this, whether she has said so in plain words or not. She knows that her mother should have a hand in controlling her too; but you, her father, have an equal share in the job. Your personal examples are very important, too, along with your rules. You won't be able to sell her any double standards on the important issues in life. She will come much closer to following what you do and what you believe than what you say about these issues.

Your daughter does not have to believe that you are the wisest man in all the world to count you as a good father. She does want to be able to come to you with important questions about life. She needs to see that you are learning and growing, too, that you are open to new ideas, new concepts.

Being a real father to your children is one job that no one else can ever do as well as you. Good fathers deserve their full share of top praise, for they are helping to build the loftiest cathedrals in the universe: young hearts and minds that are learning how to make this world a better place in which to live.

Additional Scripture Readings:
Matthew 7:15–20; John 15:1–17

Go to page 341 for your next devotional reading.

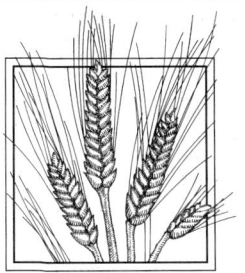

WEEKENDING

RECOGNIZE

The clear duty of real men goes beyond "live and let live." We are mandated to protect widows, orphans, the alien and all those who lack sustaining relationships. As long as men and boys fail to be protective, they will fall prey to the typical male sexual fantasy that sells [pornographic] magazines and films . . .

The only real solution is to teach boys that the source of their power is in the nurturing and protecting image of God created within them. When we express our essential nature, then substitutes, like pornographic fantasies, lose their appeal.

– E. James Wilder

REVIVE
Saturday: 1 Thessalonians 4:3–8
Sunday: James 1:22–27

Go to page 343 for your next devotional reading.

discriminated among yourselves and become judges with evil thoughts?

⁵Listen, my dear brothers: Has not God chosen those who are poor in the eyes of the world to be rich in faith and to inherit the kingdom he promised those who love him? ⁶But you have insulted the poor. Is it not the rich who are exploiting you? Are they not the ones who are dragging you into court? ⁷Are they not the ones who are slandering the noble name of him to whom you belong?

⁸If you really keep the royal law found in Scripture, "Love your neighbor as yourself,"ᵃ you are doing right. ⁹But if you show favoritism, you sin and are convicted by the law as lawbreakers. ¹⁰For whoever keeps the whole law and yet stumbles at just one point is guilty of breaking all of it. ¹¹For he who said, "Do not commit adultery,"ᵇ also said, "Do not murder."ᶜ If you do not commit adultery but do commit murder, you have become a lawbreaker.

¹²Speak and act as those who are going to be judged by the law that gives freedom, ¹³because judgment without mercy will be shown to anyone who has not been merciful. Mercy triumphs over judgment!

Faith and Deeds

¹⁴What good is it, my brothers, if a man claims to have faith but has no deeds? Can such faith save him? ¹⁵Suppose a brother or sister is without clothes and daily food. ¹⁶If one of you says to him, "Go, I wish you well; keep warm and well fed," but does nothing about his physical needs, what good is it? ¹⁷In the same way, faith by itself, if it is not accompanied by action, is dead.

¹⁸But someone will say, "You have faith; I have deeds."

Show me your faith without deeds, and I will show you my faith by what I do. ¹⁹You believe that there is one God. Good! Even the demons believe that — and shudder.

²⁰You foolish man, do you want evidence that faith without deeds is useless*d*? ²¹Was not our ancestor Abraham considered righteous for what he did when he offered his son Isaac on the altar? ²²You see that his faith and his actions were working together, and his faith was made complete by what he did. ²³And the scripture was fulfilled that says, "Abraham believed God, and it was credited to him as righteousness,"ᵉ and he was called God's friend. ²⁴You see that a person is justified by what he does and not by faith alone.

²⁵In the same way, was not even Rahab the prostitute considered righteous for what she did when she gave lodging to the spies and sent them off in a different direction? ²⁶As the body without the spirit is dead, so faith without deeds is dead.

Taming the Tongue

3 Not many of you should presume to be teachers, my brothers, because you know that we who teach will be judged more strictly. ²We all stumble in many ways. If anyone is never at fault in what he says, he is a perfect man, able to keep his whole body in check.

³When we put bits into the mouths of horses to make them obey us, we can turn the whole animal. ⁴Or take ships as an example. Although they are so large and are driven by strong winds, they are steered by a very small rudder wherever the pilot wants to go. ⁵Likewise the tongue is a small part of the body, but it makes great boasts. Consider what a great forest is set on fire by a small spark. ⁶The tongue also is a fire, a world of evil among the parts of the body. It corrupts the whole person, sets the whole course of his life on fire, and is itself set on fire by hell.

⁷All kinds of animals, birds, reptiles and creatures of the sea are being tamed and have been tamed by man, ⁸but no man can tame the tongue. It is a restless evil, full of deadly poison.

⁹With the tongue we praise our Lord and Father, and with it we curse men, who have been made in God's likeness. ¹⁰Out of the same mouth come praise and cursing. My brothers, this should not be. ¹¹Can both fresh water and salt*f* water flow from the same spring? ¹²My brothers, can a fig tree bear olives, or a grapevine bear figs? Neither can a salt spring produce fresh water.

Two Kinds of Wisdom

¹³Who is wise and understanding among you? Let him show it by his good life, by deeds done in the humility that comes from wisdom. ¹⁴But if you harbor bitter envy and selfish ambition in your

---

*a*8 Lev. 19:18   *b*11 Exodus 20:14; Deut. 5:18   *c*11 Exodus 20:13; Deut. 5:17   *d*20 Some early manuscripts *dead*   *e*23 Gen. 15:6   *f*11 Greek *bitter* (see also verse 14)

hearts, do not boast about it or deny the truth. ¹⁵Such "wisdom" does not come down from heaven but is earthly, unspiritual, of the devil. ¹⁶For where you have envy and selfish ambition, there you find disorder and every evil practice.

¹⁷But the wisdom that comes from heaven is first of all pure; then peace-loving, considerate, submissive, full of mercy and good fruit, impartial and sincere. ¹⁸Peacemakers who sow in peace raise a harvest of righteousness.

MONDAY

VERSE FOR THE DAY:
James 2:9

AUTHOR:
Paul Brand

PASSAGE FOR THE DAY:
James 2:1–11

Loyalty to the Head

THE Bible directs harsh words to those who show favoritism. James spelled out a situation we can all identify with: "Suppose a man comes into your meeting wearing a gold ring and fine clothes, and a poor man in shabby clothes also comes in. If you show special attention to the man wearing fine clothes and say, 'Here's a good seat for you,' but say to the poor man, 'You stand there,' or, 'Sit on the floor by my feet,' have you not discriminated among yourselves and become judges with evil thoughts?" He concludes, "If you show favoritism, you sin and are convicted by the law as lawbreakers. For whoever keeps the whole law and yet stumbles at just one point is guilty of breaking all of it" (James 2:2–4,9–10) . . .

In our rating-conscious society that ranks everything from baseball teams to "the best chili in New York," an attitude of relative worth can easily seep into the church of Christ. But the design of the group of people who follow Jesus should not resemble a military machine or a corporate structure. The church Jesus founded is more like a family in which the son retarded from birth has as much worth as his brother the Rhodes scholar. It is like the body composed of cells most striking in their diversity but most effective in their mutuality.

God requires only one thing of his "cells": that each person be loyal to the Head. If each cell accepts the needs of the whole Body as the purpose of its life, then the Body will live in health. It is a brilliant stroke, the only pure egalitarianism I observe in all of society. He has endowed every person in the Body with the same capacity to respond to him. In Christ's Body, a teacher of three-year-olds has the same value as a bishop, and that teacher's work may be just as significant. A widow's dollar can equal a millionaire's annuity. Shyness, beauty, eloquence, race, sophistication—none of these matter, only loyalty to the Head, and through the Head to each other.

Additional Scripture Readings:
Ephesians 4:7–16;
Colossians 1:15–20

Go to page 344 for your next devotional reading.

Submit Yourselves to God

4 What causes fights and quarrels among you? Don't they come from your desires that battle within you? **2** You want something but don't get it. You kill and covet, but you cannot have what you want. You quarrel and fight. You do not have, because you do not ask God. **3** When you ask, you do not receive, because you ask with wrong motives, that you may spend what you get on your pleasures.

4 You adulterous people, don't you know that friendship with the world is hatred toward God? Anyone who chooses to be a friend of the world becomes an enemy of God. **5** Or do you think Scripture says without reason that the spirit he

---

TUESDAY

VERSE FOR THE DAY:
James 3:17

AUTHOR:
Larry Crabb

PASSAGE FOR THE DAY:
James 3:13–18

The Deadliest Culprit

DESIRING our own good is not sinful in itself, but natural and instinctive. God gave us everything, even our very existence. He wants us to take care of what he gave us. It is the act of putting ourselves at the center of the universe, where God belongs, that is unqualified sin. This is, in fact, the very definition of sin.

When self-interest continues as the dominant commitment of our lives, when we devote our energy to serving ourselves above all others, then we are wrongly self-centered. And this form of self-interest is a far more serious and dangerous problem than the wounds we suffer at the hands of others.

But very few people even notice their commitment to self-interest, and among those who do, even fewer are deeply concerned about it. More often, self-centeredness is encouraged: "Look out for yourself. Who else is going to?" "You shouldn't have to put up with that kind of treatment." "You must learn to take care of yourself before you can properly give to others" . . .

We will not move very far in our efforts to develop good marriages until we understand that repairing a damaged sense of identity and healing the wound in our hearts is *not* the first order of business. It is rather dealing with the subtle, pervasive, stubborn commitment to ourselves.

Self-centeredness is the killer. In every bad relationship, it is the deadliest culprit. Poor communication, temper problems, unhealthy responses to dysfunctional family backgrounds, codependent relationships, and personal incompatibility —everything (unless medically caused) flows out of the cesspool of self-centeredness.

Additional Scripture Readings:
John 13:12–17; Philippians 2:1–11

Go to page 345 for your next devotional reading.

caused to live in us envies intensely?[a] ⁶But he gives us more grace. That is why Scripture says:

> "God opposes the proud
> but gives grace to the humble."[b]

⁷Submit yourselves, then, to God. Resist the devil, and he will flee from you. ⁸Come near to God and he will come near to you. Wash your hands, you sinners, and purify your hearts, you double-minded. ⁹Grieve, mourn and wail. Change your laughter to mourning and your joy to gloom. ¹⁰Humble yourselves before the Lord, and he will lift you up.

¹¹Brothers, do not slander one another. Anyone who speaks against his brother or judges him speaks against the law and judges it. When you judge the law, you are not keeping it, but sitting in judgment on it. ¹²There is only one Lawgiver and Judge, the one who is able to save and destroy. But you—who are you to judge your neighbor?

Boasting About Tomorrow

¹³Now listen, you who say, "Today or tomorrow we will go to this or that city, spend a year there, carry on business and make money." ¹⁴Why, you do not even know what will happen tomorrow. What is your life? You are a mist that appears for a little while and then vanishes. ¹⁵Instead, you ought to say, "If it is the Lord's will,

---

[a]5 Or *that God jealously longs for the spirit that he made to live in us*; or *that the Spirit he caused to live in us longs jealously*   [b]6 Prov. 3:34

WEDNESDAY

VERSE FOR THE DAY:
James 5:16

AUTHOR:
Stephen Arterburn and David Stoop

PASSAGE FOR THE DAY:
James 5:13–20

Torn Between Two . . .

IN ORDER to meet the basic psychological needs to know and be known, to love and be loved by others, men need deep caring relationships with other men. It's to this level that James instructed Christians, "Confess your sins to each other and pray for each other so that you may be healed" (James 5:16). A man who doesn't have at least one other man to whom he can be accountable regarding his failures, hurts and temptations is a prime target for masculine anger.

The angry man in our society is caught between mythical masculinity on the one side and true masculinity on the other. He feels the pressure to achieve, to earn, to conquer, to win —and to do all these things on his own. But he also feels the need to love and to nurture those he loves, and to be loved and nurtured by those who love him. He futilely attempts to reconcile the two in his own life. He is torn between being invincible and vulnerable, aloof and involved, self-serving and succoring . . . The roots of this conflict send up numerous shoots of anger-producing tendencies in his life.

Additional Scripture Readings:
Ephesians 4:22–32;
1 Thessalonians 2:6b-12

Go to page 348 for your next devotional reading.

we will live and do this or that." **16**As it is, you boast and brag. All such boasting is evil. **17**Anyone, then, who knows the good he ought to do and doesn't do it, sins.

Warning to Rich Oppressors

5 Now listen, you rich people, weep and wail because of the misery that is coming upon you. **2**Your wealth has rotted, and moths have eaten your clothes. **3**Your gold and silver are corroded. Their corrosion will testify against you and eat your flesh like fire. You have hoarded wealth in the last days. **4**Look! The wages you failed to pay the workmen who mowed your fields are crying out against you. The cries of the harvesters have reached the ears of the Lord Almighty. **5**You have lived on earth in luxury and self-indulgence. You have fattened yourselves in the day of slaughter.[a] **6**You have condemned and murdered innocent men, who were not opposing you.

Patience in Suffering

7Be patient, then, brothers, until the Lord's coming. See how the farmer waits for the land to yield its valuable crop and how patient he is for the autumn and spring rains. **8**You too, be patient and stand firm, because the Lord's coming is near. **9**Don't grumble against each other, brothers, or you will be judged. The Judge is standing at the door!

10Brothers, as an example of patience in the face of suffering, take the prophets who spoke in the name of the Lord. **11**As you know, we consider blessed those who have persevered. You have heard of Job's perseverance and have seen what the Lord finally brought about. The Lord is full of compassion and mercy.

12Above all, my brothers, do not swear—not by heaven or by earth or by anything else. Let your "Yes" be yes, and your "No," no, or you will be condemned.

The Prayer of Faith

13Is any one of you in trouble? He should pray. Is anyone happy? Let him sing songs of praise. **14**Is any one of you sick? He should call the elders of the church to pray over him and anoint him with oil in the name of the Lord. **15**And the prayer offered in faith will make the sick person well; the Lord will raise him up. If he has sinned, he will be forgiven. **16**Therefore confess your sins to each other and pray for each other so that you may be healed. The prayer of a righteous man is powerful and effective.

17Elijah was a man just like us. He prayed earnestly that it would not rain, and it did not rain on the land for three and a half years. **18**Again he prayed, and the heavens gave rain, and the earth produced its crops.

19My brothers, if one of you should wander from the truth and someone should bring him back, **20**remember this: Whoever turns a sinner from the error of his way will save him from death and cover over a multitude of sins.

---

[a]5 Or *yourselves as in a day of feasting*

PETER writes this letter to a group of Christians suffering for their faith, reminding them of how much Jesus suffered. He inspires them with hope for the future and shows them how to grow in their faith. As you read this book, decide to do your best to live a holy life as you look forward to the return of Jesus and to the reward he promises to give his followers.

1 PETER

1 Peter, an apostle of Jesus Christ,

To God's elect, strangers in the world, scattered throughout Pontus, Galatia, Cappadocia, Asia and Bithynia, ²who have been chosen according to the foreknowledge of God the Father, through the sanctifying work of the Spirit, for obedience to Jesus Christ and sprinkling by his blood:

Grace and peace be yours in abundance.

Praise to God for a Living Hope

³Praise be to the God and Father of our Lord Jesus Christ! In his great mercy he has given us new birth into a living hope through the resurrection of Jesus Christ from the dead, ⁴and into an inheritance that can never perish, spoil or fade — kept in heaven for you, ⁵who through faith are shielded by God's power until the coming of the salvation that is ready to be revealed in the last time. ⁶In this you greatly rejoice, though now for a little while you may have had to suffer grief in all kinds of trials. ⁷These have come so that your faith — of greater worth than gold, which perishes even though refined by fire — may be proved genuine and may result in praise, glory and honor when Jesus Christ is revealed. ⁸Though you have not seen him, you love him; and even though you do not see him now, you believe in him and are filled with an inexpressible and glorious joy, ⁹for you are receiving the goal of your faith, the salvation of your souls.

¹⁰Concerning this salvation, the prophets, who spoke of the grace that was to come to you, searched intently and with the greatest care, ¹¹trying to find out the time and circumstances to which the Spir-

it of Christ in them was pointing when he predicted the sufferings of Christ and the glories that would follow. [12]It was revealed to them that they were not serving themselves but you, when they spoke of the things that have now been told you by those who have preached the gospel to you by the Holy Spirit sent from heaven. Even angels long to look into these things.

Be Holy

[13]Therefore, prepare your minds for action; be self-controlled; set your hope fully on the grace to be given you when Jesus Christ is revealed. [14]As obedient children, do not conform to the evil desires you had when you lived in ignorance. [15]But just as he who called you is holy, so be holy in all you do; [16]for it is written: "Be holy, because I am holy."[a]

[17]Since you call on a Father who judges each man's work impartially, live your lives as strangers here in reverent fear. [18]For you know that it was not with per-

[a]16 Lev. 11:44,45; 19:2; 20:7

THURSDAY

VERSE FOR THE DAY:
1 Peter 1:15

AUTHOR:
Thomas Merton

PASSAGE FOR THE DAY:
1 Peter 1:13–16

Be Holy in All You Do

THE way of Christian holiness is, in any case, hard and austere. We must fast and pray. We must embrace hardship and sacrifice, for the love of Christ, and in order to improve the condition of man on earth. We may not merely enjoy the good things of life ourselves, occasionally "purifying our intention" to make sure that we are doing it all "for God." Such purely abstract and mental operations are only a pitiful excuse for mediocrity. They do not justify us in the sight of God. It is not enough to make pious gestures. Our love of God and of man cannot be merely symbolic, it has to be completely real. It is not just a mental operation, but the gift and commitment of our inmost self.

Obviously, this means going a little further than the vapid preachments of that popular religion which has led some people to believe that a "religious revival" is taking place among us. Let us not be too sure of that! The mere fact that men are frightened and insecure, that they grasp at optimistic slogans, run more frequently to church, and seek to pacify their troubled souls by cheerful and humanitarian maxims, is surely no indication that our society is becoming "religious." In fact, it may be a symptom of spiritual sickness. It is certainly a good thing to be aware of our symptoms, but that does not justify our palliating them with quack medicines. Let us not therefore delude ourselves with easy and infantile conceptions of holiness . . . Mere external respectability, without deeper or more positive moral values, brings discredit upon the Christian faith.

Additional Scripture Readings:
Matthew 23:25–28; James 2:14–26

Go to page 350 for your next devotional reading.

ishable things such as silver or gold that you were redeemed from the empty way of life handed down to you from your forefathers, **19**but with the precious blood of Christ, a lamb without blemish or defect. **20**He was chosen before the creation of the world, but was revealed in these last times for your sake. **21**Through him you believe in God, who raised him from the dead and glorified him, and so your faith and hope are in God.

22Now that you have purified yourselves by obeying the truth so that you have sincere love for your brothers, love one another deeply, from the heart.*a* **23**For you have been born again, not of perishable seed, but of imperishable, through the living and enduring word of God. **24**For,

"All men are like grass,
 and all their glory is like the flowers of the field;
the grass withers and the flowers fall,
25 but the word of the Lord stands forever."*b*

And this is the word that was preached to you.

2 Therefore, rid yourselves of all malice and all deceit, hypocrisy, envy, and slander of every kind. **2**Like newborn babies, crave pure spiritual milk, so that by it you may grow up in your salvation, **3**now that you have tasted that the Lord is good.

The Living Stone and a Chosen People

4As you come to him, the living Stone — rejected by men but chosen by God and precious to him — **5**you also, like living stones, are being built into a spiritual house to be a holy priesthood, offering spiritual sacrifices acceptable to God through Jesus Christ. **6**For in Scripture it says:

"See, I lay a stone in Zion,
 a chosen and precious cornerstone,
and the one who trusts in him
 will never be put to shame."*c*

7Now to you who believe, this stone is precious. But to those who do not believe,

"The stone the builders rejected
 has become the capstone,*d*"*e*

8and,

"A stone that causes men to stumble
 and a rock that makes them fall."*f*

They stumble because they disobey the message — which is also what they were destined for.

9But you are a chosen people, a royal priesthood, a holy nation, a people belonging to God, that you may declare the praises of him who called you out of darkness into his wonderful light. **10**Once you were not a people, but now you are the people of God; once you had not received mercy, but now you have received mercy.

11Dear friends, I urge you, as aliens and strangers in the world, to abstain from sinful desires, which war against your soul. **12**Live such good lives among the pagans that, though they accuse you of doing wrong, they may see your good deeds and glorify God on the day he visits us.

Submission to Rulers and Masters

13Submit yourselves for the Lord's sake to every authority instituted among men: whether to the king, as the supreme authority, **14**or to governors, who are sent by him to punish those who do wrong and to commend those who do right. **15**For it is God's will that by doing good you should silence the ignorant talk of foolish men. **16**Live as free men, but do not use your freedom as a cover-up for evil; live as servants of God. **17**Show proper respect to everyone: Love the brotherhood of believers, fear God, honor the king.

18Slaves, submit yourselves to your masters with all respect, not only to those who are good and considerate, but also to those who are harsh. **19**For it is commendable if a man bears up under the pain of unjust suffering because he is conscious of God. **20**But how is it to your credit if you receive a beating for doing wrong and endure it? But if you suffer for doing good and you endure it, this is commendable before God. **21**To this you were called, because Christ suffered for you, leaving you an example, that you should follow in his steps.

22"He committed no sin,
 and no deceit was found in his mouth."*g*

23When they hurled their insults at him, he did not retaliate; when he suffered, he

---

*a*22 Some early manuscripts *from a pure heart*   *b*25 Isaiah 40:6-8   *c*6 Isaiah 28:16   *d*7 Or *cornerstone*   *e*7 Psalm 118:22   *f*8 Isaiah 8:14   *g*22 Isaiah 53:9

made no threats. Instead, he entrusted himself to him who judges justly. **24**He himself bore our sins in his body on the tree, so that we might die to sins and live for righteousness; by his wounds you have been healed. **25**For you were like sheep going astray, but now you have returned to the Shepherd and Overseer of your souls.

Wives and Husbands

3 Wives, in the same way be submissive to your husbands so that, if any of them do not believe the word, they may be won over without words by the behavior of their wives, **2**when they see the purity and reverence of your lives. **3**Your beauty should not come from outward adornment, such as braided hair and the

---

FRIDAY

VERSE FOR THE DAY:
1 Peter 2:1

AUTHOR:
Mark Ritchie

PASSAGE FOR THE DAY:
1 Peter 1:22—2:3

Who's the Hypocrite?

[FOR atheist Jean-Paul Sartre,] it was a "misunderstanding" that caused something to come between him and God. It seems that as a young boy he had done something wrong (he was playing with matches and burned a rug) and while attempting to conceal the evidence, his conscience irritated him.

This was the same sort of thing I had gone through as a boy, I thought, that irritating conscience. "I felt his gaze inside my head," he wrote, "and on my hands. I whirled about in the bathroom, horribly visible, a live target." He flew into a rage at such a crude indiscretion by God and cursed him repeatedly. How could God be so crude, Sartre thought, as to invade the private mind of a small child? This "misunderstanding," as he called it, caused God to vegetate and die.

For myself, I could not possibly have been more puzzled. I certainly shared his feeling that the hypocrisy of the so-called godly made Christianity look false and God powerless. But now God was "gazing on *his* hands," irritating *him* for *his* hypocrisy, and it made him angry. He had experienced God for himself as he said, "inside my head," and he liked the idea even less.

Well, which is it, I asked myself? Are we going to disbelieve because of the hypocrisy we see in others or because God won't allow that same hypocrisy in us? It reminded me of the statement of that other famous atheist, Nietzsche, when he wrote, "If you could prove God to me, I would believe in him all the less." It almost seemed as if the closer these great thinkers came to the idea of God, the less clarity of thought they expressed. While I was impressed—in fact, amazed—at their honesty, I began to lose respect for the objectivity with which they searched for truth.

Additional Scripture Readings:
Mark 7:6–13; Romans 3:9–20

Go to page 351 for your next devotional reading.

WEEKENDING

RENEW

Develop a new kind of trust in God's presence and sovereign lordship in your life. At birth, he gives each of us a unique, authentic self. As we mature, God encourages us to discover that unique self he made each of us to be. He wants us to nurture it and then to let others see it as his handiwork . . .

Let what you do arise out of who you are. Being is more important than doing. As for me, I have decided that whatever I do for the rest of my life, it will not be in order to have an identity. It will be the result of allowing my God-given self to emerge. I'm done with posturing for a public that demands an unattainable and hypocritical perfection.
– *Stan Mooneyham*

REVIVE
Saturday: Ephesians 4:20–24
Sunday: 1 Peter 2:9–12

Go to page 352 for your next devotional reading.

wearing of gold jewelry and fine clothes. ⁴Instead, it should be that of your inner self, the unfading beauty of a gentle and quiet spirit, which is of great worth in God's sight. ⁵For this is the way the holy women of the past who put their hope in God used to make themselves beautiful. They were submissive to their own husbands, ⁶like Sarah, who obeyed Abraham and called him her master. You are her daughters if you do what is right and do not give way to fear.

⁷Husbands, in the same way be considerate as you live with your wives, and treat them with respect as the weaker partner and as heirs with you of the gracious gift of life, so that nothing will hinder your prayers.

Suffering for Doing Good

⁸Finally, all of you, live in harmony with one another; be sympathetic, love as brothers, be compassionate and humble. ⁹Do not repay evil with evil or insult with insult, but with blessing, because to this you were called so that you may inherit a blessing. ¹⁰For,

"Whoever would love life
   and see good days

MONDAY

VERSE FOR THE DAY:　　　AUTHOR:　　　PASSAGE FOR THE DAY:
1 Peter 3:7　　　　D. Stuart Briscoe　　　　1 Peter 3:1–7

Real Husbands

THIS revolutionary teaching by Peter—that women were *equally* heirs of the grace of life—amazed the men of that time. For in Peter and Paul's day, men were the legal heirs of life. They strutted around and had everything going their way. The women entertained them, met their sexual needs, managed their homes, and produced sons (and heirs). Women were locked into roles determined by the men.

Husbands, do you look at your wives from Peter's perspective? Are you as concerned about their spiritual fulfillment as you are about your own? Do you treat them with genuine respect?

Many of us men are extremely gifted at being *inconsiderate*. We fail to see the deep hurts and intense fears of our wives. We are notoriously insensitive—and the people we live with have the scars to prove it. It seems to be a characteristic of the male ego. Peter is telling us that because women are co-heirs with men of "the gracious gift of life," they are equally citizens of the kingdom of heaven.

What do *real* husbands do? They adhere to Jesus' teaching known as the Golden Rule: "Do to others as you would have them do to you" [Luke 6:31]. If husbands faithfully followed that precept in relating to their wives, the married women in our world would think they were "on the threshold of heaven, if not halfway through the door!" Men—let's become *real* husbands!

Additional Scripture Readings:　　　*Go to page 354 for your next*
Luke 6:27–36; Ephesians 5:22–33　　　　*devotional reading.*

must keep his tongue from evil
and his lips from deceitful speech.
11He must turn from evil and do good;
he must seek peace and pursue it.
12For the eyes of the Lord are on the righteous
and his ears are attentive to their prayer,
but the face of the Lord is against those who do evil."[a]

13Who is going to harm you if you are eager to do good? **14**But even if you should suffer for what is right, you are blessed. "Do not fear what they fear[b]; do not be frightened."[c] **15**But in your hearts set apart Christ as Lord. Always be prepared to give an answer to everyone who asks you to give the reason for the hope that you have. But do this with gentleness and respect, **16**keeping a clear conscience, so that those who speak maliciously against your good behavior in Christ may be ashamed of their slander. **17**It is better, if it is God's will, to suffer for doing good than for doing evil. **18**For Christ died for sins once for all, the righteous for the unrighteous, to bring you to God. He was put to death in the body but made alive by the Spirit, **19**through whom[d] also he went and preached to the spirits in prison **20**who disobeyed long ago when God waited patiently in the days of Noah while the ark was being built. In it only a few people, eight in all, were saved through water, **21**and this water symbolizes baptism that now saves you also—not the removal of dirt from the body but the pledge[e] of a good conscience toward God. It saves you by the resurrection of Jesus Christ, **22**who has gone into heaven and is at God's right hand—with angels, authorities and powers in submission to him.

Living for God

4 Therefore, since Christ suffered in his body, arm yourselves also with the same attitude, because he who has suffered in his body is done with sin. **2**As a result, he does not live the rest of his earthly life for evil human desires, but rather for the will of God. **3**For you have spent enough time in the past doing what pagans choose to do—living in debauchery, lust, drunkenness, orgies, carousing and detestable idolatry. **4**They think it strange that you do not plunge with them into the same flood of dissipation, and they heap abuse on you. **5**But they will have to give account to him who is ready to judge the living and the dead. **6**For this is the reason the gospel was preached even to those who are now dead, so that they might be judged according to men in regard to the body, but live according to God in regard to the spirit.

7The end of all things is near. Therefore be clear minded and self-controlled so that you can pray. **8**Above all, love each other deeply, because love covers over a multitude of sins. **9**Offer hospitality to one another without grumbling. **10**Each one should use whatever gift he has received to serve others, faithfully administering God's grace in its various forms. **11**If anyone speaks, he should do it as one speaking the very words of God. If anyone serves, he should do it with the strength God provides, so that in all things God may be praised through Jesus Christ. To him be the glory and the power for ever and ever. Amen.

Suffering for Being a Christian

12Dear friends, do not be surprised at the painful trial you are suffering, as though something strange were happening to you. **13**But rejoice that you participate in the sufferings of Christ, so that you may be overjoyed when his glory is revealed. **14**If you are insulted because of the name of Christ, you are blessed, for the Spirit of glory and of God rests on you. **15**If you suffer, it should not be as a murderer or thief or any other kind of criminal, or even as a meddler. **16**However, if you suffer as a Christian, do not be ashamed, but praise God that you bear that name. **17**For it is time for judgment to begin with the family of God; and if it begins with us, what will the outcome be for those who do not obey the gospel of God? **18**And,

"If it is hard for the righteous to be saved,
what will become of the ungodly and the sinner?"[f]

19So then, those who suffer according to God's will should commit themselves to their faithful Creator and continue to do good.

---

[a]12 Psalm 34:12-16   [b]14 Or *not fear their threats*   [c]14 Isaiah 8:12   [d]18,19 Or *alive in the spirit, 19through which*   [e]21 Or *response*   [f]18 Prov. 11:31

1 PETER 5

To Elders and Young Men

5 To the elders among you, I appeal as a fellow elder, a witness of Christ's sufferings and one who also will share in the glory to be revealed: ²Be shepherds of God's flock that is under your care, serving as overseers—not because you must, but because you are willing, as God wants you to be; not greedy for money, but eager to serve; ³not lording it over those entrusted to you, but being examples to the flock. ⁴And when the Chief Shepherd appears, you will receive the crown of glory that will never fade away.

⁵Young men, in the same way be submissive to those who are older. All of you, clothe yourselves with humility toward one another, because,

"God opposes the proud
but gives grace to the humble."*a*

⁶Humble yourselves, therefore, under God's mighty hand, that he may lift you up in due time. ⁷Cast all your anxiety on him because he cares for you.

⁸Be self-controlled and alert. Your ene-

a 5 Prov. 3:34

TUESDAY

VERSE FOR THE DAY:
1 Peter 5:8

AUTHOR:
Steve Farrar

PASSAGE FOR THE DAY:
1 Peter 5:8–9

Satan's Strategy

THE enemy is no fool. He has a strategically designed game plan, a diabolical method he employs time and time again. When he wants to destroy a family, he focuses on the man. For if he can neutralize the man . . . he has neutralized the family. And the damage that takes place when a man's family leadership is neutralized is beyond calculation.

Satan's approach is the same, whether he's doing combat in the church or in the family. If Satan can neutralize a pastor through financial impropriety or by a sexual escapade, he has neutralized that pastor's church as well. Not only the reputation of the pastor, but the reputation of the church has been tarnished. Satan's strategy has always been to neutralize the leaders. It works in the family, and it works in the church.

What that means is that we should *expect* to be attacked. We should *expect* extreme temptation to come our way. When you get serious about leading your family, you will be opposed.

If a man is passive and indifferent to the things of God and the spiritual leadership of his home, then attack is not necessary. He is already "neutralized" . . .

Gentlemen, I know that you love your families. You love your wife. You love your children. You would be willing to die for them. In most wars, that's what men are asked to do. They go off to war because they're willing to die for their families. That's what he would have you to do.

Additional Scripture Readings:
Proverbs 4:1–12; Ephesians 6:10–18

Go to page 357 for your next devotional reading.

my the devil prowls around like a roaring lion looking for someone to devour. ⁹Resist him, standing firm in the faith, because you know that your brothers throughout the world are undergoing the same kind of sufferings.

¹⁰And the God of all grace, who called you to his eternal glory in Christ, after you have suffered a little while, will himself restore you and make you strong, firm and steadfast. ¹¹To him be the power for ever and ever. Amen.

Final Greetings

¹²With the help of Silas,[a] whom I regard as a faithful brother, I have written to you briefly, encouraging you and testifying that this is the true grace of God. Stand fast in it.

¹³She who is in Babylon, chosen together with you, sends you her greetings, and so does my son Mark. ¹⁴Greet one another with a kiss of love.

Peace to all of you who are in Christ.

---

[a] 12 Greek *Silvanus*, a variant of *Silas*

*P*ETER *writes a second letter because false teachers are troubling the church and disturbing the faith of some by their heresy, immorality and greed. He wants Christians to grow in the knowledge of the truth of God's Word. As you read this book, remember that God will eventually win the battle against false teaching, and promise the Lord that you will study to increase your knowledge of the Bible.*

2 PETER

1 Simon Peter, a servant and apostle of Jesus Christ,

To those who through the righteousness of our God and Savior Jesus Christ have received a faith as precious as ours:

²Grace and peace be yours in abundance through the knowledge of God and of Jesus our Lord.

Making One's Calling and Election Sure

³His divine power has given us everything we need for life and godliness through our knowledge of him who called us by his own glory and goodness. ⁴Through these he has given us his very great and precious promises, so that through them you may participate in the divine nature and escape the corruption in the world caused by evil desires.

⁵For this very reason, make every effort to add to your faith goodness; and to goodness, knowledge; ⁶and to knowledge, self-control; and to self-control, perseverance; and to perseverance, godliness; ⁷and to godliness, brotherly kindness; and to brotherly kindness, love. ⁸For if you possess these qualities in increasing measure, they will keep you from being ineffective and unproductive in your knowledge of our Lord Jesus Christ. ⁹But if anyone does not have them, he is nearsighted and blind, and has forgotten that he has been cleansed from his past sins.

¹⁰Therefore, my brothers, be all the

more eager to make your calling and election sure. For if you do these things, you will never fall, **11**and you will receive a rich welcome into the eternal kingdom of our Lord and Savior Jesus Christ.

Prophecy of Scripture

12So I will always remind you of these things, even though you know them and are firmly established in the truth you now have. **13**I think it is right to refresh your memory as long as I live in the tent of this body, **14**because I know that I will soon put it aside, as our Lord Jesus Christ has made clear to me. **15**And I will make every effort to see that after my departure you will always be able to remember these things.

16We did not follow cleverly invented stories when we told you about the power and coming of our Lord Jesus Christ, but we were eyewitnesses of his majesty. **17**For he received honor and glory from God the Father when the voice came to

---

WEDNESDAY

VERSE FOR THE DAY:
2 Peter 1:1

AUTHOR:
Thomas Hale

PASSAGE FOR THE DAY:
2 Peter 1:1–2

Faith as Precious as Ours

THOMAS and Cynthia Hale, a surgeon and pediatrician respectively, moved their family to Nepal in 1970 with the understanding that they would not be allowed to "proselytize" the Nepali people.

Some may ask why we have come to Nepal if not to "proselytize" or "Christianize" the country. Our reason for coming, besides the fact that God has called us here, is to communicate the love of God to the Nepali people through our service and through our lives. We have come because God has given us a love for the people, especially for those suffering in body and spirit. This love does not arise from ourselves—it is a gift purely from God. Out of that love has grown a desire to introduce others to the person who has meant more to us than any other: Jesus Christ. To neglect sharing with our Nepali friends the joy of knowing him would make a pretense of our friendship. To withhold from them this greatest gift would be to no longer love them. And so it is not our religion that we desire to introduce to them but Jesus himself. There is no pressure, no enticement, no ulterior motive, no effort to undermine the many wonderful aspects of their own culture, which we not only admire but from which we have learned and profited. Rather we seek to work among the Nepalis as friends and equals, contributing our professional skills where needed and involving ourselves as much as possible in their national aspirations. During the course of all this, it is perfectly natural for us to share with them, as occasions arise, our hearts' deepest feelings. They can take Christ or leave him; we shall serve them regardless.

Additional Scripture Readings:
Colossians 4:2–6; 1 Peter 3:13–17

Go to page 358 for your next devotional reading.

him from the Majestic Glory, saying, "This is my Son, whom I love; with him I am well pleased."[a] [18]We ourselves heard this voice that came from heaven when we were with him on the sacred mountain.

[19]And we have the word of the prophets made more certain, and you will do well to pay attention to it, as to a light shining in a dark place, until the day dawns and the morning star rises in your hearts. [20]Above all, you must understand that no prophecy of Scripture came about by the prophet's own interpretation. [21]For prophecy never had its origin in the will of man, but men spoke from God as they were carried along by the Holy Spirit.

False Teachers and Their Destruction

2 But there were also false prophets among the people, just as there will be false teachers among you. They will secretly introduce destructive heresies, even denying the sovereign Lord who bought them—bringing swift destruction on themselves. [2]Many will follow their shameful ways and will bring the way of truth into disrepute. [3]In their greed these teachers will exploit you with stories they have made up. Their condemnation has

[a]17 Matt. 17:5; Mark 9:7; Luke 9:35

THURSDAY

VERSE FOR THE DAY:
2 Peter 1:19

AUTHOR:
Frederick Buechner

PASSAGE FOR THE DAY:
2 Peter 1:16–21

Our Very Own Story

FOR all its vast diversity and unevenness, it [the Bible] is a book with a plot and a plot that can be readily stated. God makes the world in love. For one reason or another the world chooses to reject God. God will not reject the world but continues his mysterious and relentless pursuit of it to the end of time. That is what he is doing by choosing Israel to be his special people. That is what he is doing through all the passion and poetry and invective of the prophets. That is why history plays such a crucial part in the Old Testament—all those kings and renegades and battles and invasions and apostasies —because it was precisely through people like that and events like those that God was at work, as, later, in the New Testament, he was supremely at work in the person and event of Jesus Christ. Only "*is* at work" would be the more accurate way of putting it because . . . his work goes on still, of course, and at one and the same time the Biblical past not only illumines the present but becomes itself part of that present, part of our own individual pasts. Until you can read the story of Adam and Eve, of Abraham and Sarah, of David and Bathsheba, as your own story . . . you have not really understood it. The Bible . . . is a book finally about ourselves, our own apostasies, our own battles and blessings.

Additional Scripture Readings:
Psalm 119:105–112;
2 Timothy 3:14–17

Go to page 360 for your next devotional reading.

long been hanging over them, and their destruction has not been sleeping. ⁴For if God did not spare angels when they sinned, but sent them to hell,ᵃ putting them into gloomy dungeonsᵇ to be held for judgment; ⁵if he did not spare the ancient world when he brought the flood on its ungodly people, but protected Noah, a preacher of righteousness, and seven others; ⁶if he condemned the cities of Sodom and Gomorrah by burning them to ashes, and made them an example of what is going to happen to the ungodly; ⁷and if he rescued Lot, a righteous man, who was distressed by the filthy lives of lawless men ⁸(for that righteous man, living among them day after day, was tormented in his righteous soul by the lawless deeds he saw and heard) — ⁹if this is so, then the Lord knows how to rescue godly men from trials and to hold the unrighteous for the day of judgment, while continuing their punishment.ᶜ ¹⁰This is especially true of those who follow the corrupt desire of the sinful natureᵈ and despise authority.

Bold and arrogant, these men are not afraid to slander celestial beings; ¹¹yet even angels, although they are stronger and more powerful, do not bring slanderous accusations against such beings in the presence of the Lord. ¹²But these men blaspheme in matters they do not understand. They are like brute beasts, creatures of instinct, born only to be caught and destroyed, and like beasts they too will perish.

¹³They will be paid back with harm for the harm they have done. Their idea of pleasure is to carouse in broad daylight. They are blots and blemishes, reveling in their pleasures while they feast with you.ᵉ ¹⁴With eyes full of adultery, they never stop sinning; they seduce the unstable; they are experts in greed — an accursed brood! ¹⁵They have left the straight way and wandered off to follow the way of Balaam son of Beor, who loved the wages of wickedness. ¹⁶But he was rebuked for his wrongdoing by a donkey — a beast without speech — who spoke with a man's voice and restrained the prophet's madness.

¹⁷These men are springs without water and mists driven by a storm. Blackest darkness is reserved for them. ¹⁸For they mouth empty, boastful words and, by appealing to the lustful desires of sinful human nature, they entice people who are just escaping from those who live in error. ¹⁹They promise them freedom, while they themselves are slaves of depravity — for a man is a slave to whatever has mastered him. ²⁰If they have escaped the corruption of the world by knowing our Lord and Savior Jesus Christ and are again entangled in it and overcome, they are worse off at the end than they were at the beginning. ²¹It would have been better for them not to have known the way of righteousness, than to have known it and then to turn their backs on the sacred command that was passed on to them. ²²Of them the proverbs are true: "A dog returns to its vomit,"ᶠ and, "A sow that is washed goes back to her wallowing in the mud."

The Day of the Lord

3 Dear friends, this is now my second letter to you. I have written both of them as reminders to stimulate you to wholesome thinking. ²I want you to recall the words spoken in the past by the holy prophets and the command given by our Lord and Savior through your apostles.

³First of all, you must understand that in the last days scoffers will come, scoffing and following their own evil desires. ⁴They will say, "Where is this 'coming' he promised? Ever since our fathers died, everything goes on as it has since the beginning of creation." ⁵But they deliberately forget that long ago by God's word the heavens existed and the earth was formed out of water and by water. ⁶By these waters also the world of that time was deluged and destroyed. ⁷By the same word the present heavens and earth are reserved for fire, being kept for the day of judgment and destruction of ungodly men.

⁸But do not forget this one thing, dear friends: With the Lord a day is like a thousand years, and a thousand years are like a day. ⁹The Lord is not slow in keeping his promise, as some understand slowness. He is patient with you, not wanting anyone to perish, but everyone to come to repentance.

¹⁰But the day of the Lord will come like a thief. The heavens will disappear with a roar; the elements will be destroyed by

---

ᵃ4 Greek *Tartarus*   ᵇ4 Some manuscripts *into chains of darkness*   ᶜ9 Or *unrighteous for punishment until the day of judgment*   ᵈ10 Or *the flesh*   ᵉ13 Some manuscripts *in their love feasts*   ᶠ22 Prov. 26:11

fire, and the earth and everything in it will be laid bare.[a]

[11]Since everything will be destroyed in this way, what kind of people ought you to be? You ought to live holy and godly lives [12]as you look forward to the day of God and speed its coming.[b] That day will bring about the destruction of the heavens by fire, and the elements will melt in the heat. [13]But in keeping with his promise we are looking forward to a new heaven and a new earth, the home of righteousness.

[14]So then, dear friends, since you are looking forward to this, make every effort to be found spotless, blameless and at peace with him. [15]Bear in mind that our Lord's patience means salvation, just as our dear brother Paul also wrote you with the wisdom that God gave him. [16]He writes the same way in all his letters, speaking in them of these matters. His letters contain some things that are hard to understand, which ignorant and unstable people distort, as they do the other Scriptures, to their own destruction.

[a]10 Some manuscripts *be burned up* [b]12 Or *as you wait eagerly for the day of God to come*

FRIDAY

VERSE FOR THE DAY:
2 Peter 3:11

AUTHOR:
Thomas Merton

PASSAGE FOR THE DAY:
2 Peter 3:11–14

Simply a Window

THE true saint is not one who has become convinced that he himself is holy, but one who is overwhelmed by the realization that God, and God alone, is holy. He is so awestruck with the reality of the divine holiness that he begins to see it everywhere. Eventually, he may be able to see it in himself too: but surely he will see it there last of all, because in himself he will continue to experience the nothingness, the pseudo reality of egoism and sin. Yet even in the darkness of our disposition to evil shines the presence and the mercy of the divine Savior. The saint is capable, as [Russian novelist] Dostoevski said, of loving others even in their sin. For what he sees in all things and in all men is the object of the divine compassion.

The saint, then, seeks not his own glory but the glory of God. And in order that God may be glorified in all things, the saint wishes himself to be nothing but a pure instrument of the divine will. He wants himself to be simply a window through which God's mercy shines on the world. And for this he strives to be holy. He strives to practice virtue heroically, not in order to be known as a virtuous and holy man, but in order that the goodness of God may never be obscured by any selfish act of his.

Hence it is that he who loves God, and seeks the glory of God, seeks to become, by God's grace, perfect in love, as the "heavenly Father is perfect" (Matthew 5:48).

Additional Scripture Readings:
2 Corinthians 3:12—4:6;
1 Peter 1:13–16

Go to page 362 for your next devotional reading.

2 PETER 3

¹⁷Therefore, dear friends, since you already know this, be on your guard so that you may not be carried away by the error of lawless men and fall from your secure position. ¹⁸But grow in the grace and knowledge of our Lord and Savior Jesus Christ. To him be glory both now and forever! Amen.

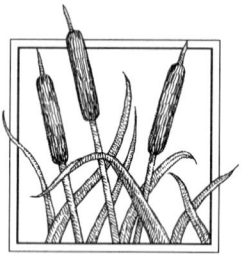

WEEKENDING

REFLECT

Redemption in Jesus Christ initiates a new life, one in which the life of God invades ours, making the passage of time take on the significance of eternity. We can see the design of history's tapestry even though the entire cloth is not yet woven, and we can be sure that the thread of our lives fits into his great design . . .

It is not that we must pump time full of life again with our own activity. That is the way the world is doing it; and rather than find life in time, the world discovers that time becomes scarce, disappears and ends in remorse. We who are alive with God's life will also have God's time. Time itself will become alive again to us. That calls for a dramatically different view of life: a releasing of our inner time with a consequent sense of fulfillment in our tasks and the expectation of a complete "coming together" of all the redeemed time of the saints at the end.

– *William T. McConnell*

REVIVE
Saturday: Ephesians 5:13–16
Sunday: 2 Peter 3:8–16

Go to page 364 for your next devotional reading.

JOHN writes this first letter to emphasize some of the same themes as his Gospel (such as "walking in the light," "knowing the truth," and "loving one another"). He does so because antichrists are promoting false views of the Son of God. As you read this book, realize how much God wants you to fight sin, to love others and to believe in the true Jesus for eternal life.

1 JOHN

The Word of Life

1 That which was from the beginning, which we have heard, which we have seen with our eyes, which we have looked at and our hands have touched—this we proclaim concerning the Word of life. ²The life appeared; we have seen it and testify to it, and we proclaim to you the eternal life, which was with the Father and has appeared to us. ³We proclaim to you what we have seen and heard, so that you also may have fellowship with us. And our fellowship is with the Father and with his Son, Jesus Christ. ⁴We write this to make our*a* joy complete.

Walking in the Light

⁵This is the message we have heard from him and declare to you: God is light; in him there is no darkness at all. ⁶If we claim to have fellowship with him yet walk in the darkness, we lie and do not live by the truth. ⁷But if we walk in the light, as he is in the light, we have fellowship with one another, and the blood of Jesus, his Son, purifies us from all*b* sin.

⁸If we claim to be without sin, we deceive ourselves and the truth is not in us. ⁹If we confess our sins, he is faithful and just and will forgive us our sins and purify us from all unrighteousness. ¹⁰If we claim

*a*4 Some manuscripts *your*   *b*7 Or *every*

we have not sinned, we make him out to be a liar and his word has no place in our lives.

2 My dear children, I write this to you so that you will not sin. But if anybody does sin, we have one who speaks to the Father in our defense—Jesus Christ, the Righteous One. **2**He is the atoning sacrifice for our sins, and not only for ours but also for*a* the sins of the whole world.

3We know that we have come to know him if we obey his commands. **4**The man who says, "I know him," but does not do what he commands is a liar, and the truth is not in him. **5**But if anyone obeys his word, God's love*b* is truly made complete in him. This is how we know we are in him: **6**Whoever claims to live in him must walk as Jesus did.

7Dear friends, I am not writing you a new command but an old one, which you have had since the beginning. This old

a2 Or *He is the one who turns aside God's wrath, taking away our sins, and not only ours but also*
b5 Or *word, love for God*

MONDAY

VERSE FOR THE DAY:
1 John 1:9

AUTHOR:
Max Lucado

PASSAGE FOR THE DAY:
1 John 1:5–10

Strange Path to Joy

A PRISON of pride is filled with self-made men and women determined to pull themselves up by their own bootstraps even if they land on their rear ends. It doesn't matter what they did or to whom they did it or where they will end up; it only matters that "I did it my way."

You've seen the prisoners. You've seen the alcoholic who won't admit his drinking problem. You've seen the woman who refuses to talk to anyone about her fears. You've seen the businessman who adamantly rejects help, even when his dreams are falling apart.

Perhaps to see such a prisoner all you have to do is look in the mirror.

"*If* we confess our sins, he is faithful and just" (1 John 1:9, [italics added]). The biggest word in Scripture just might be that two-letter one, *if*. For confessing sins—admitting failure—is exactly what prisoners of pride refuse to do . . .

To mourn for your sins is a natural outflow of poverty of spirit. The second beatitude [Blessed are those who mourn] should follow the first [Blessed are the poor in spirit]. But that's not always the case. Many deny their weakness. Many know they are wrong, yet pretend they are right. As a result, they never taste the exquisite sorrow of repentance.

Of all the paths to joy, this one has to be the strangest. True blessedness, Jesus says, begins with deep sadness.

"Blessed are those who know they are in trouble and have enough sense to admit it."

Additional Scripture Readings:
Matthew 5:1–10; Luke 18:9–14

Go to page 367 for your next devotional reading.

command is the message you have heard. ⁸Yet I am writing you a new command; its truth is seen in him and you, because the darkness is passing and the true light is already shining.

⁹Anyone who claims to be in the light but hates his brother is still in the darkness. ¹⁰Whoever loves his brother lives in the light, and there is nothing in him[a] to make him stumble. ¹¹But whoever hates his brother is in the darkness and walks around in the darkness; he does not know where he is going, because the darkness has blinded him.

¹²I write to you, dear children,
  because your sins have been
    forgiven on account of his
    name.
¹³I write to you, fathers,
  because you have known him who
    is from the beginning.
I write to you, young men,
  because you have overcome the evil
    one.
I write to you, dear children,
  because you have known the
    Father.
¹⁴I write to you, fathers,
  because you have known him who
    is from the beginning.
I write to you, young men,
  because you are strong,
  and the word of God lives in you,
  and you have overcome the evil one.

Do Not Love the World

¹⁵Do not love the world or anything in the world. If anyone loves the world, the love of the Father is not in him. ¹⁶For everything in the world—the cravings of sinful man, the lust of his eyes and the boasting of what he has and does—comes not from the Father but from the world. ¹⁷The world and its desires pass away, but the man who does the will of God lives forever.

Warning Against Antichrists

¹⁸Dear children, this is the last hour; and as you have heard that the antichrist is coming, even now many antichrists have come. This is how we know it is the last hour. ¹⁹They went out from us, but they did not really belong to us. For if they had belonged to us, they would have remained with us; but their going showed that none of them belonged to us.

²⁰But you have an anointing from the Holy One, and all of you know the truth.[b] ²¹I do not write to you because you do not know the truth, but because you do know it and because no lie comes from the truth. ²²Who is the liar? It is the man who denies that Jesus is the Christ. Such a man is the antichrist—he denies the Father and the Son. ²³No one who denies the Son has the Father; whoever acknowledges the Son has the Father also.

²⁴See that what you have heard from the beginning remains in you. If it does, you also will remain in the Son and in the Father. ²⁵And this is what he promised us—even eternal life.

²⁶I am writing these things to you about those who are trying to lead you astray. ²⁷As for you, the anointing you received from him remains in you, and you do not need anyone to teach you. But as his anointing teaches you about all things and as that anointing is real, not counterfeit—just as it has taught you, remain in him.

Children of God

²⁸And now, dear children, continue in him, so that when he appears we may be confident and unashamed before him at his coming.

²⁹If you know that he is righteous, you know that everyone who does what is right has been born of him.

3 How great is the love the Father has lavished on us, that we should be called children of God! And that is what we are! The reason the world does not know us is that it did not know him. ²Dear friends, now we are children of God, and what we will be has not yet been made known. But we know that when he appears,[c] we shall be like him, for we shall see him as he is. ³Everyone who has this hope in him purifies himself, just as he is pure.

⁴Everyone who sins breaks the law; in fact, sin is lawlessness. ⁵But you know that he appeared so that he might take away our sins. And in him is no sin. ⁶No one who lives in him keeps on sinning. No one who continues to sin has either seen him or known him.

⁷Dear children, do not let anyone lead you astray. He who does what is right is righteous, just as he is righteous. ⁸He who does what is sinful is of the devil, because the devil has been sinning from the beginning. The reason the Son of God appeared

---

[a]10 Or it   [b]20 Some manuscripts *and you know all things*   [c]2 Or *when it is made known*

was to destroy the devil's work. **9**No one who is born of God will continue to sin, because God's seed remains in him; he cannot go on sinning, because he has been born of God. **10**This is how we know who the children of God are and who the children of the devil are: Anyone who does not do what is right is not a child of God; nor is anyone who does not love his brother.

Love One Another

11This is the message you heard from the beginning: We should love one another. **12**Do not be like Cain, who belonged to the evil one and murdered his brother. And why did he murder him? Because his own actions were evil and his brother's were righteous. **13**Do not be surprised, my brothers, if the world hates you. **14**We know that we have passed from death to life, because we love our brothers. Anyone who does not love remains in death. **15**Anyone who hates his brother is a murderer, and you know that no murderer has eternal life in him.

16This is how we know what love is: Jesus Christ laid down his life for us. And we ought to lay down our lives for our brothers. **17**If anyone has material possessions and sees his brother in need but has no pity on him, how can the love of God be in him? **18**Dear children, let us not love with words or tongue but with actions and in truth. **19**This then is how we know that we belong to the truth, and how we set our hearts at rest in his presence **20**whenever our hearts condemn us. For God is greater than our hearts, and he knows everything.

21Dear friends, if our hearts do not condemn us, we have confidence before God **22**and receive from him anything we ask, because we obey his commands and do what pleases him. **23**And this is his command: to believe in the name of his Son, Jesus Christ, and to love one another as he commanded us. **24**Those who obey his commands live in him, and he in them. And this is how we know that he lives in us: We know it by the Spirit he gave us.

Test the Spirits

4 Dear friends, do not believe every spirit, but test the spirits to see whether they are from God, because many false prophets have gone out into the world. **2**This is how you can recognize the Spirit of God: Every spirit that acknowledges that Jesus Christ has come in the flesh is from God, **3**but every spirit that does not acknowledge Jesus is not from God. This is the spirit of the antichrist, which you have heard is coming and even now is already in the world.

4You, dear children, are from God and have overcome them, because the one who is in you is greater than the one who is in the world. **5**They are from the world and therefore speak from the viewpoint of the world, and the world listens to them. **6**We are from God, and whoever knows God listens to us; but whoever is not from God does not listen to us. This is how we recognize the Spirit*a* of truth and the spirit of falsehood.

God's Love and Ours

7Dear friends, let us love one another, for love comes from God. Everyone who loves has been born of God and knows God. **8**Whoever does not love does not know God, because God is love. **9**This is how God showed his love among us: He sent his one and only Son*b* into the world that we might live through him. **10**This is love: not that we loved God, but that he loved us and sent his Son as an atoning sacrifice for*c* our sins. **11**Dear friends, since God so loved us, we also ought to love one another. **12**No one has ever seen God; but if we love one another, God lives in us and his love is made complete in us.

13We know that we live in him and he in us, because he has given us of his Spirit. **14**And we have seen and testify that the Father has sent his Son to be the Savior of the world. **15**If anyone acknowledges that Jesus is the Son of God, God lives in him and he in God. **16**And so we know and rely on the love God has for us.

God is love. Whoever lives in love lives in God, and God in him. **17**In this way, love is made complete among us so that we will have confidence on the day of judgment, because in this world we are like him. **18**There is no fear in love. But perfect love drives out fear, because fear has to do with punishment. The one who fears is not made perfect in love.

19We love because he first loved us. **20**If anyone says, "I love God," yet hates his brother, he is a liar. For anyone who does not love his brother, whom he has seen,

---

a 6 Or *spirit*   *b* 9 Or *his only begotten Son*   *c* 10 Or *as the one who would turn aside his wrath, taking away*

1 JOHN 4–5

cannot love God, whom he has not seen. **21**And he has given us this command: Whoever loves God must also love his brother.

Faith in the Son of God

5 Everyone who believes that Jesus is the Christ is born of God, and everyone who loves the father loves his child as well. **2**This is how we know that we love the children of God: by loving God and carrying out his commands. **3**This is love for God: to obey his commands. And his commands are not burdensome, **4**for everyone born of God overcomes the world. This is the victory that has overcome the

---

TUESDAY

VERSE FOR THE DAY:
1 John 4:18

AUTHOR:
Daniel Taylor

PASSAGE FOR THE DAY:
1 John 4:7–21

Significant Living

I AM tempted to say that I am not genuinely afraid about anything—but that isn't true. My main fear now is insignificance. I am afraid, to put it simply, of living a life that doesn't matter. I am afraid of leaving the world exactly as I found it, no different for my having been here. I am afraid, as the writer Henry Thoreau said, of coming to the end of life and finding that I have not lived.

A lot of people say something like that these days, but they think "having lived" means having a lot of adventures or a lot of fun or a lot of money. I don't think that has much to do with it. Significant living comes from filling your life with things which last forever. That's why the usual things people seek to guarantee importance in their lives—money, fame, power—don't work very well. They all come to an end, often during the person's own life, and certainly thereafter.

What are things which last forever? Justice, mercy, forgiveness, compassion and grace are a few. Truth also lasts forever. These are all forms of the greatest value of all—love. And as you know, the source and perfect giver of love is God.

If I want my life to count, to be significant, then I will try to fill it as much as possible with these attitudes and actions . . . If you have made someone else's life better, you have done something eternal. And that means that a significant life will usually have lots of people in it. Because people are the only part of this world which will last forever . . .

This world is filled with threats—some imagined, some real —to our safety, to our sense of being okay. The ultimate security, the only true safety, is to be in right relationship with the God who is the alpha and omega, the beginning and the end. He was there before the beginning. He has no end. He has seen and suffered all. He has known our fears. He sets us free.

Additional Scripture Readings:
Hebrews 2:10–18; Revelation 1:4–8

Go to page 368 for your next devotional reading.

world, even our faith. **5**Who is it that overcomes the world? Only he who believes that Jesus is the Son of God.

6This is the one who came by water and blood—Jesus Christ. He did not come by water only, but by water and blood. And it is the Spirit who testifies, because the Spirit is the truth. **7**For there are three that testify: **8**the*a* Spirit, the water and the blood; and the three are in agreement. **9**We accept man's testimony, but God's testimony is greater because it is the testimony of God, which he has given about his Son. **10**Anyone who believes in the Son of God has this testimony in his heart. Anyone who does not believe God has made him out to be a liar, because he has not believed the testimony God has given about his Son. **11**And this is the testimony: God has given us eternal life, and this life is in his Son. **12**He who has the Son has life; he who does not have the Son of God does not have life.

Concluding Remarks

13I write these things to you who believe in the name of the Son of God so that you may know that you have eternal life. **14**This is the confidence we have in approaching God: that if we ask anything ac-

---

a7,8 Late manuscripts of the Vulgate *testify in heaven: the Father, the Word and the Holy Spirit, and these three are one.* *8And there are three that testify on earth: the* (not found in any Greek manuscript before the sixteenth century)

WEDNESDAY

VERSE FOR THE DAY:
1 John 5:3

AUTHOR:
Jerry Bridges

PASSAGE FOR THE DAY:
1 John 5:1–5

A Solid Foundation

THE practice of godliness is an exercise or discipline that focuses upon God. From this Godward attitude arise the character and conduct that we usually think of as godliness. So often we try to develop Christian character and conduct without taking the time to develop God-centered devotion. We try to please God without taking the time to walk with him and develop a relationship with him. This is impossible to do.

Consider the exacting requirements of a godly lifestyle . . . Note the totality of godliness over one's entire life . . . Nothing is excluded. God is at the center of his thoughts. His most ordinary duties are done with an eye to God's glory. In Paul's words to the Corinthians, whether he eats or drinks or whatever he does, he does it all for the glory of God (1 Corinthians 10:31).

Now it is obvious that such a God-centered lifestyle cannot be developed and maintained apart from a solid foundation of devotion to God. Only a strong personal relationship with the living God can keep such a commitment from becoming oppressive and legalistic. John writes that God's commands are not burdensome; a godly life is not wearisome, but this is true only because a godly person is first of all devoted to God.

Additional Scripture Readings:
Psalm 86:1–13; John 15:1–17

Go to page 371 for your next devotional reading.

cording to his will, he hears us. ¹⁵And if we know that he hears us—whatever we ask—we know that we have what we asked of him.

¹⁶If anyone sees his brother commit a sin that does not lead to death, he should pray and God will give him life. I refer to those whose sin does not lead to death. There is a sin that leads to death. I am not saying that he should pray about that. ¹⁷All wrongdoing is sin, and there is sin that does not lead to death.

¹⁸We know that anyone born of God does not continue to sin; the one who was born of God keeps him safe, and the evil one cannot harm him. ¹⁹We know that we are children of God, and that the whole world is under the control of the evil one. ²⁰We know also that the Son of God has come and has given us understanding, so that we may know him who is true. And we are in him who is true—even in his Son Jesus Christ. He is the true God and eternal life.

²¹Dear children, keep yourselves from idols.

*J*OHN *writes this second letter to warn the church to stand firm against false teachers and to keep loving other Christians. As you read this book, learn how to stand up for your Lord whenever you encounter false teachers.*

2 JOHN

¹The elder,

To the chosen lady and her children, whom I love in the truth—and not I only, but also all who know the truth— ²because of the truth, which lives in us and will be with us forever:

³Grace, mercy and peace from God the Father and from Jesus Christ, the Father's Son, will be with us in truth and love.

⁴It has given me great joy to find some of your children walking in the truth, just as the Father commanded us. ⁵And now, dear lady, I am not writing you a new command but one we have had from the beginning. I ask that we love one another. ⁶And this is love: that we walk in obedience to his commands. As you have heard from the beginning, his command is that you walk in love.

⁷Many deceivers, who do not acknowledge Jesus Christ as coming in the flesh, have gone out into the world. Any such person is the deceiver and the antichrist. ⁸Watch out that you do not lose what you have worked for, but that you may be rewarded fully. ⁹Anyone who runs ahead and does not continue in the teaching of Christ does not have God; whoever continues in the teaching has both the Father and the Son. ¹⁰If anyone comes to you and does not bring this teaching, do not take him into your house or welcome him. ¹¹Anyone who welcomes him shares in his wicked work.

¹²I have much to write to you, but I do not want to use paper and ink. Instead, I hope to visit you and talk with you face to face, so that our joy may be complete.

¹³The children of your chosen sister send their greetings.

THURSDAY

VERSE FOR THE DAY:
2 John 9

AUTHOR:
David Wiersbe and
Warren Wiersbe

PASSAGE FOR THE DAY:
2 John 8–9

On Gains and Losses

IN THESE two verses, the aged apostle John pointed out two special threats to the church: the danger of losing what we have gained, and the danger of making gains that are really losses. You and I certainly need discernment and wisdom to detect these dangers and overcome the enemy.

As to the first danger, John tells us, "Watch out that you do not lose what you have worked for, but that you may be rewarded fully." Sometimes we are so anxious to move forward in God's work that we fail to conserve and protect the blessings we have already received . . .

The second danger is that of making gains that are really losses. Verse 9 reads, "Anyone who runs ahead and does not continue in the teaching of Christ does not have God." This is a warning against the "progressive theology" that abandons "the faith that was once for all entrusted to the saints" (Jude 3) and ends up denying Jesus Christ. Over the centuries, more than one ministry has gone backwards by trying to move "forward" in developing a so-called up-to-date doctrinal position.

To be sure, there is always more to be learned from the Bible! And the unchanging Word of God must constantly be related to whatever new insight men discover in Scripture. But to go beyond the fundamental truths that the church holds dear is to make "gains" that are really losses. We must know the truth, live the truth, defend the truth and share the truth with others. But we must never go *beyond* that truth . . .

This is why God's work is so important, and why it demands the very best that we can give it. We are on guard duty for God, staying alert to protect our gains and rejecting profits that are really losses. If you ask, "Who is equal to such a task?" (2 Corinthians 2:16), the answer is clear: "Our competence comes from God" (2 Corinthians 3:5).

Additional Scripture Readings:
John 8:31–38; Hebrews 10:35–39

Go to page 373 for your next devotional reading.

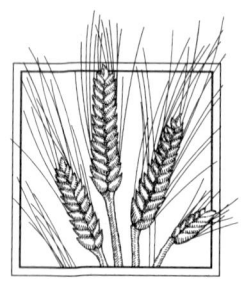

John writes this third letter to commend a church leader for his hospitality and to warn against another one who is unfriendly and even cruel. As you read this book, think how you can act as a friend toward other Christians.

3 JOHN

¹The elder,

To my dear friend Gaius, whom I love in the truth.

²Dear friend, I pray that you may enjoy good health and that all may go well with you, even as your soul is getting along well. ³It gave me great joy to have some brothers come and tell about your faithfulness to the truth and how you continue to walk in the truth. ⁴I have no greater joy than to hear that my children are walking in the truth.

⁵Dear friend, you are faithful in what you are doing for the brothers, even though they are strangers to you. ⁶They have told the church about your love. You will do well to send them on their way in a manner worthy of God. ⁷It was for the sake of the Name that they went out, receiving no help from the pagans. ⁸We ought therefore to show hospitality to such men so that we may work together for the truth.

⁹I wrote to the church, but Diotrephes, who loves to be first, will have nothing to do with us. ¹⁰So if I come, I will call attention to what he is doing, gossiping maliciously about us. Not satisfied with that, he refuses to welcome the brothers. He also stops those who want to do so and puts them out of the church.

¹¹Dear friend, do not imitate what is evil but what is good. Anyone who does what is good is from God. Anyone who does what is evil has not seen God. ¹²Demetrius is well spoken of by everyone—and even by the truth itself. We also speak well of him, and you know that our testimony is true.

¹³I have much to write you, but I do not want to do so with pen and ink. ¹⁴I hope to see you soon, and we will talk face to face.

Peace to you. The friends here send their greetings. Greet the friends there by name.

FRIDAY

VERSE FOR THE DAY:
3 John 2

AUTHOR:
D. Stuart Briscoe

PASSAGE FOR THE DAY:
3 John 1–8

Luxuries, or Necessities?

SCRIPTURE makes it very clear that our lives are lived in terms of relationships: with God and with human beings . . .

Third John is a very interesting letter. It is about the shortest book in the Bible, and over and over again in the fourteen verses is the term "dear friend." If you read this letter, you will get a very lovely picture. John, the aged apostle, writing to a group of believers, is pointing out that they are all his friends. He identifies in special ways some intimate friendships with the people there.

John is making a commitment to that fellowship of believers in general, and to individuals in the fellowship in particular, and so should we. There should be a degree in which you and I look in friendly terms toward the fellowship of believers. And when we do that, we should make a commitment to it. On the basis of the friendly commitment to the fellowship of believers, we should then be giving of ourselves in some ways so that we are building up dear-friend relationships.

If we are to know fellowship and friendship, there has to be a commitment to the fellowship as a whole, and there has to be a readiness to identify individually with people for our good and for theirs. For your good and mine, we need friendships. We need fellowships and relationships. And they don't happen by just coming into church and sitting among the people and then going back home. These friendships happen when there is commitment to the group as a whole, and when we get ourselves into situations where we can begin to nurture more personal, more intimate relationships . . .

Do you have friends? What kind of friends? Is Jesus your friend? Does God call you his friend [see James 2:23]? What kind of friends do you have? Are you cautious? Are you careful? Are you committed, and candid? These are qualities we need to have . . . Are real friends luxuries or necessities? What do you think?

Additional Scripture Readings:
John 15:9–17; 1 Peter 1:22—2:3

Go to page 374 for your next devotional reading.

WEEKENDING

REGARD

Now when the self replaces God at the center of the universe, some interesting things begin to happen. The most important . . . is that people begin to order their world according to their own wants and aspirations. This, of course, is a difficult thing to do since the people around them are doing the same thing, and since a great many things happen that are not in the least predictable. Nevertheless, the self is not easily deterred. It demands fulfillment. And fulfillment requires control. You cannot guarantee your own happiness unless you are able to control events and manage people . . .

But God cannot be controlled. And he would be within his rights to either ignore our attempts at control or simply push us and our petty little pretensions aside. But thanks be to God, he is not like that. Instead, out of his grace and mercy he periodically reminds us of the folly of our ways. And one way he has done this in my life is through my children.

– S. D. Gaede

REVIVE
Saturday: James 4:13–15
Sunday: Romans 11:33–36

Go to page 376 for your next devotional reading.

JUDE (a brother of Jesus and James) writes this short letter to warn Christians against false teachers in the church and to urge them to strengthen their faith and love. As you read this book, begin to grow in faith and love by depending on the Father, Son and Holy Spirit.

JUDE

¹Jude, a servant of Jesus Christ and a brother of James,

To those who have been called, who are loved by God the Father and kept by[a] Jesus Christ:

²Mercy, peace and love be yours in abundance.

The Sin and Doom of Godless Men

³Dear friends, although I was very eager to write to you about the salvation we share, I felt I had to write and urge you to contend for the faith that was once for all entrusted to the saints. ⁴For certain men whose condemnation was written about[b] long ago have secretly slipped in among you. They are godless men, who change the grace of our God into a license for immorality and deny Jesus Christ our only Sovereign and Lord.

⁵Though you already know all this, I want to remind you that the Lord[c] delivered his people out of Egypt, but later destroyed those who did not believe. ⁶And the angels who did not keep their positions of authority but abandoned their own home—these he has kept in darkness, bound with everlasting chains for judgment on the great Day. ⁷In a similar way, Sodom and Gomorrah and the surrounding towns gave themselves up to sexual immorality and perversion. They serve as an example of those who suffer the punishment of eternal fire.

⁸In the very same way, these dreamers pollute their own bodies, reject authority and slander celestial beings. ⁹But even the archangel Michael, when he was disputing with the devil about the body of Moses, did not dare to bring a slanderous accusation against him, but said, "The Lord rebuke you!" ¹⁰Yet these men speak abusively against whatever they do not under-

---

[a]1 Or *for;* or *in* Jesus   [b]4 Or *men who were marked out for condemnation*   [c]5 Some early manuscripts

stand; and what things they do understand by instinct, like unreasoning animals—these are the very things that destroy them.

¹¹Woe to them! They have taken the way of Cain; they have rushed for profit into Balaam's error; they have been destroyed in Korah's rebellion.

¹²These men are blemishes at your love feasts, eating with you without the slightest qualm—shepherds who feed only themselves. They are clouds without rain, blown along by the wind; autumn trees, without fruit and uprooted—twice dead. ¹³They are wild waves of the sea, foaming up their shame; wandering stars, for whom blackest darkness has been reserved forever.

¹⁴Enoch, the seventh from Adam, prophesied about these men: "See, the Lord is coming with thousands upon thousands of his holy ones ¹⁵to judge everyone, and to convict all the ungodly of all the ungodly acts they have done in the ungodly way, and of all the harsh words ungodly sinners have spoken against

---

MONDAY

VERSE FOR THE DAY:
Jude 21

AUTHOR:
A.W. Tozer

PASSAGE FOR THE DAY:
Jude 20–23

A Raging Torrent

BOTH the Old and New Testaments teach that the essence of true worship is the love of God.

Our Lord declared this to be the sum of the Law and the Prophets: "Love the Lord your God with all your heart and with all your soul and with all your mind and with all your strength" (Mark 12:30).

Now, love is both a principle and an emotion; it is something both felt and willed. It is capable of almost infinite degrees. Love in the human heart may begin so modestly as to be hardly perceptible and go on to become a raging torrent that sweeps its possessor before it in total helplessness.

Something like this must have been the experience of the Apostle Paul, for he felt it necessary to explain to his critics that his apparent madness was actually the love of God ravishing his willing heart!

In the love that any intelligent creature feels for God there must always be a measure of mystery. It is even possible that it is almost wholly mystery, and that our attempt to find reasons is merely a rationalizing of a love already mysteriously present in the heart as a result of some secret operation of the Spirit within us.

We can be certain that it is quite impossible to worship God without loving him. Scripture and reason agree to declare this. And God is never satisfied with anything less than all. This may not at first be possible, but the inward operations of the Holy Spirit will enable us in his time to offer him our poured-out fullness of love!

Additional Scripture Readings:
Psalm 18:1–6;
2 Corinthians 5:11–15

Go to page 380 for your next devotional reading.

him." ¹⁶These men are grumblers and faultfinders; they follow their own evil desires; they boast about themselves and flatter others for their own advantage.

A Call to Persevere

¹⁷But, dear friends, remember what the apostles of our Lord Jesus Christ foretold. ¹⁸They said to you, "In the last times there will be scoffers who will follow their own ungodly desires." ¹⁹These are the men who divide you, who follow mere natural instincts and do not have the Spirit.

²⁰But you, dear friends, build yourselves up in your most holy faith and pray in the Holy Spirit. ²¹Keep yourselves in God's love as you wait for the mercy of our Lord Jesus Christ to bring you to eternal life.

²²Be merciful to those who doubt; ²³snatch others from the fire and save them; to others show mercy, mixed with fear—hating even the clothing stained by corrupted flesh.

Doxology

²⁴To him who is able to keep you from falling and to present you before his glorious presence without fault and with great joy— ²⁵to the only God our Savior be glory, majesty, power and authority, through Jesus Christ our Lord, before all ages, now and forevermore! Amen.

JOHN, banished to the island of Patmos, writes what Christ reveals to him in order to comfort Christians suffering for their faith. Through visions of God in control of both the present and the future, he offers them hope, assuring them that in the end Christ will achieve victory over Satan, who is doomed to eternal punishment. As you read this book, rejoice in the awesome power of Christ, and remember that regardless of what happens now or in the future, nothing can ever separate you from his love.

REVELATION

Prologue

1 The revelation of Jesus Christ, which God gave him to show his servants what must soon take place. He made it known by sending his angel to his servant John, **²**who testifies to everything he saw—that is, the word of God and the testimony of Jesus Christ. **³**Blessed is the one who reads the words of this prophecy, and blessed are those who hear it and take to heart what is written in it, because the time is near.

Greetings and Doxology

⁴John,

To the seven churches in the province of Asia:

Grace and peace to you from him who is, and who was, and who is to come, and from the seven spirits[a] before his throne, **⁵**and from Jesus Christ, who is the faithful witness, the firstborn from the dead, and the ruler of the kings of the earth.

---

[a] 4 Or *the sevenfold Spirit*

To him who loves us and has freed us from our sins by his blood, **6**and has made us to be a kingdom and priests to serve his God and Father—to him be glory and power for ever and ever! Amen.

7Look, he is coming with the clouds,
  and every eye will see him,
even those who pierced him;
  and all the peoples of the earth will
    mourn because of him.
      So shall it be! Amen.

8"I am the Alpha and the Omega," says the Lord God, "who is, and who was, and who is to come, the Almighty."

One Like a Son of Man

9I, John, your brother and companion in the suffering and kingdom and patient endurance that are ours in Jesus, was on the island of Patmos because of the word of God and the testimony of Jesus. **10**On the Lord's Day I was in the Spirit, and I heard behind me a loud voice like a trumpet, **11**which said: "Write on a scroll what you see and send it to the seven churches: to Ephesus, Smyrna, Pergamum, Thyatira, Sardis, Philadelphia and Laodicea."

12I turned around to see the voice that was speaking to me. And when I turned I saw seven golden lampstands, **13**and among the lampstands was someone "like a son of man,"[a] dressed in a robe reaching down to his feet and with a golden sash around his chest. **14**His head and hair were white like wool, as white as snow, and his eyes were like blazing fire. **15**His feet were like bronze glowing in a furnace, and his voice was like the sound of rushing waters. **16**In his right hand he held seven stars, and out of his mouth came a sharp double-edged sword. His face was like the sun shining in all its brilliance.

17When I saw him, I fell at his feet as though dead. Then he placed his right hand on me and said: "Do not be afraid. I am the First and the Last. **18**I am the Living One; I was dead, and behold I am alive for ever and ever! And I hold the keys of death and Hades.

19"Write, therefore, what you have seen, what is now and what will take place later. **20**The mystery of the seven stars that you saw in my right hand and of the seven golden lampstands is this: The seven stars are the angels[b] of the seven churches, and the seven lampstands are the seven churches.

To the Church in Ephesus

2 "To the angel[c] of the church in Ephesus write:

These are the words of him who holds the seven stars in his right hand and walks among the seven golden lampstands: **2**I know your deeds, your hard work and your perseverance. I know that you cannot tolerate wicked men, that you have tested those who claim to be apostles but are not, and have found them false. **3**You have persevered and have endured hardships for my name, and have not grown weary.

4Yet I hold this against you: You have forsaken your first love. **5**Remember the height from which you have fallen! Repent and do the things you did at first. If you do not repent, I will come to you and remove your lampstand from its place. **6**But you have this in your favor: You hate the practices of the Nicolaitans, which I also hate.

7He who has an ear, let him hear what the Spirit says to the churches. To him who overcomes, I will give the right to eat from the tree of life, which is in the paradise of God.

To the Church in Smyrna

8"To the angel of the church in Smyrna write:

These are the words of him who is the First and the Last, who died and came to life again. **9**I know your afflictions and your poverty—yet you are rich! I know the slander of those who say they are Jews and are not, but are a synagogue of Satan. **10**Do not be afraid of what you are about to suffer. I tell you, the devil will put some of you in prison to test you, and you will suffer persecution for ten days. Be faithful, even to the point of death, and I will give you the crown of life.

11He who has an ear, let him hear what the Spirit says to the churches. He who overcomes will not be hurt at all by the second death.

---

a13 Daniel 7:13   *b20* Or *messengers*   *c1* Or *messenger*; also in verses 8, 12 and 18

To the Church in Pergamum

12"To the angel of the church in Pergamum write:

These are the words of him who has the sharp, double-edged sword. 13I know where you live—where Satan has his throne. Yet you remain true to my name. You did not renounce your faith in me, even in the days of Antipas, my faithful witness, who was put to death in your city—where Satan lives.

14Nevertheless, I have a few things against you: You have people there who hold to the teaching of Balaam, who taught Balak to entice the Israelites to sin by eating food sacrificed to idols and by committing sexual immorality. 15Likewise you also have those who hold to the teaching of the Nicolaitans. 16Repent therefore! Otherwise, I will soon come to you and will fight against them with the sword of my mouth.

17He who has an ear, let him hear

TUESDAY

VERSE FOR THE DAY:
Revelation 1:18

AUTHOR:
Dave Dravecky

PASSAGE FOR THE DAY:
Revelation 1:17–20

He Holds the Keys

AS THE baseball season ended, Giants pitcher Dave Dravecky waited for the results of a biopsy on a lump on his pitching arm.

It was an anxious time, waiting, just waiting to hear the news. When the phone rang I always wondered whether it would be the results.

Yet it was a good kind of anxiety, if I can put it that way. Just looking at [my wife] Janice reminded me how much I loved her, of how much she did for me. I stared at her and I stared at my kids, thinking they were the most beautiful sight in the entire universe. Some nights when Tiffany and Jonathan were asleep I would go into their room and listen to them slowly breathing. I thought of how often I didn't have time for them. On so many occasions, when they had asked me to play ball, I'd told them, "I'm busy reading right now; give me ten minutes"—and then the phone would ring and I never would get to play with them. During those days of waiting I did play ball, or whatever else they wanted to play.

I also thought about my eternal destination. I felt a deep sense of security there—that if I were going to die, I knew what would come next. That meant a lot to me.

I don't ordinarily think much about heaven and hell. I'm too busy keeping up with the day-to-day concerns of life. But in those days I found that my perspective shifted. Some things that mattered a lot in the day-to-day routine of living mattered much less. Some things that I seldom considered mattered a great deal more.

Additional Scripture Readings:
2 Corinthians 4:16–5:7;
Philippians 3:7–11

Go to page 382 for your next devotional reading.

what the Spirit says to the churches. To him who overcomes, I will give some of the hidden manna. I will also give him a white stone with a new name written on it, known only to him who receives it.

To the Church in Thyatira

18"To the angel of the church in Thyatira write:

These are the words of the Son of God, whose eyes are like blazing fire and whose feet are like burnished bronze. 19I know your deeds, your love and faith, your service and perseverance, and that you are now doing more than you did at first.

20Nevertheless, I have this against you: You tolerate that woman Jezebel, who calls herself a prophetess. By her teaching she misleads my servants into sexual immorality and the eating of food sacrificed to idols. 21I have given her time to repent of her immorality, but she is unwilling. 22So I will cast her on a bed of suffering, and I will make those who commit adultery with her suffer intensely, unless they repent of her ways. 23I will strike her children dead. Then all the churches will know that I am he who searches hearts and minds, and I will repay each of you according to your deeds. 24Now I say to the rest of you in Thyatira, to you who do not hold to her teaching and have not learned Satan's so-called deep secrets (I will not impose any other burden on you): 25Only hold on to what you have until I come.

26To him who overcomes and does my will to the end, I will give authority over the nations—

27'He will rule them with an iron
     scepter;
  he will dash them to pieces
     like pottery'[a]—

just as I have received authority from my Father. 28I will also give him the morning star. 29He who has an ear, let him hear what the Spirit says to the churches.

To the Church in Sardis

3 "To the angel[b] of the church in Sardis write:

These are the words of him who holds the seven spirits[c] of God and the seven stars. I know your deeds; you have a reputation of being alive, but you are dead. 2Wake up! Strengthen what remains and is about to die, for I have not found your deeds complete in the sight of my God. 3Remember, therefore, what you have received and heard; obey it, and repent. But if you do not wake up, I will come like a thief, and you will not know at what time I will come to you.

4Yet you have a few people in Sardis who have not soiled their clothes. They will walk with me, dressed in white, for they are worthy. 5He who overcomes will, like them, be dressed in white. I will never blot out his name from the book of life, but will acknowledge his name before my Father and his angels. 6He who has an ear, let him hear what the Spirit says to the churches.

To the Church in Philadelphia

7"To the angel of the church in Philadelphia write:

These are the words of him who is holy and true, who holds the key of David. What he opens no one can shut, and what he shuts no one can open. 8I know your deeds. See, I have placed before you an open door that no one can shut. I know that you have little strength, yet you have kept my word and have not denied my name. 9I will make those who are of the synagogue of Satan, who claim to be Jews though they are not, but are liars—I will make them come and fall down at your feet and acknowledge that I have loved you. 10Since you have kept my command to endure patiently, I will also keep you from the hour of trial that is going to come upon the whole world to test those who live on the earth.

11I am coming soon. Hold on to what you have, so that no one will take your crown. 12Him who overcomes I will make a pillar in the temple of my God. Never again will he leave it. I will write on him the name of my God and the name of the city of my God, the new Jerusalem, which is

---

a27 Psalm 2:9   b1 Or messenger; also in verses 7 and 14   c1 Or the sevenfold Spirit

coming down out of heaven from my God; and I will also write on him my new name. **13**He who has an ear, let him hear what the Spirit says to the churches.

To the Church in Laodicea

14"To the angel of the church in Laodicea write:

These are the words of the Amen, the faithful and true witness, the ruler of God's creation. **15**I know your deeds, that you are neither cold nor hot. I wish you were either one or the other! **16**So, because you are lukewarm—neither hot nor cold—I am about to spit you out of my mouth. **17**You say, 'I am rich; I have acquired wealth and do not need a thing.' But you do not realize that you are wretched, pitiful, poor, blind and naked. **18**I counsel you to buy from me gold refined in the fire, so you can become rich; and white clothes to wear, so you can cover your shameful nakedness; and salve to put on your eyes, so you can see.

19Those whom I love I rebuke and discipline. So be earnest, and repent.

WEDNESDAY

VERSE FOR THE DAY:
Revelation 3:1

AUTHOR:
Dietrich Bonhoeffer

PASSAGE FOR THE DAY:
Revelation 3:1–6

Grace Without Christ

CHEAP grace is the grace we bestow on ourselves. Cheap grace is the preaching of forgiveness without requiring repentance, baptism without church discipline, Communion without confession, absolution without personal confession. Cheap grace is grace without discipleship, grace without the cross, grace without Jesus Christ, living and incarnate.

Costly grace is the treasure hidden in the field; for the sake of it a man will gladly go and sell all that he has. It is the pearl of great price to buy which the merchant will sell all his goods. It is the kingly rule of Christ, for whose sake a man will pluck out the eye that causes him to stumble, it is the call of Jesus Christ at which the disciple leaves his nets and follows him.

Costly grace is the gospel which must be *sought* again and again, the gift which must be *asked* for, the door at which a man must *knock*.

Such grace is *costly* because it calls us to follow, and it is *grace* because it calls us to follow *Jesus Christ*. It is costly because it gives a man the only true life. It is costly because it condemns sin, and grace because it justifies the sinner. Above all, it is *costly* because it cost God the life of his Son: "You were bought at a price" (1 Corinthians 7:23), and what has cost God much cannot be cheap for us. Above all, it is *grace* because God did not reckon his Son too dear a price to pay for our life, but delivered him up for us. Costly grace is the Incarnation of God.

Additional Scripture Readings:
Mark 10:41–45; Romans 5:6–11

Go to page 384 for your next devotional reading.

20Here I am! I stand at the door and knock. If anyone hears my voice and opens the door, I will come in and eat with him, and he with me.

21To him who overcomes, I will give the right to sit with me on my throne, just as I overcame and sat down with my Father on his throne. **22**He who has an ear, let him hear what the Spirit says to the churches."

The Throne in Heaven

4 After this I looked, and there before me was a door standing open in heaven. And the voice I had first heard speaking to me like a trumpet said, "Come up here, and I will show you what must take place after this." **2**At once I was in the Spirit, and there before me was a throne in heaven with someone sitting on it. **3**And the one who sat there had the appearance of jasper and carnelian. A rainbow, resembling an emerald, encircled the throne. **4**Surrounding the throne were twenty-four other thrones, and seated on them were twenty-four elders. They were dressed in white and had crowns of gold on their heads. **5**From the throne came flashes of lightning, rumblings and peals of thunder. Before the throne, seven lamps were blazing. These are the seven spirits*a* of God. **6**Also before the throne there was what looked like a sea of glass, clear as crystal.

In the center, around the throne, were four living creatures, and they were covered with eyes, in front and in back. **7**The first living creature was like a lion, the second was like an ox, the third had a face like a man, the fourth was like a flying eagle. **8**Each of the four living creatures had six wings and was covered with eyes all around, even under his wings. Day and night they never stop saying:

"Holy, holy, holy
is the Lord God Almighty,
who was, and is, and is to come."

9Whenever the living creatures give glory, honor and thanks to him who sits on the throne and who lives for ever and ever, **10**the twenty-four elders fall down before him who sits on the throne, and worship him who lives for ever and ever. They lay their crowns before the throne and say:

11"You are worthy, our Lord and God,
to receive glory and honor and power,
for you created all things,
and by your will they were created and have their being."

The Scroll and the Lamb

5 Then I saw in the right hand of him who sat on the throne a scroll with writing on both sides and sealed with seven seals. **2**And I saw a mighty angel proclaiming in a loud voice, "Who is worthy to break the seals and open the scroll?" **3**But no one in heaven or on earth or under the earth could open the scroll or even look inside it. **4**I wept and wept because no one was found who was worthy to open the scroll or look inside. **5**Then one of the elders said to me, "Do not weep! See, the Lion of the tribe of Judah, the Root of David, has triumphed. He is able to open the scroll and its seven seals."

6Then I saw a Lamb, looking as if it had been slain, standing in the center of the throne, encircled by the four living creatures and the elders. He had seven horns and seven eyes, which are the seven spirits*a* of God sent out into all the earth. **7**He came and took the scroll from the right hand of him who sat on the throne. **8**And when he had taken it, the four living creatures and the twenty-four elders fell down before the Lamb. Each one had a harp and they were holding golden bowls full of incense, which are the prayers of the saints. **9**And they sang a new song:

"You are worthy to take the scroll
and to open its seals,
because you were slain,
and with your blood you purchased men for God
from every tribe and language and people and nation.
10You have made them to be a kingdom and priests to serve our God,
and they will reign on the earth."

11Then I looked and heard the voice of many angels, numbering thousands upon thousands, and ten thousand times ten thousand. They encircled the throne and the living creatures and the elders. **12**In a loud voice they sang:

"Worthy is the Lamb, who was slain,
to receive power and wealth and wisdom and strength
and honor and glory and praise!"

a 5,6 Or *the sevenfold Spirit*

¹³Then I heard every creature in heaven and on earth and under the earth and on the sea, and all that is in them, singing:

"To him who sits on the throne and to the Lamb
be praise and honor and glory and power,
for ever and ever!"

¹⁴The four living creatures said, "Amen," and the elders fell down and worshiped.

The Seals

6 I watched as the Lamb opened the first of the seven seals. Then I heard

---

THURSDAY

VERSE FOR THE DAY:
Revelation 3:20

AUTHOR:
Tim LaHaye

PASSAGE FOR THE DAY:
Revelation 3:14–22

Knock-Knock

A VERY emotionally burdened man came to Jesus Christ one night (John 3:1–13), inquiring how he might come into a personal relationship with God. Jesus said, "I tell you the truth, no one can see the kingdom of God unless he is born again." Obviously puzzled by Christ's explanation, Nicodemus asked, "How can a man be born when he is old? . . . Surely he cannot enter a second time into his mother's womb to be born!" Jesus answered, "I tell you the truth, no one can enter the kingdom of God unless he is born of water and the Spirit." The context of this passage clearly indicates that Nicodemus needed a personal spiritual experience. Just as he had been born physically to enter this world, he had to be born spiritually to fulfill his destiny and prepare for the next world. This spiritual birth of power, created by individually receiving Jesus Christ as Lord and Savior, gives a person the external power he needs to cope with his emotional problems. This is particularly true in the case of depression.

Contrary to public opinion, Jesus Christ is not automatically born within a person; otherwise he would not have need for this spiritual birth. Instead, Jesus Christ is external to man's spiritual nature, for man is born void of God. Through his Holy Spirit and the teaching of the Bible, Christ knocks at the door of man's spiritual consciousness, saying, "If anyone hears my voice and opens the door, I will come in and eat with him, and he with me" (Revelation 3:20). This promise of Christ testifies that any individual conscious of his God-void and rebellion against the will of God can invite him into his life. Christ never forces his way into an individual's life, but responds only when invited. At that moment, the individual is spiritually made alive. This gives him a consciousness for God and an increased capacity to cope with all the problems of life, including depression.

Additional Scripture Readings:
John 3:1–21; Romans 8:9–17

Go to page 395 for your next devotional reading.

one of the four living creatures say in a voice like thunder, "Come!" ²I looked, and there before me was a white horse! Its rider held a bow, and he was given a crown, and he rode out as a conqueror bent on conquest.

³When the Lamb opened the second seal, I heard the second living creature say, "Come!" ⁴Then another horse came out, a fiery red one. Its rider was given power to take peace from the earth and to make men slay each other. To him was given a large sword.

⁵When the Lamb opened the third seal, I heard the third living creature say, "Come!" I looked, and there before me was a black horse! Its rider was holding a pair of scales in his hand. ⁶Then I heard what sounded like a voice among the four living creatures, saying, "A quart*a* of wheat for a day's wages,*b* and three quarts of barley for a day's wages,*b* and do not damage the oil and the wine!"

⁷When the Lamb opened the fourth seal, I heard the voice of the fourth living creature say, "Come!" ⁸I looked, and there before me was a pale horse! Its rider was named Death, and Hades was following close behind him. They were given power over a fourth of the earth to kill by sword, famine and plague, and by the wild beasts of the earth.

⁹When he opened the fifth seal, I saw under the altar the souls of those who had been slain because of the word of God and the testimony they had maintained. ¹⁰They called out in a loud voice, "How long, Sovereign Lord, holy and true, until you judge the inhabitants of the earth and avenge our blood?" ¹¹Then each of them was given a white robe, and they were told to wait a little longer, until the number of their fellow servants and brothers who were to be killed as they had been was completed.

¹²I watched as he opened the sixth seal. There was a great earthquake. The sun turned black like sackcloth made of goat hair, the whole moon turned blood red, ¹³and the stars in the sky fell to earth, as late figs drop from a fig tree when shaken by a strong wind. ¹⁴The sky receded like a scroll, rolling up, and every mountain and island was removed from its place.

¹⁵Then the kings of the earth, the princes, the generals, the rich, the mighty, and every slave and every free man hid in caves and among the rocks of the mountains. ¹⁶They called to the mountains and the rocks, "Fall on us and hide us from the face of him who sits on the throne and from the wrath of the Lamb! ¹⁷For the great day of their wrath has come, and who can stand?"

144,000 Sealed

7 After this I saw four angels standing at the four corners of the earth, holding back the four winds of the earth to prevent any wind from blowing on the land or on the sea or on any tree. ²Then I saw another angel coming up from the east, having the seal of the living God. He called out in a loud voice to the four angels who had been given power to harm the land and the sea: ³"Do not harm the land or the sea or the trees until we put a seal on the foreheads of the servants of our God." ⁴Then I heard the number of those who were sealed: 144,000 from all the tribes of Israel.

⁵From the tribe of Judah 12,000 were sealed,
 from the tribe of Reuben 12,000,
 from the tribe of Gad 12,000,
⁶from the tribe of Asher 12,000,
 from the tribe of Naphtali 12,000,
 from the tribe of Manasseh 12,000,
⁷from the tribe of Simeon 12,000,
 from the tribe of Levi 12,000,
 from the tribe of Issachar 12,000,
⁸from the tribe of Zebulun 12,000,
 from the tribe of Joseph 12,000,
 from the tribe of Benjamin 12,000.

The Great Multitude in White Robes

⁹After this I looked and there before me was a great multitude that no one could count, from every nation, tribe, people and language, standing before the throne and in front of the Lamb. They were wearing white robes and were holding palm branches in their hands. ¹⁰And they cried out in a loud voice:

"Salvation belongs to our God,
who sits on the throne,
and to the Lamb."

¹¹All the angels were standing around the throne and around the elders and the four living creatures. They fell down on their faces before the throne and worshiped God, ¹²saying:

"Amen!
Praise and glory

---

*a*6 Greek *a choinix* (probably about a liter)   *b*6 Greek *a denarius*

and wisdom and thanks and honor
and power and strength
be to our God for ever and ever.
Amen!"

¹³Then one of the elders asked me, "These in white robes—who are they, and where did they come from?"

¹⁴I answered, "Sir, you know."

And he said, "These are they who have come out of the great tribulation; they have washed their robes and made them white in the blood of the Lamb. ¹⁵Therefore,

"they are before the throne of God
and serve him day and night in his temple;
and he who sits on the throne will spread his tent over them.
¹⁶Never again will they hunger;
never again will they thirst.
The sun will not beat upon them,
nor any scorching heat.
¹⁷For the Lamb at the center of the throne will be their shepherd;
he will lead them to springs of living water.
And God will wipe away every tear from their eyes."

The Seventh Seal and the Golden Censer

8 When he opened the seventh seal, there was silence in heaven for about half an hour.

²And I saw the seven angels who stand before God, and to them were given seven trumpets.

³Another angel, who had a golden censer, came and stood at the altar. He was given much incense to offer, with the prayers of all the saints, on the golden altar before the throne. ⁴The smoke of the incense, together with the prayers of the saints, went up before God from the angel's hand. ⁵Then the angel took the censer, filled it with fire from the altar, and hurled it on the earth; and there came peals of thunder, rumblings, flashes of lightning and an earthquake.

The Trumpets

⁶Then the seven angels who had the seven trumpets prepared to sound them.

⁷The first angel sounded his trumpet, and there came hail and fire mixed with blood, and it was hurled down upon the earth. A third of the earth was burned up,
a third of the trees were burned up, and all the green grass was burned up.

⁸The second angel sounded his trumpet, and something like a huge mountain, all ablaze, was thrown into the sea. A third of the sea turned into blood, ⁹a third of the living creatures in the sea died, and a third of the ships were destroyed.

¹⁰The third angel sounded his trumpet, and a great star, blazing like a torch, fell from the sky on a third of the rivers and on the springs of water— ¹¹the name of the star is Wormwood.ᵃ A third of the waters turned bitter, and many people died from the waters that had become bitter.

¹²The fourth angel sounded his trumpet, and a third of the sun was struck, a third of the moon, and a third of the stars, so that a third of them turned dark. A third of the day was without light, and also a third of the night.

¹³As I watched, I heard an eagle that was flying in midair call out in a loud voice: "Woe! Woe! Woe to the inhabitants of the earth, because of the trumpet blasts about to be sounded by the other three angels!"

9 The fifth angel sounded his trumpet, and I saw a star that had fallen from the sky to the earth. The star was given the key to the shaft of the Abyss. ²When he opened the Abyss, smoke rose from it like the smoke from a gigantic furnace. The sun and sky were darkened by the smoke from the Abyss. ³And out of the smoke locusts came down upon the earth and were given power like that of scorpions of the earth. ⁴They were told not to harm the grass of the earth or any plant or tree, but only those people who did not have the seal of God on their foreheads. ⁵They were not given power to kill them, but only to torture them for five months. And the agony they suffered was like that of the sting of a scorpion when it strikes a man. ⁶During those days men will seek death, but will not find it; they will long to die, but death will elude them.

⁷The locusts looked like horses prepared for battle. On their heads they wore something like crowns of gold, and their faces resembled human faces. ⁸Their hair was like women's hair, and their teeth were like lions' teeth. ⁹They had breastplates like breastplates of iron, and the sound of their wings was like the thundering of many horses and chariots rushing

---

ᵃ *11 That is, Bitterness*

into battle. ¹⁰They had tails and stings like scorpions, and in their tails they had power to torment people for five months. ¹¹They had as king over them the angel of the Abyss, whose name in Hebrew is Abaddon, and in Greek, Apollyon.[a]

¹²The first woe is past; two other woes are yet to come.

¹³The sixth angel sounded his trumpet, and I heard a voice coming from the horns[b] of the golden altar that is before God. ¹⁴It said to the sixth angel who had the trumpet, "Release the four angels who are bound at the great river Euphrates." ¹⁵And the four angels who had been kept ready for this very hour and day and month and year were released to kill a third of mankind. ¹⁶The number of the mounted troops was two hundred million. I heard their number.

¹⁷The horses and riders I saw in my vision looked like this: Their breastplates were fiery red, dark blue, and yellow as sulfur. The heads of the horses resembled the heads of lions, and out of their mouths came fire, smoke and sulfur. ¹⁸A third of mankind was killed by the three plagues of fire, smoke and sulfur that came out of their mouths. ¹⁹The power of the horses was in their mouths and in their tails; for their tails were like snakes, having heads with which they inflict injury.

²⁰The rest of mankind that were not killed by these plagues still did not repent of the work of their hands; they did not stop worshiping demons, and idols of gold, silver, bronze, stone and wood—idols that cannot see or hear or walk. ²¹Nor did they repent of their murders, their magic arts, their sexual immorality or their thefts.

The Angel and the Little Scroll

10 Then I saw another mighty angel coming down from heaven. He was robed in a cloud, with a rainbow above his head; his face was like the sun, and his legs were like fiery pillars. ²He was holding a little scroll, which lay open in his hand. He planted his right foot on the sea and his left foot on the land, ³and he gave a loud shout like the roar of a lion. When he shouted, the voices of the seven thunders spoke. ⁴And when the seven thunders spoke, I was about to write; but I heard a voice from heaven say, "Seal up what the seven thunders have said and do not write it down."

⁵Then the angel I had seen standing on the sea and on the land raised his right hand to heaven. ⁶And he swore by him who lives for ever and ever, who created the heavens and all that is in them, the earth and all that is in it, and the sea and all that is in it, and said, "There will be no more delay! ⁷But in the days when the seventh angel is about to sound his trumpet, the mystery of God will be accomplished, just as he announced to his servants the prophets."

⁸Then the voice that I had heard from heaven spoke to me once more: "Go, take the scroll that lies open in the hand of the angel who is standing on the sea and on the land."

⁹So I went to the angel and asked him to give me the little scroll. He said to me, "Take it and eat it. It will turn your stomach sour, but in your mouth it will be as sweet as honey." ¹⁰I took the little scroll from the angel's hand and ate it. It tasted as sweet as honey in my mouth, but when I had eaten it, my stomach turned sour. ¹¹Then I was told, "You must prophesy again about many peoples, nations, languages and kings."

The Two Witnesses

11 I was given a reed like a measuring rod and was told, "Go and measure the temple of God and the altar, and count the worshipers there. ²But exclude the outer court; do not measure it, because it has been given to the Gentiles. They will trample on the holy city for 42 months. ³And I will give power to my two witnesses, and they will prophesy for 1,260 days, clothed in sackcloth." ⁴These are the two olive trees and the two lampstands that stand before the Lord of the earth. ⁵If anyone tries to harm them, fire comes from their mouths and devours their enemies. This is how anyone who wants to harm them must die. ⁶These men have power to shut up the sky so that it will not rain during the time they are prophesying; and they have power to turn the waters into blood and to strike the earth with every kind of plague as often as they want.

⁷Now when they have finished their testimony, the beast that comes up from the Abyss will attack them, and overpower and kill them. ⁸Their bodies will lie in the street of the great city, which is figuratively called Sodom and Egypt, where also their Lord was crucified. ⁹For three and a

---

[a]11 *Abaddon* and *Apollyon* mean *Destroyer.*   [b]13 That is, projections

half days men from every people, tribe, language and nation will gaze on their bodies and refuse them burial. ¹⁰The inhabitants of the earth will gloat over them and will celebrate by sending each other gifts, because these two prophets had tormented those who live on the earth.

¹¹But after the three and a half days a breath of life from God entered them, and they stood on their feet, and terror struck those who saw them. ¹²Then they heard a loud voice from heaven saying to them, "Come up here." And they went up to heaven in a cloud, while their enemies looked on.

¹³At that very hour there was a severe earthquake and a tenth of the city collapsed. Seven thousand people were killed in the earthquake, and the survivors were terrified and gave glory to the God of heaven.

¹⁴The second woe has passed; the third woe is coming soon.

The Seventh Trumpet

¹⁵The seventh angel sounded his trumpet, and there were loud voices in heaven, which said:

"The kingdom of the world has
    become the kingdom of our
    Lord and of his Christ,
and he will reign for ever and ever."

¹⁶And the twenty-four elders, who were seated on their thrones before God, fell on their faces and worshiped God, ¹⁷saying:

"We give thanks to you, Lord God
    Almighty,
the One who is and who was,
because you have taken your great
    power
    and have begun to reign.
¹⁸The nations were angry;
    and your wrath has come.
The time has come for judging the
    dead,
    and for rewarding your servants the
    prophets
and your saints and those who
    reverence your name,
    both small and great—
and for destroying those who destroy
    the earth."

¹⁹Then God's temple in heaven was opened, and within his temple was seen the ark of his covenant. And there came flashes of lightning, rumblings, peals of thunder, an earthquake and a great hailstorm.

The Woman and the Dragon

12 A great and wondrous sign appeared in heaven: a woman clothed with the sun, with the moon under her feet and a crown of twelve stars on her head. ²She was pregnant and cried out in pain as she was about to give birth. ³Then another sign appeared in heaven: an enormous red dragon with seven heads and ten horns and seven crowns on his heads. ⁴His tail swept a third of the stars out of the sky and flung them to the earth. The dragon stood in front of the woman who was about to give birth, so that he might devour her child the moment it was born. ⁵She gave birth to a son, a male child, who will rule all the nations with an iron scepter. And her child was snatched up to God and to his throne. ⁶The woman fled into the desert to a place prepared for her by God, where she might be taken care of for 1,260 days.

⁷And there was war in heaven. Michael and his angels fought against the dragon, and the dragon and his angels fought back. ⁸But he was not strong enough, and they lost their place in heaven. ⁹The great dragon was hurled down—that ancient serpent called the devil, or Satan, who leads the whole world astray. He was hurled to the earth, and his angels with him.

¹⁰Then I heard a loud voice in heaven say:

"Now have come the salvation and the
    power and the kingdom of our
    God,
    and the authority of his Christ.
For the accuser of our brothers,
    who accuses them before our God
    day and night,
    has been hurled down.
¹¹They overcame him
    by the blood of the Lamb
    and by the word of their testimony;
they did not love their lives so much
    as to shrink from death.
¹²Therefore rejoice, you heavens
    and you who dwell in them!
But woe to the earth and the sea,
    because the devil has gone down to
    you!
He is filled with fury,
    because he knows that his time is
    short."

¹³When the dragon saw that he had been hurled to the earth, he pursued the woman who had given birth to the male

child. ¹⁴The woman was given the two wings of a great eagle, so that she might fly to the place prepared for her in the desert, where she would be taken care of for a time, times and half a time, out of the serpent's reach. ¹⁵Then from his mouth the serpent spewed water like a river, to overtake the woman and sweep her away with the torrent. ¹⁶But the earth helped the woman by opening its mouth and swallowing the river that the dragon had spewed out of his mouth. ¹⁷Then the dragon was enraged at the woman and went off to make war against the rest of her offspring—those who obey God's commandments and hold to the testimony of Jesus.

13 ¹And the dragon*ᵃ* stood on the shore of the sea.

The Beast out of the Sea

And I saw a beast coming out of the sea. He had ten horns and seven heads, with ten crowns on his horns, and on each head a blasphemous name. ²The beast I saw resembled a leopard, but had feet like those of a bear and a mouth like that of a lion. The dragon gave the beast his power and his throne and great authority. ³One of the heads of the beast seemed to have had a fatal wound, but the fatal wound had been healed. The whole world was astonished and followed the beast. ⁴Men worshiped the dragon because he had given authority to the beast, and they also worshiped the beast and asked, "Who is like the beast? Who can make war against him?"

⁵The beast was given a mouth to utter proud words and blasphemies and to exercise his authority for forty-two months. ⁶He opened his mouth to blaspheme God, and to slander his name and his dwelling place and those who live in heaven. ⁷He was given power to make war against the saints and to conquer them. And he was given authority over every tribe, people, language and nation. ⁸All inhabitants of the earth will worship the beast—all whose names have not been written in the book of life belonging to the Lamb that was slain from the creation of the world.*ᵇ*

⁹He who has an ear, let him hear.

¹⁰If anyone is to go into captivity,
  into captivity he will go.
If anyone is to be killed*ᶜ* with the sword,
  with the sword he will be killed.

This calls for patient endurance and faithfulness on the part of the saints.

The Beast out of the Earth

¹¹Then I saw another beast, coming out of the earth. He had two horns like a lamb, but he spoke like a dragon. ¹²He exercised all the authority of the first beast on his behalf, and made the earth and its inhabitants worship the first beast, whose fatal wound had been healed. ¹³And he performed great and miraculous signs, even causing fire to come down from heaven to earth in full view of men. ¹⁴Because of the signs he was given power to do on behalf of the first beast, he deceived the inhabitants of the earth. He ordered them to set up an image in honor of the beast who was wounded by the sword and yet lived. ¹⁵He was given power to give breath to the image of the first beast, so that it could speak and cause all who refused to worship the image to be killed. ¹⁶He also forced everyone, small and great, rich and poor, free and slave, to receive a mark on his right hand or on his forehead, ¹⁷so that no one could buy or sell unless he had the mark, which is the name of the beast or the number of his name.

¹⁸This calls for wisdom. If anyone has insight, let him calculate the number of the beast, for it is man's number. His number is 666.

The Lamb and the 144,000

14 Then I looked, and there before me was the Lamb, standing on Mount Zion, and with him 144,000 who had his name and his Father's name written on their foreheads. ²And I heard a sound from heaven like the roar of rushing waters and like a loud peal of thunder. The sound I heard was like that of harpists playing their harps. ³And they sang a new song before the throne and before the four living creatures and the elders. No one could learn the song except the 144,000 who had been redeemed from the earth. ⁴These are those who did not defile themselves with women, for they kept themselves pure. They follow the Lamb wherever he goes. They were purchased from among men and offered as firstfruits to God and the Lamb. ⁵No lie was found in their mouths; they are blameless.

ᵃ1 Some late manuscripts *And I* *ᵇ8* Or *written from the creation of the world in the book of life belonging to the Lamb that was slain* *ᶜ10* Some manuscripts *anyone kills*

The Three Angels

6Then I saw another angel flying in mid-air, and he had the eternal gospel to proclaim to those who live on the earth—to every nation, tribe, language and people. **7**He said in a loud voice, "Fear God and give him glory, because the hour of his judgment has come. Worship him who made the heavens, the earth, the sea and the springs of water."

8A second angel followed and said, "Fallen! Fallen is Babylon the Great, which made all the nations drink the maddening wine of her adulteries."

9A third angel followed them and said in a loud voice: "If anyone worships the beast and his image and receives his mark on the forehead or on the hand, **10**he, too, will drink of the wine of God's fury, which has been poured full strength into the cup of his wrath. He will be tormented with burning sulfur in the presence of the holy angels and of the Lamb. **11**And the smoke of their torment rises for ever and ever. There is no rest day or night for those who worship the beast and his image, or for anyone who receives the mark of his name." **12**This calls for patient endurance on the part of the saints who obey God's commandments and remain faithful to Jesus.

13Then I heard a voice from heaven say, "Write: Blessed are the dead who die in the Lord from now on."

"Yes," says the Spirit, "they will rest from their labor, for their deeds will follow them."

The Harvest of the Earth

14I looked, and there before me was a white cloud, and seated on the cloud was one "like a son of man"[a] with a crown of gold on his head and a sharp sickle in his hand. **15**Then another angel came out of the temple and called in a loud voice to him who was sitting on the cloud, "Take your sickle and reap, because the time to reap has come, for the harvest of the earth is ripe." **16**So he who was seated on the cloud swung his sickle over the earth, and the earth was harvested.

17Another angel came out of the temple in heaven, and he too had a sharp sickle. **18**Still another angel, who had charge of the fire, came from the altar and called in a loud voice to him who had the sharp sickle, "Take your sharp sickle and gather the clusters of grapes from the earth's vine, because its grapes are ripe." **19**The angel swung his sickle on the earth, gathered its grapes and threw them into the great winepress of God's wrath. **20**They were trampled in the winepress outside the city, and blood flowed out of the press, rising as high as the horses' bridles for a distance of 1,600 stadia.[b]

Seven Angels With Seven Plagues

15 I saw in heaven another great and marvelous sign: seven angels with the seven last plagues—last, because with them God's wrath is completed. **2**And I saw what looked like a sea of glass mixed with fire and, standing beside the sea, those who had been victorious over the beast and his image and over the number of his name. They held harps given them by God **3**and sang the song of Moses the servant of God and the song of the Lamb:

> "Great and marvelous are your deeds,
>   Lord God Almighty.
> Just and true are your ways,
>   King of the ages.
> **4**Who will not fear you, O Lord,
>   and bring glory to your name?
> For you alone are holy.
> All nations will come
>   and worship before you,
> for your righteous acts have been
>   revealed."

5After this I looked and in heaven the temple, that is, the tabernacle of the Testimony, was opened. **6**Out of the temple came the seven angels with the seven plagues. They were dressed in clean, shining linen and wore golden sashes around their chests. **7**Then one of the four living creatures gave to the seven angels seven golden bowls filled with the wrath of God, who lives for ever and ever. **8**And the temple was filled with smoke from the glory of God and from his power, and no one could enter the temple until the seven plagues of the seven angels were completed.

The Seven Bowls of God's Wrath

16 Then I heard a loud voice from the temple saying to the seven angels, "Go, pour out the seven bowls of God's wrath on the earth."

2The first angel went and poured out his bowl on the land, and ugly and painful sores broke out on the people who had the

---

[a]14 Daniel 7:13   [b]20 That is, about 180 miles (about 300 kilometers)

mark of the beast and worshiped his image.

³The second angel poured out his bowl on the sea, and it turned into blood like that of a dead man, and every living thing in the sea died.

⁴The third angel poured out his bowl on the rivers and springs of water, and they became blood. ⁵Then I heard the angel in charge of the waters say:

"You are just in these judgments,
  you who are and who were, the Holy One,
because you have so judged;
⁶for they have shed the blood of your saints and prophets,
  and you have given them blood to drink as they deserve."

⁷And I heard the altar respond:

"Yes, Lord God Almighty,
  true and just are your judgments."

⁸The fourth angel poured out his bowl on the sun, and the sun was given power to scorch people with fire. ⁹They were seared by the intense heat and they cursed the name of God, who had control over these plagues, but they refused to repent and glorify him.

¹⁰The fifth angel poured out his bowl on the throne of the beast, and his kingdom was plunged into darkness. Men gnawed their tongues in agony ¹¹and cursed the God of heaven because of their pains and their sores, but they refused to repent of what they had done.

¹²The sixth angel poured out his bowl on the great river Euphrates, and its water was dried up to prepare the way for the kings from the East. ¹³Then I saw three evil*ᵃ* spirits that looked like frogs; they came out of the mouth of the dragon, out of the mouth of the beast and out of the mouth of the false prophet. ¹⁴They are spirits of demons performing miraculous signs, and they go out to the kings of the whole world, to gather them for the battle on the great day of God Almighty.

¹⁵"Behold, I come like a thief! Blessed is he who stays awake and keeps his clothes with him, so that he may not go naked and be shamefully exposed."

¹⁶Then they gathered the kings together to the place that in Hebrew is called Armageddon.

¹⁷The seventh angel poured out his bowl into the air, and out of the temple came a loud voice from the throne, saying, "It is done!" ¹⁸Then there came flashes of lightning, rumblings, peals of thunder and a severe earthquake. No earthquake like it has ever occurred since man has been on earth, so tremendous was the quake. ¹⁹The great city split into three parts, and the cities of the nations collapsed. God remembered Babylon the Great and gave her the cup filled with the wine of the fury of his wrath. ²⁰Every island fled away and the mountains could not be found. ²¹From the sky huge hailstones of about a hundred pounds each fell upon men. And they cursed God on account of the plague of hail, because the plague was so terrible.

The Woman on the Beast

17 One of the seven angels who had the seven bowls came and said to me, "Come, I will show you the punishment of the great prostitute, who sits on many waters. ²With her the kings of the earth committed adultery and the inhabitants of the earth were intoxicated with the wine of her adulteries."

³Then the angel carried me away in the Spirit into a desert. There I saw a woman sitting on a scarlet beast that was covered with blasphemous names and had seven heads and ten horns. ⁴The woman was dressed in purple and scarlet, and was glittering with gold, precious stones and pearls. She held a golden cup in her hand, filled with abominable things and the filth of her adulteries. ⁵This title was written on her forehead:

MYSTERY
BABYLON THE GREAT
THE MOTHER OF PROSTITUTES
AND OF THE ABOMINATIONS OF THE EARTH.

⁶I saw that the woman was drunk with the blood of the saints, the blood of those who bore testimony to Jesus.

When I saw her, I was greatly astonished. ⁷Then the angel said to me: "Why are you astonished? I will explain to you the mystery of the woman and of the beast she rides, which has the seven heads and ten horns. ⁸The beast, which you saw, once was, now is not, and will come up out of the Abyss and go to his destruction. The inhabitants of the earth whose names have not been written in the book of life from the creation of the world will be astonished when they see the beast, because

---

ᵃ13 Greek *unclean*

he once was, now is not, and yet will come.

⁹"This calls for a mind with wisdom. The seven heads are seven hills on which the woman sits. ¹⁰They are also seven kings. Five have fallen, one is, the other has not yet come; but when he does come, he must remain for a little while. ¹¹The beast who once was, and now is not, is an eighth king. He belongs to the seven and is going to his destruction.

¹²"The ten horns you saw are ten kings who have not yet received a kingdom, but who for one hour will receive authority as kings along with the beast. ¹³They have one purpose and will give their power and authority to the beast. ¹⁴They will make war against the Lamb, but the Lamb will overcome them because he is Lord of lords and King of kings—and with him will be his called, chosen and faithful followers."

¹⁵Then the angel said to me, "The waters you saw, where the prostitute sits, are peoples, multitudes, nations and languages. ¹⁶The beast and the ten horns you saw will hate the prostitute. They will bring her to ruin and leave her naked; they will eat her flesh and burn her with fire. ¹⁷For God has put it into their hearts to accomplish his purpose by agreeing to give the beast their power to rule, until God's words are fulfilled. ¹⁸The woman you saw is the great city that rules over the kings of the earth."

The Fall of Babylon

18 After this I saw another angel coming down from heaven. He had great authority, and the earth was illuminated by his splendor. ²With a mighty voice he shouted:

"Fallen! Fallen is Babylon the Great!
    She has become a home for demons
and a haunt for every evilᵃ spirit,
    a haunt for every unclean and detestable bird.
³For all the nations have drunk
    the maddening wine of her adulteries.
The kings of the earth committed adultery with her,
    and the merchants of the earth grew rich from her excessive luxuries."

⁴Then I heard another voice from heaven say:

"Come out of her, my people,
    so that you will not share in her sins,
    so that you will not receive any of her plagues;
⁵for her sins are piled up to heaven,
    and God has remembered her crimes.
⁶Give back to her as she has given;
    pay her back double for what she has done.
Mix her a double portion from her own cup.
⁷Give her as much torture and grief
    as the glory and luxury she gave herself.
In her heart she boasts,
    'I sit as queen; I am not a widow,
    and I will never mourn.'
⁸Therefore in one day her plagues will overtake her:
    death, mourning and famine.
She will be consumed by fire,
    for mighty is the Lord God who judges her.

⁹"When the kings of the earth who committed adultery with her and shared her luxury see the smoke of her burning, they will weep and mourn over her. ¹⁰Terrified at her torment, they will stand far off and cry:

" 'Woe! Woe, O great city,
    O Babylon, city of power!
In one hour your doom has come!'

¹¹"The merchants of the earth will weep and mourn over her because no one buys their cargoes any more— ¹²cargoes of gold, silver, precious stones and pearls; fine linen, purple, silk and scarlet cloth; every sort of citron wood, and articles of every kind made of ivory, costly wood, bronze, iron and marble; ¹³cargoes of cinnamon and spice, of incense, myrrh and frankincense, of wine and olive oil, of fine flour and wheat; cattle and sheep; horses and carriages; and bodies and souls of men.

¹⁴"They will say, 'The fruit you longed for is gone from you. All your riches and splendor have vanished, never to be recovered.' ¹⁵The merchants who sold these things and gained their wealth from her will stand far off, terrified at her torment. They will weep and mourn ¹⁶and cry out:

" 'Woe! Woe, O great city,

ᵃ2 Greek *unclean*

dressed in fine linen, purple and scarlet,
and glittering with gold, precious stones and pearls!
¹⁷In one hour such great wealth has been brought to ruin!'

"Every sea captain, and all who travel by ship, the sailors, and all who earn their living from the sea, will stand far off. ¹⁸When they see the smoke of her burning, they will exclaim, 'Was there ever a city like this great city?' ¹⁹They will throw dust on their heads, and with weeping and mourning cry out:

" 'Woe! Woe, O great city,
where all who had ships on the sea became rich through her wealth!
In one hour she has been brought to ruin!
²⁰Rejoice over her, O heaven!
Rejoice, saints and apostles and prophets!
God has judged her for the way she treated you.' "

²¹Then a mighty angel picked up a boulder the size of a large millstone and threw it into the sea, and said:

"With such violence
the great city of Babylon will be thrown down,
never to be found again.
²²The music of harpists and musicians, flute players and trumpeters,
will never be heard in you again.
No workman of any trade
will ever be found in you again.
The sound of a millstone
will never be heard in you again.
²³The light of a lamp
will never shine in you again.
The voice of bridegroom and bride
will never be heard in you again.
Your merchants were the world's great men.
By your magic spell all the nations were led astray.
²⁴In her was found the blood of prophets and of the saints,
and of all who have been killed on the earth."

Hallelujah!

19 After this I heard what sounded like the roar of a great multitude in heaven shouting:

"Hallelujah!
Salvation and glory and power belong to our God,
² for true and just are his judgments.
He has condemned the great prostitute who corrupted the earth by her adulteries.
He has avenged on her the blood of his servants."

³And again they shouted:

"Hallelujah!
The smoke from her goes up for ever and ever."

⁴The twenty-four elders and the four living creatures fell down and worshiped God, who was seated on the throne. And they cried:

"Amen, Hallelujah!"

⁵Then a voice came from the throne, saying:

"Praise our God,
all you his servants,
you who fear him,
both small and great!"

⁶Then I heard what sounded like a great multitude, like the roar of rushing waters and like loud peals of thunder, shouting:

"Hallelujah!
For our Lord God Almighty reigns.
⁷Let us rejoice and be glad
and give him glory!
For the wedding of the Lamb has come,
and his bride has made herself ready.
⁸Fine linen, bright and clean,
was given her to wear."

(Fine linen stands for the righteous acts of the saints.)

⁹Then the angel said to me, "Write: 'Blessed are those who are invited to the wedding supper of the Lamb!' " And he added, "These are the true words of God." ¹⁰At this I fell at his feet to worship him. But he said to me, "Do not do it! I am a fellow servant with you and with your brothers who hold to the testimony of Jesus. Worship God! For the testimony of Jesus is the spirit of prophecy."

The Rider on the White Horse

¹¹I saw heaven standing open and there before me was a white horse, whose rider is called Faithful and True. With justice he judges and makes war. ¹²His eyes are like blazing fire, and on his head are many

crowns. He has a name written on him that no one knows but he himself. ¹³He is dressed in a robe dipped in blood, and his name is the Word of God. ¹⁴The armies of heaven were following him, riding on white horses and dressed in fine linen, white and clean. ¹⁵Out of his mouth comes a sharp sword with which to strike down the nations. "He will rule them with an iron scepter."ᵃ He treads the winepress of the fury of the wrath of God Almighty. ¹⁶On his robe and on his thigh he has this name written:

KING OF KINGS AND LORD OF LORDS.

¹⁷And I saw an angel standing in the sun, who cried in a loud voice to all the birds flying in midair, "Come, gather together for the great supper of God, ¹⁸so that you may eat the flesh of kings, generals, and mighty men, of horses and their riders, and the flesh of all people, free and slave, small and great."

¹⁹Then I saw the beast and the kings of the earth and their armies gathered together to make war against the rider on the horse and his army. ²⁰But the beast was captured, and with him the false prophet who had performed the miraculous signs on his behalf. With these signs he had deluded those who had received the mark of the beast and worshiped his image. The two of them were thrown alive into the fiery lake of burning sulfur. ²¹The rest of them were killed with the sword that came out of the mouth of the rider on the horse, and all the birds gorged themselves on their flesh.

The Thousand Years

20 And I saw an angel coming down out of heaven, having the key to the Abyss and holding in his hand a great chain. ²He seized the dragon, that ancient serpent, who is the devil, or Satan, and bound him for a thousand years. ³He threw him into the Abyss, and locked and sealed it over him, to keep him from deceiving the nations anymore until the thousand years were ended. After that, he must be set free for a short time.

⁴I saw thrones on which were seated those who had been given authority to judge. And I saw the souls of those who had been beheaded because of their testimony for Jesus and because of the word of God. They had not worshiped the beast or his image and had not received his mark on their foreheads or their hands. They came to life and reigned with Christ a thousand years. ⁵(The rest of the dead did not come to life until the thousand years were ended.) This is the first resurrection. ⁶Blessed and holy are those who have part in the first resurrection. The second death has no power over them, but they will be priests of God and of Christ and will reign with him for a thousand years.

Satan's Doom

⁷When the thousand years are over, Satan will be released from his prison ⁸and will go out to deceive the nations in the four corners of the earth—Gog and Magog—to gather them for battle. In number they are like the sand on the seashore. ⁹They marched across the breadth of the earth and surrounded the camp of God's people, the city he loves. But fire came down from heaven and devoured them. ¹⁰And the devil, who deceived them, was thrown into the lake of burning sulfur, where the beast and the false prophet had been thrown. They will be tormented day and night for ever and ever.

The Dead Are Judged

¹¹Then I saw a great white throne and him who was seated on it. Earth and sky fled from his presence, and there was no place for them. ¹²And I saw the dead, great and small, standing before the throne, and books were opened. Another book was opened, which is the book of life. The dead were judged according to what they had done as recorded in the books. ¹³The sea gave up the dead that were in it, and death and Hades gave up the dead that were in them, and each person was judged according to what he had done. ¹⁴Then death and Hades were thrown into the lake of fire. The lake of fire is the second death. ¹⁵If anyone's name was not found written in the book of life, he was thrown into the lake of fire.

The New Jerusalem

21 Then I saw a new heaven and a new earth, for the first heaven and the first earth had passed away, and there was no longer any sea. ²I saw the Holy City, the new Jerusalem, coming down out of heaven from God, prepared as a bride beautifully dressed for her husband. ³And I heard a loud voice from the throne

---

ᵃ 15 Psalm 2:9

| FRIDAY |

VERSE FOR THE DAY: *AUTHOR:* *PASSAGE FOR THE DAY:*
Revelation 21:4 *Gerald Oosterveen* *Revelation 21:1–5*

At Home with Jesus

GERALD Oosterveen reflects on the day his 9-year-old son Gerard was buried. Gerard had fought a courageous 39-month battle with cancer.

Parents are not supposed to bury their children. The old are not supposed to stand beside the graves of the young. It is unnatural. One is not prepared for it. The death of a child tears apart a family like the uprooting of one plant out of a cluster that have been allowed to grow together in one pot. It cannot be done. All those roots become so intertwined over the years that nothing short of violence can separate them. And it leaves all the plants stunted . . .

In the end, God will always be victorious. Satan may rampage through the world and through the souls of people, with God's inscrutable permission, and cause indescribable disaster and anguish. When he is finished, however, and arrogantly boasts to God, "Look what I've done," God will silence him with his majestic, "And now look what I can do." Then Satan will shamefacedly slink into the corners of his hell while God goes about his work of redemption and restoration.

Oh, yes, we mourn . . . But we have hope—bright hope for tomorrow, when all who trust in Jesus Christ as Savior will move beyond pain and grief forever because we shall be forever with the Lord. And it is not just some pipe dream, some opium to stupify and mislead hurting people. It is real, because Christ is real, because in our past there is a blood-stained cross on which the Prince of Glory died. Because of that bloody, pain-filled past we have hope when all things are made new and death shall be no more, nor grief, nor crying.

In a little cemetery in a small, out-of-the-way town there is a tiny marker. It bears only three lines: 1961–1970 GERARD RICHARD OOSTERVEEN "At Home With Jesus."

Of the three, the last line is the only one that really matters. The last line sums up a glorious, endless future, an adventure that for my son has only just begun. Even if he remembers his life on earth, I am sure his joy has wiped away any recollection of pain.

Additional Scripture Readings:
1 Corinthians 15:12–28;
1 Thessalonians 4:13–18

Go to page 397 for your next devotional reading.

saying, "Now the dwelling of God is with men, and he will live with them. They will be his people, and God himself will be with them and be their God. **4**He will wipe every tear from their eyes. There will be no more death or mourning or crying or pain, for the old order of things has passed away."

5He who was seated on the throne said, "I am making everything new!" Then he said, "Write this down, for these words are trustworthy and true."

6He said to me: "It is done. I am the Alpha and the Omega, the Beginning and the End. To him who is thirsty I will give to drink without cost from the spring of the water of life. **7**He who overcomes will inherit all this, and I will be his God and he will be my son. **8**But the cowardly, the unbelieving, the vile, the murderers, the sexually immoral, those who practice magic arts, the idolaters and all liars — their place will be in the fiery lake of burning sulfur. This is the second death."

9One of the seven angels who had the seven bowls full of the seven last plagues came and said to me, "Come, I will show you the bride, the wife of the Lamb." **10**And he carried me away in the Spirit to a mountain great and high, and showed me the Holy City, Jerusalem, coming down out of heaven from God. **11**It shone with the glory of God, and its brilliance was like that of a very precious jewel, like a jasper, clear as crystal. **12**It had a great, high wall with twelve gates, and with twelve angels at the gates. On the gates were written the names of the twelve tribes of Israel. **13**There were three gates on the east, three on the north, three on the south and three on the west. **14**The wall of the city had twelve foundations, and on them were the names of the twelve apostles of the Lamb.

15The angel who talked with me had a measuring rod of gold to measure the city, its gates and its walls. **16**The city was laid out like a square, as long as it was wide. He measured the city with the rod and found it to be 12,000 stadia*a* in length, and as wide and high as it is long. **17**He measured its wall and it was 144 cubits*b* thick,*c* by man's measurement, which the angel was using. **18**The wall was made of jasper, and the city of pure gold, as pure as glass. **19**The foundations of the city walls were decorated with every kind of precious stone. The first foundation was jasper, the second sapphire, the third chalcedony, the fourth emerald, **20**the fifth sardonyx, the sixth carnelian, the seventh chrysolite, the eighth beryl, the ninth topaz, the tenth chrysoprase, the eleventh jacinth, and the twelfth amethyst.*d* **21**The twelve gates were twelve pearls, each gate made of a single pearl. The great street of the city was of pure gold, like transparent glass.

22I did not see a temple in the city, because the Lord God Almighty and the Lamb are its temple. **23**The city does not need the sun or the moon to shine on it, for the glory of God gives it light, and the Lamb is its lamp. **24**The nations will walk by its light, and the kings of the earth will bring their splendor into it. **25**On no day will its gates ever be shut, for there will be no night there. **26**The glory and honor of the nations will be brought into it. **27**Nothing impure will ever enter it, nor will anyone who does what is shameful or deceitful, but only those whose names are written in the Lamb's book of life.

The River of Life

22 Then the angel showed me the river of the water of life, as clear as crystal, flowing from the throne of God and of the Lamb **2**down the middle of the great street of the city. On each side of the river stood the tree of life, bearing twelve crops of fruit, yielding its fruit every month. And the leaves of the tree are for the healing of the nations. **3**No longer will there be any curse. The throne of God and of the Lamb will be in the city, and his servants will serve him. **4**They will see his face, and his name will be on their foreheads. **5**There will be no more night. They will not need the light of a lamp or the light of the sun, for the Lord God will give them light. And they will reign for ever and ever.

6The angel said to me, "These words are trustworthy and true. The Lord, the God of the spirits of the prophets, sent his angel to show his servants the things that must soon take place."

Jesus Is Coming

7"Behold, I am coming soon! Blessed is he who keeps the words of the prophecy in this book."

---

a16 That is, about 1,400 miles (about 2,200 kilometers)   *b17* That is, about 200 feet (about 65 meters)
c17 Or *high*   *d20* The precise identification of some of these precious stones is uncertain.

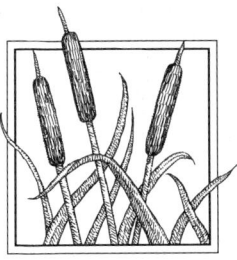

WEEKENDING

RESPOND

Father of glory, how I thank you for the assurance of heaven! While I know I could never deserve such an assurance, I'm so grateful that you even give it to me as a right because of my union with your Son, my Savior.

Thank you that while I live in the world I can seek to serve you fruitfully, and to praise you by the kind of life I live, as well as by my lips.

I long to give glory, honor and thanks to you always. May your indwelling Spirit—the Spirit of glory—ever keep before me the great privilege of being an heir of your glory, and a citizen of heaven. May my life in its praise and worship of you now be the closest possible approximation to the praise and worship of heaven.

Father, I worship and adore you, through Jesus Christ your Son. Amen.

– *Derek Prime*

REVIVE

Saturday: Colossians 3:1–4
Sunday: Revelation 4:1–11

Go to page 402 for your next devotional reading.

⁸I, John, am the one who heard and saw these things. And when I had heard and seen them, I fell down to worship at the feet of the angel who had been showing them to me. ⁹But he said to me, "Do not do it! I am a fellow servant with you and with your brothers the prophets and of all who keep the words of this book. Worship God!"

¹⁰Then he told me, "Do not seal up the words of the prophecy of this book, because the time is near. ¹¹Let him who does wrong continue to do wrong; let him who is vile continue to be vile; let him who does right continue to do right; and let him who is holy continue to be holy."

¹²"Behold, I am coming soon! My reward is with me, and I will give to everyone according to what he has done. ¹³I am the Alpha and the Omega, the First and the Last, the Beginning and the End.

¹⁴"Blessed are those who wash their robes, that they may have the right to the tree of life and may go through the gates into the city. ¹⁵Outside are the dogs, those who practice magic arts, the sexually immoral, the murderers, the idolaters and everyone who loves and practices falsehood.

¹⁶"I, Jesus, have sent my angel to give you*a* this testimony for the churches. I am the Root and the Offspring of David, and the bright Morning Star."

¹⁷The Spirit and the bride say, "Come!" And let him who hears say, "Come!" Whoever is thirsty, let him come; and whoever wishes, let him take the free gift of the water of life.

¹⁸I warn everyone who hears the words of the prophecy of this book: If anyone adds anything to them, God will add to him the plagues described in this book. ¹⁹And if anyone takes words away from this book of prophecy, God will take away from him his share in the tree of life and in the holy city, which are described in this book.

²⁰He who testifies to these things says, "Yes, I am coming soon."

Amen. Come, Lord Jesus.

²¹The grace of the Lord Jesus be with God's people. Amen.

---

a 16 The Greek is plural.

PSALMS
PROVERBS

DAVID, the shepherd boy and Israel's greatest king, writes most of the psalms. Together these 150 songs form the greatest collection of prayers ever written. A wide range of human emotion is expressed—joy, excitement, compassion, love, anger, grief, depression. As you read this book, remember that no matter what you are feeling, God wants to hear about it in your prayers to him. He promises to listen to all your concerns and to answer them for Jesus' sake.

PSALMS

BOOK I

Psalms 1–41

Psalm 1

¹Blessed is the man
  who does not walk in the counsel of the wicked
 or stand in the way of sinners
 or sit in the seat of mockers.
²But his delight is in the law of the LORD,
  and on his law he meditates day and night.
³He is like a tree planted by streams of water,
  which yields its fruit in season
  and whose leaf does not wither.
  Whatever he does prospers.

⁴Not so the wicked!
  They are like chaff
  that the wind blows away.
⁵Therefore the wicked will not stand in the judgment,
  nor sinners in the assembly of the righteous.

⁶For the LORD watches over the way of the righteous,
  but the way of the wicked will perish.

MONDAY

VERSE FOR THE DAY:
Psalm 1:3

AUTHOR:
Bill Hybels

PASSAGE FOR THE DAY:
Psalm 1:1–6

Authentic Manhood

TO A generation of men failed by their fathers and lost in a cloud of confusion, God says, "Don't spend a lifetime in aimless drifting. Don't succumb to mindless misinterpretations of masculine identity. Enter into a relationship with me, through Jesus Christ, and allow *me* to lead you into authentic manhood. Become my adopted sons and let me 're-father' you."

To say that God wants to re-father his sons is no empty cliché. Scripture repeatedly presents God's desire to be personally and intimately involved with his children. He wants to provide the warmth, affection, discipline and accountability that characterize a parent's loving relationship.

But divine re-fathering is not a simple, overnight process . . . It requires a commitment to two-way dialogue, through prayer and Bible study. It demands that sons take time to listen to the Father's guidance, and then act on it . . .

God wants to father all of us until we're dead sure of his approval, his guiding power and his promise of heaven. Why?

Because God wants us all to experience a deeper level of security. He wants emasculated men to become secure enough to confront timidity and fear, to take risks and make commitments. He wants macho men to become secure enough to crawl out from under the false pretensions and quit trying to impress people . . .

The freedom of authentic masculinity is an amazing thing to see. It produces a "divine elasticity" in men. Finally they can lead with firmness, then submit with humility. They can challenge with a cutting edge, then encourage with enthusiasm. They can fight aggressively for just causes, then moments later weep over suffering.

These are the masterpieces God had in mind when he created man. God looks at them and says, "Very good. You are magnificent creatures—and authentically male."

Additional Scripture Readings:
1 Corinthians 16:13–14;
2 Timothy 1:3–12

Go to page 404 for your next devotional reading.

Psalm 2

¹Why do the nations conspire[a]
and the peoples plot in vain?
²The kings of the earth take their stand
and the rulers gather together
against the LORD
and against his Anointed One.[b]
³"Let us break their chains," they say,
"and throw off their fetters."

⁴The One enthroned in heaven laughs;
the Lord scoffs at them.
⁵Then he rebukes them in his anger
and terrifies them in his wrath,
saying,
⁶"I have installed my King[c]
on Zion, my holy hill."

⁷I will proclaim the decree of the LORD:

He said to me, "You are my Son[d];
today I have become your Father.[e]
⁸Ask of me,
and I will make the nations your
inheritance,
the ends of the earth your
possession.
⁹You will rule them with an iron
scepter[f];
you will dash them to pieces like
pottery."

¹⁰Therefore, you kings, be wise;
be warned, you rulers of the earth.
¹¹Serve the LORD with fear
and rejoice with trembling.
¹²Kiss the Son, lest he be angry
and you be destroyed in your way,
for his wrath can flare up in a
moment.
Blessed are all who take refuge in
him.

Psalm 3

A psalm of David. When he fled from
his son Absalom.

¹O LORD, how many are my foes!
How many rise up against me!
²Many are saying of me,
"God will not deliver him." *Selah*[g]

³But you are a shield around me,
O LORD;
you bestow glory on me and lift[h]
up my head.
⁴To the LORD I cry aloud,
and he answers me from his holy
hill. *Selah*

⁵I lie down and sleep;
I wake again, because the LORD
sustains me.
⁶I will not fear the tens of thousands
drawn up against me on every side.

⁷Arise, O LORD!
Deliver me, O my God!
Strike all my enemies on the jaw;
break the teeth of the wicked.

⁸From the LORD comes deliverance.
May your blessing be on your
people. *Selah*

Psalm 4

For the director of music. With stringed
instruments. A psalm of David.

¹Answer me when I call to you,
O my righteous God.
Give me relief from my distress;
be merciful to me and hear my
prayer.

²How long, O men, will you turn my
glory into shame[i]?
How long will you love delusions
and seek false gods[j]? *Selah*
³Know that the LORD has set apart the
godly for himself;
the LORD will hear when I call to
him.

⁴In your anger do not sin;
when you are on your beds,
search your hearts and be silent.
Selah

⁵Offer right sacrifices
and trust in the LORD.

⁶Many are asking, "Who can show us
any good?"
Let the light of your face shine
upon us, O LORD.
⁷You have filled my heart with greater
joy
than when their grain and new wine
abound.

---

*a*1 Hebrew; Septuagint *rage*   *b*2 Or *anointed one*   *c*6 Or *king*   *d*7 Or *son*; also in verse 12
*e*7 Or *have begotten you*   *f*9 Or *will break them with a rod of iron*   *g*2 A word of uncertain meaning,
occurring frequently in the Psalms; possibly a musical term   *h*3 Or LORD, / *my Glorious One, who lifts*
*i*2 Or *you dishonor my Glorious One*   *j*2 Or *seek lies*

TUESDAY

VERSE FOR THE DAY: *AUTHOR:* *PASSAGE FOR THE DAY:*
Psalm 4:2 *Frederick Buechner* *Psalm 4:1–8*

The Gods Are Dying

THE gods are dying. The gods of this world are sick unto death. If someone does not believe this, the next time he happens to wake up in the great silence of the night or of the day, just listen. And after a while, at the heart of the silence, he will hear the sound that gives it away: the soft, crazy thud of the feet of the gods as they stagger across the earth; the huge white hands fluttering like moths; the little moans of bewilderment and anguish. And we all shudder at the sound because to witness the death of gods is a fearsome thing.

Which gods? The gods that we worship. The gods that our enemies worship. Their sacred names? There is Science, for one: he who was to redeem the world from poverty and disease, on whose mighty shoulders mankind was to be borne onward and upward toward the high stars. There is Communism, that holy one so terrible in his predilection for blood sacrifice but so magnificent in his promise of the messianic age: from each according to his ability, to each according to his need . . . And we must not leave out from this role of the dying what often passes for the god of the church: the god who sanctifies our foreign policy and our business methods, our political views and our racial prejudices. The god who, bless him, asks so little and promises so much: peace of mind, the end of our inferiority complexes . . .

These are the gods in whom the world has put its ultimate trust. Some of them are our particular gods, and there are plenty of others, each can name for himself. And where are they now? They are dying, dying, and their twilight thickens into night. Where is the security that they promised? Where is the peace? The terrible truth is that the gods of this world are no more worthy of our ultimate trust than are the men who created them.

Additional Scripture Readings:
Psalm 115:1–11; Romans 1:18–23

Go to page 408 for your next devotional reading.

⁸I will lie down and sleep in peace,
 for you alone, O LORD,
 make me dwell in safety.

Psalm 5

*For the director of music. For flutes.
A psalm of David.*

¹Give ear to my words, O LORD,
 consider my sighing.
²Listen to my cry for help,
 my King and my God,
 for to you I pray.
³In the morning, O LORD, you hear my voice;
 in the morning I lay my requests before you
 and wait in expectation.

⁴You are not a God who takes pleasure in evil;
 with you the wicked cannot dwell.
⁵The arrogant cannot stand in your presence;
 you hate all who do wrong.
⁶You destroy those who tell lies;
 bloodthirsty and deceitful men
 the LORD abhors.

⁷But I, by your great mercy,
 will come into your house;
 in reverence will I bow down
 toward your holy temple.
⁸Lead me, O LORD, in your righteousness
 because of my enemies—
 make straight your way before me.

⁹Not a word from their mouth can be trusted;
 their heart is filled with destruction.
 Their throat is an open grave;
 with their tongue they speak deceit.
¹⁰Declare them guilty, O God!
 Let their intrigues be their downfall.
 Banish them for their many sins,
 for they have rebelled against you.

¹¹But let all who take refuge in you be glad;
 let them ever sing for joy.
 Spread your protection over them,
 that those who love your name may rejoice in you.
¹²For surely, O LORD, you bless the righteous;
 you surround them with your favor
 as with a shield.

Psalm 6

*For the director of music. With stringed instruments. According to sheminith.ᵃ
A psalm of David.*

¹O LORD, do not rebuke me in your anger
 or discipline me in your wrath.
²Be merciful to me, LORD, for I am faint;
 O LORD, heal me, for my bones are in agony.
³My soul is in anguish.
 How long, O LORD, how long?

⁴Turn, O LORD, and deliver me;
 save me because of your unfailing love.
⁵No one remembers you when he is dead.
 Who praises you from the graveᵇ?

⁶I am worn out from groaning;
 all night long I flood my bed with weeping
 and drench my couch with tears.
⁷My eyes grow weak with sorrow;
 they fail because of all my foes.

⁸Away from me, all you who do evil,
 for the LORD has heard my weeping.
⁹The LORD has heard my cry for mercy;
 the LORD accepts my prayer.
¹⁰All my enemies will be ashamed and dismayed;
 they will turn back in sudden disgrace.

Psalm 7

A shiggaionᶜ of David, which he sang to the LORD concerning Cush, a Benjamite.

¹O LORD my God, I take refuge in you;
 save and deliver me from all who pursue me,
²or they will tear me like a lion
 and rip me to pieces with no one to rescue me.

³O LORD my God, if I have done this
 and there is guilt on my hands—
⁴if I have done evil to him who is at peace with me
 or without cause have robbed my foe—
⁵then let my enemy pursue and overtake me;

ᵃTitle: Probably a musical term   ᵇ5 Hebrew *Sheol*   ᶜTitle: Probably a literary or musical term

let him trample my life to the
    ground
and make me sleep in the dust.
                    Selah

⁶Arise, O LORD, in your anger;
    rise up against the rage of my
        enemies.
Awake, my God; decree justice.
⁷Let the assembled peoples gather
        around you.
    Rule over them from on high;
⁸ let the LORD judge the peoples.
Judge me, O LORD, according to my
        righteousness,
    according to my integrity, O Most
        High.
⁹O righteous God,
    who searches minds and hearts,
bring to an end the violence of the
        wicked
    and make the righteous secure.

¹⁰My shield[a] is God Most High,
    who saves the upright in heart.
¹¹God is a righteous judge,
    a God who expresses his wrath
        every day.
¹²If he does not relent,
    he[b] will sharpen his sword;
    he will bend and string his bow.
¹³He has prepared his deadly weapons;
    he makes ready his flaming arrows.

¹⁴He who is pregnant with evil
    and conceives trouble gives birth to
        disillusionment.
¹⁵He who digs a hole and scoops it out
    falls into the pit he has made.
¹⁶The trouble he causes recoils on
        himself;
    his violence comes down on his
        own head.

¹⁷I will give thanks to the LORD because
        of his righteousness
    and will sing praise to the name of
        the LORD Most High.

Psalm 8

For the director of music. According to
gittith.[c] A psalm of David.

¹O LORD, our Lord,
    how majestic is your name in all
        the earth!

You have set your glory
    above the heavens.
²From the lips of children and infants
    you have ordained praise[d]
because of your enemies,
    to silence the foe and the avenger.

³When I consider your heavens,
    the work of your fingers,
the moon and the stars,
    which you have set in place,
⁴what is man that you are mindful of
        him,
    the son of man that you care for
        him?
⁵You made him a little lower than the
        heavenly beings[e]
    and crowned him with glory and
        honor.

⁶You made him ruler over the works of
        your hands;
    you put everything under his feet:
⁷all flocks and herds,
    and the beasts of the field,
⁸the birds of the air,
    and the fish of the sea,
    all that swim the paths of the seas.

⁹O LORD, our Lord,
    how majestic is your name in all
        the earth!

Psalm 9[f]

For the director of music. To ,the tune
of, "The Death of the Son." A psalm
of David.

¹I will praise you, O LORD, with all my
        heart;
    I will tell of all your wonders.
²I will be glad and rejoice in you;
    I will sing praise to your name,
        O Most High.

³My enemies turn back;
    they stumble and perish before you.
⁴For you have upheld my right and my
        cause;
    you have sat on your throne,
        judging righteously.
⁵You have rebuked the nations and
        destroyed the wicked;
    you have blotted out their name for
        ever and ever.

---

a 10 Or *sovereign*   *b* 12 Or *If a man does not repent, / God*   *c* Title: Probably a musical term   *d* 2 Or *strength*   *e* 5 Or *than God*   *f* Psalms 9 and 10 may have been originally a single acrostic poem, the stanzas of which begin with the successive letters of the Hebrew alphabet. In the Septuagint they constitute one psalm.

⁶Endless ruin has overtaken the enemy,
 you have uprooted their cities;
 even the memory of them has
  perished.

⁷The LORD reigns forever;
 he has established his throne for
  judgment.
⁸He will judge the world in
  righteousness;
 he will govern the peoples with
  justice.
⁹The LORD is a refuge for the
  oppressed,
 a stronghold in times of trouble.
¹⁰Those who know your name will trust
  in you,
 for you, LORD, have never forsaken
  those who seek you.

¹¹Sing praises to the LORD, enthroned in
  Zion;
 proclaim among the nations what
  he has done.
¹²For he who avenges blood remembers;
 he does not ignore the cry of the
  afflicted.

¹³O LORD, see how my enemies
  persecute me!
 Have mercy and lift me up from the
  gates of death,
¹⁴that I may declare your praises
 in the gates of the Daughter of Zion
  and there rejoice in your salvation.
¹⁵The nations have fallen into the pit
  they have dug;
 their feet are caught in the net they
  have hidden.
¹⁶The LORD is known by his justice;
 the wicked are ensnared by the
  work of their hands.
            *Higgaion.*ᵃ *Selah*
¹⁷The wicked return to the grave,ᵇ
 all the nations that forget God.
¹⁸But the needy will not always be
  forgotten,
 nor the hope of the afflicted ever
  perish.

¹⁹Arise, O LORD, let not man triumph;
 let the nations be judged in your
  presence.
²⁰Strike them with terror, O LORD;
 let the nations know they are but
  men.   *Selah*

Psalm 10ᶜ

¹Why, O LORD, do you stand far off?
 Why do you hide yourself in times
  of trouble?

²In his arrogance the wicked man
  hunts down the weak,
 who are caught in the schemes he
  devises.
³He boasts of the cravings of his heart;
 he blesses the greedy and reviles
  the LORD.
⁴In his pride the wicked does not seek
  him;
 in all his thoughts there is no room
  for God.
⁵His ways are always prosperous;
 he is haughty and your laws are far
  from him;
 he sneers at all his enemies.
⁶He says to himself, "Nothing will
  shake me;
 I'll always be happy and never have
  trouble."

⁷His mouth is full of curses and lies
  and threats;
 trouble and evil are under his
  tongue.
⁸He lies in wait near the villages;
 from ambush he murders the
  innocent,
 watching in secret for his victims.
⁹He lies in wait like a lion in cover;
 he lies in wait to catch the helpless;
 he catches the helpless and drags
  them off in his net.
¹⁰His victims are crushed, they collapse;
 they fall under his strength.
¹¹He says to himself, "God has
  forgotten;
 he covers his face and never sees."

¹²Arise, LORD! Lift up your hand, O God.
 Do not forget the helpless.
¹³Why does the wicked man revile God?
 Why does he say to himself,
 "He won't call me to account"?
¹⁴But you, O God, do see trouble and
  grief;
 you consider it to take it in hand.
 The victim commits himself to you;
 you are the helper of the fatherless.
¹⁵Break the arm of the wicked and evil
  man;
 call him to account for his
  wickedness

ᵃ16 Or *Meditation*; possibly a musical notation   ᵇ17 Hebrew *Sheol*   ᶜPsalms 9 and 10 may have been originally a single acrostic poem, the stanzas of which begin with the successive letters of the Hebrew alphabet. In the Septuagint they constitute one psalm.

that would not be found out.

16The LORD is King for ever and ever;
the nations will perish from his land.
17You hear, O LORD, the desire of the afflicted;
you encourage them, and you listen to their cry,
18defending the fatherless and the oppressed,
in order that man, who is of the earth, may terrify no more.

WEDNESDAY

VERSE FOR THE DAY:
Psalm 10:14

AUTHOR:
Thomas Hale

PASSAGE FOR THE DAY:
Psalm 10:12–18

Pure Religion

REJECTED *by his Nepali villagers, nine-year-old Krishna asked surgeon Thomas Hale to allow him to stay at the mission hospital.*

I thought of the precedent it would set. We would be deluged with orphans the minute the word got out. Up until now we had been very careful not to get involved taking in unwanted children. Wasn't it enough to have come to this place, to care for the sick until they recovered, to feed them if they were hungry, and to pay their bills if they had no money? Did our Christian duty demand adopting them as well?

"Krishna, you must go home. Now."

He burst into tears.

My decision had been right, but I was wrong. Krishna cried for a long time. Along with his tears, he poured out his heart to me—his fears, his loneliness, his longing for a home and for affection. My mind went back to an evening some weeks earlier when I had haltingly tried to explain the meaning of James 1:27 to our Nepali Bible class: "Religion that God our Father accepts as pure and faultless is this: to look after orphans and widows in their distress and to keep oneself from being polluted by the world." That passage, I learned, is [one of only two places] in the New Testament where the word "orphan" is used. The verse had not impressed me then; in fact, I had been unable to figure out why James defined "pure and faultless" in such odd terms. As I sat there listening to Krishna, however, the verse began to take on a new meaning for me. It meant that if I were not ready to care for orphans in their distress, then there was something very wrong with my religion. Not being content with my exegesis of this verse, God seemed further to be asking me, "If you are not ready to care for *this* orphan in his distress, who are you ever going to care for?"

That day, Krishna did not return to his village.

Additional Scripture Readings:
Psalm 146; James 1:19–27

Go to page 416 for your next devotional reading.

Psalm 11

For the director of music. Of David.

¹In the LORD I take refuge.
  How then can you say to me:
  "Flee like a bird to your mountain.
²For look, the wicked bend their bows;
  they set their arrows against the strings
to shoot from the shadows
  at the upright in heart.
³When the foundations are being destroyed,
  what can the righteous do[a]?"

⁴The LORD is in his holy temple;
  the LORD is on his heavenly throne.
He observes the sons of men;
  his eyes examine them.
⁵The LORD examines the righteous,
  but the wicked[b] and those who love violence
  his soul hates.
⁶On the wicked he will rain
  fiery coals and burning sulfur;
  a scorching wind will be their lot.

⁷For the LORD is righteous,
  he loves justice;
  upright men will see his face.

Psalm 12

For the director of music. According to *sheminith.*[c] A psalm of David.

¹Help, LORD, for the godly are no more;
  the faithful have vanished from among men.
²Everyone lies to his neighbor;
  their flattering lips speak with deception.

³May the LORD cut off all flattering lips
  and every boastful tongue
⁴that says, "We will triumph with our tongues;
  we own our lips[d] — who is our master?"

⁵"Because of the oppression of the weak
  and the groaning of the needy,
I will now arise," says the LORD.
  "I will protect them from those who malign them."
⁶And the words of the LORD are flawless,
  like silver refined in a furnace of clay,
  purified seven times.

⁷O LORD, you will keep us safe
  and protect us from such people forever.
⁸The wicked freely strut about
  when what is vile is honored among men.

Psalm 13

For the director of music. A psalm of David.

¹How long, O LORD? Will you forget me forever?
  How long will you hide your face from me?
²How long must I wrestle with my thoughts
  and every day have sorrow in my heart?
  How long will my enemy triumph over me?

³Look on me and answer, O LORD my God.
  Give light to my eyes, or I will sleep in death;
⁴my enemy will say, "I have overcome him,"
  and my foes will rejoice when I fall.

⁵But I trust in your unfailing love;
  my heart rejoices in your salvation.
⁶I will sing to the LORD,
  for he has been good to me.

Psalm 14

For the director of music. Of David.

¹The fool[e] says in his heart,
  "There is no God."
They are corrupt, their deeds are vile;
  there is no one who does good.

²The LORD looks down from heaven
  on the sons of men
to see if there are any who understand,
  any who seek God.
³All have turned aside,
  they have together become corrupt;
there is no one who does good,
  not even one.

---

[a]3 Or *what is the Righteous One doing*   [b]5 Or *The LORD, the Righteous One, examines the wicked,* /
[c]Title: Probably a musical term   [d]4 Or / *our lips are our plowshares*   [e]1 The Hebrew words rendered *fool* in Psalms denote one who is morally deficient.

⁴Will evildoers never learn—
  those who devour my people as
    men eat bread
  and who do not call on the LORD?
⁵There they are, overwhelmed with
    dread,
  for God is present in the company
    of the righteous.
⁶You evildoers frustrate the plans of
    the poor,
  but the LORD is their refuge.

⁷Oh, that salvation for Israel would
    come out of Zion!
  When the LORD restores the fortunes
    of his people,
  let Jacob rejoice and Israel be glad!

Psalm 15

A psalm of David.

¹LORD, who may dwell in your
    sanctuary?
  Who may live on your holy hill?

²He whose walk is blameless
  and who does what is righteous,
  who speaks the truth from his heart
³ and has no slander on his tongue,
  who does his neighbor no wrong
  and casts no slur on his fellowman,
⁴who despises a vile man
  but honors those who fear the LORD,
  who keeps his oath
    even when it hurts,
⁵who lends his money without usury
  and does not accept a bribe against
    the innocent.

He who does these things
  will never be shaken.

Psalm 16

A miktam^a of David.

¹Keep me safe, O God,
  for in you I take refuge.

²I said to the LORD, "You are my Lord;
  apart from you I have no good
    thing."
³As for the saints who are in the land,
  they are the glorious ones in whom
    is all my delight.^{b}
⁴The sorrows of those will increase
  who run after other gods.
I will not pour out their libations of
    blood
  or take up their names on my lips.

⁵LORD, you have assigned me my
    portion and my cup;
  you have made my lot secure.
⁶The boundary lines have fallen for me
    in pleasant places;
  surely I have a delightful
    inheritance.

⁷I will praise the LORD, who counsels
    me;
  even at night my heart instructs me.
⁸I have set the LORD always before me.
  Because he is at my right hand,
  I will not be shaken.

⁹Therefore my heart is glad and my
    tongue rejoices;
  my body also will rest secure,
¹⁰because you will not abandon me to
    the grave,^{c}
  nor will you let your Holy One^d
    see decay.
¹¹You have made^e known to me the
    path of life;
  you will fill me with joy in your
    presence,
  with eternal pleasures at your right
    hand.

Psalm 17

A prayer of David.

¹Hear, O LORD, my righteous plea;
  listen to my cry.
  Give ear to my prayer—
  it does not rise from deceitful lips.
²May my vindication come from you;
  may your eyes see what is right.

³Though you probe my heart and
    examine me at night,
  though you test me, you will find
    nothing;
  I have resolved that my mouth will
    not sin.
⁴As for the deeds of men—
  by the word of your lips
  I have kept myself
    from the ways of the violent.
⁵My steps have held to your paths;
  my feet have not slipped.

⁶I call on you, O God, for you will
    answer me;

---

^{a}Title: Probably a literary or musical term ^{b}3 Or *As for the pagan priests who are in the land / and the nobles in whom all delight, I said:* ^{c}10 Hebrew *Sheol* ^{d}10 Or *your faithful one* ^{e}11 Or *You will make*

give ear to me and hear my prayer.
⁷Show the wonder of your great love,
you who save by your right hand
those who take refuge in you from
their foes.
⁸Keep me as the apple of your eye;
hide me in the shadow of your
wings
⁹from the wicked who assail me,
from my mortal enemies who
surround me.

¹⁰They close up their callous hearts,
and their mouths speak with
arrogance.
¹¹They have tracked me down, they
now surround me,
with eyes alert, to throw me to the
ground.
¹²They are like a lion hungry for prey,
like a great lion crouching in cover.

¹³Rise up, O Lord, confront them, bring
them down;
rescue me from the wicked by your
sword.
¹⁴O Lord, by your hand save me from
such men,
from men of this world whose
reward is in this life.

You still the hunger of those you
cherish;
their sons have plenty,
and they store up wealth for their
children.
¹⁵And I—in righteousness I will see
your face;
when I awake, I will be satisfied
with seeing your likeness.

Psalm 18

For the director of music. Of David the
servant of the Lord. He sang to the
Lord the words of this song when
the Lord delivered him from the hand
of all his enemies and from the
hand of Saul. He said:

¹I love you, O Lord, my strength.

²The Lord is my rock, my fortress and
my deliverer;
my God is my rock, in whom I take
refuge.
He is my shield and the horn[a] of
my salvation, my stronghold.
³I call to the Lord, who is worthy of
praise,
and I am saved from my enemies.

⁴The cords of death entangled me;
the torrents of destruction
overwhelmed me.
⁵The cords of the grave[b] coiled around
me;
the snares of death confronted me.
⁶In my distress I called to the Lord;
I cried to my God for help.
From his temple he heard my voice;
my cry came before him, into his
ears.

⁷The earth trembled and quaked,
and the foundations of the
mountains shook;
they trembled because he was
angry.
⁸Smoke rose from his nostrils;
consuming fire came from his
mouth,
burning coals blazed out of it.
⁹He parted the heavens and came
down;
dark clouds were under his feet.
¹⁰He mounted the cherubim and flew;
he soared on the wings of the wind.
¹¹He made darkness his covering, his
canopy around him—
the dark rain clouds of the sky.
¹²Out of the brightness of his presence
clouds advanced,
with hailstones and bolts of
lightning.
¹³The Lord thundered from heaven;
the voice of the Most High
resounded.[c]
¹⁴He shot his arrows and scattered the
enemies,
great bolts of lightning and routed
them.
¹⁵The valleys of the sea were exposed
and the foundations of the earth
laid bare
at your rebuke, O Lord,
at the blast of breath from your
nostrils.

¹⁶He reached down from on high and
took hold of me;
he drew me out of deep waters.
¹⁷He rescued me from my powerful
enemy,
from my foes, who were too strong
for me.

---

[a] 2 *Horn* here symbolizes strength.   [b] 5 Hebrew *Sheol*   [c] 13 Some Hebrew manuscripts and Septuagint
(see also 2 Samuel 22:14); most Hebrew manuscripts *resounded, / amid hailstones and bolts of lightning*

¹⁸They confronted me in the day of my disaster,
but the LORD was my support.
¹⁹He brought me out into a spacious place;
he rescued me because he delighted in me.

²⁰The LORD has dealt with me according to my righteousness;
according to the cleanness of my hands he has rewarded me.
²¹For I have kept the ways of the LORD;
I have not done evil by turning from my God.
²²All his laws are before me;
I have not turned away from his decrees.
²³I have been blameless before him
and have kept myself from sin.
²⁴The LORD has rewarded me according to my righteousness,
according to the cleanness of my hands in his sight.

²⁵To the faithful you show yourself faithful,
to the blameless you show yourself blameless,
²⁶to the pure you show yourself pure,
but to the crooked you show yourself shrewd.
²⁷You save the humble
but bring low those whose eyes are haughty.
²⁸You, O LORD, keep my lamp burning;
my God turns my darkness into light.
²⁹With your help I can advance against a troop*a*;
with my God I can scale a wall.

³⁰As for God, his way is perfect;
the word of the LORD is flawless.
He is a shield
for all who take refuge in him.
³¹For who is God besides the LORD?
And who is the Rock except our God?
³²It is God who arms me with strength
and makes my way perfect.
³³He makes my feet like the feet of a deer;
he enables me to stand on the heights.
³⁴He trains my hands for battle;
my arms can bend a bow of bronze.

³⁵You give me your shield of victory,
and your right hand sustains me;
you stoop down to make me great.
³⁶You broaden the path beneath me,
so that my ankles do not turn.

³⁷I pursued my enemies and overtook them;
I did not turn back till they were destroyed.
³⁸I crushed them so that they could not rise;
they fell beneath my feet.
³⁹You armed me with strength for battle;
you made my adversaries bow at my feet.
⁴⁰You made my enemies turn their backs in flight,
and I destroyed my foes.
⁴¹They cried for help, but there was no one to save them—
to the LORD, but he did not answer.
⁴²I beat them as fine as dust borne on the wind;
I poured them out like mud in the streets.

⁴³You have delivered me from the attacks of the people;
you have made me the head of nations;
people I did not know are subject to me.
⁴⁴As soon as they hear me, they obey me;
foreigners cringe before me.
⁴⁵They all lose heart;
they come trembling from their strongholds.

⁴⁶The LORD lives! Praise be to my Rock!
Exalted be God my Savior!
⁴⁷He is the God who avenges me,
who subdues nations under me,
⁴⁸ who saves me from my enemies.
You exalted me above my foes;
from violent men you rescued me.
⁴⁹Therefore I will praise you among the nations, O LORD;
I will sing praises to your name.
⁵⁰He gives his king great victories;
he shows unfailing kindness to his anointed,
to David and his descendants forever.

a29 Or can run through a barricade

Psalm 19

For the director of music. A psalm of David.

¹The heavens declare the glory of God;
  the skies proclaim the work of his hands.
²Day after day they pour forth speech;
  night after night they display knowledge.
³There is no speech or language
  where their voice is not heard.[a]
⁴Their voice[b] goes out into all the earth,
  their words to the ends of the world.

In the heavens he has pitched a tent for the sun,
⁵ which is like a bridegroom coming forth from his pavilion,
  like a champion rejoicing to run his course.
⁶It rises at one end of the heavens
  and makes its circuit to the other;
  nothing is hidden from its heat.

⁷The law of the LORD is perfect,
  reviving the soul.
The statutes of the LORD are trustworthy,
  making wise the simple.
⁸The precepts of the LORD are right,
  giving joy to the heart.
The commands of the LORD are radiant,
  giving light to the eyes.
⁹The fear of the LORD is pure,
  enduring forever.
The ordinances of the LORD are sure
  and altogether righteous.
¹⁰They are more precious than gold,
  than much pure gold;
they are sweeter than honey,
  than honey from the comb.
¹¹By them is your servant warned;
  in keeping them there is great reward.

¹²Who can discern his errors?
  Forgive my hidden faults.
¹³Keep your servant also from willful sins;
  may they not rule over me.
Then will I be blameless,
  innocent of great transgression.

¹⁴May the words of my mouth and the meditation of my heart
be pleasing in your sight,
  O LORD, my Rock and my Redeemer.

Psalm 20

For the director of music. A psalm of David.

¹May the LORD answer you when you are in distress;
  may the name of the God of Jacob protect you.
²May he send you help from the sanctuary
  and grant you support from Zion.
³May he remember all your sacrifices
  and accept your burnt offerings.
    Selah
⁴May he give you the desire of your heart
  and make all your plans succeed.
⁵We will shout for joy when you are victorious
  and will lift up our banners in the name of our God.
May the LORD grant all your requests.

⁶Now I know that the LORD saves his anointed;
  he answers him from his holy heaven
  with the saving power of his right hand.
⁷Some trust in chariots and some in horses,
  but we trust in the name of the LORD our God.
⁸They are brought to their knees and fall,
  but we rise up and stand firm.

⁹O LORD, save the king!
  Answer[c] us when we call!

Psalm 21

For the director of music. A psalm of David.

¹O LORD, the king rejoices in your strength.
  How great is his joy in the victories you give!
²You have granted him the desire of his heart

---

[a]3 Or *They have no speech, there are no words; / no sound is heard from them* [b]4 Septuagint, Jerome and Syriac; Hebrew *line* [c]9 Or *save! / O King, answer*

and have not withheld the request
  of his lips. *Selah*
³You welcomed him with rich blessings
  and placed a crown of pure gold on
    his head.
⁴He asked you for life, and you gave it
    to him—
  length of days, for ever and ever.
⁵Through the victories you gave, his
    glory is great;
  you have bestowed on him splendor
    and majesty.
⁶Surely you have granted him eternal
    blessings
  and made him glad with the joy of
    your presence.
⁷For the king trusts in the LORD;
  through the unfailing love of the
    Most High
  he will not be shaken.

⁸Your hand will lay hold on all your
    enemies;
  your right hand will seize your foes.
⁹At the time of your appearing
  you will make them like a fiery
    furnace.
  In his wrath the LORD will swallow
    them up,
  and his fire will consume them.
¹⁰You will destroy their descendants
    from the earth,
  their posterity from mankind.
¹¹Though they plot evil against you
  and devise wicked schemes, they
    cannot succeed;
¹²for you will make them turn their
    backs
  when you aim at them with drawn
    bow.

¹³Be exalted, O LORD, in your strength;
  we will sing and praise your might.

Psalm 22

*For the director of music. To the tune
of "The Doe of the Morning." A psalm
of David.*

¹My God, my God, why have you
    forsaken me?
  Why are you so far from saving me,
  so far from the words of my
    groaning?
²O my God, I cry out by day, but you
    do not answer,
  by night, and am not silent.

³Yet you are enthroned as the Holy
    One;
  you are the praise of Israel.ᵃ
⁴In you our fathers put their trust;
  they trusted and you delivered
    them.
⁵They cried to you and were saved;
  in you they trusted and were not
    disappointed.

⁶But I am a worm and not a man,
  scorned by men and despised by
    the people.
⁷All who see me mock me;
  they hurl insults, shaking their
    heads:
⁸"He trusts in the LORD;
  let the LORD rescue him.
  Let him deliver him,
  since he delights in him."

⁹Yet you brought me out of the womb;
  you made me trust in you
  even at my mother's breast.
¹⁰From birth I was cast upon you;
  from my mother's womb you have
    been my God.
¹¹Do not be far from me,
  for trouble is near
  and there is no one to help.

¹²Many bulls surround me;
  strong bulls of Bashan encircle me.
¹³Roaring lions tearing their prey
  open their mouths wide against me.
¹⁴I am poured out like water,
  and all my bones are out of joint.
  My heart has turned to wax;
  it has melted away within me.
¹⁵My strength is dried up like a
    potsherd,
  and my tongue sticks to the roof of
    my mouth;
  you lay meᵇ in the dust of death.
¹⁶Dogs have surrounded me;
  a band of evil men has encircled
    me,
  they have piercedᶜ my hands and
    my feet.
¹⁷I can count all my bones;
  people stare and gloat over me.
¹⁸They divide my garments among them
  and cast lots for my clothing.

¹⁹But you, O LORD, be not far off;
  O my Strength, come quickly to
    help me.
²⁰Deliver my life from the sword,

ᵃ3 Or *Yet you are holy, / enthroned on the praises of Israel*   ᵇ15 Or */ I am laid*   ᶜ16 Some Hebrew manuscripts, Septuagint and Syriac; most Hebrew manuscripts */ like the lion,*

my precious life from the power of the dogs.
²¹Rescue me from the mouth of the lions;
save*ᵃ* me from the horns of the wild oxen.

²²I will declare your name to my brothers;
in the congregation I will praise you.
²³You who fear the LORD, praise him!
All you descendants of Jacob, honor him!
Revere him, all you descendants of Israel!
²⁴For he has not despised or disdained
the suffering of the afflicted one;
he has not hidden his face from him
but has listened to his cry for help.

²⁵From you comes the theme of my praise in the great assembly;
before those who fear you*ᵇ* will I fulfill my vows.
²⁶The poor will eat and be satisfied;
they who seek the LORD will praise him—
may your hearts live forever!
²⁷All the ends of the earth
will remember and turn to the LORD,
and all the families of the nations
will bow down before him,
²⁸for dominion belongs to the LORD
and he rules over the nations.

²⁹All the rich of the earth will feast and worship;
all who go down to the dust will kneel before him—
those who cannot keep themselves alive.
³⁰Posterity will serve him;
future generations will be told about the Lord.
³¹They will proclaim his righteousness
to a people yet unborn—
for he has done it.

Psalm 23

A psalm of David.

¹The LORD is my shepherd, I shall not be in want.
² He makes me lie down in green pastures,
he leads me beside quiet waters,
³ he restores my soul.
He guides me in paths of righteousness
for his name's sake.
⁴Even though I walk
through the valley of the shadow of death,*ᶜ*
I will fear no evil,
for you are with me;
your rod and your staff,
they comfort me.

⁵You prepare a table before me
in the presence of my enemies.
You anoint my head with oil;
my cup overflows.
⁶Surely goodness and love will follow me
all the days of my life,
and I will dwell in the house of the LORD
forever.

Psalm 24

Of David. A psalm.

¹The earth is the LORD's, and everything in it,
the world, and all who live in it;
²for he founded it upon the seas
and established it upon the waters.

³Who may ascend the hill of the LORD?
Who may stand in his holy place?
⁴He who has clean hands and a pure heart,
who does not lift up his soul to an idol
or swear by what is false.*ᵈ*
⁵He will receive blessing from the LORD
and vindication from God his Savior.
⁶Such is the generation of those who seek him,
who seek your face, O God of Jacob.*ᵉ*   *Selah*

⁷Lift up your heads, O you gates;
be lifted up, you ancient doors,
that the King of glory may come in.
⁸Who is this King of glory?
The LORD strong and mighty,
the LORD mighty in battle.
⁹Lift up your heads, O you gates;
lift them up, you ancient doors,
that the King of glory may come in.
¹⁰Who is he, this King of glory?
The LORD Almighty—
he is the King of glory.   *Selah*

---

*a*21 Or / *you have heard*   *b*25 Hebrew *him*   *c*4 Or *through the darkest valley*   *d*4 Or *swear falsely*
*e*6 Two Hebrew manuscripts and Syriac (see also Septuagint); most Hebrew manuscripts *face, Jacob*

Psalm 25[a]

Of David.

¹To you, O LORD, I lift up my soul;
² in you I trust, O my God.
Do not let me be put to shame,
  nor let my enemies triumph over me.
³No one whose hope is in you
  will ever be put to shame,
but they will be put to shame
  who are treacherous without excuse.
⁴Show me your ways, O LORD,
  teach me your paths;
⁵guide me in your truth and teach me,
  for you are God my Savior,
  and my hope is in you all day long.
⁶Remember, O LORD, your great mercy and love,
  for they are from of old.
⁷Remember not the sins of my youth
  and my rebellious ways;
according to your love remember me,
  for you are good, O LORD.
⁸Good and upright is the LORD;

[a] This psalm is an acrostic poem, the verses of which begin with the successive letters of the Hebrew alphabet.

THURSDAY

VERSE FOR THE DAY:
Psalm 24:1

AUTHOR:
Don Wyrtzen

PASSAGE FOR THE DAY:
Psalm 24:1–10

No Loose Ends!

THE creative power of God inspires awe. I'm filled with reverent wonder as I contemplate it. To think that he spoke and worlds came into being! In contrast to God, I work with raw materials that he created. My creativity is derived from his. I put the wrapping paper and ribbon on his packages.

Several years ago, Karen and I traveled to Brazil. Along with lecturing and ministering to missionaries, we scheduled some sightseeing. I will never forget the awesome Iguacu Falls. There in the majestic grandeur of cascading water, I saw the omnipotence of the almighty God. I shouted spontaneously, "How great Thou art!"

Because the Lord made the earth and everything in it, he owns it. He founded the earth (Genesis 1) and established it upon the waters. The heathen nations feared the restless, perilous, foaming seas. But even the violent waters belong to God and reflect the variety and depth of his creative imagination.

The Lord didn't create the earth and then abandon it. He is intimately involved with sustaining it. He watches over what belongs to him. My Lord doesn't like loose ends! He not only sustains his creation; he watches over me too and allows me to reflect his creativity!

I praise you, Lord, for your incredible imagination and creativity. I thank you that I can, in a very small way, imitate it.

Additional Scripture Readings:
Psalm 104:1–30; Matthew 6:25–34

Go to page 424 for your next devotional reading.

therefore he instructs sinners in his
ways.
⁹He guides the humble in what is right
and teaches them his way.
¹⁰All the ways of the LORD are loving
and faithful
for those who keep the demands of
his covenant.
¹¹For the sake of your name, O LORD,
forgive my iniquity, though it is
great.
¹²Who, then, is the man that fears the
LORD?
He will instruct him in the way
chosen for him.
¹³He will spend his days in prosperity,
and his descendants will inherit the
land.
¹⁴The LORD confides in those who fear
him;
he makes his covenant known to
them.
¹⁵My eyes are ever on the LORD,
for only he will release my feet
from the snare.

¹⁶Turn to me and be gracious to me,
for I am lonely and afflicted.
¹⁷The troubles of my heart have
multiplied;
free me from my anguish.
¹⁸Look upon my affliction and my
distress
and take away all my sins.
¹⁹See how my enemies have increased
and how fiercely they hate me!
²⁰Guard my life and rescue me;
let me not be put to shame,
for I take refuge in you.
²¹May integrity and uprightness protect
me,
because my hope is in you.

²²Redeem Israel, O God,
from all their troubles!

Psalm 26

Of David.

¹Vindicate me, O LORD,
for I have led a blameless life;
I have trusted in the LORD
without wavering.
²Test me, O LORD, and try me,
examine my heart and my mind;
³for your love is ever before me,
and I walk continually in your truth.
⁴I do not sit with deceitful men,
nor do I consort with hypocrites;
⁵I abhor the assembly of evildoers
and refuse to sit with the wicked.
⁶I wash my hands in innocence,
and go about your altar, O LORD,
⁷proclaiming aloud your praise
and telling of all your wonderful
deeds.
⁸I love the house where you live,
O LORD,
the place where your glory dwells.

⁹Do not take away my soul along with
sinners,
my life with bloodthirsty men,
¹⁰in whose hands are wicked schemes,
whose right hands are full of bribes.
¹¹But I lead a blameless life;
redeem me and be merciful to me.

¹²My feet stand on level ground;
in the great assembly I will praise
the LORD.

Psalm 27

Of David.

¹The LORD is my light and my
salvation—
whom shall I fear?
The LORD is the stronghold of my
life—
of whom shall I be afraid?
²When evil men advance against me
to devour my flesh,*ᵃ*
when my enemies and my foes attack
me,
they will stumble and fall.
³Though an army besiege me,
my heart will not fear;
though war break out against me,
even then will I be confident.

⁴One thing I ask of the LORD,
this is what I seek:
that I may dwell in the house of the
LORD
all the days of my life,
to gaze upon the beauty of the LORD
and to seek him in his temple.
⁵For in the day of trouble
he will keep me safe in his
dwelling;
he will hide me in the shelter of his
tabernacle
and set me high upon a rock.
⁶Then my head will be exalted

---

a 2 Or *to slander me*

above the enemies who surround me;
at his tabernacle will I sacrifice with shouts of joy;
I will sing and make music to the LORD.

⁷Hear my voice when I call, O LORD;
be merciful to me and answer me.
⁸My heart says of you, "Seek his[a] face!"
Your face, LORD, I will seek.
⁹Do not hide your face from me,
do not turn your servant away in anger;
you have been my helper.
Do not reject me or forsake me,
O God my Savior.
¹⁰Though my father and mother forsake me,
the LORD will receive me.
¹¹Teach me your way, O LORD;
lead me in a straight path
because of my oppressors.
¹²Do not turn me over to the desire of my foes,
for false witnesses rise up against me,
breathing out violence.

¹³I am still confident of this:
I will see the goodness of the LORD
in the land of the living.
¹⁴Wait for the LORD;
be strong and take heart
and wait for the LORD.

Psalm 28

Of David.

¹To you I call, O LORD my Rock;
do not turn a deaf ear to me.
For if you remain silent,
I will be like those who have gone down to the pit.
²Hear my cry for mercy
as I call to you for help,
as I lift up my hands
toward your Most Holy Place.

³Do not drag me away with the wicked,
with those who do evil,
who speak cordially with their neighbors
but harbor malice in their hearts.
⁴Repay them for their deeds
and for their evil work;
repay them for what their hands have done
and bring back upon them what they deserve.
⁵Since they show no regard for the works of the LORD
and what his hands have done,
he will tear them down
and never build them up again.

⁶Praise be to the LORD,
for he has heard my cry for mercy.
⁷The LORD is my strength and my shield;
my heart trusts in him, and I am helped.
My heart leaps for joy
and I will give thanks to him in song.

⁸The LORD is the strength of his people,
a fortress of salvation for his anointed one.
⁹Save your people and bless your inheritance;
be their shepherd and carry them forever.

Psalm 29

A psalm of David.

¹Ascribe to the LORD, O mighty ones,
ascribe to the LORD glory and strength.
²Ascribe to the LORD the glory due his name;
worship the LORD in the splendor of his[b] holiness.

³The voice of the LORD is over the waters;
the God of glory thunders,
the LORD thunders over the mighty waters.
⁴The voice of the LORD is powerful;
the voice of the LORD is majestic.
⁵The voice of the LORD breaks the cedars;
the LORD breaks in pieces the cedars of Lebanon.
⁶He makes Lebanon skip like a calf,
Sirion[c] like a young wild ox.
⁷The voice of the LORD strikes
with flashes of lightning.
⁸The voice of the LORD shakes the desert;
the LORD shakes the Desert of Kadesh.

---

[a] 8 Or *To you, O my heart, he has said, "Seek my* Mount Hermon [b] 2 Or LORD *with the splendor of* [c] 6 That is,

⁹The voice of the LORD twists the oaks*a*
and strips the forests bare.
And in his temple all cry, "Glory!"

¹⁰The LORD sits*b* enthroned over the flood;
the LORD is enthroned as King forever.
¹¹The LORD gives strength to his people;
the LORD blesses his people with peace.

Psalm 30

A psalm. A song. For the dedication of the temple.*c* Of David.

¹I will exalt you, O LORD,
for you lifted me out of the depths
and did not let my enemies gloat over me.
²O LORD my God, I called to you for help
and you healed me.
³O LORD, you brought me up from the grave*d*;
you spared me from going down into the pit.

⁴Sing to the LORD, you saints of his;
praise his holy name.
⁵For his anger lasts only a moment,
but his favor lasts a lifetime;
weeping may remain for a night,
but rejoicing comes in the morning.

⁶When I felt secure, I said,
"I will never be shaken."
⁷O LORD, when you favored me,
you made my mountain*e* stand firm;
but when you hid your face,
I was dismayed.

⁸To you, O LORD, I called;
to the Lord I cried for mercy:
⁹"What gain is there in my destruction,*f*
in my going down into the pit?
Will the dust praise you?
Will it proclaim your faithfulness?
¹⁰Hear, O LORD, and be merciful to me;
O LORD, be my help."

¹¹You turned my wailing into dancing;
you removed my sackcloth and clothed me with joy,
¹²that my heart may sing to you and not be silent.
O LORD my God, I will give you thanks forever.

Psalm 31

For the director of music. A psalm of David.

¹In you, O LORD, I have taken refuge;
let me never be put to shame;
deliver me in your righteousness.
²Turn your ear to me,
come quickly to my rescue;
be my rock of refuge,
a strong fortress to save me.
³Since you are my rock and my fortress,
for the sake of your name lead and guide me.
⁴Free me from the trap that is set for me,
for you are my refuge.
⁵Into your hands I commit my spirit;
redeem me, O LORD, the God of truth.

⁶I hate those who cling to worthless idols;
I trust in the LORD.
⁷I will be glad and rejoice in your love,
for you saw my affliction
and knew the anguish of my soul.
⁸You have not handed me over to the enemy
but have set my feet in a spacious place.

⁹Be merciful to me, O LORD, for I am in distress;
my eyes grow weak with sorrow,
my soul and my body with grief.
¹⁰My life is consumed by anguish
and my years by groaning;
my strength fails because of my affliction,*g*
and my bones grow weak.
¹¹Because of all my enemies,
I am the utter contempt of my neighbors;
I am a dread to my friends—
those who see me on the street flee from me.
¹²I am forgotten by them as though I were dead;
I have become like broken pottery.
¹³For I hear the slander of many;
there is terror on every side;
they conspire against me

---

*a*9 Or LORD *makes the deer give birth*   *b*10 Or *sat*   *c*Title: Or *palace*   *d*3 Hebrew *Sheol*   *e*7 Or *hill country*   *f*9 Or *there if I am silenced*   *g*10 Or *guilt*

and plot to take my life.
¹⁴But I trust in you, O LORD;
    I say, "You are my God."
¹⁵My times are in your hands;
    deliver me from my enemies
    and from those who pursue me.
¹⁶Let your face shine on your servant;
    save me in your unfailing love.
¹⁷Let me not be put to shame, O LORD,
    for I have cried out to you;
but let the wicked be put to shame
    and lie silent in the grave.[a]
¹⁸Let their lying lips be silenced,
    for with pride and contempt
    they speak arrogantly against the
        righteous.

¹⁹How great is your goodness,
    which you have stored up for those
        who fear you,
which you bestow in the sight of men
    on those who take refuge in you.
²⁰In the shelter of your presence you
        hide them
    from the intrigues of men;
in your dwelling you keep them safe
    from accusing tongues.

²¹Praise be to the LORD,
    for he showed his wonderful love to
        me
    when I was in a besieged city.
²²In my alarm I said,
    "I am cut off from your sight!"
Yet you heard my cry for mercy
    when I called to you for help.

²³Love the LORD, all his saints!
    The LORD preserves the faithful,
    but the proud he pays back in full.
²⁴Be strong and take heart,
    all you who hope in the LORD.

Psalm 32

Of David. A *maskil.*[b]

¹Blessed is he
    whose transgressions are forgiven,
    whose sins are covered.
²Blessed is the man
    whose sin the LORD does not count
        against him
    and in whose spirit is no deceit.

³When I kept silent,
    my bones wasted away
    through my groaning all day long.

⁴For day and night
    your hand was heavy upon me;
my strength was sapped
    as in the heat of summer.   *Selah*
⁵Then I acknowledged my sin to you
    and did not cover up my iniquity.
I said, "I will confess
    my transgressions to the LORD"—
and you forgave
    the guilt of my sin.   *Selah*

⁶Therefore let everyone who is godly
        pray to you
    while you may be found;
surely when the mighty waters rise,
    they will not reach him.
⁷You are my hiding place;
    you will protect me from trouble
    and surround me with songs of
        deliverance.   *Selah*

⁸I will instruct you and teach you in
        the way you should go;
    I will counsel you and watch over
        you.
⁹Do not be like the horse or the mule,
    which have no understanding
but must be controlled by bit and
        bridle
    or they will not come to you.
¹⁰Many are the woes of the wicked,
    but the LORD's unfailing love
    surrounds the man who trusts in
        him.

¹¹Rejoice in the LORD and be glad, you
        righteous;
    sing, all you who are upright in
        heart!

Psalm 33

¹Sing joyfully to the LORD, you
        righteous;
    it is fitting for the upright to praise
        him.
²Praise the LORD with the harp;
    make music to him on the
        ten-stringed lyre.
³Sing to him a new song;
    play skillfully, and shout for joy.

⁴For the word of the LORD is right and
        true;
    he is faithful in all he does.

---

[a]17 Hebrew *Sheol*   [b]Title: Probably a literary or musical term

⁵The Lord loves righteousness and justice;
 the earth is full of his unfailing love.

⁶By the word of the Lord were the heavens made,
 their starry host by the breath of his mouth.
⁷He gathers the waters of the sea into jars*ᵃ*;
 he puts the deep into storehouses.
⁸Let all the earth fear the Lord;
 let all the people of the world revere him.
⁹For he spoke, and it came to be;
 he commanded, and it stood firm.
¹⁰The Lord foils the plans of the nations;
 he thwarts the purposes of the peoples.
¹¹But the plans of the Lord stand firm forever,
 the purposes of his heart through all generations.
¹²Blessed is the nation whose God is the Lord,
 the people he chose for his inheritance.
¹³From heaven the Lord looks down
 and sees all mankind;
¹⁴from his dwelling place he watches
 all who live on earth—
¹⁵he who forms the hearts of all,
 who considers everything they do.
¹⁶No king is saved by the size of his army;
 no warrior escapes by his great strength.
¹⁷A horse is a vain hope for deliverance;
 despite all its great strength it cannot save.
¹⁸But the eyes of the Lord are on those who fear him,
 on those whose hope is in his unfailing love,
¹⁹to deliver them from death
 and keep them alive in famine.

²⁰We wait in hope for the Lord;
 he is our help and our shield.
²¹In him our hearts rejoice,
 for we trust in his holy name.
²²May your unfailing love rest upon us, O Lord,
 even as we put our hope in you.

Psalm 34*ᵇ*

Of David. When he pretended to be insane before Abimelech, who drove him away, and he left.

¹I will extol the Lord at all times;
 his praise will always be on my lips.
²My soul will boast in the Lord;
 let the afflicted hear and rejoice.
³Glorify the Lord with me;
 let us exalt his name together.

⁴I sought the Lord, and he answered me;
 he delivered me from all my fears.
⁵Those who look to him are radiant;
 their faces are never covered with shame.
⁶This poor man called, and the Lord heard him;
 he saved him out of all his troubles.
⁷The angel of the Lord encamps around those who fear him,
 and he delivers them.

⁸Taste and see that the Lord is good;
 blessed is the man who takes refuge in him.
⁹Fear the Lord, you his saints,
 for those who fear him lack nothing.
¹⁰The lions may grow weak and hungry,
 but those who seek the Lord lack no good thing.

¹¹Come, my children, listen to me;
 I will teach you the fear of the Lord.
¹²Whoever of you loves life
 and desires to see many good days,
¹³keep your tongue from evil
 and your lips from speaking lies.
¹⁴Turn from evil and do good;
 seek peace and pursue it.

¹⁵The eyes of the Lord are on the righteous
 and his ears are attentive to their cry;
¹⁶the face of the Lord is against those who do evil,
 to cut off the memory of them from the earth.

¹⁷The righteous cry out, and the Lord hears them;
 he delivers them from all their troubles.

---

*ᵃ*7 Or *sea as into a heap*   *ᵇ*This psalm is an acrostic poem, the verses of which begin with the successive letters of the Hebrew alphabet.

¹⁸The LORD is close to the brokenhearted
and saves those who are crushed in spirit.

¹⁹A righteous man may have many troubles,
but the LORD delivers him from them all;
²⁰he protects all his bones,
not one of them will be broken.

²¹Evil will slay the wicked;
the foes of the righteous will be condemned.
²²The LORD redeems his servants;
no one will be condemned who takes refuge in him.

Psalm 35

Of David.

¹Contend, O LORD, with those who contend with me;
fight against those who fight against me.
²Take up shield and buckler;
arise and come to my aid.
³Brandish spear and javelin*ᵃ*
against those who pursue me.
Say to my soul,
"I am your salvation."

⁴May those who seek my life
be disgraced and put to shame;
may those who plot my ruin
be turned back in dismay.
⁵May they be like chaff before the wind,
with the angel of the LORD driving them away;
⁶may their path be dark and slippery,
with the angel of the LORD pursuing them.
⁷Since they hid their net for me without cause
and without cause dug a pit for me,
⁸may ruin overtake them by surprise—
may the net they hid entangle them,
may they fall into the pit, to their ruin.
⁹Then my soul will rejoice in the LORD
and delight in his salvation.
¹⁰My whole being will exclaim,
"Who is like you, O LORD?
You rescue the poor from those too strong for them,
the poor and needy from those who rob them."

¹¹Ruthless witnesses come forward;
they question me on things I know nothing about.
¹²They repay me evil for good
and leave my soul forlorn.
¹³Yet when they were ill, I put on sackcloth
and humbled myself with fasting.
When my prayers returned to me unanswered,
¹⁴ I went about mourning
as though for my friend or brother.
I bowed my head in grief
as though weeping for my mother.
¹⁵But when I stumbled, they gathered in glee;
attackers gathered against me when I was unaware.
They slandered me without ceasing.
¹⁶Like the ungodly they maliciously mocked*ᵇ*;
they gnashed their teeth at me.
¹⁷O Lord, how long will you look on?
Rescue my life from their ravages,
my precious life from these lions.
¹⁸I will give you thanks in the great assembly;
among throngs of people I will praise you.

¹⁹Let not those gloat over me
who are my enemies without cause;
let not those who hate me without reason
maliciously wink the eye.
²⁰They do not speak peaceably,
but devise false accusations
against those who live quietly in the land.
²¹They gape at me and say, "Aha! Aha!
With our own eyes we have seen it."

²²O LORD, you have seen this; be not silent.
Do not be far from me, O Lord.
²³Awake, and rise to my defense!
Contend for me, my God and Lord.
²⁴Vindicate me in your righteousness,
O LORD my God;
do not let them gloat over me.
²⁵Do not let them think, "Aha, just what we wanted!"
or say, "We have swallowed him up."

²⁶May all who gloat over my distress

ᵃ3 Or and block the way   *ᵇ16 Septuagint; Hebrew may mean ungodly circle of mockers.*

be put to shame and confusion;
may all who exalt themselves over me
  be clothed with shame and disgrace.
²⁷May those who delight in my
    vindication
  shout for joy and gladness;
may they always say, "The LORD be
    exalted,
  who delights in the well-being of his
    servant."
²⁸My tongue will speak of your
    righteousness
  and of your praises all day long.

Psalm 36

For the director of music. Of David the servant of the LORD.

¹An oracle is within my heart
  concerning the sinfulness of the
    wicked:ᵃ
There is no fear of God
  before his eyes.
²For in his own eyes he flatters himself
  too much to detect or hate his sin.
³The words of his mouth are wicked
    and deceitful;
  he has ceased to be wise and to do
    good.
⁴Even on his bed he plots evil;
  he commits himself to a sinful
    course
  and does not reject what is wrong.

⁵Your love, O LORD, reaches to the
    heavens,
  your faithfulness to the skies.
⁶Your righteousness is like the mighty
    mountains,
  your justice like the great deep.
O LORD, you preserve both man and
    beast.
⁷ How priceless is your unfailing
    love!
Both high and low among men
  findᵇ refuge in the shadow of your
    wings.
⁸They feast on the abundance of your
    house;
  you give them drink from your river
    of delights.
⁹For with you is the fountain of life;
  in your light we see light.

¹⁰Continue your love to those who
    know you,
  your righteousness to the upright in
    heart.
¹¹May the foot of the proud not come
    against me,
  nor the hand of the wicked drive
    me away.
¹²See how the evildoers lie fallen—
  thrown down, not able to rise!

Psalm 37ᶜ

Of David.

¹Do not fret because of evil men
  or be envious of those who do
    wrong;
²for like the grass they will soon
    wither,
  like green plants they will soon die
    away.

³Trust in the LORD and do good;
  dwell in the land and enjoy safe
    pasture.
⁴Delight yourself in the LORD
  and he will give you the desires of
    your heart.

⁵Commit your way to the LORD;
  trust in him and he will do this:
⁶He will make your righteousness shine
    like the dawn,
  the justice of your cause like the
    noonday sun.

⁷Be still before the LORD and wait
    patiently for him;
  do not fret when men succeed in
    their ways,
  when they carry out their wicked
    schemes.

⁸Refrain from anger and turn from
    wrath;
  do not fret—it leads only to evil.
⁹For evil men will be cut off,
  but those who hope in the LORD will
    inherit the land.

¹⁰A little while, and the wicked will be
    no more;
  though you look for them, they will
    not be found.
¹¹But the meek will inherit the land
  and enjoy great peace.

¹²The wicked plot against the righteous

ᵃ1 Or *heart: / Sin proceeds from the wicked.*   ᵇ7 Or *love, O God! / Men find*; or *love! / Both heavenly beings and men / find*   ᶜThis psalm is an acrostic poem, the stanzas of which begin with the successive letters of the Hebrew alphabet.

and gnash their teeth at them;
¹³but the Lord laughs at the wicked,
for he knows their day is coming.

¹⁴The wicked draw the sword
and bend the bow
to bring down the poor and needy,
to slay those whose ways are
upright.

¹⁵But their swords will pierce their own
hearts,
and their bows will be broken.

¹⁶Better the little that the righteous have
than the wealth of many wicked;
¹⁷for the power of the wicked will be
broken,
but the LORD upholds the righteous.

| FRIDAY |

VERSE FOR THE DAY:
Psalm 37:8

AUTHOR:
Richard P. Walters

PASSAGE FOR THE DAY:
Psalm 37:1–11

An Age of Rage

WE LIVE in an age of rage... By studying anger and its power, we can learn self-control so that we do not need to *lose* our temper in rage or *abuse* ourselves with resentment, but can *defuse* anger by resolving circumstances and then *use the energy of anger through Christlike indignation.*

The following summary, written in the form of resolutions, can form a point of departure for us as we continue with life. We should reflect prayerfully about how we can incorporate these ideals in our own lives.

- To keep my life centered on God, as best I can, recognizing that when I do not, my natural self will generate things to become angry about;
- To not condemn myself for feelings of anger;
- To do everything I can to avoid acting on the basis of anger;
- To clean up any problems I create as quickly as possible;
- To recognize God's help in this process;
- To redirect the energy of anger away from hurting people and toward improving conditions for people;
- To be sensitive to injustice and evil, learning to be angry about the misery that sin inflicts on people without becoming controlled by the anger.

It has been my observation, in counseling on problems of anger control, that each person who has sought God's help in the understanding and resolution of his or her anger has, without exception, received that help. These people have described the results as "miraculous." There is, indeed, a miracle involved. It is the miracle of God's love for us, the miracle of his redemptive grace.

Additional Scripture Readings:
Psalm 4; Ephesians 4:25—5:2

Go to page 429 for your next devotional reading.

¹⁸The days of the blameless are known to the LORD,
and their inheritance will endure forever.
¹⁹In times of disaster they will not wither;
in days of famine they will enjoy plenty.

²⁰But the wicked will perish:
The LORD's enemies will be like the beauty of the fields,
they will vanish—vanish like smoke.

²¹The wicked borrow and do not repay,
but the righteous give generously;
²²those the LORD blesses will inherit the land,
but those he curses will be cut off.

²³If the LORD delights in a man's way,
he makes his steps firm;
²⁴though he stumble, he will not fall,
for the LORD upholds him with his hand.

²⁵I was young and now I am old,
yet I have never seen the righteous forsaken
or their children begging bread.
²⁶They are always generous and lend freely;
their children will be blessed.

²⁷Turn from evil and do good;
then you will dwell in the land forever.
²⁸For the LORD loves the just
and will not forsake his faithful ones.

They will be protected forever,
but the offspring of the wicked will be cut off;
²⁹the righteous will inherit the land
and dwell in it forever.

³⁰The mouth of the righteous man utters wisdom,
and his tongue speaks what is just.
³¹The law of his God is in his heart;
his feet do not slip.

³²The wicked lie in wait for the righteous,
seeking their very lives;
³³but the LORD will not leave them in their power
or let them be condemned when brought to trial.

³⁴Wait for the LORD
and keep his way.
He will exalt you to inherit the land;
when the wicked are cut off, you will see it.

³⁵I have seen a wicked and ruthless man
flourishing like a green tree in its native soil,
³⁶but he soon passed away and was no more;
though I looked for him, he could not be found.

³⁷Consider the blameless, observe the upright;
there is a future*ᵃ* for the man of peace.
³⁸But all sinners will be destroyed;
the future*ᵇ* of the wicked will be cut off.

³⁹The salvation of the righteous comes from the LORD;
he is their stronghold in time of trouble.
⁴⁰The LORD helps them and delivers them;
he delivers them from the wicked and saves them,
because they take refuge in him.

Psalm 38

A psalm of David. A petition.

¹O LORD, do not rebuke me in your anger
or discipline me in your wrath.
²For your arrows have pierced me,
and your hand has come down upon me.
³Because of your wrath there is no health in my body;
my bones have no soundness because of my sin.
⁴My guilt has overwhelmed me
like a burden too heavy to bear.

⁵My wounds fester and are loathsome
because of my sinful folly.
⁶I am bowed down and brought very low;
all day long I go about mourning.
⁷My back is filled with searing pain;
there is no health in my body.
⁸I am feeble and utterly crushed;
I groan in anguish of heart.

---

a 37 Or there will be posterity   b 38 Or posterity

⁹All my longings lie open before you,
O Lord;
my sighing is not hidden from you.
¹⁰My heart pounds, my strength fails me;
even the light has gone from my eyes.
¹¹My friends and companions avoid me
because of my wounds;
my neighbors stay far away.
¹²Those who seek my life set their traps,
those who would harm me talk of my ruin;
all day long they plot deception.

¹³I am like a deaf man, who cannot hear,
like a mute, who cannot open his mouth;
¹⁴I have become like a man who does not hear,
whose mouth can offer no reply.
¹⁵I wait for you, O Lord;
you will answer, O Lord my God.
¹⁶For I said, "Do not let them gloat
or exalt themselves over me when my foot slips."

¹⁷For I am about to fall,
and my pain is ever with me.
¹⁸I confess my iniquity;
I am troubled by my sin.
¹⁹Many are those who are my vigorous enemies;
those who hate me without reason are numerous.
²⁰Those who repay my good with evil
slander me when I pursue what is good.

²¹O Lord, do not forsake me;
be not far from me, O my God.
²²Come quickly to help me,
O Lord my Savior.

Psalm 39

For the director of music. For Jeduthun. A psalm of David.

¹I said, "I will watch my ways
and keep my tongue from sin;
I will put a muzzle on my mouth
as long as the wicked are in my presence."
²But when I was silent and still,
not even saying anything good,
my anguish increased.
³My heart grew hot within me,
and as I meditated, the fire burned;
then I spoke with my tongue:
⁴"Show me, O Lord, my life's end
and the number of my days;
let me know how fleeting is my life.
⁵You have made my days a mere handbreadth;
the span of my years is as nothing before you.
Each man's life is but a breath. *Selah*

⁶Man is a mere phantom as he goes to and fro:
He bustles about, but only in vain;
he heaps up wealth, not knowing who will get it.

⁷"But now, Lord, what do I look for?
My hope is in you.
⁸Save me from all my transgressions;
do not make me the scorn of fools.
⁹I was silent; I would not open my mouth,
for you are the one who has done this.
¹⁰Remove your scourge from me;
I am overcome by the blow of your hand.
¹¹You rebuke and discipline men for their sin;
you consume their wealth like a moth—
each man is but a breath. *Selah*

¹²"Hear my prayer, O Lord,
listen to my cry for help;
be not deaf to my weeping.
For I dwell with you as an alien,
a stranger, as all my fathers were.
¹³Look away from me, that I may rejoice again
before I depart and am no more."

Psalm 40

For the director of music. Of David. A psalm.

¹I waited patiently for the Lord;
he turned to me and heard my cry.
²He lifted me out of the slimy pit,
out of the mud and mire;
he set my feet on a rock
and gave me a firm place to stand.
³He put a new song in my mouth,
a hymn of praise to our God.
Many will see and fear
and put their trust in the Lord.

⁴Blessed is the man
who makes the Lord his trust,
who does not look to the proud,

to those who turn aside to false
    gods.^a
⁵Many, O LORD my God,
    are the wonders you have done.
The things you planned for us
    no one can recount to you;
were I to speak and tell of them,
    they would be too many to declare.

⁶Sacrifice and offering you did not
        desire,
    but my ears you have pierced^{b,c};
burnt offerings and sin offerings
    you did not require.
⁷Then I said, "Here I am, I have
        come—
    it is written about me in the
        scroll.^d
⁸I desire to do your will, O my God;
    your law is within my heart."

⁹I proclaim righteousness in the great
        assembly;
    I do not seal my lips,
    as you know, O LORD.
¹⁰I do not hide your righteousness in
        my heart;
    I speak of your faithfulness and
        salvation.
I do not conceal your love and your
        truth
    from the great assembly.

¹¹Do not withhold your mercy from me,
        O LORD;
    may your love and your truth
        always protect me.
¹²For troubles without number surround
        me;
    my sins have overtaken me, and I
        cannot see.
They are more than the hairs of my
        head,
    and my heart fails within me.

¹³Be pleased, O LORD, to save me;
    O LORD, come quickly to help me.
¹⁴May all who seek to take my life
    be put to shame and confusion;
may all who desire my ruin
    be turned back in disgrace.
¹⁵May those who say to me, "Aha! Aha!"
    be appalled at their own shame.
¹⁶But may all who seek you
    rejoice and be glad in you;
may those who love your salvation
        always say,
    "The LORD be exalted!"

¹⁷Yet I am poor and needy;
    may the Lord think of me.
You are my help and my deliverer;
    O my God, do not delay.

Psalm 41

For the director of music. A psalm of David.

¹Blessed is he who has regard for the
        weak;
    the LORD delivers him in times of
        trouble.
²The LORD will protect him and
        preserve his life;
    he will bless him in the land
    and not surrender him to the desire
        of his foes.
³The LORD will sustain him on his
        sickbed
    and restore him from his bed of
        illness.

⁴I said, "O LORD, have mercy on me;
    heal me, for I have sinned against
        you."
⁵My enemies say of me in malice,
    "When will he die and his name
        perish?"
⁶Whenever one comes to see me,
    he speaks falsely, while his heart
        gathers slander;
    then he goes out and spreads it
        abroad.

⁷All my enemies whisper together
        against me;
    they imagine the worst for me,
        saying,
⁸"A vile disease has beset him;
    he will never get up from the place
        where he lies."
⁹Even my close friend, whom I trusted,
    he who shared my bread,
    has lifted up his heel against me.

¹⁰But you, O LORD, have mercy on me;
    raise me up, that I may repay them.
¹¹I know that you are pleased with me,
    for my enemy does not triumph
        over me.
¹²In my integrity you uphold me
    and set me in your presence
        forever.

¹³Praise be to the LORD, the God of
        Israel,
    from everlasting to everlasting.
        Amen and Amen.

---

^a4 Or *to falsehood*   ^b6 Hebrew; Septuagint *but a body you have prepared for me* (see also Symmachus and Theodotion)   ^c6 Or *opened*   ^d7 Or *come / with the scroll written for me*

BOOK II

Psalms 42–72

Psalm 42[a]

For the director of music. A *maskil*[b] of the Sons of Korah.

¹As the deer pants for streams of water,
  so my soul pants for you, O God.
²My soul thirsts for God, for the living God.
  When can I go and meet with God?
³My tears have been my food
  day and night,
while men say to me all day long,
  "Where is your God?"
⁴These things I remember
  as I pour out my soul:
how I used to go with the multitude,
  leading the procession to the house of God,
with shouts of joy and thanksgiving
  among the festive throng.

⁵Why are you downcast, O my soul?
  Why so disturbed within me?
Put your hope in God,
  for I will yet praise him,
  my Savior and ⁶my God.

My[c] soul is downcast within me;
  therefore I will remember you
from the land of the Jordan,
  the heights of Hermon—from Mount Mizar.
⁷Deep calls to deep
  in the roar of your waterfalls;
all your waves and breakers
  have swept over me.

⁸By day the LORD directs his love,
  at night his song is with me—
  a prayer to the God of my life.

⁹I say to God my Rock,
  "Why have you forgotten me?
Why must I go about mourning,
  oppressed by the enemy?"
¹⁰My bones suffer mortal agony
  as my foes taunt me,
saying to me all day long,
  "Where is your God?"

¹¹Why are you downcast, O my soul?
  Why so disturbed within me?
Put your hope in God,
  for I will yet praise him,
  my Savior and my God.

Psalm 43[a]

¹Vindicate me, O God,
  and plead my cause against an ungodly nation;
rescue me from deceitful and wicked men.
²You are God my stronghold.
  Why have you rejected me?
Why must I go about mourning,
  oppressed by the enemy?
³Send forth your light and your truth,
  let them guide me;
let them bring me to your holy mountain,
  to the place where you dwell.
⁴Then will I go to the altar of God,
  to God, my joy and my delight.
I will praise you with the harp,
  O God, my God.

⁵Why are you downcast, O my soul?
  Why so disturbed within me?
Put your hope in God,
  for I will yet praise him,
  my Savior and my God.

Psalm 44

For the director of music. Of the Sons of Korah. A *maskil.*[b]

¹We have heard with our ears, O God;
  our fathers have told us
what you did in their days,
  in days long ago.
²With your hand you drove out the nations
  and planted our fathers;
you crushed the peoples
  and made our fathers flourish.
³It was not by their sword that they won the land,
  nor did their arm bring them victory;
it was your right hand, your arm,
  and the light of your face, for you loved them.

⁴You are my King and my God,
  who decrees[d] victories for Jacob.

---

[a]In many Hebrew manuscripts Psalms 42 and 43 constitute one psalm. [b]Title: Probably a literary or musical term [c]5,6 A few Hebrew manuscripts, Septuagint and Syriac; most Hebrew manuscripts *praise him for his saving help. / ⁶O my God, my command* [d]4 Septuagint, Aquila and Syriac; Hebrew *King, O God; /*

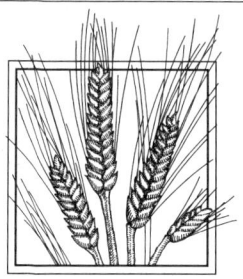

WEEKENDING

RETHINK

Is this society so far gone that it's hopeless? Have we abandoned our role model responsibilities for so long that we can't change? I don't think so. Each of us can change our own little world. Fathers who are honest with themselves will admit that we all make mistakes. We have all made bad decisions. Some of those decisions have to be reversed. If you have accepted a promotion and a transfer that takes you a step up the corporate ladder at the expense of your kids, maybe you need to think about taking a step back. More important than providing a life of ease for your kids is making sure they know you love them unconditionally.

– *Mike Singletary*

REVIVE
Saturday: Psalm 40:4–10
Sunday: 1 Corinthians 13

Go to page 433 for your next devotional reading.

⁵Through you we push back our enemies;
 through your name we trample our foes.
⁶I do not trust in my bow,
 my sword does not bring me victory;
⁷but you give us victory over our enemies,
 you put our adversaries to shame.
⁸In God we make our boast all day long,
 and we will praise your name forever. *Selah*

⁹But now you have rejected and humbled us;
 you no longer go out with our armies.
¹⁰You made us retreat before the enemy,
 and our adversaries have plundered us.
¹¹You gave us up to be devoured like sheep
 and have scattered us among the nations.
¹²You sold your people for a pittance,
 gaining nothing from their sale.

¹³You have made us a reproach to our neighbors,
 the scorn and derision of those around us.
¹⁴You have made us a byword among the nations;
 the peoples shake their heads at us.
¹⁵My disgrace is before me all day long,
 and my face is covered with shame
¹⁶at the taunts of those who reproach and revile me,
 because of the enemy, who is bent on revenge.

¹⁷All this happened to us,
 though we had not forgotten you
 or been false to your covenant.
¹⁸Our hearts had not turned back;
 our feet had not strayed from your path.
¹⁹But you crushed us and made us a haunt for jackals
 and covered us over with deep darkness.

²⁰If we had forgotten the name of our God
 or spread out our hands to a foreign god,
²¹would not God have discovered it,
 since he knows the secrets of the heart?
²²Yet for your sake we face death all day long;
 we are considered as sheep to be slaughtered.

²³Awake, O Lord! Why do you sleep?
 Rouse yourself! Do not reject us forever.
²⁴Why do you hide your face
 and forget our misery and oppression?

²⁵We are brought down to the dust;
 our bodies cling to the ground.
²⁶Rise up and help us;
 redeem us because of your unfailing love.

Psalm 45

For the director of music. To the tune of, "Lilies." Of the Sons of Korah. A *maskil.*ᵃ A wedding song.

¹My heart is stirred by a noble theme
 as I recite my verses for the king;
 my tongue is the pen of a skillful writer.

²You are the most excellent of men
 and your lips have been anointed with grace,
 since God has blessed you forever.
³Gird your sword upon your side, O mighty one;
 clothe yourself with splendor and majesty.
⁴In your majesty ride forth victoriously
 in behalf of truth, humility and righteousness;
 let your right hand display awesome deeds.
⁵Let your sharp arrows pierce the hearts of the king's enemies;
 let the nations fall beneath your feet.
⁶Your throne, O God, will last for ever and ever;
 a scepter of justice will be the scepter of your kingdom.
⁷You love righteousness and hate wickedness;
 therefore God, your God, has set you above your companions
 by anointing you with the oil of joy.
⁸All your robes are fragrant with myrrh and aloes and cassia;
 from palaces adorned with ivory

ᵃ Title: Probably a literary or musical term

the music of the strings makes you glad.
⁹Daughters of kings are among your honored women;
at your right hand is the royal bride in gold of Ophir.

¹⁰Listen, O daughter, consider and give ear:
Forget your people and your father's house.
¹¹The king is enthralled by your beauty; honor him, for he is your lord.
¹²The Daughter of Tyre will come with a gift,ᵃ
men of wealth will seek your favor.

¹³All glorious is the princess within ⌊her chamber⌋;
her gown is interwoven with gold.
¹⁴In embroidered garments she is led to the king;
her virgin companions follow her and are brought to you.
¹⁵They are led in with joy and gladness; they enter the palace of the king.

¹⁶Your sons will take the place of your fathers;
you will make them princes throughout the land.
¹⁷I will perpetuate your memory through all generations;
therefore the nations will praise you for ever and ever.

Psalm 46

For the director of music. Of the Sons of Korah. According to *alamoth.*ᵇ A song.

¹God is our refuge and strength, an ever-present help in trouble.
²Therefore we will not fear, though the earth give way
and the mountains fall into the heart of the sea,
³though its waters roar and foam and the mountains quake with their surging. *Selah*

⁴There is a river whose streams make glad the city of God,
the holy place where the Most High dwells.
⁵God is within her, she will not fall; God will help her at break of day.
⁶Nations are in uproar, kingdoms fall; he lifts his voice, the earth melts.

⁷The LORD Almighty is with us; the God of Jacob is our fortress. *Selah*

⁸Come and see the works of the LORD, the desolations he has brought on the earth.
⁹He makes wars cease to the ends of the earth;
he breaks the bow and shatters the spear,
he burns the shieldsᶜ with fire.
¹⁰"Be still, and know that I am God;
I will be exalted among the nations,
I will be exalted in the earth."

¹¹The LORD Almighty is with us; the God of Jacob is our fortress. *Selah*

Psalm 47

For the director of music. Of the Sons of Korah. A psalm.

¹Clap your hands, all you nations; shout to God with cries of joy.
²How awesome is the LORD Most High, the great King over all the earth!
³He subdued nations under us, peoples under our feet.
⁴He chose our inheritance for us, the pride of Jacob, whom he loved. *Selah*

⁵God has ascended amid shouts of joy, the LORD amid the sounding of trumpets.
⁶Sing praises to God, sing praises; sing praises to our King, sing praises.

⁷For God is the King of all the earth; sing to him a psalmᵈ of praise.
⁸God reigns over the nations; God is seated on his holy throne.
⁹The nobles of the nations assemble as the people of the God of Abraham,
for the kingsᵉ of the earth belong to God;
he is greatly exalted.

Psalm 48

A song. A psalm of the Sons of Korah.

¹Great is the LORD, and most worthy of praise,

ᵃ12 Or *A Tyrian robe is among the gifts* ᵇTitle: Probably a musical term ᶜ9 Or *chariots* ᵈ7 Or *a maskil* (probably a literary or musical term) ᵉ9 Or *shields*

in the city of our God, his holy
  mountain.
2It is beautiful in its loftiness,
  the joy of the whole earth.
Like the utmost heights of Zaphon*a* is
    Mount Zion,
  the*b* city of the Great King.
3God is in her citadels;
  he has shown himself to be her
    fortress.

4When the kings joined forces,
  when they advanced together,
5they saw ¸her¸ and were astounded;
  they fled in terror.
6Trembling seized them there,
  pain like that of a woman in labor.
7You destroyed them like ships of
    Tarshish
  shattered by an east wind.

8As we have heard,
  so have we seen
in the city of the LORD Almighty,
  in the city of our God:
God makes her secure forever. *Selah*

9Within your temple, O God,
  we meditate on your unfailing love.
10Like your name, O God,
  your praise reaches to the ends of
    the earth;
  your right hand is filled with
    righteousness.
11Mount Zion rejoices,
  the villages of Judah are glad
  because of your judgments.

12Walk about Zion, go around her,
  count her towers,
13consider well her ramparts,
  view her citadels,
  that you may tell of them to the
    next generation.
14For this God is our God for ever and
    ever;
  he will be our guide even to the
    end.

Psalm 49

*For the director of music. Of the Sons of
Korah. A psalm.*

1Hear this, all you peoples;
  listen, all who live in this world,
2both low and high,
  rich and poor alike:
3My mouth will speak words of
    wisdom;
  the utterance from my heart will
    give understanding.
4I will turn my ear to a proverb;
  with the harp I will expound my
    riddle:

5Why should I fear when evil days
    come,
  when wicked deceivers surround
    me —
6those who trust in their wealth
  and boast of their great riches?
7No man can redeem the life of
    another
  or give to God a ransom for
    him —
8the ransom for a life is costly,
  no payment is ever enough —
9that he should live on forever
  and not see decay.

10For all can see that wise men die;
  the foolish and the senseless alike
    perish
  and leave their wealth to others.
11Their tombs will remain their
    houses*c* forever,
  their dwellings for endless
    generations,
  though they had*d* named lands
    after themselves.

12But man, despite his riches, does not
    endure;
  he is*e* like the beasts that perish.

13This is the fate of those who trust in
    themselves,
  and of their followers, who approve
    their sayings.   *Selah*
14Like sheep they are destined for the
    grave,*f*
  and death will feed on them.
The upright will rule over them in the
    morning;
  their forms will decay in the
    grave,*f*
  far from their princely mansions.
15But God will redeem my life*g* from
    the grave;
  he will surely take me to himself.
        Selah

---

*a*2 *Zaphon* can refer to a sacred mountain or the direction north. *b*2 Or *earth, / Mount Zion, on the
northern side / of the* *c*11 Septuagint and Syriac; Hebrew *In their thoughts their houses will remain*
*d*11 Or */ for they have* *e*12 Hebrew; Septuagint and Syriac read verse 12 the same as verse 20.
*f*14 Hebrew *Sheol*; also in verse 15 *g*15 Or *soul*

¹⁶Do not be overawed when a man grows rich,
  when the splendor of his house increases;
¹⁷for he will take nothing with him when he dies,
  his splendor will not descend with him.
¹⁸Though while he lived he counted himself blessed—
  and men praise you when you prosper—
¹⁹he will join the generation of his fathers,
  who will never see the light ₍of life₎.
²⁰A man who has riches without understanding
  is like the beasts that perish.

Psalm 50

A psalm of Asaph.

¹The Mighty One, God, the LORD,
  speaks and summons the earth
  from the rising of the sun to the place where it sets.
²From Zion, perfect in beauty,
  God shines forth.
³Our God comes and will not be silent;

MONDAY

VERSE FOR THE DAY: Psalm 49:20

AUTHOR: Don Wyrtzen

PASSAGE FOR THE DAY: Psalm 49:16–20

Eternity's Values in View

THE finite nature of wealth . . .

I must admit that I, along with many others, have been charmed by "Tinseltown." The accouterments of success seem so appealing that it's pretty easy to fall for those less-than-subtle advertising ploys touting fancy foreign engineering or the architectural wonders of some luxury house. Even in church we sometimes focus on the trappings—lavish sanctuaries, fine pipe organs, plush carpeting. When materialism and personal pride fuse together, we're all in grave danger of neglecting or even forgetting God!

Thoughts of death and the prospect of eternity, however, can abruptly change one's focus, perspective and priorities. The psalmist reminds us that, no matter how imposing the wealthy and powerful may appear, "they can't take it with them."

In this life the wealthy often inspire awe, admiration and praise. But this adulation will be short-lived. The possessions that are the basis of their pride and self-aggrandizement will not survive past the grave. Verse 20 describes the final state of the man who leaves God out of his life. Without understanding, he is like the beasts that perish. His power, influence and wealth won't carry any weight in eternity.

Lord, may I learn to live always, not for this life only, but with "eternity's values in view."

Additional Scripture Readings:
Psalm 73:1–20;
1 Timothy 6:3–10

Go to page 436 for your next devotional reading.

a fire devours before him,
and around him a tempest rages.
⁴He summons the heavens above,
and the earth, that he may judge his people:
⁵"Gather to me my consecrated ones,
who made a covenant with me by sacrifice."
⁶And the heavens proclaim his righteousness,
for God himself is judge. *Selah*

⁷"Hear, O my people, and I will speak,
O Israel, and I will testify against you:
I am God, your God.
⁸I do not rebuke you for your sacrifices
or your burnt offerings, which are ever before me.
⁹I have no need of a bull from your stall
or of goats from your pens,
¹⁰for every animal of the forest is mine,
and the cattle on a thousand hills.
¹¹I know every bird in the mountains,
and the creatures of the field are mine.
¹²If I were hungry I would not tell you,
for the world is mine, and all that is in it.
¹³Do I eat the flesh of bulls
or drink the blood of goats?
¹⁴Sacrifice thank offerings to God,
fulfill your vows to the Most High,
¹⁵and call upon me in the day of trouble;
I will deliver you, and you will honor me."

¹⁶But to the wicked, God says:

"What right have you to recite my laws
or take my covenant on your lips?
¹⁷You hate my instruction
and cast my words behind you.
¹⁸When you see a thief, you join with him;
you throw in your lot with adulterers.
¹⁹You use your mouth for evil
and harness your tongue to deceit.
²⁰You speak continually against your brother
and slander your own mother's son.
²¹These things you have done and I kept silent;
you thought I was altogether[a] like you.
But I will rebuke you
and accuse you to your face.

²²"Consider this, you who forget God,
or I will tear you to pieces, with none to rescue:
²³He who sacrifices thank offerings honors me,
and he prepares the way
so that I may show him[b] the salvation of God."

Psalm 51

For the director of music. A psalm of David. When the prophet Nathan came to him after David had committed adultery with Bathsheba.

¹Have mercy on me, O God,
according to your unfailing love;
according to your great compassion
blot out my transgressions.
²Wash away all my iniquity
and cleanse me from my sin.

³For I know my transgressions,
and my sin is always before me.
⁴Against you, you only, have I sinned
and done what is evil in your sight,
so that you are proved right when you speak
and justified when you judge.
⁵Surely I was sinful at birth,
sinful from the time my mother conceived me.
⁶Surely you desire truth in the inner parts[c];
you teach[d] me wisdom in the inmost place.

⁷Cleanse me with hyssop, and I will be clean;
wash me, and I will be whiter than snow.
⁸Let me hear joy and gladness;
let the bones you have crushed rejoice.
⁹Hide your face from my sins
and blot out all my iniquity.

¹⁰Create in me a pure heart, O God,
and renew a steadfast spirit within me.
¹¹Do not cast me from your presence
or take your Holy Spirit from me.

---

[a] 21 Or *thought the 'I AM' was*   [b] 23 Or *and to him who considers his way / I will show*   [c] 6 The meaning of the Hebrew for this phrase is uncertain.   [d] 6 Or *you desired . . . ; / you taught*

¹²Restore to me the joy of your salvation
and grant me a willing spirit, to sustain me.

¹³Then I will teach transgressors your ways,
and sinners will turn back to you.
¹⁴Save me from bloodguilt, O God,
the God who saves me,
and my tongue will sing of your righteousness.
¹⁵O Lord, open my lips,
and my mouth will declare your praise.
¹⁶You do not delight in sacrifice, or I would bring it;
you do not take pleasure in burnt offerings.
¹⁷The sacrifices of God are[a] a broken spirit;
a broken and contrite heart,
O God, you will not despise.

¹⁸In your good pleasure make Zion prosper;
build up the walls of Jerusalem.
¹⁹Then there will be righteous sacrifices,
whole burnt offerings to delight you;
then bulls will be offered on your altar.

Psalm 52

For the director of music. A *maskil*[b] of David. When Doeg the Edomite had gone to Saul and told him: "David has gone to the house of Ahimelech."

¹Why do you boast of evil, you mighty man?
Why do you boast all day long,
you who are a disgrace in the eyes of God?
²Your tongue plots destruction;
it is like a sharpened razor,
you who practice deceit.
³You love evil rather than good,
falsehood rather than speaking the truth. *Selah*
⁴You love every harmful word,
O you deceitful tongue!

⁵Surely God will bring you down to everlasting ruin:
He will snatch you up and tear you from your tent;
he will uproot you from the land of the living. *Selah*
⁶The righteous will see and fear;
they will laugh at him, saying,
⁷"Here now is the man
who did not make God his stronghold
but trusted in his great wealth
and grew strong by destroying others!"

⁸But I am like an olive tree
flourishing in the house of God;
I trust in God's unfailing love
for ever and ever.
⁹I will praise you forever for what you have done;
in your name I will hope, for your name is good.
I will praise you in the presence of your saints.

Psalm 53

For the director of music. According to *mahalath*.[c] A *maskil*[b] of David.

¹The fool says in his heart,
"There is no God."
They are corrupt, and their ways are vile;
there is no one who does good.

²God looks down from heaven
on the sons of men
to see if there are any who understand,
any who seek God.
³Everyone has turned away,
they have together become corrupt;
there is no one who does good,
not even one.

⁴Will the evildoers never learn—
those who devour my people as men eat bread
and who do not call on God?
⁵There they were, overwhelmed with dread,
where there was nothing to dread.
God scattered the bones of those who attacked you;

---

[a] 17 Or *My sacrifice, O God, is* [b] Title: Probably a literary or musical term [c] Title: Probably a musical term

PSALMS 53–54

you put them to shame, for God despised them.

⁶Oh, that salvation for Israel would come out of Zion!
When God restores the fortunes of his people,
let Jacob rejoice and Israel be glad!

*a*Title: Probably a literary or musical term

Psalm 54

For the director of music. With stringed instruments. A *maskil*[a] of David. When the Ziphites had gone to Saul and said, "Is not David hiding among us?"

¹Save me, O God, by your name;
vindicate me by your might.

TUESDAY

VERSE FOR THE DAY:
Psalm 51:1

AUTHOR:
Larry Crabb

PASSAGE FOR THE DAY:
Psalm 51:1–17

A Path Leading Downward

REPENTANT people realize that inexcusable wrong can either be judged or forgiven, never understood and overlooked, and so they beg for forgiveness with no thought of deserving it. Truly repentant people are the ones who begin to grasp God's amazing grace, the ones who know that they need only confess to experience the forgiveness that is always there in infinite supply.

Whether we are adulterers or thoughtless spouses, the problem with all of us is that we stubbornly regard our interpersonal failures not as *inexcusably selfish choices*, but as *understandable mistakes*. The things our spouses do to us seem more like the former; the things we do to them more like the latter.

Excuse-making has been a natural tendency in people ever since Adam blamed Eve and Eve blamed the snake. Without some means of self-justification, we would be forced to face ourselves squarely as we really are, corrupt by God's standards and deserving punishment.

And seeing ourselves as we are would mean taking our place as condemned sinners, worthy of judgment, powerless to improve ourselves, humbled that our very best deeds provide no defense, and utterly at the mercy of a righteously angry Judge. This doesn't sound like much fun. Surely the path to the top would never begin with a descent *this* steep! How can joy emerge from such misery?

Perhaps the hardest thing to get through our brain-damaged heads (when Adam fell, he must have fallen on his head) is that this painful point of nakedness and humility is not only where life begins, but also where joyful growth continues.

Additional Scripture Readings:
Romans 3:9–26; 1 John 1:5–10

Go to page 438 for your next devotional reading.

²Hear my prayer, O God;
   listen to the words of my mouth.

³Strangers are attacking me;
   ruthless men seek my life—
   men without regard for God. *Selah*

⁴Surely God is my help;
   the Lord is the one who sustains me.

⁵Let evil recoil on those who slander me;
   in your faithfulness destroy them.

⁶I will sacrifice a freewill offering to you;
   I will praise your name, O LORD,
   for it is good.
⁷For he has delivered me from all my troubles,
   and my eyes have looked in triumph on my foes.

Psalm 55

For the director of music. With stringed instruments. A *maskil*ᵃ of David.

¹Listen to my prayer, O God,
   do not ignore my plea;
² hear me and answer me.
My thoughts trouble me and I am distraught
³ at the voice of the enemy,
   at the stares of the wicked;
for they bring down suffering upon me
   and revile me in their anger.

⁴My heart is in anguish within me;
   the terrors of death assail me.
⁵Fear and trembling have beset me;
   horror has overwhelmed me.
⁶I said, "Oh, that I had the wings of a dove!
   I would fly away and be at rest—
⁷I would flee far away
   and stay in the desert; *Selah*
⁸I would hurry to my place of shelter,
   far from the tempest and storm."

⁹Confuse the wicked, O Lord, confound their speech,
   for I see violence and strife in the city.
¹⁰Day and night they prowl about on its walls;
   malice and abuse are within it.
¹¹Destructive forces are at work in the city;
   threats and lies never leave its streets.

¹²If an enemy were insulting me,
   I could endure it;
if a foe were raising himself against me,
   I could hide from him.
¹³But it is you, a man like myself,
   my companion, my close friend,
¹⁴with whom I once enjoyed sweet fellowship
   as we walked with the throng at the house of God.

¹⁵Let death take my enemies by surprise;
   let them go down alive to the grave,ᵇ
   for evil finds lodging among them.

¹⁶But I call to God,
   and the LORD saves me.
¹⁷Evening, morning and noon
   I cry out in distress,
   and he hears my voice.
¹⁸He ransoms me unharmed
   from the battle waged against me,
   even though many oppose me.
¹⁹God, who is enthroned forever,
   will hear them and afflict them— *Selah*
men who never change their ways
   and have no fear of God.

²⁰My companion attacks his friends;
   he violates his covenant.
²¹His speech is smooth as butter,
   yet war is in his heart;
his words are more soothing than oil,
   yet they are drawn swords.

²²Cast your cares on the LORD
   and he will sustain you;
he will never let the righteous fall.
²³But you, O God, will bring down the wicked
   into the pit of corruption;
bloodthirsty and deceitful men
   will not live out half their days.

But as for me, I trust in you.

ᵃTitle: Probably a literary or musical term   ᵇ15 Hebrew *Sheol*

Psalm 56

For the director of music. To the tune of, "A Dove on Distant Oaks." Of David. A *miktam.*[a] When the Philistines had seized him in Gath.

¹Be merciful to me, O God, for men hotly pursue me;
  all day long they press their attack.
²My slanderers pursue me all day long;
  many are attacking me in their pride.

³When I am afraid,
  I will trust in you.
⁴In God, whose word I praise,
  in God I trust; I will not be afraid.
  What can mortal man do to me?

⁵All day long they twist my words;
  they are always plotting to harm me.
⁶They conspire, they lurk,
  they watch my steps,
  eager to take my life.
⁷On no account let them escape;

[a] Title: Probably a literary or musical term

WEDNESDAY

VERSE FOR THE DAY:　　AUTHOR:　　PASSAGE FOR THE DAY:
Psalm 55:13　　David W. Smith　　Psalm 55:1–14

Be Men of Faithfulness

BIBLICAL friendship calls for faithfulness. Circumstances should not affect our consistency. In Romans 12:15 Paul tells us to "rejoice with those who rejoice; mourn with those who mourn" . . .

Faithfulness is critical to a close relationship because we depend on those who are close to us. Christ's deepest hurts occurred within his circle of closest companions, and David was wounded emotionally more by the treachery of his close friends than by the efforts of his enemies. He laments in Psalm 55:12–14, "If an enemy were insulting me, I could endure it; if a foe were raising himself against me, I could hide from him. But it is you, a man like myself, my companion, my close friend, with whom I once enjoyed sweet fellowship as we walked with the throng at the house of God." Paul too was left to stand alone when he was deserted by Demas and others (2 Timothy 4:10).

A faithful friend keeps confidences. In Proverbs we read that "a perverse man stirs up dissension, and a gossip separates close friends" (16:28). And in 17:9, "He who covers over an offense promotes love, but whoever repeats the matter separates close friends."

Entering friendship involves revealing yourself in confidence to another, and thus becoming vulnerable. This is as it should be, but it is what makes betrayal so evil and faithfulness so virtuous.

Additional Scripture Readings:
Psalm 41; John 13:18–30

Go to page 442 for your next devotional reading.

in your anger, O God, bring down
   the nations.
⁸Record my lament;
   list my tears on your scroll ᵃ—
   are they not in your record?

⁹Then my enemies will turn back
   when I call for help.
   By this I will know that God is for
      me.
¹⁰In God, whose word I praise,
   in the LORD, whose word I praise—
¹¹in God I trust; I will not be afraid.
   What can man do to me?

¹²I am under vows to you, O God;
   I will present my thank offerings to
      you.
¹³For you have delivered me ᵇ from
      death
   and my feet from stumbling,
   that I may walk before God
   in the light of life. ᶜ

Psalm 57

For the director of music. ⌊To the tune
of⌋ "Do Not Destroy." Of David. A
miktam. ᵈ When he had fled from Saul
into the cave.

¹Have mercy on me, O God, have
      mercy on me,
   for in you my soul takes refuge.
   I will take refuge in the shadow of
      your wings
   until the disaster has passed.

²I cry out to God Most High,
   to God, who fulfills ⌊his purpose⌋ for
      me.
³He sends from heaven and saves me,
   rebuking those who hotly pursue
      me;   *Selah*
   God sends his love and his
      faithfulness.

⁴I am in the midst of lions;
   I lie among ravenous beasts—
   men whose teeth are spears and
      arrows,
   whose tongues are sharp swords.

⁵Be exalted, O God, above the heavens;
   let your glory be over all the earth.

⁶They spread a net for my feet—
   I was bowed down in distress.
   They dug a pit in my path—
   but they have fallen into it
      themselves.   *Selah*

⁷My heart is steadfast, O God,
   my heart is steadfast;
   I will sing and make music.
⁸Awake, my soul!
   Awake, harp and lyre!
   I will awaken the dawn.

⁹I will praise you, O Lord, among the
      nations;
   I will sing of you among the
      peoples.
¹⁰For great is your love, reaching to the
      heavens;
   your faithfulness reaches to the
      skies.

¹¹Be exalted, O God, above the heavens;
   let your glory be over all the earth.

Psalm 58

For the director of music. ⌊To the tune
of⌋ "Do Not Destroy." Of David.
A miktam. ᵈ

¹Do you rulers indeed speak justly?
   Do you judge uprightly among men?
²No, in your heart you devise injustice,
   and your hands mete out violence
      on the earth.
³Even from birth the wicked go astray;
   from the womb they are wayward
      and speak lies.
⁴Their venom is like the venom of a
      snake,
   like that of a cobra that has stopped
      its ears,
⁵that will not heed the tune of the
      charmer,
   however skillful the enchanter may
      be.

⁶Break the teeth in their mouths,
      O God;
   tear out, O LORD, the fangs of the
      lions!
⁷Let them vanish like water that flows
      away;
   when they draw the bow, let their
      arrows be blunted.
⁸Like a slug melting away as it moves
      along,
   like a stillborn child, may they not
      see the sun.

⁹Before your pots can feel ⌊the heat of⌋
      the thorns—

ᵃ8 Or / *put my tears in your wineskin*   ᵇ13 Or *my soul*   ᶜ13 Or *the land of the living*   ᵈTitle:
Probably a literary or musical term

whether they be green or dry—the
wicked will be swept away.*a*
¹⁰The righteous will be glad when they
are avenged,
when they bathe their feet in the
blood of the wicked.
¹¹Then men will say,
"Surely the righteous still are
rewarded;
surely there is a God who judges
the earth."

Psalm 59

For the director of music. ₍To the tune
of₎ "Do Not Destroy." Of David. A
miktam.b When Saul had sent men to
watch David's house in order to kill him.

¹Deliver me from my enemies, O God;
protect me from those who rise up
against me.
²Deliver me from evildoers
and save me from bloodthirsty men.

³See how they lie in wait for me!
Fierce men conspire against me
for no offense or sin of mine,
O LORD.
⁴I have done no wrong, yet they are
ready to attack me.
Arise to help me; look on my
plight!
⁵O LORD God Almighty, the God of
Israel,
rouse yourself to punish all the
nations;
show no mercy to wicked traitors.
Selah

⁶They return at evening,
snarling like dogs,
and prowl about the city.
⁷See what they spew from their
mouths—
they spew out swords from their
lips,
and they say, "Who can hear us?"
⁸But you, O LORD, laugh at them;
you scoff at all those nations.

⁹O my Strength, I watch for you;
you, O God, are my fortress, ¹⁰my
loving God.

God will go before me
and will let me gloat over those
who slander me.

¹¹But do not kill them, O Lord our
shield,*c*
or my people will forget.
In your might make them wander
about,
and bring them down.
¹²For the sins of their mouths,
for the words of their lips,
let them be caught in their pride.
For the curses and lies they utter,
¹³ consume them in wrath,
consume them till they are no more.
Then it will be known to the ends of
the earth
that God rules over Jacob. *Selah*

¹⁴They return at evening,
snarling like dogs,
and prowl about the city.
¹⁵They wander about for food
and howl if not satisfied.
¹⁶But I will sing of your strength,
in the morning I will sing of your
love;
for you are my fortress,
my refuge in times of trouble.

¹⁷O my Strength, I sing praise to you;
you, O God, are my fortress, my
loving God.

Psalm 60

For the director of music. To ₍the tune
of₎ "The Lily of the Covenant." A
miktamb of David. For teaching. When
he fought Aram Naharaim*d* and Aram
Zobah,*e* and when Joab returned and
struck down twelve thousand Edomites
in the Valley of Salt.

¹You have rejected us, O God, and
burst forth upon us;
you have been angry—now restore
us!
²You have shaken the land and torn it
open;
mend its fractures, for it is quaking.
³You have shown your people
desperate times;
you have given us wine that makes
us stagger.

⁴But for those who fear you, you have
raised a banner
to be unfurled against the bow.
Selah

---

*a*9 The meaning of the Hebrew for this verse is uncertain.   *b*Title: Probably a literary or musical term
*c*11 Or *sovereign*   *d*Title: That is, Arameans of Northwest Mesopotamia   *e*Title: That is, Arameans of
central Syria

5 Save us and help us with your right hand,
that those you love may be delivered.
6 God has spoken from his sanctuary:
"In triumph I will parcel out Shechem
and measure off the Valley of Succoth.
7 Gilead is mine, and Manasseh is mine;
Ephraim is my helmet,
Judah my scepter.
8 Moab is my washbasin,
upon Edom I toss my sandal;
over Philistia I shout in triumph."

9 Who will bring me to the fortified city?
Who will lead me to Edom?
10 Is it not you, O God, you who have rejected us
and no longer go out with our armies?
11 Give us aid against the enemy,
for the help of man is worthless.
12 With God we will gain the victory,
and he will trample down our enemies.

Psalm 61

For the director of music. With stringed instruments. Of David.

1 Hear my cry, O God;
listen to my prayer.

2 From the ends of the earth I call to you,
I call as my heart grows faint;
lead me to the rock that is higher than I.
3 For you have been my refuge,
a strong tower against the foe.

4 I long to dwell in your tent forever
and take refuge in the shelter of your wings. *Selah*
5 For you have heard my vows, O God;
you have given me the heritage of those who fear your name.

6 Increase the days of the king's life,
his years for many generations.
7 May he be enthroned in God's presence forever;

appoint your love and faithfulness to protect him.
8 Then will I ever sing praise to your name
and fulfill my vows day after day.

Psalm 62

For the director of music. For Jeduthun. A psalm of David.

1 My soul finds rest in God alone;
my salvation comes from him.
2 He alone is my rock and my salvation;
he is my fortress, I will never be shaken.

3 How long will you assault a man?
Would all of you throw him down—
this leaning wall, this tottering fence?
4 They fully intend to topple him from his lofty place;
they take delight in lies.
With their mouths they bless,
but in their hearts they curse. *Selah*

5 Find rest, O my soul, in God alone;
my hope comes from him.
6 He alone is my rock and my salvation;
he is my fortress, I will not be shaken.
7 My salvation and my honor depend on God[a];
he is my mighty rock, my refuge.
8 Trust in him at all times, O people;
pour out your hearts to him,
for God is our refuge. *Selah*

9 Lowborn men are but a breath,
the highborn are but a lie;
if weighed on a balance, they are nothing;
together they are only a breath.
10 Do not trust in extortion
or take pride in stolen goods;
though your riches increase,
do not set your heart on them.

11 One thing God has spoken,
two things have I heard:
that you, O God, are strong,
12 and that you, O Lord, are loving.
Surely you will reward each person according to what he has done.

---

[a] 7 Or / *God Most High is my salvation and my honor*

Psalm 63

A psalm of David. When he was in the Desert of Judah.

¹O God, you are my God,
 earnestly I seek you;
my soul thirsts for you,
 my body longs for you,
in a dry and weary land
 where there is no water.
²I have seen you in the sanctuary
 and beheld your power and your glory.
³Because your love is better than life,
 my lips will glorify you.
⁴I will praise you as long as I live,
 and in your name I will lift up my hands.
⁵My soul will be satisfied as with the richest of foods;

THURSDAY

VERSE FOR THE DAY:
Psalm 63:8

AUTHOR:
Charles Spurgeon

PASSAGE FOR THE DAY:
Psalm 63:1–8

Under the Shadow

LIVE by the day—aye, by the hour. Put not trust in frames and feelings. Care more for a grain of faith than a ton of excitement. Trust in God alone, and lean not on the reeds of human help. Be not surprised when friends fail you: it is a failing world. Never count upon immutability in a man: inconstancy you may reckon upon without fear of disappointment. The disciples of Jesus forsook him; be not amazed if your adherents wander away to other teachers: as they were not your all when with you, all is not gone from you with their departure.

Serve God with all your might while the candle is burning, and then when it goes out for a season, you will have the less to regret. Be content to be nothing, for that is what you are. When your own emptiness is painfully forced upon your consciousness, chide yourself that you ever dreamed of being full, except in the Lord. Set small store by present rewards; be grateful for earnests by the way, but look for the recompensing joy hereafter. Continue with double earnestness to serve your Lord when no visible result is before you. Any simpleton can follow the narrow path in the light: faith's rare wisdom enables us to march on in the dark with infallible accuracy, since she places her hand in that of her great Guide. Between this and heaven there may be rougher weather yet, but it is all provided for by our covenant Head.

In nothing let us be turned aside from the path which the divine call has urged us to pursue. Come fair or come foul, the pulpit is our watchtower, and the ministry our warfare; be it ours, when we cannot see the face of God, to trust under the shadow of his wings.

Additional Scripture Readings:
Psalm 17:6–15; John 10:22–30

Go to page 444 for your next devotional reading.

with singing lips my mouth will
   praise you.
⁶On my bed I remember you;
   I think of you through the watches
      of the night.
⁷Because you are my help,
   I sing in the shadow of your wings.
⁸My soul clings to you;
   your right hand upholds me.

⁹They who seek my life will be
      destroyed;
   they will go down to the depths of
      the earth.
¹⁰They will be given over to the sword
   and become food for jackals.

¹¹But the king will rejoice in God;
   all who swear by God's name will
      praise him,
   while the mouths of liars will be
      silenced.

Psalm 64

For the director of music. A psalm
of David.

¹Hear me, O God, as I voice my
      complaint;
   protect my life from the threat of
      the enemy.
²Hide me from the conspiracy of the
      wicked,
   from that noisy crowd of evildoers.

³They sharpen their tongues like
      swords
   and aim their words like deadly
      arrows.
⁴They shoot from ambush at the
      innocent man;
   they shoot at him suddenly, without
      fear.

⁵They encourage each other in evil
      plans,
   they talk about hiding their snares;
   they say, "Who will see them^a?"
⁶They plot injustice and say,
   "We have devised a perfect plan!"
   Surely the mind and heart of man
      are cunning.

⁷But God will shoot them with arrows;
   suddenly they will be struck down.
⁸He will turn their own tongues against
      them
   and bring them to ruin;
   all who see them will shake their
      heads in scorn.

⁹All mankind will fear;
   they will proclaim the works of God
   and ponder what he has done.
¹⁰Let the righteous rejoice in the LORD
   and take refuge in him;
   let all the upright in heart praise
      him!

Psalm 65

For the director of music. A psalm
of David. A song.

¹Praise awaits^b you, O God, in Zion;
   to you our vows will be fulfilled.
²O you who hear prayer,
   to you all men will come.
³When we were overwhelmed by sins,
   you forgave^c our transgressions.
⁴Blessed are those you choose
   and bring near to live in your
      courts!
We are filled with the good things of
      your house,
   of your holy temple.

⁵You answer us with awesome deeds of
      righteousness,
   O God our Savior,
the hope of all the ends of the earth
   and of the farthest seas,
⁶who formed the mountains by your
      power,
   having armed yourself with
      strength,
⁷who stilled the roaring of the seas,
   the roaring of their waves,
   and the turmoil of the nations.
⁸Those living far away fear your
      wonders;
   where morning dawns and evening
      fades
   you call forth songs of joy.

⁹You care for the land and water it;
   you enrich it abundantly.
The streams of God are filled with
      water
   to provide the people with grain,
   for so you have ordained it.^{d}
¹⁰You drench its furrows
   and level its ridges;
   you soften it with showers
   and bless its crops.
¹¹You crown the year with your bounty,

---

^{a}5 Or *us* ^{b}1 Or *befits*; the meaning of the Hebrew for this word is uncertain. ^{c}3 Or *made atonement for* ^{d}9 Or *for that is how you prepare the land*

and your carts overflow with
    abundance.
¹²The grasslands of the desert overflow;
    the hills are clothed with gladness.
¹³The meadows are covered with flocks
    and the valleys are mantled with
        grain;
    they shout for joy and sing.

Psalm 66

*For the director of music. A song.
A psalm.*

¹Shout with joy to God, all the earth!
² Sing the glory of his name;
    make his praise glorious!
³Say to God, "How awesome are your
        deeds!
    So great is your power
    that your enemies cringe before
        you.
⁴All the earth bows down to you;
    they sing praise to you,
    they sing praise to your name." *Selah*

⁵Come and see what God has done,
    how awesome his works in man's
        behalf!
⁶He turned the sea into dry land,
    they passed through the waters on
        foot—
    come, let us rejoice in him.
⁷He rules forever by his power,
    his eyes watch the nations—
    let not the rebellious rise up against
        him. *Selah*

FRIDAY

VERSE FOR THE DAY: *AUTHOR:* *PASSAGE FOR THE DAY:*
Psalm 65:8 W. Phillip Keller Psalm 65:5–13

Our Father's World

HAVE we, as a people, so immersed in our science and tough technology, lost touch with the earth our Father formed? It is remarkable to recall how often Christ himself referred to such natural objects as sheep, birds, flowers, grass, seed, soil, fish and trees. He used them in his many parables. He explained the most profound spiritual truths through natural processes.

Part of our problem is that most of us do not really believe he created all the majestic and complex diversity of the earth. In our schools and institutions, through books, films and the media, we have been seduced to believe the earth in all its glory has emerged from oblivion by pure chance. We are convinced it is the end product of a blind evolutionary process that appears headed back to oblivion. No wonder our world is so deep in despair, so sad and forlorn in its futility.

But for a tiny handful of us this is still "My Father's World." We know assuredly that it is he who brought it into being. We are acutely aware that he cares for it deeply. He knows the most minute detail of every bird, flower or tree upon it. They are his. He is theirs. And amid all the lovely interaction between Creator and creation he speaks to me. Therein lies part of his wonder, awe and inspiration.

Additional Scripture Readings:
Psalm 95; Matthew 10:29–31

*Go to page 445 for your next
devotional reading.*

WEEKENDING

REFLECT

The sooner a man becomes satisfied with what he has and stops comparing his financial scorecard and trophies with those of other men, the better he will feel about himself. The apostle Paul states: "I have learned to be content whatever the circumstances. I know what it is to be in need, and I know what it is to have plenty. I have learned the secret of being content in any and every situation, whether well fed or hungry, whether living in plenty or in want" (Philippians 4:11–12). Men who opt to be satisfied with what they possess will have more time and energy for the kinds of nurturing relationships that will meet their basic needs.

– *Stephen Arterburn and David Stoop*

REVIVE
Saturday: 1 Timothy 6:3–10
Sunday: Hebrews 13:5–6

Go to page 447 for your next devotional reading.

⁸Praise our God, O peoples,
  let the sound of his praise be heard;
⁹he has preserved our lives
  and kept our feet from slipping.
¹⁰For you, O God, tested us;
  you refined us like silver.
¹¹You brought us into prison
  and laid burdens on our backs.
¹²You let men ride over our heads;
  we went through fire and water,
  but you brought us to a place of
    abundance.

¹³I will come to your temple with burnt
    offerings
  and fulfill my vows to you—
¹⁴vows my lips promised and my mouth
    spoke
  when I was in trouble.
¹⁵I will sacrifice fat animals to you
  and an offering of rams;
  I will offer bulls and goats. *Selah*

¹⁶Come and listen, all you who fear
    God;
  let me tell you what he has done
    for me.
¹⁷I cried out to him with my mouth;
  his praise was on my tongue.
¹⁸If I had cherished sin in my heart,
  the Lord would not have listened;
¹⁹but God has surely listened
  and heard my voice in prayer.
²⁰Praise be to God,
  who has not rejected my prayer
  or withheld his love from me!

Psalm 67

For the director of music. With stringed
instruments. A psalm. A song.

¹May God be gracious to us and bless
    us
  and make his face shine upon us,
                                          Selah
²that your ways may be known on
    earth,
  your salvation among all nations.

³May the peoples praise you, O God;
  may all the peoples praise you.
⁴May the nations be glad and sing for
    joy,
  for you rule the peoples justly
  and guide the nations of the earth.
                                          Selah
⁵May the peoples praise you, O God;
  may all the peoples praise you.

⁶Then the land will yield its harvest,
  and God, our God, will bless us.
⁷God will bless us,
  and all the ends of the earth will
    fear him.

Psalm 68

For the director of music. Of David.
A psalm. A song.

¹May God arise, may his enemies be
    scattered;
  may his foes flee before him.
²As smoke is blown away by the wind,
  may you blow them away;
  as wax melts before the fire,
  may the wicked perish before God.
³But may the righteous be glad
  and rejoice before God;
  may they be happy and joyful.

⁴Sing to God, sing praise to his name,
  extol him who rides on the
    clouds*ᵃ*—
  his name is the LORD—
  and rejoice before him.
⁵A father to the fatherless, a defender
    of widows,
  is God in his holy dwelling.
⁶God sets the lonely in families,*ᵇ*
  he leads forth the prisoners with
    singing;
  but the rebellious live in a
    sun-scorched land.

⁷When you went out before your
    people, O God,
  when you marched through the
    wasteland,   *Selah*
⁸the earth shook,
  the heavens poured down rain,
  before God, the One of Sinai,
  before God, the God of Israel.
⁹You gave abundant showers, O God;
  you refreshed your weary
    inheritance.
¹⁰Your people settled in it,
  and from your bounty, O God, you
    provided for the poor.

¹¹The Lord announced the word,
  and great was the company of those
    who proclaimed it:
¹²"Kings and armies flee in haste;
  in the camps men divide the
    plunder.

---

*ᵃ*4 Or / *prepare the way for him who rides through the deserts*   *ᵇ*6 Or *the desolate in a homeland*

¹³Even while you sleep among the campfires,ᵃ
the wings of ⸤my⸥ dove are sheathed with silver,
its feathers with shining gold."
¹⁴When the Almightyᵇ scattered the kings in the land,
it was like snow fallen on Zalmon.

¹⁵The mountains of Bashan are majestic mountains;
rugged are the mountains of Bashan.
¹⁶Why gaze in envy, O rugged mountains,
at the mountain where God chooses to reign,
where the Lord himself will dwell forever?
¹⁷The chariots of God are tens of thousands
and thousands of thousands;
the Lord ⸤has come⸥ from Sinai into his sanctuary.
¹⁸When you ascended on high,
you led captives in your train;
you received gifts from men,
even fromᶜ the rebellious—
that you,ᵈ O Lord God, might dwell there.

ᵃ13 Or *saddlebags*   ᵇ14 Hebrew *Shaddai*   ᶜ18 Or *gifts for men, / even*   ᵈ18 Or *they*

MONDAY

VERSE FOR THE DAY:
Psalm 66:10

AUTHOR:
Joe Gibbs

PASSAGE FOR THE DAY:
Psalm 66:8–12

Through Deep Waters

NATIONAL Football League coach Joe Gibbs prayed fervently as doctors removed a tumor from inside his wife's skull. She survived the operation and recuperated, yet part of her face remains paralyzed.

"I belong to God," she says. "And I believe he allows things to come into our lives for a reason. Just because I don't know the reason doesn't mean there isn't one. Maybe this has just made me more sensitive to other people with problems."

She's dealing with it. It's been more than ten years now and is part of our lives. I'm proud to introduce her anywhere. Surgery may have slightly altered her looks, but it did not change her character. She's still Pat.

I'll tell you, going through something like that with the person you love sure makes losing a football game seem trivial. I had asked God why he had let me endure that horrible season in Tampa, and why I had been so blind and faithless when I had no peace about his leading me to San Diego. In a small way, I think, he was preparing me for this real trial.

There would be other difficulties in my life but none as difficult or scary as almost losing my wife. I still had a lot to learn about priorities and my faith and my ego, but I could never again say that God hadn't led me through some deep waters to strengthen me for when those new lessons came.

Additional Scripture Readings:
Romans 8:18–28; 1 Peter 1:3–9

Go to page 455 for your next devotional reading.

¹⁹Praise be to the Lord, to God our
    Savior,
  who daily bears our burdens. *Selah*
²⁰Our God is a God who saves;
  from the Sovereign LORD comes
    escape from death.

²¹Surely God will crush the heads of his
    enemies,
  the hairy crowns of those who go
    on in their sins.
²²The Lord says, "I will bring them from
    Bashan;
  I will bring them from the depths of
    the sea,
²³that you may plunge your feet in the
    blood of your foes,
  while the tongues of your dogs have
    their share."

²⁴Your procession has come into view,
    O God,
  the procession of my God and King
    into the sanctuary.
²⁵In front are the singers, after them the
    musicians;
  with them are the maidens playing
    tambourines.
²⁶Praise God in the great congregation;
  praise the LORD in the assembly of
    Israel.
²⁷There is the little tribe of Benjamin,
    leading them,
  there the great throng of Judah's
    princes,
  and there the princes of Zebulun
    and of Naphtali.

²⁸Summon your power, O God*ᵃ*;
  show us your strength, O God, as
    you have done before.
²⁹Because of your temple at Jerusalem
  kings will bring you gifts.
³⁰Rebuke the beast among the reeds,
  the herd of bulls among the calves
    of the nations.
  Humbled, may it bring bars of silver.
  Scatter the nations who delight in
    war.
³¹Envoys will come from Egypt;
  Cush*ᵇ* will submit herself to God.

³²Sing to God, O kingdoms of the earth,
  sing praise to the Lord,   *Selah*
³³to him who rides the ancient skies
    above,
  who thunders with mighty voice.
³⁴Proclaim the power of God,
  whose majesty is over Israel,
  whose power is in the skies.
³⁵You are awesome, O God, in your
    sanctuary;
  the God of Israel gives power and
    strength to his people.

Praise be to God!

Psalm 69

For the director of music. To the tune
of "Lilies." Of David.

¹Save me, O God,
  for the waters have come up to my
    neck.
²I sink in the miry depths,
  where there is no foothold.
  I have come into the deep waters;
  the floods engulf me.
³I am worn out calling for help;
  my throat is parched.
  My eyes fail,
  looking for my God.
⁴Those who hate me without reason
  outnumber the hairs of my head;
  many are my enemies without cause,
  those who seek to destroy me.
  I am forced to restore
  what I did not steal.

⁵You know my folly, O God;
  my guilt is not hidden from you.

⁶May those who hope in you
  not be disgraced because of me,
    O Lord, the LORD Almighty;
  may those who seek you
  not be put to shame because of me,
    O God of Israel.
⁷For I endure scorn for your sake,
  and shame covers my face.
⁸I am a stranger to my brothers,
  an alien to my own mother's sons;
⁹for zeal for your house consumes me,
  and the insults of those who insult
    you fall on me.
¹⁰When I weep and fast,
  I must endure scorn;
¹¹when I put on sackcloth,
  people make sport of me.
¹²Those who sit at the gate mock me,
  and I am the song of the drunkards.

¹³But I pray to you, O LORD,
  in the time of your favor;
  in your great love, O God,
  answer me with your sure salvation.
¹⁴Rescue me from the mire,

ᵃ28 Many Hebrew manuscripts, Septuagint and Syriac; most Hebrew manuscripts *Your God has summoned power for you*   *ᵇ31* That is, the upper Nile region

do not let me sink;
deliver me from those who hate me,
  from the deep waters.
¹⁵Do not let the floodwaters engulf me
  or the depths swallow me up
  or the pit close its mouth over me.
¹⁶Answer me, O LORD, out of the
    goodness of your love;
  in your great mercy turn to me.
¹⁷Do not hide your face from your
    servant;
  answer me quickly, for I am in
    trouble.
¹⁸Come near and rescue me;
  redeem me because of my foes.

¹⁹You know how I am scorned,
    disgraced and shamed;
  all my enemies are before you.
²⁰Scorn has broken my heart
    and has left me helpless;
  I looked for sympathy, but there was
    none,
  for comforters, but I found none.
²¹They put gall in my food
  and gave me vinegar for my thirst.

²²May the table set before them become
    a snare;
  may it become retribution and^a a
    trap.
²³May their eyes be darkened so they
    cannot see,
  and their backs be bent forever.
²⁴Pour out your wrath on them;
  let your fierce anger overtake them.
²⁵May their place be deserted;
  let there be no one to dwell in their
    tents.
²⁶For they persecute those you wound
  and talk about the pain of those you
    hurt.
²⁷Charge them with crime upon crime;
  do not let them share in your
    salvation.
²⁸May they be blotted out of the book
    of life
  and not be listed with the righteous.

²⁹I am in pain and distress;
  may your salvation, O God, protect
    me.

³⁰I will praise God's name in song
  and glorify him with thanksgiving.
³¹This will please the LORD more than
    an ox,
  more than a bull with its horns and
    hoofs.
³²The poor will see and be glad —
  you who seek God, may your hearts
    live!
³³The LORD hears the needy
  and does not despise his captive
    people.

³⁴Let heaven and earth praise him,
  the seas and all that move in them,
³⁵for God will save Zion
  and rebuild the cities of Judah.
Then people will settle there and
    possess it;
³⁶ the children of his servants will
    inherit it,
  and those who love his name will
    dwell there.

Psalm 70

*For the director of music. Of David.
A petition.*

¹Hasten, O God, to save me;
  O LORD, come quickly to help me.
²May those who seek my life
  be put to shame and confusion;
  may all who desire my ruin
  be turned back in disgrace.
³May those who say to me, "Aha!
    Aha!"
  turn back because of their shame.
⁴But may all who seek you
  rejoice and be glad in you;
  may those who love your salvation
    always say,
    "Let God be exalted!"

⁵Yet I am poor and needy;
  come quickly to me, O God.
You are my help and my deliverer;
  O LORD, do not delay.

Psalm 71

¹In you, O LORD, I have taken refuge;
  let me never be put to shame.
²Rescue me and deliver me in your
    righteousness;
  turn your ear to me and save me.
³Be my rock of refuge,
  to which I can always go;
  give the command to save me,
  for you are my rock and my
    fortress.
⁴Deliver me, O my God, from the hand
    of the wicked,
  from the grasp of evil and cruel
    men.

---

^{a}22 Or *snare / and their fellowship become*

⁵For you have been my hope,
O Sovereign Lord,
my confidence since my youth.
⁶From birth I have relied on you;
you brought me forth from my
mother's womb.
I will ever praise you.
⁷I have become like a portent to many,
but you are my strong refuge.
⁸My mouth is filled with your praise,
declaring your splendor all day
long.

⁹Do not cast me away when I am old;
do not forsake me when my
strength is gone.
¹⁰For my enemies speak against me;
those who wait to kill me conspire
together.
¹¹They say, "God has forsaken him;
pursue him and seize him,
for no one will rescue him."
¹²Be not far from me, O God;
come quickly, O my God, to help
me.
¹³May my accusers perish in shame;
may those who want to harm me
be covered with scorn and disgrace.

¹⁴But as for me, I will always have
hope;
I will praise you more and more.
¹⁵My mouth will tell of your
righteousness,
of your salvation all day long,
though I know not its measure.
¹⁶I will come and proclaim your mighty
acts, O Sovereign Lord;
I will proclaim your righteousness,
yours alone.
¹⁷Since my youth, O God, you have
taught me,
and to this day I declare your
marvelous deeds.
¹⁸Even when I am old and gray,
do not forsake me, O God,
till I declare your power to the next
generation,
your might to all who are to come.

¹⁹Your righteousness reaches to the
skies, O God,
you who have done great things.
Who, O God, is like you?
²⁰Though you have made me see
troubles, many and bitter,
you will restore my life again;
from the depths of the earth
you will again bring me up.
²¹You will increase my honor
and comfort me once again.

²²I will praise you with the harp
for your faithfulness, O my God;
I will sing praise to you with the lyre,
O Holy One of Israel.
²³My lips will shout for joy
when I sing praise to you—
I, whom you have redeemed.
²⁴My tongue will tell of your righteous
acts
all day long,
for those who wanted to harm me
have been put to shame and
confusion.

Psalm 72

Of Solomon.

¹Endow the king with your justice,
O God,
the royal son with your
righteousness.
²He will*a* judge your people in
righteousness,
your afflicted ones with justice.
³The mountains will bring prosperity to
the people,
the hills the fruit of righteousness.
⁴He will defend the afflicted among the
people
and save the children of the needy;
he will crush the oppressor.

⁵He will endure*b* as long as the sun,
as long as the moon, through all
generations.
⁶He will be like rain falling on a mown
field,
like showers watering the earth.
⁷In his days the righteous will flourish;
prosperity will abound till the moon
is no more.

⁸He will rule from sea to sea
and from the River*c* to the ends of
the earth.*d*
⁹The desert tribes will bow before him
and his enemies will lick the dust.
¹⁰The kings of Tarshish and of distant
shores
will bring tribute to him;
the kings of Sheba and Seba
will present him gifts.
¹¹All kings will bow down to him
and all nations will serve him.

---

*a*2 Or *May he;* similarly in verses 3-11 and 17   *b*5 Septuagint; Hebrew *You will be feared*   *c*8 That is, the Euphrates   *d*8 Or *the end of the land*

¹²For he will deliver the needy who cry out,
  the afflicted who have no one to help.
¹³He will take pity on the weak and the needy
  and save the needy from death.
¹⁴He will rescue them from oppression and violence,
  for precious is their blood in his sight.

¹⁵Long may he live!
  May gold from Sheba be given him.
  May people ever pray for him
  and bless him all day long.
¹⁶Let grain abound throughout the land;
  on the tops of the hills may it sway.
  Let its fruit flourish like Lebanon;
  let it thrive like the grass of the field.
¹⁷May his name endure forever;
  may it continue as long as the sun.

All nations will be blessed through him,
  and they will call him blessed.

¹⁸Praise be to the LORD God, the God of Israel,
  who alone does marvelous deeds.
¹⁹Praise be to his glorious name forever;
  may the whole earth be filled with his glory.
    Amen and Amen.

²⁰This concludes the prayers of David son of Jesse.

BOOK III

Psalms 73–89

Psalm 73

A psalm of Asaph.

¹Surely God is good to Israel,
  to those who are pure in heart.

²But as for me, my feet had almost slipped;
  I had nearly lost my foothold.
³For I envied the arrogant
  when I saw the prosperity of the wicked.

⁴They have no struggles;
  their bodies are healthy and strong.[a]
⁵They are free from the burdens common to man;
  they are not plagued by human ills.
⁶Therefore pride is their necklace;
  they clothe themselves with violence.
⁷From their callous hearts comes iniquity[b];
  the evil conceits of their minds know no limits.
⁸They scoff, and speak with malice;
  in their arrogance they threaten oppression.
⁹Their mouths lay claim to heaven,
  and their tongues take possession of the earth.
¹⁰Therefore their people turn to them
  and drink up waters in abundance.[c]
¹¹They say, "How can God know?
  Does the Most High have knowledge?"

¹²This is what the wicked are like—
  always carefree, they increase in wealth.

¹³Surely in vain have I kept my heart pure;
  in vain have I washed my hands in innocence.
¹⁴All day long I have been plagued;
  I have been punished every morning.

¹⁵If I had said, "I will speak thus,"
  I would have betrayed your children.
¹⁶When I tried to understand all this,
  it was oppressive to me
¹⁷till I entered the sanctuary of God;
  then I understood their final destiny.

¹⁸Surely you place them on slippery ground;
  you cast them down to ruin.
¹⁹How suddenly are they destroyed,
  completely swept away by terrors!
²⁰As a dream when one awakes,
  so when you arise, O Lord,
  you will despise them as fantasies.

²¹When my heart was grieved
  and my spirit embittered,
²²I was senseless and ignorant;

---

a 4 With a different word division of the Hebrew; Masoretic Text *struggles at their death; / their bodies are healthy*   *b 7* Syriac (see also Septuagint); Hebrew *Their eyes bulge with fat*   *c 10* The meaning of the Hebrew for this verse is uncertain.

I was a brute beast before you.

²³Yet I am always with you;
 you hold me by my right hand.
²⁴You guide me with your counsel,
 and afterward you will take me into glory.
²⁵Whom have I in heaven but you?
 And earth has nothing I desire besides you.
²⁶My flesh and my heart may fail,
 but God is the strength of my heart and my portion forever.

²⁷Those who are far from you will perish;
 you destroy all who are unfaithful to you.
²⁸But as for me, it is good to be near God.
 I have made the Sovereign Lord my refuge;
 I will tell of all your deeds.

Psalm 74

A maskil[a] of Asaph.

¹Why have you rejected us forever, O God?
 Why does your anger smolder against the sheep of your pasture?
²Remember the people you purchased of old,
 the tribe of your inheritance, whom you redeemed—
 Mount Zion, where you dwelt.
³Turn your steps toward these everlasting ruins,
 all this destruction the enemy has brought on the sanctuary.

⁴Your foes roared in the place where you met with us;
 they set up their standards as signs.
⁵They behaved like men wielding axes to cut through a thicket of trees.
⁶They smashed all the carved paneling with their axes and hatchets.
⁷They burned your sanctuary to the ground;
 they defiled the dwelling place of your Name.
⁸They said in their hearts, "We will crush them completely!"
 They burned every place where God was worshiped in the land.
⁹We are given no miraculous signs;
 no prophets are left,
 and none of us knows how long this will be.
¹⁰How long will the enemy mock you, O God?
 Will the foe revile your name forever?
¹¹Why do you hold back your hand, your right hand?
 Take it from the folds of your garment and destroy them!

¹²But you, O God, are my king from of old;
 you bring salvation upon the earth.
¹³It was you who split open the sea by your power;
 you broke the heads of the monster in the waters.
¹⁴It was you who crushed the heads of Leviathan
 and gave him as food to the creatures of the desert.
¹⁵It was you who opened up springs and streams;
 you dried up the ever flowing rivers.
¹⁶The day is yours, and yours also the night;
 you established the sun and moon.
¹⁷It was you who set all the boundaries of the earth;
 you made both summer and winter.

¹⁸Remember how the enemy has mocked you, O Lord,
 how foolish people have reviled your name.
¹⁹Do not hand over the life of your dove to wild beasts;
 do not forget the lives of your afflicted people forever.
²⁰Have regard for your covenant,
 because haunts of violence fill the dark places of the land.
²¹Do not let the oppressed retreat in disgrace;
 may the poor and needy praise your name.

²²Rise up, O God, and defend your cause;
 remember how fools mock you all day long.
²³Do not ignore the clamor of your adversaries,
 the uproar of your enemies, which rises continually.

---

[a] Title: Probably a literary or musical term

Psalm 75

For the director of music. To the tune of "Do Not Destroy." A psalm of Asaph. A song.

¹We give thanks to you, O God,
  we give thanks, for your Name is near;
  men tell of your wonderful deeds.

²You say, "I choose the appointed time;
  it is I who judge uprightly.
³When the earth and all its people quake,
  it is I who hold its pillars firm.
      Selah
⁴To the arrogant I say, 'Boast no more,'
  and to the wicked, 'Do not lift up your horns.
⁵Do not lift your horns against heaven;
  do not speak with outstretched neck.' "

⁶No one from the east or the west
  or from the desert can exalt a man.
⁷But it is God who judges:
  He brings one down, he exalts another.
⁸In the hand of the LORD is a cup
  full of foaming wine mixed with spices;
 he pours it out, and all the wicked of the earth
  drink it down to its very dregs.

⁹As for me, I will declare this forever;
  I will sing praise to the God of Jacob.
¹⁰I will cut off the horns of all the wicked,
  but the horns of the righteous will be lifted up.

Psalm 76

For the director of music. With stringed instruments. A psalm of Asaph. A song.

¹In Judah God is known;
  his name is great in Israel.
²His tent is in Salem,
  his dwelling place in Zion.
³There he broke the flashing arrows,
  the shields and the swords, the weapons of war.   *Selah*

⁴You are resplendent with light,
  more majestic than mountains rich with game.
⁵Valiant men lie plundered,
  they sleep their last sleep;
 not one of the warriors
  can lift his hands.
⁶At your rebuke, O God of Jacob,
  both horse and chariot lie still.
⁷You alone are to be feared.
  Who can stand before you when you are angry?
⁸From heaven you pronounced judgment,
  and the land feared and was quiet—

⁹when you, O God, rose up to judge,
  to save all the afflicted of the land.
      Selah
¹⁰Surely your wrath against men brings you praise,
  and the survivors of your wrath are restrained.[a]

¹¹Make vows to the LORD your God and fulfill them;
 let all the neighboring lands
  bring gifts to the One to be feared.
¹²He breaks the spirit of rulers;
  he is feared by the kings of the earth.

Psalm 77

For the director of music. For Jeduthun. Of Asaph. A psalm.

¹I cried out to God for help;
  I cried out to God to hear me.
²When I was in distress, I sought the Lord;
  at night I stretched out untiring hands
  and my soul refused to be comforted.

³I remembered you, O God, and I groaned;
  I mused, and my spirit grew faint.
      Selah
⁴You kept my eyes from closing;
  I was too troubled to speak.
⁵I thought about the former days,
  the years of long ago;
⁶I remembered my songs in the night.
  My heart mused and my spirit inquired:

⁷"Will the Lord reject forever?
  Will he never show his favor again?
⁸Has his unfailing love vanished forever?
  Has his promise failed for all time?
⁹Has God forgotten to be merciful?

---

[a] 10 Or *Surely the wrath of men brings you praise, / and with the remainder of wrath you arm yourself*

Has he in anger withheld his
compassion?" *Selah*

¹⁰Then I thought, "To this I will appeal:
the years of the right hand of the
Most High."
¹¹I will remember the deeds of the
LORD;
yes, I will remember your miracles
of long ago.
¹²I will meditate on all your works
and consider all your mighty deeds.

¹³Your ways, O God, are holy.
What god is so great as our God?
¹⁴You are the God who performs
miracles;
you display your power among the
peoples.
¹⁵With your mighty arm you redeemed
your people,
the descendants of Jacob and
Joseph. *Selah*

¹⁶The waters saw you, O God,
the waters saw you and writhed;
the very depths were convulsed.
¹⁷The clouds poured down water,
the skies resounded with thunder;
your arrows flashed back and forth.
¹⁸Your thunder was heard in the
whirlwind,
your lightning lit up the world;
the earth trembled and quaked.
¹⁹Your path led through the sea,
your way through the mighty
waters,
though your footprints were not
seen.

²⁰You led your people like a flock
by the hand of Moses and Aaron.

Psalm 78

A maskil[a] of Asaph.

¹O my people, hear my teaching;
listen to the words of my mouth.
²I will open my mouth in parables,
I will utter hidden things, things
from of old—
³what we have heard and known,
what our fathers have told us.
⁴We will not hide them from their
children;
we will tell the next generation
the praiseworthy deeds of the LORD,
his power, and the wonders he has
done.

⁵He decreed statutes for Jacob
and established the law in Israel,
which he commanded our forefathers
to teach their children,
⁶so the next generation would know
them,
even the children yet to be born,
and they in turn would tell their
children.
⁷Then they would put their trust in
God
and would not forget his deeds
but would keep his commands.
⁸They would not be like their
forefathers—
a stubborn and rebellious
generation,
whose hearts were not loyal to God,
whose spirits were not faithful to
him.

⁹The men of Ephraim, though armed
with bows,
turned back on the day of battle;
¹⁰they did not keep God's covenant
and refused to live by his law.
¹¹They forgot what he had done,
the wonders he had shown them.
¹²He did miracles in the sight of their
fathers
in the land of Egypt, in the region
of Zoan.
¹³He divided the sea and led them
through;
he made the water stand firm like a
wall.
¹⁴He guided them with the cloud by day
and with light from the fire all
night.
¹⁵He split the rocks in the desert
and gave them water as abundant
as the seas;
¹⁶he brought streams out of a rocky
crag
and made water flow down like
rivers.

¹⁷But they continued to sin against him,
rebelling in the desert against the
Most High.
¹⁸They willfully put God to the test
by demanding the food they craved.
¹⁹They spoke against God, saying,
"Can God spread a table in the
desert?
²⁰When he struck the rock, water
gushed out,
and streams flowed abundantly.

---

[a] Title: Probably a literary or musical term

But can he also give us food?
Can he supply meat for his people?"
²¹When the LORD heard them, he was very angry;
his fire broke out against Jacob,
and his wrath rose against Israel,
²²for they did not believe in God
or trust in his deliverance.
²³Yet he gave a command to the skies above
and opened the doors of the heavens;
²⁴he rained down manna for the people to eat,
he gave them the grain of heaven.
²⁵Men ate the bread of angels;
he sent them all the food they could eat.
²⁶He let loose the east wind from the heavens
and led forth the south wind by his power.
²⁷He rained meat down on them like dust,
flying birds like sand on the seashore.
²⁸He made them come down inside their camp,
all around their tents.
²⁹They ate till they had more than enough,
for he had given them what they craved.
³⁰But before they turned from the food they craved,
even while it was still in their mouths,
³¹God's anger rose against them;
he put to death the sturdiest among them,

TUESDAY

VERSE FOR THE DAY:
Psalm 78:4

AUTHOR:
James Dobson

PASSAGE FOR THE DAY:
Psalm 78:1–8

Passing the Baton

[A FATHER'S] most important responsibility, I believe, is to communicate the real meaning of Christianity to his children. This mission can be likened to a three-man relay race. First, your father runs his lap around the track, carrying the baton, which represents the gospel of Jesus Christ. At the appropriate moment, he hands the baton to you, and you begin your journey around the track. Then finally, the time will come when you must get the baton safely in the hands of your children. But as any track coach will testify, *relay races are won or lost in the transfer of the baton.* There is a critical moment when all can be lost by a fumble or miscalculation. The baton is rarely dropped on the back side of the track when the runner has it firmly in his grasp. If failure is to occur, it will probably happen in the exchange between generations.

According to the Christian values that govern my life, my most important reason for living is to get the baton, the gospel, safely in the hands of my children. Of course, I want to place it in as many other hands as possible; *nevertheless, my number one responsibility is to evangelize my own children.* I hope millions of other fathers agree with that ultimate priority.

Additional Scripture Readings:
Psalm 145:1–7; 2 Timothy 3:14–4:2

Go to page 460 for your next devotional reading.

cutting down the young men of Israel.
³²In spite of all this, they kept on sinning;
in spite of his wonders, they did not believe.
³³So he ended their days in futility and their years in terror.
³⁴Whenever God slew them, they would seek him;
they eagerly turned to him again.
³⁵They remembered that God was their Rock,
that God Most High was their Redeemer.
³⁶But then they would flatter him with their mouths,
lying to him with their tongues;
³⁷their hearts were not loyal to him, they were not faithful to his covenant.
³⁸Yet he was merciful;
he forgave their iniquities
and did not destroy them.
Time after time he restrained his anger
and did not stir up his full wrath.
³⁹He remembered that they were but flesh,
a passing breeze that does not return.

⁴⁰How often they rebelled against him in the desert
and grieved him in the wasteland!
⁴¹Again and again they put God to the test;
they vexed the Holy One of Israel.
⁴²They did not remember his power—
the day he redeemed them from the oppressor,
⁴³the day he displayed his miraculous signs in Egypt,
his wonders in the region of Zoan.
⁴⁴He turned their rivers to blood;
they could not drink from their streams.
⁴⁵He sent swarms of flies that devoured them,
and frogs that devastated them.
⁴⁶He gave their crops to the grasshopper,
their produce to the locust.
⁴⁷He destroyed their vines with hail and their sycamore-figs with sleet.
⁴⁸He gave over their cattle to the hail, their livestock to bolts of lightning.
⁴⁹He unleashed against them his hot anger,
his wrath, indignation and hostility—
a band of destroying angels.
⁵⁰He prepared a path for his anger;
he did not spare them from death
but gave them over to the plague.
⁵¹He struck down all the firstborn of Egypt,
the firstfruits of manhood in the tents of Ham.
⁵²But he brought his people out like a flock;
he led them like sheep through the desert.
⁵³He guided them safely, so they were unafraid;
but the sea engulfed their enemies.
⁵⁴Thus he brought them to the border of his holy land,
to the hill country his right hand had taken.
⁵⁵He drove out nations before them
and allotted their lands to them as an inheritance;
he settled the tribes of Israel in their homes.

⁵⁶But they put God to the test
and rebelled against the Most High;
they did not keep his statutes.
⁵⁷Like their fathers they were disloyal and faithless,
as unreliable as a faulty bow.
⁵⁸They angered him with their high places;
they aroused his jealousy with their idols.
⁵⁹When God heard them, he was very angry;
he rejected Israel completely.
⁶⁰He abandoned the tabernacle of Shiloh,
the tent he had set up among men.
⁶¹He sent the ark of his might into captivity,
his splendor into the hands of the enemy.
⁶²He gave his people over to the sword;
he was very angry with his inheritance.
⁶³Fire consumed their young men,
and their maidens had no wedding songs;
⁶⁴their priests were put to the sword,
and their widows could not weep.

⁶⁵Then the Lord awoke as from sleep,
as a man wakes from the stupor of wine.
⁶⁶He beat back his enemies;
he put them to everlasting shame.

⁶⁷Then he rejected the tents of Joseph,
  he did not choose the tribe of
    Ephraim;
⁶⁸but he chose the tribe of Judah,
  Mount Zion, which he loved.
⁶⁹He built his sanctuary like the heights,
  like the earth that he established
    forever.
⁷⁰He chose David his servant
  and took him from the sheep pens;
⁷¹from tending the sheep he brought
    him
  to be the shepherd of his people
    Jacob,
  of Israel his inheritance.
⁷²And David shepherded them with
    integrity of heart;
  with skillful hands he led them.

Psalm 79

A psalm of Asaph.

¹O God, the nations have invaded your
    inheritance;
  they have defiled your holy temple,
  they have reduced Jerusalem to
    rubble.
²They have given the dead bodies of
    your servants
  as food to the birds of the air,
  the flesh of your saints to the beasts
    of the earth.
³They have poured out blood like
    water
  all around Jerusalem,
  and there is no one to bury the
    dead.
⁴We are objects of reproach to our
    neighbors,
  of scorn and derision to those
    around us.

⁵How long, O Lord? Will you be angry
    forever?
  How long will your jealousy burn
    like fire?
⁶Pour out your wrath on the nations
  that do not acknowledge you,
  on the kingdoms
  that do not call on your name;
⁷for they have devoured Jacob
  and destroyed his homeland.
⁸Do not hold against us the sins of the
    fathers;
  may your mercy come quickly to
    meet us,
  for we are in desperate need.

⁹Help us, O God our Savior,
  for the glory of your name;
  deliver us and forgive our sins
    for your name's sake.
¹⁰Why should the nations say,
  "Where is their God?"
  Before our eyes, make known among
    the nations
  that you avenge the outpoured
    blood of your servants.
¹¹May the groans of the prisoners come
    before you;
  by the strength of your arm
  preserve those condemned to die.

¹²Pay back into the laps of our
    neighbors seven times
  the reproach they have hurled at
    you, O Lord.
¹³Then we your people, the sheep of
    your pasture,
  will praise you forever;
  from generation to generation
  we will recount your praise.

Psalm 80

*For the director of music. To the tune
of, "The Lilies of the Covenant."
Of Asaph. A psalm.*

¹Hear us, O Shepherd of Israel,
  you who lead Joseph like a flock;
  you who sit enthroned between the
    cherubim, shine forth
² before Ephraim, Benjamin and
    Manasseh.
  Awaken your might;
  come and save us.

³Restore us, O God;
  make your face shine upon us,
  that we may be saved.

⁴O Lord God Almighty,
  how long will your anger smolder
  against the prayers of your people?
⁵You have fed them with the bread of
    tears;
  you have made them drink tears by
    the bowlful.
⁶You have made us a source of
    contention to our neighbors,
  and our enemies mock us.

⁷Restore us, O God Almighty;
  make your face shine upon us,
  that we may be saved.

⁸You brought a vine out of Egypt;
  you drove out the nations and
    planted it.
⁹You cleared the ground for it,
  and it took root and filled the land.

¹⁰The mountains were covered with its shade,
the mighty cedars with its branches.
¹¹It sent out its boughs to the Sea,ᵃ
its shoots as far as the River.ᵇ

¹²Why have you broken down its walls
so that all who pass by pick its grapes?
¹³Boars from the forest ravage it
and the creatures of the field feed on it.
¹⁴Return to us, O God Almighty!
Look down from heaven and see!
Watch over this vine,
¹⁵ the root your right hand has planted,
the sonᶜ you have raised up for yourself.

¹⁶Your vine is cut down, it is burned with fire;
at your rebuke your people perish.
¹⁷Let your hand rest on the man at your right hand,
the son of man you have raised up for yourself.
¹⁸Then we will not turn away from you;
revive us, and we will call on your name.

¹⁹Restore us, O LORD God Almighty;
make your face shine upon us,
that we may be saved.

Psalm 81

For the director of music. According to gittith.ᵈ Of Asaph.

¹Sing for joy to God our strength;
shout aloud to the God of Jacob!
²Begin the music, strike the tambourine,
play the melodious harp and lyre.

³Sound the ram's horn at the New Moon,
and when the moon is full, on the day of our Feast;
⁴this is a decree for Israel,
an ordinance of the God of Jacob.
⁵He established it as a statute for Joseph
when he went out against Egypt,
where we heard a language we did not understand.ᵉ

⁶He says, "I removed the burden from their shoulders;
their hands were set free from the basket.
⁷In your distress you called and I rescued you,
I answered you out of a thundercloud;
I tested you at the waters of Meribah.   *Selah*

⁸"Hear, O my people, and I will warn you—
if you would but listen to me, O Israel!
⁹You shall have no foreign god among you;
you shall not bow down to an alien god.
¹⁰I am the LORD your God,
who brought you up out of Egypt.
Open wide your mouth and I will fill it.

¹¹But my people would not listen to me;
Israel would not submit to me.
¹²So I gave them over to their stubborn hearts
to follow their own devices.

¹³"If my people would but listen to me,
if Israel would follow my ways,
¹⁴how quickly would I subdue their enemies
and turn my hand against their foes!
¹⁵Those who hate the LORD would cringe before him,
and their punishment would last forever.
¹⁶But you would be fed with the finest of wheat;
with honey from the rock I would satisfy you."

Psalm 82

A psalm of Asaph.

¹God presides in the great assembly;
he gives judgment among the "gods":

²"How long will youᶠ defend the unjust
and show partiality to the wicked?   *Selah*

³Defend the cause of the weak and fatherless;

ᵃ11 Probably the Mediterranean   ᵇ11 That is, the Euphrates   ᶜ15 Or *branch*   ᵈTitle: Probably a musical term   ᵉ5 Or */ and we heard a voice we had not known*   ᶠ2 The Hebrew is plural.

maintain the rights of the poor and
    oppressed.
⁴Rescue the weak and needy;
    deliver them from the hand of the
        wicked.

⁵"They know nothing, they understand
        nothing.
    They walk about in darkness;
    all the foundations of the earth are
        shaken.

⁶"I said, 'You are "gods";
    you are all sons of the Most High.'
⁷But you will die like mere men;
    you will fall like every other ruler."

⁸Rise up, O God, judge the earth,
    for all the nations are your
        inheritance.

Psalm 83

A song. A psalm of Asaph.

¹O God, do not keep silent;
    be not quiet, O God, be not still.
²See how your enemies are astir,
    how your foes rear their heads.
³With cunning they conspire against
        your people;
    they plot against those you cherish.
⁴"Come," they say, "let us destroy them
        as a nation,
    that the name of Israel be
        remembered no more."

⁵With one mind they plot together;
    they form an alliance against you—
⁶the tents of Edom and the Ishmaelites,
    of Moab and the Hagrites,
⁷Gebal,ᵃ Ammon and Amalek,
    Philistia, with the people of Tyre.
⁸Even Assyria has joined them
    to lend strength to the descendants
        of Lot.   *Selah*

⁹Do to them as you did to Midian,
    as you did to Sisera and Jabin at the
        river Kishon,
¹⁰who perished at Endor
    and became like refuse on the
        ground.
¹¹Make their nobles like Oreb and Zeeb,
    all their princes like Zebah and
        Zalmunna,
¹²who said, "Let us take possession
    of the pasturelands of God."

¹³Make them like tumbleweed, O my
        God,
    like chaff before the wind.
¹⁴As fire consumes the forest
    or a flame sets the mountains
        ablaze,
¹⁵so pursue them with your tempest
    and terrify them with your storm.
¹⁶Cover their faces with shame
    so that men will seek your name,
        O LORD.

¹⁷May they ever be ashamed and
        dismayed;
    may they perish in disgrace.
¹⁸Let them know that you, whose name
        is the LORD—
    that you alone are the Most High
        over all the earth.

Psalm 84

*For the director of music. According to
gittith.ᵇ Of the Sons of Korah. A psalm.*

¹How lovely is your dwelling place,
    O LORD Almighty!
²My soul yearns, even faints,
    for the courts of the LORD;
    my heart and my flesh cry out
        for the living God.

³Even the sparrow has found a home,
    and the swallow a nest for herself,
    where she may have her young—
    a place near your altar,
    O LORD Almighty, my King and my
        God.
⁴Blessed are those who dwell in your
        house;
    they are ever praising you.   *Selah*

⁵Blessed are those whose strength is in
        you,
    who have set their hearts on
        pilgrimage.
⁶As they pass through the Valley of
        Baca,
    they make it a place of springs;
    the autumn rains also cover it with
        pools.ᶜ
⁷They go from strength to strength,
    till each appears before God in Zion.

⁸Hear my prayer, O LORD God
        Almighty;
    listen to me, O God of Jacob.   *Selah*
⁹Look upon our shield,ᵈ O God;
    look with favor on your anointed
        one.

ᵃ7 That is, Byblos   ᵇTitle: Probably a musical term   ᶜ6 Or *blessings*   ᵈ9 Or *sovereign*

¹⁰Better is one day in your courts
  than a thousand elsewhere;
I would rather be a doorkeeper in the
    house of my God
  than dwell in the tents of the
    wicked.
¹¹For the LORD God is a sun and shield;
  the LORD bestows favor and honor;
  no good thing does he withhold
    from those whose walk is blameless.

¹²O LORD Almighty,
  blessed is the man who trusts in
    you.

WEDNESDAY

VERSE FOR THE DAY:
Psalm 84:10

AUTHOR:
Don Wyrtzen

PASSAGE FOR THE DAY:
Psalm 84:8–12

A Worthy Walk

THESE verses are both a comfort and a challenge. I know I've been "set apart" to Christian service in the ministry of music, but sometimes low-grade motivation obscures my vision. The enchantment of conducting a professional orchestra for the first time, seeing my first published song, listening to my first record have faded, and I'm faced with the daily grind. I must work harder to keep the excitement and creative-energy level high.

The psalmist has no such fears or insecurities. His rock-solid devotion to God supersedes all other concerns. He knows he has been set apart ("anointed") by the Lord, and he is utterly committed to his calling (v. 9). In fact, if necessary, he is willing to serve in some menial position ("a doorkeeper") in the house of the Lord rather than to live in the lavish tents of the wicked (v. 10).

In verse 11 we learn the reason for such devotion. The Lord is pictured as a "sun and shield." He offers warmth, blessing, protection and prosperity. He does not withhold anything good from those whose walk with him is blameless—"a spotless walk, conduct ordered according to God's will, and a truth-loving mode of thought."

Now that the musical honeymoon is over, I need to be more committed, to persist and persevere in practicing my craft. I need to exercise discipline as I'm enjoying inspiration. I also need to follow the example of my ancient colleague—turn to my Source and spend more time in meaningful interaction with his people. Out of the rich texture of meaningful human relationships come songs that touch the heart.

O Lord, today I rededicate my life to your service. Be my sun and shield, and give me the satisfaction of knowing that my walk is worthy of my calling.

Additional Scripture Readings:
Psalm 27; 2 John 4–6

Go to page 465 for your next devotional reading.

Psalm 85

For the director of music. Of the Sons of Korah. A psalm.

¹You showed favor to your land,
O LORD;
   you restored the fortunes of Jacob.
²You forgave the iniquity of your
      people
   and covered all their sins.   Selah
³You set aside all your wrath
   and turned from your fierce anger.

⁴Restore us again, O God our Savior,
   and put away your displeasure
      toward us.
⁵Will you be angry with us forever?
   Will you prolong your anger
      through all generations?
⁶Will you not revive us again,
   that your people may rejoice in
      you?
⁷Show us your unfailing love, O LORD,
   and grant us your salvation.

⁸I will listen to what God the LORD will
      say;
   he promises peace to his people, his
      saints—
   but let them not return to folly.
⁹Surely his salvation is near those who
      fear him,
   that his glory may dwell in our
      land.

¹⁰Love and faithfulness meet together;
   righteousness and peace kiss each
      other.
¹¹Faithfulness springs forth from the
      earth,
   and righteousness looks down from
      heaven.
¹²The LORD will indeed give what is
      good,
   and our land will yield its harvest.
¹³Righteousness goes before him
   and prepares the way for his steps.

Psalm 86

A prayer of David.

¹Hear, O LORD, and answer me,
   for I am poor and needy.
²Guard my life, for I am devoted to
      you.
   You are my God; save your servant
      who trusts in you.
³Have mercy on me, O Lord,
   for I call to you all day long.
⁴Bring joy to your servant,
   for to you, O Lord,
   I lift up my soul.

⁵You are forgiving and good, O Lord,
   abounding in love to all who call to
      you.
⁶Hear my prayer, O LORD;
   listen to my cry for mercy.
⁷In the day of my trouble I will call to
      you,
   for you will answer me.

⁸Among the gods there is none like
      you, O Lord;
   no deeds can compare with yours.
⁹All the nations you have made
   will come and worship before you,
      O Lord;
   they will bring glory to your name.
¹⁰For you are great and do marvelous
      deeds;
   you alone are God.

¹¹Teach me your way, O LORD,
   and I will walk in your truth;
give me an undivided heart,
   that I may fear your name.
¹²I will praise you, O Lord my God,
   with all my heart;
   I will glorify your name forever.
¹³For great is your love toward me;
   you have delivered me from the
      depths of the grave.ᵃ

¹⁴The arrogant are attacking me, O God;
   a band of ruthless men seeks my
      life—
   men without regard for you.
¹⁵But you, O Lord, are a compassionate
      and gracious God,
   slow to anger, abounding in love
      and faithfulness.
¹⁶Turn to me and have mercy on me;
   grant your strength to your servant
   and save the son of your
      maidservant.ᵇ
¹⁷Give me a sign of your goodness,
   that my enemies may see it and be
      put to shame,
   for you, O LORD, have helped me
      and comforted me.

Psalm 87

Of the Sons of Korah. A psalm. A song.

¹He has set his foundation on the holy
      mountain;

ᵃ13 Hebrew *Sheol*   ᵇ16 Or *save your faithful son*

2 the LORD loves the gates of Zion
more than all the dwellings of
Jacob.
³Glorious things are said of you,
O city of God: *Selah*
⁴"I will record Rahab*a* and Babylon
among those who acknowledge
me —
Philistia too, and Tyre, along with
Cush*b* —
and will say, 'This*c* one was born
in Zion.' "

⁵Indeed, of Zion it will be said,
"This one and that one were born
in her,
and the Most High himself will
establish her."
⁶The LORD will write in the register of
the peoples:
"This one was born in Zion." *Selah*
⁷As they make music they will sing,
"All my fountains are in you."

Psalm 88

A song. A psalm of the Sons of Korah.
For the director of music. According to
mahalath leannoth.d A *maskile* of
Heman the Ezrahite.

¹O LORD, the God who saves me,
day and night I cry out before you.
²May my prayer come before you;
turn your ear to my cry.

³For my soul is full of trouble
and my life draws near the grave.*f*
⁴I am counted among those who go
down to the pit;
I am like a man without strength.
⁵I am set apart with the dead,
like the slain who lie in the grave,
whom you remember no more,
who are cut off from your care.

⁶You have put me in the lowest pit,
in the darkest depths.
⁷Your wrath lies heavily upon me;
you have overwhelmed me with all
your waves. *Selah*
⁸You have taken from me my closest
friends
and have made me repulsive to
them.
I am confined and cannot escape;
⁹ my eyes are dim with grief.

I call to you, O LORD, every day;
I spread out my hands to you.
¹⁰Do you show your wonders to the
dead?
Do those who are dead rise up and
praise you? *Selah*
¹¹Is your love declared in the grave,
your faithfulness in Destruction*g*?
¹²Are your wonders known in the place
of darkness,
or your righteous deeds in the land
of oblivion?

¹³But I cry to you for help, O LORD;
in the morning my prayer comes
before you.
¹⁴Why, O LORD, do you reject me
and hide your face from me?

¹⁵From my youth I have been afflicted
and close to death;
I have suffered your terrors and am
in despair.
¹⁶Your wrath has swept over me;
your terrors have destroyed me.
¹⁷All day long they surround me like a
flood;
they have completely engulfed me.
¹⁸You have taken my companions and
loved ones from me;
the darkness is my closest friend.

Psalm 89

A *maskile* of Ethan the Ezrahite.

¹I will sing of the LORD's great love
forever;
with my mouth I will make your
faithfulness known through all
generations.
²I will declare that your love stands
firm forever,
that you established your
faithfulness in heaven itself.

³You said, "I have made a covenant
with my chosen one,
I have sworn to David my servant,
⁴'I will establish your line forever
and make your throne firm through
all generations.' " *Selah*

⁵The heavens praise your wonders,
O LORD,
your faithfulness too, in the
assembly of the holy ones.

---

*a*4 A poetic name for Egypt   *b*4 That is, the upper Nile region   *c*4 Or *"O Rahab and Babylon, / Philistia, Tyre and Cush, / I will record concerning those who acknowledge me: / 'This*   *d*Title: Possibly a tune, "The Suffering of Affliction"   *e*Title: Probably a literary or musical term   *f*3 Hebrew *Sheol*   *g*11 Hebrew *Abaddon*

⁶For who in the skies above can compare with the LORD?
Who is like the LORD among the heavenly beings?
⁷In the council of the holy ones God is greatly feared;
he is more awesome than all who surround him.
⁸O LORD God Almighty, who is like you?
You are mighty, O LORD, and your faithfulness surrounds you.

⁹You rule over the surging sea;
when its waves mount up, you still them.
¹⁰You crushed Rahab like one of the slain;
with your strong arm you scattered your enemies.
¹¹The heavens are yours, and yours also the earth;
you founded the world and all that is in it.
¹²You created the north and the south;
Tabor and Hermon sing for joy at your name.
¹³Your arm is endued with power;
your hand is strong, your right hand exalted.

¹⁴Righteousness and justice are the foundation of your throne;
love and faithfulness go before you.
¹⁵Blessed are those who have learned to acclaim you,
who walk in the light of your presence, O LORD.
¹⁶They rejoice in your name all day long;
they exult in your righteousness.
¹⁷For you are their glory and strength,
and by your favor you exalt our horn.[a]
¹⁸Indeed, our shield[b] belongs to the LORD,
our king to the Holy One of Israel.

¹⁹Once you spoke in a vision,
to your faithful people you said:
"I have bestowed strength on a warrior;
I have exalted a young man from among the people.
²⁰I have found David my servant;
with my sacred oil I have anointed him.
²¹My hand will sustain him;
surely my arm will strengthen him.
²²No enemy will subject him to tribute;
no wicked man will oppress him.
²³I will crush his foes before him
and strike down his adversaries.
²⁴My faithful love will be with him,
and through my name his horn[c] will be exalted.
²⁵I will set his hand over the sea,
his right hand over the rivers.
²⁶He will call out to me, 'You are my Father,
my God, the Rock my Savior.'
²⁷I will also appoint him my firstborn,
the most exalted of the kings of the earth.
²⁸I will maintain my love to him forever,
and my covenant with him will never fail.
²⁹I will establish his line forever,
his throne as long as the heavens endure.

³⁰"If his sons forsake my law
and do not follow my statutes,
³¹if they violate my decrees
and fail to keep my commands,
³²I will punish their sin with the rod,
their iniquity with flogging;
³³but I will not take my love from him,
nor will I ever betray my faithfulness.
³⁴I will not violate my covenant
or alter what my lips have uttered.
³⁵Once for all, I have sworn by my holiness—
and I will not lie to David—
³⁶that his line will continue forever
and his throne endure before me like the sun;
³⁷it will be established forever like the moon,
the faithful witness in the sky."
Selah

³⁸But you have rejected, you have spurned,
you have been very angry with your anointed one.
³⁹You have renounced the covenant with your servant
and have defiled his crown in the dust.
⁴⁰You have broken through all his walls
and reduced his strongholds to ruins.
⁴¹All who pass by have plundered him;
he has become the scorn of his neighbors.

---

a 17 Horn here symbolizes strong one.   *b 18 Or sovereign*   *c 24 Horn here symbolizes strength.*

⁴²You have exalted the right hand of his foes;
  you have made all his enemies rejoice.
⁴³You have turned back the edge of his sword
  and have not supported him in battle.
⁴⁴You have put an end to his splendor
  and cast his throne to the ground.
⁴⁵You have cut short the days of his youth;
  you have covered him with a mantle of shame.   *Selah*

⁴⁶How long, O L ORD? Will you hide yourself forever?
  How long will your wrath burn like fire?
⁴⁷Remember how fleeting is my life.
  For what futility you have created all men!
⁴⁸What man can live and not see death,
  or save himself from the power of the grave*a*?   *Selah*
⁴⁹O Lord, where is your former great love,
  which in your faithfulness you swore to David?
⁵⁰Remember, Lord, how your servant has*b* been mocked,
  how I bear in my heart the taunts of all the nations,
⁵¹the taunts with which your enemies have mocked, O L ORD,
  with which they have mocked every step of your anointed one.

⁵²Praise be to the L ORD forever!
  Amen and Amen.

BOOK IV

Psalms 90–106

Psalm 90

A prayer of Moses the man of God.

¹Lord, you have been our dwelling place
  throughout all generations.
²Before the mountains were born
  or you brought forth the earth and the world,
  from everlasting to everlasting you are God.

³You turn men back to dust,
  saying, "Return to dust, O sons of men."
⁴For a thousand years in your sight
  are like a day that has just gone by,
  or like a watch in the night.
⁵You sweep men away in the sleep of death;
  they are like the new grass of the morning—
⁶though in the morning it springs up new,
  by evening it is dry and withered.

⁷We are consumed by your anger
  and terrified by your indignation.
⁸You have set our iniquities before you,
  our secret sins in the light of your presence.
⁹All our days pass away under your wrath;
  we finish our years with a moan.
¹⁰The length of our days is seventy years—
  or eighty, if we have the strength;
  yet their span*c* is but trouble and sorrow,
  for they quickly pass, and we fly away.

¹¹Who knows the power of your anger?
  For your wrath is as great as the fear that is due you.
¹²Teach us to number our days aright,
  that we may gain a heart of wisdom.

¹³Relent, O L ORD! How long will it be?
  Have compassion on your servants.
¹⁴Satisfy us in the morning with your unfailing love,
  that we may sing for joy and be glad all our days.
¹⁵Make us glad for as many days as you have afflicted us,
  for as many years as we have seen trouble.
¹⁶May your deeds be shown to your servants,
  your splendor to their children.

¹⁷May the favor*d* of the Lord our God rest upon us;
  establish the work of our hands for us—
  yes, establish the work of our hands.

---

a 48 Hebrew *Sheol*   *b* 50 Or *your servants have*   *c* 10 Or *yet the best of them*   *d* 17 Or *beauty*

Psalm 91

¹He who dwells in the shelter of the Most High
will rest in the shadow of the Almighty.ᵃ

²I will sayᵇ of the LORD, "He is my refuge and my fortress,
my God, in whom I trust."

³Surely he will save you from the fowler's snare

ᵃ1 Hebrew *Shaddai*   ᵇ2 Or *He says*

THURSDAY

VERSE FOR THE DAY:
Psalm 90:17

AUTHOR:
Ted Engstrom and David Juroe

PASSAGE FOR THE DAY:
Psalm 90:13–17

Work Benches and Altars

FOR millions, work is a drudgery, a grim necessity. Many hate their work every day of their lives and many find escapes in harmful ways to counterbalance the drudgery. Ask career counselors. Some estimate that as high as 90 percent of the labor market see themselves as *victims*, trapped in an unfulfilled daily round of work.

Certainly if Christianity is going to be relevant, it must have something to say about this problem area. There is a Christian philosophy of the family, education and history. Why not a Christian philosophy or theology of work?

One unfortunate development during the long history of the Christian church was the view during the Medieval period that there was a separation of the laity and the clergy. This difference between the sacred and secular callings still exists. In the architecture of early European cathedrals a screen separated the people from the priests because of the common view which held that working people had not been called of God in their tasks as clergy had. Therefore, they had to worship apart.

Martin Luther saw the fallacy in this and courageously spoke out against it. He tore down this screen, and from him we get the idea of "vocational guidance." He said that man, in his worthier callings, is called just as surely as a man who is called to the priesthood or ministry.

Christianity . . . has always provided a connection between work and worship. Men can dignify labor by doing ordinary things, but as redeemed persons. There lies the difference, and this is where the drudgery dissipates—God is in it. That means that every work bench in a plant is an altar! The psalmist says, "May the favor of the Lord our God rest upon us; establish the work of our hands for us" (Psalm 90:17). So you see, we can please the Lord by our work.

Additional Scripture Readings:
2 Thessalonians 3:6–15;
1 Peter 4:7–11

Go to page 467 for your next devotional reading.

and from the deadly pestilence.
⁴He will cover you with his feathers,
and under his wings you will find refuge;
his faithfulness will be your shield and rampart.
⁵You will not fear the terror of night,
nor the arrow that flies by day,
⁶nor the pestilence that stalks in the darkness,
nor the plague that destroys at midday.
⁷A thousand may fall at your side,
ten thousand at your right hand,
but it will not come near you.
⁸You will only observe with your eyes
and see the punishment of the wicked.

⁹If you make the Most High your dwelling—
even the LORD, who is my refuge—
¹⁰then no harm will befall you,
no disaster will come near your tent.
¹¹For he will command his angels concerning you
to guard you in all your ways;
¹²they will lift you up in their hands,
so that you will not strike your foot against a stone.
¹³You will tread upon the lion and the cobra;
you will trample the great lion and the serpent.

¹⁴"Because he loves me," says the LORD, "I will rescue him;
I will protect him, for he acknowledges my name.
¹⁵He will call upon me, and I will answer him;
I will be with him in trouble,
I will deliver him and honor him.
¹⁶With long life will I satisfy him
and show him my salvation."

Psalm 92

A psalm. A song. For the Sabbath day.

¹It is good to praise the LORD
and make music to your name, O Most High,
²to proclaim your love in the morning
and your faithfulness at night,
³to the music of the ten-stringed lyre
and the melody of the harp.
⁴For you make me glad by your deeds, O LORD;
I sing for joy at the works of your hands.
⁵How great are your works, O LORD,
how profound your thoughts!
⁶The senseless man does not know,
fools do not understand,
⁷that though the wicked spring up like grass
and all evildoers flourish,
they will be forever destroyed.

⁸But you, O LORD, are exalted forever.

⁹For surely your enemies, O LORD,
surely your enemies will perish;
all evildoers will be scattered.
¹⁰You have exalted my horn[a] like that of a wild ox;
fine oils have been poured upon me.
¹¹My eyes have seen the defeat of my adversaries;
my ears have heard the rout of my wicked foes.

¹²The righteous will flourish like a palm tree,
they will grow like a cedar of Lebanon;
¹³planted in the house of the LORD,
they will flourish in the courts of our God.
¹⁴They will still bear fruit in old age,
they will stay fresh and green,
¹⁵proclaiming, "The LORD is upright;
he is my Rock, and there is no wickedness in him."

Psalm 93

¹The LORD reigns, he is robed in majesty;
the LORD is robed in majesty
and is armed with strength.
The world is firmly established;
it cannot be moved.
²Your throne was established long ago;
you are from all eternity.

³The seas have lifted up, O LORD,
the seas have lifted up their voice;
the seas have lifted up their pounding waves.
⁴Mightier than the thunder of the great waters,
mightier than the breakers of the sea—
the LORD on high is mighty.

---

[a] 10 *Horn* here symbolizes strength.

Psalm 94

5Your statutes stand firm;
  holiness adorns your house
  for endless days, O LORD.

1O LORD, the God who avenges,
  O God who avenges, shine forth.
2Rise up, O Judge of the earth;
  pay back to the proud what they deserve.
3How long will the wicked, O LORD,
  how long will the wicked be jubilant?

4They pour out arrogant words;
  all the evildoers are full of boasting.

5They crush your people, O LORD;
  they oppress your inheritance.
6They slay the widow and the alien;
  they murder the fatherless.
7They say, "The LORD does not see;
  the God of Jacob pays no heed."

8Take heed, you senseless ones among the people;
  you fools, when will you become wise?
9Does he who implanted the ear not hear?
  Does he who formed the eye not see?
10Does he who disciplines nations not punish?

FRIDAY

VERSE FOR THE DAY:
Psalm 91:11

AUTHOR:
Billy Graham

PASSAGE FOR THE DAY:
Psalm 91:9–16

Nearer Than You Think

REPORTS continually flow to my attention from many places around the world telling of visitors of the angelic order appearing, ministering, fellowshiping and disappearing. They warn of God's impending judgment; they spell out the tenderness of his love; they meet a desperate need; then they are gone. Of one thing we can be sure: angels never draw attention to themselves but ascribe glory to God and press his message upon the hearers as a delivering and sustaining word of the highest order.

Demonic activity and Satan worship are on the increase in all parts of the world. The devil is alive and more at work than at any other time. The Bible says that since he realizes his time is short, his activity will increase. Through his demonic influences, he does succeed in turning many away from true faith; but we can still say that his evil activities are countered for the people of God by his ministering spirits, the holy ones of the angelic order. They are vigorous in delivering the heirs of salvation from the stratagems of evil men. They cannot fail.

Believers, look up—take courage. The angels are nearer than you think. For after all, "God will command his angels concerning you to guard you in all your ways; they will lift you up in their hands, so that you will not strike your foot against a stone" (Psalm 91:11–12).

Additional Scripture Readings:
Ephesians 6:10–18; Hebrews 1:1–14

Go to page 470 for your next devotional reading.

Does he who teaches man lack knowledge?
¹¹The LORD knows the thoughts of man;
he knows that they are futile.

¹²Blessed is the man you discipline, O LORD,
the man you teach from your law;
¹³you grant him relief from days of trouble,
till a pit is dug for the wicked.
¹⁴For the LORD will not reject his people;
he will never forsake his inheritance.
¹⁵Judgment will again be founded on righteousness,
and all the upright in heart will follow it.

¹⁶Who will rise up for me against the wicked?
Who will take a stand for me against evildoers?
¹⁷Unless the LORD had given me help,
I would soon have dwelt in the silence of death.
¹⁸When I said, "My foot is slipping,"
your love, O LORD, supported me.
¹⁹When anxiety was great within me,
your consolation brought joy to my soul.

²⁰Can a corrupt throne be allied with you—
one that brings on misery by its decrees?
²¹They band together against the righteous
and condemn the innocent to death.
²²But the LORD has become my fortress,
and my God the rock in whom I take refuge.
²³He will repay them for their sins
and destroy them for their wickedness;
the LORD our God will destroy them.

Psalm 95

¹Come, let us sing for joy to the LORD;
let us shout aloud to the Rock of our salvation.
²Let us come before him with thanksgiving
and extol him with music and song.

³For the LORD is the great God,
the great King above all gods.
⁴In his hand are the depths of the earth,
and the mountain peaks belong to him.
⁵The sea is his, for he made it,
and his hands formed the dry land.

⁶Come, let us bow down in worship,
let us kneel before the LORD our Maker;
⁷for he is our God
and we are the people of his pasture,
the flock under his care.

Today, if you hear his voice,
⁸ do not harden your hearts as you did at Meribah,ᵃ
as you did that day at Massahᵇ in the desert,
⁹where your fathers tested and tried me,
though they had seen what I did.
¹⁰For forty years I was angry with that generation;
I said, "They are a people whose hearts go astray,
and they have not known my ways."
¹¹So I declared on oath in my anger,
"They shall never enter my rest."

Psalm 96

¹Sing to the LORD a new song;
sing to the LORD, all the earth.
²Sing to the LORD, praise his name;
proclaim his salvation day after day.
³Declare his glory among the nations,
his marvelous deeds among all peoples.

⁴For great is the LORD and most worthy of praise;
he is to be feared above all gods.
⁵For all the gods of the nations are idols,
but the LORD made the heavens.
⁶Splendor and majesty are before him;
strength and glory are in his sanctuary.

⁷Ascribe to the LORD, O families of nations,
ascribe to the LORD glory and strength.
⁸Ascribe to the LORD the glory due his name;
bring an offering and come into his courts.
⁹Worship the LORD in the splendor of hisᶜ holiness;

ᵃ8 Meribah means *quarreling*.   ᵇ8 Massah means *testing*.   ᶜ9 Or LORD *with the splendor of*

tremble before him, all the earth.
¹⁰Say among the nations, "The LORD reigns."
The world is firmly established, it cannot be moved;
he will judge the peoples with equity.
¹¹Let the heavens rejoice, let the earth be glad;
let the sea resound, and all that is in it;
¹² let the fields be jubilant, and everything in them.
Then all the trees of the forest will sing for joy;
¹³ they will sing before the LORD, for he comes,
he comes to judge the earth.
He will judge the world in righteousness
and the peoples in his truth.

Psalm 97

¹The LORD reigns, let the earth be glad;
let the distant shores rejoice.

²Clouds and thick darkness surround him;
righteousness and justice are the foundation of his throne.
³Fire goes before him
and consumes his foes on every side.
⁴His lightning lights up the world;
the earth sees and trembles.
⁵The mountains melt like wax before the LORD,
before the Lord of all the earth.
⁶The heavens proclaim his righteousness,
and all the peoples see his glory.

⁷All who worship images are put to shame,
those who boast in idols—
worship him, all you gods!

⁸Zion hears and rejoices
and the villages of Judah are glad
because of your judgments, O LORD.
⁹For you, O LORD, are the Most High over all the earth;
you are exalted far above all gods.

¹⁰Let those who love the LORD hate evil,
for he guards the lives of his faithful ones
and delivers them from the hand of the wicked.
¹¹Light is shed upon the righteous
and joy on the upright in heart.
¹²Rejoice in the LORD, you who are righteous,
and praise his holy name.

Psalm 98

A psalm.

¹Sing to the LORD a new song,
for he has done marvelous things;
his right hand and his holy arm
have worked salvation for him.
²The LORD has made his salvation known
and revealed his righteousness to the nations.
³He has remembered his love
and his faithfulness to the house of Israel;
all the ends of the earth have seen
the salvation of our God.

⁴Shout for joy to the LORD, all the earth,
burst into jubilant song with music;
⁵make music to the LORD with the harp,
with the harp and the sound of singing,
⁶with trumpets and the blast of the ram's horn—
shout for joy before the LORD, the King.

⁷Let the sea resound, and everything in it,
the world, and all who live in it.
⁸Let the rivers clap their hands,
let the mountains sing together for joy;
⁹let them sing before the LORD,
for he comes to judge the earth.
He will judge the world in righteousness
and the peoples with equity.

Psalm 99

¹The LORD reigns,
let the nations tremble;
he sits enthroned between the cherubim,
let the earth shake.
²Great is the LORD in Zion;
he is exalted over all the nations.
³Let them praise your great and awesome name—
he is holy.

⁴The King is mighty, he loves justice—

WEEKENDING

RECHARGE

It is important for us to grasp the truth that there is no shame in neediness. For those of us who were raised to appear strong, neediness is a horrible condition from which we turn away. We don't mind giving generously or acting with compassion toward those who are needy around us, but we don't let ourselves get to the place where we must receive help from others. This fear of unmet needs can drive us to acquire, achieve and accumulate symbols of satisfaction . . .

These symbols of satisfaction, while holding at bay our gnawing sense of insecurity and self-doubt, also can cloud our view of what is important. They may also inhibit our pursuing the very things we need most in life: relationships in which we are known intimately, in which we share vulnerably, and in which we discover love and accountability.

– *John F. Westfall*

REVIVE
Saturday: 1 Corinthians 1:26–31
Sunday: Philippians 4:10–20

Go to page 474 for your next devotional reading.

you have established equity;
in Jacob you have done
what is just and right.
⁵Exalt the LORD our God
and worship at his footstool;
he is holy.

⁶Moses and Aaron were among his
priests,
Samuel was among those who
called on his name;
they called on the LORD
and he answered them.
⁷He spoke to them from the pillar of
cloud;
they kept his statutes and the
decrees he gave them.

⁸O LORD our God,
you answered them;
you were to Israel*a* a forgiving God,
though you punished their
misdeeds.*b*
⁹Exalt the LORD our God
and worship at his holy mountain,
for the LORD our God is holy.

Psalm 100

A psalm. For giving thanks.

¹Shout for joy to the LORD, all the
earth.
² Worship the LORD with gladness;
come before him with joyful songs.
³Know that the LORD is God.
It is he who made us, and we are
his*c*;
we are his people, the sheep of his
pasture.

⁴Enter his gates with thanksgiving
and his courts with praise;
give thanks to him and praise his
name.
⁵For the LORD is good and his love
endures forever;
his faithfulness continues through
all generations.

Psalm 101

Of David. A psalm.

¹I will sing of your love and justice;
to you, O LORD, I will sing praise.
²I will be careful to lead a blameless
life—
when will you come to me?

I will walk in my house
with blameless heart.
³I will set before my eyes
no vile thing.

The deeds of faithless men I hate;
they will not cling to me.
⁴Men of perverse heart shall be far
from me;
I will have nothing to do with evil.

⁵Whoever slanders his neighbor in
secret,
him will I put to silence;
whoever has haughty eyes and a
proud heart,
him will I not endure.

⁶My eyes will be on the faithful in the
land,
that they may dwell with me;
he whose walk is blameless
will minister to me.

⁷No one who practices deceit
will dwell in my house;
no one who speaks falsely
will stand in my presence.

⁸Every morning I will put to silence
all the wicked in the land;
I will cut off every evildoer
from the city of the LORD.

Psalm 102

A prayer of an afflicted man. When he is
faint and pours out his lament before
the LORD.

¹Hear my prayer, O LORD;
let my cry for help come to you.
²Do not hide your face from me
when I am in distress.
Turn your ear to me;
when I call, answer me quickly.

³For my days vanish like smoke;
my bones burn like glowing embers.
⁴My heart is blighted and withered like
grass;
I forget to eat my food.
⁵Because of my loud groaning
I am reduced to skin and bones.
⁶I am like a desert owl,
like an owl among the ruins.
⁷I lie awake; I have become
like a bird alone on a roof.
⁸All day long my enemies taunt me;
those who rail against me use my
name as a curse.

a8 Hebrew *them*   *b8* Or / *an avenger of the wrongs done to them*   *c3* Or *and not we ourselves*

⁹For I eat ashes as my food
and mingle my drink with tears
¹⁰because of your great wrath,
for you have taken me up and
thrown me aside.
¹¹My days are like the evening shadow;
I wither away like grass.

¹²But you, O LORD, sit enthroned
forever;
your renown endures through all
generations.
¹³You will arise and have compassion
on Zion,
for it is time to show favor to her;
the appointed time has come.
¹⁴For her stones are dear to your
servants;
her very dust moves them to pity.
¹⁵The nations will fear the name of the
LORD,
all the kings of the earth will revere
your glory.
¹⁶For the LORD will rebuild Zion
and appear in his glory.
¹⁷He will respond to the prayer of the
destitute;
he will not despise their plea.

¹⁸Let this be written for a future
generation,
that a people not yet created may
praise the LORD:
¹⁹"The LORD looked down from his
sanctuary on high,
from heaven he viewed the earth,
²⁰to hear the groans of the prisoners
and release those condemned to
death."
²¹So the name of the LORD will be
declared in Zion
and his praise in Jerusalem
²²when the peoples and the kingdoms
assemble to worship the LORD.

²³In the course of my life[a] he broke
my strength;
he cut short my days.
²⁴So I said:
"Do not take me away, O my God,
in the midst of my days;
your years go on through all
generations.
²⁵In the beginning you laid the
foundations of the earth,
and the heavens are the work of
your hands.
²⁶They will perish, but you remain;
they will all wear out like a
garment.
Like clothing you will change them
and they will be discarded.
²⁷But you remain the same,
and your years will never end.
²⁸The children of your servants will live
in your presence;
their descendants will be
established before you."

Psalm 103

Of David.

¹Praise the LORD, O my soul;
all my inmost being, praise his holy
name.
²Praise the LORD, O my soul,
and forget not all his benefits—
³who forgives all your sins
and heals all your diseases,
⁴who redeems your life from the pit
and crowns you with love and
compassion,
⁵who satisfies your desires with good
things
so that your youth is renewed like
the eagle's.

⁶The LORD works righteousness
and justice for all the oppressed.

⁷He made known his ways to Moses,
his deeds to the people of Israel:
⁸The LORD is compassionate and
gracious,
slow to anger, abounding in love.
⁹He will not always accuse,
nor will he harbor his anger forever;
¹⁰he does not treat us as our sins
deserve
or repay us according to our
iniquities.
¹¹For as high as the heavens are above
the earth,
so great is his love for those who
fear him;
¹²as far as the east is from the west,
so far has he removed our
transgressions from us.
¹³As a father has compassion on his
children,
so the LORD has compassion on
those who fear him;
¹⁴for he knows how we are formed,
he remembers that we are dust.
¹⁵As for man, his days are like grass,

---

[a] 23 Or *By his power*

he flourishes like a flower of the
  field;
¹⁶the wind blows over it and it is gone,
  and its place remembers it no more.
¹⁷But from everlasting to everlasting
  the LORD's love is with those who
    fear him,
  and his righteousness with their
    children's children—
¹⁸with those who keep his covenant
  and remember to obey his precepts.

¹⁹The LORD has established his throne in
    heaven,
  and his kingdom rules over all.

²⁰Praise the LORD, you his angels,
  you mighty ones who do his
    bidding,
  who obey his word.
²¹Praise the LORD, all his heavenly hosts,
  you his servants who do his will.
²²Praise the LORD, all his works
  everywhere in his dominion.

Praise the LORD, O my soul.

Psalm 104

¹Praise the LORD, O my soul.

O LORD my God, you are very great;
  you are clothed with splendor and
    majesty.
²He wraps himself in light as with a
    garment;
  he stretches out the heavens like a
    tent
³   and lays the beams of his upper
      chambers on their waters.
  He makes the clouds his chariot
  and rides on the wings of the wind.
⁴He makes winds his messengers,ᵃ
  flames of fire his servants.

⁵He set the earth on its foundations;
  it can never be moved.
⁶You covered it with the deep as with a
    garment;
  the waters stood above the
    mountains.
⁷But at your rebuke the waters fled,
  at the sound of your thunder they
    took to flight;
⁸they flowed over the mountains,
  they went down into the valleys,
  to the place you assigned for them.
⁹You set a boundary they cannot cross;
  never again will they cover the
    earth.

¹⁰He makes springs pour water into the
    ravines;
  it flows between the mountains.
¹¹They give water to all the beasts of
    the field;
  the wild donkeys quench their
    thirst.
¹²The birds of the air nest by the
    waters;
  they sing among the branches.
¹³He waters the mountains from his
    upper chambers;
  the earth is satisfied by the fruit of
    his work.
¹⁴He makes grass grow for the cattle,
  and plants for man to cultivate—
  bringing forth food from the earth:
¹⁵wine that gladdens the heart of man,
  oil to make his face shine,
  and bread that sustains his heart.
¹⁶The trees of the LORD are well
    watered,
  the cedars of Lebanon that he
    planted.
¹⁷There the birds make their nests;
  the stork has its home in the pine
    trees.
¹⁸The high mountains belong to the
    wild goats;
  the crags are a refuge for the
    coneys.ᵇ

¹⁹The moon marks off the seasons,
  and the sun knows when to go
    down.
²⁰You bring darkness, it becomes night,
  and all the beasts of the forest
    prowl.
²¹The lions roar for their prey
  and seek their food from God.
²²The sun rises, and they steal away;
  they return and lie down in their
    dens.
²³Then man goes out to his work,
  to his labor until evening.

²⁴How many are your works, O LORD!
  In wisdom you made them all;
  the earth is full of your creatures.
²⁵There is the sea, vast and spacious,
  teeming with creatures beyond
    number—
  living things both large and small.
²⁶There the ships go to and fro,
  and the leviathan, which you
    formed to frolic there.

²⁷These all look to you

ᵃ4 Or *angels*   ᵇ18 That is, the hyrax or rock badger

to give them their food at the
proper time.
²⁸When you give it to them,
they gather it up;
when you open your hand,
they are satisfied with good things.
²⁹When you hide your face,
they are terrified;
when you take away their breath,
they die and return to the dust.
³⁰When you send your Spirit,
they are created,
and you renew the face of the earth.

³¹May the glory of the LORD endure
forever;
may the LORD rejoice in his works—
³²he who looks at the earth, and it
trembles,

MONDAY

VERSE FOR THE DAY:
Psalm 103:15

AUTHOR:
James Dobson

PASSAGE FOR THE DAY:
Psalm 103:1–22

A Better Way

I HAVE examined America's breathless lifestyle and find it to be *unacceptable*. At forty-three years of age (I would be forty-four but I was sick a year), I have been thinking about the stages of my earthly existence and what they will represent at its conclusion. There was a time when all of my friends were graduating from high school. Then I recall so many who entered colleges around the country. And alas, I lived through a phase when everyone seemed to be getting married. Then a few years later, we were besieged by baby shower announcements. You see, my generation is slowly but relentlessly moving through the decades, as have 2,400 generations that preceded it. Now, it occurs to me that a time will soon come when my friends will be dying. ["Wasn't it tragic what happened to Charles Painter yesterday?"]

My aunt, Naomi Dobson, wrote me shortly before her death in 1978. She said, "It seems like every day another of my close friends either passes away or is afflicted with a terrible disease." Obviously, she was in that final phase of her generation. Now she is also gone.

What does this have to do with my life today? How does it relate to yours? I'm suggesting that we stop and consider the brevity of our years on earth, perhaps finding new motivation to preserve the values that will endure. Why should we work ourselves into an early grave, missing those precious moments with loved ones who crave our affection and attention? It is a question that every man and woman should consider.

Let me offer this final word of encouragement for those who are determined to slow the pace: once you get out from under constant pressure, you'll wonder why you drove yourself so hard for all those years. *There is a better way!*

Additional Scripture Readings:
Psalm 90:1–12; James 4:13–17

*Go to page 481 for your next
devotional reading.*

who touches the mountains, and they smoke.

³³I will sing to the Lord all my life;
 I will sing praise to my God as long as I live.
³⁴May my meditation be pleasing to him,
 as I rejoice in the Lord.
³⁵But may sinners vanish from the earth
 and the wicked be no more.

Praise the Lord, O my soul.

Praise the Lord.ᵃ

Psalm 105

¹Give thanks to the Lord, call on his name;
 make known among the nations what he has done.
²Sing to him, sing praise to him;
 tell of all his wonderful acts.
³Glory in his holy name;
 let the hearts of those who seek the Lord rejoice.
⁴Look to the Lord and his strength;
 seek his face always.

⁵Remember the wonders he has done,
 his miracles, and the judgments he pronounced,
⁶O descendants of Abraham his servant,
 O sons of Jacob, his chosen ones.
⁷He is the Lord our God;
 his judgments are in all the earth.

⁸He remembers his covenant forever,
 the word he commanded, for a thousand generations,
⁹the covenant he made with Abraham,
 the oath he swore to Isaac.
¹⁰He confirmed it to Jacob as a decree,
 to Israel as an everlasting covenant:
¹¹"To you I will give the land of Canaan
 as the portion you will inherit."

¹²When they were but few in number,
 few indeed, and strangers in it,
¹³they wandered from nation to nation,
 from one kingdom to another.
¹⁴He allowed no one to oppress them;
 for their sake he rebuked kings:
¹⁵"Do not touch my anointed ones;
 do my prophets no harm."

¹⁶He called down famine on the land
 and destroyed all their supplies of food;
¹⁷and he sent a man before them—
 Joseph, sold as a slave.
¹⁸They bruised his feet with shackles,
 his neck was put in irons,
¹⁹till what he foretold came to pass,
 till the word of the Lord proved him true.
²⁰The king sent and released him,
 the ruler of peoples set him free.
²¹He made him master of his household,
 ruler over all he possessed,
²²to instruct his princes as he pleased
 and teach his elders wisdom.

²³Then Israel entered Egypt;
 Jacob lived as an alien in the land of Ham.
²⁴The Lord made his people very fruitful;
 he made them too numerous for their foes,
²⁵whose hearts he turned to hate his people,
 to conspire against his servants.
²⁶He sent Moses his servant,
 and Aaron, whom he had chosen.
²⁷They performed his miraculous signs among them,
 his wonders in the land of Ham.
²⁸He sent darkness and made the land dark—
 for had they not rebelled against his words?
²⁹He turned their waters into blood,
 causing their fish to die.
³⁰Their land teemed with frogs,
 which went up into the bedrooms of their rulers.
³¹He spoke, and there came swarms of flies,
 and gnats throughout their country.
³²He turned their rain into hail,
 with lightning throughout their land;
³³he struck down their vines and fig trees
 and shattered the trees of their country.
³⁴He spoke, and the locusts came,
 grasshoppers without number;
³⁵they ate up every green thing in their land,
 ate up the produce of their soil.
³⁶Then he struck down all the firstborn in their land,
 the firstfruits of all their manhood.

ᵃ35 Hebrew *Hallelu Yah*; in the Septuagint this line stands at the beginning of Psalm 105.

⁳⁷He brought out Israel, laden with silver and gold,
and from among their tribes no one faltered.
³⁸Egypt was glad when they left,
because dread of Israel had fallen on them.
³⁹He spread out a cloud as a covering,
and a fire to give light at night.
⁴⁰They asked, and he brought them quail
and satisfied them with the bread of heaven.
⁴¹He opened the rock, and water gushed out;
like a river it flowed in the desert.

⁴²For he remembered his holy promise
given to his servant Abraham.
⁴³He brought out his people with rejoicing,
his chosen ones with shouts of joy;
⁴⁴he gave them the lands of the nations,
and they fell heir to what others had toiled for—
⁴⁵that they might keep his precepts
and observe his laws.

Praise the Lord.[a]

Psalm 106

¹Praise the Lord.[b]

Give thanks to the Lord, for he is good;
his love endures forever.
²Who can proclaim the mighty acts of the Lord
or fully declare his praise?
³Blessed are they who maintain justice,
who constantly do what is right.
⁴Remember me, O Lord, when you show favor to your people,
come to my aid when you save them,
⁵that I may enjoy the prosperity of your chosen ones,
that I may share in the joy of your nation
and join your inheritance in giving praise.

⁶We have sinned, even as our fathers did;
we have done wrong and acted wickedly.
⁷When our fathers were in Egypt,
they gave no thought to your miracles;
they did not remember your many kindnesses,
and they rebelled by the sea, the Red Sea.[c]
⁸Yet he saved them for his name's sake,
to make his mighty power known.
⁹He rebuked the Red Sea, and it dried up;
he led them through the depths as through a desert.
¹⁰He saved them from the hand of the foe;
from the hand of the enemy he redeemed them.
¹¹The waters covered their adversaries;
not one of them survived.
¹²Then they believed his promises
and sang his praise.

¹³But they soon forgot what he had done
and did not wait for his counsel.
¹⁴In the desert they gave in to their craving;
in the wasteland they put God to the test.
¹⁵So he gave them what they asked for,
but sent a wasting disease upon them.

¹⁶In the camp they grew envious of Moses
and of Aaron, who was consecrated to the Lord.
¹⁷The earth opened up and swallowed Dathan;
it buried the company of Abiram.
¹⁸Fire blazed among their followers;
a flame consumed the wicked.

¹⁹At Horeb they made a calf
and worshiped an idol cast from metal.
²⁰They exchanged their Glory
for an image of a bull, which eats grass.
²¹They forgot the God who saved them,
who had done great things in Egypt,
²²miracles in the land of Ham
and awesome deeds by the Red Sea.
²³So he said he would destroy them—
had not Moses, his chosen one,
stood in the breach before him
to keep his wrath from destroying them.

---

[a]45 Hebrew *Hallelu Yah*   [b]1 Hebrew *Hallelu Yah*; also in verse 48   [c]7 Hebrew *Yam Suph*; that is, Sea of Reeds; also in verses 9 and 22

²⁴Then they despised the pleasant land;
 they did not believe his promise.
²⁵They grumbled in their tents
 and did not obey the LORD.
²⁶So he swore to them with uplifted hand
 that he would make them fall in the desert,
²⁷make their descendants fall among the nations
 and scatter them throughout the lands.

²⁸They yoked themselves to the Baal of Peor
 and ate sacrifices offered to lifeless gods;
²⁹they provoked the LORD to anger by their wicked deeds,
 and a plague broke out among them.
³⁰But Phinehas stood up and intervened,
 and the plague was checked.
³¹This was credited to him as righteousness
 for endless generations to come.

³²By the waters of Meribah they angered the LORD,
 and trouble came to Moses because of them;
³³for they rebelled against the Spirit of God,
 and rash words came from Moses' lips.*ᵃ*

³⁴They did not destroy the peoples
 as the LORD had commanded them,
³⁵but they mingled with the nations
 and adopted their customs.
³⁶They worshiped their idols,
 which became a snare to them.
³⁷They sacrificed their sons
 and their daughters to demons.
³⁸They shed innocent blood,
 the blood of their sons and daughters,
 whom they sacrificed to the idols of Canaan,
 and the land was desecrated by their blood.
³⁹They defiled themselves by what they did;
 by their deeds they prostituted themselves.

⁴⁰Therefore the LORD was angry with his people
 and abhorred his inheritance.
⁴¹He handed them over to the nations,
 and their foes ruled over them.
⁴²Their enemies oppressed them
 and subjected them to their power.
⁴³Many times he delivered them,
 but they were bent on rebellion
 and they wasted away in their sin.

⁴⁴But he took note of their distress
 when he heard their cry;
⁴⁵for their sake he remembered his covenant
 and out of his great love he relented.
⁴⁶He caused them to be pitied
 by all who held them captive.

⁴⁷Save us, O LORD our God,
 and gather us from the nations,
that we may give thanks to your holy name
 and glory in your praise.

⁴⁸Praise be to the LORD, the God of Israel,
 from everlasting to everlasting.
Let all the people say, "Amen!"

Praise the LORD.

BOOK V

Psalms 107–150

Psalm 107

¹Give thanks to the LORD, for he is good;
 his love endures forever.
²Let the redeemed of the LORD say this—
 those he redeemed from the hand of the foe,
³those he gathered from the lands,
 from east and west, from north and south.*ᵇ*

⁴Some wandered in desert wastelands,
 finding no way to a city where they could settle.
⁵They were hungry and thirsty,
 and their lives ebbed away.
⁶Then they cried out to the LORD in their trouble,
 and he delivered them from their distress.
⁷He led them by a straight way
 to a city where they could settle.

ᵃ33 Or *against his spirit, / and rash words came from his lips*   *ᵇ3* Hebrew *north and the sea*

⁸Let them give thanks to the LORD for his unfailing love
and his wonderful deeds for men,
⁹for he satisfies the thirsty
and fills the hungry with good things.

¹⁰Some sat in darkness and the deepest gloom,
prisoners suffering in iron chains,
¹¹for they had rebelled against the words of God
and despised the counsel of the Most High.
¹²So he subjected them to bitter labor;
they stumbled, and there was no one to help.
¹³Then they cried to the LORD in their trouble,
and he saved them from their distress.
¹⁴He brought them out of darkness and the deepest gloom
and broke away their chains.
¹⁵Let them give thanks to the LORD for his unfailing love
and his wonderful deeds for men,
¹⁶for he breaks down gates of bronze
and cuts through bars of iron.

¹⁷Some became fools through their rebellious ways
and suffered affliction because of their iniquities.
¹⁸They loathed all food
and drew near the gates of death.
¹⁹Then they cried to the LORD in their trouble,
and he saved them from their distress.
²⁰He sent forth his word and healed them;
he rescued them from the grave.
²¹Let them give thanks to the LORD for his unfailing love
and his wonderful deeds for men.
²²Let them sacrifice thank offerings
and tell of his works with songs of joy.

²³Others went out on the sea in ships;
they were merchants on the mighty waters.
²⁴They saw the works of the LORD,
his wonderful deeds in the deep.
²⁵For he spoke and stirred up a tempest
that lifted high the waves.
²⁶They mounted up to the heavens and went down to the depths;
in their peril their courage melted away.
²⁷They reeled and staggered like drunken men;
they were at their wits' end.
²⁸Then they cried out to the LORD in their trouble,
and he brought them out of their distress.
²⁹He stilled the storm to a whisper;
the waves of the sea were hushed.
³⁰They were glad when it grew calm,
and he guided them to their desired haven.
³¹Let them give thanks to the LORD for his unfailing love
and his wonderful deeds for men.
³²Let them exalt him in the assembly of the people
and praise him in the council of the elders.

³³He turned rivers into a desert,
flowing springs into thirsty ground,
³⁴and fruitful land into a salt waste,
because of the wickedness of those who lived there.
³⁵He turned the desert into pools of water
and the parched ground into flowing springs;
³⁶there he brought the hungry to live,
and they founded a city where they could settle.
³⁷They sowed fields and planted vineyards
that yielded a fruitful harvest;
³⁸he blessed them, and their numbers greatly increased,
and he did not let their herds diminish.

³⁹Then their numbers decreased, and they were humbled
by oppression, calamity and sorrow;
⁴⁰he who pours contempt on nobles
made them wander in a trackless waste.
⁴¹But he lifted the needy out of their affliction
and increased their families like flocks.
⁴²The upright see and rejoice,
but all the wicked shut their mouths.

⁴³Whoever is wise, let him heed these things
and consider the great love of the LORD.

Psalm 108

A song. A psalm of David.

1My heart is steadfast, O God;
  I will sing and make music with all my soul.
2Awake, harp and lyre!
  I will awaken the dawn.
3I will praise you, O LORD, among the nations;
  I will sing of you among the peoples.
4For great is your love, higher than the heavens;
  your faithfulness reaches to the skies.
5Be exalted, O God, above the heavens,
  and let your glory be over all the earth.

6Save us and help us with your right hand,
  that those you love may be delivered.
7God has spoken from his sanctuary:
  "In triumph I will parcel out Shechem
  and measure off the Valley of Succoth.
8Gilead is mine, Manasseh is mine;
  Ephraim is my helmet,
  Judah my scepter.
9Moab is my washbasin,
  upon Edom I toss my sandal;
  over Philistia I shout in triumph."

10Who will bring me to the fortified city?
  Who will lead me to Edom?
11Is it not you, O God, you who have rejected us
  and no longer go out with our armies?
12Give us aid against the enemy,
  for the help of man is worthless.
13With God we will gain the victory,
  and he will trample down our enemies.

Psalm 109

For the director of music. Of David. A psalm.

1O God, whom I praise,
  do not remain silent,
2for wicked and deceitful men have opened their mouths against me;
  they have spoken against me with lying tongues.
3With words of hatred they surround me;
  they attack me without cause.
4In return for my friendship they accuse me,
  but I am a man of prayer.
5They repay me evil for good,
  and hatred for my friendship.

6Appoint*a* an evil man*b* to oppose him;
  let an accuser*c* stand at his right hand.
7When he is tried, let him be found guilty,
  and may his prayers condemn him.
8May his days be few;
  may another take his place of leadership.
9May his children be fatherless
  and his wife a widow.
10May his children be wandering beggars;
  may they be driven*d* from their ruined homes.
11May a creditor seize all he has;
  may strangers plunder the fruits of his labor.
12May no one extend kindness to him
  or take pity on his fatherless children.
13May his descendants be cut off,
  their names blotted out from the next generation.
14May the iniquity of his fathers be remembered before the LORD;
  may the sin of his mother never be blotted out.
15May their sins always remain before the LORD,
  that he may cut off the memory of them from the earth.

16For he never thought of doing a kindness,
  but hounded to death the poor
  and the needy and the brokenhearted.
17He loved to pronounce a curse—
  may it*e* come on him;
  he found no pleasure in blessing—
  may it be*f* far from him.
18He wore cursing as his garment;
  it entered into his body like water,

---

*a*6 Or *They say:, "Appoint* (with quotation marks at the end of verse 19) *b*6 Or *the Evil One* *c*6 Or *let Satan* *d*10 Septuagint; Hebrew *sought* *e*17 Or *curse, / and it has* *f*17 Or *blessing, / and it is*

into his bones like oil.
¹⁹May it be like a cloak wrapped about him,
like a belt tied forever around him.
²⁰May this be the LORD's payment to my accusers,
to those who speak evil of me.

²¹But you, O Sovereign LORD,
deal well with me for your name's sake;
out of the goodness of your love, deliver me.
²²For I am poor and needy,
and my heart is wounded within me.
²³I fade away like an evening shadow;
I am shaken off like a locust.
²⁴My knees give way from fasting;
my body is thin and gaunt.
²⁵I am an object of scorn to my accusers;
when they see me, they shake their heads.

²⁶Help me, O LORD my God;
save me in accordance with your love.
²⁷Let them know that it is your hand,
that you, O LORD, have done it.
²⁸They may curse, but you will bless;
when they attack they will be put to shame,
but your servant will rejoice.
²⁹My accusers will be clothed with disgrace
and wrapped in shame as in a cloak.

³⁰With my mouth I will greatly extol the LORD;
in the great throng I will praise him.
³¹For he stands at the right hand of the needy one,
to save his life from those who condemn him.

Psalm 110

Of David. A psalm.

¹The LORD says to my Lord:
"Sit at my right hand
until I make your enemies
a footstool for your feet."

²The LORD will extend your mighty scepter from Zion;
you will rule in the midst of your enemies.
³Your troops will be willing
on your day of battle.
Arrayed in holy majesty,
from the womb of the dawn
you will receive the dew of your youth.^a

⁴The LORD has sworn
and will not change his mind:
"You are a priest forever,
in the order of Melchizedek."

⁵The Lord is at your right hand;
he will crush kings on the day of his wrath.
⁶He will judge the nations, heaping up the dead
and crushing the rulers of the whole earth.
⁷He will drink from a brook beside the way^b;
therefore he will lift up his head.

Psalm 111^c

¹Praise the LORD.^d

I will extol the LORD with all my heart
in the council of the upright and in the assembly.

²Great are the works of the LORD;
they are pondered by all who delight in them.
³Glorious and majestic are his deeds,
and his righteousness endures forever.
⁴He has caused his wonders to be remembered;
the LORD is gracious and compassionate.
⁵He provides food for those who fear him;
he remembers his covenant forever.
⁶He has shown his people the power of his works,
giving them the lands of other nations.
⁷The works of his hands are faithful and just;
all his precepts are trustworthy.

---

^a3 Or / *your young men will come to you like the dew*   ^b7 Or / *The One who grants succession will set him in authority*   ^cThis psalm is an acrostic poem, the lines of which begin with the successive letters of the Hebrew alphabet.   ^d1 Hebrew *Hallelu Yah*

⁸They are steadfast for ever and ever,
  done in faithfulness and
    uprightness.
⁹He provided redemption for his
    people;
  he ordained his covenant forever—
  holy and awesome is his name.

¹⁰The fear of the LORD is the beginning
    of wisdom;
  all who follow his precepts have
    good understanding.
  To him belongs eternal praise.

Psalm 112[a]

¹Praise the LORD.[b]

Blessed is the man who fears the
    LORD,
  who finds great delight in his
    commands.

²His children will be mighty in the
    land;
  the generation of the upright will be
    blessed.
³Wealth and riches are in his house,

---

[a] This psalm is an acrostic poem, the lines of which begin with the successive letters of the Hebrew alphabet.   [b] 1 Hebrew *Hallelu Yah*

TUESDAY

VERSE FOR THE DAY:
Psalm 111:10

AUTHOR:
Don Wyrtzen

PASSAGE FOR THE DAY:
Psalm 111:5–10

The Obvious Outcome

THE psalmist develops his theme very specifically here. Our compassionate and gracious Lord has expressed himself by helping his people—by providing a daily supply of food, by remembering his covenant and keeping his promises to make them victorious in conquest, by bequeathing to them the heathen lands around them, by revealing his power. And wonder of wonders, when they continued to grumble and complain against him, he provided a way back to him—a plan of redemption and forgiveness!

My Lord is no less active in my life today. He provides for my basic needs—food, shelter, clothing—by allowing me to serve him through meaningful and fulfilling work. He has blessed me with rich personal relationships with my family and intimate friends. To guide me in facing the hassles of daily living, he has sent his Holy Spirit, and I find myself clinging to him every day.

The conclusion of this psalm reminds me of Proverbs 1:7: "The fear (awesome respect) of the LORD is the beginning of knowledge." It seems that following his precepts in obedience should be the obvious outcome of my gratitude for all he's done for me!

I pray that you will fill me with an awesome respect for you, Lord, so that it will be the most natural thing in the world to obey your rules for right living!

Additional Scripture Readings:
Psalm 19:7–14; John 14:15–21

Go to page 483 for your next devotional reading.

and his righteousness endures
  forever.
⁴Even in darkness light dawns for the
    upright,
  for the gracious and compassionate
    and righteous man.ᵃ
⁵Good will come to him who is
    generous and lends freely,
  who conducts his affairs with
    justice.
⁶Surely he will never be shaken;
  a righteous man will be
    remembered forever.
⁷He will have no fear of bad news;
  his heart is steadfast, trusting in the
    Lord.
⁸His heart is secure, he will have no
    fear;
  in the end he will look in triumph
    on his foes.
⁹He has scattered abroad his gifts to
    the poor,
  his righteousness endures forever;
  his hornᵇ will be lifted high in
    honor.
¹⁰The wicked man will see and be
    vexed,
  he will gnash his teeth and waste
    away;
  the longings of the wicked will
    come to nothing.

Psalm 113

¹Praise the Lord.ᶜ

Praise, O servants of the Lord,
  praise the name of the Lord.
²Let the name of the Lord be praised,
  both now and forevermore.
³From the rising of the sun to the place
    where it sets,
  the name of the Lord is to be
    praised.
⁴The Lord is exalted over all the
    nations,
  his glory above the heavens.
⁵Who is like the Lord our God,
  the One who sits enthroned on
    high,
⁶who stoops down to look
  on the heavens and the earth?

⁷He raises the poor from the dust
  and lifts the needy from the ash
    heap;
⁸he seats them with princes,
  with the princes of their people.
⁹He settles the barren woman in her
    home
  as a happy mother of children.

Praise the Lord.

Psalm 114

¹When Israel came out of Egypt,
  the house of Jacob from a people of
    foreign tongue,
²Judah became God's sanctuary,
  Israel his dominion.

³The sea looked and fled,
  the Jordan turned back;
⁴the mountains skipped like rams,
  the hills like lambs.

⁵Why was it, O sea, that you fled,
  O Jordan, that you turned back,
⁶you mountains, that you skipped like
    rams,
  you hills, like lambs?

⁷Tremble, O earth, at the presence of
    the Lord,
  at the presence of the God of Jacob,
⁸who turned the rock into a pool,
  the hard rock into springs of water.

Psalm 115

¹Not to us, O Lord, not to us
  but to your name be the glory,
  because of your love and
    faithfulness.

²Why do the nations say,
  "Where is their God?"
³Our God is in heaven;
  he does whatever pleases him.
⁴But their idols are silver and gold,
  made by the hands of men.
⁵They have mouths, but cannot speak,
  eyes, but they cannot see;
⁶they have ears, but cannot hear,
  noses, but they cannot smell;
⁷they have hands, but cannot feel,
  feet, but they cannot walk;
  nor can they utter a sound with
    their throats.
⁸Those who make them will be like
    them,
  and so will all who trust in them.

⁹O house of Israel, trust in the Lord—
  he is their help and shield.
¹⁰O house of Aaron, trust in the Lord—

ᵃ4 Or / for ₜhe Lord, is gracious and compassionate and righteous   ᵇ9 Horn here symbolizes dignity.
ᶜ1 Hebrew Hallelu Yah; also in verse 9

WEDNESDAY

VERSE FOR THE DAY:
Psalm 115:8

AUTHOR:
Doug Sherman and
Wiliam Hendricks

PASSAGE FOR THE DAY:
Psalm 115:2–8

Worshiping Work

MANY workers today are sacrificing themselves on the altar of work. They tolerate immensely harmful symptoms such as anger, chemical dependencies and loneliness in a blind pursuit of self-fulfillment through career success. This may be pathological—but it is also idolatrous! Such a person *worships* his career as though it were a god.

But like all idols, work is impotent in the face of true human need. As Psalm 115:4–7 puts it: "Their idols are silver and gold, made by the hands of men. They have mouths, but cannot speak, eyes, but they cannot see; they have ears, but cannot hear, noses, but they cannot smell; they have hands, but cannot feel, feet, but they cannot walk; nor can they utter a sound with their throats."

In other words, idols are powerless. And work as an idol is just as powerless. Worst of all, those who worship work as an idol are defenseless in the face of true need. In the psalmist's words, "Those who make them will be like them, and so will all who trust in them" (115:8).

I have seen this happen. I have sat with grown men, exceptionally powerful men in business, and watched them weep as they told me their tragic stories, some with personal lives shattered, others with families in shambles, perhaps their character debased or their business in doubt or their circumstances out of control. None of their professional accomplishments, none of the machinery of their companies, none of their wealth is of the slightest help. They are in deep trouble and their god is impotent.

I grieve with such men and women. They have chosen the wrong god. Of course, I also respect the fact that the same thing could happen to me as to anyone. It happens when we take God's gift of work and begin to worship and serve it rather than Christ.

Additional Scripture Readings:
Matthew 6:19–24; Luke 10:38–42

Go to page 486 for your next devotional reading.

he is their help and shield.
¹¹You who fear him, trust in the Lord—
he is their help and shield.

¹²The Lord remembers us and will bless us:
He will bless the house of Israel,
he will bless the house of Aaron,
¹³he will bless those who fear the Lord—
small and great alike.

¹⁴May the Lord make you increase,
both you and your children.
¹⁵May you be blessed by the Lord,
the Maker of heaven and earth.

¹⁶The highest heavens belong to the Lord,
but the earth he has given to man.
¹⁷It is not the dead who praise the Lord,
those who go down to silence;
¹⁸it is we who extol the Lord,
both now and forevermore.

Praise the Lord.[a]

Psalm 116

¹I love the Lord, for he heard my voice;
he heard my cry for mercy.
²Because he turned his ear to me,
I will call on him as long as I live.

³The cords of death entangled me,
the anguish of the grave[b] came upon me;
I was overcome by trouble and sorrow.
⁴Then I called on the name of the Lord:
"O Lord, save me!"

⁵The Lord is gracious and righteous;
our God is full of compassion.
⁶The Lord protects the simplehearted;
when I was in great need, he saved me.

⁷Be at rest once more, O my soul,
for the Lord has been good to you.

⁸For you, O Lord, have delivered my soul from death,
my eyes from tears,
my feet from stumbling,
⁹that I may walk before the Lord
in the land of the living.
¹⁰I believed; therefore[c] I said,
"I am greatly afflicted."
¹¹And in my dismay I said,
"All men are liars."

¹²How can I repay the Lord
for all his goodness to me?
¹³I will lift up the cup of salvation
and call on the name of the Lord.
¹⁴I will fulfill my vows to the Lord
in the presence of all his people.

¹⁵Precious in the sight of the Lord
is the death of his saints.
¹⁶O Lord, truly I am your servant;
I am your servant, the son of your maidservant[d];
you have freed me from my chains.

¹⁷I will sacrifice a thank offering to you
and call on the name of the Lord.
¹⁸I will fulfill my vows to the Lord
in the presence of all his people,
¹⁹in the courts of the house of the Lord—
in your midst, O Jerusalem.

Praise the Lord.[a]

Psalm 117

¹Praise the Lord, all you nations;
extol him, all you peoples.
²For great is his love toward us,
and the faithfulness of the Lord endures forever.

Praise the Lord.[a]

Psalm 118

¹Give thanks to the Lord, for he is good;
his love endures forever.

²Let Israel say:
"His love endures forever."
³Let the house of Aaron say:
"His love endures forever."
⁴Let those who fear the Lord say:
"His love endures forever."

⁵In my anguish I cried to the Lord,
and he answered by setting me free.
⁶The Lord is with me; I will not be afraid.
What can man do to me?
⁷The Lord is with me; he is my helper.
I will look in triumph on my enemies.

⁸It is better to take refuge in the Lord
than to trust in man.

---

[a] 18,19,2 Hebrew *Hallelu Yah*   [b] 3 Hebrew *Sheol*   [c] 10 Or *believed even when*   [d] 16 Or *servant,
your faithful son*

⁹It is better to take refuge in the Lord
    than to trust in princes.

¹⁰All the nations surrounded me,
    but in the name of the Lord I cut
        them off.
¹¹They surrounded me on every side,
    but in the name of the Lord I cut
        them off.
¹²They swarmed around me like bees,
    but they died out as quickly as
        burning thorns;
    in the name of the Lord I cut them
        off.

¹³I was pushed back and about to fall,
    but the Lord helped me.
¹⁴The Lord is my strength and my song;
    he has become my salvation.

¹⁵Shouts of joy and victory
    resound in the tents of the
        righteous:
    "The Lord's right hand has done
        mighty things!
¹⁶   The Lord's right hand is lifted high;
    the Lord's right hand has done
        mighty things!"

¹⁷I will not die but live,
    and will proclaim what the Lord has
        done.
¹⁸The Lord has chastened me severely,
    but he has not given me over to
        death.

¹⁹Open for me the gates of
        righteousness;
    I will enter and give thanks to the
        Lord.
²⁰This is the gate of the Lord
    through which the righteous may
        enter.
²¹I will give you thanks, for you
        answered me;
    you have become my salvation.

²²The stone the builders rejected
    has become the capstone;
²³the Lord has done this,
    and it is marvelous in our eyes.
²⁴This is the day the Lord has made;
    let us rejoice and be glad in it.

²⁵O Lord, save us;
    O Lord, grant us success.
²⁶Blessed is he who comes in the name
        of the Lord.
    From the house of the Lord we
        bless you.ᵃ

²⁷The Lord is God,
    and he has made his light shine
        upon us.
    With boughs in hand, join in the
        festal procession
    upᵇ to the horns of the altar.

²⁸You are my God, and I will give you
        thanks;
    you are my God, and I will exalt
        you.

²⁹Give thanks to the Lord, for he is
        good;
    his love endures forever.

Psalm 119ᶜ

א Aleph

¹Blessed are they whose ways are
        blameless,
    who walk according to the law of
        the Lord.
²Blessed are they who keep his statutes
    and seek him with all their heart.
³They do nothing wrong;
    they walk in his ways.
⁴You have laid down precepts
    that are to be fully obeyed.
⁵Oh, that my ways were steadfast
    in obeying your decrees!
⁶Then I would not be put to shame
    when I consider all your commands.
⁷I will praise you with an upright heart
    as I learn your righteous laws.
⁸I will obey your decrees;
    do not utterly forsake me.

ב Beth

⁹How can a young man keep his way
        pure?
    By living according to your word.
¹⁰I seek you with all my heart;
    do not let me stray from your
        commands.
¹¹I have hidden your word in my heart
    that I might not sin against you.
¹²Praise be to you, O Lord;
    teach me your decrees.
¹³With my lips I recount
    all the laws that come from your
        mouth.
¹⁴I rejoice in following your statutes
    as one rejoices in great riches.
¹⁵I meditate on your precepts
    and consider your ways.

ᵃ26 The Hebrew is plural.   ᵇ27 Or *Bind the festal sacrifice with ropes / and take it*   ᶜThis psalm is an acrostic poem; the verses of each stanza begin with the same letter of the Hebrew alphabet.

16I delight in your decrees;
I will not neglect your word.

ג Gimel

17Do good to your servant, and I will live;
I will obey your word.
18Open my eyes that I may see wonderful things in your law.
19I am a stranger on earth;
do not hide your commands from me.
20My soul is consumed with longing
for your laws at all times.
21You rebuke the arrogant, who are cursed

THURSDAY

VERSE FOR THE DAY:
Psalm 119:16

AUTHOR:
Charles Colson

PASSAGE FOR THE DAY:
Psalm 119:9–16

Truth in a Fast-food World

WE TAKE our stand not on the shifting sands of secular relativism but on the holy and inerrant Word of God. Decisions in the world are made on the basis of expedience and changing sociological factors. But the Word is unchanging, immutable, and without it we Christians have nothing.

Taking our stand on Biblical truth can be our only defense against our culture's penchant to reduce all issues to simplistic suppositions and glib answers. We impatiently expect to get solutions to the most profound ambiguities of life the same way we drive up to the fast-food counter: one double burger, chocolate shake, and an order of fries. We are faddists. Just look at the rash of new diets and instant physical-conditioning courses that week after week dominate our bestseller lists.

The problem is, that "easy-answer" mentality is invading the Christian church: we want scorecards by which we can instantly rate our politicians, new catchy acronyms for salvation, time-saving techniques for discipleship. But formulas don't convert people; slick slogans and cute phrases are no substitute for hard spiritual truth.

In our well-intentioned effort to reach unsaved masses, we often make the gospel message itself sound easy, unthreatening, a painless answer to all life's ills. We portray a loving God who forgives all and asks nothing in return. Now, that may tickle the ears of this pleasure-seeking generation, but it is nothing less than heresy.

We must challenge presuppositions—not only of society as a whole but of the evangelical subculture as well. The gospel of Jesus Christ must be the bad news of the conviction of sin before it can be the Good News of redemption. The truth is revealed in God's Holy Word; life can be lived only in absolute and disciplined submission to its authority.

Additional Scripture Readings:
John 8:31–41; 2 Timothy 3:14–17

Go to page 489 for your next devotional reading.

and who stray from your
  commands.
²²Remove from me scorn and contempt,
  for I keep your statutes.
²³Though rulers sit together and slander
    me,
  your servant will meditate on your
    decrees.
²⁴Your statutes are my delight;
  they are my counselors.

ד Daleth

²⁵I am laid low in the dust;
  preserve my life according to your
    word.
²⁶I recounted my ways and you
    answered me;
  teach me your decrees.
²⁷Let me understand the teaching of
    your precepts;
  then I will meditate on your
    wonders.
²⁸My soul is weary with sorrow;
  strengthen me according to your
    word.
²⁹Keep me from deceitful ways;
  be gracious to me through your law.
³⁰I have chosen the way of truth;
  I have set my heart on your laws.
³¹I hold fast to your statutes, O Lord;
  do not let me be put to shame.
³²I run in the path of your commands,
  for you have set my heart free.

ה He

³³Teach me, O Lord, to follow your
    decrees;
  then I will keep them to the end.
³⁴Give me understanding, and I will
    keep your law
  and obey it with all my heart.
³⁵Direct me in the path of your
    commands,
  for there I find delight.
³⁶Turn my heart toward your statutes
  and not toward selfish gain.
³⁷Turn my eyes away from worthless
    things;
  preserve my life according to your
    word.ᵃ
³⁸Fulfill your promise to your servant,
  so that you may be feared.
³⁹Take away the disgrace I dread,
  for your laws are good.
⁴⁰How I long for your precepts!
  Preserve my life in your
    righteousness.

ו Waw

⁴¹May your unfailing love come to me,
    O Lord,
  your salvation according to your
    promise;
⁴²then I will answer the one who taunts
    me,
  for I trust in your word.
⁴³Do not snatch the word of truth from
    my mouth,
  for I have put my hope in your
    laws.
⁴⁴I will always obey your law,
  for ever and ever.
⁴⁵I will walk about in freedom,
  for I have sought out your precepts.
⁴⁶I will speak of your statutes before
    kings
  and will not be put to shame,
⁴⁷for I delight in your commands
  because I love them.
⁴⁸I lift up my hands toᵇ your
    commands, which I love,
  and I meditate on your decrees.

ז Zayin

⁴⁹Remember your word to your servant,
  for you have given me hope.
⁵⁰My comfort in my suffering is this:
  Your promise preserves my life.
⁵¹The arrogant mock me without
    restraint,
  but I do not turn from your law.
⁵²I remember your ancient laws,
    O Lord,
  and I find comfort in them.
⁵³Indignation grips me because of the
    wicked,
  who have forsaken your law.
⁵⁴Your decrees are the theme of my
    song
  wherever I lodge.
⁵⁵In the night I remember your name,
    O Lord,
  and I will keep your law.
⁵⁶This has been my practice:
  I obey your precepts.

ח Heth

⁵⁷You are my portion, O Lord;
  I have promised to obey your
    words.
⁵⁸I have sought your face with all my
    heart;
  be gracious to me according to your
    promise.

ᵃ37 Two manuscripts of the Masoretic Text and Dead Sea Scrolls; most manuscripts of the Masoretic Text *life in your way*   ᵇ48 Or *for*

⁵⁹I have considered my ways
  and have turned my steps to your statutes.
⁶⁰I will hasten and not delay
  to obey your commands.
⁶¹Though the wicked bind me with ropes,
  I will not forget your law.
⁶²At midnight I rise to give you thanks
  for your righteous laws.
⁶³I am a friend to all who fear you,
  to all who follow your precepts.
⁶⁴The earth is filled with your love, O LORD;
  teach me your decrees.

ט Teth

⁶⁵Do good to your servant
  according to your word, O LORD.
⁶⁶Teach me knowledge and good judgment,
  for I believe in your commands.
⁶⁷Before I was afflicted I went astray,
  but now I obey your word.
⁶⁸You are good, and what you do is good;
  teach me your decrees.
⁶⁹Though the arrogant have smeared me with lies,
  I keep your precepts with all my heart.
⁷⁰Their hearts are callous and unfeeling,
  but I delight in your law.
⁷¹It was good for me to be afflicted
  so that I might learn your decrees.
⁷²The law from your mouth is more precious to me
  than thousands of pieces of silver and gold.

י Yodh

⁷³Your hands made me and formed me;
  give me understanding to learn your commands.
⁷⁴May those who fear you rejoice when they see me,
  for I have put my hope in your word.
⁷⁵I know, O LORD, that your laws are righteous,
  and in faithfulness you have afflicted me.
⁷⁶May your unfailing love be my comfort,
  according to your promise to your servant.
⁷⁷Let your compassion come to me that I may live,
  for your law is my delight.
⁷⁸May the arrogant be put to shame for wronging me without cause;
  but I will meditate on your precepts.
⁷⁹May those who fear you turn to me,
  those who understand your statutes.
⁸⁰May my heart be blameless toward your decrees,
  that I may not be put to shame.

כ Kaph

⁸¹My soul faints with longing for your salvation,
  but I have put my hope in your word.
⁸²My eyes fail, looking for your promise;
  I say, "When will you comfort me?"
⁸³Though I am like a wineskin in the smoke,
  I do not forget your decrees.
⁸⁴How long must your servant wait?
  When will you punish my persecutors?
⁸⁵The arrogant dig pitfalls for me,
  contrary to your law.
⁸⁶All your commands are trustworthy;
  help me, for men persecute me without cause.
⁸⁷They almost wiped me from the earth,
  but I have not forsaken your precepts.
⁸⁸Preserve my life according to your love,
  and I will obey the statutes of your mouth.

ל Lamedh

⁸⁹Your word, O LORD, is eternal;
  it stands firm in the heavens.
⁹⁰Your faithfulness continues through all generations;
  you established the earth, and it endures.
⁹¹Your laws endure to this day,
  for all things serve you.
⁹²If your law had not been my delight,
  I would have perished in my affliction.
⁹³I will never forget your precepts,
  for by them you have preserved my life.
⁹⁴Save me, for I am yours;
  I have sought out your precepts.
⁹⁵The wicked are waiting to destroy me,
  but I will ponder your statutes.

⁹⁶To all perfection I see a limit;
 but your commands are boundless.

מ Mem

⁹⁷Oh, how I love your law!
 I meditate on it all day long.
⁹⁸Your commands make me wiser than my enemies,
 for they are ever with me.
⁹⁹I have more insight than all my teachers,
 for I meditate on your statutes.
¹⁰⁰I have more understanding than the elders,
 for I obey your precepts.
¹⁰¹I have kept my feet from every evil path
 so that I might obey your word.
¹⁰²I have not departed from your laws,
 for you yourself have taught me.
¹⁰³How sweet are your words to my taste,
 sweeter than honey to my mouth!
¹⁰⁴I gain understanding from your precepts;
 therefore I hate every wrong path.

נ Nun

¹⁰⁵Your word is a lamp to my feet
 and a light for my path.
¹⁰⁶I have taken an oath and confirmed it,
 that I will follow your righteous laws.
¹⁰⁷I have suffered much;
 preserve my life, O LORD, according to your word.
¹⁰⁸Accept, O LORD, the willing praise of my mouth,
 and teach me your laws.
¹⁰⁹Though I constantly take my life in my hands,
 I will not forget your law.
¹¹⁰The wicked have set a snare for me,
 but I have not strayed from your precepts.

FRIDAY

VERSE FOR THE DAY: Psalm 119:96

AUTHOR: Tom Landry

PASSAGE FOR THE DAY: Psalm 119:89–96

Life Within Limits

MOST successful [football] players not only accept rules and limitations, I believe they need them. In fact, I believe players are free to perform at their best only when they know what the expectations are, where the limits stand.

I see this as a Biblical principle that also applies to life, a principle our society as a whole has forgotten. You can't enjoy true freedom without limits.

We often resent rules because they limit what we can do. Yet without the rules that define a football game, you can't play the game, let alone enjoy it. The same thing is true in life. To live and enjoy the freedom we have in America, we have to live by the rules of society. To live life to its fullest and truly enjoy it, we need to understand and abide by the rules God spells out in the Bible. God isn't out to spoil our fun; he knows that life without limits results in anarchy and misery. It's only when we have absolute limits that we can be truly free to enjoy the best life has to offer.

Additional Scripture Readings:
Romans 6:15–23; 1 John 2:3–8

Go to page 493 for your next devotional reading.

¹¹¹Your statutes are my heritage forever;
  they are the joy of my heart.
¹¹²My heart is set on keeping your decrees
  to the very end.

ס Samekh

¹¹³I hate double-minded men,
  but I love your law.
¹¹⁴You are my refuge and my shield;
  I have put my hope in your word.
¹¹⁵Away from me, you evildoers,
  that I may keep the commands of my God!
¹¹⁶Sustain me according to your promise, and I will live;
  do not let my hopes be dashed.
¹¹⁷Uphold me, and I will be delivered;
  I will always have regard for your decrees.
¹¹⁸You reject all who stray from your decrees,
  for their deceitfulness is in vain.
¹¹⁹All the wicked of the earth you discard like dross;
  therefore I love your statutes.
¹²⁰My flesh trembles in fear of you;
  I stand in awe of your laws.

ע Ayin

¹²¹I have done what is righteous and just;
  do not leave me to my oppressors.
¹²²Ensure your servant's well-being;
  let not the arrogant oppress me.
¹²³My eyes fail, looking for your salvation,
  looking for your righteous promise.
¹²⁴Deal with your servant according to your love
  and teach me your decrees.
¹²⁵I am your servant; give me discernment
  that I may understand your statutes.
¹²⁶It is time for you to act, O LORD;
  your law is being broken.
¹²⁷Because I love your commands more than gold, more than pure gold,
¹²⁸and because I consider all your precepts right,
  I hate every wrong path.

פ Pe

¹²⁹Your statutes are wonderful;
  therefore I obey them.
¹³⁰The unfolding of your words gives light;
  it gives understanding to the simple.
¹³¹I open my mouth and pant,
  longing for your commands.
¹³²Turn to me and have mercy on me,
  as you always do to those who love your name.
¹³³Direct my footsteps according to your word;
  let no sin rule over me.
¹³⁴Redeem me from the oppression of men,
  that I may obey your precepts.
¹³⁵Make your face shine upon your servant
  and teach me your decrees.
¹³⁶Streams of tears flow from my eyes,
  for your law is not obeyed.

צ Tsadhe

¹³⁷Righteous are you, O LORD,
  and your laws are right.
¹³⁸The statutes you have laid down are righteous;
  they are fully trustworthy.
¹³⁹My zeal wears me out,
  for my enemies ignore your words.
¹⁴⁰Your promises have been thoroughly tested,
  and your servant loves them.
¹⁴¹Though I am lowly and despised,
  I do not forget your precepts.
¹⁴²Your righteousness is everlasting
  and your law is true.
¹⁴³Trouble and distress have come upon me,
  but your commands are my delight.
¹⁴⁴Your statutes are forever right;
  give me understanding that I may live.

ק Qoph

¹⁴⁵I call with all my heart; answer me, O LORD,
  and I will obey your decrees.
¹⁴⁶I call out to you; save me
  and I will keep your statutes.
¹⁴⁷I rise before dawn and cry for help;
  I have put my hope in your word.
¹⁴⁸My eyes stay open through the watches of the night,
  that I may meditate on your promises.
¹⁴⁹Hear my voice in accordance with your love;
  preserve my life, O LORD, according to your laws.
¹⁵⁰Those who devise wicked schemes are near,
  but they are far from your law.
¹⁵¹Yet you are near, O LORD,
  and all your commands are true.

¹⁵²Long ago I learned from your statutes
  that you established them to last
  forever.

ר Resh

¹⁵³Look upon my suffering and
  deliver me,
  for I have not forgotten your law.
¹⁵⁴Defend my cause and redeem me;
  preserve my life according to your
  promise.
¹⁵⁵Salvation is far from the wicked,
  for they do not seek out your
  decrees.
¹⁵⁶Your compassion is great, O LORD;
  preserve my life according to your
  laws.
¹⁵⁷Many are the foes who persecute me,
  but I have not turned from your
  statutes.
¹⁵⁸I look on the faithless with loathing,
  for they do not obey your word.
¹⁵⁹See how I love your precepts;
  preserve my life, O LORD, according
  to your love.
¹⁶⁰All your words are true;
  all your righteous laws are eternal.

ש Sin and Shin

¹⁶¹Rulers persecute me without cause,
  but my heart trembles at your word.
¹⁶²I rejoice in your promise
  like one who finds great spoil.
¹⁶³I hate and abhor falsehood
  but I love your law.
¹⁶⁴Seven times a day I praise you
  for your righteous laws.
¹⁶⁵Great peace have they who love your
  law,
  and nothing can make them
  stumble.
¹⁶⁶I wait for your salvation, O LORD,
  and I follow your commands.
¹⁶⁷I obey your statutes,
  for I love them greatly.
¹⁶⁸I obey your precepts and your
  statutes,
  for all my ways are known to you.

ת Taw

¹⁶⁹May my cry come before you,
  O LORD;
  give me understanding according to
  your word.
¹⁷⁰May my supplication come before
  you;
  deliver me according to your
  promise.
¹⁷¹May my lips overflow with praise,
  for you teach me your decrees.
¹⁷²May my tongue sing of your word,
  for all your commands are
  righteous.
¹⁷³May your hand be ready to help me,
  for I have chosen your precepts.
¹⁷⁴I long for your salvation, O LORD,
  and your law is my delight.
¹⁷⁵Let me live that I may praise you,
  and may your laws sustain me.
¹⁷⁶I have strayed like a lost sheep.
  Seek your servant,
  for I have not forgotten your
  commands.

Psalm 120

A song of ascents.

¹I call on the LORD in my distress,
  and he answers me.
²Save me, O LORD, from lying lips
  and from deceitful tongues.

³What will he do to you,
  and what more besides, O deceitful
  tongue?
⁴He will punish you with a warrior's
  sharp arrows,
  with burning coals of the broom
  tree.

⁵Woe to me that I dwell in Meshech,
  that I live among the tents of Kedar!
⁶Too long have I lived
  among those who hate peace.
⁷I am a man of peace;
  but when I speak, they are for war.

Psalm 121

A song of ascents.

¹I lift up my eyes to the hills—
  where does my help come from?
²My help comes from the LORD,
  the Maker of heaven and earth.

³He will not let your foot slip—
  he who watches over you will not
  slumber;
⁴indeed, he who watches over Israel
  will neither slumber nor sleep.

⁵The LORD watches over you—
  the LORD is your shade at your right
  hand;

⁶the sun will not harm you by day,
nor the moon by night.

⁷The LORD will keep you from all harm—
he will watch over your life;
⁸the LORD will watch over your coming and going
both now and forevermore.

Psalm 122

A song of ascents. Of David.

¹I rejoiced with those who said to me,
"Let us go to the house of the LORD."
²Our feet are standing
in your gates, O Jerusalem.

³Jerusalem is built like a city
that is closely compacted together.
⁴That is where the tribes go up,
the tribes of the LORD,
to praise the name of the LORD
according to the statute given to Israel.
⁵There the thrones for judgment stand,
the thrones of the house of David.

⁶Pray for the peace of Jerusalem:
"May those who love you be secure.
⁷May there be peace within your walls
and security within your citadels."
⁸For the sake of my brothers and friends,
I will say, "Peace be within you."
⁹For the sake of the house of the LORD our God,
I will seek your prosperity.

Psalm 123

A song of ascents.

¹I lift up my eyes to you,
to you whose throne is in heaven.
²As the eyes of slaves look to the hand of their master,
as the eyes of a maid look to the hand of her mistress,
so our eyes look to the LORD our God,
till he shows us his mercy.

³Have mercy on us, O LORD, have mercy on us,
for we have endured much contempt.
⁴We have endured much ridicule from the proud,
much contempt from the arrogant.

Psalm 124

A song of ascents. Of David.

¹If the LORD had not been on our side—
let Israel say—
²if the LORD had not been on our side when men attacked us,
³when their anger flared against us,
they would have swallowed us alive;
⁴the flood would have engulfed us,
the torrent would have swept over us,
⁵the raging waters
would have swept us away.

⁶Praise be to the LORD,
who has not let us be torn by their teeth.
⁷We have escaped like a bird
out of the fowler's snare;
the snare has been broken,
and we have escaped.
⁸Our help is in the name of the LORD,
the Maker of heaven and earth.

Psalm 125

A song of ascents.

¹Those who trust in the LORD are like Mount Zion,
which cannot be shaken but endures forever.
²As the mountains surround Jerusalem,
so the LORD surrounds his people
both now and forevermore.

³The scepter of the wicked will not remain
over the land allotted to the righteous,
for the righteous might use their hands to do evil.

⁴Do good, O LORD, to those who are good,
to those who are upright in heart.
⁵But those who turn to crooked ways
the LORD will banish with the evildoers.

Peace be upon Israel.

WEEKENDING

REALIZE

When you teach your children what God's Word has to say about troubled times, you're providing a lamp to their feet (Psalm 119:105). Biblical principles are like powerful flashlights that can light up even the darkest trial your children may experience.

Because you know this, you can verbally and nonverbally convey this message to your children as they watch your response to their trials. And you can also ask them if they are willing to look for what God has to teach them in the difficulty they've experienced.
– *Gary Smalley and John Trent*

REVIVE
Saturday: Hebrews 10:32–39
Sunday: 1 Peter 4:12–19

Go to page 495 for your next devotional reading.

Psalm 126

A song of ascents.

¹When the LORD brought back the
    captives to*ᵃ* Zion,
  we were like men who dreamed.*ᵇ*
²Our mouths were filled with laughter,
    our tongues with songs of joy.
  Then it was said among the nations,
    "The LORD has done great things for
        them."
³The LORD has done great things for us,
    and we are filled with joy.

⁴Restore our fortunes,*ᶜ* O LORD,
    like streams in the Negev.
⁵Those who sow in tears
    will reap with songs of joy.
⁶He who goes out weeping,
    carrying seed to sow,
  will return with songs of joy,
    carrying sheaves with him.

Psalm 127

A song of ascents. Of Solomon.

¹Unless the LORD builds the house,
    its builders labor in vain.
  Unless the LORD watches over the city,
    the watchmen stand guard in vain.
²In vain you rise early
    and stay up late,
  toiling for food to eat—
    for he grants sleep to*ᵈ* those he
        loves.

³Sons are a heritage from the LORD,
    children a reward from him.
⁴Like arrows in the hands of a warrior
    are sons born in one's youth.
⁵Blessed is the man
    whose quiver is full of them.
  They will not be put to shame
    when they contend with their
        enemies in the gate.

Psalm 128

A song of ascents.

¹Blessed are all who fear the LORD,
    who walk in his ways.
²You will eat the fruit of your labor;
    blessings and prosperity will be
        yours.
³Your wife will be like a fruitful vine
    within your house;
  your sons will be like olive shoots
    around your table.
⁴Thus is the man blessed
    who fears the LORD.

⁵May the LORD bless you from Zion
    all the days of your life;
  may you see the prosperity of
        Jerusalem,
⁶   and may you live to see your
        children's children.

Peace be upon Israel.

Psalm 129

A song of ascents.

¹They have greatly oppressed me from
    my youth—
  let Israel say—
²they have greatly oppressed me from
    my youth,
  but they have not gained the victory
    over me.
³Plowmen have plowed my back
    and made their furrows long.
⁴But the LORD is righteous;
    he has cut me free from the cords
        of the wicked.

⁵May all who hate Zion
    be turned back in shame.
⁶May they be like grass on the roof,
    which withers before it can grow;
⁷with it the reaper cannot fill his
        hands,
    nor the one who gathers fill his
        arms.
⁸May those who pass by not say,
    "The blessing of the LORD be upon
        you;
  we bless you in the name of the
        LORD."

Psalm 130

A song of ascents.

¹Out of the depths I cry to you,
    O LORD;
² O Lord, hear my voice.
  Let your ears be attentive
    to my cry for mercy.

³If you, O LORD, kept a record of sins,
    O Lord, who could stand?
⁴But with you there is forgiveness;
    therefore you are feared.

ᵃ1 Or LORD *restored the fortunes of*   *ᵇ1* Or *men restored to health*   *ᶜ4* Or *Bring back our captives*
ᵈ2 Or *eat—* / *for while they sleep he provides for*

⁵I wait for the LORD, my soul waits,
  and in his word I put my hope.
⁶My soul waits for the Lord
  more than watchmen wait for the morning,
  more than watchmen wait for the morning.

⁷O Israel, put your hope in the LORD,
  for with the LORD is unfailing love
  and with him is full redemption.
⁸He himself will redeem Israel
  from all their sins.

MONDAY

VERSE FOR THE DAY:
Psalm 127:1

AUTHOR:
Charles Swindoll

PASSAGE FOR THE DAY:
Psalm 127:1–5

A Home Where Love Thrives

THE first two verses of Psalm 127 are the piers and beams of the home, the foundation from which all else derives its stability and security.

"Unless the Lord builds the house, its builders labor in vain. Unless the Lord watches over the city, the watchmen stand guard in vain."

Solomon, the writer of this psalm, compares the home to a city. When an ancient city was built, it was not uncommon for its walls to be finished first to keep out the enemy. If the people trusted in the walls to protect them, to give them security, their trust was misplaced, creating only a false sense of security. Likewise, walls we erect around our families and possessions offer only an illusion of security. Like Jericho's walls, they can tumble as quickly as a shout. For ultimately, it is not the watchman or the walls that protect the city; it is the *Lord*. "The name of the LORD is a strong tower; the righteous run to it and are safe" (Proverbs 18:10). In the same sense, unless a husband and wife trust in God, their work and their watchfulness are wasted.

In verse 2, Solomon qualifies the phrase *in vain*:

"In vain you rise early and stay up late, toiling for food to eat—"

Many feel that by working longer hours they can provide more things to bring happiness to their home or afford a nicer, newer home in hopes that it will bring happiness . . . It doesn't satisfy that empty longing in the pit of our soul, that longing for a home, a *real* home—a home where love thrives, lush and fragrant. The reason why it's futile burning the candle at both ends—rising early, staying up late—is that God, not our labors, is the source of our blessing, as verse 2 indicates: "for he grants sleep to those he loves" [or, as the alternate translation reads, "for while they sleep he provides for those he loves"].

Additional Scripture Readings:
Psalm 37:1–9; Matthew 6:25–34

Go to page 496 for your next devotional reading.

Psalm 131

A song of ascents. Of David.

¹My heart is not proud, O LORD,
  my eyes are not haughty;
I do not concern myself with great
    matters
  or things too wonderful for me.
²But I have stilled and quieted my
    soul;
  like a weaned child with its
    mother,
  like a weaned child is my soul
    within me.
³O Israel, put your hope in the LORD
  both now and forevermore.

Psalm 132

A song of ascents.

¹O LORD, remember David
  and all the hardships he endured.
²He swore an oath to the LORD
  and made a vow to the Mighty One
    of Jacob:
³"I will not enter my house
  or go to my bed—
⁴I will allow no sleep to my eyes,

TUESDAY

VERSE FOR THE DAY: *AUTHOR:* *PASSAGE FOR THE DAY:*
Psalm 130:1 Donald Bloesch *Psalm 130:1–8*

Empty-handed Praying

THE Biblical Christian can only pray empty-handed, as the thirteenth-century Dominican preacher William Peraldus expressed it. Or, as Augustine observed, "The best disposition for praying is that of being desolate, forsaken, stripped of everything." Unlike the ritualist, we know that any sacrifice we bring before God is stained by sin and therefore unworthy of acceptance apart from the mediation and intercession of Jesus Christ. Our hope depends not on the right technique or the proper phrase or gesture, which borders on magic, but on the promises of God to look with favor on those who throw themselves on his mercy and who acknowledge the efficacy of the atoning sacrifice of his Son, Jesus Christ, for their redemption.

As I see it, true prayer is neither mystical rapture nor ritual observance nor philosophical reflection: it is the outpouring of the soul before a living God, the crying to God "out of the depths." Such prayer can only be uttered by one convicted of sin by the grace of God and moved to confession by the Spirit of God. True prayer is an encounter with the Holy in which we realize not only our creatureliness and guilt but also the joy of knowing that our sins are forgiven through the atoning death of the divine Savior, Jesus Christ. In such an encounter, we are impelled not only to bow before God and seek his mercy but also to offer thanksgiving for grace that goes out to undeserving sinners.

Additional Scripture Readings: *Go to page 501 for your next*
Psalm 142; Philippians 4:4–7 *devotional reading.*

no slumber to my eyelids,
5till I find a place for the LORD,
a dwelling for the Mighty One of
Jacob."

6We heard it in Ephrathah,
we came upon it in the fields of
Jaar*a; b*
7"Let us go to his dwelling place;
let us worship at his footstool —
8arise, O LORD, and come to your
resting place,
you and the ark of your might.
9May your priests be clothed with
righteousness;
may your saints sing for joy."

10For the sake of David your servant,
do not reject your anointed one.

11The LORD swore an oath to David,
a sure oath that he will not revoke:
"One of your own descendants
I will place on your throne —
12if your sons keep my covenant
and the statutes I teach them,
then their sons will sit
on your throne for ever and ever."

13For the LORD has chosen Zion,
he has desired it for his dwelling:
14"This is my resting place for ever and
ever;
here I will sit enthroned, for I have
desired it —
15I will bless her with abundant
provisions;
her poor will I satisfy with food.
16I will clothe her priests with salvation,
and her saints will ever sing for joy.

17"Here I will make a horn*c* grow for
David
and set up a lamp for my anointed
one.
18I will clothe his enemies with shame,
but the crown on his head will be
resplendent."

Psalm 133

A song of ascents. Of David.

1How good and pleasant it is
when brothers live together in
unity!
2It is like precious oil poured on the
head,
running down on the beard,
running down on Aaron's beard,
down upon the collar of his robes.
3It is as if the dew of Hermon
were falling on Mount Zion.
For there the LORD bestows his
blessing,
even life forevermore.

Psalm 134

A song of ascents.

1Praise the LORD, all you servants of
the LORD
who minister by night in the house
of the LORD.
2Lift up your hands in the sanctuary
and praise the LORD.

3May the LORD, the Maker of heaven
and earth,
bless you from Zion.

Psalm 135

1Praise the LORD.*d*

Praise the name of the LORD;
praise him, you servants of the
LORD,
2you who minister in the house of the
LORD,
in the courts of the house of our
God.

3Praise the LORD, for the LORD is good;
sing praise to his name, for that is
pleasant.
4For the LORD has chosen Jacob to be
his own,
Israel to be his treasured
possession.

5I know that the LORD is great,
that our Lord is greater than all
gods.
6The LORD does whatever pleases him,
in the heavens and on the earth,
in the seas and all their depths.
7He makes clouds rise from the ends of
the earth;
he sends lightning with the rain
and brings out the wind from his
storehouses.

8He struck down the firstborn of Egypt,
the firstborn of men and animals.
9He sent his signs and wonders into
your midst, O Egypt,

---

a6 That is, Kiriath Jearim (quotes around verses 7-9)   *b6* Or *heard of it in Ephrathah, / we found it in the fields of Jaar.* (And no quotes around verses 7-9)   *c17 Horn* here symbolizes strong one, that is, king.   *d1* Hebrew *Hallelu Yah*; also in verses 3 and 21

against Pharaoh and all his servants.
¹⁰He struck down many nations
and killed mighty kings—
¹¹Sihon king of the Amorites,
Og king of Bashan
and all the kings of Canaan—
¹²and he gave their land as an inheritance,
an inheritance to his people Israel.

¹³Your name, O LORD, endures forever,
your renown, O LORD, through all generations.
¹⁴For the LORD will vindicate his people
and have compassion on his servants.

¹⁵The idols of the nations are silver and gold,
made by the hands of men.
¹⁶They have mouths, but cannot speak,
eyes, but they cannot see;
¹⁷they have ears, but cannot hear,
nor is there breath in their mouths.
¹⁸Those who make them will be like them,
and so will all who trust in them.

¹⁹O house of Israel, praise the LORD;
O house of Aaron, praise the LORD;
²⁰O house of Levi, praise the LORD;
you who fear him, praise the LORD.
²¹Praise be to the LORD from Zion,
to him who dwells in Jerusalem.

Praise the LORD.

Psalm 136

¹Give thanks to the LORD, for he is good.
His love endures forever.
²Give thanks to the God of gods.
His love endures forever.
³Give thanks to the Lord of lords:
His love endures forever.

⁴to him who alone does great wonders,
His love endures forever.
⁵who by his understanding made the heavens,
His love endures forever.
⁶who spread out the earth upon the waters,
His love endures forever.
⁷who made the great lights—
His love endures forever.
⁸the sun to govern the day,
His love endures forever.
⁹the moon and stars to govern the night;
His love endures forever.

¹⁰to him who struck down the firstborn of Egypt
His love endures forever.
¹¹and brought Israel out from among them
His love endures forever.
¹²with a mighty hand and outstretched arm;
His love endures forever.

¹³to him who divided the Red Sea[a] asunder
His love endures forever.
¹⁴and brought Israel through the midst of it,
His love endures forever.
¹⁵but swept Pharaoh and his army into the Red Sea;
His love endures forever.

¹⁶to him who led his people through the desert,
His love endures forever.
¹⁷who struck down great kings,
His love endures forever.
¹⁸and killed mighty kings—
His love endures forever.
¹⁹Sihon king of the Amorites
His love endures forever.
²⁰and Og king of Bashan—
His love endures forever.
²¹and gave their land as an inheritance,
His love endures forever.
²²an inheritance to his servant Israel;
His love endures forever.

²³to the One who remembered us in our low estate
His love endures forever.
²⁴and freed us from our enemies,
His love endures forever.
²⁵and who gives food to every creature.
His love endures forever.

²⁶Give thanks to the God of heaven.
His love endures forever.

Psalm 137

¹By the rivers of Babylon we sat and wept
when we remembered Zion.
²There on the poplars
we hung our harps,
³for there our captors asked us for songs,

---

[a]13 Hebrew *Yam Suph*; that is, Sea of Reeds; also in verse 15

our tormentors demanded songs of
joy;
they said, "Sing us one of the songs
of Zion!"

⁴How can we sing the songs of the
Lord
while in a foreign land?
⁵If I forget you, O Jerusalem,
may my right hand forget ⌊its skill⌋.
⁶May my tongue cling to the roof of
my mouth
if I do not remember you,
if I do not consider Jerusalem
my highest joy.

⁷Remember, O Lord, what the
Edomites did
on the day Jerusalem fell.
"Tear it down," they cried,
"tear it down to its foundations!"

⁸O Daughter of Babylon, doomed to
destruction,
happy is he who repays you
for what you have done to us—
⁹he who seizes your infants
and dashes them against the rocks.

Psalm 138

Of David.

¹I will praise you, O Lord, with all my
heart;
before the "gods" I will sing your
praise.
²I will bow down toward your holy
temple
and will praise your name
for your love and your faithfulness,
for you have exalted above all things
your name and your word.
³When I called, you answered me;
you made me bold and
stouthearted.

⁴May all the kings of the earth praise
you, O Lord,
when they hear the words of your
mouth.
⁵May they sing of the ways of the
Lord,
for the glory of the Lord is great.

⁶Though the Lord is on high, he looks
upon the lowly,
but the proud he knows from afar.
⁷Though I walk in the midst of trouble,
you preserve my life;
you stretch out your hand against the
anger of my foes,
with your right hand you save me.
⁸The Lord will fulfill ⌊his purpose⌋ for
me;
your love, O Lord, endures
forever—
do not abandon the works of your
hands.

Psalm 139

For the director of music. Of David.
A psalm.

¹O Lord, you have searched me
and you know me.
²You know when I sit and when I rise;
you perceive my thoughts from afar.
³You discern my going out and my
lying down;
you are familiar with all my ways.
⁴Before a word is on my tongue
you know it completely, O Lord.

⁵You hem me in—behind and before;
you have laid your hand upon me.
⁶Such knowledge is too wonderful for
me,
too lofty for me to attain.

⁷Where can I go from your Spirit?
Where can I flee from your
presence?
⁸If I go up to the heavens, you are
there;
if I make my bed in the depths,ᵃ
you are there.
⁹If I rise on the wings of the dawn,
if I settle on the far side of the sea,
¹⁰even there your hand will guide me,
your right hand will hold me fast.
¹¹If I say, "Surely the darkness will hide
me
and the light become night around
me,"
¹²even the darkness will not be dark to
you;
the night will shine like the day,
for darkness is as light to you.

¹³For you created my inmost being;
you knit me together in my
mother's womb.
¹⁴I praise you because I am fearfully
and wonderfully made;
your works are wonderful,
I know that full well.
¹⁵My frame was not hidden from you

ᵃ 8 Hebrew *Sheol*

when I was made in the secret
  place.
When I was woven together in the
  depths of the earth,
¹⁶ your eyes saw my unformed body.
All the days ordained for me
  were written in your book
  before one of them came to be.

¹⁷How precious to*a* me are your
  thoughts, O God!
  How vast is the sum of them!
¹⁸Were I to count them,
  they would outnumber the grains of
    sand.
  When I awake,
  I am still with you.

¹⁹If only you would slay the wicked,
  O God!
  Away from me, you bloodthirsty
    men!
²⁰They speak of you with evil intent;
  your adversaries misuse your name.
²¹Do I not hate those who hate you,
  O LORD,
  and abhor those who rise up against
    you?
²²I have nothing but hatred for them;
  I count them my enemies.

²³Search me, O God, and know my
  heart;
  test me and know my anxious
    thoughts.
²⁴See if there is any offensive way in
  me,
  and lead me in the way everlasting.

Psalm 140

For the director of music. A psalm
of David.

¹Rescue me, O LORD, from evil men;
  protect me from men of violence,
²who devise evil plans in their hearts
  and stir up war every day.
³They make their tongues as sharp as a
    serpent's;
  the poison of vipers is on their lips.
          Selah

⁴Keep me, O LORD, from the hands of
  the wicked;
  protect me from men of violence
  who plan to trip my feet.

⁵Proud men have hidden a snare for
  me;
  they have spread out the cords of
    their net
  and have set traps for me along my
    path.   *Selah*

⁶O LORD, I say to you, "You are my
  God."
  Hear, O LORD, my cry for mercy.
⁷O Sovereign LORD, my strong deliverer,
  who shields my head in the day of
    battle—
⁸do not grant the wicked their desires,
  O LORD;
  do not let their plans succeed,
  or they will become proud.   *Selah*

⁹Let the heads of those who surround
  me
  be covered with the trouble their
    lips have caused.
¹⁰Let burning coals fall upon them;
  may they be thrown into the fire,
  into miry pits, never to rise.
¹¹Let slanderers not be established in
  the land;
  may disaster hunt down men of
    violence.

¹²I know that the LORD secures justice
  for the poor
  and upholds the cause of the needy.
¹³Surely the righteous will praise your
  name
  and the upright will live before you.

Psalm 141

A psalm of David.

¹O LORD, I call to you; come quickly to
  me.
  Hear my voice when I call to you.
²May my prayer be set before you like
  incense;
  may the lifting up of my hands be
    like the evening sacrifice.

³Set a guard over my mouth, O LORD;
  keep watch over the door of my
    lips.
⁴Let not my heart be drawn to what is
  evil,
  to take part in wicked deeds
  with men who are evildoers;
  let me not eat of their delicacies.

---

a 17 Or concerning

⁵Let a righteous man*ᵃ* strike me—it is
    a kindness;
  let him rebuke me—it is oil on my
    head.
  My head will not refuse it.

  Yet my prayer is ever against the
    deeds of evildoers;
⁶ their rulers will be thrown down
    from the cliffs,
  and the wicked will learn that my
    words were well spoken.
⁷They will say, "As one plows and
    breaks up the earth,
  so our bones have been scattered at
    the mouth of the grave.*ᵇ*"

⁸But my eyes are fixed on you,
    O Sovereign LORD;
  in you I take refuge—do not give
    me over to death.
⁹Keep me from the snares they have
    laid for me,
  from the traps set by evildoers.
¹⁰Let the wicked fall into their own
    nets,
  while I pass by in safety.

ᵃ5 Or *Let the Righteous One*   *ᵇ7* Hebrew *Sheol*

WEDNESDAY

VERSE FOR THE DAY:
Psalm 139:1

AUTHOR:
W. Phillip Keller

PASSAGE FOR THE DAY:
Psalm 139:1–24

He Knows Me

AS HE [God] begins to share life with us, we really are astonished to discover how well he already knows all about us. He, and only he, is totally familiar with all the intimate intricacies of my genetic makeup. He understands all the unique characteristics which have been inherited from my parents and grandparents. He knows my distinctive and special personality. Because of such incredible insight he understands my behavior far better than any human being. So he deals with me fairly.

Precisely the same principle applies to his comprehension of all the social and unique environmental influences which have shaped my character and molded my mind from birth. I am not an enigma to him. I am one whom he has known since conception. Consequently, he does not reject or despise me. Rather, he begins now to re-create me in his own lovely likeness.

Likewise with my mind, my emotions, my will (heart). He perceives clearly why I think as I do; why I feel as I do in interaction with others; why I make the choices I do from day to day. In all these complex activities, he does not come to condemn me. He comes instead to change and re-direct my energies, my decisions, into noble purposes and lofty service. Bless his Name!

Additional Scripture Readings:
Romans 8:18–27; Ephesians 2:8–10

*Go to page 503 for your next
devotional reading.*

Psalm 142

A *maskil*[a] of David. When he was in the cave. A prayer.

¹I cry aloud to the LORD;
  I lift up my voice to the LORD for mercy.
²I pour out my complaint before him;
  before him I tell my trouble.

³When my spirit grows faint within me,
  it is you who know my way.
In the path where I walk
  men have hidden a snare for me.
⁴Look to my right and see;
  no one is concerned for me.
I have no refuge;
  no one cares for my life.

⁵I cry to you, O LORD;
  I say, "You are my refuge,
  my portion in the land of the living."
⁶Listen to my cry,
  for I am in desperate need;
rescue me from those who pursue me,
  for they are too strong for me.
⁷Set me free from my prison,
  that I may praise your name.

Then the righteous will gather about me
  because of your goodness to me.

Psalm 143

A psalm of David.

¹O LORD, hear my prayer,
  listen to my cry for mercy;
in your faithfulness and righteousness
  come to my relief.
²Do not bring your servant into judgment,
  for no one living is righteous before you.

³The enemy pursues me,
  he crushes me to the ground;
he makes me dwell in darkness
  like those long dead.
⁴So my spirit grows faint within me;
  my heart within me is dismayed.

⁵I remember the days of long ago;
  I meditate on all your works
  and consider what your hands have done.
⁶I spread out my hands to you;
  my soul thirsts for you like a parched land. *Selah*

⁷Answer me quickly, O LORD;
  my spirit fails.
Do not hide your face from me
  or I will be like those who go down to the pit.
⁸Let the morning bring me word of your unfailing love,
  for I have put my trust in you.
Show me the way I should go,
  for to you I lift up my soul.
⁹Rescue me from my enemies, O LORD,
  for I hide myself in you.
¹⁰Teach me to do your will,
  for you are my God;
may your good Spirit
  lead me on level ground.

¹¹For your name's sake, O LORD,
  preserve my life;
in your righteousness, bring me out of trouble.
¹²In your unfailing love, silence my enemies;
  destroy all my foes,
  for I am your servant.

Psalm 144

Of David.

¹Praise be to the LORD my Rock,
  who trains my hands for war,
  my fingers for battle.
²He is my loving God and my fortress,
  my stronghold and my deliverer,
my shield, in whom I take refuge,
  who subdues peoples[b] under me.

³O LORD, what is man that you care for him,
  the son of man that you think of him?
⁴Man is like a breath;
  his days are like a fleeting shadow.

⁵Part your heavens, O LORD, and come down;
  touch the mountains, so that they smoke.
⁶Send forth lightning and scatter the enemies;
  shoot your arrows and rout them.
⁷Reach down your hand from on high;
  deliver me and rescue me
from the mighty waters,
  from the hands of foreigners

---

[a] Title: Probably a literary or musical term [b] 2 Many manuscripts of the Masoretic Text, Dead Sea Scrolls, Aquila, Jerome and Syriac; most manuscripts of the Masoretic Text *subdues my people*

⁸whose mouths are full of lies,
　whose right hands are deceitful.

⁹I will sing a new song to you, O God;
　on the ten-stringed lyre I will make
　　music to you,
¹⁰to the One who gives victory to kings,
　who delivers his servant David from
　　the deadly sword.

¹¹Deliver me and rescue me
　from the hands of foreigners
　whose mouths are full of lies,
　whose right hands are deceitful.

¹²Then our sons in their youth
　will be like well-nurtured plants,
　and our daughters will be like pillars
　　carved to adorn a palace.
¹³Our barns will be filled
　with every kind of provision.
Our sheep will increase by thousands,
　by tens of thousands in our fields;
¹⁴　our oxen will draw heavy loads.ᵃ
There will be no breaching of walls,

a 14 Or our chieftains will be firmly established

THURSDAY

VERSE FOR THE DAY:　　　　*AUTHOR:*　　　　*PASSAGE FOR THE DAY:*
Psalm 143:8　　　　　　　*Don Wyrtzen*　　　　　　*Psalm 143:1–12*

On Level Ground

AT THE moment of rebirth, when the human spirit is "yielded and still," the Holy Spirit moves in to make his home and to provide assistance for our pilgrimage with God.

Even David anticipated something of this divine exchange, I think. His despairing prayer, filled with strong, virile verbs, is the night sky against which the dazzling stars of God's grace through his Spirit are displayed.

Guide—David prays, "Show me the way" (v. 8), sensing that God's guiding Spirit will not leave him stranded, nor remove him from the unfailing love that is everlasting.

Enabler—"Rescue me from my enemies" (v. 9), he continues. It is the Spirit of God who enables and empowers. David's many military coups were a result of divine intervention by the Enabler.

Teacher—"Teach me to do your will ... may your good Spirit lead me on level ground" (v. 10). The Holy Spirit is our Teacher/Interpreter. It is he who explains spiritual mysteries and levels the ground of our understanding.

Comforter—"For your name's sake, O LORD, preserve my life ... bring me out of trouble" (v. 11). God's Spirit whispers words of encouragement and calls to our minds his mighty works in our behalf. He banishes discouragement and puts a song in our hearts!

O Lord, fill me with your Spirit today. Guide me, enable me, teach me, comfort me. I need help as I continue my pilgrimage.

Additional Scripture Readings:　　　　*Go to page 508 for your next*
John 16:5–16;　　　　　　　　　　　　　　*devotional reading.*
1 Corinthians 12:1–11

no going into captivity,
no cry of distress in our streets.

¹⁵Blessed are the people of whom this is true;
blessed are the people whose God is the LORD.

Psalm 145[a]

A psalm of praise. Of David.

¹I will exalt you, my God the King;
I will praise your name for ever and ever.
²Every day I will praise you
and extol your name for ever and ever.

³Great is the LORD and most worthy of praise;
his greatness no one can fathom.
⁴One generation will commend your works to another;
they will tell of your mighty acts.
⁵They will speak of the glorious splendor of your majesty,
and I will meditate on your wonderful works.[b]
⁶They will tell of the power of your awesome works,
and I will proclaim your great deeds.
⁷They will celebrate your abundant goodness
and joyfully sing of your righteousness.

⁸The LORD is gracious and compassionate,
slow to anger and rich in love.
⁹The LORD is good to all;
he has compassion on all he has made.
¹⁰All you have made will praise you, O LORD;
your saints will extol you.
¹¹They will tell of the glory of your kingdom
and speak of your might,
¹²so that all men may know of your mighty acts
and the glorious splendor of your kingdom.
¹³Your kingdom is an everlasting kingdom,
and your dominion endures through all generations.

The LORD is faithful to all his promises
and loving toward all he has made.[c]
¹⁴The LORD upholds all those who fall
and lifts up all who are bowed down.
¹⁵The eyes of all look to you,
and you give them their food at the proper time.
¹⁶You open your hand
and satisfy the desires of every living thing.

¹⁷The LORD is righteous in all his ways
and loving toward all he has made.
¹⁸The LORD is near to all who call on him,
to all who call on him in truth.
¹⁹He fulfills the desires of those who fear him;
he hears their cry and saves them.
²⁰The LORD watches over all who love him,
but all the wicked he will destroy.

²¹My mouth will speak in praise of the LORD.
Let every creature praise his holy name
for ever and ever.

Psalm 146

¹Praise the LORD.[d]

Praise the LORD, O my soul.
² I will praise the LORD all my life;
I will sing praise to my God as long as I live.

³Do not put your trust in princes,
in mortal men, who cannot save.
⁴When their spirit departs, they return to the ground;
on that very day their plans come to nothing.

⁵Blessed is he whose help is the God of Jacob,
whose hope is in the LORD his God,
⁶the Maker of heaven and earth,
the sea, and everything in them—
the LORD, who remains faithful forever.

---

[a] This psalm is an acrostic poem, the verses of which (including verse 13b) begin with the successive letters of the Hebrew alphabet. [b] 5 Dead Sea Scrolls and Syriac (see also Septuagint); Masoretic Text *On the glorious splendor of your majesty / and on your wonderful works I will meditate* [c] 13 One manuscript of the Masoretic Text, Dead Sea Scrolls and Syriac (see also Septuagint); most manuscripts of the Masoretic Text do not have the last two lines of verse 13. [d] 1 Hebrew *Hallelu Yah*; also in verse 10

⁷He upholds the cause of the oppressed
 and gives food to the hungry.
The LORD sets prisoners free,
⁸ the LORD gives sight to the blind,
 the LORD lifts up those who are bowed down,
 the LORD loves the righteous.
⁹The LORD watches over the alien
 and sustains the fatherless and the widow,
 but he frustrates the ways of the wicked.

¹⁰The LORD reigns forever,
 your God, O Zion, for all generations.

Praise the LORD.

Psalm 147

¹Praise the LORD.[a]

How good it is to sing praises to our God,
 how pleasant and fitting to praise him!

²The LORD builds up Jerusalem;
 he gathers the exiles of Israel.
³He heals the brokenhearted
 and binds up their wounds.
⁴He determines the number of the stars
 and calls them each by name.
⁵Great is our Lord and mighty in power;
 his understanding has no limit.
⁶The LORD sustains the humble
 but casts the wicked to the ground.

⁷Sing to the LORD with thanksgiving;
 make music to our God on the harp.
⁸He covers the sky with clouds;
 he supplies the earth with rain
 and makes grass grow on the hills.
⁹He provides food for the cattle
 and for the young ravens when they call.

¹⁰His pleasure is not in the strength of the horse,
 nor his delight in the legs of a man;
¹¹the LORD delights in those who fear him,
 who put their hope in his unfailing love.

¹²Extol the LORD, O Jerusalem;
 praise your God, O Zion,
¹³for he strengthens the bars of your gates
 and blesses your people within you.
¹⁴He grants peace to your borders
 and satisfies you with the finest of wheat.

¹⁵He sends his command to the earth;
 his word runs swiftly.
¹⁶He spreads the snow like wool
 and scatters the frost like ashes.
¹⁷He hurls down his hail like pebbles.
 Who can withstand his icy blast?
¹⁸He sends his word and melts them;
 he stirs up his breezes, and the waters flow.

¹⁹He has revealed his word to Jacob,
 his laws and decrees to Israel.
²⁰He has done this for no other nation;
 they do not know his laws.

Praise the LORD.

Psalm 148

¹Praise the LORD.[b]

Praise the LORD from the heavens,
 praise him in the heights above.
²Praise him, all his angels,
 praise him, all his heavenly hosts.
³Praise him, sun and moon,
 praise him, all you shining stars.
⁴Praise him, you highest heavens
 and you waters above the skies.
⁵Let them praise the name of the LORD,
 for he commanded and they were created.
⁶He set them in place for ever and ever;
 he gave a decree that will never pass away.

⁷Praise the LORD from the earth,
 you great sea creatures and all ocean depths,
⁸lightning and hail, snow and clouds,
 stormy winds that do his bidding,
⁹you mountains and all hills,
 fruit trees and all cedars,
¹⁰wild animals and all cattle,
 small creatures and flying birds,
¹¹kings of the earth and all nations,
 you princes and all rulers on earth,
¹²young men and maidens,
 old men and children.

¹³Let them praise the name of the LORD,
 for his name alone is exalted;

---

[a]1 Hebrew *Hallelu Yah*; also in verse 20   [b]1 Hebrew *Hallelu Yah*; also in verse 14

his splendor is above the earth and
  the heavens.
¹⁴He has raised up for his people a
    horn,ᵃ
  the praise of all his saints,
  of Israel, the people close to his
    heart.

Praise the Lord.

Psalm 149

¹Praise the Lord.ᵇ

Sing to the Lord a new song,
  his praise in the assembly of the
    saints.
²Let Israel rejoice in their Maker;
  let the people of Zion be glad in
    their King.
³Let them praise his name with
    dancing
  and make music to him with
    tambourine and harp.
⁴For the Lord takes delight in his
    people;
  he crowns the humble with
    salvation.
⁵Let the saints rejoice in this honor
  and sing for joy on their beds.

⁶May the praise of God be in their
    mouths
  and a double-edged sword in their
    hands,
⁷to inflict vengeance on the nations
  and punishment on the peoples,
⁸to bind their kings with fetters,
  their nobles with shackles of iron,
⁹to carry out the sentence written
    against them.
  This is the glory of all his saints.

Praise the Lord.

Psalm 150

¹Praise the Lord.ᶜ

Praise God in his sanctuary;
  praise him in his mighty heavens.
²Praise him for his acts of power;
  praise him for his surpassing
    greatness.
³Praise him with the sounding of the
    trumpet,
  praise him with the harp and lyre,
⁴praise him with tambourine and
    dancing,
  praise him with the strings and
    flute,
⁵praise him with the clash of cymbals,
  praise him with resounding
    cymbals.

⁶Let everything that has breath praise
  the Lord.

Praise the Lord.

ᵃ14 *Horn* here symbolizes strong one, that is, king. ᵇ1 Hebrew *Hallelu Yah*; also in verse 9
ᶜ1 Hebrew *Hallelu Yah*; also in verse 6

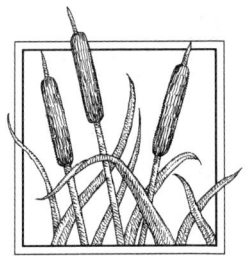

*S*OLOMON *"spoke three thousand proverbs" (1 Kings 4:32), many of which are collected in this book. These wise sayings describe patterns that operate in everyday life, offering us advice on how to conduct ourselves in various situations. Solomon's fundamental instruction is to fear and trust the Lord. As you read this book, remember that God has something to say about every aspect of your life; seek his wisdom in the decisions you must make each day.*

PROVERBS

Prologue: Purpose and Theme

1 The proverbs of Solomon son of David, king of Israel:

²for attaining wisdom and discipline;
    for understanding words of insight;
³for acquiring a disciplined and
        prudent life,
    doing what is right and just and
        fair;
⁴for giving prudence to the simple,
    knowledge and discretion to the
        young—
⁵let the wise listen and add to their
        learning,
    and let the discerning get
        guidance—
⁶for understanding proverbs and
        parables,
    the sayings and riddles of the wise.
⁷The fear of the LORD is the beginning
        of knowledge,

but fools[a] despise wisdom and discipline.

Exhortations to Embrace Wisdom

Warning Against Enticement

⁸Listen, my son, to your father's instruction
and do not forsake your mother's teaching.
⁹They will be a garland to grace your head
and a chain to adorn your neck.

¹⁰My son, if sinners entice you,
do not give in to them.
¹¹If they say, "Come along with us;

[a] 7 The Hebrew words rendered *fool* in Proverbs, and often elsewhere in the Old Testament, denote one who is morally deficient.

FRIDAY

VERSE FOR THE DAY:
Proverbs 1:7

AUTHOR:
D. Bruce Lockerbie

PASSAGE FOR THE DAY:
Proverbs 1:1–7

Discretion to the Young

HOW can we prevent ourselves from creating resentment in our children? Only by obeying the Word of God and staking our lives on its truth. If indeed "the fear of the Lord is the beginning of knowledge" (Proverbs 1:7), then before any father can dispense advice on "doing what is right and just and fair" (Proverbs 1:3), he himself must know the meaning of that reverential awe and the wisdom to which it leads.

The goal of a father's godly instruction must be this spiritual insight called in Proverbs wisdom, knowledge or understanding. But this wisdom isn't a scholastic accomplishment measured by high scores on the College Boards or admission to an Ivy League college. The true test of knowledge, according to Proverbs, goes beyond academic achievement to moral responsibility. It zeroes in on decision-making and shows itself best in the disciplining of the character; this results in "a disciplined and prudent life." To live prudently means to think clearly about one's choices and arrive at decisions controlled not by whim or appetite but by an understanding of the difference between right and wrong. This is what Proverbs also calls "discretion" or "discernment."

What we're talking about, then, is instruction that prepares a child to make wise choices, to be discreet and discerning. Such instruction doesn't presume that the child somehow already knows what's best ... So, from the earliest years, children must be taught and trained to tell the truth rather than lies; to respect the property of others rather than take for themselves; to keep from harming anyone else; to hold the miracle of life, whether animal, vegetable or human life, in highest regard.

Additional Scripture Readings:
Proverbs 3:1–18; James 3:13–18

Go to page 510 for your next devotional reading.

let's lie in wait for someone's blood,
  let's waylay some harmless soul;
¹²let's swallow them alive, like the grave,ᵃ
  and whole, like those who go down to the pit;
¹³we will get all sorts of valuable things
  and fill our houses with plunder;
¹⁴throw in your lot with us,
  and we will share a common purse"—
¹⁵my son, do not go along with them,
  do not set foot on their paths;
¹⁶for their feet rush into sin,
  they are swift to shed blood.
¹⁷How useless to spread a net
  in full view of all the birds!
¹⁸These men lie in wait for their own blood;
  they waylay only themselves!
¹⁹Such is the end of all who go after ill-gotten gain;
  it takes away the lives of those who get it.

Warning Against Rejecting Wisdom

²⁰Wisdom calls aloud in the street,
  she raises her voice in the public squares;
²¹at the head of the noisy streetsᵇ she cries out,
  in the gateways of the city she makes her speech:

²²"How long will you simple onesᶜ love your simple ways?
  How long will mockers delight in mockery
  and fools hate knowledge?
²³If you had responded to my rebuke,
  I would have poured out my heart to you
  and made my thoughts known to you.
²⁴But since you rejected me when I called
  and no one gave heed when I stretched out my hand,
²⁵since you ignored all my advice
  and would not accept my rebuke,
²⁶I in turn will laugh at your disaster;
  I will mock when calamity overtakes you—
²⁷when calamity overtakes you like a storm,
  when disaster sweeps over you like a whirlwind,
  when distress and trouble overwhelm you.

²⁸"Then they will call to me but I will not answer;
  they will look for me but will not find me.
²⁹Since they hated knowledge
  and did not choose to fear the LORD,
³⁰since they would not accept my advice
  and spurned my rebuke,
³¹they will eat the fruit of their ways
  and be filled with the fruit of their schemes.
³²For the waywardness of the simple will kill them,
  and the complacency of fools will destroy them;
³³but whoever listens to me will live in safety
  and be at ease, without fear of harm."

Moral Benefits of Wisdom

2 My son, if you accept my words
  and store up my commands within you,
²turning your ear to wisdom
  and applying your heart to understanding,
³and if you call out for insight
  and cry aloud for understanding,
⁴and if you look for it as for silver
  and search for it as for hidden treasure,
⁵then you will understand the fear of the LORD
  and find the knowledge of God.
⁶For the LORD gives wisdom,
  and from his mouth come knowledge and understanding.
⁷He holds victory in store for the upright,
  he is a shield to those whose walk is blameless,
⁸for he guards the course of the just
  and protects the way of his faithful ones.

⁹Then you will understand what is right and just
  and fair—every good path.
¹⁰For wisdom will enter your heart,
  and knowledge will be pleasant to your soul.
¹¹Discretion will protect you,
  and understanding will guard you.

ᵃ 12 Hebrew *Sheol*   ᵇ 21 Hebrew; Septuagint / *on the tops of the walls*   ᶜ 22 The Hebrew word rendered *simple* in Proverbs generally denotes one without moral direction and inclined to evil.

WEEKENDING

RETHINK

The home is the greenhouse where godly wisdom is cultivated. The power of consistent Christian living in the context of family relationships is the primary spiritual classroom for authentic Christianity. The home is where the majority of behavioral traits—good and bad—are learned, reinforced and passed along to future generations . . .

A home is . . . filled with fragrant and appealing spiritual riches when each member adopts a servant's spirit. Most family arguments and dissension stem from a failure to yield personal rights. A person filled with the Spirit of Christ strongly desires to serve. He does not seek to establish his own emotional turf but freely edifies and encourages other family members through his servant spirit.
– *Charles Stanley*

REVIVE
Saturday: Mark 9:33–37
Sunday: Philippians 2:1–11

Go to page 511 for your next devotional reading.

PROVERBS 2

¹²Wisdom will save you from the ways
of wicked men,
from men whose words are
perverse,
¹³who leave the straight paths
to walk in dark ways,
¹⁴who delight in doing wrong
and rejoice in the perverseness of
evil,
¹⁵whose paths are crooked
and who are devious in their
ways.

¹⁶It will save you also from the
adulteress,
from the wayward wife with her
seductive words,
¹⁷who has left the partner of her youth

MONDAY

VERSE FOR THE DAY:
Proverbs 2:6

AUTHOR:
Steve Farrar

PASSAGE FOR THE DAY:
Proverbs 2:1–11

Save the Boys

WE SAVE our boys by giving them a role model to follow. When our boys have a clear role model, they intuitively know how to function when they assume the responsibility of marriage and parenting. But in their generation, there are too many crippled boys who have no idea what it is to be a man.

It is my God-appointed task to ensure that my sons will be ready to lead a family. I must equip them to that end. Little boys are the hope of the next generation. They are the fathers of tomorrow. They must know who they are and what they are to do. They must see their role model in action. That's how they will know what it means to be a male. That puts the ball in my court . . . and in yours . . .

It's our job to save the boys. So the question is, how are we going to do that? My boys are eight and five. I've got ten years left with John before he heads out to college, thirteen with Josh. That time is simply going to fly by. So I must have a pretty clear idea of what I need to teach them during those remaining years. I must ask myself: *What do I specifically need to do in order to train them to become leaders of their families?*

I have five goals for saving my boys. It is my job as their father to model for them the importance of

- knowing and obeying Jesus Christ,
- knowing and displaying godly character,
- knowing and loving my wife,
- knowing and loving my children, and
- knowing my gifts and abilities, so I can work hard and effectively in an area of strength, rather than weakness, and contribute effectively to the lives of others—and have a little fun at the same time.

Additional Scripture Readings:
Philippians 3:7–11; 1 Peter 4:7–11

Go to page 513 for your next devotional reading.

and ignored the covenant she made
before God.^a
¹⁸For her house leads down to death
and her paths to the spirits of the
dead.
¹⁹None who go to her return
or attain the paths of life.

²⁰Thus you will walk in the ways of
good men
and keep to the paths of the
righteous.
²¹For the upright will live in the land,
and the blameless will remain in it;
²²but the wicked will be cut off from
the land,
and the unfaithful will be torn from
it.

Further Benefits of Wisdom

3 My son, do not forget my teaching,
but keep my commands in your
heart,
²for they will prolong your life many
years
and bring you prosperity.

³Let love and faithfulness never leave
you;
bind them around your neck,
write them on the tablet of your
heart.
⁴Then you will win favor and a good
name
in the sight of God and man.

⁵Trust in the Lord with all your heart
and lean not on your own
understanding;
⁶in all your ways acknowledge him,
and he will make your paths
straight.^b

⁷Do not be wise in your own eyes;
fear the Lord and shun evil.
⁸This will bring health to your body
and nourishment to your bones.

⁹Honor the Lord with your wealth,
with the firstfruits of all your crops;
¹⁰then your barns will be filled to
overflowing,
and your vats will brim over with
new wine.

¹¹My son, do not despise the Lord's
discipline
and do not resent his rebuke,
¹²because the Lord disciplines those he
loves,
as a father^c the son he delights in.

¹³Blessed is the man who finds wisdom,
the man who gains understanding,
¹⁴for she is more profitable than silver
and yields better returns than gold.
¹⁵She is more precious than rubies;
nothing you desire can compare
with her.
¹⁶Long life is in her right hand;
in her left hand are riches and
honor.
¹⁷Her ways are pleasant ways,
and all her paths are peace.
¹⁸She is a tree of life to those who
embrace her;
those who lay hold of her will be
blessed.

¹⁹By wisdom the Lord laid the earth's
foundations,
by understanding he set the
heavens in place;
²⁰by his knowledge the deeps were
divided,
and the clouds let drop the dew.

²¹My son, preserve sound judgment and
discernment,
do not let them out of your sight;
²²they will be life for you,
an ornament to grace your neck.
²³Then you will go on your way in
safety,
and your foot will not stumble;
²⁴when you lie down, you will not be
afraid;
when you lie down, your sleep will
be sweet.
²⁵Have no fear of sudden disaster
or of the ruin that overtakes the
wicked,
²⁶for the Lord will be your confidence
and will keep your foot from being
snared.

²⁷Do not withhold good from those who
deserve it,
when it is in your power to act.
²⁸Do not say to your neighbor,
"Come back later; I'll give it
tomorrow"—
when you now have it with
you.

²⁹Do not plot harm against your
neighbor,
who lives trustfully near you.
³⁰Do not accuse a man for no reason—
when he has done you no harm.
³¹Do not envy a violent man
or choose any of his ways,

---

^a17 Or *covenant of her God*   ^b6 Or *will direct your paths*   ^c12 Hebrew; Septuagint / *and he punishes*

³²for the LORD detests a perverse man
but takes the upright into his
confidence.

³³The LORD's curse is on the house of
the wicked,
but he blesses the home of the
righteous.
³⁴He mocks proud mockers
but gives grace to the humble.
³⁵The wise inherit honor,
but fools he holds up to shame.

Wisdom Is Supreme

4 Listen, my sons, to a father's
instruction;
pay attention and gain
understanding.
²I give you sound learning,

TUESDAY

VERSE FOR THE DAY:
Proverbs 3:6

AUTHOR:
Bill Hybels

PASSAGE FOR THE DAY:
Proverbs 3:1–6

An Endangered Trait

WE USED to play a game at summer camp in which we would blindfold one of the kids and have him or her run through a wooded area, relying on a friend for verbal directions to help navigate. "Turn to the left; there's a tree coming!" "There's a log in front of you—*jump!*" Some kids would not trust the verbal directions whatsoever. They would shuffle their feet and walk very slowly, even though their friends were shouting that the way was clear. Other kids would trot along, and a few would go like gangbusters. All the kids, though, had to fight the urge to tear off the blindfold so that they could see what was ahead. It takes a great deal of courage to follow another person's lead.

As Christians, we sometimes feel like those blindfolded children. Paul says in 2 Corinthians 5:7, "We live by faith, not by sight." We are not alone in the woods, though—God will direct our paths. But following Jesus Christ demands an enormous amount of courage. Quite often his leadings sound illogical, irrational, countercultural. Sometimes he is so challenging that I say, "No, I think I'll just crawl back into my shell and play it safe." Then a voice inside me says, "Where's your courage, Hybels? Get up and walk. You can trust God."

Cowards do not last long on their spiritual pilgrimages. They shrivel up and disappear. It takes enormous courage to repent and become a Christian. It takes enormous courage to follow God's leadings in the Christian life. Some of his callings demand the best that you can summon. Some of his tests stretch you to the limit. Some of his adventures evoke great fears and doubts. Truly, spiritual courage is on the endangered character-quality list.

Additional Scripture Readings:
1 Corinthians 16:13–14;
2 Peter 1:3–11

*Go to page 516 for your next
devotional reading.*

so do not forsake my teaching.
³When I was a boy in my father's house,
still tender, and an only child of my mother,
⁴he taught me and said,
"Lay hold of my words with all your heart;
keep my commands and you will live.
⁵Get wisdom, get understanding;
do not forget my words or swerve from them.
⁶Do not forsake wisdom, and she will protect you;
love her, and she will watch over you.
⁷Wisdom is supreme; therefore get wisdom.
Though it cost all you have,ᵃ get understanding.
⁸Esteem her, and she will exalt you;
embrace her, and she will honor you.
⁹She will set a garland of grace on your head
and present you with a crown of splendor."

¹⁰Listen, my son, accept what I say,
and the years of your life will be many.
¹¹I guide you in the way of wisdom
and lead you along straight paths.
¹²When you walk, your steps will not be hampered;
when you run, you will not stumble.
¹³Hold on to instruction, do not let it go;
guard it well, for it is your life.
¹⁴Do not set foot on the path of the wicked
or walk in the way of evil men.
¹⁵Avoid it, do not travel on it;
turn from it and go on your way.
¹⁶For they cannot sleep till they do evil;
they are robbed of slumber till they make someone fall.
¹⁷They eat the bread of wickedness
and drink the wine of violence.

¹⁸The path of the righteous is like the first gleam of dawn,
shining ever brighter till the full light of day.
¹⁹But the way of the wicked is like deep darkness;
they do not know what makes them stumble.

²⁰My son, pay attention to what I say;
listen closely to my words.
²¹Do not let them out of your sight,
keep them within your heart;
²²for they are life to those who find them
and health to a man's whole body.
²³Above all else, guard your heart,
for it is the wellspring of life.
²⁴Put away perversity from your mouth;
keep corrupt talk far from your lips.
²⁵Let your eyes look straight ahead,
fix your gaze directly before you.
²⁶Make levelᵇ paths for your feet
and take only ways that are firm.
²⁷Do not swerve to the right or the left;
keep your foot from evil.

Warning Against Adultery

5 My son, pay attention to my wisdom,
listen well to my words of insight,
²that you may maintain discretion
and your lips may preserve knowledge.
³For the lips of an adulteress drip honey,
and her speech is smoother than oil;
⁴but in the end she is bitter as gall,
sharp as a double-edged sword.
⁵Her feet go down to death;
her steps lead straight to the grave.ᶜ
⁶She gives no thought to the way of life;
her paths are crooked, but she knows it not.

⁷Now then, my sons, listen to me;
do not turn aside from what I say.
⁸Keep to a path far from her,
do not go near the door of her house,
⁹lest you give your best strength to others
and your years to one who is cruel,
¹⁰lest strangers feast on your wealth
and your toil enrich another man's house.
¹¹At the end of your life you will groan,
when your flesh and body are spent.
¹²You will say, "How I hated discipline!
How my heart spurned correction!
¹³I would not obey my teachers

ᵃ7 Or *Whatever else you get*   ᵇ26 Or *Consider the*   ᶜ5 Hebrew *Sheol*

or listen to my instructors.
¹⁴I have come to the brink of utter ruin
in the midst of the whole
assembly."

¹⁵Drink water from your own cistern,
running water from your own well.
¹⁶Should your springs overflow in the
streets,
your streams of water in the public
squares?
¹⁷Let them be yours alone,
never to be shared with strangers.
¹⁸May your fountain be blessed,
and may you rejoice in the wife of
your youth.
¹⁹A loving doe, a graceful deer—
may her breasts satisfy you always,
may you ever be captivated by her
love.
²⁰Why be captivated, my son, by an
adulteress?
Why embrace the bosom of another
man's wife?

²¹For a man's ways are in full view of
the LORD,
and he examines all his paths.
²²The evil deeds of a wicked man
ensnare him;
the cords of his sin hold him fast.
²³He will die for lack of discipline,
led astray by his own great folly.

Warnings Against Folly

6 My son, if you have put up security
for your neighbor,
if you have struck hands in pledge
for another,
²if you have been trapped by what you
said,
ensnared by the words of your
mouth,
³then do this, my son, to free yourself,
since you have fallen into your
neighbor's hands:
Go and humble yourself;
press your plea with your neighbor!
⁴Allow no sleep to your eyes,
no slumber to your eyelids.
⁵Free yourself, like a gazelle from the
hand of the hunter,
like a bird from the snare of the
fowler.

⁶Go to the ant, you sluggard;
consider its ways and be wise!
⁷It has no commander,
no overseer or ruler,
⁸yet it stores its provisions in summer
and gathers its food at harvest.

⁹How long will you lie there, you
sluggard?
When will you get up from your
sleep?
¹⁰A little sleep, a little slumber,
a little folding of the hands to
rest—
¹¹and poverty will come on you like a
bandit
and scarcity like an armed man.[a]

¹²A scoundrel and villain,
who goes about with a corrupt
mouth,
¹³ who winks with his eye,
signals with his feet
and motions with his fingers,
¹⁴ who plots evil with deceit in his
heart—
he always stirs up dissension.
¹⁵Therefore disaster will overtake him in
an instant;
he will suddenly be destroyed—
without remedy.

¹⁶There are six things the LORD hates,
seven that are detestable to him:
¹⁷ haughty eyes,
a lying tongue,
hands that shed innocent blood,
¹⁸ a heart that devises wicked
schemes,
feet that are quick to rush into
evil,
¹⁹ a false witness who pours out lies
and a man who stirs up
dissension among brothers.

Warning Against Adultery

²⁰My son, keep your father's commands
and do not forsake your mother's
teaching.
²¹Bind them upon your heart forever;
fasten them around your neck.
²²When you walk, they will guide you;
when you sleep, they will watch
over you;
when you awake, they will speak to
you.
²³For these commands are a lamp,
this teaching is a light,
and the corrections of discipline
are the way to life,
²⁴keeping you from the immoral
woman,

---

[a] 11 Or *like a vagrant / and scarcity like a beggar*

from the smooth tongue of the
wayward wife.
²⁵Do not lust in your heart after her
beauty
or let her captivate you with her
eyes,
²⁶for the prostitute reduces you to a loaf
of bread,
and the adulteress preys upon your
very life.
²⁷Can a man scoop fire into his lap
without his clothes being burned?
²⁸Can a man walk on hot coals
without his feet being scorched?
²⁹So is he who sleeps with another
man's wife;
no one who touches her will go
unpunished.

³⁰Men do not despise a thief if he steals
to satisfy his hunger when he is
starving.
³¹Yet if he is caught, he must pay
sevenfold,
though it costs him all the wealth of
his house.
³²But a man who commits adultery
lacks judgment;
whoever does so destroys himself.
³³Blows and disgrace are his lot,
and his shame will never be wiped
away;
³⁴for jealousy arouses a husband's
fury,
and he will show no mercy when
he takes revenge.
³⁵He will not accept any compensation;

WEDNESDAY

VERSE FOR THE DAY:
Proverbs 6:20

AUTHOR:
Charles Swindoll

PASSAGE FOR THE DAY:
Proverbs 6:20–29

He Gives Us Boys

THROUGHOUT history, long before the marines, God has been looking for a few good men:

"For the eyes of the LORD range throughout the earth to strengthen those whose hearts are fully committed to him" (2 Chronicles 16:9a).

"I looked for a man among them who would build up the wall and stand before me in the gap" (Ezekiel 22:30a).

God, give us men. Give us Noahs, to whom you can trust your mighty plans; give us Abrahams, who are willing to leave home and homeland to follow your call; give us Josephs, who would rather endure prison than violate one of your commands; give us Moseses, who are willing to stand as your mouthpiece against the most powerful leaders in all the world; give us Daniels, who would rather face a lions' den than compromise their faith; *God, give us men.* However, the reality is that God *does not* give us men—he gives us *boys*. To us, as parents, he gives the task of forging these boys into men. To help equip us for that task, God has provided the book of Proverbs, which is largely the advice of a father to his son... Our children are our legacy. As a parent, are you taking that thought seriously?

Additional Scripture Readings:
Psalm 127:1–5; Proverbs 1:8–19

Go to page 523 for your next devotional reading.

he will refuse the bribe, however great it is.

Warning Against the Adulteress

7 My son, keep my words
and store up my commands within you.
²Keep my commands and you will live;
guard my teachings as the apple of your eye.
³Bind them on your fingers;
write them on the tablet of your heart.
⁴Say to wisdom, "You are my sister,"
and call understanding your kinsman;
⁵they will keep you from the adulteress,
from the wayward wife with her seductive words.

⁶At the window of my house
I looked out through the lattice.
⁷I saw among the simple,
I noticed among the young men,
a youth who lacked judgment.
⁸He was going down the street near her corner,
walking along in the direction of her house
⁹at twilight, as the day was fading,
as the dark of night set in.

¹⁰Then out came a woman to meet him,
dressed like a prostitute and with crafty intent.
¹¹(She is loud and defiant,
her feet never stay at home;
¹²now in the street, now in the squares,
at every corner she lurks.)
¹³She took hold of him and kissed him
and with a brazen face she said:

¹⁴"I have fellowship offerings[a] at home;
today I fulfilled my vows.
¹⁵So I came out to meet you;
I looked for you and have found you!
¹⁶I have covered my bed
with colored linens from Egypt.
¹⁷I have perfumed my bed
with myrrh, aloes and cinnamon.
¹⁸Come, let's drink deep of love till morning;
let's enjoy ourselves with love!
¹⁹My husband is not at home;
he has gone on a long journey.
²⁰He took his purse filled with money
and will not be home till full moon."

²¹With persuasive words she led him astray;
she seduced him with her smooth talk.
²²All at once he followed her
like an ox going to the slaughter,
like a deer[b] stepping into a noose[c]
²³ till an arrow pierces his liver,
like a bird darting into a snare,
little knowing it will cost him his life.

²⁴Now then, my sons, listen to me;
pay attention to what I say.
²⁵Do not let your heart turn to her ways
or stray into her paths.
²⁶Many are the victims she has brought down;
her slain are a mighty throng.
²⁷Her house is a highway to the grave,[d]
leading down to the chambers of death.

Wisdom's Call

8 Does not wisdom call out?
Does not understanding raise her voice?
²On the heights along the way,
where the paths meet, she takes her stand;
³beside the gates leading into the city,
at the entrances, she cries aloud:
⁴"To you, O men, I call out;
I raise my voice to all mankind.
⁵You who are simple, gain prudence;
you who are foolish, gain understanding.
⁶Listen, for I have worthy things to say;
I open my lips to speak what is right.
⁷My mouth speaks what is true,
for my lips detest wickedness.
⁸All the words of my mouth are just;
none of them is crooked or perverse.
⁹To the discerning all of them are right;
they are faultless to those who have knowledge.
¹⁰Choose my instruction instead of silver,
knowledge rather than choice gold,
¹¹for wisdom is more precious than rubies,

---

a14 Traditionally *peace offerings*   *b22* Syriac (see also Septuagint); Hebrew *fool*   *c22* The meaning of the Hebrew for this line is uncertain.   *d27* Hebrew *Sheol*

and nothing you desire can compare
with her.
¹²"I, wisdom, dwell together with
prudence;
I possess knowledge and discretion.
¹³To fear the LORD is to hate evil;
I hate pride and arrogance,
evil behavior and perverse speech.
¹⁴Counsel and sound judgment are
mine;
I have understanding and power.
¹⁵By me kings reign
and rulers make laws that are just;
¹⁶by me princes govern,
and all nobles who rule on earth.*ᵃ*
¹⁷I love those who love me,
and those who seek me find me.
¹⁸With me are riches and honor,
enduring wealth and prosperity.
¹⁹My fruit is better than fine gold;
what I yield surpasses choice silver.
²⁰I walk in the way of righteousness,
along the paths of justice,
²¹bestowing wealth on those who love
me
and making their treasuries full.

²²"The LORD brought me forth as the
first of his works,*ᵇ,ᶜ*
before his deeds of old;
²³I was appointed*ᵈ* from eternity,
from the beginning, before the
world began.
²⁴When there were no oceans, I was
given birth,
when there were no springs
abounding with water;
²⁵before the mountains were settled in
place,
before the hills, I was given birth,
²⁶before he made the earth or its fields
or any of the dust of the world.
²⁷I was there when he set the heavens
in place,
when he marked out the horizon on
the face of the deep,
²⁸when he established the clouds above
and fixed securely the fountains of
the deep,
²⁹when he gave the sea its boundary
so the waters would not overstep
his command,
and when he marked out the
foundations of the earth.
³⁰ Then I was the craftsman at his
side.

I was filled with delight day after day,
rejoicing always in his presence,
³¹rejoicing in his whole world
and delighting in mankind.

³²"Now then, my sons, listen to me;
blessed are those who keep my
ways.
³³Listen to my instruction and be wise;
do not ignore it.
³⁴Blessed is the man who listens to me,
watching daily at my doors,
waiting at my doorway.
³⁵For whoever finds me finds life
and receives favor from the LORD.
³⁶But whoever fails to find me harms
himself;
all who hate me love death."

Invitations of Wisdom and of Folly

9 Wisdom has built her house;
she has hewn out its seven pillars.
²She has prepared her meat and mixed
her wine;
she has also set her table.
³She has sent out her maids, and she
calls
from the highest point of the city.
⁴"Let all who are simple come in here!"
she says to those who lack
judgment.
⁵"Come, eat my food
and drink the wine I have mixed.
⁶Leave your simple ways and you will
live;
walk in the way of understanding.

⁷"Whoever corrects a mocker invites
insult;
whoever rebukes a wicked man
incurs abuse.
⁸Do not rebuke a mocker or he will
hate you;
rebuke a wise man and he will love
you.
⁹Instruct a wise man and he will be
wiser still;
teach a righteous man and he will
add to his learning.

¹⁰"The fear of the LORD is the beginning
of wisdom,
and knowledge of the Holy One is
understanding.
¹¹For through me your days will be
many,
and years will be added to your life.

ᵃ16 Many Hebrew manuscripts and Septuagint; most Hebrew manuscripts *and nobles—all righteous rulers*
ᵇ22 Or *way;* or *dominion*   *ᶜ22* Or *The LORD possessed me at the beginning of his work;* or *The LORD brought me forth at the beginning of his work*   *ᵈ23* Or *fashioned*

¹²If you are wise, your wisdom will reward you;
if you are a mocker, you alone will suffer."

¹³The woman Folly is loud;
she is undisciplined and without knowledge.
¹⁴She sits at the door of her house,
on a seat at the highest point of the city,
¹⁵calling out to those who pass by,
who go straight on their way.
¹⁶"Let all who are simple come in here!"
she says to those who lack judgment.
¹⁷"Stolen water is sweet;
food eaten in secret is delicious!"
¹⁸But little do they know that the dead are there,
that her guests are in the depths of the grave.ᵃ

Proverbs of Solomon

10 The proverbs of Solomon:

A wise son brings joy to his father,
but a foolish son grief to his mother.

²Ill-gotten treasures are of no value,
but righteousness delivers from death.

³The LORD does not let the righteous go hungry
but he thwarts the craving of the wicked.

⁴Lazy hands make a man poor,
but diligent hands bring wealth.

⁵He who gathers crops in summer is a wise son,
but he who sleeps during harvest is a disgraceful son.

⁶Blessings crown the head of the righteous,
but violence overwhelms the mouth of the wicked.ᵇ

⁷The memory of the righteous will be a blessing,
but the name of the wicked will rot.

⁸The wise in heart accept commands,
but a chattering fool comes to ruin.

⁹The man of integrity walks securely,
but he who takes crooked paths will be found out.

¹⁰He who winks maliciously causes grief,
and a chattering fool comes to ruin.

¹¹The mouth of the righteous is a fountain of life,
but violence overwhelms the mouth of the wicked.

¹²Hatred stirs up dissension,
but love covers over all wrongs.

¹³Wisdom is found on the lips of the discerning,
but a rod is for the back of him who lacks judgment.

¹⁴Wise men store up knowledge,
but the mouth of a fool invites ruin.

¹⁵The wealth of the rich is their fortified city,
but poverty is the ruin of the poor.

¹⁶The wages of the righteous bring them life,
but the income of the wicked brings them punishment.

¹⁷He who heeds discipline shows the way to life,
but whoever ignores correction leads others astray.

¹⁸He who conceals his hatred has lying lips,
and whoever spreads slander is a fool.

¹⁹When words are many, sin is not absent,
but he who holds his tongue is wise.

²⁰The tongue of the righteous is choice silver,
but the heart of the wicked is of little value.

²¹The lips of the righteous nourish many,
but fools die for lack of judgment.

²²The blessing of the LORD brings wealth,
and he adds no trouble to it.

²³A fool finds pleasure in evil conduct,
but a man of understanding delights in wisdom.

²⁴What the wicked dreads will overtake him;
what the righteous desire will be granted.

ᵃ18 Hebrew *Sheol* ᵇ6 Or *but the mouth of the wicked conceals violence*; also in verse 11

²⁵When the storm has swept by, the
    wicked are gone,
but the righteous stand firm forever.

²⁶As vinegar to the teeth and smoke to
    the eyes,
so is a sluggard to those who send
    him.

²⁷The fear of the LORD adds length to
    life,
but the years of the wicked are cut
    short.

²⁸The prospect of the righteous is joy,
but the hopes of the wicked come
    to nothing.

²⁹The way of the LORD is a refuge for
    the righteous,
but it is the ruin of those who do
    evil.

³⁰The righteous will never be uprooted,
but the wicked will not remain in
    the land.

³¹The mouth of the righteous brings
    forth wisdom,
but a perverse tongue will be cut
    out.

³²The lips of the righteous know what is
    fitting,
but the mouth of the wicked only
    what is perverse.

11 The LORD abhors dishonest
    scales,
but accurate weights are his delight.

²When pride comes, then comes
    disgrace,
but with humility comes wisdom.

³The integrity of the upright guides
    them,
but the unfaithful are destroyed by
    their duplicity.

⁴Wealth is worthless in the day of
    wrath,
but righteousness delivers from
    death.

⁵The righteousness of the blameless
    makes a straight way for them,
but the wicked are brought down
    by their own wickedness.

⁶The righteousness of the upright
    delivers them,
but the unfaithful are trapped by
    evil desires.

⁷When a wicked man dies, his hope
    perishes;
all he expected from his power
    comes to nothing.

⁸The righteous man is rescued from
    trouble,
and it comes on the wicked instead.

⁹With his mouth the godless destroys
    his neighbor,
but through knowledge the
    righteous escape.

¹⁰When the righteous prosper, the city
    rejoices;
when the wicked perish, there are
    shouts of joy.

¹¹Through the blessing of the upright a
    city is exalted,
but by the mouth of the wicked it is
    destroyed.

¹²A man who lacks judgment derides
    his neighbor,
but a man of understanding holds
    his tongue.

¹³A gossip betrays a confidence,
but a trustworthy man keeps a
    secret.

¹⁴For lack of guidance a nation falls,
but many advisers make victory
    sure.

¹⁵He who puts up security for another
    will surely suffer,
but whoever refuses to strike hands
    in pledge is safe.

¹⁶A kindhearted woman gains respect,
but ruthless men gain only wealth.

¹⁷A kind man benefits himself,
but a cruel man brings trouble on
    himself.

¹⁸The wicked man earns deceptive
    wages,
but he who sows righteousness
    reaps a sure reward.

¹⁹The truly righteous man attains life,
but he who pursues evil goes to his
    death.

²⁰The LORD detests men of perverse
    heart
but he delights in those whose ways
    are blameless.

²¹Be sure of this: The wicked will not
    go unpunished,
but those who are righteous will go
    free.

²²Like a gold ring in a pig's snout

is a beautiful woman who shows no discretion.

²³The desire of the righteous ends only in good,
but the hope of the wicked only in wrath.

²⁴One man gives freely, yet gains even more;
another withholds unduly, but comes to poverty.

²⁵A generous man will prosper;
he who refreshes others will himself be refreshed.

²⁶People curse the man who hoards grain,
but blessing crowns him who is willing to sell.

²⁷He who seeks good finds goodwill,
but evil comes to him who searches for it.

²⁸Whoever trusts in his riches will fall,
but the righteous will thrive like a green leaf.

²⁹He who brings trouble on his family will inherit only wind,
and the fool will be servant to the wise.

³⁰The fruit of the righteous is a tree of life,
and he who wins souls is wise.

³¹If the righteous receive their due on earth,
how much more the ungodly and the sinner!

12 Whoever loves discipline loves knowledge,
but he who hates correction is stupid.

²A good man obtains favor from the LORD,
but the LORD condemns a crafty man.

³A man cannot be established through wickedness,
but the righteous cannot be uprooted.

⁴A wife of noble character is her husband's crown,
but a disgraceful wife is like decay in his bones.

⁵The plans of the righteous are just,
but the advice of the wicked is deceitful.

⁶The words of the wicked lie in wait for blood,
but the speech of the upright rescues them.

⁷Wicked men are overthrown and are no more,
but the house of the righteous stands firm.

⁸A man is praised according to his wisdom,
but men with warped minds are despised.

⁹Better to be a nobody and yet have a servant
than pretend to be somebody and have no food.

¹⁰A righteous man cares for the needs of his animal,
but the kindest acts of the wicked are cruel.

¹¹He who works his land will have abundant food,
but he who chases fantasies lacks judgment.

¹²The wicked desire the plunder of evil men,
but the root of the righteous flourishes.

¹³An evil man is trapped by his sinful talk,
but a righteous man escapes trouble.

¹⁴From the fruit of his lips a man is filled with good things
as surely as the work of his hands rewards him.

¹⁵The way of a fool seems right to him,
but a wise man listens to advice.

¹⁶A fool shows his annoyance at once,
but a prudent man overlooks an insult.

¹⁷A truthful witness gives honest testimony,
but a false witness tells lies.

¹⁸Reckless words pierce like a sword,
but the tongue of the wise brings healing.

¹⁹Truthful lips endure forever,
but a lying tongue lasts only a moment.

²⁰There is deceit in the hearts of those who plot evil,

but joy for those who promote peace.

²¹No harm befalls the righteous,
but the wicked have their fill of trouble.

²²The LORD detests lying lips,
but he delights in men who are truthful.

²³A prudent man keeps his knowledge to himself,
but the heart of fools blurts out folly.

²⁴Diligent hands will rule,
but laziness ends in slave labor.

²⁵An anxious heart weighs a man down,
but a kind word cheers him up.

²⁶A righteous man is cautious in friendship,[a]
but the way of the wicked leads them astray.

²⁷The lazy man does not roast[b] his game,
but the diligent man prizes his possessions.

²⁸In the way of righteousness there is life;
along that path is immortality.

13

A wise son heeds his father's instruction,
but a mocker does not listen to rebuke.

²From the fruit of his lips a man enjoys good things,
but the unfaithful have a craving for violence.

³He who guards his lips guards his life,
but he who speaks rashly will come to ruin.

⁴The sluggard craves and gets nothing,
but the desires of the diligent are fully satisfied.

⁵The righteous hate what is false,
but the wicked bring shame and disgrace.

⁶Righteousness guards the man of integrity,
but wickedness overthrows the sinner.

⁷One man pretends to be rich, yet has nothing;
another pretends to be poor, yet has great wealth.

⁸A man's riches may ransom his life,
but a poor man hears no threat.

⁹The light of the righteous shines brightly,
but the lamp of the wicked is snuffed out.

¹⁰Pride only breeds quarrels,
but wisdom is found in those who take advice.

¹¹Dishonest money dwindles away,
but he who gathers money little by little makes it grow.

¹²Hope deferred makes the heart sick,
but a longing fulfilled is a tree of life.

¹³He who scorns instruction will pay for it,
but he who respects a command is rewarded.

¹⁴The teaching of the wise is a fountain of life,
turning a man from the snares of death.

¹⁵Good understanding wins favor,
but the way of the unfaithful is hard.[c]

¹⁶Every prudent man acts out of knowledge,
but a fool exposes his folly.

¹⁷A wicked messenger falls into trouble,
but a trustworthy envoy brings healing.

¹⁸He who ignores discipline comes to poverty and shame,
but whoever heeds correction is honored.

¹⁹A longing fulfilled is sweet to the soul,
but fools detest turning from evil.

²⁰He who walks with the wise grows wise,
but a companion of fools suffers harm.

²¹Misfortune pursues the sinner,
but prosperity is the reward of the righteous.

---

[a]26 Or *man is a guide to his neighbor*   [b]27 The meaning of the Hebrew for this word is uncertain.
[c]15 Or *unfaithful does not endure*

²²A good man leaves an inheritance for his children's children,
but a sinner's wealth is stored up for the righteous.

²³A poor man's field may produce abundant food,
but injustice sweeps it away.

²⁴He who spares the rod hates his son,
but he who loves him is careful to discipline him.

²⁵The righteous eat to their hearts' content,
but the stomach of the wicked goes hungry.

14 The wise woman builds her house,
but with her own hands the foolish one tears hers down.

²He whose walk is upright fears the LORD,
but he whose ways are devious despises him.

THURSDAY

VERSE FOR THE DAY:
Proverbs 13:11

AUTHOR:
Ron Blue

PASSAGE FOR THE DAY:
Proverbs 13:7–11

Lesson on Stewardship

RECENTLY I was walking from the Sunday morning worship service to my Sunday school class when a teacher stopped me to ask if I could help him with his lesson on stewardship for that morning. The class was to start in just a few minutes, but I agreed to tell him all I could in that brief time. I said a quick prayer asking for wisdom and the thought came to my mind that my basic message is threefold.

1. God owns it all.
2. Money is never an end in itself, but is merely a resource used to accomplish other goals and obligations.
3. Spend less than you earn and do it for a long time, and you will be financially successful.

There is tremendous freedom of mind in knowing and believing that God owns it all, and that money is nothing more than a resource provided by God to allow us to accomplish his purposes on this earth.

Is it wrong then to have a long-term goal of financial independence? I believe not—unless financial independence is defined as having enough to be independent from God. This whole question is really one of "How much is enough?"

How do you achieve one or more of the long-term goals, such as financial independence, college education, improving your lifestyle, getting out of debt, making major contributions or starting your own business? The answer is simple—spend less than you earn and do it for a long time—or as the Bible says, "He who gathers money little by little makes it grow" (Proverbs 13:11).

Additional Scripture Readings:
Proverbs 10:4; 1 Timothy 6:17–19

Go to page 526 for your next devotional reading.

³A fool's talk brings a rod to his back,
  but the lips of the wise protect
    them.

⁴Where there are no oxen, the manger
    is empty,
  but from the strength of an ox
    comes an abundant harvest.

⁵A truthful witness does not deceive,
  but a false witness pours out lies.

⁶The mocker seeks wisdom and finds
    none,
  but knowledge comes easily to the
    discerning.

⁷Stay away from a foolish man,
  for you will not find knowledge on
    his lips.

⁸The wisdom of the prudent is to give
    thought to their ways,
  but the folly of fools is deception.

⁹Fools mock at making amends for sin,
  but goodwill is found among the
    upright.

¹⁰Each heart knows its own bitterness,
  and no one else can share its joy.

¹¹The house of the wicked will be
    destroyed,
  but the tent of the upright will
    flourish.

¹²There is a way that seems right to a
    man,
  but in the end it leads to death.

¹³Even in laughter the heart may ache,
  and joy may end in grief.

¹⁴The faithless will be fully repaid for
    their ways,
  and the good man rewarded for his.

¹⁵A simple man believes anything,
  but a prudent man gives thought to
    his steps.

¹⁶A wise man fears the LORD and shuns
    evil,
  but a fool is hotheaded and
    reckless.

¹⁷A quick-tempered man does foolish
    things,
  and a crafty man is hated.

¹⁸The simple inherit folly,
  but the prudent are crowned with
    knowledge.

¹⁹Evil men will bow down in the
    presence of the good,
  and the wicked at the gates of the
    righteous.

²⁰The poor are shunned even by their
    neighbors,
  but the rich have many friends.

²¹He who despises his neighbor sins,
  but blessed is he who is kind to the
    needy.

²²Do not those who plot evil go astray?
  But those who plan what is good
    find*a* love and faithfulness.

²³All hard work brings a profit,
  but mere talk leads only to poverty.

²⁴The wealth of the wise is their crown,
  but the folly of fools yields folly.

²⁵A truthful witness saves lives,
  but a false witness is deceitful.

²⁶He who fears the LORD has a secure
    fortress,
  and for his children it will be a
    refuge.

²⁷The fear of the LORD is a fountain of
    life,
  turning a man from the snares of
    death.

²⁸A large population is a king's glory,
  but without subjects a prince is
    ruined.

²⁹A patient man has great
    understanding,
  but a quick-tempered man displays
    folly.

³⁰A heart at peace gives life to the body,
  but envy rots the bones.

³¹He who oppresses the poor shows
    contempt for their Maker,
  but whoever is kind to the needy
    honors God.

³²When calamity comes, the wicked are
    brought down,
  but even in death the righteous
    have a refuge.

³³Wisdom reposes in the heart of the
    discerning
  and even among fools she lets
    herself be known.*b*

³⁴Righteousness exalts a nation,
  but sin is a disgrace to any people.

---

*a*22 Or *show*   *b*33 Hebrew; Septuagint and Syriac / *but in the heart of fools she is not known*

³⁵A king delights in a wise servant,
  but a shameful servant incurs his wrath.

15

¹A gentle answer turns away wrath,
  but a harsh word stirs up anger.

²The tongue of the wise commends knowledge,
  but the mouth of the fool gushes folly.

³The eyes of the LORD are everywhere,
  keeping watch on the wicked and the good.

⁴The tongue that brings healing is a tree of life,
  but a deceitful tongue crushes the spirit.

⁵A fool spurns his father's discipline,
  but whoever heeds correction shows prudence.

⁶The house of the righteous contains great treasure,
  but the income of the wicked brings them trouble.

⁷The lips of the wise spread knowledge;
  not so the hearts of fools.

⁸The LORD detests the sacrifice of the wicked,
  but the prayer of the upright pleases him.

⁹The LORD detests the way of the wicked
  but he loves those who pursue righteousness.

¹⁰Stern discipline awaits him who leaves the path;
  he who hates correction will die.

¹¹Death and Destruction[a] lie open before the LORD—
  how much more the hearts of men!

¹²A mocker resents correction;
  he will not consult the wise.

¹³A happy heart makes the face cheerful,
  but heartache crushes the spirit.

¹⁴The discerning heart seeks knowledge,
  but the mouth of a fool feeds on folly.

¹⁵All the days of the oppressed are wretched,
  but the cheerful heart has a continual feast.

¹⁶Better a little with the fear of the LORD
  than great wealth with turmoil.

¹⁷Better a meal of vegetables where there is love
  than a fattened calf with hatred.

¹⁸A hot-tempered man stirs up dissension,
  but a patient man calms a quarrel.

¹⁹The way of the sluggard is blocked with thorns,
  but the path of the upright is a highway.

²⁰A wise son brings joy to his father,
  but a foolish man despises his mother.

²¹Folly delights a man who lacks judgment,
  but a man of understanding keeps a straight course.

²²Plans fail for lack of counsel,
  but with many advisers they succeed.

²³A man finds joy in giving an apt reply—
  and how good is a timely word!

²⁴The path of life leads upward for the wise
  to keep him from going down to the grave.[b]

²⁵The LORD tears down the proud man's house
  but he keeps the widow's boundaries intact.

²⁶The LORD detests the thoughts of the wicked,
  but those of the pure are pleasing to him.

²⁷A greedy man brings trouble to his family,
  but he who hates bribes will live.

²⁸The heart of the righteous weighs its answers,
  but the mouth of the wicked gushes evil.

²⁹The LORD is far from the wicked
  but he hears the prayer of the righteous.

---

[a]11 Hebrew *Sheol* and *Abaddon*   [b]24 Hebrew *Sheol*

30 A cheerful look brings joy to the heart,
and good news gives health to the bones.

31 He who listens to a life-giving rebuke
will be at home among the wise.

32 He who ignores discipline despises himself,
but whoever heeds correction gains understanding.

33 The fear of the Lord teaches a man wisdom,*a*
and humility comes before honor.

16 To man belong the plans of the heart,
but from the Lord comes the reply of the tongue.

2 All a man's ways seem innocent to him,
but motives are weighed by the Lord.

a33 Or Wisdom teaches the fear of the Lord

FRIDAY

VERSE FOR THE DAY:
Proverbs 15:10

AUTHOR:
Reggie White

PASSAGE FOR THE DAY:
Proverbs 15:7–10

Accountability

AFTER the Lord, I'm first of all accountable to my wife, Sara. I know I can depend on her to tell it like it is. God always uses Sara to affirm or negate whatever may surface in my life. Spiritually, I'm also accountable to some Christian friends who give me sound spiritual guidance . . .

Any one of them can talk to me for just a few minutes and discern whether I'm walking close to the Lord or if I might just need a spiritual kick in the seat of my pants. I can really count on them to tell me when I'm straying off the path—whether I ask to do so or not.

Who holds you accountable? You need someone to whom you can pour out your deepest thoughts and heartaches . . .

We all have blind spots, areas in our lives that hinder our spiritual growth, but areas we cannot see. For example, we may express anger to others in a manner that is actually verbally abusive. We feel justified in our correction of them, but another believer can help us understand that our words should be the kind to inspire a positive response. In other words, there is a better way to express our anger, and we may need help finding that way.

If we are not accountable to someone else, we may never understand why people reject our advice. We must learn to accept constructive criticism ourselves. We set ourselves up for the problems in our lives that way. We have to understand the truth of the proverb: "Stern discipline awaits him who leaves the path; he who hates correction will die" (Proverbs 15:10).

Additional Scripture Readings:
Proverbs 5:7–23; Hebrews 12:4–13

Go to page 529 for your next devotional reading.

³Commit to the LORD whatever you do,
and your plans will succeed.

⁴The LORD works out everything for his own ends—
even the wicked for a day of disaster.

⁵The LORD detests all the proud of heart.
Be sure of this: They will not go unpunished.

⁶Through love and faithfulness sin is atoned for;
through the fear of the LORD a man avoids evil.

⁷When a man's ways are pleasing to the LORD,
he makes even his enemies live at peace with him.

⁸Better a little with righteousness
than much gain with injustice.

⁹In his heart a man plans his course,
but the LORD determines his steps.

¹⁰The lips of a king speak as an oracle,
and his mouth should not betray justice.

¹¹Honest scales and balances are from the LORD;
all the weights in the bag are of his making.

¹²Kings detest wrongdoing,
for a throne is established through righteousness.

¹³Kings take pleasure in honest lips;
they value a man who speaks the truth.

¹⁴A king's wrath is a messenger of death,
but a wise man will appease it.

¹⁵When a king's face brightens, it means life;
his favor is like a rain cloud in spring.

¹⁶How much better to get wisdom than gold,
to choose understanding rather than silver!

¹⁷The highway of the upright avoids evil;
he who guards his way guards his life.

¹⁸Pride goes before destruction,
a haughty spirit before a fall.

¹⁹Better to be lowly in spirit and among the oppressed
than to share plunder with the proud.

²⁰Whoever gives heed to instruction prospers,
and blessed is he who trusts in the LORD.

²¹The wise in heart are called discerning,
and pleasant words promote instruction.*a*

²²Understanding is a fountain of life to those who have it,
but folly brings punishment to fools.

²³A wise man's heart guides his mouth,
and his lips promote instruction.*b*

²⁴Pleasant words are a honeycomb,
sweet to the soul and healing to the bones.

²⁵There is a way that seems right to a man,
but in the end it leads to death.

²⁶The laborer's appetite works for him;
his hunger drives him on.

²⁷A scoundrel plots evil,
and his speech is like a scorching fire.

²⁸A perverse man stirs up dissension,
and a gossip separates close friends.

²⁹A violent man entices his neighbor
and leads him down a path that is not good.

³⁰He who winks with his eye is plotting perversity;
he who purses his lips is bent on evil.

³¹Gray hair is a crown of splendor;
it is attained by a righteous life.

³²Better a patient man than a warrior,
a man who controls his temper than one who takes a city.

³³The lot is cast into the lap,
but its every decision is from the LORD.

17

Better a dry crust with peace and quiet

---

a21 Or words make a man persuasive   *b23 Or mouth / and makes his lips persuasive* than a house full of feasting,^a with strife.

²A wise servant will rule over a disgraceful son,
and will share the inheritance as one of the brothers.

³The crucible for silver and the furnace for gold,
but the LORD tests the heart.

⁴A wicked man listens to evil lips;
a liar pays attention to a malicious tongue.

⁵He who mocks the poor shows contempt for their Maker;
whoever gloats over disaster will not go unpunished.

⁶Children's children are a crown to the aged,
and parents are the pride of their children.

⁷Arrogant[b] lips are unsuited to a fool—
how much worse lying lips to a ruler!

⁸A bribe is a charm to the one who gives it;
wherever he turns, he succeeds.

⁹He who covers over an offense promotes love,
but whoever repeats the matter separates close friends.

¹⁰A rebuke impresses a man of discernment
more than a hundred lashes a fool.

¹¹An evil man is bent only on rebellion;
a merciless official will be sent against him.

¹²Better to meet a bear robbed of her cubs
than a fool in his folly.

¹³If a man pays back evil for good,
evil will never leave his house.

¹⁴Starting a quarrel is like breaching a dam;
so drop the matter before a dispute breaks out.

¹⁵Acquitting the guilty and condemning the innocent—
the LORD detests them both.

¹⁶Of what use is money in the hand of a fool,
since he has no desire to get wisdom?

¹⁷A friend loves at all times,
and a brother is born for adversity.

¹⁸A man lacking in judgment strikes hands in pledge
and puts up security for his neighbor.

¹⁹He who loves a quarrel loves sin;
he who builds a high gate invites destruction.

²⁰A man of perverse heart does not prosper;
he whose tongue is deceitful falls into trouble.

²¹To have a fool for a son brings grief;
there is no joy for the father of a fool.

²²A cheerful heart is good medicine,
but a crushed spirit dries up the bones.

²³A wicked man accepts a bribe in secret
to pervert the course of justice.

²⁴A discerning man keeps wisdom in view,
but a fool's eyes wander to the ends of the earth.

²⁵A foolish son brings grief to his father
and bitterness to the one who bore him.

²⁶It is not good to punish an innocent man,
or to flog officials for their integrity.

²⁷A man of knowledge uses words with restraint,
and a man of understanding is even-tempered.

²⁸Even a fool is thought wise if he keeps silent,
and discerning if he holds his tongue.

18

An unfriendly man pursues selfish ends;
he defies all sound judgment.

²A fool finds no pleasure in understanding
but delights in airing his own opinions.

---

^a1 Hebrew *sacrifices*   ^b7 Or *Eloquent*

WEEKENDING

RESOLVE

Most of us are poor listeners. Since our mind moves forward faster than the words to which we are listening, we are frequently preparing something to say when we should be listening . . .

Are we aware of our listening biases? Many of us tune out children or old people. For years many women have complained that men do not listen to them as carefully as they listen to other men. When we are angry about something, do we carefully listen to an explanation?

The world aches for good listeners. Many doctors report that they daily see patients who have nothing physically wrong with them. They merely need someone to listen to them.

– *William E. Diehl*

REVIVE
Saturday: Proverbs 18:13
Sunday: James 1:19–21

Go to page 532 for your next devotional reading.

³When wickedness comes, so does contempt,
and with shame comes disgrace.

⁴The words of a man's mouth are deep waters,
but the fountain of wisdom is a bubbling brook.

⁵It is not good to be partial to the wicked
or to deprive the innocent of justice.

⁶A fool's lips bring him strife,
and his mouth invites a beating.

⁷A fool's mouth is his undoing,
and his lips are a snare to his soul.

⁸The words of a gossip are like choice morsels;
they go down to a man's inmost parts.

⁹One who is slack in his work
is brother to one who destroys.

¹⁰The name of the Lord is a strong tower;
the righteous run to it and are safe.

¹¹The wealth of the rich is their fortified city;
they imagine it an unscalable wall.

¹²Before his downfall a man's heart is proud,
but humility comes before honor.

¹³He who answers before listening—
that is his folly and his shame.

¹⁴A man's spirit sustains him in sickness,
but a crushed spirit who can bear?

¹⁵The heart of the discerning acquires knowledge;
the ears of the wise seek it out.

¹⁶A gift opens the way for the giver
and ushers him into the presence of the great.

¹⁷The first to present his case seems right,
till another comes forward and questions him.

¹⁸Casting the lot settles disputes
and keeps strong opponents apart.

¹⁹An offended brother is more unyielding than a fortified city,
and disputes are like the barred gates of a citadel.

²⁰From the fruit of his mouth a man's stomach is filled;
with the harvest from his lips he is satisfied.

²¹The tongue has the power of life and death,
and those who love it will eat its fruit.

²²He who finds a wife finds what is good
and receives favor from the Lord.

²³A poor man pleads for mercy,
but a rich man answers harshly.

²⁴A man of many companions may come to ruin,
but there is a friend who sticks closer than a brother.

19

Better a poor man whose walk is blameless
than a fool whose lips are perverse.

²It is not good to have zeal without knowledge,
nor to be hasty and miss the way.

³A man's own folly ruins his life,
yet his heart rages against the Lord.

⁴Wealth brings many friends,
but a poor man's friend deserts him.

⁵A false witness will not go unpunished,
and he who pours out lies will not go free.

⁶Many curry favor with a ruler,
and everyone is the friend of a man who gives gifts.

⁷A poor man is shunned by all his relatives—
how much more do his friends avoid him!
Though he pursues them with pleading,
they are nowhere to be found.[a]

⁸He who gets wisdom loves his own soul;
he who cherishes understanding prospers.

⁹A false witness will not go unpunished,
and he who pours out lies will perish.

¹⁰It is not fitting for a fool to live in luxury—

---

[a] 7 The meaning of the Hebrew for this sentence is uncertain.

how much worse for a slave to rule
over princes!

¹¹A man's wisdom gives him patience;
it is to his glory to overlook an
offense.

¹²A king's rage is like the roar of a lion,
but his favor is like dew on the
grass.

¹³A foolish son is his father's ruin,
and a quarrelsome wife is like a
constant dripping.

¹⁴Houses and wealth are inherited from
parents,
but a prudent wife is from the LORD.

¹⁵Laziness brings on deep sleep,
and the shiftless man goes hungry.

¹⁶He who obeys instructions guards his
life,
but he who is contemptuous of his
ways will die.

¹⁷He who is kind to the poor lends to
the LORD,
and he will reward him for what he
has done.

¹⁸Discipline your son, for in that there
is hope;
do not be a willing party to his
death.

¹⁹A hot-tempered man must pay the
penalty;
if you rescue him, you will have to
do it again.

²⁰Listen to advice and accept
instruction,
and in the end you will be wise.

²¹Many are the plans in a man's heart,
but it is the LORD's purpose that
prevails.

²²What a man desires is unfailing
love*a*;
better to be poor than a liar.

²³The fear of the LORD leads to life:
Then one rests content, untouched
by trouble.

²⁴The sluggard buries his hand in the
dish;
he will not even bring it back to his
mouth!

²⁵Flog a mocker, and the simple will
learn prudence;
rebuke a discerning man, and he
will gain knowledge.

²⁶He who robs his father and drives out
his mother
is a son who brings shame and
disgrace.

²⁷Stop listening to instruction, my son,
and you will stray from the words
of knowledge.

²⁸A corrupt witness mocks at justice,
and the mouth of the wicked gulps
down evil.

²⁹Penalties are prepared for mockers,
and beatings for the backs of fools.

20 Wine is a mocker and beer a
brawler;
whoever is led astray by them is not
wise.

²A king's wrath is like the roar of a
lion;
he who angers him forfeits his life.

³It is to a man's honor to avoid strife,
but every fool is quick to quarrel.

⁴A sluggard does not plow in season;
so at harvest time he looks but
finds nothing.

⁵The purposes of a man's heart are
deep waters,
but a man of understanding draws
them out.

⁶Many a man claims to have unfailing
love,
but a faithful man who can find?

⁷The righteous man leads a blameless
life;
blessed are his children after him.

⁸When a king sits on his throne to
judge,
he winnows out all evil with his eyes.

⁹Who can say, "I have kept my heart
pure;
I am clean and without sin"?

¹⁰Differing weights and differing
measures—
the LORD detests them both.

¹¹Even a child is known by his actions,
by whether his conduct is pure and
right.

---

a22 Or *A man's greed is his shame*

¹²Ears that hear and eyes that see—
the Lord has made them both.

¹³Do not love sleep or you will grow poor;
stay awake and you will have food to spare.

¹⁴"It's no good, it's no good!" says the buyer;
then off he goes and boasts about his purchase.

¹⁵Gold there is, and rubies in abundance,
but lips that speak knowledge are a rare jewel.

¹⁶Take the garment of one who puts up security for a stranger;
hold it in pledge if he does it for a wayward woman.

MONDAY

VERSE FOR THE DAY:
Proverbs 20:7

AUTHOR:
Larry Burkett

PASSAGE FOR THE DAY:
Proverbs 20:6–7

Instilling Basic Values

GOD'S instructions are neither complicated nor harsh. In fact, they are designed to free us, not bind us to a set of rigid do's and don'ts. The difficulty is that most American families have been duped into a life of "get rich quick" that includes the way we buy homes, cars, clothes and food. God's principles in the area of finances have been largely ignored for the last forty years, and now we are reaping what has been sown.

I read an article in a business magazine that vividly brought this into focus. It seems that the largest mail order seed company in the country decided to go out of business, despite the fact that sales were higher than ever. Unfortunately, so were nonpayments by their mail order sales force. For nearly fifty years, the company had been supplying seeds to children who would sell them door-to-door, mostly in rural communities, to raise money. In recent years, the nonpayment rate to the company had risen steadily, until in 1981, it reached 70 percent. The average age of these delinquent salesmen was ten years! The final straw came when the company attempted to contact the parents, hoping they would help in collection, only to discover that the parents actually encouraged the kids.

The symptom described is nonpayment of a just debt, but the problem runs much deeper. It involves basic values that parents fail to instill in their children. It's an attitude that my rights come before others. The lack of integrity in the parents is reflected and amplified in the lives of their children.

It's unfortunate that later these parents probably won't understand why irresponsible children become irresponsible adults. *"The righteous man leads a blameless life; blessed are his children after him"* [Proverbs 20:7, italics added].

Additional Scripture Readings:
Ephesians 6:1–4; Titus 2:6–8

Go to page 534 for your next devotional reading.

¹⁷Food gained by fraud tastes sweet to a man,
   but he ends up with a mouth full of gravel.

¹⁸Make plans by seeking advice;
   if you wage war, obtain guidance.

¹⁹A gossip betrays a confidence;
   so avoid a man who talks too much.

²⁰If a man curses his father or mother,
   his lamp will be snuffed out in pitch darkness.

²¹An inheritance quickly gained at the beginning
   will not be blessed at the end.

²²Do not say, "I'll pay you back for this wrong!"
   Wait for the LORD, and he will deliver you.

²³The LORD detests differing weights,
   and dishonest scales do not please him.

²⁴A man's steps are directed by the LORD.
   How then can anyone understand his own way?

²⁵It is a trap for a man to dedicate something rashly
   and only later to consider his vows.

²⁶A wise king winnows out the wicked;
   he drives the threshing wheel over them.

²⁷The lamp of the LORD searches the spirit of a man[a];
   it searches out his inmost being.

²⁸Love and faithfulness keep a king safe;
   through love his throne is made secure.

²⁹The glory of young men is their strength,
   gray hair the splendor of the old.

³⁰Blows and wounds cleanse away evil,
   and beatings purge the inmost being.

21

The king's heart is in the hand of the LORD;
   he directs it like a watercourse wherever he pleases.

²All a man's ways seem right to him,
   but the LORD weighs the heart.

³To do what is right and just
   is more acceptable to the LORD than sacrifice.

⁴Haughty eyes and a proud heart,
   the lamp of the wicked, are sin!

⁵The plans of the diligent lead to profit
   as surely as haste leads to poverty.

⁶A fortune made by a lying tongue
   is a fleeting vapor and a deadly snare.[b]

⁷The violence of the wicked will drag them away,
   for they refuse to do what is right.

⁸The way of the guilty is devious,
   but the conduct of the innocent is upright.

⁹Better to live on a corner of the roof
   than share a house with a quarrelsome wife.

¹⁰The wicked man craves evil;
   his neighbor gets no mercy from him.

¹¹When a mocker is punished, the simple gain wisdom;
   when a wise man is instructed, he gets knowledge.

¹²The Righteous One[c] takes note of the house of the wicked
   and brings the wicked to ruin.

¹³If a man shuts his ears to the cry of the poor,
   he too will cry out and not be answered.

¹⁴A gift given in secret soothes anger,
   and a bribe concealed in the cloak pacifies great wrath.

¹⁵When justice is done, it brings joy to the righteous
   but terror to evildoers.

¹⁶A man who strays from the path of understanding
   comes to rest in the company of the dead.

¹⁷He who loves pleasure will become poor;
   whoever loves wine and oil will never be rich.

---

[a] 27 Or *The spirit of man is the LORD's lamp*   [b] 6 Some Hebrew manuscripts, Septuagint and Vulgate; most Hebrew manuscripts *vapor for those who seek death*   [c] 12 Or *The righteous man*

¹⁸The wicked become a ransom for the righteous,
and the unfaithful for the upright.

¹⁹Better to live in a desert
than with a quarrelsome and ill-tempered wife.

²⁰In the house of the wise are stores of choice food and oil,
but a foolish man devours all he has.

²¹He who pursues righteousness and love
finds life, prosperity[a] and honor.

²²A wise man attacks the city of the mighty
and pulls down the stronghold in which they trust.

a21 Or righteousness

TUESDAY

VERSE FOR THE DAY:
Proverbs 21:5

AUTHOR:
Ron Blue

PASSAGE FOR THE DAY:
Proverbs 21:5–6

Trust Her Intuition

NO ONE has ever come to the office or sent a proposal and said, "Let me show you a bad deal." On the front end, every business and investment deal is a good one. It only went bad later! What makes investment and business debts so difficult to evaluate and reject are that they are all presented as good deals, and a person would be foolish to turn them down. Therefore, there never seems to be economic justification alone for turning them down.

This is one of the reasons why I feel it is so important to apply the rule that a husband and wife have perfect unity on their debt decisions. God has granted to women a special sense, which some have called intuition, that cannot be explained, but in many cases, it has kept a husband from making a poor decision . . .

I give two general rules in this area. First of all, if you cannot explain the deal or investment to your wife in such a way that she totally understands it, don't do it. Second, even if you can explain it so that she totally understands it, but she feels uneasy or unsure in any way about it, don't do it. Granted, you may pass up many opportunities. However, one of the surest ways to financial success is to avoid the major mistakes, because not only do you have to make up for the lost investment, but also you lose the earnings that this money could have generated, and the earnings that the earnings could have generated, and the earnings that the earnings that the earnings could have generated, and so on. Again, the Biblical counsel is sound: "He who gathers money little by little makes it grow" (Proverbs 13:11). Or . . . "Get rich slow."

Additional Scripture Readings:
Psalm 37:1–9; Proverbs 13:11

Go to page 536 for your next devotional reading.

²³He who guards his mouth and his tongue
  keeps himself from calamity.

²⁴The proud and arrogant man—
    "Mocker" is his name;
  he behaves with overweening pride.

²⁵The sluggard's craving will be the death of him,
  because his hands refuse to work.
²⁶All day long he craves for more,
  but the righteous give without sparing.

²⁷The sacrifice of the wicked is detestable—
  how much more so when brought with evil intent!

²⁸A false witness will perish,
  and whoever listens to him will be destroyed forever.[a]

²⁹A wicked man puts up a bold front,
  but an upright man gives thought to his ways.

³⁰There is no wisdom, no insight, no plan
  that can succeed against the LORD.

³¹The horse is made ready for the day of battle,
  but victory rests with the LORD.

22 A good name is more desirable than great riches;
  to be esteemed is better than silver or gold.

²Rich and poor have this in common:
  The LORD is the Maker of them all.

³A prudent man sees danger and takes refuge,
  but the simple keep going and suffer for it.

⁴Humility and the fear of the LORD
  bring wealth and honor and life.

⁵In the paths of the wicked lie thorns and snares,
  but he who guards his soul stays far from them.

⁶Train[b] a child in the way he should go,
  and when he is old he will not turn from it.

⁷The rich rule over the poor,
  and the borrower is servant to the lender.

⁸He who sows wickedness reaps trouble,
  and the rod of his fury will be destroyed.

⁹A generous man will himself be blessed,
  for he shares his food with the poor.

¹⁰Drive out the mocker, and out goes strife;
  quarrels and insults are ended.

¹¹He who loves a pure heart and whose speech is gracious
  will have the king for his friend.

¹²The eyes of the LORD keep watch over knowledge,
  but he frustrates the words of the unfaithful.

¹³The sluggard says, "There is a lion outside!"
  or, "I will be murdered in the streets!"

¹⁴The mouth of an adulteress is a deep pit;
  he who is under the LORD's wrath will fall into it.

¹⁵Folly is bound up in the heart of a child,
  but the rod of discipline will drive it far from him.

¹⁶He who oppresses the poor to increase his wealth
  and he who gives gifts to the rich—
  both come to poverty.

Sayings of the Wise

¹⁷Pay attention and listen to the sayings of the wise;
  apply your heart to what I teach,
¹⁸for it is pleasing when you keep them in your heart
  and have all of them ready on your lips.
¹⁹So that your trust may be in the LORD,
  I teach you today, even you.
²⁰Have I not written thirty[c] sayings for you,
  sayings of counsel and knowledge,
²¹teaching you true and reliable words,

---

[a] 28 Or / but the words of an obedient man will live on not written excellent   [b] 6 Or Start   [c] 20 Or not formerly written; or

so that you can give sound answers to him who sent you?

²²Do not exploit the poor because they are poor
and do not crush the needy in court,
²³for the LORD will take up their case
and will plunder those who plunder them.

²⁴Do not make friends with a hot-tempered man,
do not associate with one easily angered,
²⁵or you may learn his ways
and get yourself ensnared.

²⁶Do not be a man who strikes hands in pledge
or puts up security for debts;

WEDNESDAY

VERSE FOR THE DAY:
Proverbs 22:6

AUTHOR:
Charles Swindoll

PASSAGE FOR THE DAY:
Proverbs 22:4–6

Understanding the Bents

PROVERBS 22:6 is key in understanding the process of knowing and raising your child:

"Train a child in the way he should go, and when he is old he will not turn from it."

The verse doesn't mean "train up a child as you see him." Rather, "if you want your training to be meaningful and wise, be observant and discover your child's way, and adapt your training accordingly." Strengthening this idea is the word *way*. This Hebrew term literally means "road" or "path." Metaphorically, it is "a characteristic." Therefore, the thought is, "according to his characteristic, his manner." In Proverbs 22:6, the word *way* is used in the same sense: "Train up a child in keeping with his characteristics." And his characteristics are distinct and set. There is a bent already established within every child God places in our care. Each is not, in fact, a pliable lump of clay but has been bent, prescribed according to a predetermined pattern. For example, perhaps you have several children in your home. If not, perhaps you were from a home of several children. One may be creative; another, practical. One may be intelligent; another, just average. One may be outgoing; another, withdrawn. Whatever the case, they're all individuals. They weren't created on the assembly line. They were handcrafted, individually, by God . . .

Invariably, parents make two common mistakes. First, they use the same approach with all their children. Secondly, they compare them with other children. Both mistakes stem from not knowing them, from failing to see their individual bents. Consequently, the crucial concern for us as parents is to understand what the bents are in each of our children.

Additional Scripture Readings:
Psalm 139:1–16;
1 Corinthians 12:14–26

Go to page 539 for your next devotional reading.

²⁷if you lack the means to pay,
  your very bed will be snatched from
    under you.

²⁸Do not move an ancient boundary
    stone
  set up by your forefathers.

²⁹Do you see a man skilled in his work?
  He will serve before kings;
  he will not serve before obscure
    men.

23 When you sit to dine with a
    ruler,
  note well what^a is before you,
²and put a knife to your throat
  if you are given to gluttony.
³Do not crave his delicacies,
  for that food is deceptive.

⁴Do not wear yourself out to get rich;
  have the wisdom to show restraint.
⁵Cast but a glance at riches, and they
    are gone,
  for they will surely sprout wings
  and fly off to the sky like an eagle.

⁶Do not eat the food of a stingy man,
  do not crave his delicacies;
⁷for he is the kind of man
  who is always thinking about the
    cost.^{b}
"Eat and drink," he says to you,
  but his heart is not with you.
⁸You will vomit up the little you have
    eaten
  and will have wasted your
    compliments.

⁹Do not speak to a fool,
  for he will scorn the wisdom of
    your words.

¹⁰Do not move an ancient boundary
    stone
  or encroach on the fields of the
    fatherless,
¹¹for their Defender is strong;
  he will take up their case against
    you.

¹²Apply your heart to instruction
  and your ears to words of
    knowledge.

¹³Do not withhold discipline from a
    child;
  if you punish him with the rod, he
    will not die.
¹⁴Punish him with the rod
  and save his soul from death.^{c}

¹⁵My son, if your heart is wise,
  then my heart will be glad;
¹⁶my inmost being will rejoice
  when your lips speak what is right.

¹⁷Do not let your heart envy sinners,
  but always be zealous for the fear
    of the LORD.
¹⁸There is surely a future hope for you,
  and your hope will not be cut off.

¹⁹Listen, my son, and be wise,
  and keep your heart on the right
    path.
²⁰Do not join those who drink too much
    wine
  or gorge themselves on meat,
²¹for drunkards and gluttons become
    poor,
  and drowsiness clothes them in
    rags.

²²Listen to your father, who gave you
    life,
  and do not despise your mother
    when she is old.
²³Buy the truth and do not sell it;
  get wisdom, discipline and
    understanding.
²⁴The father of a righteous man has
    great joy;
  he who has a wise son delights in
    him.
²⁵May your father and mother be glad;
  may she who gave you birth
    rejoice!

²⁶My son, give me your heart
  and let your eyes keep to my ways,
²⁷for a prostitute is a deep pit
  and a wayward wife is a narrow
    well.
²⁸Like a bandit she lies in wait,
  and multiplies the unfaithful among
    men.

²⁹Who has woe? Who has sorrow?
  Who has strife? Who has
    complaints?
  Who has needless bruises? Who has
    bloodshot eyes?
³⁰Those who linger over wine,
  who go to sample bowls of mixed
    wine.
³¹Do not gaze at wine when it is red,
  when it sparkles in the cup,
  when it goes down smoothly!
³²In the end it bites like a snake

---

^{a}1 Or *who* ^{b}7 Or *for as he thinks within himself, / so he is*; or *for as he puts on a feast, / so he is*
^{c}14 Hebrew *Sheol*

and poisons like a viper.
³³Your eyes will see strange sights
and your mind imagine confusing
things.
³⁴You will be like one sleeping on the
high seas,
lying on top of the rigging.
³⁵"They hit me," you will say, "but I'm
not hurt!
They beat me, but I don't feel it!
When will I wake up
so I can find another drink?"

24 Do not envy wicked men,
do not desire their company;
²for their hearts plot violence,
and their lips talk about making
trouble.

³By wisdom a house is built,
and through understanding it is
established;
⁴through knowledge its rooms are filled
with rare and beautiful treasures.

⁵A wise man has great power,
and a man of knowledge increases
strength;
⁶for waging war you need guidance,
and for victory many advisers.

⁷Wisdom is too high for a fool;
in the assembly at the gate he has
nothing to say.

⁸He who plots evil
will be known as a schemer.
⁹The schemes of folly are sin,
and men detest a mocker.

¹⁰If you falter in times of trouble,
how small is your strength!

¹¹Rescue those being led away to death;
hold back those staggering toward
slaughter.
¹²If you say, "But we knew nothing
about this,"
does not he who weighs the heart
perceive it?
Does not he who guards your life
know it?
Will he not repay each person
according to what he has done?

¹³Eat honey, my son, for it is good;
honey from the comb is sweet to
your taste.
¹⁴Know also that wisdom is sweet to
your soul;
if you find it, there is a future hope
for you,
and your hope will not be cut off.

¹⁵Do not lie in wait like an outlaw
against a righteous man's
house,
do not raid his dwelling place;
¹⁶for though a righteous man falls seven
times, he rises again,
but the wicked are brought down
by calamity.

¹⁷Do not gloat when your enemy falls;
when he stumbles, do not let your
heart rejoice,
¹⁸or the LORD will see and disapprove
and turn his wrath away from him.

¹⁹Do not fret because of evil men
or be envious of the wicked,
²⁰for the evil man has no future hope,
and the lamp of the wicked will be
snuffed out.

²¹Fear the LORD and the king, my son,
and do not join with the rebellious,
²²for those two will send sudden
destruction upon them,
and who knows what calamities
they can bring?

Further Sayings of the Wise

²³These also are sayings of the wise:

To show partiality in judging is not
good:
²⁴Whoever says to the guilty, "You are
innocent"—
peoples will curse him and nations
denounce him.
²⁵But it will go well with those who
convict the guilty,
and rich blessing will come upon
them.

²⁶An honest answer
is like a kiss on the lips.

²⁷Finish your outdoor work
and get your fields ready;
after that, build your house.

²⁸Do not testify against your neighbor
without cause,
or use your lips to deceive.
²⁹Do not say, "I'll do to him as he has
done to me;
I'll pay that man back for what he
did."

³⁰I went past the field of the sluggard,
past the vineyard of the man who
lacks judgment;
³¹thorns had come up everywhere,
the ground was covered with weeds,
and the stone wall was in ruins.

32 I applied my heart to what I observed
and learned a lesson from what I
saw:
33 A little sleep, a little slumber,
a little folding of the hands to
rest—
34 and poverty will come on you like a
bandit
and scarcity like an armed man.*a*

More Proverbs of Solomon

25 These are more proverbs of Solomon, copied by the men of Hezekiah king of Judah:

2 It is the glory of God to conceal a
matter;
to search out a matter is the glory
of kings.

3 As the heavens are high and the earth
is deep,
so the hearts of kings are
unsearchable.

4 Remove the dross from the silver,
and out comes material for*b* the
silversmith;
5 remove the wicked from the king's
presence,

a34 Or *like a vagrant / and scarcity like a beggar*   *b4* Or *comes a vessel from*

THURSDAY

VERSE FOR THE DAY:
Proverbs 24:33

AUTHOR:
Gary Smalley and John Trent

PASSAGE FOR THE DAY:
Proverbs 24:33–34

The Gift of Honor

WE [SOUND] the call for parents to join the battle against a major destroyer of children—their feeling valueless and insignificant. We can't stress enough how important each day is in waging this war. If we sit back, fold our hands, and neglect building self-worth in our children, one day King Solomon's words may come true in their lives or our own. When this wise king wrote about the sluggard, he made this comment:

"A little sleep, a little slumber, a little folding of the hands to rest—and poverty will come on you like a bandit and scarcity like an armed man."

If we act like tourists or sluggards when it comes to building value into our children, heartache may enter our homes as stealthily as a prowler, or discouragement may burst upon us as forcefully as an armed man.

No matter how old your children are, it's never too late to unfold your hands and start honoring them. When you consistently apply this concept, you save them the heartache of damaged relationships, and you also give them the foundation they will need to truly value God, themselves and others.

Parents, do your children (and yourself) a great favor. Give them a gift that can strengthen them their entire lives—a gift that can continue to build up and bless your children and even your grandchildren—*the gift of honor.*

Additional Scripture Readings:
Proverbs 4:1–27; Mark 10:13–16

Go to page 546 for your next devotional reading.

and his throne will be established
through righteousness.

⁶Do not exalt yourself in the king's
presence,
and do not claim a place among
great men;
⁷it is better for him to say to you,
"Come up here,"
than for him to humiliate you
before a nobleman.

What you have seen with your eyes
⁸ do not bring*a* hastily to court,
for what will you do in the end
if your neighbor puts you to shame?

⁹If you argue your case with a
neighbor,
do not betray another man's
confidence,
¹⁰or he who hears it may shame you
and you will never lose your bad
reputation.

¹¹A word aptly spoken
is like apples of gold in settings of
silver.

¹²Like an earring of gold or an
ornament of fine gold
is a wise man's rebuke to a listening
ear.

¹³Like the coolness of snow at harvest
time
is a trustworthy messenger to those
who send him;
he refreshes the spirit of his
masters.

¹⁴Like clouds and wind without rain
is a man who boasts of gifts he
does not give.

¹⁵Through patience a ruler can be
persuaded,
and a gentle tongue can break a
bone.

¹⁶If you find honey, eat just enough—
too much of it, and you will vomit.
¹⁷Seldom set foot in your neighbor's
house—
too much of you, and he will hate
you.

¹⁸Like a club or a sword or a sharp
arrow
is the man who gives false
testimony against his neighbor.

¹⁹Like a bad tooth or a lame foot
is reliance on the unfaithful in times
of trouble.

²⁰Like one who takes away a garment
on a cold day,
or like vinegar poured on soda,
is one who sings songs to a heavy
heart.

²¹If your enemy is hungry, give him
food to eat;
if he is thirsty, give him water to
drink.
²²In doing this, you will heap burning
coals on his head,
and the LORD will reward you.

²³As a north wind brings rain,
so a sly tongue brings angry looks.

²⁴Better to live on a corner of the roof
than share a house with a
quarrelsome wife.

²⁵Like cold water to a weary soul
is good news from a distant land.

²⁶Like a muddied spring or a polluted
well
is a righteous man who gives way
to the wicked.

²⁷It is not good to eat too much honey,
nor is it honorable to seek one's
own honor.

²⁸Like a city whose walls are broken
down
is a man who lacks self-control.

26 Like snow in summer or rain in
harvest,
honor is not fitting for a fool.

²Like a fluttering sparrow or a darting
swallow,
an undeserved curse does not come
to rest.

³A whip for the horse, a halter for the
donkey,
and a rod for the backs of fools!

⁴Do not answer a fool according to his
folly,
or you will be like him yourself.

⁵Answer a fool according to his folly,
or he will be wise in his own eyes.

⁶Like cutting off one's feet or drinking
violence
is the sending of a message by the
hand of a fool.

a 7,8 Or nobleman / on whom you had set your eyes. / ⁸Do not go

⁷Like a lame man's legs that hang limp
  is a proverb in the mouth of a fool.

⁸Like tying a stone in a sling
  is the giving of honor to a fool.

⁹Like a thornbush in a drunkard's hand
  is a proverb in the mouth of a fool.

¹⁰Like an archer who wounds at random
  is he who hires a fool or any
    passer-by.

¹¹As a dog returns to its vomit,
  so a fool repeats his folly.

¹²Do you see a man wise in his own
    eyes?
  There is more hope for a fool than
    for him.

¹³The sluggard says, "There is a lion in
    the road,
  a fierce lion roaming the streets!"

¹⁴As a door turns on its hinges,
  so a sluggard turns on his bed.

¹⁵The sluggard buries his hand in the
    dish;
  he is too lazy to bring it back to his
    mouth.

¹⁶The sluggard is wiser in his own eyes
  than seven men who answer
    discreetly.

¹⁷Like one who seizes a dog by the ears
  is a passer-by who meddles in a
    quarrel not his own.

¹⁸Like a madman shooting
    firebrands or deadly arrows
¹⁹is a man who deceives his neighbor
  and says, "I was only joking!"

²⁰Without wood a fire goes out;
  without gossip a quarrel dies down.

²¹As charcoal to embers and as wood to
    fire,
  so is a quarrelsome man for
    kindling strife.

²²The words of a gossip are like choice
    morsels;
  they go down to a man's inmost
    parts.

²³Like a coating of glaze*ᵃ* over
    earthenware
  are fervent lips with an evil heart.

²⁴A malicious man disguises himself
    with his lips,
  but in his heart he harbors deceit.

²⁵Though his speech is charming, do
    not believe him,
  for seven abominations fill his
    heart.

²⁶His malice may be concealed by
    deception,
  but his wickedness will be exposed
    in the assembly.

²⁷If a man digs a pit, he will fall into it;
  if a man rolls a stone, it will roll
    back on him.

²⁸A lying tongue hates those it hurts,
  and a flattering mouth works ruin.

27 Do not boast about tomorrow,
  for you do not know what a day
    may bring forth.

²Let another praise you, and not your
    own mouth;
  someone else, and not your own
    lips.

³Stone is heavy and sand a burden,
  but provocation by a fool is heavier
    than both.

⁴Anger is cruel and fury overwhelming,
  but who can stand before jealousy?

⁵Better is open rebuke
  than hidden love.

⁶Wounds from a friend can be trusted,
  but an enemy multiplies kisses.

⁷He who is full loathes honey,
  but to the hungry even what is
    bitter tastes sweet.

⁸Like a bird that strays from its nest
  is a man who strays from his home.

⁹Perfume and incense bring joy to the
    heart,
  and the pleasantness of one's friend
    springs from his earnest
    counsel.

¹⁰Do not forsake your friend and the
    friend of your father,
  and do not go to your brother's
    house when disaster strikes
    you—
  better a neighbor nearby than a
    brother far away.

¹¹Be wise, my son, and bring joy to my
    heart;
  then I can answer anyone who
    treats me with contempt.

---

a23 With a different word division of the Hebrew; Masoretic Text *of silver dross*

¹²The prudent see danger and take refuge,
  but the simple keep going and suffer for it.

¹³Take the garment of one who puts up security for a stranger;
  hold it in pledge if he does it for a wayward woman.

¹⁴If a man loudly blesses his neighbor early in the morning,
  it will be taken as a curse.

¹⁵A quarrelsome wife is like a constant dripping on a rainy day;
¹⁶restraining her is like restraining the wind
  or grasping oil with the hand.

¹⁷As iron sharpens iron,
  so one man sharpens another.

¹⁸He who tends a fig tree will eat its fruit,
  and he who looks after his master will be honored.

¹⁹As water reflects a face,
  so a man's heart reflects the man.

²⁰Death and Destruction[a] are never satisfied,
  and neither are the eyes of man.

²¹The crucible for silver and the furnace for gold,
  but man is tested by the praise he receives.

²²Though you grind a fool in a mortar, grinding him like grain with a pestle,
  you will not remove his folly from him.

²³Be sure you know the condition of your flocks,
  give careful attention to your herds;
²⁴for riches do not endure forever,
  and a crown is not secure for all generations.
²⁵When the hay is removed and new growth appears
  and the grass from the hills is gathered in,
²⁶the lambs will provide you with clothing,
  and the goats with the price of a field.
²⁷You will have plenty of goats' milk to feed you and your family
  and to nourish your servant girls.

28 The wicked man flees though no one pursues,
  but the righteous are as bold as a lion.

²When a country is rebellious, it has many rulers,
  but a man of understanding and knowledge maintains order.

³A ruler[b] who oppresses the poor
  is like a driving rain that leaves no crops.

⁴Those who forsake the law praise the wicked,
  but those who keep the law resist them.

⁵Evil men do not understand justice,
  but those who seek the LORD understand it fully.

⁶Better a poor man whose walk is blameless
  than a rich man whose ways are perverse.

⁷He who keeps the law is a discerning son,
  but a companion of gluttons disgraces his father.

⁸He who increases his wealth by exorbitant interest
  amasses it for another, who will be kind to the poor.

⁹If anyone turns a deaf ear to the law,
  even his prayers are detestable.

¹⁰He who leads the upright along an evil path
  will fall into his own trap,
  but the blameless will receive a good inheritance.

¹¹A rich man may be wise in his own eyes,
  but a poor man who has discernment sees through him.

¹²When the righteous triumph, there is great elation;
  but when the wicked rise to power, men go into hiding.

¹³He who conceals his sins does not prosper,
  but whoever confesses and renounces them finds mercy.

¹⁴Blessed is the man who always fears the LORD,

---

a20 Hebrew *Sheol and Abaddon*   *b3* Or *A poor man*

but he who hardens his heart falls
into trouble.

¹⁵Like a roaring lion or a charging bear
is a wicked man ruling over a
helpless people.

¹⁶A tyrannical ruler lacks judgment,
but he who hates ill-gotten gain will
enjoy a long life.

¹⁷A man tormented by the guilt of
murder
will be a fugitive till death;
let no one support him.

¹⁸He whose walk is blameless is kept
safe,
but he whose ways are perverse will
suddenly fall.

¹⁹He who works his land will have
abundant food,
but the one who chases fantasies
will have his fill of poverty.

²⁰A faithful man will be richly blessed,
but one eager to get rich will not go
unpunished.

²¹To show partiality is not good—
yet a man will do wrong for a piece
of bread.

²²A stingy man is eager to get rich
and is unaware that poverty awaits
him.

²³He who rebukes a man will in the end
gain more favor
than he who has a flattering tongue.

²⁴He who robs his father or mother
and says, "It's not wrong"—
he is partner to him who destroys.

²⁵A greedy man stirs up dissension,
but he who trusts in the LORD will
prosper.

²⁶He who trusts in himself is a fool,
but he who walks in wisdom is kept
safe.

²⁷He who gives to the poor will lack
nothing,
but he who closes his eyes to them
receives many curses.

²⁸When the wicked rise to power,
people go into hiding;
but when the wicked perish, the
righteous thrive.

29 A man who remains stiff-necked
after many rebukes
will suddenly be destroyed—
without remedy.

²When the righteous thrive, the people
rejoice;
when the wicked rule, the people
groan.

³A man who loves wisdom brings joy
to his father,
but a companion of prostitutes
squanders his wealth.

⁴By justice a king gives a country
stability,
but one who is greedy for bribes
tears it down.

⁵Whoever flatters his neighbor
is spreading a net for his feet.

⁶An evil man is snared by his own sin,
but a righteous one can sing and be
glad.

⁷The righteous care about justice for
the poor,
but the wicked have no such
concern.

⁸Mockers stir up a city,
but wise men turn away anger.

⁹If a wise man goes to court with a
fool,
the fool rages and scoffs, and there
is no peace.

¹⁰Bloodthirsty men hate a man of
integrity
and seek to kill the upright.

¹¹A fool gives full vent to his anger,
but a wise man keeps himself under
control.

¹²If a ruler listens to lies,
all his officials become wicked.

¹³The poor man and the oppressor have
this in common:
The LORD gives sight to the eyes of
both.

¹⁴If a king judges the poor with fairness,
his throne will always be secure.

¹⁵The rod of correction imparts wisdom,
but a child left to himself disgraces
his mother.

¹⁶When the wicked thrive, so does sin,
but the righteous will see their
downfall.

¹⁷Discipline your son, and he will give
you peace;
he will bring delight to your soul.

¹⁸Where there is no revelation, the
    people cast off restraint;
  but blessed is he who keeps the
    law.

¹⁹A servant cannot be corrected by mere
    words;
  though he understands, he will not
    respond.

²⁰Do you see a man who speaks in
    haste?
  There is more hope for a fool than
    for him.

²¹If a man pampers his servant from
    youth,
  he will bring grief[a] in the end.

²²An angry man stirs up dissension,
  and a hot-tempered one commits
    many sins.

²³A man's pride brings him low,
  but a man of lowly spirit gains
    honor.

²⁴The accomplice of a thief is his own
    enemy;
  he is put under oath and dare not
    testify.

²⁵Fear of man will prove to be a snare,
  but whoever trusts in the LORD is
    kept safe.

²⁶Many seek an audience with a ruler,
  but it is from the LORD that man
    gets justice.

²⁷The righteous detest the dishonest;
  the wicked detest the upright.

Sayings of Agur

30 The sayings of Agur son of Jakeh—
    an oracle[b]:

This man declared to Ithiel,
  to Ithiel and to Ucal:[c]

²"I am the most ignorant of men;
  I do not have a man's
    understanding.
³I have not learned wisdom,
  nor have I knowledge of the Holy
    One.
⁴Who has gone up to heaven and come
    down?
  Who has gathered up the wind in
    the hollow of his hands?
  Who has wrapped up the waters in
    his cloak?
  Who has established all the ends of
    the earth?
  What is his name, and the name of
    his son?
  Tell me if you know!

⁵"Every word of God is flawless;
  he is a shield to those who take
    refuge in him.
⁶Do not add to his words,
  or he will rebuke you and prove
    you a liar.

⁷"Two things I ask of you, O LORD;
  do not refuse me before I die:
⁸Keep falsehood and lies far from me;
  give me neither poverty nor riches,
  but give me only my daily bread.
⁹Otherwise, I may have too much and
    disown you
  and say, 'Who is the LORD?'
  Or I may become poor and steal,
    and so dishonor the name of my
      God.

¹⁰"Do not slander a servant to his
    master,
  or he will curse you, and you will
    pay for it.

¹¹"There are those who curse their
    fathers
  and do not bless their mothers;
¹²those who are pure in their own eyes
  and yet are not cleansed of their
    filth;
¹³those whose eyes are ever so haughty,
  whose glances are so disdainful;
¹⁴those whose teeth are swords
  and whose jaws are set with knives
  to devour the poor from the earth,
    the needy from among mankind.

¹⁵"The leech has two daughters.
  'Give! Give!' they cry.

"There are three things that are never
    satisfied,
  four that never say, 'Enough!':
¹⁶the grave,[d] the barren womb,
  land, which is never satisfied with
    water,
  and fire, which never says,
    'Enough!'

¹⁷"The eye that mocks a father,
  that scorns obedience to a mother,

---

[a]21 The meaning of the Hebrew for this word is uncertain.   [b]1 Or *Jakeh of Massa*   [c]1 Masoretic Text; with a different word division of the Hebrew *declared, "I am weary, O God; / I am weary, O God, and faint.*   [d]16 Hebrew *Sheol*

will be pecked out by the ravens of
    the valley,
  will be eaten by the vultures.

¹⁸"There are three things that are too
    amazing for me,
  four that I do not understand:
¹⁹the way of an eagle in the sky,
  the way of a snake on a rock,
  the way of a ship on the high seas,
  and the way of a man with a
    maiden.

²⁰"This is the way of an adulteress:
  She eats and wipes her mouth
  and says, 'I've done nothing wrong.'

²¹"Under three things the earth
    trembles,
  under four it cannot bear up:
²²a servant who becomes king,
  a fool who is full of food,
²³an unloved woman who is married,
  and a maidservant who displaces
    her mistress.

²⁴"Four things on earth are small,
  yet they are extremely wise:
²⁵Ants are creatures of little strength,
  yet they store up their food in the
    summer;
²⁶coneys*a* are creatures of little power,
  yet they make their home in the
    crags;
²⁷locusts have no king,
  yet they advance together in ranks;
²⁸a lizard can be caught with the hand,
  yet it is found in kings' palaces.

²⁹"There are three things that are stately
    in their stride,
  four that move with stately bearing:
³⁰a lion, mighty among beasts,
  who retreats before nothing;
³¹a strutting rooster, a he-goat,
  and a king with his army around
    him.*b*

³²"If you have played the fool and
    exalted yourself,
  or if you have planned evil,
  clap your hand over your mouth!
³³For as churning the milk produces
    butter,
  and as twisting the nose produces
    blood,
  so stirring up anger produces strife."

Sayings of King Lemuel

31 The sayings of King Lemuel—an
  oracle*c* his mother taught him:

²"O my son, O son of my womb,
  O son of my vows,*d*
³do not spend your strength on
    women,
  your vigor on those who ruin kings.

⁴"It is not for kings, O Lemuel—
  not for kings to drink wine,
  not for rulers to crave beer,
⁵lest they drink and forget what the
    law decrees,
  and deprive all the oppressed of
    their rights.
⁶Give beer to those who are perishing,
  wine to those who are in anguish;
⁷let them drink and forget their poverty
  and remember their misery no
    more.

⁸"Speak up for those who cannot speak
    for themselves,
  for the rights of all who are
    destitute.
⁹Speak up and judge fairly;
  defend the rights of the poor and
    needy."

Epilogue: The Wife of Noble Character

¹⁰*e*A wife of noble character who can
    find?
  She is worth far more than rubies.
¹¹Her husband has full confidence in
    her
  and lacks nothing of value.
¹²She brings him good, not harm,
  all the days of her life.
¹³She selects wool and flax
  and works with eager hands.
¹⁴She is like the merchant ships,
  bringing her food from afar.
¹⁵She gets up while it is still dark;
  she provides food for her family
  and portions for her servant girls.
¹⁶She considers a field and buys it;
  out of her earnings she plants a
    vineyard.
¹⁷She sets about her work vigorously;
  her arms are strong for her tasks.
¹⁸She sees that her trading is profitable,
  and her lamp does not go out at
    night.

---

a26 That is, the hyrax or rock badger   *b31* Or *king secure against revolt*   *c1* Or *of Lemuel king of Massa, which*   *d2* Or */ the answer to my prayers*   *e10* Verses 10-31 are an acrostic, each verse beginning with a successive letter of the Hebrew alphabet.

¹⁹In her hand she holds the distaff
and grasps the spindle with her
fingers.
²⁰She opens her arms to the poor
and extends her hands to the needy.
²¹When it snows, she has no fear for
her household;
for all of them are clothed in
scarlet.
²²She makes coverings for her bed;
she is clothed in fine linen and
purple.
²³Her husband is respected at the city
gate,
where he takes his seat among the
elders of the land.
²⁴She makes linen garments and sells
them,
and supplies the merchants with
sashes.
²⁵She is clothed with strength and
dignity;
she can laugh at the days to come.
²⁶She speaks with wisdom,
and faithful instruction is on her
tongue.
²⁷She watches over the affairs of her
household
and does not eat the bread of
idleness.
²⁸Her children arise and call her
blessed;
her husband also, and he praises
her:
²⁹"Many women do noble things,
but you surpass them all."

FRIDAY

VERSE FOR THE DAY:
Proverbs 31:10

AUTHOR:
Joe Gibbs

PASSAGE FOR THE DAY:
Proverbs 31:10–31

Praising Your Wife

[MY WIFE] Pat is perfect for me and always has been. During our long courtship after meeting in high school, we had our ups and downs and our fights. But we always knew we would wind up married, best friends, and partners for life. She has a great sense of humor and gift of gab. We enjoy each other and we enjoy life. I can't imagine life without her . . .

In the eyes of the world, she's in the background. Her work is not as visible, and thus, to some people, not as important. But my work would be nothing without a wife like her. What most people don't realize is that something is as true in my family as it is in almost any man's family: What our wives do and have done is much more valuable in terms of eternity than anything we could ever do. Ten years from now my name may appear in the Redskin Hall of Fame because my teams have won a lot of football games. That will be my legacy. By then I will be a fan, going to games and cheering along with everyone else. I have no illusions about that.

But Pat's accomplishments, unknown to most people, will be honored for eternity. She's been father and mother to our boys while I spent months leaving the house early and getting home late, investing my time in a game.

Additional Scripture Readings:
Proverbs 12:4; 1 Peter 3:1–6

Go to page 2 for your next devotional reading.

30Charm is deceptive, and beauty is fleeting;
but a woman who fears the Lord is to be praised.

31Give her the reward she has earned,
and let her works bring her praise at the city gate.

WEIGHTS AND MEASURES

The figures of the table are calculated on the basis of a shekel equaling 11.5 grams, a cubit equaling 18 inches and an ephah equaling 22 liters. The quart referred to is either a dry quart (slightly larger than a liter) or a liquid quart (slightly smaller than a liter), whichever is applicable. The ton referred to in the footnotes is the American ton of 2,000 pounds.

This table is based upon the best available information, but it is not intended to be mathematically precise; like the measurement equivalents in the footnotes, it merely gives approximate amounts and distances. Weights and measures differed somewhat at various times and places in the ancient world. There is uncertainty particularly about the ephah and the bath; further discoveries may give more light on these units of capacity.

	BIBLICAL UNIT		APPROXIMATE AMERICAN EQUIVALENT	APPROXIMATE METRIC EQUIVALENT
WEIGHTS	talent	*(60 minas)*	75 pounds	34 kilograms
	mina	*(50 shekels)*	1 1/4 pounds	0.6 kilogram
	shekel	*(2 bekas)*	2/5 ounce	11.5 grams
	pim	*(2/3 shekel)*	1/3 ounce	7.6 grams
	beka	*(10 gerahs)*	1/5 ounce	5.5 grams
	gerah		1/50 ounce	0.6 gram
LENGTH	cubit		18 inches	0.5 meter
	span		9 inches	23 centimeters
	handbreadth		3 inches	8 centimeters
CAPACITY Dry Measure	cor [homer]	*(10 ephahs)*	6 bushels	220 liters
	lethek	*(5 ephahs)*	3 bushels	110 liters
	ephah	*(10 omers)*	3/5 bushel	22 liters
	seah	*(1/3 ephah)*	7 quarts	7.3 liters
	omer	*(1/10 ephah)*	2 quarts	2 liters
	cab	*(1/18 ephah)*	1 quart	1 liter
Liquid Measure	bath	*(1 ephah)*	6 gallons	22 liters
	hin	*(1/6 bath)*	4 quarts	4 liters
	log	*(1/72 bath)*	1/3 quart	0.3 liter

ACKNOWLEDGMENTS INDEX

Page 2: Taken from THE MISUNDERSTOOD MAN by Walter Trobisch. Copyright © 1983 by InterVarsity Christian Fellowship of the USA. Used by permission.
Page 4: Taken from IMMANUEL: REFLECTIONS ON THE LIFE OF CHRIST by Michael Card. Copyright © 1990 by Michael Card. Used by permission of Thomas Nelson Publishers.
Page 7: Taken from LIFE AND HOLINESS by Thomas Merton. Copyright © 1963 by the Abbey of Gethsemani, Inc. Used by permission.
Page 9: Taken from LIGHT FROM LIGHT by Jack Perry. Copyright © 1987 by Jack Perry. Used by permission of Zondervan Publishing House.
Page 11: Taken from TOM LANDRY: AN AUTOBIOGRAPHY by Tom Landry with Gregg Lewis. Copyright © 1990 by Tom Landry. Used by permission of Zondervan Publishing House.
Page 13: Taken from THE APPLAUSE OF HEAVEN by Max Lucado. Copyright © 1990 by Max Lucado. Used by permission of Word, Inc., Dallas, Texas.
Page 14: Taken from DARE TO BE DIFFERENT by Charles Colson. Copyright © 1986 by SP Publications, Inc. Used by permission.
Page 18: Taken from THE COST OF DISCIPLESHIP by Dietrich Bonhoeffer. Copyright © 1959 by SCM Press, Ltd. Used by permission of Macmillan Publishing Company.
Page 23: Taken from DON'T LET THE GOATS EAT THE LOQUAT TREES by Thomas Hale. Copyright © 1986 by Thomas Hale, Jr. Used by permission of Zondervan Publishing House.
Page 27: Taken from WHEN A LOVED ONE DIES by Philip W. Williams. Copyright © 1976 by Augsburg Publishing House. Used by permission of Augsburg Fortress.
Page 29: Taken from WHO YOU ARE WHEN NO ONE'S LOOKING by Bill Hybels. Copyright © 1987 by Bill Hybels. Used by permission of InterVarsity Press, P.O. Box 1400, Downers Grove, IL 60515.
Page 31: Taken from FORGIVE AND FORGET by Lewis B. Smedes. Copyright © 1984 by Lewis B. Smedes. Used by permission of HarperCollins Publishers.
Page 33: Taken from SINGLETARY ON SINGLETARY by Mike Singletary with Jerry Jenkins. Copyright © 1991 by Mike Singletary and Jerry B. Jenkins. Used by permission of Thomas Nelson Publishers.
Page 37: Taken from TRUE BELIEVERS DON'T ASK WHY by John Fischer. Copyright © 1989 by John Fischer. Used by permission of Bethany House Publishers.
Page 48: Taken from THE COST OF DISCIPLESHIP by Dietrich Bonhoeffer. Copyright © 1959 by SCM Press, Ltd. Used by permission of Macmillan Publishing Company.
Page 50: Taken from THE ANGRY MAN by Stephen Arterburn and David Stoop. Copyright © 1991 by Stephen Arterburn and David Stoop. Used by permission of Word, Inc., Dallas, Texas.
Page 53: Taken from BEING THE REAL FATHER NOW THAT YOUR TEENAGER WILL NEED by John Crawford. Copyright © 1968 by Fortress Press. Used by permission of Augsburg Fortress.
Page 57: Taken from SEE YOU AT THE HOUSE by Bob Benson. Copyright © 1989 by Generoux Nelson, a division of Thomas Nelson Publishers. Used by permission.
Page 59: Taken from FRIENDSHIP by Jim Conway. Copyright © 1989 by Jim Conway. Used by permission of Zondervan Publishing House.
Page 61: Taken from SEX, STRENGTH AND THE SECRETS OF BECOMING A MAN by Donald M. Joy. Copyright © 1990 by Donald M. Joy. Used by permission of Regal Books, Ventura, CA 93003.
Page 63: Taken from MASTER YOUR MONEY by Ron Blue. Copyright © 1986 by Ronald W. Blue. Used by permission of Thomas Nelson Publishers.
Page 66: Taken from DON'T LET THE GOATS EAT THE LOQUAT TREES by Thomas Hale. Copyright © 1986 by Thomas Hale, Jr. Used by permission of Zondervan Publishing House.
Page 75: Taken from BEING THE REAL FATHER NOW THAT YOUR TEENAGER WILL NEED by John Crawford. Copyright © 1968 by Fortress Press. Used by permission of Augsburg Fortress.
Page 77: Taken from REVERSED THUNDER by Eugene H. Peterson. Copyright © 1988 by Eugene H. Peterson. Used by permission of HarperCollins Publishers.
Page 79: Taken from THE APPLAUSE OF HEAVEN by Max Lucado. Copyright © 1990 by Max Lucado. Used by permission of Word, Inc., Dallas, Texas.
Page 84: Taken from TRUE BELIEVERS DON'T ASK WHY by John Fischer. Copyright © 1989 by John Fischer. Used by permission of Bethany House Publishers.
Page 86: Taken from HOW TO WIN OVER DEPRESSION by Tim LaHaye. Copyright © 1974 by The Zondervan Corporation. Used by permission.
Page 88: Taken from WHAT IT MEANS TO BE REAL by D. Stuart Briscoe. Copyright © 1988 by D. Stuart Briscoe. Published by Word, Inc. Used by permission.
Page 90: Taken from WHEN A LOVED ONE DIES by Philip W. Williams. Copyright © 1976 by Augsburg Publishing House. Used by permission of Augsburg Fortress.
Page 94: Taken from INTIMATE MOMENTS WITH THE SAVIOR by Ken Gire. Copyright © 1989 by Ken Gire. Used by permission of Zondervan Publishing House.
Page 98: Taken from MASTER YOUR MONEY by Ron Blue. Copyright © 1986 by Ronald W. Blue. Used by permission of Thomas Nelson Publishers.
Page 104: Taken from WHO YOU ARE WHEN NO ONE'S LOOKING by Bill Hybels. Copyright © 1987 by Bill Hybels. Used by permission of InterVarsity Press, P.O. Box 1400, Downers Grove, IL 60515.
Page 107: Taken from DON'T LET THE GOATS EAT THE LOQUAT TREES by Thomas Hale. Copyright © 1986 by Thomas Hale, Jr. Used by permission of Zondervan Publishing House.
Page 109: Taken from FRIENDSHIP by Jim Conway. Copyright © 1989 by Jim Conway. Used by permission of Zondervan Publishing House.
Page 115: Taken from MEN AND WOMEN by Lawrence J. Crabb, Jr. Copyright © 1991 by Dr. Lawrence J. Crabb, Jr. Used by permission of Zondervan Publishing House.
Page 117: Taken from MOURNING INTO DANCING by Walter Wangerin, Jr. Copyright © 1992 by Walter Wangerin, Jr. Used by permission of Zondervan Publishing House.
Page 121: Taken from THE ANGRY MAN by Stephen Arterburn and David Stoop. Copyright © 1991 by Stephen Arterburn and David Stoop. Used by permission of Word, Inc., Dallas, Texas.
Page 123: Taken from FRIENDSHIP by Jim Conway. Copyright © 1989 by Jim Conway. Used by permission of Zondervan Publishing House.

ACKNOWLEDGMENTS INDEX

Page 125: Taken from WHAT IT MEANS TO BE REAL by D. Stuart Briscoe. Copyright © 1988 by D. Stuart Briscoe. Published by Word, Inc. Used by permission.

Page 127: Taken from IMMANUEL: REFLECTIONS ON THE LIFE OF CHRIST by Michael Card. Copyright © 1990 by Michael Card. Used by permission of Thomas Nelson Publishers.

Page 131: Taken from THE APPLAUSE OF HEAVEN by Max Lucado. Copyright © 1990 by Max Lucado. Used by permission of Word, Inc., Dallas, Texas.

Page 133: Taken from LIFE IN THE SLOW LANE by S.D. Gaede. Copyright © 1991 by S.D. Gaede. Used by permission of Zondervan Publishing House.

Page 135: Taken from GOD IN THE PITS by Mark A. Ritchie. Copyright © 1989,1990 by Mark A. Ritchie. Used by permission of Thomas Nelson Publishers.

Page 137: Taken from HOW TO WIN OVER DEPRESSION by Tim LaHaye. Copyright © 1974 by The Zondervan Corporation. Used by permission.

Page 140: Taken from GRIEF by Haddon W. Robinson. Copyright © 1974 by The Christian Medical Society. Assigned to The Zondervan Corporation, 1976. Used by permission.

Page 143: Taken from DAILY THOUGHTS FOR DISCIPLES by Oswald Chambers. Copyright © 1990 by Oswald Chambers Publications Association 1976. Used by permission of Discovery House Publishers.

Page 146: Taken from THE MAN IN THE MIRROR by Patrick Morley. Copyright © 1989 by Patrick Morley. Published by Wolgemuth and Hyatt, Publishers. Used by permission of Thomas Nelson Publishers.

Page 147: Taken from LET'S LISTEN TO JESUS by Reuben Welch. Revised editions Copyright © 1985,1988 by The Zondervan Corporation. Used by permission.

Page 149: Taken from FEARFULLY AND WONDERFULLY MADE by Dr. Paul Brand and Philip Yancey. Copyright © 1980 by Paul Brand and Philip Yancey. Used by permission of Zondervan Publishing House.

Page 154: Taken from IMMANUEL: REFLECTIONS ON THE LIFE OF CHRIST by Michael Card. Copyright © 1990 by Michael Card. Used by permission of Thomas Nelson Publishers.

Page 157: Taken from REGGIE WHITE: MINISTER OF DEFENSE by Reggie White with Terry Hill. Copyright © 1991 by Reggie White with Terry Hill. Used by permission of Word, Inc., Dallas, Texas.

Page 162: Taken from PERSPECTIVE by Richard C. Halverson. Copyright © 1957,1985 by Cowman Publishing Company. Used by permission of Zondervan Publishing House.

Page 168: Taken from FROM ASHES TO GLORY by Bill McCartney with Dave Diles. Copyright © 1990 by Bill McCartney. Used by permission of Thomas Nelson Publishers.

Page 170: Taken from THE SIGNATURE OF JESUS by Brennan Manning. Copyright © 1992 by Brennan Manning. Published by Multnomah Press. Used by permission of Questar Publishers.

Page 172: Taken from FORGIVENESS by Charles Stanley. Copyright © 1987 by Charles Stanley. Used by permission of Thomas Nelson Publishers.

Page 176: Taken from FROM ASHES TO GLORY by Bill McCartney with Dave Diles. Copyright © 1990 by Bill McCartney. Used by permission of Thomas Nelson Publishers.

Page 181: Taken from TOM LANDRY: AN AUTOBIOGRAPHY by Tom Landry with Gregg Lewis. Copyright © 1990 by Tom Landry. Used by permission of Zondervan Publishing House.

Page 185: Taken from THE MAN IN THE MIRROR by Patrick Morley. Copyright © 1989 by Patrick Morley. Published by Wolgemuth and Hyatt, Publishers. Used by permission of Thomas Nelson Publishers.

Page 188: Taken from THE APPLAUSE OF HEAVEN by Max Lucado. Copyright © 1990 by Max Lucado. Used by permission of Word, Inc., Dallas, Texas.

Page 193: Taken from JUST BETWEEN FATHER & SON by E. James Wilder. Copyright © 1990 by E. James Wilder. Used by permission of InterVarsity Press, P.O. Box 1400, Downers Grove, IL 60515.

Page 198: Taken from TRUE BELIEVERS DON'T ASK WHY by John Fischer. Copyright © 1989 by John Fischer. Used by permission of Bethany House Publishers.

Page 200: Taken from MEN AND WOMEN by Lawrence J. Crabb, Jr. Copyright © 1991 by Dr. Lawrence J. Crabb, Jr. Used by permission of Zondervan Publishing House.

Page 202: Taken from MERE CHRISTIANITY by C.S. Lewis. Copyright © 1942, 1943, 1944 and 1952 by C.S. Lewis Pte. Ltd. Used by permission of Collins Fount, an imprint of HarperCollins Publishers Limited.

Page 204: Taken from THE GIFT OF HONOR by Gary Smalley and John Trent. Copyright © 1987 by Gary Smalley and John Trent. Used by permission of Thomas Nelson Publishers.

Page 206: Taken from THE PRACTICE OF GODLINESS by Jerry Bridges. Copyright © 1983 by Jerry Bridges. Used by permission of NavPress.

Page 208: Taken from DANCING INTO ZION by Judson B. Edwards. Copyright © 1986 by Judson Edwards. Used by permission of Zondervan Publishing House.

Page 209: Taken from IMMANUEL: REFLECTIONS ON THE LIFE OF CHRIST by Michael Card. Copyright © 1990 by Michael Card. Used by permission of Thomas Nelson Publishers.

Page 211: Taken from CORRESPONDENCE WITH A CRIPPLE FROM TARSUS by H. Beecher Hicks, Jr. Copyright © 1990 by H. Beecher Hicks, Jr. Used by permission of Zondervan Publishing House.

Page 215: Taken from WHEN A LOVED ONE DIES by Philip W. Williams. Copyright © 1976 by Augsburg Publishing House. Used by permission of Augsburg Fortress.

Page 221: Taken from POINT MAN by Steve Farrar. Copyright © 1990 by Steve Farrar. Published by Multnomah Press. Used by permission of Questar Publishers.

Page 223: Taken from LIFE AND HOLINESS by Thomas Merton. Copyright © 1963 by the Abbey of Gethsemani, Inc. Used by permission.

Page 225: Taken from IMMANUEL: REFLECTIONS ON THE LIFE OF CHRIST by Michael Card. Copyright © 1990 by Michael Card. Used by permission of Thomas Nelson Publishers.

Page 225: Taken from SEX, STRENGTH AND THE SECRETS OF BECOMING A MAN by Donald M. Joy. Copyright © 1990 by Donald M. Joy. Used by permission of Regal Books, Ventura, CA 93003.

Page 226: Taken from STRONG MEN, WEAK MEN by Leonard LeSourd. Copyright © 1990 by Leonard LeSourd. Published by Chosen Books. Used by permission of Baker Book House.

Page 230: Taken from CHERISHABLE: LOVE AND MARRIAGE by David Augsburger. Copyright © 1971 by Herald Press. Used by permission.

Page 232: Taken from FEARFULLY AND WONDERFULLY MADE by Dr. Paul Brand and Philip Yancey. Copyright © 1980 by Paul Brand and Philip Yancey. Used by permission of Zondervan Publishing House.

Page 233: Taken from MEN AND WOMEN by Lawrence J. Crabb, Jr. Copyright © 1991 by Dr. Lawrence J. Crabb, Jr. Used by permission of Zondervan Publishing House.

Page 235: Taken from WHEN A LOVED ONE DIES by Philip W. Williams. Copyright © 1976 by Augsburg Publishing House. Used by permission of Augsburg Fortress.

Page 237: Taken from EPISTLES/NOW by Leslie Brandt. Copyright © 1974,1976 by Concordia Publishing House. Used by permission.

ACKNOWLEDGMENTS INDEX 551

Page 238: Taken from WHO YOU ARE WHEN NO ONE'S LOOKING by Bill Hybels. Copyright © 1987 by Bill Hybels. Used by permission of InterVarsity Press, P.O. Box 1400, Downers Grove, IL 60515.

Page 241: Taken from THE PROBLEM OF PAIN by C.S. Lewis. Copyright © 1940 by C.S. Lewis Pte. Ltd. Used by permission of Collins Fount, an imprint of HarperCollins Publishers Limited.

Page 245: Taken from FEARFULLY AND WONDERFULLY MADE by Dr. Paul Brand and Philip Yancey. Copyright © 1980 by Paul Brand and Philip Yancey. Used by permission of Zondervan Publishing House.

Page 247: Taken from LETTERS TO MY CHILDREN by Daniel Taylor. Copyright © 1989 by Daniel Taylor. Used by permission of InterVarsity Press, P.O. Box 1400, Downers Grove, IL 60515.

Page 249: Taken from STRONG MEN, WEAK MEN by Leonard LeSourd. Copyright © 1990 by Leonard LeSourd. Published by Chosen Books. Used by permission of Baker Book House.

Page 251: Taken from TRAVELING LIGHT by Eugene H. Peterson. Copyright © 1988 by Eugene H. Peterson. Used by permission.

Page 251: Taken from A PRETTY GOOD PERSON by Lewis B. Smedes. Copyright © 1990 by Lewis B. Smedes. Used by permission of HarperCollins Publishers.

Page 252: Taken from FATHERLOVE by D. Bruce Lockerbie. Copyright © 1981 by D. Bruce Lockerbie. Used by permission of Doubleday, a division of Bantam Doubleday Dell Publishing Group, Inc.

Page 255: Taken from GOD IS MY DELIGHT by W. Phillip Keller. Copyright © 1991 by W. Phillip Keller and published by Kregel Publications, a division of Kregel, Inc., P.O. Box 2607, Grand Rapids, MI 49501. Used by permission.

Page 257: Taken from YOUR WORK MATTERS TO GOD by Doug Sherman and William Hendricks. Copyright © 1987 by Doug Sherman and William Hendricks. Used by permission of NavPress.

Page 259: Taken from CHERISHABLE: LOVE AND MARRIAGE by David Augsburger. Copyright © 1971 by Herald Press. Used by permission.

Page 264: Taken from GOD IN THE PITS by Mark A. Ritchie. Copyright © 1989,1990 by Mark A. Ritchie. Used by permission of Thomas Nelson Publishers.

Page 266: Taken from GROWING STRONG IN THE SEASONS OF LIFE by Charles R. Swindoll. Copyright © 1983 by Charles R. Swindoll. Published by Multnomah Press. Used by permission of Questar Publishers.

Page 267: Taken from FEARFULLY AND WONDERFULLY MADE by Dr. Paul Brand and Philip Yancey. Copyright © 1980 by Paul Brand and Philip Yancey. Used by permission of Zondervan Publishing House.

Page 269: Taken from SINGLETARY ON SINGLETARY by Mike Singletary with Jerry Jenkins. Copyright © 1991 by Mike Singletary and Jerry B. Jenkins. Used by permission of Thomas Nelson Publishers.

Page 270: Taken from THE ANGRY MAN by Stephen Arterburn and David Stoop. Copyright © 1991 by Stephen Arterburn and David Stoop. Used by permission of Word, Inc., Dallas, Texas.

Page 273: Taken from LETTERS TO MY CHILDREN by Daniel Taylor. Copyright © 1989 by Daniel Taylor. Used by permission of InterVarsity Press, P.O. Box 1400, Downers Grove, IL 60515.

Page 275: Taken from LOVE FOR A LIFETIME by James C. Dobson. Copyright © 1987 by James C. Dobson. Published by Multnomah Press. Used by permission of Questar Publishers.

Page 276: Taken from THE POWER DELUSION by Tony Campolo. Copyright © 1983 by SP Publications, Inc. Used by permission.

Page 277: Taken from WHEN A LOVED ONE DIES by Philip W. Williams. Copyright © 1976 by Augsburg Publishing House. Used by permission of Augsburg Fortress.

Page 279: Taken from LISTENING TO YOUR LIFE by Frederick Buechner. Copyright © 1992 by Frederick Buechner. Used by permission of HarperCollins Publishers.

Page 281: Taken from TRUE BELIEVERS DON'T ASK WHY by John Fischer. Copyright © 1989 by John Fischer. Used by permission of Bethany House Publishers.

Page 283: Taken from COME BEFORE WINTER by Charles R. Swindoll. Copyright © 1985 by Charles R. Swindoll, Inc. Published by Multnomah Press. Used by permission of Questar Publishers.

Page 284: Taken from MARRIAGE IS FOR LIVING compiled by Bruce Larson. Excerpt from "When the Wine Runs Out" by G.R. Slater. Copyright © 1968 by Zondervan Publishing House. Used by permission.

Page 286: Taken from LAUGHTER, JOY, AND HEALING by Donald E. Demaray. Copyright © 1986 by Baker Book House Company. Used by permission.

Page 287: Taken from REGGIE WHITE: MINISTER OF DEFENSE by Reggie White with Terry Hill. Copyright © 1991 by Reggie White with Terry Hill. Used by permission of Word, Inc., Dallas, Texas.

Page 289: Taken from SINGLETARY ON SINGLETARY by Mike Singletary with Jerry Jenkins. Copyright © 1991 by Mike Singletary and Jerry B. Jenkins. Used by permission of Thomas Nelson Publishers.

Page 291: Taken from LOVE FOR A LIFETIME by James C. Dobson. Copyright © 1987 by James C. Dobson. Published by Multnomah Press. Used by permission of Questar Publishers.

Page 292: Taken from LETTERS TO MY CHILDREN by Daniel Taylor. Copyright © 1989 by Daniel Taylor. Used by permission of InterVarsity Press, P.O. Box 1400, Downers Grove, IL 60515.

Page 295: Taken from LISTENING TO YOUR LIFE by Frederick Buechner. Copyright © 1992 by Frederick Buechner. Used by permission of HarperCollins Publishers.

Page 296: Taken from LAMENT FOR A SON by Nicholas Wolterstorff. Copyright © 1987 by Wm. B. Eerdmans Publishing Co. Used by permission.

Page 297: Taken from LIFE AND HOLINESS by Thomas Merton. Copyright © 1963 by the Abbey of Gethsemani, Inc. Used by permission.

Page 300: Taken from FRIENDSHIP by Jim Conway. Copyright © 1989 by Jim Conway. Used by permission of Zondervan Publishing House.

Page 302: Taken from GUIDING TEEN-AGERS TO MATURITY by J.H. Waterink. Copyright © 1969 by Zondervan Publishing House. Used by permission.

Page 303: Taken from YOUR WORK MATTERS TO GOD by Doug Sherman and William Hendricks. Copyright © 1987 by Doug Sherman and William Hendricks. Used by permission of NavPress.

Page 305: Taken from OUT OF THE BLUE by Orel Hershiser. Copyright © 1989 by Orel Leonard Hershiser IV. Published by Wolgemuth and Hyatt, Publishers. Used by permission of Leader Enterprises, Inc.

Page 306: Taken from USING YOUR MONEY WISELY by Larry Burkett. Copyright © 1985 by Christian Financial Concepts. Used by permission.

Page 308: Taken from OUT OF THE BLUE by Orel Hershiser. Copyright © 1989 by Orel Leonard Hershiser IV. Published by Wolgemuth and Hyatt, Publishers. Used by permission of Leader Enterprises, Inc.

Page 309: Taken from OUT OF THE BLUE by Orel Hershiser. Copyright © 1989 by Orel Leonard Hershiser IV. Published by Wolgemuth and Hyatt, Publishers. Used by permission of Leader Enterprises, Inc.

Page 311: Taken from THE COST OF DISCIPLESHIP by Dietrich Bonhoeffer. Copyright © 1959 by SCM Press, Ltd. Used by permission of Macmillan Publishing Company.

Page 314: Taken from OUT OF THE BLUE by Orel Hershiser. Copyright © 1989 by Orel Leonard Hershiser IV. Published by Wolgemuth and Hyatt, Publishers. Used by permission of Leader Enterprises, Inc.

ACKNOWLEDGMENTS INDEX

Page 315: Taken from COMEBACK by Dave Dravecky with Tim Stafford. Copyright © 1990 by Dave Dravecky. Used by permission of Zondervan Publishing House

Page 318: Taken from PSALMS OF MY LIFE by Joseph Bayly, available at your local Christian bookstore. Copyright © 1987 by the estate of Joseph Bayly. Used by permission of David C. Cook Publishing Co.

Page 319: Taken from FORGIVENESS by Charles Stanley. Copyright © 1987 by Charles Stanley. Used by permission of Thomas Nelson Publishers.

Page 322: Taken from FAITH FOR THE JOURNEY by Reuben R. Welch. Copyright © 1988 by Reuben R. Welch. Used by permission of Zondervan Publishing House.

Page 324: Taken from FRIENDSHIP by Jim Conway. Copyright © 1989 by Jim Conway. Used by permission of Zondervan Publishing House.

Page 326: Taken from REGGIE WHITE: MINISTER OF DEFENSE by Reggie White with Terry Hill. Copyright © 1991 by Reggie White with Terry Hill. Used by permission of Word, Inc., Dallas, Texas.

Page 329: Taken from THE COST OF DISCIPLESHIP by Dietrich Bonhoeffer. Copyright © 1959 by SCM Press, Ltd. Used by permission of Macmillan Publishing Company.

Page 331: Taken from COLORING OUTSIDE THE LINES by John F. Westfall. Copyright © 1991 by John F. Westfall. Used by permission of HarperCollins Publishers.

Page 331: Taken from PRAY TO WIN by Pat Boone. Copyright © 1980 by Pat Boone. Used by permission.

Page 333: Taken from REGGIE WHITE: MINISTER OF DEFENSE by Reggie White with Terry Hill. Copyright © 1991 by Reggie White with Terry Hill. Used by permission of Word, Inc., Dallas, Texas.

Page 335: Taken from THE PRACTICE OF GODLINESS by Jerry Bridges. Copyright © 1983 by Jerry Bridges. Used by permission of NavPress.

Page 336: Taken from COMEBACK by Dave Dravecky with Tim Stafford. Copyright © 1990 by Dave Dravecky. Used by permission of Zondervan Publishing House

Page 339: Taken from THE GIFT OF HONOR by Gary Smalley and John Trent. Copyright © 1987 by Gary Smalley and John Trent. Used by permission of Thomas Nelson Publishers.

Page 340: Taken from BEING THE REAL FATHER NOW THAT YOUR TEENAGER WILL NEED by John Crawford. Copyright © 1968 by Fortress Press. Used by permission of Augsburg Fortress.

Page 341: Taken from JUST BETWEEN FATHER & SON by E. James Wilder. Copyright © 1990 by E. James Wilder. Used by permission of InterVarsity Press, P.O. Box 1400, Downers Grove, IL 60515.

Page 343: Taken from FEARFULLY AND WONDERFULLY MADE by Dr. Paul Brand and Philip Yancey. Copyright © 1980 by Paul Brand and Philip Yancey. Used by permission of Zondervan Publishing House.

Page 344: Taken from MEN AND WOMEN by Lawrence J. Crabb, Jr. Copyright © 1991 by Dr. Lawrence J. Crabb, Jr. Used by permission of Zondervan Publishing House.

Page 345: Taken from THE ANGRY MAN by Stephen Arterburn and David Stoop. Copyright © 1991 by Stephen Arterburn and David Stoop. Used by permission of Word, Inc., Dallas, Texas.

Page 348: Taken from LIFE AND HOLINESS by Thomas Merton. Copyright © 1963 by the Abbey of Gethsemani, Inc. Used by permission.

Page 350: Taken from GOD IN THE PITS by Mark A. Ritchie. Copyright © 1989,1990 by Mark A. Ritchie. Used by permission of Thomas Nelson Publishers.

Page 351: Taken from DANCING ON THE STRAIT AND NARROW by Stan Mooneyham. Copyright © 1989 by W. Stanley Mooneyham. Used by permission.

Page 352: Taken from WHAT IT MEANS TO BE REAL by D. Stuart Briscoe. Copyright © 1988 by D. Stuart Briscoe. Published by Word, Inc. Used by permission.

Page 354: Taken from POINT MAN by Steve Farrar. Copyright © 1990 by Steve Farrar. Published by Multnomah Press. Used by permission of Questar Publishers.

Page 357: Taken from DON'T LET THE GOATS EAT THE LOQUAT TREES by Thomas Hale. Copyright © 1986 by Thomas Hale, Jr. Used by permission of Zondervan Publishing House.

Page 358: Taken from LISTENING TO YOUR LIFE by Frederick Buechner. Copyright © 1992 by Frederick Buechner. Used by permission of HarperCollins Publishers.

Page 360: Taken from LIFE AND HOLINESS by Thomas Merton. Copyright © 1963 by the Abbey of Gethsemani, Inc. Used by permission.

Page 362: Taken from THE GIFT OF TIME by William McConnell. Copyright © 1983 by InterVarsity Christian Fellowship of the USA. Used by permission.

Page 364: Taken from THE APPLAUSE OF HEAVEN by Max Lucado. Copyright © 1990 by Max Lucado. Used by permission of Word, Inc., Dallas, Texas.

Page 367: Taken from LETTERS TO MY CHILDREN by Daniel Taylor. Copyright © 1989 by Daniel Taylor. Used by permission of InterVarsity Press, P.O. Box 1400, Downers Grove, IL 60515.

Page 368: Taken from THE PRACTICE OF GODLINESS by Jerry Bridges. Copyright © 1983 by Jerry Bridges. Used by permission of NavPress.

Page 371: Taken from DEVOTIONAL TALKS FOR PEOPLE WHO DO GOD'S BUSINESS by David W. Wiersbe and Warren W. Wiersbe. Copyright © 1986 by Baker Book House Company. Used by permission.

Page 373: Taken from WHAT IT MEANS TO BE REAL by D. Stuart Briscoe. Copyright © 1988 by D. Stuart Briscoe. Published by Word, Inc. Used by permission.

Page 374: Taken from LIFE IN THE SLOW LANE by S.D. Gaede. Copyright © 1991 by S.D. Gaede. Used by permission of Zondervan Publishing House.

Page 376: Taken from RENEWED DAY BY DAY by A.W. Tozer. Copyright © 1980 by Christian Publications, Inc. Used by permission.

Page 380: Taken from COMEBACK by Dave Dravecky with Tim Stafford. Copyright © 1990 by Dave Dravecky. Used by permission of Zondervan Publishing House

Page 382: Taken from THE COST OF DISCIPLESHIP by Dietrich Bonhoeffer. Copyright © 1959 by SCM Press, Ltd. Used by permission of Macmillan Publishing Company.

Page 388: Taken from HOW TO WIN OVER DEPRESSION by Tim LaHaye. Copyright © 1974 by The Zondervan Corporation. Used by permission.

Page 395: Taken from TOO EARLY FROST by Gerald Oosterveen. Copyright © 1988 by Gerald Oosterveen. Used by permission of Zondervan Publishing House.

Page 397: Taken from CREATED TO PRAISE by Derek Prime. Copyright © 1981 by Derek Prime. Used by permission.

Page 402: Taken from HONEST TO GOD? by Bill Hybels. Copyright © 1990 by Bill Hybels. Used by permission of Zondervan Publishing House.

Page 404: Taken from LISTENING TO YOUR LIFE by Frederick Buechner. Copyright © 1992 by Frederick Buechner. Used by permission of HarperCollins Publishers.

Page 408: Taken from DON'T LET THE GOATS EAT THE LOQUAT TREES by Thomas Hale. Copyright © 1986 by Thomas Hale, Jr. Used by permission of Zondervan Publishing House.

ACKNOWLEDGMENTS INDEX

Page 416: Taken from A MUSICIAN LOOKS AT THE PSALMS by Don Wyrtzen. Copyright © 1988 by Donald J. Wyrtzen. Used by permission of Zondervan Publishing House.
Page 424: Taken from ANGER: YOURS AND MINE AND WHAT TO DO ABOUT IT by Richard P. Walters. Copyright © 1981 by The Zondervan Corporation. Used by permission.
Page 429: Taken from SINGLETARY ON SINGLETARY by Mike Singletary with Jerry Jenkins. Copyright © 1991 by Mike Singletary and Jerry B. Jenkins. Used by permission of Thomas Nelson Publishers.
Page 433: Taken from A MUSICIAN LOOKS AT THE PSALMS by Don Wyrtzen. Copyright © 1988 by Donald J. Wyrtzen. Used by permission of Zondervan Publishing House.
Page 436: Taken from MEN AND WOMEN by Lawrence J. Crabb, Jr. Copyright © 1991 by Dr. Lawrence J. Crabb, Jr. Used by permission of Zondervan Publishing House.
Page 438: Taken from MEN WITHOUT FRIENDS by David W. Smith. Copyright © 1990 by David W. Smith. Used by permission of Thomas Nelson Publishers.
Page 442: Taken from LECTURES TO MY STUDENTS by Charles Spurgeon. Used by permission of HarperCollins Publishers Limited.
Page 444: Taken from GOD IS MY DELIGHT by W. Phillip Keller. Copyright © 1991 by W. Phillip Keller and published by Kregel Publications, a division of Kregel, Inc., P.O. Box 2607, Grand Rapids, MI 49501. Used by permission.
Page 445: Taken from THE ANGRY MAN by Stephen Arterburn and David Stoop. Copyright © 1991 by Stephen Arterburn and David Stoop. Used by permission of Word, Inc., Dallas, Texas.
Page 447: Taken from JOE GIBBS: FOURTH AND ONE by Joe Gibbs with Jerry Jenkins. Copyright © 1991 by Joe J. Gibbs and Jerry B. Jenkins. Used by permission of Thomas Nelson Publishers.
Page 455: Taken from STRAIGHT TALK TO MEN AND THEIR WIVES by James C. Dobson. Copyright © 1980. Published by Word, Inc., Dallas Texas. Used by permission.
Page 460: Taken from A MUSICIAN LOOKS AT THE PSALMS by Don Wyrtzen. Copyright © 1988 by Donald J. Wyrtzen. Used by permission of Zondervan Publishing House.
Page 465: Taken from FOR THE WORKAHOLIC I LOVE by Ted W. Engstrom and David J. Juroe. Copyright © 1979 by Ted W. Engstrom and David J. Juroe. Published by Fleming H. Revell Company. Used by permission of Baker Book House.
Page 467: Taken from ANGELS by Billy Graham. Copyright © 1975, 1986 by Billy Graham. Used by permission of Word, Inc., Dallas, Texas.
Page 470: Taken from COLORING OUTSIDE THE LINES by John F. Westfall. Copyright © 1991 by John F. Westfall. Used by permission of HarperCollins Publishers.
Page 474: Taken from STRAIGHT TALK TO MEN AND THEIR WIVES by James C. Dobson. Copyright © 1980. Published by Word, Inc., Dallas Texas. Used by permission.
Page 481: Taken from A MUSICIAN LOOKS AT THE PSALMS by Don Wyrtzen. Copyright © 1988 by Donald J. Wyrtzen. Used by permission of Zondervan Publishing House.
Page 483: Taken from YOUR WORK MATTERS TO GOD by Doug Sherman and William Hendricks. Copyright © 1987 by Doug Sherman and William Hendricks. Used by permission of NavPress.
Page 486: Taken from DARE TO BE DIFFERENT by Charles Colson. Copyright © 1986 by SP Publications, Inc. Used by permission.
Page 489: Taken from TOM LANDRY: AN AUTOBIOGRAPHY by Tom Landry with Gregg Lewis. Copyright © 1990 by Tom Landry. Used by permission of Zondervan Publishing House.
Page 493: Taken from THE GIFT OF HONOR by Gary Smalley and John Trent. Copyright © 1987 by Gary Smalley and John Trent. Used by permission of Thomas Nelson Publishers.
Page 495: Taken from the Bible study guide YOU AND YOUR CHILD by Charles R. Swindoll. Copyright © 1973,1977,1979,1986; pages 1–3,15–16, and 67–68. Published by Insight for Living, Anaheim, CA 92806. All rights reserved. Used by permission.
Page 496: Taken from THE STRUGGLE OF PRAYER by Donald G. Bloesch. Copyright © 1980 by Donald G. Bloesch. Used by permission of HarperCollins Publishers.
Page 501: Taken from GOD IS MY DELIGHT by W. Phillip Keller. Copyright © 1991 by W. Phillip Keller and published by Kregel Publications, a division of Kregel, Inc., P.O. Box 2607, Grand Rapids, MI 49501. Used by permission.
Page 503: Taken from A MUSICIAN LOOKS AT THE PSALMS by Don Wyrtzen. Copyright © 1988 by Donald J. Wyrtzen. Used by permission of Zondervan Publishing House.
Page 508: Taken from FATHERLOVE by D. Bruce Lockerbie. Copyright © 1981 by D. Bruce Lockerbie. Used by permission of Doubleday, a division of Bantam Doubleday Dell Publishing Group, Inc.
Page 510: Taken from A TOUCH OF HIS WISDOM by Charles Stanley. Copyright © 1992 by Charles Stanley. Used by permission of Zondervan Publishing House.
Page 511: Taken from POINT MAN by Steve Farrar. Copyright © 1990 by Steve Farrar. Published by Multnomah Press. Used by permission of Questar Publishers.
Page 513: Taken from WHO YOU ARE WHEN NO ONE'S LOOKING by Bill Hybels. Copyright © 1987 by Bill Hybels. Used by permission of InterVarsity Press, P.O. Box 1400 Downers Grove, IL 60515.
Page 516: Taken from the Bible study guide YOU AND YOUR CHILD by Charles R. Swindoll. Copyright © 1973,1977,1979,1986; pages 1–3,15–16, and 67–68. Published by Insight for Living, Anaheim, CA 92806. All rights reserved. Used by permission.
Page 523: Taken from MASTER YOUR MONEY by Ron Blue. Copyright © 1986 by Ronald W. Blue. Used by permission of Thomas Nelson Publishers.
Page 526: Taken from REGGIE WHITE: MINISTER OF DEFENSE by Reggie White with Terry Hill. Copyright © 1991 by Reggie White with Terry Hill. Used by permission of Word, Inc., Dallas, Texas.
Page 529: Taken from THE MONDAY CONNECTION by William E. Diehl. Copyright © 1991 by William E. Diehl. Used by permission of HarperCollins Publishers.
Page 532: Taken from USING YOUR MONEY WISELY by Larry Burkett. Copyright © 1985 by Christian Financial Concepts. Used by permission.
Page 534: Taken from MASTER YOUR MONEY by Ron Blue. Copyright © 1986 by Ronald W. Blue. Used by permission of Thomas Nelson Publishers.
Page 536: Taken from the Bible study guide YOU AND YOUR CHILD by Charles R. Swindoll. Copyright © 1973,1977,1979,1986; pages 1–3,15–16, and 67–68. Published by Insight for Living, Anaheim, CA 92806. All rights reserved. Used by permission.
Page 539: Taken from THE GIFT OF HONOR by Gary Smalley and John Trent. Copyright © 1987 by Gary Smalley and John Trent. Used by permission of Thomas Nelson Publishers.
Page 546: Taken from JOE GIBBS: FOURTH AND ONE by Joe Gibbs with Jerry Jenkins. Copyright © 1991 by Joe J. Gibbs and Jerry B. Jenkins. Used by permission of Thomas Nelson Publishers.

Every effort has been made to give proper credit for each devotion used. If any error or inaccuracy is noted, please inform the publishers.

READING PLAN

God's Word is full of promises, encouragement and guidance for you. This reading plan gives you a simple structure for reading through the New Testament, Psalms and Proverbs in one year.

JANUARY	A.M.	P.M.
1	Matt 1	Prov 1:1–7
2	Matt 2	Prov 1:8–19
3	Matt 3	Prov 1:20–33
4	Matt 4	Prov 2:1–11
5	Matt 5	Prov 2:12–22
6	Matt 6	Prov 3:1–4
7	Matt 7	Prov 3:5–10
8	Matt 8	Prov 3:11–18
9	Matt 9	Prov 3:19–26
10	Matt 10	Prov 3:27–35
11	Matt 11	Prov 4:1–9
12	Matt 12	Prov 4:10–19
13	Matt 13:1–52	Prov 4:20–27
14	Matt 13:53–14:36	Prov 5:1–6
15	Matt 15	Prov 5:7–14
16	Matt 16	Prov 5:15–23
17	Matt 17	Prov 6:1–5
18	Matt 18	Prov 6:6–11
19	Matt 19:1–20:16	Prov 6:12–15
20	Matt 20:17–21:17	Prov 6:16–19
21	Matt 21:18–46	Prov 6:20–29
22	Matt 22:1–40	Prov 6:30–35
23	Matt 22:41–23:38	Prov 7:1–5
24	Matt 24:1–44	Prov 7:6–23
25	Matt 24:45–25:30	Prov 7:24–27
26	Matt 25:31–26:16	Prov 8:1–11
27	Matt 26:17–56	Prov 8:12–21
28	Matt 26:57–75	Prov 8:22–36
29	Matt 27:1–31	Prov 9:1–6
30	Matt 27:32–66	Prov 9:7–12
31	Matt 28	Prov 9:13–18

FEBRUARY	A.M.	P.M.
1	Mark 1:1–20	Prov 10:1–5
2	Mark 1:21–45	Prov 10:6–11
3	Mark 2	Prov 10:12–16
4	Mark 3:1–19	Prov 10:17–23
5	Mark 3:20–35	Prov 10:24–27
6	Mark 4:1–34	Prov 10:28–32
7	Mark 4:35–5:20	Prov 11:1–4
8	Mark 5:21–43	Prov 11:5–9
9	Mark 6:1–13	Prov 11:10–14
10	Mark 6:14–29	Prov 11:15–19
11	Mark 6:30–56	Prov 11:20–26
12	Mark 7:1–23	Prov 11:27–31
13	Mark 7:24–37	Prov 12:1–6
14	Mark 8:1–21	Prov 12:7–10
15	Mark 8:22–9:13	Prov 12:11–14
16	Mark 9:14–50	Prov 12:15–22
17	Mark 10:1–31	Prov 12:23–28
18	Mark 10:32–52	Prov 13:1–6
19	Mark 11:1–19	Prov 13:7–12
20	Mark 11:20–12:12	Prov 13:13–18
21	Mark 12:13–44	Prov 13:19–25
22	Mark 13	Prov 14:1–4
23	Mark 14:1–26	Prov 14:5–9
24	Mark 14:27–52	Prov 14:10–18
25	Mark 14:53–72	Prov 14:19–24
26	Mark 15:1–20	Prov 14:25–30
27	Mark 15:21–47	Prov 14:31–35
28	Mark 16	Prov 15:1–4

READING PLAN

MARCH	A.M.	P.M.
1	Luke 1:1–38	Prov 15:5–10
2	Luke 1:39–56	Prov 15:11–19
3	Luke 1:57–80	Prov 15:20–24
4	Luke 2	Prov 15:25–29
5	Luke 3	Prov 15:30–33
6	Luke 4	Prov 16:1–5
7	Luke 5	Prov 16:6–9
8	Luke 6:1–16	Prov 16:10–15
9	Luke 6:17–49	Prov 16:16–19
10	Luke 7:1–35	Prov 16:20–24
11	Luke 7:36–50	Prov 16:25–28
12	Luke 8	Prov 16:29–33
13	Luke 9:1–36	Prov 17:1–5
14	Luke 9:37–62	Prov 17:6–10
15	Luke 10	Prov 17:11–15
16	Luke 11	Prov 17:16–21
17	Luke 12	Prov 17:22–28
18	Luke 13	Prov 18:1–7
19	Luke 14	Prov 18:8–15
20	Luke 15	Prov 18:16–19
21	Luke 16	Prov 18:20–24
22	Luke 17	Prov 19:1–6
23	Luke 18	Prov 19:7–12
24	Luke 19	Prov 19:13–19
25	Luke 20	Prov 19:20–29
26	Luke 21:1–36	Prov 20:1–5
27	Luke 21:37–22:23	Prov 20:6–12
28	Luke 22:24–53	Prov 20:13–19
29	Luke 22:54–23:25	Prov 20:20–25
30	Luke 23:26–56	Prov 20:26–30
31	Luke 24	Prov 21:1–8

MAY	A.M.	P.M.
1	Acts 1	Prov 28:1–5
2	Acts 2	Prov 28:6–10
3	Acts 3:1–4:4	Prov 28:11–14
4	Acts 4:5–37	Prov 28:15–22
5	Acts 5:1–11	Prov 28:23–28
6	Acts 5:12–6:7	Prov 29:1–6
7	Acts 6:8–8:1a	Prov 29:7–11
8	Acts 8:1b–40	Prov 29:12–16
9	Acts 9	Prov 29:17–21
10	Acts 10	Prov 29:22–27
11	Acts 11	Prov 30:1–4
12	Acts 12	Prov 30:5–9
13	Acts 13	Prov 30:10–14
14	Acts 14	Prov 30:15–17
15	Acts 15:1–21	Prov 30:18–23
16	Acts 15:22–41	Prov 30:24–28
17	Acts 16:1–15	Prov 30:29–33
18	Acts 16:16–40	Prov 31:1–9
19	Acts 17	Prov 31:10–31
20	Acts 18	Psa 1
21	Acts 19:1–22	Psa 2
22	Acts 19:23–41	Psa 3
23	Acts 20	Psa 4
24	Acts 21:1–36	Psa 5
25	Acts 21:37–22:29	Psa 6
26	Acts 22:30–23:35	Psa 7:1–9
27	Acts 24	Psa 7:10–17
28	Acts 25:1–22	Psa 8
29	Acts 25:23–26:32	Psa 9:1–10
30	Acts 27	Psa 9:11–20
31	Acts 28	Psa 10

APRIL	A.M.	P.M.
1	John 1:1–28	Prov 21:9–16
2	John 1:29–51	Prov 21:17–24
3	John 2	Prov 21:25–31
4	John 3	Prov 22:1–5
5	John 4:1–42	Prov 22:6–9
6	John 4:43–54	Prov 22:10–16
7	John 5	Prov 22:17–21
8	John 6:1–21	Prov 22:22–29
9	John 6:22–65	Prov 23:1–8
10	John 6:66–7:13	Prov 23:9–14
11	John 7:14–44	Prov 23:15–21
12	John 7:45–8:11	Prov 23:22–28
13	John 8:12–30	Prov 23:29–35
14	John 8:31–59	Prov 24:1–7
15	John 9	Prov 24:8–12
16	John 10:1–21	Prov 24:13–22
17	John 10:22–42	Prov 24:23–29
18	John 11	Prov 24:30–34
19	John 12:1–36	Prov 25:1–5
20	John 12:37–50	Prov 25:6–12
21	John 13:1–30	Prov 25:13–20
22	John 13:31–14:31	Prov 25:21–28
23	John 15	Prov 26:1–10
24	John 16	Prov 26:11–16
25	John 17	Prov 26:17–22
26	John 18	Prov 26:23–28
27	John 19:1–27	Prov 27:1–7
28	John 19:28–42	Prov 27:8–11
29	John 20	Prov 27:12–18
30	John 21	Prov 27:19–27

JUNE	A.M.	P.M.
1	Rom 1:1–17	Psa 11
2	Rom 1:18–32	Psa 12
3	Rom 2:1–16	Psa 13
4	Rom 2:17–29	Psa 14
5	Rom 3:1–20	Psa 15
6	Rom 3:21–31	Psa 16
7	Rom 4:1–12	Psa 17
8	Rom 4:13–25	Psa 18:1–19
9	Rom 5:1–11	Psa 18:20–29
10	Rom 5:12–21	Psa 18:30–36
11	Rom 6:1–14	Psa 18:37–50
12	Rom 6:15–23	Psa 19
13	Rom 7:1–6	Psa 20
14	Rom 7:7–25	Psa 21
15	Rom 8:1–17	Psa 22:1–11
16	Rom 8:18–39	Psa 22:12–24
17	Rom 9:1–29	Psa 22:25–31
18	Rom 9:30–10:21	Psa 23
19	Rom 11:1–10	Psa 24
20	Rom 11:11–24	Psa 25:1–7
21	Rom 11:25–36	Psa 25:8–15
22	Rom 12:1–8	Psa 25:16–22
23	Rom 12:9–21	Psa 26
24	Rom 13:1–7	Psa 27
25	Rom 13:8–14	Psa 28
26	Rom 14:1–12	Psa 29
27	Rom 14:13–23	Psa 30
28	Rom 15:1–13	Psa 31:1–8
29	Rom 15:14–33	Psa 31:9–18
30	Rom 16	Psa 31:19–24

READING PLAN

JULY

	A.M.	P.M.
1	1 Cor 1:1—2:5	Psa 32
2	1 Cor 2:5–16	Psa 33:1–11
3	1 Cor 3	Psa 33:12–22
4	1 Cor 4	Psa 34:1–10
5	1 Cor 5	Psa 34:11–22
6	1 Cor 6	Psa 35:1–18
7	1 Cor 7	Psa 35:19–28
8	1 Cor 8	Psa 36
9	1 Cor 9	Psa 37:1–22
10	1 Cor 10:1—11:1	Psa 37:23–40
11	1 Cor 11:2–34	Psa 38
12	1 Cor 12:1–31a	Psa 39
13	1 Cor 12:31b—13:13	Psa 40:1–10
14	1 Cor 14:1–25	Psa 40:11–17
15	1 Cor 14:26–40	Psa 41
16	1 Cor 15:1–34	Psa 42
17	1 Cor 15:35–58	Psa 43
18	1 Cor 16	Psa 44:1–8
19	2 Cor 1:1—2:11	Psa 44:9–26
20	2 Cor 2:12—3:18	Psa 45
21	2 Cor 4	Psa 46
22	2 Cor 5:1–10	Psa 47
23	2 Cor 5:11—6:2	Psa 48
24	2 Cor 6:3—7:1	Psa 49:1–15
25	2 Cor 7:2–16	Psa 49:16–20
26	2 Cor 8:1–15	Psa 50
27	2 Cor 8:16—9:15	Psa 51
28	2 Cor 10	Psa 52
29	2 Cor 11:1–15	Psa 53
30	2 Cor 11:16—12:10	Psa 54
31	2 Cor 12:11—13:14	Psa 55

SEPTEMBER

	A.M.	P.M.
1	1 Thess 1	Psa 78:40–55
2	1 Thess 2:1–16	Psa 78:56–72
3	1 Thess 2:17—3:13	Psa 79
4	1 Thess 4:1–12	Psa 80
5	1 Thess 4:13–18	Psa 81
6	1 Thess 5:1–11	Psa 82
7	1 Thess 5:12–28	Psa 83
8	2 Thess 1	Psa 84
9	2 Thess 2:1–12	Psa 85
10	2 Thess 2:13—3:5	Psa 86
11	2 Thess 3:6–18	Psa 87
12	1 Tim 1:1–11	Psa 88
13	1 Tim 1:12–20	Psa 89:1–13
14	1 Tim 2	Psa 89:14–29
15	1 Tim 3	Psa 89:30–45
16	1 Tim 4:1–10	Psa 89:46–52
17	1 Tim 4:11—5:8	Psa 90
18	1 Tim 5:9—6:2	Psa 91
19	1 Tim 6:3–10	Psa 92
20	1 Tim 6:11–21	Psa 93
21	2 Tim 1:1–14	Psa 94:1–15
22	2 Tim 1:15—2:13	Psa 94:16–23
23	2 Tim 2:14–26	Psa 95
24	2 Tim 3:1–9	Psa 96
25	2 Tim 3:10—4:8	Psa 97
26	2 Tim 4:9–22	Psa 98
27	Titus 1	Psa 99
28	Titus 2	Psa 100
29	Titus 3	Psa 101
30	Philemon	Psa 102:1–17

AUGUST

	A.M.	P.M.
1	Gal 1	Psa 56
2	Gal 2	Psa 57
3	Gal 3:1–14	Psa 58
4	Gal 3:15–25	Psa 59:1–9
5	Gal 3:26—4:20	Psa 59:10–17
6	Gal 4:21—5:15	Psa 60
7	Gal 5:16–26	Psa 61
8	Gal 6	Psa 62
9	Eph 1:1–14	Psa 63
10	Eph 1:15–23	Psa 64
11	Eph 2:1–10	Psa 65
12	Eph 2:11–22	Psa 66:1–7
13	Eph 3	Psa 66:8–20
14	Eph 4:1–16	Psa 67
15	Eph 4:17—5:2	Psa 68:1–18
16	Eph 5:3–20	Psa 68:19–35
17	Eph 5:21–33	Psa 69:1–18
18	Eph 6:1–9	Psa 69:19–36
19	Eph 6:10–24	Psa 70
20	Php 1	Psa 71:1–18
21	Php 2:1–11	Psa 71:19–24
22	Php 2:12–18	Psa 72
23	Php 2:19–30	Psa 73:1–20
24	Php 3:1–14	Psa 73:21–28
25	Php 3:15—4:9	Psa 74:1–11
26	Php 4:10–23	Psa 74:12–23
27	Col 1:1–14	Psa 75
28	Col 1:15—2:5	Psa 76
29	Col 2:6–23	Psa 77
30	Col 3:1—4:1	Psa 78:1–8
31	Col 4:2–18	Psa 78:9–39

OCTOBER

	A.M.	P.M.
1	Heb 1	Psa 102:18–28
2	Heb 2:1–4	Psa 103:1–18
3	Heb 2:5–18	Psa 103:19–22
4	Heb 3:1–6	Psa 104:1–23
5	Heb 3:7–19	Psa 104:24–35
6	Heb 4:1–13	Psa 105:1–22
7	Heb 4:14—5:10	Psa 105:23–45
8	Heb 5:11—6:12	Psa 106:1–5
9	Heb 6:13–20	Psa 106:6–31
10	Heb 7:1–10	Psa 106:32–48
11	Heb 7:11–28	Psa 107:1–3
12	Heb 8	Psa 107:4–9
13	Heb 9:1–10	Psa 107:10–16
14	Heb 9:11–28	Psa 107:17–22
15	Heb 10:1–18	Psa 107:23–32
16	Heb 10:19–39	Psa 107:33–43
17	Heb 11:1–16	Psa 108
18	Heb 11:17–40	Psa 109:1–20
19	Heb 12:1–13	Psa 109:21–31
20	Heb 12:14–29	Psa 110
21	Heb 13	Psa 111
22	James 1:1–18	Psa 112
23	James 1:19–27	Psa 113
24	James 2:1–13	Psa 114
25	James 2:14–26	Psa 115
26	James 3:1–12	Psa 116:1–6
27	James 3:13—4:3	Psa 116:7–14
28	James 4:4–12	Psa 116:15–19
29	James 4:13—5:6	Psa 117
30	James 5:7–12	Psa 118:1–7
31	James 5:13–20	Psa 118:8–14

READING PLAN

NOVEMBER	A.M.	P.M.
1	1 Pet 1:1–12	Psa 118:15–21
2	1 Pet 1:13–2:3	Psa 118:22–29
3	1 Pet 2:4–12	Psa 119:1–8
4	1 Pet 2:13–25	Psa 119:9–16
5	1 Pet 3:1–7	Psa 119:17–24
6	1 Pet 3:8–22	Psa 119:25–32
7	1 Pet 4:1–11	Psa 119:33–40
8	1 Pet 4:12–19	Psa 119:41–48
9	1 Pet 5	Psa 119:49–56
10	2 Pet 1:1–11	Psa 119:57–64
11	2 Pet 1:12–21	Psa 119:65–72
12	2 Pet 2:1–9	Psa 119:73–80
13	2 Pet 2:10–22	Psa 119:81–88
14	2 Pet 3:1–9	Psa 119:89–96
15	2 Pet 3:10–18	Psa 119:97–104
16	1 John 1:1–4	Psa 119:105–112
17	1 John 1:5–2:2	Psa 119:113–120
18	1 John 2:3–11	Psa 119:121–128
19	1 John 2:12–17	Psa 119:129–136
20	1 John 2:18–27	Psa 119:137–144
21	1 John 2:28–3:10	Psa 119:145–152
22	1 John 3:11–24	Psa 119:153–160
23	1 John 4:1–6	Psa 119:161–168
24	1 John 4:7–21	Psa 119:169–176
25	1 John 5:1–12	Psa 120
26	1 John 5:13–21	Psa 121
27	2 John	Psa 122
28	3 John	Psa 123
29	Jude 1–16	Psa 124
30	Jude 17–25	Psa 125

DECEMBER	A.M.	P.M.
1	Rev 1:1–8	Psa 126
2	Rev 1:9–20	Psa 127
3	Rev 2:1–11	Psa 128
4	Rev 2:12–29	Psa 129
5	Rev 3:1–6	Psa 130
6	Rev 3:7–13	Psa 131
7	Rev 3:14–22	Psa 132
8	Rev 4	Psa 133
9	Rev 5	Psa 134
10	Rev 6	Psa 135:1–12
11	Rev 7	Psa 135:13–21
12	Rev 8	Psa 136
13	Rev 9	Psa 137
14	Rev 10	Psa 138
15	Rev 11:1–14	Psa 139:1–16
16	Rev 11:15–19	Psa 139:17–24
17	Rev 12:1–13:1a	Psa 140
18	Rev 13:1b–10	Psa 141
19	Rev 13:11–18	Psa 142
20	Rev 14	Psa 143
21	Rev 15	Psa 144
22	Rev 16	Psa 145:1–7
23	Rev 17	Psa 145:8–13a
24	Rev 18	Psa 145:13b–21
25	Rev 19:1–10	Psa 146
26	Rev 19:11–21	Psa 147:1–6
27	Rev 20:1–6	Psa 147:7–11
28	Rev 20:7–15	Psa 147:12–20
29	Rev 21:1–8	Psa 148
30	Rev 21:9–27	Psa 149
31	Rev 22	Psa 150

AUTHOR BIOGRAPHIES

This index gives you information about each contributor and tells you where his devotions can be found.

Stephen Arterburn is founder and chairman of New Life Treatment Centers, Inc. He is the author of *Growing Up Addicted* and *Addicted to "Love."* Among his other books are *The Angry Man*, written with David Stoop. *Devotions are found on pages 50, 121, 270, 345, 445.*

David Augsburger holds a Ph.D. degree in pastoral psychotherapy and family therapy from the School of Theology at Claremont, California. He has written many books, including *Caring Enough to Confront* and *When Enough Is Enough*. *Devotions are found on pages 230, 259.*

Joseph Bayly was the first director of InterVarsity Press and later filled several key positions at David C. Cook Publishing Company, including service as president. The author of several books, including *A View from the Hearse* and *Psalms of My Life*, he died in 1986, joining three sons who preceded him in death. *A devotion is found on page 318.*

Bob Benson, the son of a religious music publisher, was one of the Christian world's leading publishing executives, serving for almost 20 years at The John T. Benson Publishing Company in Nashville, Tennessee, before pursuing speaking and writing on a full-time basis. The author of six books, he succumbed to cancer in March, 1986. *A devotion is found on page 57.*

Donald Bloesch, a widely respected scholar and a prolific author, is a professor of theology at the University of Dubuque Theological Seminary in Dubuque, Iowa. Among his many books are *The Christian Life and Salvation* and *The Essentials of Evangelical Theology*. *A devotion is found on page 496.*

Ron Blue, a Certified Public Accountant, is a managing partner of Christian Financial Management, an Atlanta-based firm. He has more than twenty years' experience in helping people plan for their financial future. He has written *Master Your Money* and *Managing Your Money*. *Devotions are found on pages 63, 98, 523, 534.*

Dietrich Bonhoeffer was a German Lutheran pastor and theologian who was arrested in 1943 for his involvement in the Confessing Church and in anti-Nazi activities in wartime Germany. On April 9, 1945, he was hanged in a concentration camp. His books include *The Cost of Discipleship* and *Life Together*. *Devotions are found on pages 18, 48, 311, 329, 382.*

Pat Boone is a recording artist, author and speaker who has achieved long-lasting success in the entertainment world. Boone, who lives with his wife Shirley in Beverly Hills, is the father of four daughters. He has written a number of books, including *A New Song* and *Pray to Win*. *A devotion is found on page 331.*

Paul Brand, now retired, served as Chief of the Rehabilitative branch of the U.S. Public Health Service Hospital in Carville, Louisiana. He is known for his brilliant work as a hand surgeon. With Philip Yancey he has written *Fearfully and Wonderfully Made* and *In His Image*. *Devotions are found on pages 149, 232, 245, 267, 343.*

Leslie Brandt has had a powerful ministry through his work as an evangelist, retreat leader and author. He is the author of numerous books, including *Psalms/Now*, *Jesus/Now* and *God Is Here—Let's Celebrate*. *A devotion is found on page 237.*

Jerry Bridges is Vice President of Corporate Affairs of The Navigators, a parachurch organization. He has served on its staff in some capacity since 1955. Among the books he has written are *Transforming Grace*, *The Pursuit of Holiness*, and *The Practice of Godliness*. *Devotions are found on pages 206, 335, 368.*

D. Stuart Briscoe is the author of more than a dozen books and the senior pastor of Elmbrook Church in Waukesha, Wisconsin. Born in England, he was with The Torchbearers missionary fellowship before coming to the U.S. Among his books are *Getting into God* and *What It Means to Be Real*. *Devotions are found on pages 88, 125, 352, 373.*

Frederick Buechner, called by USA Today "one of our most original storytellers," is a critically acclaimed author of more than 20 novels and nonfiction works, including *The Book of Bebb*, *Godric*, *Wishful Thinking*, and *The Alphabet of Grace*. A Presbyterian minister, he lives in Vermont. *Devotions are found on pages 279, 295, 358, 404.*

Larry Burkett is founder and president of Financial Concepts, Inc., a ministry dedicated to teaching and counseling on God's principles of finance. He is the author of a number of best-selling, award-winning books, including *The Coming Economic Earthquake*, *Investing for the Future*, and *Debt-Free Living*. *Devotions are found on pages 306, 532.*

Tony Campolo is professor of sociology at Eastern College in St. Davids, Pennsylvania. A leader in evangelical social action, he has written several books, including *The Kingdom of God Is a Party* and *Wake Up America!* *A devotion is found on page 276.*

AUTHOR BIOGRAPHIES

Michael Card is a singer/songwriter whose song "El Shaddai" was rated the number one song of the decade by Christian radio broadcasters. He has a master's degree in Biblical Studies from Western Kentucky University. In addition to writing songs, Card studies and teaches the Bible. He is the author of *Immanuel* and *The Promise*. Devotions are found on pages 4, 127, 154, 209, 225.

Oswald Chambers was a Bible teacher, conference leader and YMCA chaplain. After his death his widow compiled his writings in *My Utmost for His Highest*, *Daily Thoughts for Disciples* and other popular devotional books. A devotion is found on page 143.

Charles W. Colson served as Special Counsel to President Richard M. Nixon from 1969 to 1973. He is founder and chairman of the board of Prison Fellowship Ministries, an international prison outreach. His books include: *Born Again*, *Kingdoms in Conflict*, and *The Body*. Devotions are found on pages 14, 486.

Jim Conway is co-founder and president of Christian Living Resources/Mid-Life Dimensions, a non-profit organization. He is the author of a number of books, including *Men in Mid-Life Crisis* and *Friendship*. With his wife Sally he has written *Your Marriage Can Survive Mid-Life Crisis*. Devotions are found on pages 59, 109, 123, 300, 324.

Larry Crabb is founder and director of the Institute of Biblical Counseling, a ministry committed to training Christians to resolve life's problems using Biblical principles. He is also professor of Biblical Counseling at Colorado Christian University, and the author of many books, including *Inside Out* and *Men and Women*. Devotions are found on pages 115, 200, 233, 344, 436.

John E. Crawford was a professor of psychology who in his varied career worked as a college director of guidance and a director of research, as well as a consulting psychologist for children. He developed the "Crawford Spatial Relations Test " and wrote ten books, including *Being the Real Father Now That Your Teenager Will Need*. Devotions are found on pages 53, 75, 340.

Donald E. Demaray is professor of preaching at Asbury Theological Seminary. He has written, edited or compiled more than 20 books, including *A Guide to Happiness*, *Alive to God Through Praise*, and *Laughter, Joy and Healing*. A devotion is found on page 286.

William E. Diehl is the president of Riverbend Resource Center, Inc., a management consulting firm. He was manager of sales for Bethlehem Steel for 32 years. He is the author of *In Search of Faithfulness*, *Thank God It's Monday*, and *The Monday Connection*. A devotion is found on page 529.

James Dobson is founder and president of Focus on the Family, a non-profit organization that produces his nationally syndicated radio program. Among his books are *Hide or Seek*, *Straight Talk to Men and Their Wives*, *Dare to Discipline*, and *Love for a Lifetime*. Devotions are found on pages 275, 291, 455, 474.

Dave Dravecky is a former San Francisco Giants baseball pitcher who returned to the game after a cancerous tumor was removed from his pitching arm. He gained national recognition for his comeback and for the dramatic way his arm broke during his second game back. He is the author of *Comeback* and *When You Can't Come Back*, written with his wife Jan. Devotions are on pages 315, 336, 380.

Judson Edwards is pastor of the Heritage Baptist Church in Webster, Texas. He is the author of several books, including *Dancing to Zion* and *Regaining Control of Your Life*. A devotion is found on page 208.

Ted Engstrom is President Emeritus of World Vision, a Christian humanitarian organization. He previously served as president of Youth for Christ International and as general manager of Zondervan Publishing House. He is the author of 36 books, including *The Making of a Christian Leader* and *The Pursuit of Excellence*. A devotion is found on page 465.

Steve Farrar is president of Strategic Living, based in Dallas, Texas. He has earned a doctorate from Dallas Theological Seminary. He and his wife speak across the United States in the Family Life Marriage Conferences. He is the author of *Point Man*. Devotions are found on pages 221, 354, 511.

John Fischer is a pioneer in contemporary Christian music. He has been a performing and recording artist for over twenty years. For several years his columns have appeared in the periodical *Contemporary Christian Music*. He is the author of three books, including *Real Christians Don't Dance* and *Making Real What I Already Believe*. Devotions are found on pages 37, 84, 198, 281.

Stan D. Gaede is Professor of Sociology at Gordon College in Wenham, Massachusetts. The father of three children, he has written several books, including *Belonging*, *Life in the Slow Lane*, and *Where Gods May Dwell*. Devotions are found on pages 133, 374.

Joe Gibbs not only led his football team to the most victories in Washington Redskin history, his record as head coach was one of the most successful ever in the National Football League's history. His autobiography is entitled *Fourth and One*. Devotions are found on pages 447, 546.

Ken Gire is a writer living in Fullerton, California, with his wife and four children. He is an award-winning author of such books as *Intimate Moments with the Savior*, *Incredible Moments with the Savior*, and *A Father's Gift*. A devotion is found on page 94.

Billy Graham has quite possibly reached more people with the gospel than any other person on earth. In addition to being an international evangelist, he is an accomplished author, whose best-selling books include *Answers to Life's Questions*, *Peace with God*, and *The Secret of Happiness*. A devotion is found on page 467.

AUTHOR BIOGRAPHIES

Thomas Hale, a surgeon, and his wife Cynthia, a pediatrician, are medical missionaries and have lived in Nepal since 1970. He is the author of two books on their adventures in Nepal: *Don't Let the Goats Eat the Loquat Trees* and *On The Far Side of Liglig Mountain*. Devotions are found on pages 23, 66, 107, 357, 408.

Richard Halverson is chaplain of the United States Senate and former pastor of Fourth Presbyterian Church in Washington, D.C. He has written several books, including *Man to Man* and *Manhood with Meaning*. A devotion is found on page 162.

William Hendricks is the president of a communications development group in Dallas, Texas, and the co-author of seven books, including *Living by the Book*, written with Howard Hendricks. He has written several books with Doug Sherman, including *Your Work Matters to God*. Devotions are found on pages 257, 303, 483.

Orel Hershiser is a major league baseball pitcher for the Los Angeles Dodgers. In 1988 he won the National League Cy Young Award and was named Most Valuable Player in the World Series. At the same time he was named The Sporting News's Major League Player of the year and the Associated Press Professional Athlete of the Year. His autobiography is entitled *Out of the Blue*. Devotion are found on pages 305, 308, 309, 314.

H. Beecher Hicks, Jr., is Senior Minister of Metropolitan Baptist Church in Washington, D.C. A graduate of Colgate Rochester Divinity School, he is the author of several books, including *Preaching Through a Storm* and *Correspondence with a Cripple from Tarsus*. A devotion is found on page 211.

Bill Hybels is pastor of Willow Creek Community Church, which over the past ten years has grown from a fellowship of 125 people to one of over 9,000. He is the author of many books, including *Descending into Greatness* and *Honest to God?* With his wife Lynne he has written *Fit to Be Tied*. Devotions are found on pages 29, 104, 238, 402, 513.

Donald M. Joy is professor of Human Development and Christian Education at Asbury Theological Seminary. He is the author of more than ten books, including *Bonding: Relationships in the Image of God* and *Unfinished Business*. Devotions are found on pages 61, 225.

David Juroe is a family counselor with the Yorba Park Medical Group in Orange, California. He has written *Successful Stepparenting* and, with Ted Engstrom, *For the Workaholic I Love*. A devotion is found on page 465.

W. Phillip Keller is a Canadian citizen and the son of missionaries to Kenya. He has lived in various places around the world and now makes his home in British Columbia. He is the author of over 35 books, the most popular of which is *A Shepherd Looks at Psalm 23*. Devotions are found on pages 255, 444, 501.

Tim LaHaye is founder and president of Family Life Ministries in Washington D.C., and the author of numerous books, including *Spirit-controlled Temperament* and *How to Win Over Depression*. With his wife Beverly he has written *The Act of Marriage*. Devotions are found on pages 86, 137, 384.

Tom Landry is the revolutionary former football coach of the Dallas Cowboys. A Texas native, he coached for the New York Giants football team until becoming the Cowboys' first and only coach until 1989. During his tenure, he led the team to an impressive 271–180–6 record. His autobiography is entitled *Tom Landry*. Devotions are found on pages 11, 181, 489.

Leonard E. LeSourd is Chairman of the Board of Directors of Breakthrough, an intercessory prayer ministry. A writer and editor, he has edited hundreds of books and is the author of numerous others, including *Strong Men, Weak Men*. Devotions are found on pages 226, 249.

C.S. Lewis was a professor of Medieval and Renaissance Literature at Cambridge University, Cambridge, England. He is the author of numerous books, including *Mere Christianity*, *The Screwtape Letters*, *The Chronicles of Narnia*, and *The Problem of Pain*. Devotions are found on pages 202, 241.

D. Bruce Lockerbie was affiliated with Wheaton College before joining the Stony Brook School, where he held the positions of chairman of the Fine Arts department and dean of the faculty, and, more recently, Scholar in Residence. He has written over 30 books, including *Fatherlove*. Devotions are found on pages 252, 508.

Max Lucado pastors the Oak Hills Church of Christ in San Antonio, Texas, and lectures at conferences. He is the author of numerous books, including: *No Wonder They Call Him the Savior*, *The Applause of Heaven*, and *In the Eye of the Storm*. Devotions are found on pages 13, 79, 131, 188, 364.

Brennan Manning, who lives with his wife Rosalyn in New Orleans, spends six months each year on the road directing spiritual retreats and proclaiming God's unconditional love. His books include *Lion and Lamb*, *The Ragamuffin Gospel*, and *The Signature of Jesus*. A devotion is found on page 170.

Bill McCartney is head football coach at the University of Colorado. Following the 1989 season, he was named United Press International Coach of the Year. He is the founder of Promise Keepers, a national ministry geared to instructing men in their growth in Christlike masculinity. His autobiography is entitled, *From Ashes to Glory*. Devotions are found on pages 168, 176.

William McConnell served as a staff worker for InterVarsity campus ministry before living in Brazil, South America, where he worked with the Bible University Alliance. He is now Assistant to the President of In-

AUTHOR BIOGRAPHIES

terVarsity Christian Fellowship in Madison, Wisconsin, and is the author of *The Gift of Time*. A devotion is found on page 362.

Thomas Merton was a poet, author and clergyman born in France. He taught at Columbia and St. Bonaventure Universities and worked at a Catholic settlement house in Harlem before joining the Trappist monastery in Gethsemane, Kentucky. Among his books are *Seeds of Contemplation*. *Devotions are found on pages 7, 223, 297, 348, 360.*

Stan Mooneyham was the former president of World Vision, a Christian humanitarian organization. He had also served as special assistant to Billy Graham. He wrote several books, including *What Do You Say to a Hungry World?* and *Dancing on the Strait and Narrow*. *A devotion is found on page 351.*

Patrick M. Morley is founder, chairman and president of Morley Properties, Inc. He teaches a weekly men's Bible study near his home in central Florida, and is the author of *The Man in the Mirror* and *The Rest of Your Life*. *Devotions are found on pages 146, 185.*

Gerald Oosterveen is a pastor with experience in parish ministry and chaplaincy ministries. He has most recently served as a hospital chaplain. He is the author of *Serving Mentally Impaired Persons* and *Too Early Frost*. *A devotion is found on page 395.*

Eugene Peterson served as a pastor for many years in Bel Air, Maryland, and is now on the faculty at Regent College in Vancouver, B.C., Canada, where he helps students in their devotional and practical approach to God. He has written many books, including *Reversed Thunder* and *Answering God*. *Devotions are found on pages 77, 251.*

Jack Perry had a distinguished diplomatic career that included service as a political officer in U.S. embassies in Moscow and Paris and as U.S. ambassador to Bulgaria. He teaches political science and is the director of the Dean Rusk Program in International Studies at Davidson College. He has written *Light from Light*. *A devotion is found on page 9.*

Derek Prime serves as minister of Charlotte Chapel, Edinburgh. He is the author of *Created to Praise*. *A devotion is found on page 397.*

Mark A. Ritchie is a commodities trader on the Chicago Board of Trade and the author of *God in the Pits*. *Devotions are found on pages 135, 264, 350.*

Haddon W. Robinson, former president of Denver Theological Seminary, is distinguished professor of preaching at Gordon-Conwell Seminary in South Hamilton, Massachusetts. He is the author of *Decision Making by the Book* and *Biblical Preaching*. *A devotion is found on page 140.*

Doug Sherman is president and founder of Career Impact Ministries. He is the author of *How to Keep Your Head Up When Your Job's Got You Down*. The books he has written with William Hendricks include *How to Balance Competing Time Demands* and *Your Work Matters to God*. *Devotions are found on pages 257, 303, 483.*

Mike Singletary played middle linebacker for the Chicago Bears football team for 12 seasons. He earned the National Football League's "Defensive Player of the Year" award in 1984, 1985 and 1988, and was named the "1990 NFL Man of the Year" for his on-field performance and dedicated community service. He is the author of two books: *Calling the Shots* and *Singletary on Singletary*. *Devotions are found on pages 33, 269, 289, 429.*

G.R. Slater served as minister of St. Matthew's United Church in Toronto, Ontario, Canada, and was a contributor to *Marriage Is for Living*. *A devotion is found on page 284.*

Gary Smalley was a family life pastor and is now president of Today's Family, based in Phoenix, Arizona. He is the author of a number of books, including *If Only He Knew* and *Joy That Lasts*. With John Trent he has written *The Gift of Honor* and *The Hidden Value of a Man*. *Devotions are found on pages 204, 339, 493, 539.*

Lewis B. Smedes is Professor Emeritus at Fuller Theological Seminary in Pasadena, California, where he served as professor of philosophy and integration. He is the award-winning author of nine books, including *Choices* and *Forgive and Forget*. *Devotions are found on pages 31, 251.*

David W. Smith is superintendent of schools at the Delphi School Corporation in Delphi, Indiana. A respected lecturer in the fields of social science and education, he has been a guest on "Focus on the Family" and NBC's "Today" show. He is the author of *Men Without Friends* and *Choosing Your Child's School*. *A devotion is found on page 438.*

Charles H. Spurgeon was pastor of New Park Street Baptist Church in London, England, for 38 years and the founder of the Pastor's College, where he instructed over 900 men for the ministry. He had over 1,900 different sermons published during his lifetime, and he has written many books, including *Morning and Evening* and *Lectures to My Students*. *A devotion is found on page 442.*

Charles Stanley is senior pastor of the 10,000-member First Baptist Church in Atlanta, Georgia, and the broadcast teacher on "In Touch," a national television and radio program. He has written numerous books, including *A Touch of His Wisdom* and *A Touch of His Freedom*. *Devotions are found on pages 172, 319, 510.*

David Stoop is a psychologist and co-director of the Minirth-Meier Clinic West. He is the author of *Hope* for the *Perfectionist* and *Self Talk*. Together with Stephen Arterburn he has written *When Someone You Love Is Someone You Hate* and *The Angry Man*. *Devotions are found on pages 50, 121, 270, 345, 445.*

Charles R. Swindoll is pastor of First Evangelical Free Church in Fullerton, California. His "Insight for Living" radio broadcasts are heard nationwide, and he is the author of numerous books, including *Improving Your Serve* and *Laugh Again*. *Devotions are found on pages 266, 283, 495, 516, 536.*

Daniel Taylor is associate professor of English at Bethel College in St. Paul, Minnesota. Married and the father of four children, he is the author of *The Myth of Certainty* and *Letters to My Children*. *Devotions are found on pages 247, 273, 292, 367.*

A.W. Tozer was born in Pennsylvania in 1897 and was a pastor of the Christian and Missionary Alliance from 1919 until his death in 1963. His books include *The Divine Conquest, Christ the Eternal Song*, and *The Knowledge of the Holy*. *A devotion is found on page 376.*

John Trent is associate director of Today's Family, based in Phoenix, Arizona. Previously he served as a family life pastor for eight years. He is the author of *Growing Together*. With Gary Smalley, he has written *The Gift of Honor* and *The Hidden Value of a Man*. *Devotions are found on pages 204, 339, 493, 539.*

Walter Trobisch had a profound impact on numerous people in his ministry of writing and lecturing, which took him around the world. Until his death in 1979, he lived with his wife Ingrid in Austria, where he carried on a huge counseling service by mail. Among the books he wrote were *I Loved a Girl* and *The Misunderstood Man*. *A devotion is found on page 2.*

Richard Walters has had broad and varied experience in his career as a psychologist, serving in such settings as psychiatric hospitals, general hospitals, local churches and now as a professor of psychology at Bellhaven College in Jackson, Mississippi. He is the author of *Forgive and Be Free* and *The Escape Trap*. *A devotion is found on page 424.*

Walter Wangerin, Jr., is a prolific writer, the author of such books as *The Book of the Dun Cow, Reliving the Passion*, and *Mourning into Dancing*. A Lutheran pastor, he currently occupies the Jochum Chair at Valparaiso University. *A devotion is found on page 117.*

J.H. Waterink was an internationally known educator and psychologist, who spent 35 years as Professor of Education and Psychology at the Free University of Amsterdam. He is the author of many books, including *Guiding Teen-agers to Maturity* and *Leading Little Ones to Jesus*. *A devotion is found on page 302.*

Reuben Welch joined the faculty at Point Loma Nazarene College in San Diego in 1960 as associate professor of religion. A popular conference speaker, he is the author of several books, including *Faith for the Journey* and *Let's Listen to Jesus*. *Devotions are found on pages 147, 322.*

John Westfall, the co-host and co-producer of the radio show, "Everyday People," is the author of *Coloring Outside the Lines* and *Enough Is Enough*. He and his family live in Walnut Creek, California. *Devotions are found on pages 331, 470.*

Reggie White was a defensive lineman for the Green Bay Packers football team. He was an All-American lineman for the University of Tennessee and a member of the Philadelphia Eagles from 1985–1992. He is a perennial All-Pro and is regularly a league leader in sacks. He has written *Minister of Defense*. *Devotions are found on pages 157, 287, 326, 333, 526.*

David Wiersbe is pastor of Hope Evangelical Free Church in Roscoe, Illinois. He is the co-author, with Warren Wiersbe, of *Devotional Talks for People Who Do God's Business* and *Comforting the Bereaved*. *A devotion is found on page 371.*

Warren Wiersbe is the general director and Bible teacher of Back to the Bible, speaking regularly on the daily program, which originates in Lincoln, Nebraska. He is the author of more than 80 books, including his BE series of expositional commentaries on the Bible. *A devotion is found on page 371.*

E. James Wilder is an ordained minister and a licensed clinical psychologist, serving as assistant director of Shepherd's House Counseling Center in Van Nuys, California. He is the author of *Just between Father & Son*. *Devotions are found on pages 193, 341.*

Philip W. Williams is an ordained American Lutheran minister who has worked as an assistant church pastor and as a hospital director of pastoral care and associate director of clinical pastoral education. He is the author of *When a Loved One Dies* and *Water for Our Wilderness*. *Devotions are found on pages 27, 90, 215, 235, 277.*

Nicholas Wolterstorff is a well-known Christian philosopher and author who taught for many years at Calvin College in Grand Rapids, Michigan. He is now professor of philosophical theology at Yale Divinity School. Among the books he has written are *Lament for a Son* and *Reason within the Bounds of Religion*. *A devotion is found on page 296.*

Don Wyrtzen received an early start in music, radio and television under the care of his father, Jack Wyrtzen, founder of Word of Life International. He has arranged and composed more than 200 anthems and sacred songs and has written *A Musician Looks at the Psalms*. *Devotions are found on pages 416, 433, 460, 481, 503.*

SUBJECT INDEX

SUBJECT INDEX This subject index lists topics and sends you to those places where you can find devotions related to those topics.

Abundance, 98
Acceptance, 2, 109, 318
Accountability, 526
Angels, 467
Anger, 121, 204, 270, 345, 424
Authority of Jesus, 48
Baptism, 223
Belief, 11, 162, 176, 264, 314, 333, 350
Biblical truth, 486
Bitterness, 319
Borrowing money, 98
Careerism, 483
Celibacy, 61, 226
Character, 181, 204, 368
Children, 380
Christian community, 14
Christmas, 127
Christ's birth, 79
Christ's body, 149, 232, 245, 267
Church, 149, 154
Comfort, 13, 77
Commitment, 221
Compassion, 57, 255, 341
Confession, 424
Conflict, 284
Contentment, 445
Courage, 238, 402, 513
Creation, 416, 444
Daughters, 53, 75, 340
Death, 27, 90, 215, 235, 273, 277, 296, 380, 395
Dependence on God, 198, 241
Depression, 137
Devotion, 162, 226, 368, 460
Discipleship, 18, 23, 107, 170, 329
Eternal life, 397
Eternity, 362
Evangelism, 237, 455
Failure, 225, 305, 322, 336
Faith, 27, 176, 305, 309, 329, 442
Faithfulness, 438
Family, 510
Fatherhood, 4, 53, 75, 133, 252, 302, 318, 339, 340, 429, 455, 495, 508, 511, 516, 532, 539
Favoritism, 343
Fear, 336
Fear of the Lord, 206
Forgiveness, 31, 37, 135, 172, 319, 436
Freedom, 84, 135
Friendship, 59, 238, 324, 373, 438
Gentleness, 266
Giving, 107, 247, 251, 257
Goals, 86

Godliness, 368
God's constancy, 336
God's love, 66, 206, 209, 276, 315
God's plan, 211
God's presence, 168
God's provision, 133, 303, 481
God's will, 9, 11
God's Word, 311, 326, 358, 493
God's work, 371
Grace, 143, 225, 382, 496
Gratitude, 251, 286
Grief, 90, 117, 140
Growing older, 474
Guilt, 90
Headship, 230, 259
Holiness, 7, 335, 348, 360
Holy Spirit, 503
Home, 495
Honor, 539
Hope, 395
Humility, 125, 275, 276
Hunger, 23
Husbanding, 33, 352
Identity, 50
Idolatry, 404
Incarnation, 4, 127
Integrity, 532
Knowing God, 147
Known by God, 501
Light, 7
Listening, 529
Love, 90, 109, 208, 233, 237
Loving God, 376
Lust, 283
Marriage, 221, 230, 233, 238, 249, 259, 269, 275, 284, 291, 344, 352, 534, 546
Masculinity, 2, 88, 125, 193, 266, 270, 341, 345, 351, 402
Maturity, 300, 351
Meekness, 79
Mentoring, 345
Mercy, 324, 360
Missions, 66, 357
Money, 86, 534
Neediness, 470
Nurture, 270
Obedience, 48, 481
Orphans, 408
Pain, 13, 204, 215, 241, 339
Parents, 123
Perfectionism, 300
Perspective, 77, 380, 433
Power, 374
Prayer, 249, 279, 292, 331, 335, 496

SUBJECT INDEX

Pride, 364
Priorities, 11, 433, 447
Proclaiming the Word, 157, 287
Providence, 416
Questions, 84, 198, 281
Rat race, 185
Rebirth, 123, 245, 384
Relationship, 84, 238
Repentance, 364, 436
Respect, 302
Responsibility, 408
Riches, 86
Righteousness, 131
Role models, 289, 429, 511
Salvation, 188, 202, 206
Satan worship, 467
Self-centeredness, 115, 200, 344, 374
Self-examination, 37, 193
Selflessness, 208
Servanthood, 33, 63, 230, 259, 269, 305, 510
Service, 465
Sex, 61
Sexual restraint, 61, 283, 291
Significance, 146, 367
Sin, 188, 223, 343, 344, 486
Sons, 516
Sons of God, 223
Sorrow, 13
Spiritual hunger, 94, 137
Spiritual leadership, 354
Spiritual life, 297, 384
Spiritual warfare, 249, 354
Stewardship, 523
Strength, 18, 305, 339
Success, 63
Suffering, 9, 154, 339, 493
Time, 362
Treasures, 63
Trials, 168, 442, 447
Trust, 404, 513
Truth, 281
Value, 539
Victory, 117, 235, 295
Vision, 29, 88, 104
Vulnerability, 125, 470
Wealth, 107, 306, 523
Wisdom, 508, 510
Witness, 14, 157, 287, 308
Work, 185, 257, 295, 297, 303, 465, 474, 483, 495
Worry, 279
Worship, 94, 149, 267, 376, 397